VISIBLE
WOMEN

VISIBLE WOMEN

New Essays on American Activism

Edited by
Nancy A. Hewitt and Suzanne Lebsock

UNIVERSITY OF ILLINOIS PRESS
Urbana and Chicago

© 1993 by the Board of Trustees of the University of Illinois
Manufactured in the United States of America
1   2   3   4   5   C   P   5   4   3   2   1

This book is printed on acid-free paper.

Library of Congress Cataloging-in-Publication Data

Visible women : new essays on American activism / edited by Nancy A.
  Hewitt and Suzanne Lebsock.
      p.   cm. — (Women in American history)
  Includes bibliographical references and index.
  ISBN 0-252-01771-4 (alk. paper). — ISBN 0-252-06333-3 (alk. paper
  : pbk.)
  1. Women—United States. 2. Women—United States—Social
conditions. 3. Women in politics—United States. 4. Feminism—
United States. I. Hewitt, Nancy A., 1951-   . II. Lebsock,
Suzanne. III. Series.
HQ1421.V57   1993
305.4'0973—dc20   93-18538
                                                                        CIP

To Anne Firor Scott

Contents

Acknowledgments   xi

Introduction   1

Part 1. Formal Politics: Ideologies and Strategies   15

Taking the Law into Our Own Hands:
Bradwell, Minor, and Suffrage Militance in the 1870s   19
Ellen Carol DuBois

Rebecca Latimer Felton and the Problem of "Protection"
in the New South   41
LeeAnn Whites

Woman Suffrage and White Supremacy: A Virginia Case Study   62
Suzanne Lebsock

Women's History and Political History: Some Thoughts
on Progressivism and the New Deal   101
William H. Chafe

Women's History and Political Theory: Toward a Feminist
Approach to Public Life   119
Sara M. Evans

**Part 2. Economic Justice: Representation and
        Mobilization**   141

Needlewomen and the Vicissitudes of Modern Life: A Study
of Middle-Class Construction in the Antebellum Northeast   145
Mari Jo Buhle

O. Delight Smith's Progressive Era: Labor, Feminism, and
Reform in the Urban South   166
Jacquelyn Dowd Hall

In Pursuit of Power: The Political Economy
of Women's Activism in Twentieth-Century Tampa   199
Nancy A. Hewitt

The Housewives' League of Detroit: Black Women
and Economic Nationalism   223
Darlene Clark Hine

Part 3. The Politics of Reform: Tensions and Contradictions   243

The Cost of Club Work, the Price of Black Feminism   247
Deborah Gray White

Bridging Chasms: Community and the Southern YWCA   270
Marion W. Roydhouse

"Each One Is Dependent on the Other":
Southern Churchwomen, Racial Reform, and
the Process of Transformation, 1880–1940   296
Mary E. Frederickson

Giving Women a Future: Alice Fletcher,
the "Woman Question," and "Indian Reform"   325
Dolores Janiewski

Part 4. The Politics of Knowledge: Exemplary Lives   345

"Why Should Girls Be Learn'd and Wise?":
The Unfinished Work of Alice Mary Baldwin   349
Linda K. Kerber

Invincible Woman: Anne Firor Scott   383
Nancy Weiss Malkiel

Contributors   393

Index   397

Acknowledgments

We would like to thank Cynthia Herrup, who first suggested that we edit a volume in honor of Anne Firor Scott, and our colleagues and friends at Rutgers University and the University of South Florida, who provided encouragement as we worked on the manuscript. We are grateful to Duke University and the University of North Carolina at Chapel Hill for bringing us together for the final stages of manuscript preparation, which were eased immensely by the deft copyediting of Jane Mohraz and the editorial support of Carole Appel. We would also like to thank Stacy Braukman, Jennifer Ritterhouse, and Kathy Wallerstein, who helped us complete the footnote checking and the index. Our deepest gratitude is reserved for our cocontributors and for our friend and mentor, Anne Firor Scott.

Introduction

Among Anne Firor Scott's many published works, there are three whose titles crystallize her profound concern over the traditional invisibility of women in history: "On Seeing and Not Seeing," "Making the Invisible Woman Visible," and "Most Invisible of All."[1] It is no accident that Scott has written evocatively of vision and blindness in history, for Scott, from the beginning, was herself a seer. When other historians encountered evidence of women's activism in the Progressive Era South, they either did not see it at all or assumed it was too trivial for words. Anne Scott saw the same evidence and sought out more, in time grasped its significance, had the nerve to start publishing it in the early 1960s, and became a major figure in setting off a revolution in the writing and teaching of history.

We call this collection of essays *Visible Women* in recognition of Anne Scott's persistent concern with historical vision. Our title is also intended as a statement about the astonishing increase in our knowledge since Scott first faced the void more than thirty years ago. Scott herself is responsible for much of this increase, as she has continued to break new ground, national as well as southern. At the same time, an ever larger group of younger scholars, inspired by Scott's example as well as her direct encouragement, have added their diverse contributions to the burgeoning whole. In this book we bring together some of their most recent work, original essays that say something about the present state of the art and about scholarship still to come.

The fact that these essays converge on women's activism signals a decisive shift in the center of gravity of research on women. The women's history mansion has always had many rooms, but since about 1980 a growing number of them have been occupied by scholars intent on understanding the scope and meaning of women's public and political action. This is a happy vindication of Scott's long-standing and primary commitment to recovering the actions of women who changed themselves, who changed the prospects for other women, and who did their best to change the world. To be sure, in her wide-ranging scholarly career, Anne Scott has at times written about the lives of women centered on domestic endeavors. Her unforgettable portrait of Jane Mecom, for example, uses the letters of an eighteenth-century woman to remind us of the importance of the "small events of which great events are composed." The first segment of *The Southern Lady* re-creates the lives of elite antebellum women who were confined to household and church.[2] But even here, there is the underlying suggestion of a preferable public life. How, Scott asks, would Jane Mecom's experience have been different had she, like her brother Ben Franklin, possessed maleness as well as formidable talents? Scott's antebellum ladies tried earnestly to find contentment in their circumscribed lives. But they often failed, and their story was in many ways a prologue to the more dynamic narrative of change as "door after door" flew open during the Civil War and in its wake.

Anne Scott's favorite subjects were, and are, women who got things done—individual women with exceptional force of character, and women's organizations in which ordinary mortals could accomplish things in concert. At first, few readers were predisposed to believe that any of these women mattered very much, and Scott developed some interesting rhetorical strategies for their remedial education. One was to rank the woman in question with a string of eminent men. The pacifist convictions of Jane Addams, Scott wrote, were very like those of St. Francis, Gandhi, and Tolstoy. Emma Willard was placed in the company of Jefferson and Lincoln.[3] Another tactic was to attach dignified language to behavior that others might play for laughs. In introducing the women who took axes to the saloons in the 1850s, Scott categorized their action in the spirit that they themselves would have, as "civil disobedience."[4]

By the time Scott was ready to write *Natural Allies* (1991), there was also a more direct case to be made for the significance of women's voluntary associations. As she conducted research on all parts of the country, Scott found women's groups everywhere, from the 1790s on. They were truly countless, and even Scott was surprised at their reach and their variety. *Natural Allies* maps them, examines their evolution over time, speculates on their founders' motives, explores their character, both national and local, and, above all, makes claims for their importance. There can be no doubt that voluntary associations were the major vehicles for expanding the rights and the efficacy of American women. This in itself would have had major ripple effects on the rest of the citizenry, but Scott goes on to claim their direct impact on the development of American society at large. Associated women helped shape the class structure. They democratized the political order. They built a whole range of community institutions that are now taken for granted. They largely invented progressivism; in that era more than any other, they spotted emergent social problems, proposing and often enacting practical solutions. The welfare state as it emerged in the early twentieth century was largely their creation, as agencies of government assumed responsibility for many of the programs originally instituted by voluntary associations.

These are large claims, and some of the essays in the present volume make claims that are larger still—and raise important questions about how we conceptualize women's participation in American political life. It seems clear enough that the traditional boundaries of political history will no longer do. What we call politics must be expanded beyond electioneering and the conduct of formal governance to encompass the colossal efforts of organized women. As William H. Chafe contends, this has potentially dramatic consequences for our understanding of periods of reform like the Progressive Era. Progressivism emerged from the confluence of two broad streams of political action—one largely male and the other largely female, each with its distinctive aims, values, tactics, and style. If we further understand that white, middle-class progressives, both male and female, tended to converge in their condescension toward African Americans and the working class, then progressivism makes new sense; we have a better grasp of its breadth, its legendary contradictions, its achievements, and its failures—as well as its links to the revival of reform under the New Deal. Ellen Carol DuBois offers another example of how an analysis of women's politics can give us fresh perspective on subjects of longer-standing interest to historians. Between 1869 and 1875, suffragists tried to make the case that women were already entitled to vote under the Fourteenth and Fifteenth amendments to the U.S. Constitution. When the U.S. Supreme Court decisively rejected their arguments, it was a turning point in the history of feminism. The decision, however, did not affect women alone. It also helped pave the way for the Court's ultimate refusal to uphold the voting rights of southern freedmen.

Attention to women's voluntary associations, in short, can and does change our understanding of American political history. Sara M. Evans proposes yet another use for the history of women's organizations: in that history lie the materials for a new theory of public life. Voluntary associations, Evans suggests, are a third sort of human space—neither private, nor entirely public, but linking the two and containing characteristics of both. They are schools in which women and men learn the skills needed for effective public participation. They potentially constitute an arena in which citizen decision making may thrive.

As our claims for the importance of women activists become bolder, it matters all the more that we understand their political practice. Most of the women portrayed in this book were indeed visible women, at least locally, and while their actual power varied a great deal, all contributed something—language, vision, action—to the politics of some larger community. Most of them faced choices, often dilemmas, about how to enact their ambitions for women within a society deeply divided by class and race. From their dilemmas we seek instruction. In the past decade, in history and across the disciplines that constitute the interdisciplinary field of women's studies, feminist scholars (including some of the authors in this book) have made urgent pleas for studies that pay serious attention to race and to class as well as gender. In this volume, some of the early results are in. As we might expect from so broad a charge, those results are varied, complex, and in places replete with irony. We have no single conclusion, but we think it might be useful to create some categories, to identify some approaches and themes that emerge from these essays.

First, much depends on social location. In the history of women's activism, there has been a fundamental distinction between those who do not have the luxury of race or class privilege and those who do. For women of the latter group, it was possible to cast their struggle in the relatively simple terms of gender alone: women contended with men, who needed to be improved but not empowered because they had too much power already. The irony here is that the women who have mounted the most global critique of male privilege have typically been those with the greatest access to it. Female activists who were white and relatively well-off could often tap male resources, ranging from hefty personal incomes to the funds and prestige of government agencies.

A different dynamic was set in motion by African Americans, working-class women, and many other groups whose feminism was not underwritten by race, ethnic, or class privilege. Their immediate social landscape included men and boys—kin, neighbors, coworkers—who were themselves exploited. Moreover, it did not escape their notice that high-status women—usually white and middle or upper class—often benefited from that exploitation and in some cases went out of their way to perpetuate it. These were the materials for a feminist theory that sorted women into particular groups and understood their needs and aspirations as shaped by race and class hierarchies as well as by gender. These were also the materials for a feminist practice that encompassed, even fused with, campaigns for economic justice, racial justice, or both.

The Housewives' League of Detroit is a case in point. It is also a lesson in visibility, since Darlene Clark Hine is the first scholar to see the Housewives' League and to enter it into the historical record. Organized by African American club women in 1930, the Housewives' League mobilized thousands of Detroit homemakers in an effort to curb the combined ravages of racial discrimination and the Great Depression. Consumer power was key; the idea was to patronize black-owned businesses and black professionals and to boycott white-owned businesses unless they employed blacks. What sort of philosophy was this? In Hine's words, the Housewives' League empowered women and at the same time "remained securely attached to concern for home, family, and community uplift." This organization, in short, exhibited "a communal womanist consciousness."

"Womanism," it turns out, has a longer history than most of us know. Many of us were introduced to the term in the 1980s through essays by Alice Walker and Elsa Barkley Brown. As early as 1909, however, O. Delight Smith deployed the term to help convey her own conviction that the progress of women was inseparable from that of the larger community, the community in this instance defined as the labor movement. Smith was white, a telegrapher by trade, and a labor organizer in Atlanta. As Jacquelyn Dowd Hall tells us, Smith was a passionate advocate of economic independence for wage-earning women and of full union recognition for working-class wives, whose labor and consciousness as consumers were vital to the welfare of all. As a "labor feminist," Smith insisted that feminism was best served by labor organization; she believed that the trade union, including men but cured of its sexism, would be the primary agent of women's freedom. Should anyone still think of feminism as the property of middle-class women working through single-sex organizations, Hall's essay makes it clear we must think again.

So does Nancy A. Hewitt's analysis of Tampa, Florida, in the early twentieth century, a study that discerns several distinct patterns of women's activism in a single multiracial city. Among Tampa's activists were thousands of "Latin" women—Cubans and Italians associated with the city's immense cigar industry. As cigarworkers and workers' wives, they entered politics via labor militance, enacted in solidarity with men through a series of strikes and crucial strike support services. Interestingly enough, as Latin women continued on a trajectory of rising visibility, their labor militance came to incorporate new dimensions of gender consciousness, exhibited in a women's wildcat strike and in the use of a new women's rights rhetoric. By 1920 they had earned increased respect from male co-unionists and were poised to enter a phase of intense organization building in the 1920s.

Not that any of this was easy. As Deborah Gray White writes in her essay on African American club women, there was a kind of seamlessness in their agenda: "As they saw it, what they did for women they did for the race, what they did for the race they did for all classes of the race, and when they worked for all classes, they worked for black women and black men." When club women moved to implementation, however, tensions along gender and class lines often arose. Women's claims to leadership drew resentment from some black men, who were themselves under seige in this era of disfranchisement and lynching. As for priorities, club women's number one goal was the protection of black women and girls from sexual assault and slander, but others found this a less serious and less urgent concern. Nor were the values and life-styles of middle-class club women a perfect match with those of the lower-class women they sought to uplift. And always there were new attacks and insults from the white world. As White explains it, genuine unity often was not possible. This was a structural problem, the product of treble oppression, and club women simply had to withstand the resulting tensions.

To bring these histories to light is a matter of simple justice. But it is more, a move in the direction of greater wisdom as well as fairness, a step that allows us, in Jacquelyn Hall's words, "to expand our own imaginative boundaries." As we have just seen, our vision of women's activism undergoes a marked expansion, and we see decidedly more complex patterns when we study activists who operated from a position of race or class disadvantage. The richness of such studies has suggested the wider utility of a "difference" analysis, "difference" in this instance referring to divisions among various groups of women. (In other contexts the "difference" label refers to divisions between the sexes.) Hence another frontier: what happens when we beam questions about race and class on past crusades in which the protagonists were largely women of privilege?

Several of the essays in this collection ask those questions in a southern context; one salutary effect of our burgeoning interest in race has been a burst of work on the South, which despite all of Anne Scott's efforts has been an underdeveloped region in women's history. The South in the late nineteenth century and early twentieth presents historians with extraordinary challenges. This was perhaps the greatest age ever for activism among women (and this means women of almost every description); at the same time it has been called the "nadir" for black southerners, an era of rape, lynching, disfranchisement, and legally mandated segregation, all of which was fueled by a white supremacist discourse whose perniciousness knew no limits. Here, if anywhere, is interesting ground for reconnoitering junctions of gender and race.

LeeAnn Whites probes the thought of Rebecca Latimer Felton, the Georgia temperance organizer and suffragist introduced initially to modern readers by Anne Scott in *The Southern Lady*. Felton was the first woman to take a seat in the U.S. Senate. She was by then eighty-seven, and it was a strictly ceremonial occasion, meant to cap a truly formidable public career. For us, it may be especially telling that this was the woman the white South sent to Washington. By birth a member of the antebellum elite, Felton fashioned herself after the war as a champion of ordinary white women, of poor white girls in need of education, of isolated and drudging white farm wives. In the abstract, her larger program bore an eerie resemblance to that of the black club women described by Deborah White. Felton, too, worked simultaneously to uplift the poor, to empower women, and to strengthen the race. The difference was that for Felton race work meant not only working for the interests of her own group but also deliberately debasing the other; when Felton spoke to the vulnerability of white women, she repeatedly invoked the image of the shiftless black laborer, the lurking rapist. Could there be such a thing as white supremacist womanism?

The point, in any case, is that one did not have to be an African American to do race work; white women did race work, too, whether they were aware of it or not. Fortunately, Rebecca Felton was not the only model. When her generation departed the scene, leadership passed to women too young to have experienced the cataclysms of Civil War and Reconstruction. While some whites in this new generation echoed Felton (and worse), others found new ways to negotiate the deep social divisions of their region, occasionally in cautious alliances with African Americans. Here we present three case studies: of reform-minded Methodists, of the southern YWCA, and of Virginia suffragists, all of whom were first put on the historian's map by Anne Scott. Taken together, they point to some room for maneuver within a larger context of overarching and overwhelming racial division.

The church provided one space where experimentation was possible. As Anne Scott has recently warned, it is not smart to underestimate the power of religion as a motivating force for social change;[5] Mary Frederickson's essay in this volume underscores the point. Among the most successful pioneers in early twentieth-century interracial cooperation were Methodist women, members of the Colored Methodist Episcopal Church and the white Methodist Episcopal Church, South. Frederickson casts the relationship between black and white churchwomen as one of mutual dependency, which is not to say equality. These women were able to work together in the age of maximum segregation by developing rituals that preserved the appearance of white authority and superior wisdom, when in fact African American women were instructing whites and directing the investment of funds in specific projects that were implemented by black people in black communities. Women in the Colored Methodist Episcopal Church also moved first on the question of laity rights for women within the denomination, opening discussion on that issue many years before their white counterparts did.

Under the mantle of churchly respectability, then, forward-thinking Methodist women launched some relatively effective ventures in interracial cooperation. Their successes can be attributed in part to their tactical skill, but it should also be said that their projects could be dismissed by contemporaries as unrelated to the exercise of real power. When the economic and political stakes went up, the chances for bridging the racial divide ranged from slim to nonexistent. In her essay on the southern Young Women's Christian Association, Marion Roydhouse asks whether and how women of the Y were able to overcome barriers of class and race. On the question of class, she finds, white Y organizers were perpetually embattled but partially successful in terms of both ideology and human contact. Under YWCA auspices, workers met face-to-face with middle-class college students and board members. In a region famous for its hostility to organized labor, Y consciousness-raising also brought some middle-class women around to support protective legislation and even collective bargaining. When it came to race, however, there was no comparable progress. There were African American Y branches in many southern cities, but these were generally underfunded and subordinate to the "main" (white) organization. Events that brought black and white Y members together were extremely rare, a situation that would not change until the 1940s.

When political power was at issue, all doors to interracial cooperation slammed shut, or at least that is the lesson from Virginia. In an essay that situates the history of woman suffrage in the mire of local politics, Suzanne Lebsock studies the ways in which white supremacy infected the debates over granting the vote to women. In Virginia, the antisuffragists largely made the rules, partly because they were so powerful (their numbers included most of the politicians and public officials) and partly because they were willing to go lower than the suffragists were when it came to racialist rhetoric. Having set off alarms that woman suffrage would destroy white supremacy, the antis had everyone else in a box. White suffrage activists opted for a strategy of denial, arguing that woman suffrage was not relevant to white supremacy and posed no danger to it. Black Virginians, meanwhile, could only damage the woman suffrage cause by speaking for it; as a consequence, there were no black organizations promoting woman suffrage, at least none that was visible to white people. Note the contrast with the YWCA, the churches, the temperance and club movements, all of which encompassed black organizations as well as white ones. In formal politics, it seems, the practice of white supremacy was of a special order. After the Nineteenth Amendment was ratified in 1920, African American women in Virginia cities did organize voter registration campaigns, and some white suffragists helped to launch the interracial movement. It would be a long time, however, before any group of white women would lend public support to black women's quest for full citizenship.

Some barriers were clearly more formidable than others. Some people were also better than others at getting past them. Marion Roydhouse writes, for example, about Lois MacDonald, a member of the college YWCA who learned about working-class life by getting a job in an Atlanta textile factory and living in a bug-ridden boardinghouse—a "Church Home," no less, sponsored by middle-class women who had no idea of the conditions there until MacDonald enlightened them. Activism put many thousands of women at risk to learn new, unsettling, possibly galvanizing things about other groups and about the social order. We cannot yet say why some women were able to see while others were not, but we can offer instructive examples of women with exceptional vision.

Dolores Janiewski introduces us to Alice Cunningham Fletcher, feminist, ethnographer, reformer, and in the 1880s and 1890s an agent of the U.S. government assigned to divide western tribal lands into individual freeholds. For a white person in that time, Fletcher had unusual regard for Native Americans; she devoted much of her life to the study and observation of indigenous cultures and, in her own words, "sometimes succeeded in twisting around to the Indian view." She had, moreover, a gender analysis. Fletcher believed that the status of women was high in traditional Native American societies, and she feared for the loss of that status as more Native Americans adopted the essentials of the Euroamerican system. Nevertheless, Fletcher was personally responsible for speeding that process, taking charge of land allotments first among the Omaha and later the Winnebago and Nez Perce; to the end of her life she stuck to her conviction, common among progressive whites at the time, that Native Americans were best served by turning themselves into farmers and farmers' wives on parcels of land they individually owned. Fletcher's was a life of massive contradiction. As Janiewski explains, her commitment to improving women's lot was in direct conflict with her commitments as a professional and reformer, and this conflict was not resolved. As historians of women have increasingly taken up the study of race and class, it has become possible to speak of identity as multiple. Alice Fletcher, too, offers a case of multiple (and as it happens, conflicting) identities, but notice that in this case the warring identities—feminist and careerist—were chosen ones. In our continuing explorations of identity in history, it might be useful to think through how identities that were chosen may have differed from those that were in some sense given or imposed.

Complex as Alice Fletcher's vision was (and it was complex—on top of everything else, it included a streak of maternalist condescension), she can at least be credited with seeing beyond the epidemic racism of her time and searching for language in which her vision could be effectively expressed. A roughly comparable case can be made for middle-class philanthropists and novelists who took up the cause of impoverished needlewomen in the era before the Civil War. According to Mari Jo Buhle, both writers and reformers moved from their observations of the female poor to a rejection of prevailing theory on poverty, theory that held the poor responsible for their own misery. The novelists went further, and in stories recounting the trials of destitute wage laborers, they provided a counterpoint to their era's dominant discourse of gender relations—the discourse of "stable domesticity," as Buhle calls it. In the novels, domesticity was anything but stable; women and children were shown to be the main victims of the extraordinary volatility of the economy; and the protagonists were in fact pushed out of the home into the relatively public world of wage labor. Although these melodramas were ostensibly descriptive of working-class life, Buhle reads them for what they reveal about the concerns of the middle class as they were formulated at mid-century and reformulated by century's end. Implicit in this essay is a point about sources as well as substance: read with the requisite subtlety, popular fiction can be as suggestive as "harder" sources for revealing relationships between class and gender.

One last commentary on vision comes from Linda K. Kerber, whose essay-within-an-essay takes up the life of the historian Alice Mary Baldwin and the long history of women's intellect in the United States. Baldwin's career was in some ways a success story. She earned her Ph.D. in 1926, published a book on New England ministers in the Revolution that became the standard work on the subject, and served for many years as dean of the Woman's College of Duke University. Her story was also one of frustration; like many academic women of her generation, she was virtually forced into an administrative career, which in her case involved a series of losing battles on behalf of equality for Trinity's women. These demoralizing struggles left her little time for research. Such scholarship as she managed to produce had virtually no audience and was not published.

"Much depends, in any life, on timing."[6] Those are Anne Scott's words, written initially in an essay on Emma Willard but equally to the point for Alice Mary Baldwin and Anne Scott herself. The subject of Baldwin's unconventional, unpublished research was the history of women, specifically the intellectual history of women in early America. Taking Baldwin's essays and notes as a starting point, Linda Kerber goes on to sketch a broad history, from the eighteenth century to the twentieth, of the "continuing quest by determined women to claim access to books, instruction, and opportunity to interpret, always resisting the assumption . . . that women's minds are naturally suited merely to the trivial." The careers of Alice Baldwin and Anne Scott together chart a sea change in the second half of the twentieth century. Baldwin died in 1961, leaving behind a sealed manuscript memoir detailing her painful encounters with sexism at Duke. Scott joined the Duke history faculty that year and shortly thereafter began publishing essays on women. She went on to establish women's history as a teaching field, she worked for women in the university and in the state of North Carolina, and she became a national, eventually international, leader in the development of women's history as a scholarly endeavor. She retired from Duke in 1991 with every honor the university could bestow.

Small wonder that in her biographical pieces, Scott concentrated on figures like Jane Addams, Emma Willard, and most recently Janie Porter Barrett—all extraordinary individuals who seized a moment, proposed momentous innovations without alienating the powerful, invented new careers, and built new institutions.[7] The final essay in this volume, written by Nancy Weiss Malkiel on behalf of all the authors, is a personal appreciation of Anne Scott's phenomenal work for women and women's history. Explicit in this essay is our gratitude for all that Anne Scott has done. Implicit is a message about the social production of knowledge. Our society's body of available historical knowledge now includes an enormous and growing fund of knowledge about women and gender. This could not have happened in the absence of a flourishing women's movement, nor could it have happened had pioneers like Anne Scott not envisioned the development of the field as a huge, open, even messy enterprise requiring the best efforts of many minds. Scott was and is a key figure in connecting one scholar to another, across the country and across generations, and she has invested a great deal of energy in helping other historians secure academic appointments and fellowships so their research may thrive. We have only to contrast our experience with that of Alice Mary Baldwin to apprehend the magnitude of the advance.

Still, as Linda Kerber writes, it remains to be seen whether higher education can "provide understanding of the world in which the record of women's experience, needs, and accomplishments is regarded with as much respect and pride as the record of men is." The full integration of women into history as it is commonly understood is probably a long way off, and in many respects it is out of our hands. As historians of women, however, we can try to speed the process by writing accessible prose and broadcasting our knowledge in forms likely to reach a wide public. Once again, Anne Scott has much to teach us—about writing with clarity, grace, humor, and remarkable economy. Here is a representative sentence from Scott's 1963 essay on Jane Addams: "To be born in Illinois in 1860 was to bridge two eras." In exactly twelve words, Scott not only brought Addams into the world but also placed her in the great sweep of nineteenth-century events. Scott is persistently attentive to readers' needs for the large view, and she is always on the lookout for ways to explain to modern people what was different about the past. In a lecture on aging, Scott found a novel way to suggest just how youthful the American population was in the time of George Washington. "Being president," she wrote, "must have been something like being head of Boys' Town."[8] Any author agonizing over how, precisely, to conclude or begin a book should go back to *The Southern Lady* and read the last sentence and the first two.

Reaching a wider public is also a matter of form. Anne Scott has written textbooks for high school students and for college use. She has also written a good deal of biography, which is the form of history that students and the general public most want to read. Among professional historians biography has had a rather dubious reputation; this was especially the case in women's history in the 1970s, when historians of women were warned away from studies of "women worthies" in favor of other approaches that presumably had greater analytical significance. Anne Scott, however, has sided with the public. She has been a practitioner and a champion of biography, both individual and collective. Who else would devote a summer to reading all 1,359 sketches in *Notable American Women?* We hope the biographical pieces in this volume affirm Scott's belief in the value of the exemplary life.

At this writing, Scott has just completed a new book that brings together her interests in biography, the South, education, and links from one generation to the next. *Unheard Voices,* a title very much in the Scott tradition, is a study of five historians who in the 1920s, 1930s, and 1940s pioneered the scholarly study of southern women.[9] All were qualified for regular faculty appointments in colleges or universities; none was offered such an appointment; all were women; four of the five were completely unsung in their own time. It is impossible to emerge from this account without a sense of mourning for talent wasted. Scott's book at least reprints their pioneering work and recovers those five lives.

Let us keep at it. We dedicate this book to Anne Firor Scott in the hope that many Americans will one day find the past richly populated with women—audible and visible—who made a difference.

NOTES

1. Anne Firor Scott, "On Seeing and Not Seeing: A Case of Historical Invisibility," *Journal of American History* 71 (June 1984): 7–21; "Making the Invisible Woman Visible: An Essay Review," *Journal of Southern History* 38 (November 1972): 629–38; "Most Invisible of All: Black Women's Voluntary Associations," *Journal of Southern History* 56 (February 1990): 3–22. *Making the Invisible Woman Visible* is also the title of Scott's collected essays (Urbana: University of Illinois Press, 1984).

2. Anne Firor Scott, "Self-Portraits: Three Women," in *Making the Invisible Woman Visible,* 12; *The Southern Lady: From Pedestal to Politics, 1830–1930* (Chicago: University of Chicago Press, 1970).

3. Scott, *Making the Invisible Woman Visible,* 137, 42, 46. The essays on Jane Addams and Emma Willard were originally published in 1963 and 1978, respectively.

4. Anne Firor Scott, *Natural Allies: Women's Associations in American History* (Urbana: University of Illinois Press, 1991), 45.

5. Ibid., 182.

6. Scott, *Making the Invisible Woman Visible,* 38.

7. The Barrett sketch appears in John T. Kneebone, Brent Tarter, and Sandra Gioia Treadway, eds., *Dictionary of Virginia Biography* (Richmond: Virginia State Library, forthcoming).

8. Scott, *Making the Invisible Woman Visible,* 108, 323–24.

9. Anne Firor Scott, *Unheard Voices: The First Historians of Southern Women* (Charlottesville: University Press of Virginia, 1993).

Part 1

Formal Politics:
Ideologies and Strategies

In *English Social History,* completed in 1944, G. M. Trevelyan claimed that "social history might be defined negatively as the history of a people with the politics left out." Two decades later women's historians began challenging this dichotomy between social and political analysis. Many of the classic texts in the field—Eleanor Flexner's *Century of Struggle,* Aileen Kraditor's *Ideas of the Woman Suffrage Movement,* Anne Firor Scott's *Southern Lady,* and Gerda Lerner's *Black Women in White America*—showcased American women's struggles to gain first-class citizenship. Granted that other scholars went on to concentrate on domesticity and the private sphere, the problem was less women's historians' lack of concern with politics than it was political historians' lack of concern with women. Gradually the evidence accumulated of the myriad ways that women shaped and were shaped by legislative and judicial initiatives and social and political movements. By the 1980s, feminist scholars had demonstrated women's centrality in the antebellum crusades for social reform, Progressive Era battles for social justice, and post–World War II movements of social protest.

Recently, in the face of a conservative resurgence in U.S. politics, women's historians have begun to look more closely at those who opposed expanded roles and rights for women. Though not the focus of any single essay in this collection, the forces supporting the sexual status quo are explored as part of the larger story of campaigns for women's equality. Ellen Carol DuBois, for instance, demonstrates that in the late nineteenth century, as in the late twentieth, one of the strongest guarantors of sexual and racial hierarchy was the U.S. Supreme Court. Yet there were also women among those who opposed efforts on behalf of rights for their sex. The antisuffragist forces explored by Suzanne Lebsock included both prominent male politicians and affluent female advocates of the existing gender hierarchy; the opponents of women's education noted by Linda K. Kerber in a later section of this volume sought to control and constrain not only actions that might challenge existing relations of power but also thinking about such actions. Then there were those—such as Rebecca Latimer Felton—who straddled the line, seeking expanded rights for some (all classes of white women) while denying those same rights to others (black women and men).

Authors in this section, and throughout the volume, note the tensions among women pursuing political agendas rooted in their racial, class, and gender identities. Such recognition of diversity and dissension greatly complicates the portrait of women's political agency. Attention to these divisions, however, has encouraged us to rethink activist women's relations with their male counterparts, allowing us to paint a much more nuanced portrait of coalitions and conflicts, successes and failures, intentions and outcomes. In the process, we come to recognize the ways that the study of women transforms our understanding of some of the most fundamental developments in American political history. For instance, the fight by pioneer suffragists to gain the vote for women through the Fourteenth and Fifteenth amendments emerges as key to interpretations of constitutional law regarding race and rights. Highlighting the voting protests of the early 1870s, Ellen Carol DuBois calls attention to women's political inventiveness and its impact on the legal environment in which definitions of citizenship for all persons were recast during Reconstruction.

In the South, the cross currents of race, class, and gender relations generated by the Civil War created a particularly treacherous terrain on which to carve out a new balance between rights and responsibilities, protection and independence, for blacks and whites, women and men. LeeAnn Whites probes the contradictory efforts of Rebecca Latimer Felton to expand the political influence of Georgia women. Felton asserted white women's heightened need for protection, while at the same time she recognized their war-induced independence. Her success as a politician, culminating in her ceremonial appointment to the Senate at age eighty-seven, demonstrates both the possibilities and limits of women's public activism so long as it remained entangled within the confines of the South's traditional race and gender hierarchies. Yet Felton's "militant commitment to domestic defense" led her to advocate not only greater equality between the sexes in the family but also increased intervention by the state to ensure women's rights.

Suzanne Lebsock examines a generation of Virginia women who

alternately championed and challenged state power and regional conventions of race and gender relations as they struggled to redefine their relation to electoral politics. Challenging conventional wisdom, Lebsock argues that it was *anti*suffragists who bore primary (though not total) responsibility for infusing racist arguments into the woman suffrage debate. At the same time, she sketches the double bind that kept African Americans from participating in the suffrage controversy. Finally, after probing Virginia women's various positions on rights and race, she urges us to employ political labels—such as progressive—in ways appropriate to particular historical contexts, even as we seek to illuminate issues relevant to our own time and place.

Closing out the section on formal politics, William H. Chafe and Sara M. Evans shift our view back to the national arena, illustrating how such case studies as those presented here allow us to rethink the trajectory of political history and the conceptualization of political theory. In reexamining progressivism and the New Deal through the lenses of race, class, and gender, women's historians, according to Chafe, have reconfigured the chronology of twentieth-century political history, transformed our understanding of the Progressive Era's contradictory impulses, and remapped the paths along which the New Deal and the modern welfare state emerged in the United States. Evans, building on the analysis of female voluntarism offered by Chafe, works toward a new theory of public life. For Evans, voluntary associations—rooted in the personal relations of family and community and reaching out to the institutions of political power and public policy—serve as schools for democracy. Here, women and men, but particularly women, make the connections between private needs and public resources; here, then, historians and theorists can make the fullest connections between the new social history and traditional political history.

Taking the Law into Our Own Hands: *Bradwell, Minor,* and Suffrage Militance in the 1870s

Ellen Carol DuBois

Among the most contested elements of the Constitution have been the Reconstruction amendments, and a crucial aspect of that contest has been the relation of the Fourteenth Amendment to women's rights. This essay addresses the early history of women's rights claims to the Fourteenth and Fifteenth amendments. It explores the legal arguments with which woman suffragists approached the Reconstruction amendments, the popular support and militant activism they inspired, and the role that the defeat of women's rights claims played in the larger history of Reconstruction constitutionalism. This mid-nineteenth-century episode in women's rights history was extremely brief, but it reverberates richly with many important and perplexing issues facing feminist thinkers and activists today. At various moments during which I worked on this essay, I felt that this material provided the historical key to current debates within feminism over "equality," over "rights," and over "politics."

Here, in the post–Civil War years, we can see proponents of women's rights as they move from universal to particularistic arguments, providing us with the Gilded Age equivalent of the shift from "equality" to "difference" in the feminism of our own time. While many of my contemporaries emphasize the abstract and "male" character of such universalistic categories as "person" or "citizen," I have chosen to stress the many costs to the women's rights tradition of moving away from such frameworks—however "hegemonic" they may seem to our postmodern consciousness—which have helped situate women's emancipation in the larger context of humanity's freedom.[1]

Here, too, we can trace the course of the demands of a disempowered group based on the venerable but problematic constitutional concept of "rights." Of late, "rights arguments" have been criticized, not only by conservatives but also by those on the left, for the assumption that entitlement inheres "naturally" in individuals, flourishing in a "private" realm that must be protected from interference, by others and by the state. Such a concept of "rights," it is argued, masks the workings of power and favors those already privileged by existing social and political structures—men, white people, and the propertied.[2] But this episode in women's rights, perhaps the entire tradition, treats rights quite differently: as something to be won and exercised collectively rather than individually; as the object of political struggle as much as of judicial resolution; as that which government affirmatively establishes rather than negatively shields; and above all as that which has greatest meaning not to the powerful, who already enjoy their entitlements, but to the powerless, who have yet to have their full place in society recognized.

Finally, this episode has implications for the character and place of the "political" in women's history. While women's historians have deepened our knowledge of the public activism of women, even—or especially—before their enfranchisement, much of this scholarship has followed what is called (in shorthand) "the separate spheres" model. Women, it is argued, have had—and may still have—their own political culture distinct from men's, and they have chosen to work for their own and society's better- ment by embracing different institutions, following different rules, and adhering to different political values.[3] This essay suggests that to the degree that nineteenth-century women abandoned a political terrain also occupied by men—of partisan power and judicial contest—they were driven from it by defeat and forced to pursue politics by other, more indirect means. This essay considers women as they attempted to march into power directly, through the main political entrance, rather than indirectly, through the backdoor of the nursery or kitchen.

Most histories of women's rights—my own included—have emphasized the initial rage of women's rights leaders at the Radical Republican authors of the Fourteenth and Fifteenth amendments. In 1865 Elizabeth Cady Stanton was horrified to discover what she called "the word male" in proposals for a Fourteenth Amendment. The second section of the amendment defines the basis of congressional representation as "male persons over the age of twenty-one" and in doing so makes the first reference to sex anywhere in the Constitution. The passage of the Fif- teenth Amendment in 1869, a much more powerful constitutional defense of political equality, only deepened the anger of women's rights advo- cates because it did not include sex among its prohibited disfranchisements.[4]

In 1869 the crisis split suffragists into two camps—the National Woman Suffrage Association, which protested the omission of women from the Reconstruction amendments, and the American Woman Suffrage Associa- tion, which accepted the deferral of their claims. This part of the story is well known to students of woman suffrage, as is the National Association's concentration, through most of its twenty-one-year life (in 1890 it amalgamated with the American Association), on securing a separate amendment enfranchising women. Inasmuch as the form that federal woman suffrage ultimately took was precisely a separate constitutional amendment —the Nineteenth, ratified in 1920—this strategy is taken as the entirety of woman suffragists' constitutional claims. Yet, in the first few years after the passage of the Fourteenth and Fifteenth amendments, suffragists in the National Association camp energetically pursued another constitutional approach. They proposed a broad and inclusive construction of the Fourteenth and Fifteenth amendments, under which, they claimed, women were already enfranchised. This constitutional strategy, known at the time as the New Departure, laid the basis for the subsequent focus on a separate woman suffrage amendment, even as it embodied a radical democratic vision that the latter approach did not have.[5]

While the Fourteenth Amendment was in the process of being ratified, woman suffragists concentrated on its second clause, because of the offensive reference to "male persons." This phrase was included by the amendment's framers because in 1867 there was an active movement demanding the franchise for women, and it would no longer do to use such gender neutral terms as "person" to mean only men.[6] Yet such explicit exclusions of particular groups from the universal blessings of American democracy were not at all in the egalitarian spirit of the age. Perhaps it was for this reason that in writing the first section of the Fourteenth Amendment, which defines federal citizenship, the framers could not bring themselves to speak of races or sexes but instead relied on the abstractions of "persons" and "citizens." In other words, the universalities of the first section of the Fourteenth Amendment, where federal citizenship is established, run headlong into the sex-based restrictions of the second section, where voting rights are limited. Those Reconstruction Era feminists angered at the restrictive clause quickly recognized these contradictions and became determined to get women's rights demands included in the broadest possible construction of the terms "persons" and "citizens" in the first section, to use, in other words, the first section to defeat the second.

After the Fifteenth Amendment was finally ratified, the suffragists of the National Association therefore shifted from the claim that the Reconstruction amendments excluded women and began to argue instead that they were broad enough to include women's rights along with those of the freedmen. This strategic turn, known within woman suffrage circles as the New Departure,[7] was first outlined in October 1869 by a husband

and wife team of Missouri suffragists, Francis and Virginia Minor. They offered an elaborate and elegant interpretation of the Constitution to demonstrate that women already had the right to vote. Their construction rested on a consistent perspective on the whole Constitution, but especially on a broad interpretation of the Fourteenth Amendment.[8]

The Minors' first premise was that popular sovereignty preceded and underlay constitutional authority. In exchange for creating government, the people expected protection of their preeminent and natural rights. This is a familiar element of revolutionary ideology. Their second premise was to equate the power of the *federal* government with the defense of individual rights, to regard federal power as positive.[9] Historically, the federal government had been regarded as the enemy of rights; the Bill of Rights protects individual rights by enjoining the federal government from infringing on them. In the wake of the devastating experience of secession, the Fourteenth Amendment reversed the order, relying on federal power to protect its citizens against the tyrannical action of the states. The Minors thus argued in good Radical Reconstruction fashion that national citizenship had finally been established as supreme by the first section of the Fourteenth Amendment: "the immunities and privileges of American citizenship, however defined, are national in character and paramount to all state authority."

A third element in the Minors' case was that the benefits of national citizenship were equally the rights of all. This too bore the mark of the Reconstruction Era. In the words of the amendment, "all persons born or naturalized in the United States" were equally entitled to the privileges and protections of national citizenship; there were no additional qualifications. In the battle for the rights of the black man, the rights of all had been secured. The war had expanded the rights of "proud white man" to all those who had historically been deprived of them, or so these radical reconstructionists believed.[10] In other words, the historic claim of asserting *individual* rights was becoming the modern one of realizing *equal* rights, especially for the lowly.

Finally, the Minors argued that the right to vote was one of the basic privileges and immunities of national citizenship. This was both the most controversial and the most important part of the New Departure constitutional construction. Popular sovereignty had always included an implicit theory of political power. The Minors' New Departure argument took this article of popular faith, reinterpreted it in light of Reconstruction Era egalitarianism, and gave it constitutional expression to produce a theory of universal rights to the suffrage. The New Departure case for universal suffrage brought together the Fourteenth Amendment, which nationalized citizenship and linked it to federal power, and the Fifteenth

Amendment, which shifted the responsibility for the suffrage from the state to the national government.[11] This theory of the suffrage underlay much of the case for black suffrage as well, but because the drive for black suffrage was so intertwined with Republican partisan interest, it was woman suffrage, which had no such political thrust behind it, that generated the most formal constitutional expression of this Reconstruction Era faith in political equality.

The New Departure was not simply a lawyer's exercise in constitutional exegesis. Reconstruction was an age of popular constitutionalism. Although presented in formal, constitutional terms, what the Minors had to say had much support among the rank and file of the women's rights movement. The underlying spirit of the Minors' constitutional arguments was militant and activist. The basic message was that the vote was already women's right; they merely had to take it. The New Departure took on meaning precisely because of this direct action element. Many women took the argument to heart and went to the polls, determined to vote. By 1871 hundreds of women were trying to register and vote in dozens of towns all over the country.[12] In 1871 in Philadelphia, to take one of many examples, Carrie Burnham, an unmarried tax-paying woman, got as far as having her name registered on the voting rolls. When her vote was refused, she formed the Citizens Suffrage Association of Philadelphia, dedicated not only to the defense of women's political rights but also to the greater truth that the right to vote was inherent, not bestowed. If the contrary were true, if the right to vote were a gift, this "implied a right lodged somewhere in society, which society had never acquired by any direct concession from the people." Such a theory of political power was patently tyrannical.[13]

That the first examples of women's direct action voting occurred in 1868 and 1869, before the Minors made their formal constitutional argument, suggests that the New Departure grew out of a genuinely popular political faith. In 1868 in the radical, spiritualist town of Vineland, New Jersey, almost two hundred women cast their votes into a separate ballot box and then tried to get them counted along with the men's. "The platform was crowded with earnest refined intellectual women, who feel it was good for them to be there," the *Revolution* reported. "One beautiful girl said 'I feel so much stronger for having voted.' "[14] The Vineland women repeated the effort for several years, and the ballot box eventually became an icon, which the local historical society still owns. From Vineland, the idea of women's voting spread to nearby towns, including Roseville, where, despite the American Association's official disinterest in the New Departure, Lucy Stone and her mother tried—but failed—to register their votes.

On the other side of the continent, Mary Olney Brown also decided she had the right to vote because the legislature of Washington Territory had passed an act giving "all white American citizens above the age of twenty-one years the right to vote." She wrote to other "prominent women urging them to go out and vote at the coming election . . . [but] I was looked upon as a fanatic and the idea of woman voting was regarded as an absurdity." "Many [women] wished to vote . . . ," she decided, "[but] had not the courage to go to the polls in defiance of custom." Finally, in 1869, she went to the polls with her husband, daughter, and son-in-law. Election officials threatened that she would not be "treated as a lady."

> Summoning all my strength, I walked up to the desk behind which sat the august officers of election, and presented my vote. . . . I was pompously met with the assertion, "You are not an American citizen; hence not entitled to vote." . . . I said . . . "I claim to be an American citizen, and a native-born citizen at that; and I wish to show you from the fourteenth amendment to the constitution of the United States, that women are not only citizens having the con-stitutional right to vote, but also that our territorial election law gives women the privilege of exercising that right." . . . I went on to show them that the . . . emancipation of the Southern slaves threw upon the country a class of people, who, like the women of the nation, owed allegiance to the government, but whose citizen-ship was not recognized. To settle this question, the fourteenth amendment was adopted.

Whereupon, the local election official, "with great dignity of manner and an immense display of ignorance," insisted "that the laws of congress don't extend over Washington territory" and refused her vote. When Brown was refused again, two years later, she concluded, "It amounts to this: the law gives women the right to vote in this territory, and you three men who have been appointed to receive our votes, sit here and arbitrar-ily refuse to take them, giving no reason why, only that you have decided not to take the women's votes. There is no law to sustain you in this usurpation of power."[15]

News of the efforts of women to register and vote spread through formal and informal means. Women's rights and mainstream journals reported on them, but information also might have been passed by word of mouth through networks of activists. Many sisters and friends, often in different states, turn up in the stories of New Departure voting women. In her account, Mary Olney Brown tells of her sister, who was inspired by her efforts to try to vote in a nearby town. Brown's sister took a different approach and was more successful. Eager to vote in a school election, she and her friends prepared a special dinner for election officials. "When the voting was resumed, the women, my sister being the first, handed in their ballots as if they had always been accustomed to voting. One lady, Mrs. Sargent, seventy-two years old, said she thanked the Lord that he had let her live until she could vote."[16]

The voting women of the 1870s often went to the polls in groups. They believed in the suffrage as an individual right but an individual right that would be achieved and experienced collectively. The most famous of these voting groups was the nearly fifty local activists, friends, and relatives who joined Susan B. Anthony in attempting to vote in Rochester, New York, in 1872. Virginia Minor herself was swept up in this collective activism. When she and some of her friends, all suffrage activists and Republican partisans, tried to register in St. Louis and were refused, she sued.

The congressional passage of the Enforcement Act in May 1870 to strengthen the Fifteenth Amendment greatly accelerated women's direct action voting. The Enforcement Act was meant to enforce the freedmen's political rights by providing recourse to the federal courts and penalties against local election officials who refused the lawful votes of citizens. Women who wanted to vote saw the act as a way to use the power of the federal government for their own benefit. Benjamin Quarles reports that freedwomen in South Carolina were encouraged by Freedmen's Bureau officials to attempt to vote by appealing to the Enforcement Act.[17] Some election officials responded to the Enforcement Act by accepting women's votes. When Nanette Gardner went to vote in Detroit in 1871, the ward official in her district was sympathetic to her protest and accepted her vote. The same man accepted Gardner's vote again in 1872, and she presented him with "a beautiful banner of white satin, trimmed with gold fringe on which was inscribed . . . 'To Peter Hill, Alderman of the Ninth Ward, Detroit. . . . By recognizing civil liberty and equality for woman, he has placed the last and brightest jewel on the brow of Michigan.' "[18]

Most local officials, however, refused to accept women's votes. While Nanette Gardner voted successfully in Detroit, her friend Catherine Stebbins (the daughter of one of the Rochester voters) was turned away in the next ward. When Mary Brown's vote was refused in Olympia, she concluded that politicians more powerful than the local committeemen had decided to resist women's direct action efforts to vote and that "money was pledged in case of prosecution." In Santa Cruz, California, when Ellen Van Valkenberg was similarly turned back at the polls, she became the first woman to sue an election official under the Enforcement Act for refusing her vote.[19] By 1871 numerous New Departure woman suffrage cases were making their way through the federal courts.

Meanwhile, the New Departure gained an advocate who moved it from the local level into national politics: Victoria Woodhull. In January of 1871 Woodhull appeared before the House Judiciary Committee to make the constitutional case for women's right to vote. No woman had ever before been invited to address a committee of the U.S. Congress. Her appearance was sponsored by Massachusetts Republican Benjamin Butler, who may have helped her outline her constitutional case. The deeply felt conviction about women's rights underlying her argument was undoubtedly her own, however. Her memorial asked Congress to pass legislation clarifying the right of all women to vote under the new Reconstruction amendments.[20] The major difference between Woodhull and the Minors was tactical; she urged women to turn to Congress to resolve the question, while they relied on the courts.

Like all New Departure advocates, Woodhull embraced the premise that popular sovereignty was absolute: "the sovereign power of this country is perpetual in the politically-organized people of the United States, and can neither be relinquished nor abandoned by any portion of them." Her case for woman suffrage was simple and, from a Radical Reconstruction perspective, virtually unassailable: inasmuch as the first section of the Fourteenth Amendment made no reference to sex, women along with men were citizens of the United States, and foremost among the "privileges and immunities" of national citizenship was the right to vote.[21] Like the Minors, Woodhull argued that the Fourteenth Amendment established the supremacy of national over state citizenship and the obligation of the federal government to protect the rights of all citizens equally.

Woodhull also argued from the Fifteenth Amendment, which she interpreted broadly, that voting is "a Right, not a privilege of citizens of the United States."[22] She directly confronted the most obvious objection to this interpretation, that the Fifteenth Amendment specifically prohibits only disfranchisements by race, color, and previous condition. First, she argued, the amendment's wording does not bestow the right to vote but assumes it to be preexisting. Although it explicitly prohibited certain disfranchisements, Woodhull argued that it could not be read to implicitly permit others. Second, the Fifteenth Amendment forbids disfranchisement "under three distinct conditions, in all of which," Woodhull argued, "woman is distinctly embraced." In other words, "a race comprises all the people, male and female." Woodhull here seems to grasp what many modern white feminists are still struggling to understand, that counterposing the discriminations of race and sex obscures the experience of those who suffer both, that is, black women. Finally, Woodhull argued for her broad construction of the right of suffrage on the grounds of what she called "the blending of [the Constitution's] various parts," that is, the relation between the Fourteenth Amendment, which nationalizes citizenship and links it to the power of the federal government, and the Fifteenth Amendment, which shifts the responsibility for the suffrage from the state to the national government.[23]

The first official reaction to the New Departure came in response to Woodhull's memorial. The House Judiciary Committee issued two conflicting reports on the constitutional issues she raised.[24] Here we begin to see that debate over the feminists' particular constitutional arguments was inseparable from questions of the larger meaning of the Reconstruction amendments. The Majority Report rejected Woodhull's claims. Its author was John Bingham, one of the framers of the Fourteenth Amendment. Although Bingham conceded that women enjoyed the privileges of U.S. citizenship along with men, he disagreed that the Fourteenth Amendment added anything new to the content of national citizenship or altered the relationship between national and state citizenship. The Minority Report, signed by William Loughridge of Iowa and Benjamin Butler of Massachusetts, supported Woodhull's memorial and the generous and radical interpretation of the amendments on which it relied. The Minority Report interpreted the Fourteenth Amendment broadly, arguing that it was intended "to secure the natural rights of citizens as well as their equal capacities before the law." The Majority Report rejected Woodhull's argument that the Fifteenth Amendment shifted responsibility for the suffrage from the state to the national level, while the Minority Report agreed that the Fifteenth Amendment "clearly recognizes the right to vote, as one of the rights of a citizen of the United States."[25] "Thus it can be seen," Woodhull observed archly, "that equally able men differ upon a simple point of Constitutional Law."[26]

The mere fact of a congressional hearing was a victory for woman suffrage leaders, and the language of constitutional principle was an improvement over the semisexual innuendo with which their claims were often met.[27] The favorable Minority Report meant that some of the leaders of the Republican party supported women's rights claims on the Constitution. In 1871 two committee rooms in the Capitol were put at the disposal of the suffragists to facilitate their lobbying efforts.[28] "Could you feel the atmosphere of . . . Congress, to-day, you would not doubt what the end must be, nor that it will be very soon," Isabella Beecher Hooker wrote.[29] The National Woman Suffrage Association urged women to put pressure on their congressmen to support the Butler Report, as well as to continue trying to vote and to work through the courts.[30]

It was in this context, as Republicans struggled over the claims of the New Departure and suffragists grew hopeful, that the issue of "free love" was raised. The sexual discourse that soon surrounded the New Departure played a role in shaping the political context and therefore the constitutional outcome. Woodhull is generally remembered in the history books not for her powerful constitutional arguments but for her shady sexual reputation. These sexual issues, however, were introduced not by Woodhull but by her opponents, who saw in them a way to divert attention from the constitutional arguments she made. Republican newspapers, notably the *New York Tribune,* accused Woodhull of multiple marriages, bigamy, and advocacy of free love.[31] Suffrage leaders allied with Woodhull were either accused of sharing her "free love" sentiments or warned against the consequences of associating with disreputable women. As in other times, when politicians cannot face the genuine issues before them, the importance of "character" was asserted. "Men judge men's conventions not more by the formal platform they present than by . . . the character of those who are prominent in the proceedings," a New York periodical solemnly warned.[32]

Rather than react defensively to the attacks on her, Woodhull embraced the "free love" opprobrium with which she was charged. To her, the principles at the heart of sexual life were the same as those at the heart of political life, and the true basis of marriage was the same as the true basis of republican government: individual rights. Groping for a way to express her conviction that women, whether married or unmarried, must have unqualified control over their own reproductive and sexual lives, she used the language of Reconstruction constitutionalism to proclaim the doctrine of rights to and over one's own person. "Yes I am a Free lover," Woodhull responded to a heckler at one of her speeches. "I have an *inalienable, constitutional* and *natural* right to love whom I may, . . . to *change* that love *every day* if I please, . . . and it is your *duty* not only to *accord* [me my right], but, as a community, to see that I am protected in it."[33]

Such sex radicalism was not the predominant strain in nineteenth-century feminist circles. Most of the New Departure leaders (with the significant exception of Elizabeth Cady Stanton) were closer to the Victorian stereotype than Woodhull was, and they believed that the sex impulse must be tamed, not constitutionally secured. Nonetheless, even these "pious" women defended their alliance with Woodhull and rejected the conventional moral divide that separated "good" women from "bad." "God has raised up Woodhull to embody all questions of fellowship in political work [among] women irrespective of character," declared Isabella Beecher Hooker.[34] Instead of joining in a crusade against the immorality of women, New Departure suffragists began to attack the "hypocrisy" of men. Woodhull had been "raised up of God," Paulina Wright Davis claimed, to expose the perfidy of "a class that no one dares touch," men who said one thing and did another, men in power.[35] They shifted accusations of immorality not only from women to men but also from sexuality to politics. The true prostitutes, Woodhull asserted, were Republican leaders, who sold out principles for party power and wealth.[36]

In late 1871, in the midst of this increasingly sexualized political context, the first New Departure cases began to reach the dockets of the federal courts. One was the case of Sara Spencer and seventy other women from the District of Columbia, who sued election officials under the Enforcement Act for refusing to permit them to vote. The District of Columbia was a deliberate choice for testing the New Departure argument. There, as advocates of black suffrage had first realized in 1867, the power of the federal government over the suffrage was not complicated by questions of dual sovereignty and states rights.[37]

In October Judge Cartter of the Supreme Court of the District of Columbia ruled against Spencer. Cartter conceded that the Fourteenth Amendment included women along with men in the privileges and immunities of national citizenship; however, he rejected the democratic theory of suffrage on which the case rested. To concede that voting was a right was, in his opinion, to open the door to anarchy and would "involve the destruction of civil government." "The right of all men to vote is as fully recognized in the population of our large centres and cities as can well be done," wrote Cartter. "The result . . . is political profligacy and violence verging upon anarchy."[38] The larger context of the opinion, therefore, was anxiety about democratic politics, and Cartter's concern for the proper position of women in society was secondary. This was true of the entire New Departure debate (and perhaps of judicial disposition of women's rights claims more generally); it was conducted primarily in terms of "rights," not woman's sphere. What was claimed or denied for women was claimed or denied for all citizens, especially those previously excluded from rights due them. Whether this was because the question of women's place was subsumed in a more general struggle for political democracy or because sex-prejudice was still unspeakable in constitutional terms, the consequence was the same: denying women the rights they claimed under general provisions weakened those provisions in general.

The observation that general questions of constitutional rights had

overtaken the specific discourse on woman's place is even clearer in the
next major New Departure decision, the *Myra Bradwell* case. *Bradwell*
was the first case touching on the New Departure to reach the Supreme
Court. In 1869 Myra Bradwell, a Chicago feminist and pioneering woman
lawyer, was refused admission to the Illinois bar. The grounds on which
the state supreme court refused her application, along with the initial
brief that Bradwell submitted in response, were concerned entirely with
coverture, that is, with the question of the disabilities of married women
before the law. By the time Bradwell brought her case before the U.S.
Supreme Court in October 1871, she had changed the terms radically.
Her case was no longer about coverture but had been reformulated in
entirely New Departure terms. Her brief argued that her right to practice
law was a citizen's right and that Illinois's action in refusing her was
prohibited by the Fourteenth Amendment. As for coverture, she asserted
that "the great innovation of the XIV Amendment . . . sweeps away the
principles of the common law," so that even reforms of married women's
property rights were no longer necessary. The *Bradwell* case is one of the
few concerning women's rights commonly included in the history of
constitutional law, but in my opinion it is not correctly situated, since it is
usually cited to illustrate judicial assumptions about woman's place rather
than the constitutional issues of citizenship on which it was actually
argued and decided.[39]

Bradwell's case was closely watched by suffragists as an indication of
how much support to expect from the Republican party. Bradwell was
represented before the Supreme Court by Senator Matthew Carpenter,
one of the major second-generation leaders of the Republican party.
While Carpenter took up Bradwell's case and argued it in strong Fourteenth Amendment terms, he prefaced his case with an equally strong
argument about why the right to vote was not covered by the Reconstruction amendments. He insisted, in other words, on a distinction between
civil and political rights. While the federal government protected civil
rights, women's as well as men's, Carpenter argued, the suffrage remained
under the control of the states, beyond the lawful interference of federal
power.[40]

Suffragists were understandably confused by the way Carpenter argued
Bradwell's case. Was it an indication that Republican leaders were in
favor of the New Departure or against it? Stanton allowed herself to be
encouraged; if women were covered along with men under the Fourteenth Amendment, wasn't the fundamental point of equal rights won?[41]
Victoria Woodhull, however, saw it differently; she argued that women
might be admitted to the benefits of the postwar amendments only to
find those amendments so narrowed that they bestowed virtually nothing

at all, certainly not political rights. She charged that Republicans, "frightened by the grandeur and the extent" of the amendments they had enacted, had retreated to the enemies' doctrine of states' rights, where their own greatest achievements would ultimately be undone.[42]

The Supreme Court held back its decision on *Bradwell* until after the election. To trace the final judicial disposition of the suffragists' constitutional arguments, we have to understand what was at stake in this election and what a Republican victory would mean. The election of 1872 was a crisis for the Republicans.[43] In June 1872 an important group of reformers split off from regular Republicans to run an independent presidential campaign. These political rebels, the Liberal Republicans, based their revolt on the old opposition between central government and individual rights. From the perspective of feminists, who were also looking for a political alternative to the regular Republicans, the terms of the bolt were particularly disappointing. Feminists had learned from freedmen to see the federal government not as a threat to their rights but as the agency for winning them.

To add insult to injury, the Liberal Republicans picked as their candidate Horace Greeley, a man who had made his opposition to woman suffrage clear many years before. Infuriated by the nomination of Greeley, many New Departure suffragists campaigned actively for Ulysses Grant in 1872.[44] The regular Republicans cultivated their support, sending them about the country on official speaking tours and inserting a timid little reference to "additional rights" for women in their platform, a plank so insignificant that suffragists called it a "splinter." Holding off a decision on *Bradwell* was consistent with this temporary friendliness. Anthony expected that if Republicans won, they would reward women with the suffrage by recognizing the New Departure claims. She was so sure that when she came home from her last speaking tour on election day, she gathered together friends and relatives and went down to her local polling place to submit her vote for Grant. Although the local Republican official accepted the votes of fifteen of the demonstrators, including Anthony,[45] a few weeks later a U.S. marshall came to her house and arrested her for violation of federal law—the Enforcement Act.

Anthony's arrest was a signal that the Republicans were ready to dispose of the New Departure. Because she was the most famous woman suffragist in the nation, there is good reason to suspect her arrest had been authorized at the highest level of government. The conduct of her trial several months later reinforces this suspicion. The trial was moved from her home county, where she had lectured extensively to educate potential jurors, to another venue. The judge was no small-town jurist but a recent appointee to the U.S. Supreme Court. He refused to submit the case to the jury, instead directing a guilty verdict from the bench, a practice that was later found unconstitutional. Years later, Anthony's lawyer observed, "There never was a trial in the country with one half the importance of Miss Anthony's. . . . If Anthony had won her case on the merit it would have revolutionized the suffrage of the country. . . . There was a prearranged determination to convict her. A jury trial was dangerous and so the Constitution was deliberately and openly violated." Anthony was not even permitted to appeal.[46]

In general, the outcome of the election cleared the way for the Republican party to retreat from the radical implications of the postwar amendments. There is a link between the judicial dismissal of the feminists' New Departure and the larger repudiation of the postwar amendments. It is embodied in the fact that the Supreme Court's opinions on *Bradwell* and on the *Slaughterhouse* cases were delivered on the same day in 1873. *Slaughterhouse* is generally considered the fundamental Fourteenth Amendment Supreme Court decision. The case involved a group of Louisiana butchers who challenged a state law regulating their occupation on the grounds that it violated their rights as federal citizens (to practice their vocation—the same issue as *Bradwell*) and that the Fourteenth Amendment established the supremacy of national over state citizenship.[47]

Six months after the election, the Court delivered negative opinions in both cases, interpreting the Fourteenth Amendment very narrowly and finding it inapplicable in both cases. The case that the Court lingered over was *Slaughterhouse*.[48] By a bare majority, it ruled that the amendment's intent was only to ensure "the freedom of the slave race" and that it did not transfer the jurisdiction over fundamental civil rights from state to federal government. The opinion in *Bradwell* covered much less territory but did so by a larger majority. The Court merely rejected the claim that the right to practice law was one of the privileges and immunities of federal citizenship protected by the amendment. Beyond that, the Court simply commented that "the opinion just delivered in the Slaughterhouse Cases . . . renders elaborate argument in the present case unnecessary."[49] We should not be misled by this preemptory dismissal, however. The very interpretation under which the *Slaughterhouse* cases had been decided, that the Fourteenth Amendment was limited to matters of race and did not elevate national over state citizenship, had first been articulated in 1871 in the Majority Report of the House Judiciary Committee, rejecting Victoria Woodhull's claim that the Fourteenth Amendment guaranteed her right to vote.

The Supreme Court ruled conclusively against the New Departure two years later, in 1875. The case in which it did so was *Minor v.*

Happersett, brought, appropriately enough, by Virginia Minor, the woman who had first argued that as a citizen of the United States, she was constitutionally protected in her right to vote. Like Anthony, Minor had tried to vote in the 1872 election, but when her vote was refused, she brought suit under the Enforcement Act. The Missouri courts ruled against her, and she appealed to the U.S. Supreme Court on the grounds that constitutional protections of the citizen's right to vote invalidated any state regulations to the contrary. The Court ruled unanimously against her. Since the *Slaughterhouse* and *Bradwell* cases had disposed of the first element of the New Departure, that the Fourteenth Amendment established the supremacy of national citizenship, the decision in *Minor* concentrated on the second assertion, that suffrage was a right of citizenship. On this, the Court ruled starkly that "the Constitution of the United States does not confer the right of suffrage upon any one."[50]

Here, too, there was an intimate link between the fate of woman suffragists' constitutional claims and that of the Reconstruction amendments in general. The day after the Court delivered its opinion in *Minor,* it heard arguments in *United States v. Cruikshank.* In this case and in the *United States v. Reese,* black men for the first time brought suit under the Enforcement Act for protection of their political rights under the Fourteenth and Fifteenth amendments, and the Court ruled against them. In the process of ruling against the plaintiffs, the Court found the Enforcement Act, under which both feminists and freedmen had sought protection, unconstitutional. Citing the recent decision in *Minor,* the Court ruled that inasmuch as the Constitution did not bestow the suffrage on anyone, the federal courts were outside their jurisdiction in protecting the freedmen's political rights.

The rejection of woman suffrage arguments on the grounds that the Fifteenth Amendment was only intended to forbid disfranchisement by race paved the way for a reading of the Fifteenth Amendment that was so narrow it did not even protect the freedmen themselves. In its decision in *United States v. Reese,* the Court argued that the plaintiff, although a black man, had not proved that his vote was denied on the grounds of race and so was not covered by constitutional protections. Eventually, of course, the freedmen were effectively disfranchised on grounds of income, residence, and education, all surrogates for race. Anthony had anticipated this connection. At her own trial, she predicted that the general narrowing of the Reconstruction amendments would follow on the heels of the repudiation of women's claims of equal rights under them. "If we once establish the false principle, that United States citizenship does not carry with it the right to vote in every state in this Union," she said, "there is no end to the petty freaks and cunning devices that will be resorted to to exclude one and another class of citizens from the right of suffrage."[51]

Three years after the *Minor* defeat, suffragists began their pursuit of a separate constitutional amendment to prohibit disfranchisement on account of sex. At many levels, this was a less radical strategy. With the defeat of the New Departure, winning the vote for women was no longer tied to an overall democratic interpretation of the Constitution. To the degree that the struggle for women's votes was not strategically linked to the general defense of political democracy, that its goal was "woman suffrage" not "universal suffrage," elitist and racist tendencies faced fewer barriers, had freer reign, and imparted a more conservative character to suffragism over the next half-century.

Yet, despite this very important strategic shift, the New Departure period left a deep mark on the history of feminism. From time to time, some suffragist would see possibilities in the existing propositions of the Constitution and propose some clever legal mechanism for exploiting them.[52] Even direct action voting never completely died away. Twenty years after the *Minor* decision, Elizabeth Grannis of New York City made her eighth attempt to register to vote.[53] Certainly the larger spirit of militant direct action resurfaced in a spectacular way in the last decade of the American suffrage movement. The deepest mark of the New Departure, however, was to make women's rights and political equality indelibly constitutional issues. As Susan B. Anthony wrote, she "had learned . . . through the passage of the Fourteenth and Fifteenth amendments that it had been possible to amend [the Constitution] in such a way as to enfranchise an entire new class of voters."[54] The *Minor* case, the historian Norma Basch has observed, "drew the inferiority of women's status out of the grooves of common law assumptions and state provisions and thrust it into the maelstrom of constitutional conflict. The demand for woman suffrage . . . acquired a contentious national life."[55]

NOTES

1. The literature generated by the contemporary feminist debate on equality versus difference is enormous. Two excellent analyses by historians are Linda Gordon, "On Difference," *Genders* 10 (Spring 1991): 91-111; and Joan Scott, "Deconstructing Equality-versus-Difference; or the Uses of Poststructuralist Theory for Feminism," *Feminist Studies* 14 (Spring 1988): 33-50. Jean Beth Elshtain criticizes the appropriateness of "androgynous" concepts for feminist analysis; see, for instance, "Against Androgyny," *Telos* 47 (1981): 5-21. In a recent article, Lisa Vogel explores the implications of this debate for feminist legal scholarship:

"Debating Difference: Feminism, Pregnancy, and the Workplace," *Feminist Studies* 16 (Spring 1990): 9-32.

2. For a sampling of critical legal studies scholarship on the limitations of rights thinking, see Mark Tushnet, "An Essay on Rights," *Texas Law Review* 62 (May 1984): 1386; and Peter Gabel, "The Phenomenology of Rights Consciousness and the Pact of Withdrawn Selves," ibid., 1563-99. Frances Olsen develops the implications of this perspective for feminism; see "Statutory Rape: A Feminist Critique of Rights Analysis," *Texas Law Review* 63 (October 1984): 387-42. From the perspective of a woman of color, Patricia Williams criticizes this dismissal of rights consciousness; see "Alchemical Notes: Reconstructed Ideals from Deconstructed Rights," *Harvard Civil Rights Civil Liberties Law Review* 22 (Spring 1987): 401-33. From the perspective of political philosophy, Nancy Fraser considers the translation of "needs claims" frequently made on women's behalf into "rights claims"; see "Struggle over Needs: Outline of a Socialist-Feminist Critical Theory of Late-Capitalist Political Culture," in *Women, the State, and Welfare,* ed. Linda Gordon (Madison: University of Wisconsin Press, 1990), 199-225.

3. Paula Baker made this argument most forcefully for the pre-1920 period; see "The Domestication of Politics: Women and American Political Society, 1780-1920," *American Historical Review* 89 (June 1984): 620-47. The implications of her argument for the existence of a separate women's political culture after 1920 are ambiguous. Susan Ware, in her biography of Molly Dewson (*Partner and I: Molly Dewson, Feminism, and New Deal Politics* [New Haven, Conn.: Yale University Press, 1987]), adapts Baker's argument to the post-1920 era. For a complex and interesting overview of the historical literature on woman's sphere and women's political involvement, see Lori Ginzberg, "Introduction," in *Women and the Work of Benevolence* (New Haven, Conn.: Yale University Press, 1990). In her focus on the continuing importance of women's voluntary organizations in the post-suffrage period, Anne Firor Scott herself is inclined to accept the importance of a distinct women's political culture after, as well as before, the Nineteenth Amendment; see her *Natural Allies: Women's Associations in American History* (Urbana: University of Illinois Press, 1991).

4. Ellen Carol DuBois, *Feminism and Suffrage: The Emergence of an Independent Women's Movement in America, 1848-1869* (Ithaca, N.Y.: Cornell University Press, 1978); Elizabeth Cady Stanton, *Eighty Years and More: Reminiscences, 1815-1897,* ed. Ellen Carol DuBois (Boston: Northeastern University Press, 1993 [1898]), 242. In the context of women's history, emphasizing the opposition of woman suffrage leaders to the Fourteenth and Fifteenth amendments has highlighted the collapse of the prewar abolitionist unity of women's rights and black rights and the rise of a new racism in the woman suffrage movement.

5. The constitutional issues raised by the "New Departure" became, like virtually every other political issue, an element in the American/National split. To distinguish itself from the National Association and the New Departure constitutional strategy it advocated, the American Association advocated a separate woman suffrage constitutional amendment throughout the early 1870s.

Ironically, this proposal for what would have then been a Sixteenth Amendment had first been made by Elizabeth Stanton in 1869 as a protest against the "manhood suffrage" of the Fifteenth Amendment, then still pending. But just as the original National proposal for a woman suffrage amendment was primarily a protest against the black suffrage amendment rather than a strategy in its own right, so the American's advocacy of it was primarily a protest against the New Departure approach. Full-fledged advocacy of a separate woman suffrage amendment did not begin until the late 1870s, when it became the trademark demand of the National. The American, again seeking to distinguish itself from its rival, focused its energies on state suffrage campaigns. See Elizabeth C. Stanton, Susan B. Anthony, and Matilda J. Gage, eds. *History of Woman Suffrage*, vol. 2 (Rochester, N.Y.: Susan B. Anthony, 1881), 350-55, 802-17 (hereafter cited as HWS).

6. Stanton, *Eighty Years and More*, 242.

7. HWS, vol. 2, 407-520; Ida Husted Harper, ed., *Life and Work of Susan B. Anthony*, vol. 1 (Indianapolis: Bowen-Merrill, 1899), 409-48.

8. HWS, vol. 2, 407-10; on the Minors, see Louise R. Noun, *Strong Minded Women: The Emergence of the Woman Suffrage Movement in Iowa* (Ames: Iowa State University Press, 1969), 168-69.

9. David Montgomery notes the importance of this Reconstruction Era shift in attitude to the positive state in *Beyond Equality: Labor and the Radical Republicans, 1862-1872* (New York: Random House, 1967), 80-81.

10. On this aspect of Reconstruction Era constitutional thought, see Judith A. Baer, *Equality under the Constitution: Reclaiming the Fourteenth Amendment* (Ithaca, N.Y.: Cornell University Press, 1983).

11. While the Fifteenth Amendment was still pending, the Minors found an alternative constitutional basis for their claim that suffrage was a natural right in the frequently cited 1820 case *Corfield v. Coryell*, which included the franchise as one of the privileges and immunities protected in Article IV.

12. In New Hampshire in 1870, Matilda Ricker tried to vote (HWS, vol. 2, 586-87). In New York in 1871, Matilda Joslyn Gage tried to vote in Fayetteville, and a group of women, led by Louise Mansfield, tried to vote in Nyack (HWS, vol. 3, 406; Isabelle K. Savelle, *Ladies' Lib: How Rockland Women Got the Vote* [New York: Rockland Historical Society, 1979], 13-16); in New York City, Victoria Woodhull and Tennessee Claflin tried to vote (Johanna Johnston, *Mrs. Satan* [New York: Popular Library, 1967], 110). In Connecticut, Anna Middlebrook and nineteen others tried to vote in Bridgeport, and Louise Mateen led a group in Hadlyone (*Woodhull and Claflin's Weekly*, April 22, 1871, 5). In Hyde Park, Illinois, also in 1871, Catherine Waite, wife of an important Republican politician, tried to vote (HWS, vol. 2, 601, and vol. 3, 571-72); and in California, her sister-in-law, Mrs. Van Valkenburg, tried in the same year (HWS, vol. 3, 766).

13. HWS, vol. 3, 461-62; see also HWS, vol. 2, 600-601.

14. Eleanor Flexner, *Century of Struggle: The Women's Rights Movement in the United States* (Cambridge, Mass.: Belknap Press, 1959), 168, citing the *Revolution*, November 19, 1868, 307. On the links between spiritualism and

women's rights, see Anne Braude, *Radical Spirits: Spiritualism and Women's Rights in Nineteenth Century America* (Boston: Beacon, 1991).

15. HWS, vol. 3, 780-86.

16. Ibid., 784.

17. Benjamin Quarles, "Frederick Douglass and the Woman's Rights Movement," *Journal of Negro History* 25 (June 1940): 35.

18. HWS, vol. 3, 523-24.

19. Ibid., 766.

20. Ibid., vol. 2, 443-48.

21. "The Constitution defines a woman born or naturalized in the United States, and subject to the jurisdiction thereof, to be a citizen. It recognizes the right of citizens to vote." Ibid., 445.

22. Victoria C. Woodhull, *Constitutional Equality: A Lecture Delivered at Lincoln Hall, Washington, D.C., February 16, 1871* (New York: Journeymen Printers Co-operative Association, 1871).

23. HWS, vol. 2, 445-46. The comment on "blending" was made in Woodhull's arguments in support of her congressional memorial. These are available in Victoria Woodhull, *The Argument for Woman's Electoral Rights under Amendments XIV and XV of the Constitution of the United States* (London: G. Norman and Son, 1887), 44.

24. Both reports can be found in HWS, vol. 2, 461-82.

25. Ibid., 469, 478. In support of their interpretation, they cited the federal district court's decision in what was called the *Crescent City* case, later renamed the *Slaughterhouse* cases.

26. Woodhull, *Constitutional Equality*, 4.

27. Martha Wright complained to Elizabeth Stanton about a congressman who "said rudely to Mrs. Davis & Mrs. Griffing, 'You just call on us because you like to,'" to which Mrs. Griffing answered "'We call on you, because it is the only way known to us, to present our appeal to you,' & Mrs. Davis said 'You must remember that we are your constituents.'" Wright to Stanton, December 29, 1870, Garrison Family Collection, Smith College, Northampton, Mass.

28. HWS, vol. 2, 489.

29. Isabella Beecher Hooker to the Editor, *Independent*, February 11, 1871, reprinted in *Woodhull and Claflin's Weekly*, March 4, 1871, 10.

30. Ibid.; *An Appeal to the Women of the United States by the National Woman Suffrage and Educational Committee* (Hartford, Conn.: National Woman Suffrage Association, April 19, 1871).

31. Woodhull's response to the charges can be found in the *New York World*, May 22, 1871, 3. A close study of "free love" attacks on Frances Wright in the 1820s would probably show a similar pattern.

32. "The Voice of Apollo Hall," *Every Saturday*, June 17, 1871, 554.

33. Victoria C. Woodhull, *The Principles of Social Freedom, Delivered in New York City, November 20, 1871* (New York: Woodhull, Claflin and Company, 1871), 23-24.

34. Isabella Beecher Hooker to Anna E. Dickenson, April 22, [1871], box 9, Dickenson Papers, Library of Congress, Washington, D.C.

35. Paulina Wright Davis to Woodhull, May 29, 1871, Victoria Woodhull Martin Collection, Southern Illinois University, Carbondale.

36. Victoria C. Woodhull, "The Speech of Victoria C. Woodhull before the National Woman's Suffrage Convention at Apollo Hall, May 11, 1871," reprinted in Woodhull, *The Argument for Women's Electoral Rights,* 137.

37. HWS, vol. 2, 587-99. Spencer's lawyer was Arthur Riddle, former congressman from Ohio and one of Woodhull's advisers. Riddle emphasized the relationship between the Fourteenth and Fifteenth amendments. The Fifteenth Amendment, he contended, was only important inasmuch as it invalidated what he called "the mischief" of the second section of the Fourteenth. Inasmuch as the right to vote is assumed to exist by the Fifteenth Amendment, it was actually conferred by the first section of the Fourteenth.

38. Ibid., 598.

39. Ibid., 622. The opinion in *Bradwell* that is usually cited is not the terse dismissal of the Fourteenth Amendment argument that settled the case, but an individual concurring opinion by Justice Bradley that addressed the coverture issues that Bradwell had removed from her argument.

40. HWS, vol. 2, 618.

41. Elizabeth Cady Stanton, "Argument before the Senate Judiciary Committee," January 11, 1872, reprinted in *Woodhull and Claflin's Weekly,* January 27, 1872, 7; see also Stanton to Woodhull, December 29, [1872], Stanton Miscellaneous Papers, New York Public Library, New York.

42. Woodhull anticipated that if a narrow construction of the Fifteenth Amendment was adopted, if the southern states were only forbidden to disfranchise the freedmen "because they belonged to the African race, they might have invented any other reason and excluded them in spite of Congress. If this doctrine prevail, I do not see why the States may not . . . find reasons to exclude every negro in them from the ballot." Victoria Woodhull, *Carpenter and Cartter Reviewed: A Speech before the National Suffrage Association at Lincoln Hall, Washington, D.C., January 10, 1872* (New York: Woodhull, Claflin and Company, 1872), 20.

43. Montgomery, *Beyond Equality,* 379-86.

44. "We must make it hot for the Cincinnatians for their neglect to recognize us." Anthony to Stanton, July 10, 1872, box 38, National American Woman Suffrage Association Papers, Library of Congress.

45. Nancy A. Hewitt, *Women's Activism and Social Change: Rochester, New York, 1822-1872* (Ithaca, N.Y.: Cornell University Press, 1984), 211. Anthony to Stanton, November 5, 1872, Harper Papers, Huntington Library, San Marino, Calif.: "Well I have been & gone & done it!! positively voted the republican ticket strait this A.M. at 7 o'clock & *swore my vote in at that.* Was registered on Friday & 15 other women followed suit in this ward. Then on Sunday others some 20 or thirty other women *tried to register,* but all save two were refused. All my three sisters voted. Rhoda De Garmo too. Amy Post was

rejected & she will immediately bring action against the registrars. . . . I hope the morning's telegrams will tell of many women all over the country trying to vote. It is splendid that without any concert of action so many should have moved here. . . . If only *now all the woman suffrage women* would work to this end, of *enforcing* the *existing constitutional* supremacy of *national law* over state law, what strides we might make this very winter. But I'm awful tired—for five days I have been on the constant run, but to splendid purpose, so all right. I hope you voted too."

46. Harper, ed., *The Life and Work of Susan B. Anthony*, vol. 1, 423-53. The case was heard before Judge Ward Hunt, appointed to the Supreme Court in December 1872 at the suggestion of Roscoe Conkling. Charles Fairman, *History of the Supreme Court*, vol. 7 (New York: Macmillan, 1987), 224. Hunt voted with the majority in the *Slaughterhouse* cases. Anthony was sure that Conkling was responsible for his decision against her. Harper, ed., *The Life and Work of Susan B. Anthony*, vol. 1, 441.

47. Moreover, Matthew Carpenter, who had been Myra Bradwell's counsel, was counsel for the *defendants* in the *Slaughterhouse* cases. On the surface, this appears inconsistent: Carpenter argued for the applicability of the Fourteenth Amendment in *Bradwell*, but he argued against it in *Slaughterhouse*. I think there is a consistency in his position, though, especially when we remember how much of his argument in *Bradwell* was against the inclusion of the suffrage in the "privileges and immunities" of the Fourteenth Amendment; the consistency resides in Carpenter's determination, on behalf of the Republican leadership, to control and limit the breadth of the Fourteenth Amendment. Fairman, *History of the Supreme Court*, 285. Carpenter's argument in *Slaughterhouse* can be found in 21 Court Reporters Lawyers Edition, 399-401 (1872).

48. 16 Wall. 36 (1873). The language of the *Slaughterhouse* opinion frequently identifies races with men; for instance, since "the laws were administered by the white man alone . . . a race of men distinctively marked as was the negro" could not expect justice. I presume such language was not accidental but reflected the coexistence of arguments that women were persons also, or, as Victoria Woodhull had said, that "races contain both men and women."

49. 16 Wall. 130 (1873).

50. HWS, vol. 2, 734-42.

51. Ibid., 641.

52. The most important of these was Catherine McCullough's successful argument that the Constitution permitted states legislatively to enfranchise voters for presidential electors. This argument for "presidential suffrage" seems to have begun with Henry Blackwell in the 1890s. In 1914 Illinois passed a "presidential suffrage" law, giving women votes in the 1916 presidential election. See Steven W. Buechler, *The Transformation of the Woman Suffrage Movement: The Case of Illinois, 1850-1920* (New Brunswick, N.J.: Rutgers University Press, 1986), 174-76.

53. Unidentified clipping, vol. 12, p. 75, Susan B. Anthony Memorial Library Collection, Huntington Library, San Marino, Calif.

54. HWS, vol. 4, 10.

55. Norma Basch, "Reconstructing Female Citizenship" (Paper delivered at Women and the Constitution Conference, American University and the Smithsonian, October 1987).

Rebecca Latimer Felton
and the Problem of "Protection"
in the New South

LeeAnn Whites

On November 21, 1922, women packed the galleries of the U.S. Senate. Delegations from every women's organization in Washington were present for the introduction of the first woman senator ever. Hale and hearty despite her eighty-seven years, the new junior senator from Georgia rose to give her maiden speech. "The women of the country have reason to rejoice," she asserted. "This day a door has been opened to them that never was opened before."[1] Rebecca Latimer Felton had particular reason to rejoice, and to be proud, for not only was she the first woman to be so honored but, equally important to her, she was a woman of the South, of Georgia. As she later wrote, "It meant that a woman reared in the sheltered security of an antebellum plantation was to be the first of her sex to sit in the U.S. Senate. It was hard to realize.... Who in that day would have had the hardihood to predict that the time would come when Georgia women would hold public office?"[2]

Who would have had the hardihood to predict it even two years earlier, when the South, almost to a state, refused to ratify the Nineteenth Amendment? And who would have looked to the state of Georgia, whose legislators had rushed to be the first to go on record in opposition to the amendment?[3] Perhaps only Rebecca Felton herself, long a power in state Democratic circles, even without the vote, and savvy in the ways of southern politics and southern gender relations. Having grown up in the antebellum South, she understood the intensity of planter-class men's commitment to the protection and the subordination of their women. Having endured the hard years of Civil War and Reconstruction, she also understood the personal and economic necessities that had led to the new public roles that women took on during those years.[4] How to reconcile the old values of protection and seclusion with the new realities of independence and public status for women? This was the critical problem of elite southern gender relations in the late nineteenth-century South. It was in this context that Felton carved out a new role for herself. In negotiating these contradictory cross currents, she found a place for herself and for women of her class and race. She emerged as one of the preeminent new women of the New South.[5]

At first glance, Rebecca Latimer Felton's early life course gives little indication of her eventual emergence as a leading spokesperson for women's rights.[6] Born in 1835 on her family's plantation in DeKalb County, she grew up in a prosperous planter family. The oldest of the four Latimer children, she was particularly close to her father. Eventually, he sent her to live with kinfolk in the town of Madison so she could attend the Female College there and acquire the best higher education then available to women in the state. Upon graduating at age seventeen, Rebecca Latimer promptly married the graduation speaker, William Felton, a man of many talents: medical doctor, minister, planter, and politician.

For Rebecca Latimer Felton, the role of the plantation mistress, which she took up at eighteen, was one to which she had been reared. It was the life of her mother and her grandmother before her and the one she assumed her daughters would occupy after her. Even toward the end of her long life, in what had become a much different South, she continued to see the antebellum plantation mistress as a feminine ideal. "The mother of eleven children," she wrote of her grandmother, "her industry, her management and her executive ability in caring for and carrying out her household affairs are still wonderful memories." Such women presented, in Felton's estimation, *the* model for womanly endeavor and as such provided her with "examples in my own extended life."[7]

By the same token, Rebecca Latimer Felton's male ideal remained in many ways that of the antebellum planter class, men like her grandfather and father, whom she described as being as hardworking and as industrious as their wives. Her grandfather ran a grain mill and sawmill, along with his plantation, and her father combined plantation work with management of a tavern and local store. In Felton's recollection, these men cast a long shadow, a shadow that kept their women in the shade of the plantation, sheltered from the outside world. "The wife and mother," she wrote, "were like plants in the deep forest. Their softness and dependence were derived from the shade. A woman's home was the center as well as the circumference of her efforts for civilization or humanity."[8]

In her book *The Southern Lady*, Anne Scott has discussed the apparently contradictory role of the antebellum plantation mistress, caught between her authority and responsibility within the plantation and her subordination to the planter within both the household and the public arena.[9] Although some planter-class women expressed their discontent with this role through private outpourings in their diaries, Felton, at least in retrospect, understood that elite women's subordination was the price they paid for their class and race privileges. Few women anywhere, Felton argued, could lay claim to such a retinue of "servants," to such an extended domestic place. "No wonder," she concluded, "matrimony was the goal of the average woman's existence." The only acceptable alternative was that of the schoolmistress, and even she "usually married some man with slaves to wait on her." Better to be subordinate but wealthy, in Felton's view, than to be independent and poor.[10]

The planter's public power redounded to the private advantage of the lady. Her public subordination to him not only signified her recognition of his public position but also announced the extent of her own private domain. Through her exaggerated deference and public incapacity, the lady expressed the extent of her own domestic authority. To violate one's place in this world was to break an unspoken agreement, an implicit social balance of power. Only through a studied acceptance of one's place and a strict delineation of its limits could harmony reign. Precisely because elite women's class and racial authority was so substantial within the confines of the plantation, gendered proscriptions against activities outside of it were necessarily all the more intense. As George Fitzhugh so aptly put it in analyzing the nature of "women's rights" in the antebellum South, "In truth, woman, like children, has but one right, and that is the right to protection. The right to protection involves the obligation to obey. . . . If she be obedient, she is in little danger of maltreatment; if she stands upon her rights, is coarse and masculine, man loathes and despises her, and ends by abusing her."[11]

According to Rebecca Felton, women of the planter class rarely broke their end of this agreement. They "obeyed," that is, they minded their place. The rupturing of elite gender relations was the result of the hubris of planter-class men rather than the insubordination of planter-class women.[12] It was planter men who refused to compromise on the issue of slavery, who masterminded secession, and who thereby set in motion a series of events that would forever undermine their ability to offer "protection" to their dependents. It was the wholesale destruction wrought by the Civil War, especially the death and crippling of so many fighting men and the loss of their property in slaves, that eroded the privileged position of planter-class women, rendering them vulnerable to the forces that had long molded the lives of most southern women.

For women of the planter class, the decline of male protection and women's exposure to economic hardship were thus inextricably fused through the crucible of Civil War. Rebecca Felton repeatedly described the impact of the war in terms of her own unprotected "exposure" to the elemental forces of nature. "The War," she wrote, "broke on the South like a thunder clap from an almost clear sky" and brought with it a "four year hail storm."[13] The location of the Felton plantation, outside Cartersville in North Georgia and near a major railroad line, did indeed put them in the center of the storm. A main line of supply for the army of the West, the railroad brought the war to Cartersville early through an almost constant stream of soldiers and supplies and, increasingly, through the return of the wounded and dead. Felton suddenly found herself in the public arena, not as a result of any rejection of her domestic status but in an effort to protect it. There was now an entire army to care for, and women's place was where the hungry, ill clad, and wounded were. Felton helped organize the local Ladies Aid Society and became its first president. Members met the trains, provided food, and took in wounded soldiers who would not survive the rest of the trip. She cut up her dresses for uniforms and ended the war in homespun. Running out of coffee, sugar, and salt, she found substitutes.

Eventually, the strategic location of the Felton plantation made it necessary for Rebecca herself to find refuge. Her husband, who was then serving as a Confederate surgeon, was able to secure an old farm outside Macon. Here Rebecca, her two children, and what remained of their slaves lived out the last year of the war. What began with the loss of her private domestic status and the stripping of her household to support the war effort would finally end with the virtual destruction of life on the plantation as she had known it. Invading troops razed the buildings, the slaves were emancipated, and her two surviving children died in the last year of the war from tainted water supplies and epidemic disease.[14]

To rehabilitate their plantation after the war, Rebecca and William Felton opened a school. Their neighbors were so impoverished that they frequently paid their children's tuition by working to rebuild the Felton's plantation. In the context of their common struggles, Rebecca Felton came to understand and in some sense to identify with the experience of her yeomen neighbors. She particularly identified with the plight of the women, perhaps widowed and most certainly rendered destitute by the war, who faced an even harder lot than she, "forced to work in the field," as she wrote, "or worse."[15]

The bonds forged with other Confederate women in the heat of battle were thus strengthened in the lingering misery of the postwar era; they would come to form the basis for Felton's political activities for the rest of her life. Left to their own devices, women like Rebecca Felton had become a "wonder to themselves."[16] Not only could they support themselves but they could even aspire to making a vital contribution to the well-being of the less advantaged members of their own sex. As much as Felton came to value this new independence among women, however, she feared with a passion the economic necessity, the threat of "exposure" that drove it on. More than ever she valued her own domestic privilege, what was left of it.

Rebecca Latimer Felton was of two minds. Like other women throughout history, she agonized over the trade-offs between freedom and protection.[17] That which was "progressive" in her looked to the expansion of her own autonomy and that of other women as well. That which was fearful and threatened looked back longingly to the old days when protection and seclusion had been the experience of women of her race and class. She railed at those she held responsible for its decline. And who was responsible? Felton never answered this question in a consistent fashion, anymore than she ever made a clean break with the desirability of male "protection." As the years passed and elite women emerged more securely as public figures in their own right, Felton did begin to argue with mounting forcefulness that it was the men of her class who were responsible, because they were the ones who had allowed the profitability of slavery and the lure of the market to override their sense of responsibility to domestic dependents. The domestically responsible course, according to Felton, would have been to compromise with the North and agree to gradual and compensated emancipation. Instead, having grown "overblown" with their own self-importance, slaveowning men recklessly threw the entire plantation world into the crucible of war.[18]

At her most independent and outspoken, Felton was inclined to expound on the shortcomings of male dominance at great length. When confronted with the economic vulnerability that these shortcomings had created for women, however, she concluded that some male protection was preferable to none at all. To salvage what little remained of antebellum "protection," she was inclined to limit her criticism of patriarchal social relations, or at least to exempt those few individual men, like her father and husband, who initially opposed secession. In her dependent, vulnerable persona, she was inclined to criticize not patriarchy per se but those individual men whom she regarded as inadequate or downright dangerous. Gingerly criticizing hotheaded secessionists, she reserved her greatest ire for those two-faced scalawags who supported Reconstruction governments and the empowerment of black freedmen. To Felton, the very existence of free blacks, not to mention their assumption of political authority, was a constant reminder of all the ways in which the planter patriarchy had failed.

Indeed, it was freedmen who engendered Felton's most intense feelings of animosity in the postwar context. Unable to confront fully the white man's failure to live up to his domestic responsibilities, she became preoccupied with the freedman's failure to live up to his. In her view, the decline of plantation life and the loss of the protected status it afforded plantation mistresses came to rest squarely on the shoulders of the ex-slaves, whose insubordination and refusal to work were safer targets for her frustrated outrage than were the men of her own class. Indeed, Felton's racial politics reflected her own experience of class power and gendered subordination. When the ownership of slaves had enabled the planter to shelter the women of his family on the plantation, Felton had perceived black slaves as diligent and loyal members of her world. In her reminiscences, the typical slave was the female domestic, who symbolized not only the planter's authority but the authority of the mistress as well. When the fall of slavery left her husband and others of his class economically and politically exposed, the prototypical black became the shiftless male laborer—a dangerous, threatening, foreboding figure, whom she envisioned as fundamentally out of his place in the postwar world, plundering her fields rather than laboring diligently in them.[19]

The collapse of the slave-based plantation economy created a virtually irreconcilable tension for Felton. Her desire for gender equity was countered by the devastating economic vulnerability she witnessed among the women around her, particularly among those who were without male "protection." It was this tension that drove her into the political arena. In the summer of 1874 William Felton entered the race for the U.S. Congress as an Independent, committed to representing the interests of the yeoman farmer in his upcountry county, Bartow. Rebecca Felton began her political career in support of her husband's candidacy, by acting as his campaign manager, scheduling his speaking engagements, arranging to have others speak for him, and writing numerous letters to the local press in response to attacks on his positions. For the Feltons, one legacy of the new womanly roles opened during the war was the possibility for a new kind of partnership in postwar politics. William Felton not only accommodated himself to his wife's new public activities but also actively facilitated her further political development. It was widely rumored, for instance, that Rebecca Felton not only wrote newspaper editorials in the doctor's defense, which she signed "Plowboy" or "Bartow," but wrote parts of his speeches as well.[20]

If this partnership reflected the possibilities created for more equitable relations between the sexes in the postwar South, the hostile public response reflected the larger social limitations imposed on couples that assumed such relative gender equality. Widespread derision of Rebecca Felton's participation in her husband's campaign reflected the fact that although new roles for women created the opportunity for more equitable gender relations, they were even more certain to create a gender backlash, particularly among economically and psychologically diminished men. Having been forced by the exigencies of the period to give up some aspects of their former dominance, many southern men clung with increased insistence to those forms that remained. The political sphere was the one arena to which women had virtually no entree in the 1870s and 1880s, and most southern white males, defeated and defensive, intended to maintain their sexual prerogatives there. As Rebecca Felton herself recalled, "I was called a 'petticoat reformer' and subject to plenty of ridicule, in public and in private."[21] Her husband was subject to ridicule as well. One local paper went so far as to entitle the announcement of William Felton's reelection to the U.S. Congress in 1878 "Mrs. Felton and Doctor Reelected."[22]

Beyond a certain point, the hostility Rebecca Felton's political assistance engendered became a liability to her husband and outweighed the benefits that her intelligence, argumentative skill, and political savvy brought. There were real limits to the degree to which William Felton's private acceptance and public support of her work could counteract the impact of a hostile public. Gender norms in the larger society thus set limits on the extent of equity between even the Feltons. Rebecca Felton could contribute her prodigious pen to her husband's speeches, but she had to mask her contributions and certainly could not speak for herself. She could write flaming editorials in defense of his campaign for the "plow boys" of Bartow County, but she could not sign those editorials in her own name. The Feltons' partnership was necessarily based on supporting the development of William Felton's career and the interests of William Felton's yeoman constituency. The emergence of Rebecca Felton's *own* political career awaited the development of a new political constituency in Georgia, a constituency that was shortly to take form throughout the New South.

It was the Woman's Christian Temperance Union (WCTU) that would provide Felton with an audience of her own for the first time. In 1881 Frances Willard, president of the WCTU, made her first southern organizing tour. Friends and supporters tried to dissuade her from making the trip in the first place. As one friend counseled, "It will be a most disastrous failure, for there are three great disadvantages under which you will labor—to go there as a woman, a Northern woman, and a Northern temperance woman."[23] Willard was therefore pleased at the warm reception her plea for home protection received from southern audiences. She was particularly heartened when Rebecca Latimer Felton joined the WCTU in 1886. Felton was a great asset to the fledgling organization, and the benefits were more than reciprocated. Regularly touring the state, she gave rousing speeches for the cause, holding forth against public ridicule and demonstrating that her powers as a speaker, if anything, exceeded her abilities in cold print. By the end of the decade, she had become one of the organization's most prominent orators.[24]

As important as the WCTU was for Felton's development as a public political figure, it was even more important for the way it allowed her to address the gender issue at the center of her concerns—the question of home protection. For Felton, the "drink demon" became a metaphor for the social consequences that the decline of the power of the individual planter and of agricultural life in general in the South had unleashed. In the burgeoning anonymity of the city and with the expansion of free labor, Felton found a threatening world, one full of the "glow of factory furnaces" and the "whirl of machinery." This was a world where a woman could not walk down a street in safety and where her children were particularly exposed and vulnerable. "Tonight," as she told one temperance audience, "there is not a city in Georgia where a decent woman's child can go, and be safe in its streets from the danger and temptation of liquor saloons."[25]

While the Civil War had dealt a crippling blow to the power of white southern men to protect their women, Felton now argued that the "drink demon" constituted an even more formidable threat. Drink promised to destroy what little protection remained to women and children by turning their fathers, husbands, and sons into useless drunkards. According to Felton, the temperance issue revealed the continuing, and in some ways increasingly critical, gap between the rightful place of domesticity in society and its subordinated second-class status in actuality. For a few "sin-cursed dollars," contended Felton, state legislators were even willing to bargain away the well-being of the entire younger generation. "I see them sell a license," she told her audience, "which says to the liquor dealer, you can for such a length of time destroy every man you can reach—not excepting my own son." "Friends, neighbors, citizens," queried Felton in one temperance speech, "what is this curse that walks in darkness and wastes at noonday? . . . Is it not the unholy *gain* that follows liquor selling—and the eternal loss that follows liquor drinking? . . . Oh Men of Georgia, when your hearts prompted you to legislate for hound dogs, and sand hill gophers—why haven't you protected your own offspring? It is this failure to protect that has raised the outcry of temperance women."[26]

As with the issue of slavery, the lure of profit continued to override and undercut men's allegiance to the domestic interests of their families and society as a whole. Now matters were far worse, though. At least under slavery, the subordination of elite women's domestic sphere had been in some measure balanced by the extraordinary profitability of the planter's economic system. Class privilege had served to soften the impact of domestic subordination. In the face of their declining economic position, Felton insisted that elite men now needed to legislate domestic "protection" through the agency of the state. No longer capable of simply controlling their own plantations as relatively self-contained social worlds, they were now called upon to actively represent the domestic interests of their women and children in the political arena. In her temperance speeches around the state, Felton encouraged men to cast their votes for properly "feminized" candidates: "Vote for true men—men who will do your will—men pledged to your protection. Oh Men of Georgia! Your votes will either make or unmake the boys of this generation. This is a crisis. Stand to your homes and vote for no man who will not pledge himself to save these boys."[27]

Insofar as men had failed to take up her challenge and represent women's domestic interests politically, they had, according to Felton, "impeached their own manhood." Women were left with no alternative but to enter the political arena themselves and lobby for a policy of prohibition in defense of their maternal roles. As in the case of women's wartime organization into Ladies Aid societies, public organizational activity under such circumstances did not constitute a rejection of motherhood. Quite the contrary, according to Felton, it manifested the reemergence of a similar kind of militant commitment to domestic defense, an "organized mother love . . . ," "Mother love . . . stung to desperation . . . ," a "Mother love grown bold in its agony. . . ."[28]

The WCTU's politics of empowering motherhood brought elite southern women like Rebecca Felton to the threshold of an exciting but paradoxical new world. Achieving a free and independent motherhood required a precarious balancing act for female politicians with gender as the key to their agenda. While history had taught elite women of Felton's generation that they had to be prepared to earn their own living, the meager prospects for real autonomy for women in the straitened postwar economy led them back to the desirability of access to male income. Felton therefore hesitated to advocate that young women set their sights on the acquisition of a career. She was more eager to see the basic structure of the family, especially the white farm family, reformed along more gender equitable lines.

In the 1890s she took up speaking to rural audiences on the critical but undervalued role of women on the family farm. She urged farmers to recognize the contribution their wives made to farm operation. "In this day of scarce labor, I'd like to know what a farm in Georgia would amount to, as a home, unless there was a woman on it." Farmers, according to Felton, should discard the old adage "A dog, a woman and a walnut tree: The more you beat them the better they be" and replace it with greater respect and appreciation for wives and mothers. Rather than devote all his time and energy to his marketable crops, the farmer should realize that "the best crop a man ever raised in all his life was a crop of good obedient children."[29]

In 1891 Felton proposed a program to the state agricultural society that she called the "Wife's Farm." In recognition of the wife's contribution to the family farm, every farmer in the state should pledge himself to work a portion of his land as his "Wife's Farm." While the wife cooked the husband's breakfast, Felton suggested to her rural audiences, the husband should be out laboring in her fields. Felton assumed that the product of the "Wife's Farm" would be crops for home consumption rather than market production. In this way, the farmer could confront the "vexed question of commercial independence" while promoting the "contentment and happiness of the household."[30] A more balanced relationship between the interests of the family and the demands of the market would be the ultimate result of an agricultural system grounded in gender equity.

Felton claimed that the underlying message of domestic gender equity she offered her farmer audiences of the 1890s was similar to the advice she would have given the men of the antebellum planter class some thirty years earlier, had they asked. Confronted with the specter of a mounting agricultural depression, Felton herself saw the same dark vision: a vision in which southern agriculture and domesticity were undermined by white men's determination to pursue profit in the market at any human cost. Like the antebellum planter, the postwar farmer continued to orient himself toward a fickle market economy at the expense of the more solid and enduring interests of his family. Just as the planter's war had rendered him unable to protect his dependents, so the persistence of a market-oriented culture was once again threatening the very perpetuation of the farm family, leaving lower-class women and children unprotected and exposed.

In the aftermath of Civil War, when Felton herself felt overwhelmingly threatened, she focused her own fears onto the freedman. Unable to blame the husband who could no longer support her as he once had been able to do, she displaced her anger on the freedman who refused to return to his "place" in the postwar order of things. Once again, in the serious agricultural depression of the 1890s, her efforts to seek the roots of the problem in a diagnosis of gender imbalance and a program of domestic reform ended in race baiting. Felton was ultimately reduced to holding the black population, especially black men, responsible for the dire condition of white farm life. Since the most pressing need of the farm population was a "feeling of security in the homes we inhabit, where wives and daughters can be safely protected," it was all too easy to absolve the farmer for his failure to provide these and to visualize danger in terms of the threat of assault and rape on the part of black men. "I know of no evil, which more unsettles farm values and drives farmers to towns and other occupations than this lurking dread of outrage upon their helpless ones—in their homes and on the highways."[31]

Just how far out of balance Felton perceived southern gender relations to be in the 1890s can be seen in the lengths to which she took this argument. Poor white farm women in the 1890s were considerably more "vulnerable" and "exposed" than women of Felton's class had ever been, even in the darkest days of Reconstruction. During the 1890s it seemed to Felton that poor white women were losing their economic security and that their very lives and physical safety were in jeopardy. In the image of the rape of a poor farm woman on an isolated and desolate country road or homestead, Felton found a graphically explicit and emotionally explosive symbol to express the intensity of her fears for the sanctity of motherhood and the necessity for domestic reform.

Despite her best efforts to promote the elevation of motherhood and the realm of reproduction within the farm family, the condition of farm women and children appeared only to deteriorate in the 1890s. If farm men would not or could not sustain their wives and children in a progressive fashion, who or what could? In fact, the failure of gender reform in the countryside caused Felton to appeal with ever more conviction and intensity to the membership of elite women's voluntary organizations. Both because of their dedication to empowering motherhood and because of their commitment to the supremacy of their race, elite white women should throw themselves into reform efforts to improve the lot of rural women and children. The best vehicle to achieve such reform, Felton argued in speech after speech, was to be found in the expansion of educational opportunities for poor youth, especially poor white girls. "Why do I particularly mention poor white girls?," she questioned an audience of the United Daughters of the Confederacy. "Because," she answered, "these girls are the coming mothers of the great majority of the Anglo-Saxon race in the South. The future of the race for the next fifty years is in their hands."[32]

By raising the specter of "race degeneration" in the impoverishment and powerlessness of white motherhood and by pointing to elite women as the only group likely to carry out the reforms necessary to improve the status of these women, Felton lent increased urgency and larger social significance to the organizational activities of elite white women. Should gender reform fail among the mass of the white population, the threat to the entire social structure was so critical that even the voluntary activities of elite women's organizations were not sufficient to the task at hand. Government intervention was required to place a floor below which white motherhood could not be allowed to sink. As much as elite women were the critical actors in voluntary familial reform activity, they were, like the WCTU before them, even more important as the key political pressure group that would move the government to regulate the family in the interests of an improved domestic life. In particular, women's organizations had to pressure the state government to pass compulsory education laws. It was not enough to improve the quality of rural schools. Children must be required to attend them. Furthermore, the ability of men and women to enter the familial relationship in the first place must be regulated by raising the age of consent and requiring marriage licenses and health certificates: "It will always be the intelligent home life of the nation which will hold our ship of state to its moorings as a republic—and we can all appreciate the necessity of protecting home life and domestic interests. I believe as a method for the prevention of crime and for the protection of the helpless and innocent safeguards should be thrown around the issuance of marriage permits, known as marriage licenses. . . . A health certificate should have been required a hundred years ago—for the protection of the unborn."[33]

Ultimately, Felton was prepared to go so far as to demand sterilization for those women who were, in her opinion, incapable of maintaining a respectable family life. "Perhaps you may decide that my plan is too radical, but I do believe that a criminal woman should be made immune to childbearing as a punishment for crime," Felton asserted to her audience. Although she did not single out black women explicitly here, it would appear that Felton did have them particularly in mind when she proposed this scheme. Although she desired to "throw around another woman's daughter the safeguards which that less fortunate child needs" if the child was white, in the case of "erring" black women, she advocated compulsory curtailment of all reproductive capacity.[34] If the basis for racial superiority was grounded in an empowered white motherhood, as Rebecca Felton assumed, then the supposed racial inferiority of the black population must be reflected in a highly disorganized black motherhood and family. As she concluded in this speech,

We have a problem to work out in this country—as to the best methods for the intelligent education of the colored race amongst us. That it is a serious problem no one will deny. Until we can find clean living, as a rule, and not simply as an exception in the colored homes of this country, we are simply walking over a hidden crater which may do as much general damage as Mt. Pelee did in the island of Martinique. The plan of prevention of crime, by making criminals immune to the propagation of their own species, would go very far towards shutting off an influx of infanticides and brazen prostitution among the ignorant and shameless.[35]

Government intervention to protect white women and children and the actual elimination of some black women's ability to reproduce would, according to Felton, create the kind of motherhood that was critical to the larger economic, social, and political well-being of the South. It was precisely at this juncture of class, race, and gender relations in the late 1890s that Felton came to commit herself publicly to suffrage for white women. Instead of supporting suffrage for women out of a recognition of the common interests of all women, regardless of race, or the desirability of autonomy for women for its own sake, Felton advocated the enfranchisement of white women precisely because she perceived them to be so vulnerable and threatened in a world where only they could be relied upon to protect their own domestic interests. She quickly became one of the most prominent spokespersons for the movement in the state. Like so many others in the North and South, her arguments in favor of the vote for women were not explicitly racist, but they were clearly exclusionary, couched in terms of empowering native-born white women to defend the greater interests of their motherhood.[36]

Indeed, Felton's commitment to white women's suffrage was a result of what she perceived to be a lifetime of failure on the part of white men to protect their wives and daughters and to give them sufficient space to discharge their maternal role. In Felton's view, when offered a choice between the interests of motherhood and the family or of profit and the market, most southern men had consistently chosen the latter, even when womanhood had been "exposed" as a result. The issue of woman suffrage offered southern men one last opportunity to redress the failure of their fathers and grandfathers by empowering their wives and daughters to represent directly the interests of domesticity. Although the "failure of statesmanship" that led to the Civil War was a result of white southern men's inability to recognize that "the time had come in the Providence of God to give every human life a chance for freedom," Felton hoped that the intervening generation of men had learned a lesson and would not engage in another "vain effort to hold . . . property rights," this time by continuing to control women rather than slaves.[37]

Fathers, according to Felton, should give their daughters the vote because they recognized the limits of their own ability to protect them and saw that they would be most effectively protected when empowered politically to protect themselves, especially against the power of an abusive mate.[38] Indeed, making women into citizens would create the basis for a more equitable and companionate relationship between husband and wife. Political gender equity would underwrite the construction of the family in its "best form," as a "school for tenderness—for sympathy—for self-sacrifice—for forgetfulness of self—and honest dealing as to privileges between husband and wife." The days of the "fox-hunting, hard drinking—high playing—reckless living country squire," who "played the tyrant in his home," were gone. They were as gone as the days of "our great-grandmothers," who were "too busy with the spinning wheel and the loom to trouble their minds with elections and taxes."[39]

Rebecca Felton's hopes for a progressive politics of gender in the New South were to be disappointed when Georgia's legislators revealed themselves to be singularly recalcitrant. Even after the national Democratic party adopted woman suffrage as a part of its presidential platform in 1916, Georgia legislators continued to object almost to a man. In Felton's mind, this behavior was reminiscent of that manifested by their fathers and grandfathers over fifty years before. By turning their backs on the national Democratic party, Georgia legislators had once again, Felton declared, "become a law unto yourself." History was apparently repeating itself. Prominent Georgia antisuffragist Mildred Rutherford testified before the legislature that a vote for the Nineteenth Amendment was tantamount to a vote for the Fifteenth, because granting the franchise to black women would serve to reopen the whole question of enfranchising black men. Nothing could be further from the truth, Felton countered before the state legislative committee. Instead of contributing to the decline of white supremacy by politically empowering the black population, the vote for women would make a critical contribution to it by empowering white motherhood.[40]

As elsewhere in the South, it was antisuffragists who first introduced racist arguments into the suffrage campaign, and, as elsewhere, Georgia's representatives supported the antisuffrage position by an overwhelming majority. According to Felton, this failure of state legislators to grant the vote to white women actually constituted a refusal to treat them as other than slaves. Although southern representatives tried to argue that they opposed the passage of the Nineteenth Amendment because of their "steadfast belief in states rights—their exalted and virginal devotion to the principle—handed down from father to son—ever since the Civil War," the real reason Georgia legislators refused to support suffrage for women, according to Felton, had nothing to do with defending states' rights or even white supremacy. The real reason was because these men were committed to their grandfathers' gender politics, which had now become hopelessly obsolete. "The truth of the whole business lies in their determination to hold the whip hand over the wives and mothers of the South!" They, however, would learn the same lesson that their grandfathers had before them: "I predict that woman suffrage will come to the South—despite the drastic and frantic opposition of nine-tenths of the Southern Democrats in Congress—at this time. They seem to be the lineal and legal heirs to all the *political debris of secession....* They forget that the world is enfranchising its women as an act of right and justice.... It is their ignorance of what the world is doing—that now obsesses them."[41]

Knowledge of what the world was doing was to come to the state legislators of Georgia sooner than perhaps even Rebecca Latimer Felton could have hoped. On August 26, 1920, the Nineteenth Amendment was finally ratified. That which Georgia state legislators had claimed to fear most, the forcible arrival of woman suffrage through a federal amendment, had come to pass. The response of the entrenched political powers was a curious one. The state that had rushed to go on record first in opposition to the passage of the Nineteenth Amendment made even better speed in moving to be the first state to place a woman in the U.S. Senate. When Tom Watson, a longtime political ally of the Feltons, died with his term in the U.S. Senate unfinished in 1922, it provided Governor Thomas Hardwick of Georgia with the requisite opportunity. He initially offered the appointment to Watson's wife, Georgia Durham Watson, but she declined the honor. He then offered the appointment to Rebecca Latimer Felton, who accepted.

Felton was immediately flooded with congratulatory mail, not only from the state of Georgia but from across the country as well. One correspondent wrote that the appointment had "taken New York by surprise and has electrified her. Men and women alike are thrilled and enthusiastic."[42] Not only was the appointment "well earned," concluded a second correspondent, but it constituted an honor to all women. It was "one of the signs of the times; the hand-writing is on the wall. Women are rapidly coming into their own."[43] The newly formed National Woman's Party responded to the appointment by asking Rebecca Felton to join their list of "eminent women" and to accept the honorary chairmanship of their political council. As the vice president of the party, Alice Paul concluded, "Now that you are the first woman Senator your name has exceedingly great weight and we hope you will be willing to lend it to this campaign to secure a better lot for all women."[44]

For all her justified pride in the honor, Rebecca Latimer Felton must have been of two minds regarding the appointment. It reflected a due recognition of her political contributions to the state, and perhaps more important the changed status of women that had been effected as a result, but it was only a temporary, symbolic appointment, and her first Senate speech was also to be her last. As one correspondent pointed out, "Mr. Hardwick knows that Mrs. Felton has a following and Power in Georgia Superior to any Woman in the State, This Bunch of Flowers that He has tossed at your Feet does not cost Him anything yet, Since Women have been given the Franchise, His little Stunt is a Ballot winner. . . . Now Mrs. Felton, Why not you run for the U.S. Senate?"[45] Why not, indeed? The appointment was in fact a half gesture of the sort that Felton had come to expect from the southern male establishment over a long and active political life. As such, it reflected the ambiguous state of southern gender relations, even after sixty years of crisis and change. The secluded status of elite white women had indeed ended, and nothing marked that fact more clearly than Rebecca Felton rising to give her acceptance speech on the floor of the U.S. Senate. Nevertheless, the purely symbolic nature of her appointment also reflected the reality that no clear-cut public position or power for women had yet emerged in the South.[46]

Just as the South was forever remaining old while becoming new, so, ever since the collapse of the traditional order during the Civil War and Reconstruction, had the new southern woman remained subordinate while becoming liberated. The ambivalent and contradictory story of Rebecca Latimer Felton should give us some idea of why this was the case. The life of this archetypal woman reformer reveals the dynamic of progressive self-assertion and reactionary resistance characteristic of the larger social order that she steadfastly sought to change. The very forces spurring the development of independence and autonomy among elite white women in the postwar South were at the same time frequently the bedrock of conservatism and reaction that impelled them backwards to nostalgia for the hierarchies of patriarchy and race. The decline of the social and economic power of the planter class, which opened the door for the emergence of greater equity between the sexes, simultaneously reinforced the value of home "protection" and thus the ideal of gender dominance by men. White southerners' commitment to the "supremacy" of their race could be enlisted by gender reformers like Rebecca Felton to support the politics of empowering white motherhood. The larger consequence of the rigid racial hierarchy that emerged after the collapse of slavery was to deny the rights of black women as citizens and as mothers. Nevertheless, it was this denial that served to rationalize state legislators' opposition to granting the vote to white women as well. Ironic as it may appear in light of the Georgia legislature's refusal to ratify the Nineteenth Amendment less than three years earlier, the token appointment of Rebecca Felton as the first woman to sit in the U.S. Senate was perhaps the most fitting expression of the pattern of elite white gender relations that had developed in the postbellum South. As an honor graciously bestowed on her by her governor, not a right that Felton herself had earned, it marked the end, not the beginning, of a notable political career.

NOTES

This essay is a shortened version of a longer piece that has benefited greatly from the careful reading of many scholars. In particular, I would like to thank Susan Bordo, Jean Friedman, Jacquelyn Hall, Michael Johnson, Theodore Koditschek, Carol Montgomery, Nell Irvin Painter, Anne Scott, Anastatia Sims, and Peter Wallenstein. I am further indebted to Mary Robertson and the Georgia Historical Society for providing me with the opportunity to present this version of the piece before a lively and enthusiastic audience. Finally, I would like to thank the editors of this volume, Nancy Hewitt and Suzanne Lebsock, along with Tom Alexander, Catherine Clinton, and Elizabeth Turner, for their helpful comments and editorial improvements on this version.

1. Rebecca Latimer Felton, *The Romantic Story of Georgia's Women* (Atlanta: Atlanta Georgian and Sunday American, 1930), 44.

2. Ibid., 45.

3. See A. Elizabeth Taylor, "Development of the Woman's Suffrage Movement in Georgia," *Georgia Historical Quarterly* 62 (December 1958): 339-54, and "The Last Phase of the Women's Suffrage Movement in Georgia," *Georgia Historical Quarterly* 63 (March 1959): 11-28.

4. For a discussion of the centrality of protection to antebellum white gender relations, see Bertram Wyatt-Brown, *Southern Honor: Ethics and Behavior in the Old South* (New York: Oxford University Press, 1982). For the ways in which the Civil War stressed the quid pro quo of white southern gender relations, see Victoria E. Bynum, "War within a War: Women's Participation in the Revolt of the North Carolina Piedmont, 1863-1865," *Frontiers* 4, no. 3 (1987): 43-49; Drew Faust, "Altars of Sacrifice: Confederate Women and Narratives of War," *Journal of American History* 76, no. 4 (1990): 1200-1228; Donna D. Krug, "The Folks Back Home: The Confederate Homefront during the Civil War" (Ph.D. diss., University of California, Irvine, 1990); and LeeAnn Whites, "Gender and the Origins of the New South: Augusta, Georgia, 1860-1900 (Chapel Hill: University of North Carolina Press, forthcoming).

5. The outcome of this wartime rupturing of antebellum gender roles is contested. In her pathbreaking study, *The Southern Lady: From Pedestal to Politics, 1830-1930* (Chicago: University of Chicago Press, 1970), Anne Scott

argued that the Civil War "opened every door" for elite white southern women. More recently, historians have argued in a more pessimistic vein. Suzanne Lebsock, *The Free Women of Petersburg: Status and Culture in a Southern Town, 1784-1860* (New York: W. W. Norton, 1984), suggests that impoverished and defeated white men were not inclined to tolerate increased gender equity with any more equanimity than they greeted the prospect of racial equity. Jean Friedman, *The Enclosed Garden: Women and Community in the Evangelical South, 1830-1900* (Chapel Hill: University of North Carolina Press, 1985), and George Rable, *Civil Wars: Women and the Crisis of Southern Nationalism* (Urbana: University of Illinois Press, 1989), have carried this line of argument further and suggested that the autonomous roles women took up in the context of war had little lasting impact on postwar gender relations. More attention to the experience of individual women whose experience spanned the period may help sort out the nature of the relationship between persistence and change in women's roles and gender relations as well. See Kathleen Berkeley, "Elizabeth Avery Merriwether, 'An Advocate for Her Sex': Feminism and Conservatism in the Post Civil War South," *Tennessee Historical Quarterly* 43 (Winter 1984): 390-407; Joan Cashin, "Varina Howell Davis," in *Portraits of American Women: From Settlement to Present,* ed. G. J. Barker-Benfield and Catherine Clinton (New York: St. Martin's, 1991), 259-75; and Nell Irvin Painter, "The Journal of Ella Gertrude Clanton Thomas: An Educated White Woman in the Eras of Slavery, War and Reconstruction," in *The Secret Eye: The Journal of Ella Gertrude Clanton Thomas, 1848-1889,* ed. Virginia Ingraham Burr (Chapel Hill: University of North Carolina Press, 1990), 1-67.

    6. Treatments of Rebecca Latimer Felton's political career focus almost exclusively on her work in the "male" political arena. See John E. Talmadge, *Rebecca Latimer Felton: Nine Stormy Decades* (Athens: University of Georgia Press, 1960). See also Josephine Bone Floyd, "Rebecca Latimer Felton, Political Independent," *Georgia Historical Quarterly* 30 (March 1946): 14-34, and "Rebecca Latimer Felton, Champion of Women's Rights," *Georgia Historical Quarterly* 30 (June 1946): 81-104. This focus ignores both the domestic impetus for Felton's participation in the formally constituted male political arena and the interrelated emergence of a whole world of female political activity on Felton's part in the Ladies Aid societies, Ladies Memorial Association, the United Daughters of the Confederacy, the Woman's Christian Temperance Union, the General Federation of Women's Clubs, as well as the Georgia Woman's Suffrage Association. Anne Scott first outlined this road from "pedestal to politics" among elite white southern women in *The Southern Lady.* See also Friedman, *The Enclosed Garden,* 110-30; Kathleen Berkeley, " 'The Ladies Want to Bring Reform to the Public Schools': Public Education and Women's Rights in the Post Civil War South," *History of Education Quarterly* 44 (Spring 1984): 45-58; LeeAnn Whites, "The Charitable and the Poor: The Emergence of Domestic Politics in Augusta, Georgia, 1860-1880," *Journal of Social History* 17 (Summer 1984): 601-15; and Anastatia Sims, "Feminism and Femininity in the New South: White Women's Organizations in North Carolina, 1883-1930" (Ph.D. diss., University of North Carolina at Chapel Hill, 1985).

7. Rebecca Latimer Felton, *Country Life in Georgia in the Days of My Youth* (Atlanta: Index Printing, 1919), 29.

8. Rebecca Latimer Felton, "Impact of the Civil War on Women," May 20, 1892, Felton Papers, Special Collections, University of Georgia, Athens, Ga.

9. Scott, *The Southern Lady,* 3–22. See also Catherine Clinton, *Plantation Mistress: Woman's World in the Old South* (New York: Pantheon Books, 1982).

10. Felton, *Country Life,* 25. See also Felton, "Impact of the Civil War on Women." For a more general discussion of the ways race and class position tended to override gender identification, see Jacqueline Jones, *Labor of Love, Labor of Sorrow: Black Women, Work and the Family, from Slavery to the Present* (New York: Basic Books, 1985); and Elizabeth Fox-Genovese, *Within the Plantation Household: Black and White Women of the Old South* (Chapel Hill: University of North Carolina Press, 1989).

11. George Fitzhugh, *Sociology for the South or the Failure of Free Society* (New York: L. B. Franklin, 1966), 213–14.

12. Felton, *Country Life,* 79–94.

13. Ibid., 104.

14. In her recollections Felton gives a graphic description of the state in which she found her plantation upon returning home: "I never saw the home any more until August, 1865. When I reached the gate I picked up the springs that had been a part of my dead child's fine baby carriage, also the arm of a large parlor mahogany chair that had also burned. Desolation and destruction everywhere, bitter, grinding poverty—slaves all gone, money also." Felton, *Country Life,* 89.

15. Rebecca Latimer Felton, "Education of Veteran's Daughters," 1893, Felton Papers. For a further discussion of Felton's politics in relation to lower-class white women, see LeeAnn Whites, "The DeGraffenried Controversy: Race, Class, and Gender in the New South," *Journal of Southern History* 54 (August 1988): 449–78. The fact that Felton came to identify with lower-class white women in the context of her own class fall does not mean that the sentiment was reciprocated. For a discussion of the difference class location could make in the political commitments of southern women, see Jacquelyn Dowd Hall, "O. Delight Smith's Progressive Era: Labor, Feminism, and Reform in the Urban South," herein; Dolores Janiewski, *Sisterhood Denied: Race, Gender, and Class in a New South Community* (Philadelphia: Temple University Press, 1985); and Stephanie McCurry, "Their Ways Were Not Our Ways" (Paper delivered at the Southern Historical Association Meeting, Houston, Tex., 1985).

16. Felton, "Impact of the Civil War on Women." See also Rebecca Latimer Felton, "Southern Womanhood in Wartimes," n.d., Felton Papers.

17. For a further discussion of this dilemma in the particular context of the nineteenth-century South, see Suzanne Lebsock's analysis of the position of free black women in antebellum Petersburg in *The Free Women of Petersburg,* 87–111. For a similar discussion in a different time and place, see Judith Bennett, "'History that Stands Still': Women's Work in the European Past," *Feminist Studies* 14 (Summer 1988): 269–83.

18. Felton, *Country Life,* 88.

19. Felton was inclined to use the same incidents from her life over and over

again to illustrate her arguments. In the case of displacing responsibility for the decline of the planter class onto black men, her favorite example was a story of crop theft. Felton, *Country Life,* 57–59.

20. Talmadge, *Rebecca Latimer Felton,* chap. 5.

21. Felton, *Romantic Story,* 227.

22. Talmadge, *Rebecca Latimer Felton,* 83.

23. Frances Willard, *Woman and Temperance or the Work and Workers of the WCTU* (Hartford, Conn.: Park Publishing, 1883), 570.

24. Lula Barnes Ansley, *History of the Georgia Woman's Christian Temperance Union from Its Organization, 1883–1907* (Columbus, Ga.: Gilbert, 1914), 58. For a further discussion of the Georgia Woman's Christian Temperance Union in the nineteenth century, see Henry Anselm Scomp, *King Alcohol in the Realm of King Cotton* (Chicago: Blåkely, 1888), 677–78; and, more generally, Ruth Bordin, *Woman and Temperance: The Quest for Power and Liberty, 1873–1900* (Philadelphia: Temple University Press, 1981).

25. Rebecca Latimer Felton, "Temperance," 1892, Felton Papers.

26. Ibid. For a discussion of the centrality of drink to southern male culture, see Ted Ownby, *Subduing Satan: Religion, Recreation, and Manhood in the Rural South, 1865–1920* (Chapel Hill: University of North Carolina Press, 1990).

27. Felton, "Temperance."

28. Ibid.

29. Rebecca Latimer Felton, "Southern Women and Farm Life," n.d., Felton Papers.

30. Rebecca Latimer Felton, "The Before Breakfast Club," 1891, Felton Papers.

31. Felton, "Southern Women and Farm Life." Joel Williamson, *The Crucible of Race: Black-White Relations in the American South since Emancipation* (New York: Oxford University Press, 1984), discusses this incident. For a further discussion of race, gender, and the lynching of black men, see Jacquelyn Dowd Hall, *Revolt against Chivalry: Jessie Daniel Ames and the Women's Campaign against Lynching* (New York: Columbia University Press, 1979).

32. Felton, "The Education of Veteran's Daughters." See also "The Duty and Obligation that Lies on Southern Women," n.d., Felton Papers.

33. Rebecca Latimer Felton, "Rescue Work," n.d., Felton Papers. See also "The Problems that Interest Motherhood," in Felton, *Country Life,* 279–83.

34. Felton, "Rescue Work."

35. Ibid.

36. See, for example, Rebecca Latimer Felton, "Votes for Women," n.d., Felton Papers, and "Why Am I a Suffragist? The Subjection of Women and the Enfranchisement of Women," in Felton, *Country Life,* 246–60.

37. Felton, "Votes for Women." In retrospect, clear parallels can be drawn between southern black women's efforts to organize to protect themselves against abusive white men or against debilitating stereotypes in their own communities and the organizing efforts of southern white women like Felton, even though white women rarely recognized the similarities between them at the time. See

Darlene Clark Hine, "'We Specialize in the Wholly Impossible': The Philanthropic Work of Black Women," in *Lady Bountiful Revisited: Women, Philanthropy and Power*, ed. Kathleen McCarthy (New Brunswick, N.J.: Rutgers University Press, 1990), 70-93; Anne Firor Scott, "Most Invisible of All: Black Women's Voluntary Organizations," *Journal of Southern History* 61 (February 1990): 3-22; and Deborah Gray White, "The Cost of Club Work, the Price of Black Feminism," herein.

    38. Felton, "Votes For Women."

    39. Ibid.

    40. Rebecca Latimer Felton, "Southern Congressman Opposing Equal Suffrage," n.d., Felton Papers. For a further discussion of the relationship between the woman suffrage movement and the politics of white supremacy in the South, see Marjorie Spruill Wheeler, *New Women of the New South: The Leaders of the Woman Suffrage Movement in the Southern States* (Oxford: Oxford University Press, 1993); and Suzanne Lebsock, "Woman Suffrage and White Supremacy: A Virginia Case Study," herein.

    41. Felton, "Southern Congressman Opposing Equal Suffrage."

    42. Corinne Stecker Smith to Rebecca Latimer Felton, October 7, 1922, Felton Papers.

    43. Henrietta Grossman to Rebecca Latimer Felton, October 3, 1922, Felton Papers.

    44. Alice Paul to Rebecca Latimer Felton, October 27, 1922, Felton Papers.

    45. F. A. Powell to Rebecca Latimer Felton, October 7, 1922, Felton Papers. For a further discussion of the ways in which political expediency would momentarily elevate white women's political status in the South, see Judith McArthur, "Democrats Divided: Why The Texas Legislature Gave Women Primary Suffrage in 1918" (Paper delivered at the Southern Historical Meeting, Fort Worth, Tex., 1991).

    46. As one correspondent described the situation, "Woman is not what she once was, pure and good, and bless her, the fault is not hers that she has changed. Time was when man was her sword and her provider and she, perforce, was above the ten commandments, but man failed, and she was compelled to become her own sword and provider so man and woman instead of being one, became competitors. . . . Alas! The race of Toombs, of Webster and of Calhoun has run out. That is the reason that Women feel impelled to go into politics. Why don't you say it?" H. L. Trisler to Rebecca Latimer Felton, October 27, 1922, Felton Papers.

Woman Suffrage and White Supremacy: A Virginia Case Study

Suzanne Lebsock

> I think that as women we should be most prayerfully careful lest, in the future, women—whether coloured women or white women who are merely poor—should be able to say that we had betrayed their interests and excluded them from freedom.
>
> —Mary Johnston to Lila Meade Valentine, 1913

This letter from the novelist Mary Johnston to the president of Virginia's Equal Suffrage League was remarkable.[1] It was remarkable in its attention to poor women and women of color, an intriguing contrast to the gross and overt racism that prevailed among white Virginians—and to the bigotry and elitism we have come to expect from white southern suffragists. Even more remarkable was the way in which race and class figured in Johnston's sense of history in the making. Johnston foresaw a day when privileged suffragists would be harshly judged if they sold out black women and the white poor to press their own claims to the vote.

Mary Johnston proved to be right, although not specifically for Virginia. Virginia suffragists have escaped judgment because their existence has simply been erased. Despite the fact that contemporary newspapers were filled with suffrage news, editorials, debates, and jokes, and despite the rich archival sources that have been available for decades, no study of the Virginia woman suffrage movement has ever been published.[2] Nor does woman suffrage appear prominently in the standard Virginia political histories of the period.[3]

The woman suffrage movement at large, meanwhile, has come in for a good deal of criticism, both for the white leaders' shabby treatment of African American suffragists and for the willingness of many prominent white suffragists to exploit racist arguments when it seemed advantageous to do so. Suffragists from all parts of the country were implicated in such behavior.[4] The South, however, has landed in its usual spot, with southern suffragists assigned primary responsibility for the movement's racist thought and policy. Indeed, the southern woman suffrage movement has achieved its greatest fame as a purveyor of white supremacy.

The book most important to this understanding of the South is Aileen S. Kraditor's *Ideas of the Woman Suffrage Movement, 1890-1920,* first published in 1965 and still the major work on the ideology of the suffragists and their opponents. The "principal argument" of the southern suffragists, Kraditor contended, was that granting the ballot to women would enhance white political power in the southern states. Since there were more white women in the South than black women and black men put together, votes cast by white women would more than offset any votes cast by black people, and thus white supremacy would be secured.

Kraditor further challenged the democratic credentials of the white suffragists—and here she included northerners who exploited fears about the immigrant vote—by collapsing distinctions between suffragists and antisuffragists. According to Kraditor, suffragists and antis were all pretty much alike when it came to dealing with voters they considered undesirable, whether those voters were black or foreign-born. All agreed that some groups were unfit to vote; the main disagreement was how to prevent them from attaining real power, with suffragists arguing that votes for women would mean that more of the "right" people would be voting, while antis predicted that more of the "wrong" people would vote. On this issue the differences between the suffragists and their opponents were merely tactical.[5]

Kraditor's characterization of the white suffragists has had a great deal of staying power, for reasons both internal and external to her book. Kraditor's central concern was the evolution of social movements over time, and the theme of her book was how the woman suffrage movement transformed its ideology to win. In a sentence, the rationale for women's voting changed from "justice" to "expediency." Of all the appeals to expediency, white supremacy was the ugliest, and given the abolitionist beginnings of the women's rights movement, recourse to white supremacist arguments seemed to present a particularly dramatic departure. Kraditor's treatment of white supremacy, in other words, gave racism an important place in an elegant larger thesis about ideological change. Added to the power of her thesis was the evidence of a very good historian at work. Kraditor's reading of the sources was rigorous and complex, her prose dispassionate and sure. Her audience in the late 1960s, moreover, was already convinced that southern progressivism had been for whites only.[6] More recently the Kraditor thesis has played well to a different house, as historians of women have paid increased attention to division and conflict between groups of women, especially along the

lines of race. Small wonder that Kraditor's suffragist-as-racist has dominated the historiographical landscape for more than twenty-five years.

Aileen Kraditor's disclosures of racism in the woman suffrage movement were important in 1965, and they remain so today. But Kraditor's
book was a first take, not the last word, and it was based on the
pronouncements of a fairly small and exclusive club, the leaders in the
national woman suffrage movement.[7] What happens when we move to
the context in which the southern suffragists actually operated, the arena
of local and state politics? And what happens when we open the stage to
a wider range of southern characters?

The plot, first of all, gets thicker, and we find ourselves viewing a
drama that has neither the simplicity nor the elegance of the Kraditor
thesis. My reconsideration of the relationship between woman suffrage
and white supremacy began in 1983, when I took my first look in the
Virginia Woman Suffrage Collection in the Virginia State Library and
Archives. In these papers, racialist arguments were surprisingly sparse.
Had some liberal soul sifted and sanitized the collection? Not likely. The
papers were still stored in the transfer cases in which they had arrived in
the 1930s, their original chaos perfectly preserved, along with some
broken glass, dead bugs, and rusty "Votes for Women" buttons. The
condition of the papers was eloquent testimony to Virginia officialdom's
attitude toward the history of women. The content of the papers was
more difficult to interpret.

It was certain that Kraditor's thesis was not sustained, at least not in
any clear-cut way. The white women in Virginia who became suffragists
did not do so out of a desire to preserve white supremacy, nor did they
use any white supremacist argument as their principal argument. Moreover,
there were readily discernible differences between the suffragists and the
antisuffragists, with the antis emerging as the more flagrant white
supremacists. Still, the white suffragists did generate some racialist
propaganda, and even had they not, we would still have to take into
account the fact that in a state whose population was 30 percent African
American, white people did almost all the talking. All of this was sufficiently
intriguing to send me back to the archives and newspapers.

In this essay, I try to make the resulting evidence speak to three main
questions. First, how important were white supremacist arguments relative to other kinds? Second is the issue of culpability. To the degree that
white supremacy did inform the woman suffrage debates, who was
responsible for it, and what sort of damage did it do? Third, how might
the evidence generated by these debates advance the larger project of
understanding how gender and race have operated simultaneously in our
past?

As befits a complicated story, the answers will make more sense after the evidence is put forward, but some conclusions can be offered here. If we measure the importance of a particular argument by the sheer volume of ink devoted to it, then white supremacy had a varied career as an issue in the woman suffrage debates, waxing stronger as the suffrage movement picked up steam. In the beginning, race was scarcely mentioned. By 1915 the antisuffragists succeeded in making white supremacy *an* issue, arguing that woman suffrage would doom a large part of Virginia to black control at the polls. In the last two years of the campaign, the antis succeeded in making white supremacy an issue of considerable importance. The principal actors in the story of woman suffrage and white supremacy, in other words, were the antisuffragists. The antis introduced the white supremacy issue; as time went on they pressed it with increasing intensity and disregard for truth; and they refused to give it up, even after the Nineteenth Amendment was ratified. Responsibility for the white supremacist dimensions of the woman suffrage debates rests squarely on the shoulders of the antis.

It rests more ambiguously on the white suffragists, whose behavior needs to be examined bifocally. With one lens trained on the egalitarian standards of the present, it is possible to make a substantial list of ways in which the white suffragists failed to measure up. From first to last, the white suffragists saw white supremacy as a bogus issue, and they countered with a strategy of denial, arguing in most instances that white supremacy was simply not in danger and thus should not stand in the way of votes for women. They did not disavow white supremacy itself, and this by present standards must be judged a failure of major proportions. At the same time, we need a second lens for distance, to focus and clarify the standards and practicalities of southern politics in the early twentieth century. By local white standards (of which the antis' poisonous polemics were a good example), the suffragists' strategy of denial was a moderate approach. To understand just how low the antis would go does not excuse the suffragists, but it helps us locate them on a political spectrum that would have been meaningful to white southerners at the time.

Understanding the depths of the antisuffragists' unremitting bigotry also helps us locate black Virginians in the woman suffrage controversy. To resume the theatrical metaphor, there were numerous black characters on stage, but none of them had speaking parts. After the antisuffragists linked woman suffrage to the demise of white supremacy, there was nothing an African American could say that would help the woman suffrage cause. The apparent consequence was a black stance that stressed deeds over words. Once the Nineteenth Amendment was ratified, African Americans in the cities organized voter registration drives among women. Until that time, they tended to keep their own counsel.

One last question is how this whole complicated story might affect the ways we think about the connections between race and gender in more general theoretical terms. Since answers to this question involve considerable abstraction, I want to take them up after presenting further evidence. The remainder of this essay proceeds in three parts. First is a narrative of the rise of the white supremacist attack on woman suffrage and the white suffragists' formulation of a standard counterattack. Both are set in motion against a larger context that includes the progress of the Equal Suffrage League, the checkered career of woman suffrage resolutions in the General Assembly of Virginia, and the changing repertoire of suffrage arguments that were not overtly connected with race. The second segment takes a closer look at racialist rhetoric, particularly that of the white suffragists, and addresses the issue of how that rhetoric should be judged. Central to this analysis is the contention that the antis' aggressive racism constrained the options available to all other players, including the white suffragists and black persons on either side of the woman suffrage issue. Third is the denouement, an analysis of how the major parties to the controversy behaved after the Nineteenth Amendment was ratified and an inspection of voter registration figures to assess the immediate impact of woman suffrage on white supremacy in Virginia.

From 1870 on, Virginia women had made sporadic attempts to form woman suffrage organizations,[8] but not until 1909 was the first sustained organization founded. The timing was important, for in 1909, when the Equal Suffrage League of Virginia was launched, the political momentum in Virginia was decidedly undemocratic. The new century had opened with a resolute, relentless, and successful effort to destroy black political power. The central achievement of this movement was the constitution of 1902, written with the explicit purpose of disfranchising black men. A great many lower-class whites were also disfranchised— enough to arouse suspicions that the constitutional convention's unspoken purpose was to demolish the Republican party. The 1902 constitution, in any case, threatened to disfranchise so many whites that the framers did not dare submit it to the voters. They simply promulgated it as the supreme law of the commonwealth.[9]

In one stroke, the Virginia electorate was cut in half, and the number of eligible black voters was radically reduced, from about 147,000 to roughly 21,000. The stage was set for the triumph of a Democratic party machine dedicated to white supremacy, minimal government, and keeping itself in power. But even though the machine—or "the Organization," as its leaders preferred to call it—had succeeded in winning control of the state, the men who ran the state felt they could never do enough to secure their position. Despite the virtual elimination of black men as a force in Virginia elections, race baiting was still a campaign commonplace. Both parties, moreover, moved to eliminate any residual black influence from within their ranks. The Democrats saw to it that no blacks could vote in their primaries. The desperate white Republicans, who had traditionally relied on substantial black support, tried to purge their remaining black members, hoping in that way to attract white defectors from the Democrats.[10] This was bigotry that did not quit.

Given this context, the most striking feature of race issues in the debates over woman suffrage was the infrequency with which they were raised. From January 1912, when woman suffrage was brought before the Virginia legislature for the first time, to March 1920, when the legislature defeated woman suffrage for the last time, the *Richmond Times-Dispatch* published more than four hundred letters to the editor (pro and con) regarding votes for women. Eight percent of those letters made explicit mention of the race question. In the same period, the *Times-Dispatch* printed more than two hundred editorials (mostly con) on woman suffrage. Only 4 percent of them explicitly mentioned the alleged menace of the black voter—and this in a newspaper in which racist insults were standard fare.

Other hunting grounds yield even less in the way of white supremacist arguments. There was nothing about race in the special suffrage edition of the *Richmond News Leader* published in 1914, nor was there anything about black votes in the suffragists' own shortlived newspaper, the *Virginia Suffrage News*. The *Times-Dispatch* reported on all the annual conventions of the Equal Suffrage League of Virginia and printed dozens of routine summaries of speeches delivered at meetings of the Equal Suffrage League of Richmond. If anyone breathed a word about race, it was not reported here. Finally, in the archives of the Norfolk Equal Suffrage League there is a paper listing planks in the antisuffrage platform, and they are labeled "Stock arguments we had to meet over & over." None of them concerned white supremacy.[11]

The great bulk of woman suffrage propaganda, both pro and anti, conveyed the same arguments that predominated in the rest of the country—a phenomenon abetted by the fact that both sides bought leaflets in bulk from national headquarters. Suffragists contended the vote was a natural right; antis countered it was a privilege. Suffragists and antis went back and forth about whether the vote would make women better mothers and what the vote would do to, or for, the home. They debated whether women could do more for reform with the vote or without it—interestingly many antis shared the suffragists' assumption that women *should* work for reform—and in that connection the two sides offered differing interpretations of legislation enacted in states where women already had the vote. They wrangled over the question of whether women really wanted the vote and whether it mattered whether women wanted it. They fought over the question of whether woman suffrage was inevitable.

The entry of the United States into World War I provided more grist for both mills. Suffragists contended that women had earned the vote by their prodigious war service, and they repeatedly cited the recommendation of Virginia-born President Woodrow Wilson that women be enfranchised as a war measure. To antis, Wilson's recommendation was evidence that he had lived away from Virginia for too long. They dusted off the ancient argument that only those who could fight should be able to vote. And increasingly they resorted to guilt by association, accusing suffragists of being cozy with socialists, anarchists, and Bolsheviks. All these arguments came straight from the national book, and together they accounted for most of the ink and oratory devoted to woman suffrage in Virginia.

There were also issues with more local resonance. One was states' rights, which is taken up later. Another was the question, Would Thomas Jefferson be a woman suffragist if he were alive today? Anyone inclined to belittle such questions should keep in mind that Virginia legislators, when speaking before their colleagues, could still count on ritual applause when they invoked the name of Jefferson, or Patrick Henry, or Robert E. Lee. Suffragists and antis both hitched their causes to the veneration of revolutionary and Confederate heroes, sometimes by emphasizing their literal descent from the founding fathers. The suffragist Lucy Randolph Mason had a particularly illustrious ancestry that included John Marshall and George Mason. In an interview recorded more than forty years after the woman suffrage question was settled, Adèle Clark was still reciting Lucy Mason's genealogy.[12]

Finally, there was the white supremacist argument. The antis started it and elaborated on it in increasingly scurrilous ways as the woman suffrage movement gathered strength in Virginia and won more victories in other states. Then in 1920 Tennessee put the Nineteenth Amendment over the top, and woman suffrage was imposed on Virginia by national action. Instead of dropping their white supremacy theme, the resourceful former antis found new uses for it.

Before proceeding with this story, it would be helpful to identify the protagonists. Unless otherwise specified, *suffragists* refers to activists in the Equal Suffrage League of Virginia.[13] All were women, all were white, and they tended to be members of socially prominent (though not always wealthy) families. A high proportion of them lived in Richmond. There were local leagues in most of the larger towns, however, and there were pockets of suffrage activity in all kinds of places. Although officers of both state and local leagues were female, they sought allies among men and won the support of labor leaders, some liberal clergymen, a few public officials, and a very occasional newspaper editor. There were black advocates of woman suffrage as well, but for reasons that will become apparent, they rarely spoke within the hearing of white people.

The antisuffragists are in some ways more difficult to identify than the suffragists and in other ways easier. The Virginia Association Opposed to Woman Suffrage organized in 1912, when woman suffrage first came before the General Assembly. Like the Equal Suffrage League, this association was centered in Richmond, and it was made up of prominent white women, who (unlike the suffragists) took care to list the names of their prominent husbands. Their workings, however, were very shadowy. If they kept papers, they have never come to light, and it is thus impossible to know how much of the political work of antisuffrage was actually accomplished by the Virginia Association. Certainly there were legions of powerful Virginians who were willing to speak against woman suffrage, quite independently of any group organized specifically for that purpose. For these reasons, *antisuffragists,* or *antis,* in this essay refers not only to the leaders of the antisuffrage association but also to a congeries of Virginians who went on public record against votes for women. Altogether the antisuffrage forces were a formidable group, counting among them most of Virginia's newspaper editors, several well-known clergymen and writers, Virginia's governors, its U.S. senators, almost all the men Virginians sent to the U.S. House of Representatives, and most members of the General Assembly.

All of the known antis were white, with the exception of Nannie Goode of Boydton, Virginia, who was a story in herself. In 1913 the *Richmond News Leader* sponsored an essay contest, offering a ten-dollar prize for the best attack on woman suffrage. Out of 625 entries, Nannie Goode's was judged the best; Goode took a medical approach, suggesting that voting would be "an unwise expenditure of nerve energy." The *News Leader* announced the winner and asked her to send in her photograph so that it could be published. She obliged, but no photograph ever appeared. Some months later, it came to light that Nannie Goode was a woman of color, "which," as one suffragist wrote to another, "explains why the Antis of Richmond were denied the inspiration of gazing upon her likeness." The *News Leader* maintained an embarrassed silence. The black press got hold of the story and had a wonderful time.[14]

The relatively good humor that surrounded the Nannie Goode episode was an indicator of the state of the debates. Woman suffrage was not yet linked in any significant way to white supremacy. In these early days of the suffrage campaign, Virginians for the first time in the history of the commonwealth engaged in a serious, vigorous, extended, and highly publicized debate about the status of women and the relation of women to the polity. The discussion crescendoed early in 1912 and again in 1914, when the General Assembly was in session. In both sessions the woman suffrage amendment was trounced; in 1912 the House vote was 12 to 85, and the amendment failed again in 1914 by a vote of 13 to 74. The leaders of the Equal Suffrage League took what comfort they could from the fact that their cause was still young, and they resolved to make a better showing in the next legislature by dint of diligent organizing, district by district.[15]

During these early debates, white supremacist arguments were sporadic and few, and the suffragists ignored them. In 1913, for example, the *Times-Dispatch* printed a letter from William Watts Parker. Parker was an elderly physician who had opinions on just about everything, and for decades he had been firing them off to the newspapers. In this instance he identified woman suffrage as the cause of interracial marriages. "Look at the thousands of marriages in the North and West of white women and negroes, and getting worse every day!" Parker's rantings about the New Woman were by this time legendary, and the suffragists apparently paid no attention.[16]

Nor did they pay much attention to the white supremacy issue when it was first raised by legislators. A canvass by local suffragists on the eve of the 1914 legislative session evoked this response from Saxon W. Holt, a senator from Newport News: "I feel that if woman sufferage was adopted in Virginia, the results would be, that it would be hard to get the white women of the State to go to the poles and vote, when they would have to come in contact with negro women, and conditions that frequently surround the poles that would be objectionable to them." State headquarters in Richmond advised the suffragists in Newport News not to worry: "His objections in regard to the negro woman and 'location of the polls' are so easily answered."[17] As long as racist attacks on woman suffrage remained scattered, the suffragists avoided answering in kind. In 1915, however, antisuffragists gave their argument a sharper focus and brought it closer to home. This time the suffragists took the bait, and the relationship of woman suffrage to white supremacy entered a new phase.

The key document was an editorial by Alfred Williams in the *Richmond Evening Journal*. Williams invoked "figures and facts," "actual facts," and multiple "hard facts," all of which boiled down to the single "hard fact" that "twenty-nine counties of Virginia would be condemned by woman suffrage to colored rule and five others would be in serious peril of it with woman suffrage." The figures came from the census of 1910; Williams arranged them in a neat column and reasoned that wherever black females outnumbered white, woman suffrage would result in black rule. Williams contrasted his alleged facts with the desires of the suffragists, who as women could not be expected to understand practical politics and who would likely "fall back on the traditional conclusive feminine argument 'because.' " "No other argument," Williams continued, " . . . is quite so convincing or fascinating as that word 'because,' accompanied by some pouting of alluring and scarlet lips—especially if there be dimples by way of re-enforcement." But facts had to be faced. Otherwise, Williams concluded, "the Democratic party and white rule in Virginia will be swinging on a mighty thin line."[18]

Clearly the antis thought they could score with this argument. Williams's editorial found its way into other Virginia newspapers, and it was reprinted as a broadside for distribution in other southern states.[19] The suffragists decided they had to respond. They wrote letters to editors, and for the first time they published a flyer on the alleged "menace to white supremacy." The suffragists produced these with characteristic deliberation. They did a census analysis of their own; they consulted lawyers, including the state attorney general (no difficult trick in the small world of Richmond's elite—the Equal Suffrage League's press coordinator was the attorney general's sister); and they wrote measured rebuttals.[20] In the process they formulated the arguments that would serve them for the rest of the woman suffrage campaign.

The suffragists' central contention was that white supremacy was not endangered and therefore not an issue. In two-thirds of Virginia's counties, there were white majorities. In the counties with black majorities, the voting qualifications in the state constitution would apply to women as they already applied to men. The constitution provided for a cumulative poll tax. The constitution also required a literacy test; here the suffragists pointed out that the black illiteracy rate was 22 percent, compared with 8 percent among whites. There was a further provision in the constitution that had never even been used. If whites in a particular county believed themselves in danger of losing their electoral majority, they could petition for a special act of the legislature imposing an additional requirement that voters own property worth $250. That act would apply only to the county that petitioned for it. Since this had never yet been deemed necessary, the suffragists had a hard time believing white supremacy was in jeopardy.[21]

Indeed, the suffragists saw white supremacy as a bogus issue—and they said so in their private correspondence as consistently as they did in their public pronouncements. Lila Meade Valentine, president of the Equal Suffrage League, called the white supremacy scare "nonsense," "the last stand of the antis." Jessie Townsend, president of the Norfolk league, called it an "old bugaboo." Mary Johnston wrote, "If it wasn't the negro woman (Poor soul!) it would be something else—any thing or everything—far-fetchedness wouldn't matter."[22] Farfetchedness, as we shall see, in fact did not matter to the antis. It did matter to the suffragists, who relied on careful preparation and authoritative texts. "Do not have a public debate on this subject until you are thoroughly posted by some good constitutional lawyer," wrote Valentine to Townsend. "By all means keep a copy of the Va. Constitution close at hand."[23]

By such means the suffragists hoped to settle the white supremacy question once and for all. "We are in the last stages of a controversy about the negro vote," came the inside word from headquarters, "and feel much indebted to Mr. Alfred Williams, editor of the Richmond Journal, for attacking us."[24] The antis, however, were not about to let the white supremacy issue die. In January 1916 the General Assembly again convened in regular session, and for the first time white supremacy was prominent in a legislative debate on woman suffrage.

Hugh White of Rockbridge led the charge. As the *Times-Dispatch* reported it, White read from "a nationally circulated negro periodical [probably *The Crisis*]. Here it was brought out that the negro race has much the same fight for recognition on its hands as have white women. Every argument for woman suffrage, warned Mr. White, is also an argument for negro suffrage." Another newspaper reported White's comments thus: "He said equal suffrage rights would mean equal race rights, and would tend to a reversal to barbarism, since it would strip woman of her refinement." While he was at it, White contributed his bit to the male antis' stock of observations on female appearance: "Where equal suffrage prevails women have wrinkles and lines in their faces, he said, and have hawk-like faces."[25]

The woman suffrage resolution did surprisingly well in the 1916 session, losing in the House by the relatively close vote of 40 to 52. It is not clear why. Certainly the suffragists had worked hard. Lila Meade Valentine had made personal appearances all over the state, organizing new local leagues and rejuvenating older ones. By 1916 almost every town in Virginia with more than twenty-five hundred residents had a suffrage league. Suffragists were supplying suffrage news to more than forty newspapers. In any case, the leaders of the Equal Suffrage League were jubilant to have come so far in so short a time; they called the House vote "our victorious defeat."[26]

Little did they know that 40 to 52 was the best woman suffrage would ever do in Virginia (at least until 1952, when the General Assembly at last roused itself and ratified the Nineteenth Amendment). Woman suffrage did not come to a vote in the legislature again until 1919, and by that time a great deal had changed. First, there was World War I and in its wake a red scare, a season of deadly racial violence, and a surge of hope for a new world order. All of this provided material for the ongoing suffrage debate. Second, at the urging of the National American Woman Suffrage Association, the Equal Suffrage League of Virginia lined up behind Carrie Chapman Catt's "Winning Plan." That meant quietly putting aside the campaign for a state woman suffrage amendment and joining in a highly disciplined national campaign for the passage of an amendment to the U.S. Constitution.[27] Nothing could have made the antisuffragists happier. Here was an opportunity to divert the debate from woman suffrage itself to the hallowed ground of states' rights. The antis took full advantage of the opportunity and in so doing moved questions about race closer to the center of the debate.

As the suffragists pointed out, the federal amendment—commonly called the Anthony Amendment—did not directly enfranchise anyone. It merely stated that citizens could not be denied the vote on the basis of sex, and it gave Congress the power to enforce that principle. Careful antisuffragists thus argued that the danger of the woman suffrage amendment lay in its power as a precedent. If the federal government was allowed to interfere with the state's power to define its electorate in one way, it might be more likely to interfere with the state's powers in yet other ways. It might, for example, opt for enforcement of the Fifteenth Amendment (which denied states the power to deny citizens the vote on the basis of race). It might impose universal suffrage. It had happened before, during Reconstruction. What was to stop it from happening again?

As a rule, however, the antisuffragists were not careful. By June 1919, when suffrage forces at last pushed the Anthony Amendment through the U.S. Senate, the *Times-Dispatch* was arguing that the amendment would directly enfranchise millions of black women. Significantly, the *Times-Dispatch* also warned that woman suffrage would spell the end of school segregation and every other form of Jim Crow legislation. This was a marked departure from the antis' earlier tendency to construe white supremacy narrowly, that is, as a matter of numerical superiority at the polls. Late in 1919 and in 1920, as the Anthony Amendment was presented to the Virginia General Assembly for ratification, the antis' rhetoric grew ever more global and apocalyptic. Woman suffrage would mean black supremacy in politics and, as the president of the Virginia Association Opposed to Woman Suffrage wrote, "racial social equality and the intermarriage of whites and blacks."[28] Woman suffrage, moreover, was already responsible for the race riots that racked the country in 1919. "Race rioting in Arkansas," one anti told the State Democratic Committee, "is the direct result of equal suffrage. . . . " Woman suffrage, another anti claimed, "means race and sex war!"[29]

How low would the antis go? Antisuffrage prose reached its nadir in an eye-catching newspaper advertisement that appeared immediately before the legislature took action in the late summer of 1919. "What causes race riots? In Chicago it was POLITICS. . . . In Washington and Knoxville it was AROUSED BY ATTACKS ON WOMEN. As a thinking citizen, with an understanding of the laws of cause and effect, YOU KNOW THAT RACE RIOTS WILL INCREASE IF THERE IS MORE POLITICS BETWEEN THE RACES AND IF WOMEN ARE MIXED UP IN POLITICS!"[30]

The very next day the Anthony Amendment came before the Virginia House of Delegates, and it was trounced. This was more than a defeat. It was a resounding defeat, meant to echo across the nation. The deed was done by means of a resolution that declared the federal amendment "an unwarranted, unnecessary, undemocratic and dangerous interference with the rights reserved to the States," and it called upon "our sister States of the Union" to join in resistance to all such measures.[31] Although the vote was not close—61 to 21—the suffragists pressed on, hoping the General Assembly would come around once it became clear that ratification was inevitable. As Lila Meade Valentine wrote to the state senator from Fauquier, "How will the women of Virginia feel should they owe their political liberty to the men of other states, instead of to Virginians?" The senator was not moved, nor were most of his colleagues. In 1920 the Virginia House approved a resolution rejecting the Anthony Amendment 62 to 22, while the Senate vote was 24 to 10. The General Assembly then completed its work on woman suffrage by passing the "machinery" bill. The bill stipulated that should the federal amendment be ratified by action of other states, the voting restrictions then in force for Virginia men would be applied to women as well.[32]

Was it racism that defeated woman suffrage in Virginia? There is no clear answer to this question. On the one hand, the antis did exploit white anxieties to the hilt, and in the final months of the campaign suffragists could occasionally be found expressing the private opinion that "our worst stumbling block" was fear of the black voter.[33] On the other hand, the Virginia General Assembly had already demonstrated its willingness to thwart feminist aspirations, quite apart from any controversies about race relations or states' rights. The campaign for a state-supported "coordinate college" for women had commanded the support of almost every white women's organization in the state. It went without saying that this college would admit white students only, but it too was rejected in one legislative session after another.[34] If anything in Virginia was ever overdetermined, it was opposition to women's rights.

What is clear is that the antisuffragists' willingness to voice and exploit racist feeling had profound effects on the terms of the debate. For their part, the antis as a group were willing to say anything that might strengthen their cause; there were no minimal standards of either decency or truthfulness to which they held themselves or anyone else. The range of responses available to white suffragists and to African Americans was consequently narrow. The white suffragists, unwilling to get in the gutter with the antis, opted for a complex politics of distance and denial. Black Virginians were almost completely silenced.

One further example of antisuffrage tactics will help clarify the suffragists' options. After 1918 the antisuffragists increasingly expanded their accusations beyond the realm of electoral politics and into the equally explosive territory of "social equality." Carrie Chapman Catt, who came to Richmond in 1920 to address the General Assembly, was subjected to the full treatment. Catt was the president of the National American Woman Suffrage Association (NAWSA), and in her long career as a suffragist she had said many different things to many sorts of audiences. In recent years she has been routinely chastised by historians for using nativist and racist appeals for woman suffrage.[35] She arrived in Richmond, however, to find the House chamber blanketed with leaflets entitled "The 'Three Immediate Women Friends' of the Anthony Family." A portrait of Catt was followed by a portrait of Anna Howard Shaw, the former president of NAWSA, which was in turn placed beside a portrait of "Mrs. R. Jerome Jeffrey (Negro)." Mrs. Jeffrey, the caption explained, was "Often 'Guest in Anthony Home' with Mrs. Shaw and Mrs. Carrie Chapman Catt, President of National Woman Suffrage Association, to which all Southern Suffragettes belong." Completing the leaflet's front page were two quotations in large type. From Catt: "Suffrage Democracy Knows no Bias of Race, Color, Creed, or Sex." From Susan B. Anthony: "Look not to Greece or Rome for heroes, nor to Jerusalem or Mecca for saints, but for all the higher virtues of heroism, let us WORSHIP the black man at our feet."[36]

Let it be emphasized that the antis assumed these quotations and associations to be self-evidently devastating to the suffrage cause. If a woman suffragist suggested that votes for women would or should empower any black women (to say nothing of black men), she played right into the hands of the antis. So did any white suffragist who associated with black people or organizations on a footing of anything like equality.

This was the context for the Equal Suffrage League's complicity in

NAWSA's 1919 decision on the application of a federation of black women's organizations for cooperating membership. When the Northeastern Federation of Women's Clubs first applied for affiliation, NAWSA tried to persuade them to withdraw their application. That failing, NAWSA headquarters polled its own executive council, which included Lila Meade Valentine. In a private letter Valentine recommended against acceptance of the application, in the process producing the most explicit extant statement of the Equal Suffrage League's stance on race politics. "As I understand it," Valentine wrote, "the National is organized for the purpose of securing the right of suffrage for all women. I believe that all women, white or black, who meet the qualifications for suffrage in any State should have that right," Valentine continued, and then she turned practical politician:

> but in working to secure that right, we should exercise common sense, and not complicate our efforts and add to the difficulties of the task by injecting elements of discord. As you know, the negro is the one remaining argument against suffrage in the Southern States and our work in behalf of the federal amendment, already meeting great opposition because of that element, would be rendered immeasurably more difficult by admitting a large body of negro women to membership in the National at this time. This is not a matter of principle but of expediency, and I trust that the National Board will see fit to regard it as such. . . . [37]

Aileen Kraditor could not have put it better herself. Expediency prevailed, the Northeastern Federation was denied cooperating membership in NAWSA, and we are left with a set of questions about how to evaluate the white suffragists' decisions—not only their rejection of the Northeastern Federation but their entire strategy of denial.

It might be helpful to further clarify their options. In Virginia the power was on the side of white supremacy, and given the antis' willingness to exploit any resonances between woman suffrage and black suffrage, white woman suffragists were presented with a stark choice: they could distance their cause from the aspirations of black Virginians and thereby preserve some chance of victory, or they could acknowledge the legitimate interests of black women and doom their movement to certain failure. To put it another way, they could deny that white supremacy was in danger, or they could hush up and go home.

There was also a third road, a road not taken: they could have attempted to outbait the antis. One ironic development in the twisted history of antisuffrage thinking was that to argue that woman suffrage was dangerous, the antis had to pay tribute to the potential good citizenship of black women, at the same time disparaging the character of black men. "We have managed the men," said the *Newport News Daily Press*, "but could we manage the women? It is a different proposition. We believe that most of the women would qualify, and we further believe that they would persuade many of the men to qualify; and pay their poll taxes for them if need be." The *Winchester Evening Star* printed a similar prediction: "The negro woman, as a rule, is ahead of the negro man. She is the wage-earner, and as such has the rule over the more indolent negro man. He may stay away from the polls, but she won't." An antisuffrage legislator claimed that black women would "face twenty-five shotguns" to vote.[38]

Given this line of argument, the most effective counterattack available to the white suffragists was the defamation of the black woman's character. The culture of early twentieth-century America abounded with negative stereotypes of black women, and it would have been easy for the suffragists to deploy them, to paint black women as ignorant or irresponsible, as lazy or loose.[39] But this the suffragists did not do, either publicly or in their letters to one another. When in the last months of the campaign the antis succeeded in making race a "stumbling block" to woman suffrage, the suffragists could have blamed Virginia's black population. Instead, they placed the blame where it belonged, on the antisuffragists.

The white suffragists, in other words, occupied a middling place—a far cry from the theoretical egalitarianism that currently dominates feminism but also well removed from the shrieking racism of the antis. That middle ground bears further exploration. I have so far emphasized the constraints on the Equal Suffrage League, constraints imposed by the tactics of the antis and by the conservatism that prevailed among Virginia's voters and legislators. It is important to recognize, however, that the suffragists had some rhetorical latitude. They spoke on street corners and from automobiles, they handed out fliers by the hundreds, they fed news to the press, and although they failed to carry the day for woman suffrage, they contributed to the shape of the political universe in which all Virginians moved. How, in matters respecting race, do we evaluate those contributions?

The first thing to remember is that the white suffragists typically did not talk about race at all; it takes a certain intellectual agility to hold onto that fact while simultaneously attempting to evaluate the racialist arguments they did make. Meanwhile, if we are going to make moral judgments—and how can we not?—it would seem worthwhile to devise standards that are explicit and appropriate to the compromised situation in which the suffragists found themselves. For example, were their claims true or at least plausible? Second, did the suffragists accommodate white supremacy in a minimalist way, or did they pander to it or in some other way legitimate it? Third, did they leave open the possibility that black women might vote in significant numbers, or did they tend to foreclose that possibility?

Since I have already taken pains to demonstrate how low the anti-suffragists would go, it seems only fair to do likewise with the white suffragists. Among the ugliest and most opportunistic statements to be found in the extant prosuffrage literature is this sentence in an undated pamphlet issued under the imprimatur of the Equal Suffrage League: "It must be remembered that the white woman of the South is now the political subject of the negro sovereign, and there she will remain until some power lifts her from that humiliating position." This was the Virginia suffragists' most obnoxious rendition of an argument that had been formulated by northern women's rights advocates as early as 1848.[40] It was, simply put, untrue; certainly it ran against the grain of the suffragists' more commonplace claim that black male voters were not sovereign anywhere. Moreover, it evoked a fictional social dynamic parallel to the one that had historically been used to justify lynching: some unnamed power was called upon to rescue helpless white womanhood from powerful black men. The best that can be said for this sort of appeal is that the suffragists did not use it very often and that when they did, they usually phrased it in a way that was at least technically true. For example, a newspaper advertisement placed by the Equal Suffrage League in 1919 stated, "At present the Constitution of Virginia places women of both races in a position of political inferiority to negro men."[41] Even in this less provocative and more accurate rendition, this appeal pandered to white supremacist ideology.

The suffragists' primary argument with respect to race, meanwhile, had a more elastic character and a more complex career. The suffragists' central contention, once again, was one of denial: woman suffrage would not endanger whites' control of the ballot box. In its original form this was a strictly defensive argument that rendered no judgment on the justice of white supremacy itself. Thus in 1915, in response to the antis' charges that woman suffrage would subject some thirty counties to black rule, the Equal Suffrage League issued a small pamphlet called *Voting Qualifications in Virginia,* which was nothing if not matter of fact. "As these laws restrict the negro man's vote," the pamphlet explained, "it stands to reason that they will also restrict the negro woman's vote."[42]

But what a difference a few words could make. Early in 1916 the Equal Suffrage League issued a new flier, presumably for the benefit of the General Assembly then in session. *Equal Suffrage and the Negro Vote* repeated the arguments of the earlier pamphlet but with some brief additions. Most important was the final sentence: "We are secure from negro domination now—then, even more."[43] These ten words put an entirely different stamp on the suffragists' constitutional argument. They promised that woman suffrage would actually increase the margin of white voting strength; they implied that white supremacy was a good thing; and the use of "we" placed the Equal Suffrage League squarely within the community of whites who had an interest in maintaining white supremacy.

It is not surprising that such phrases should appear in a literature manufactured for the purpose of neutralizing the antis' allegations about the dangers woman suffrage posed to white supremacy. More surprising were statements to the effect that with woman suffrage, voting qualifications would and should operate in ways that were race blind. Mary Pollard Clarke put the question in 1915: "Does not everybody agree in this enlightened age that the educated, property-holding negro should have a chance to vote? Can any white man or white woman claim the right of citizenship for himself or herself and deny it to the negro man or woman of intelligence and attainment?"[44] This formulation was evidently too liberal for public consumption and apparently did not appear in print again. Subsequent statements about the evenhandedness of the law—and the consequent irrelevance of race—tended to be phrased negatively, in terms of the groups that would not qualify to vote. As Adèle Clark asserted in a broadside of 1919, voting qualifications "will operate to eliminate the illiterate and irresponsible women of both races, as they now eliminate the illiterate and irresponsible men of both races."[45]

Adèle Clark was surely aware that the election laws of Virginia were not impartially applied; to suggest that they were was to slight the injustices suffered by members of all the cheated groups—black men chiefly but poorer white men as well and some hapless Republicans. Moreover, Mary Pollard Clarke wrapped her plea for the black voter "of intelligence and attainment" in a larger package that assured readers that white supremacy was in no trouble whatever.[46]

All of which adds urgency to the question, What did the white suffragists *really* think? Not one of these articulate women left a document that tells. It may be that they did not know. The politics of denial had two dimensions. One, as we have repeatedly seen, was the belief that white supremacy was a bogus issue, stirred up by the antis to camouflage the real issues at stake in the campaign. The second dimension of denial grew out of the first: having decided from the beginning that race was not a genuine issue, the suffragists excused themselves from grappling with it in any thoughtful way. Lila Meade Valentine believed in the "principle" that black women should be able to vote where they met the state qualifications. But what should those qualifications be? Because they were women, the suffragists were exempted from struggling with that question, which for the time being had been settled by the framers of the 1902 constitution. Because the suffragists were white in a time of declining black political power, they could agitate for the vote without ever having to explain themselves to black Virginians. The suffragists operated in a zone in which they were immune from the necessity of articulating principle—a reminder, if one is needed, of how both the spoken and the unspoken can be conditioned by political circumstance.

This was even more acutely the case for African Americans. In the North and West there was substantial black support for woman suffrage— and also enough opposition to make for lively debate within black communities.[47] In Virginia, however, the tactics of the antis put blacks in an impossible position, one that made taking a public stand, whether advocacy or opposition, extremely awkward. To oppose woman suffrage in public was to align oneself with the white antis and their boundless exploitation of the race issue. A black person who supported woman suffrage, meanwhile, could only damage the cause by saying so; recall Hugh White waving *The Crisis* about during his antisuffrage peroration in the House of Delegates.

There was the further consideration that woman suffrage was unlikely to make a dramatic difference in the power of the black electorate. The *Planet,* Richmond's African American weekly, made the point in 1919, shortly after the General Assembly torpedoed the Anthony Amendment: "White folks down here are opposing woman suffrage because colored women will have the right to vote. They argue that the preponderance of colored women in some counties will show itself at the polls. We used to think so too, but a bitter experience has taught us otherwise." Even the votes of whites were discounted (or miscounted) if they went against the interests of the dominant party, the *Planet* went on. "The talk about majority rule is a joke and the colored folks of the Southland know it," said the *Planet.* " 'Quit your kidding.' "[48]

From this tough-minded critique, one might extrapolate a certain lukewarmness on the subject of votes for women. This, however, is a guess. The (male) editors of Virginia's black newspapers printed occasional woman suffrage news, and they sometimes commented on the behavior of the protagonists. On the justice or wisdom of woman suffrage itself, however, the black press took no position.[49]

As for the opinions of Virginia's black women, we have only a few tantalizing clues. In 1912 the National Association of Colored Women held its biennial convention in Hampton, Virginia. In the course of addressing the convention on "Woman and Business," Maggie Lena

Walker, the Richmond banker, insurance executive, and community leader, injected a single sentence on behalf of woman suffrage. Women were rebelling against their unjust wages, Walker asserted, "yet Capital is deaf—and will never hear their cries, until the women force Capital to hear them at the ballot box, and to be just and honest to them as to the men." The *Southern Workman,* the magazine published by Hampton Institute, praised the speech but did not report its slant on woman suffrage.[50] A small news item in the *Richmond Planet* suggests that Walker had company. In 1916 the *Planet* reported the outcome of a women's basketball game between two teams of black public school teachers; the contest was billed as the Feminists vs. the Suffragists.[51]

Such are the fragments from which we attempt to reconstruct black women's political consciousness. In a 1989 essay, the historian Elsa Barkley Brown enlists the career of Maggie Lena Walker in an exploration of the concept of "womanism." As Brown aptly charges, feminist scholars and activists have operated largely without reference to black women's experience, and as a result they tend to assume that gender struggles and race struggles can be separated from each other and opposed to one another. Black women's activism, when it has been noticed, has thus frequently been misconstrued. Black women who stood up for the race, women like Maggie Walker, are not ranked among the great figures of the women's rights tradition; they are seen as having devoted themselves to the black struggle, not women's struggle. Likewise, issues vitally concerning justice to people of color are defined as issues of race or of nation, not as women's issues, and therefore are thought to lie beyond the legitimate reach of feminism.

It is in an attempt to leave behind these false dichotomies that some black women have abandoned the term *feminism* and have opted instead for *womanism,* which suggests the inseparability of gender and race. In Brown's essay, this inseparability has at least three dimensions: first, black women experience their blackness and femaleness simultaneously, not sequentially; second, black women often experience racism and sexism simultaneously; and third, black women have centered their political consciousness on "the idea that women's struggle and race struggle were not two separate phenomena but one indivisible whole."[52] As exemplars of womanist consciousness, Brown singles out Maggie Walker and the women and men Walker mobilized in Richmond's black community.

When we put questions about the separability of gender and race on the same docket with the Virginia woman suffrage controversy, the two play off one another in interesting ways—and return us to the importance of specific political contexts. It is striking that in Maggie Walker's extant speeches there is much on the power of women, actual and potential, and very little on woman suffrage. This dearth of commentary on the vote could be a mere accident, for much that Walker said was not preserved or has not yet come to light. It would also make sense as strategic self-censorship. In Maggie Walker's Virginia there were two groups that shared the premise that woman's struggle and the race struggle were inseparable. One group centered around Walker. The other we have already met, the white supremacist antis. "Every argument for woman suffrage," as Hugh White said, "is also an argument for negro suffrage." Depending on who deployed it, the doctrine of inseparability could be progressive, egalitarian, and, in Brown's phrasing, holistic. Or it could be hierarchical, reactionary, and exclusive. Since the antisuffragists took this lower road, it would stand to reason that Walker would want to deprive them of additional ammunition.

So did the white suffragists, who occupied a distinctive piece of conceptual ground, arguing that race and gender issues were eminently separable—specifically, that Virginia could institute "equal" suffrage for women without materially increasing the political power of blacks as a group. This argument drew its force from two factors. First, the white suffragists were compelled to use it to survive as a movement; once the antis conflated woman suffrage with a revolution in race relations, the Equal Suffrage League had to make the separability argument or else throw in the towel. Second, the suffragists' argument on the simplest level turned out to be true. Votes for women, as we shall soon see, did not empower black Virginians as a group; woman suffrage did not operate on so dramatic a scale. Black women in Virginia cities, however, were quite willing to engage in the politics of the smaller gain, to attempt to use the vote for whatever it might prove to be worth.

Woman suffrage came to Virginia in 1920, after thirty-six other states ratified the Nineteenth Amendment to the U.S. Constitution. Ratification was completed in late August; in Virginia, women were given one month to register to vote in the November elections. Very quickly, woman suffrage moved out of the realm of the hypothetical, its dimensions to be decided in the hundreds of locations throughout the commonwealth, where treasurers collected poll taxes and registrars screened potential voters.

In the course of this first registration period, black women, white suffragists, and the defeated antisuffragists all revealed themselves more fully. With the Nineteenth Amendment ratified, it was no longer necessary for black Virginians to be so quiet or for white suffragists to be so cautious. Nor should it have been necessary for the antis to continue to beat the drums of white supremacy. The antis, however, were not improved by defeat; in the registration scenes of September 1920, they found new occasions for setting off racist alarms. This was largely in response to the initiatives of black women, who organized voter registration campaigns and qualified in impressive numbers in several cities. Small towns and rural areas, as we shall soon see, presented an altogether different picture. The shape of local politics played a decisive role in the registration rates of black women and white women as well.

The record of the white suffragists, meanwhile, was mixed. Having invested a great deal in the argument that woman suffrage would not endanger white supremacy, the suffragists felt vindicated by the final outcome. In the end the overall voting power of black people in Virginia did not increase, and that seems to have been all right with the white suffragists. At the same time, a number of suffragists turned up among the South's most forward-thinking white people. In the early 1920s small groups of white southerners joined with black leaders, together arguing that social progress depended on greater justice for black people and on greater contact and frank discussions between the representatives of the two races. In the Virginia wing of this fledgling interracial movement, a high proportion of the white women had been active in the Equal Suffrage League of Virginia.

When the registration books were opened in early September, Virginia women initially presented themselves in modest numbers. With about two weeks to go, however, observers in many parts of the state reported surges of applicants. In Richmond, the *Times-Dispatch* called the numbers "amazing" and "phenomenal."[53] The editor of the *Times-Dispatch* had every reason to be impressed, having claimed to the last ditch that white women did not want the vote and would not exercise it if they had it. Once the women of Richmond proved the contrary, the *Times-Dispatch* began to keep daily tabs on the proceedings at city hall.

Like other papers, the *Times-Dispatch* kept an especially close watch on the number of black registrants. On September 12 the black attorney Giles B. Jackson convened a committee of professional and activist women, who selected Maggie Walker as their chair. Within a few days, the committee organized the first of several mass meetings. Diverse white women's organizations had in the meantime been conducting campaigns of their own, and the results were immediately felt at city hall. "Swamped by a rush of women voters, both white and colored," the *News Leader* reported, "Central Registrar William S. Woodson threw up his hands this morning and called for help." A second room and a deputy were found so that the crowd could be segregated. "It was impossible for Central Registrar Woodson to supervise so many, and as a result the whole throng, white and colored, were milling about giving each other aid, suggestion and instructions, regardless of the plain provision of the constitution." Despite the confusion, 276 women were registered that day.[54]

The real rush was yet to come. On September 20 more than five hundred women were registered, with over a hundred still waiting in line when the registrars closed for the day. On September 21 over seven hundred were registered, and the pace continued at from six to eight hundred a day, with as many as three hundred applicants still waiting in line at day's end. On the final day, October 2, registrations at city hall topped a thousand.[55]

The accelerated pace of registration was made possible in part by the appointment of three white women deputies to handle white applicants. After the deputies were sworn in, Maggie Walker pressed one official after another to have black deputies appointed as well. When Walker failed, the African American social worker and community organizer Ora Brown Stokes took up the effort. With her compatriots in the Richmond Neighborhood Association, Stokes petitioned the registrar to appoint black deputies but to no avail.[56] The registration line for blacks would continue to move more slowly than that for whites, both because of the shortage of personnel and because black women's applications were more frequently challenged. Consequently, black women were more likely than whites to find themselves still waiting when registration was shut down for the day. The registrar did extend the hours of business in the final two days of registration, a belated response to requests from white women's groups. When all the paperwork was complete, the total registration of the black women of Richmond was 2,410. The total for white women was 10,645.[57]

A casual reader of the newspapers might have concluded that the numbers were just the reverse. As soon as the organization of Richmond's black women began to show results, some white newspapers turned to distortion. "NEGRO WOMEN CONTINUE TO OUTNUMBER WHITE IN ATTEMPTING TO QUALIFY," screamed the headline of the *Richmond News Leader.* The article itself said that three-quarters of the registrants that day were white. Newspapers in other parts of the state nevertheless picked up the hysterical headline. As the *Newport News Daily Press* put it, "Negro Women Swamp State Registrar's Office." "More Negro Women Than White," said the *Index-Appeal* of Petersburg. The front page in Front Royal read "White Women Kept Out." The *Danville Register* claimed that black women in Richmond outnumbered white registrants; the *Roanoke World News* said black women were qualifying "in far greater numbers" than were whites; and the *Norfolk Virginian-Pilot* supplied a ratio of three to one.[58]

Where the newspapers left off, the Democratic party began. Or rather, the Democratic leadership suddenly discovered the virtues of woman suffrage, and the press helped "the Organization" reach its female constituency. At the very center of the party's pitch to white women was white supremacy. As the chairman of the Richmond City Democratic Committee phrased it, "It is the duty of every woman who regards the domination of the white race as essential to the welfare of the Southland to qualify for the ballot. . . . "[59] A comparable call went out from Rorer James, chairman of the state central committee, who instructed the chairmen of all county and city committees to get white women registered in response to the "desperate efforts" of the black women of Richmond to register. The officials of the party were assisted by the Virginia Association Opposed to Woman Suffrage, whose president called for conservative women to qualify "in view of the fact that colored women are registering in large numbers. . . . "[60]

Notice the facility with which the Democrats shifted gears. The great majority of Democratic politicians and most of the Democratic press had opposed woman suffrage, and they had made free use of white supremacist arguments to try fending it off. When woman suffrage came to Virginia anyway, the Democrats were in the discomfiting position of having done nothing to earn the loyalty of new women voters. Out once again came the threats to white supremacy, exaggerated this time to scare white women into behaving like good Democrats. After registration was complete, some Democrats went further and tried to discipline the new voters by suggesting that women would not be able to vote in the 1921 Democratic primary unless they voted a straight ticket in November.[61]

Were white women persuaded by these appeals? Registration figures do not tell. They do make it plain, however, that the forces of white supremacy were highly resilient in the face of woman suffrage. Everywhere in Virginia, white women were able to register in greater numbers than black women, both absolutely and relatively. Male dominance proved almost as durable. Nowhere did women emerge as the majority of registered voters, even though women were a numerical majority in many Virginia cities.

Within these general patterns there were some interesting variations. For both black and white women, urban residence made a big difference. In most rural counties the proportion of black women who registered was 5 percent or less of the black adult female population; the comparable figure for white women was anywhere from about 8 percent to 20 percent.[62] Both groups did much better in the cities. In Richmond, for example, the 2,410 black women who registered represented 12.5 percent of the black adult female population; the comparable figure for white women was 26.8 percent.[63]

The reasons for this urban-rural difference are not hard to figure out. Citizens newly eligible to register to vote are most likely to actually register when shown the ropes by someone who already knows how it's done. Organizing a voter registration campaign was easier in town, where the population was dense, communications were speedy, and networks of organizations stood ready to be mobilized. The law also favored the urban citizen. Virginia lawmakers had intentionally made the registration process complicated. One had to locate the county or city treasurer, pay one's poll tax, and then proceed with receipt in hand to find the registrar. In the largest cities, this was not usually difficult; the registrar was required to sit for thirty days in a centrally located public building. In the country, registration was handled in local precincts by registrars who were required to sit for only one day out of the thirty-day registration period. They were not required to announce when that day might be or where they might be located. As Adèle Clark later recalled, "Our rural women had a lot of trouble running all over the county trying to catch the registrars, who were out plowing or fishing or doing various things."[64] Once the registrar was located, he had considerable latitude in deciding whether a given applicant was indeed literate; applicants were required to record a number of facts about themselves without prompting from anyone.

Obviously these factors could be manipulated to encourage some applicants and discourage others; in a rural district, all the registrar had to do to defeat a black woman's effort to register was to pretend he wasn't home when he saw her coming down the road. There is no hard evidence on exactly how it was done, but it could hardly have been coincidental that black women's registration rates tended to be lowest in the most heavily black counties. In King William County, for example, where just over half the residents were black, only 2.5 percent of adult black females were registered. Other black-majority counties posted even smaller figures: 2.0 percent in Nansemond, 1.7 percent in Caroline, 0.3 percent in Southampton, 0.2 in Powhatan, 0.1 percent in Essex, and zero in Dinwiddie.[65]

By the same token, black women's registration rates were higher where the total number of blacks in the population was relatively small and where competition between Democrats and Republicans was keen enough to encourage the Republican leaders to cultivate their black constituencies. The highest registration rates in the state, for both black and white women, posted in Clifton Forge. There the three factors of urbanization, a large white majority, and a scrappy bunch of Republicans converged; 32.8 percent of black women registered (94 out of 287), while the comparable figure for white women was a close 35.5 percent (508 out of 1,429).[66]

Even with these relatively high rates of black registration, however, the white majority was slightly larger than it had been. The Equal Suffrage League had argued all along that woman suffrage was no threat to white supremacy; this had been their central, unifying contention with respect to race. When actual registration figures became available, the white suffragists were thoroughly vindicated. At the same time, the suffragists' old strategy of denial became obsolete. By late September it was clear that there would be some black women voters in Virginia and that there would be significant concentrations of them in several cities. To say that they were insufficiently numerous to undo white supremacy was not to say what the Equal Suffrage League's stance toward them should be. Had Lila Meade Valentine not been critically ill, she might have exerted some leadership in this respect. As it was, no single attitude or policy arose to replace the Equal Suffrage League's well-worn strategy.

Several different strands of behavior were thus observable among the white suffragists in the fall of 1920. One tendency was to express satisfaction in their hour of vindication. The most extreme instance of this came in a letter from the headquarters secretary in Richmond to a suffragist in Lynchburg: "Yes, it is very gratifying to know that the white women registered in such large numbers—so much larger numbers than the negro women. This fortunately has been the case all over the State." The secretary went on, demonstrating her supreme insensitivity to the situation of Virginia's black women: "The negro women registered in small numbers wherever they took the trouble to register at all. In many places not a one even tried to register."[67]

If this letter was a good example of a kind of thoughtless delight at having bested the antis, it was also a fair example of what racial segregation had wrought: a sense on the white suffragists' part of vast distances between black women and themselves, a sense of distance that was undoubtedly reinforced by the suffragists' earlier refusal to identify with black aspirations for the vote. One of the most interesting developments of the postratification period was a conscious effort on the part of some white suffragists to reverse the trend and to begin bridging the distances. Among the first to try was Martha Chamberlayne McNeill. In September, when the press attempted to scare white women into registering by raising alarms about the number of black women lined up at city hall, McNeill wrote to the *Times-Dispatch* in protest: "it seems an unwise and unkind method to call white women to their duty by an effort to arouse race antagonism, and by casting aspersions on the negro women of our community." McNeill enumerated the many contributions of Richmond's black women to the recent war effort, and she claimed black leaders in turn understood "that the white women active in public and benevolent work have always been keenly interested in the betterment of the condition of the negro population. Therefore, it seems an especially dangerous and ill-considered thing to foment ill-feeling between the women of the two races, and thus shake the confidence of the colored women in their white friends." McNeill concluded, "By the law of majority rule the white people, men and women, may peaceably and properly maintain white supremacy. Their duty is clear: without excitement and without ill-feeling, but with full realization of their obligation and responsibilities to both races for the good of all, white men and white women should in full strength register before October 2."[68]

Her conclusion was paternalistic, to say the least, and its reassurances with respect to white supremacy were probably intended to diffuse the risks she had taken in the earlier paragraphs. But Martha McNeill at least put her money where her mouth was. She was involved in one of Virginia's most important early experiments in interracial cooperation, having served on the interracial board of the Industrial Home School for Girls, a reformatory for young black women founded by Janie Porter Barrett and the Virginia Federation of Colored Women's Clubs.[69] As the 1920 elections approached, it was McNeill who put Richmond's white suffragists in touch with Ora Brown Stokes and several other African American woman suffragists. As Adèle Clark later told it, "threats of bloodshed and riot and everything else" were flying about Richmond, so she and Nora Houston invited the black leadership to their studio (since they were painters, they thought they could make this daring move and have it chalked up to artistic eccentricity) to discuss what they might do. It was agreed that the white women would find cars and cruise the polling places on election day. Clark and friends kept their promise, and, as Clark told it, black women voted without incident.[70]

Clark did not specify exactly who was threatening violence against whom, but it is clear that the persistence of black women in the registration lines had an unsettling and ultimately positive impact on thoughtful whites, not unlike the impact of the new militance of African American soldiers who had returned from the war. White suffragists like Adèle Clark and Nora Houston felt compelled to make some sort of effort to reach their counterparts in black Richmond, and before long they were joined by a number of their suffrage colleagues in a more systematic movement for interracial cooperation. Of the thirty-four white women who were identified as leaders in the interracial movement of the 1920s, more than one-third had been active in the Equal Suffrage League. The antis were nowhere to be found. None of the women who were publicly identified as antisuffragists before 1920 appeared after 1920 on the rosters of Virginia's interracial organizations.[71]

In organizations like the Urban League and the Women's Section of the Commission on Interracial Cooperation, black and white women pursued a wide-ranging agenda for social action. They worked on health, recreation, housing, and education. They condemned new white supremacist groups like the revived Ku Klux Klan and the Anglo Saxon Leagues. They spoke out against lynching and the sexual exploitation of black women.[72]

In these endeavors they were sometimes joined by organizations that remained exclusively white. In September 1921 the Virginia League of Women Voters, the successor organization to the Equal Suffrage League, passed a resolution "Strongly Condemning Organizations That Breed Class, Race, or Religious Hatred."[73] "But we never had the nerve to enroll the Negro women in the League of Women Voters," as Adèle Clark confessed. "I've always regretted it, but we just couldn't bring the middle-of-the-road thinkers to the point of bringing the Negro women in."[74]

In the 1920s, as before, the white woman suffragists negotiated a middling course. After 1920 that course included significant and open cooperation with leading black Virginians, who in turn challenged the white women to enlarge their democratic vision. Virginia's Janie Porter Barrett, for example, joined other southern black club women in 1921 in asking "that white women, for the protection of their homes as well as ours indicate their sanction of the ballot for all citizens as representing government by the sober, reasoned and deliberate judgment of all the people."[75] That far the white suffragists were unwilling to go. The interracial movement took up many issues, and suffragists like Adèle Clark and Lucy Randolph Mason did some quiet citizenship work among black women.[76] The whites as a group, however, would not risk open advocacy of greater voting rights for black people.

It is important that we hold this failing firmly in mind. If one of the functions of history is to serve as social criticism—and for feminists, as self-criticism—it is essential to take a long look at the suffragists' failures, to measure their motives and actions against what we conceive to be ideal feminist practice. It will not do to stop here, however. In feminist scholarship there is a tendency to beam most of our attention on the advocates of women's rights, from whom we expect much, while their adversaries, from whom we expect little, get off the hook. I am suggesting that we pay more attention to the adversaries and to the specific and evolving political worlds in which the woman suffragists and their opponents did daily battle.

While this should clarify our analysis of the means by which woman suffragists attempted to advance their cause, we also need to look at the results. Here again, we need a vision that can acknowledge modest achievements even while it encompasses vast failures. Virginia was a bastion of white supremacy in 1919, and black women had no voice in formal politics. By the end of 1920 Virginia was still a bastion of white supremacy, but several thousand black women had achieved the dignity of citizenship, they had acquired a new instrument of resistance, and a select few had gained new channels into national political councils, chiefly through the Republican party.[77] In some cases they were able to seize the moment and push beyond the vote itself. In 1921, for example, Maggie Walker ran for state office; she ran for superintendent of public instruction on an all-black ticket of dissident Republicans.[78] The "Lily Blacks" could not hope to win, but Walker's candidacy forced everyone who read the news to cope at least momentarily with the image of a black woman seeking high office. Before 1920 putting Walker on the ticket would not have even been thinkable. In its immediate results, woman suffrage made electoral politics more inclusive. That is more than can be said for anything else in Virginia politics for many decades.

NOTES

For support of the research on which this essay is based, I am grateful to the American Association for State and Local History, Rutgers University, and the Woodrow Wilson International Center for Scholars.

1. Mary Johnston to Lila Meade Valentine, January 5, 1913, Lila Meade Valentine Papers, Virginia Historical Society, Richmond, Va.

2. There are, however, a few published biographical treatments of woman suffrage leaders. A forthcoming book by Marjorie Spruill Wheeler, *New Women of the New South: The Leaders of the Woman Suffrage Movement in the Southern States* (New York: Oxford University Press), deals at length with Lila Meade Valentine and Mary Johnston. See also Wheeler's recent "Mary Johnston, Suffragist," *Virginia Magazine of History and Biography* 100 (January 1992): 99-118. There are two biographical articles on Valentine: [Elizabeth Dabney Coleman], "Genteel Crusader," *Virginia Cavalcade* 4 (Autumn 1954): 29-32; Lloyd C. Taylor, Jr., "Lila Meade Valentine: The FFV as Reformer," *Virginia Magazine of History and Biography* 70 (October 1962): 471-87. Elsa Barkley Brown challenges conventional assumptions about who should be categorized as a woman suffragist in "Womanist Consciousness: Maggie Lena Walker and the Independent Order of Saint Luke," *Signs* 14 (Spring 1989): 610-33. There are also several useful unpublished masters theses: Anne Hamilton Stites, "The Inconceivable Revolution in Virginia 1870-1920" (University of Richmond, 1965); Carol Jean Clare, "The Woman Suffrage Movement in Virginia: Its Nature,

Rationale, and Tactics" (University of Virginia, 1968); Charlotte Jean Shelton, "Woman Suffrage and Virginia Politics, 1909-1920" (University of Virginia, 1969); and Trudy J. Hanmer, "A Divine Discontent: Mary Johnston and Woman Suffrage in Virginia" (University of Virginia, 1972). Suzanne Lebsock, *Virginia Women, 1600-1945: "A Share of Honour"* (Richmond: Virginia State Library, 1987), gives a brief history of the woman suffrage movement, placing it in the context of other women's reform causes of the period.

3. Woman suffrage receives bare mention in Allen W. Moger, *Virginia: Bourbonism to Byrd, 1870-1925* (Charlottesville: University Press of Virginia, 1968), 295, 328-29; and Raymond H. Pulley, *Old Virginia Restored: An Interpretation of the Progressive Impulse, 1870-1930* (Charlottesville: University Press of Virginia, 1968), 150.

4. Aileen S. Kraditor, *Up from the Pedestal: Selected Writings in the History of American Feminism* (Chicago: Quadrangle Books, 1968), 253-65; Gerda Lerner, *Black Women in White America: A Documentary History* (New York: Pantheon Books, 1972), 321; Rosalyn Terborg-Penn, "Discrimination against Afro-American Women in the Woman's Movement, 1830-1920," in *The Afro-American Woman: Struggles and Images,* ed. Sharon Harley and Rosalyn Terborg-Penn (Port Washington, N.Y.: Kennikat Press, 1978), 17-27; Angela Y. Davis, *Women, Race and Class* (New York: Random House, 1981), 70-86; Paula Giddings, *When and Where I Enter: The Impact of Black Women on Race and Sex in America* (New York: William Morrow, 1984), 159-70; Barbara Hilkert Andolsen, *"Daughters of Jefferson, Daughters of Bootblacks": Racism and American Feminism* (Macon, Ga.: Mercer University Press, 1986).

5. Aileen S. Kraditor, *The Ideas of the Woman Suffrage Movement, 1890-1920* (New York: Columbia University Press, 1965), 32, 165, 185. Anne Firor Scott, *The Southern Lady: From Pedestal to Politics, 1830-1930* (Chicago: University of Chicago Press, 1970), 181-83, challenged Kraditor's argument but does not seem to have dislodged it.

6. Many historians will recognize "Progressivism—For Whites Only" as a chapter title in C. Vann Woodward's monumental *Origins of the New South, 1877-1913* (Baton Rouge: Louisiana State University Press, 1951).

7. Kraditor concentrated on women who repeatedly held national office in the National American Woman Suffrage Association (NAWSA), a decision that for most purposes was probably sensible. For the South, however, it produced the odd couple of Kate Gordon of Louisiana and Laura Clay of Kentucky. Both women were professional southerners, women whose stature in the national movement depended on their persuading nonsoutherners that they held the keys to the peculiarities and mysteries of their region. This strategy naturally increased their attention to race. It also failed, sooner in Gordon's case (she was the more extreme) and later in Clay's. Both ended their woman suffrage careers confused and alienated, not only from NAWSA but also from the mainstream of southern suffragists. A more detailed and nuanced analysis of Clay may be found in Paul E. Fuller, *Laura Clay and the Woman's Rights Movement* (Lexington: University Press of Kentucky, 1975). On Gordon, see Kenneth R. Johnson, "Kate Gordon

and the Woman Suffrage Movement in the South," *Journal of Southern History* 38 (August 1972): 365-92. Both Clay and Gordon are major figures in Wheeler's *New Women of the New South.*

8. Elizabeth Cady Stanton, Susan B. Anthony, and Matilda Joslyn Gage, eds., *History of Woman Suffrage,* vol. 3 (Rochester, N.Y.: Susan B. Anthony, 1886), 823-24; Susan B. Anthony and Ida Husted Harper, *History of Woman Suffrage,* vol. 4 (Rochester, N.Y.: Susan B. Anthony, 1902), 964-66; *Richmond State,* April 24, 1896. See also the theses by Clare, Shelton, and Stites cited in note 2.

9. Andrew Buni, *The Negro in Virginia Politics, 1902-1965* (Charlottesville: University Press of Virginia, 1967), 13-19; J. Morgan Kousser, *The Shaping of Southern Politics: Suffrage Restriction and the Establishment of the One-Party South* (New Haven, Conn.: Yale University Press, 1974), 171-81; Moger, *Virginia: Bourbonism to Byrd,* 181-202; Pulley, *Old Virginia Restored,* 66-91.

10. Buni, *The Negro in Virginia Politics,* 24-93, gives the fullest account.

11. *Richmond News Leader,* May 2, 1914. The papers of the Norfolk Equal Suffrage League are located in the Virginia Woman Suffrage Collection in the Virginia State Library and Archives, Richmond, Va. Because the collection was organized after I went through it, I am unable to give specific locations for particular documents within the collection.

12. Adèle Clark Interview by Winston Broadfoot, February 28, 1964, 3, Southern Oral History Program Collection, Southern Historical Collection, University of North Carolina-Chapel Hill. See also John A. Salmond, *Miss Lucy of the CIO: The Life and Times of Lucy Randolph Mason, 1882-1959* (Athens: University of Georgia Press, 1988). Among the best pedigreed of the suffragists, Mason was also the most radical, devoting the second half of her career to the southern labor movement.

13. The Equal Suffrage League was affiliated with the National American Woman Suffrage Association. A small group of Virginians affiliated with NAWSA's rival organization, the Congressional Union (CU). Their activities can be documented in part through the hostile remarks made about them by Lila Meade Valentine and other Equal Suffrage League officers, who believed that the CU's militant tactics were particularly damaging to the woman suffrage cause in a conservative state like Virginia. Valentine made public disavowals of CU tactics on several occasions.

14. Typescript copy of the *Richmond News Leader* article (first quotation) and letter of Alice O. Taylor to Jessie E. Townsend, July 6, 1914 (second quotation), Virginia Woman Suffrage Collection; clipping from *Baltimore* [?] *Afro-American,* Peabody Clippings 231, Hampton University Archives, Hampton, Va.; clipping from *Norfolk Journal and Guide,* June 27, 1914, Adèle Clark Papers, Virginia Commonwealth University, Richmond, Va.

15. The debate was not always serious. Equal Suffrage League secretary Alice O. Taylor contrasted the respectful demeanor of the House in 1912 to their performance in 1914, in which the members, egged on by the speaker, were "jesting, laughing sneering and being generally so disorderly that the patrons of the measure could scarcely be heard." Taylor to Jessie E. Townsend, March 19, 1914, Virginia Woman Suffrage Collection.

16. *Richmond Times-Dispatch,* April 23, 1913. An earlier controversy over allowing Virginia women to practice medicine and law had prompted Parker to write *The Woman's Place. Her Position in the Christian World. The Problem Considered under Four Grand Heads—Woman Outstripped by Man, Even in Domestic Handiwork* (Richmond: n.p., 1892).

17. Saxon W. Holt to Mrs. A. J. Hauser, December 16, 1913, Virginia Woman Suffrage Collection; Alice O. Taylor [?] to Mrs. A. J. Hauser, Adèle Clark Papers.

18. Broadside in the Virginia Woman Suffrage Collection.

19. See, for example, the *Newport News Daily Press,* May 6, 1915. The broadside was headlined "Virginia Warns Her People Against Woman Suffrage— Twenty-Nine Counties would Go Under Negro Rule—Over Sixty Counties in the State of Georgia—The Entire State of Mississippi—What of Your State? Isn't It About Time for Reflecting Men and Women to Think—And Act?" Virginia Woman Suffrage Collection.

20. The attorney general was John Garland Pollard, who was later elected governor. The press coordinator for the Equal Suffrage League was Mary Pollard (Mrs. G. Harvey) Clarke, who was also the author of the flyer *Equal Suffrage and the Negro Vote,* which can be found in the Virginia Woman Suffrage Collection. The collection also contains clippings of letters to editors by Adèle Clark and Alice Overby Taylor. Taylor's response was particularly interesting; applying Williams's logic to men, she suggested that the "negro problem" could be solved by disfranchising all the men in black-majority counties.

21. This position was spelled out by the Equal Suffrage League in an undated pamphlet entitled *Voting Qualifications in Virginia,* Virginia Woman Suffrage Papers, and in the undated flier *Equal Suffrage and the Negro Vote.*

22. Lila Meade Valentine to Jessie E. Townsend, April 10, 1915 (Valentine wrote two letters to Townsend dated April 10; "nonsense" appears in one and "last stand" appears in the other), Virginia Woman Suffrage Collection; Jessie Townsend to Alice O. Taylor, April 13, 1915, Adèle Clark Papers; Mary Johnston to Lila Meade Valentine, January 5, 1913, Lila Meade Valentine Papers. Later references in a similar vein include one to the "negro bogey" in a letter of E. Virginia Smith to Thomas Martin, January 19, 1918, Roberta Wellford Papers, University of Virginia, Charlottesville, Va.

23. Valentine to Townsend, April 10, 1915 (as above, each of the two April 10 letters contains one of the quotations), Virginia Woman Suffrage Collection.

24. Alice O. Taylor to Jessie E. Townsend, April 16, 1915, Adèle Clark Papers.

25. *Richmond Times-Dispatch,* February 19, 1916; *Newport News Daily Press,* February 19, 1916. The issue from which White read was probably *The Crisis* 4 (September 1912): 234, which carried an editorial corresponding to White's description. This issue also contained a symposium on woman suffrage, as did *The Crisis* 10 (August 1915): 178-92. For an analysis of antisuffragists' use of caricature in England, see Lisa Tickner, *The Spectacle of Women: Imagery of the Suffrage Campaign 1907-14* (Chicago: University of Chicago Press, 1988), 160-67.

26. [?] to Mrs. B. M. Hagan, March 8, 1916, Adèle Clark Papers.

27. From the beginning, the Equal Suffrage League advocated agitation on both state and federal amendments, much to the disappointment of Kate Gordon, whose Southern States Woman Suffrage Conference adamantly opposed the federal amendment. In practice, the Equal Suffrage League put most of its effort into a state amendment until after the "victorious defeat" of 1916. Later in 1916 the Equal Suffrage League threw in its lot with the national's new drive for the federal amendment. It is not completely clear why the league made such a risky move, but several motives are plausible. One was the fear that Virginia women would never be enfranchised any other way. As Elizabeth Otey put it, "Anybody with one eye and half sense would know that the state of Virginia wasn't going to give it to us...." Transcript of Interview with Elizabeth Otey by Charlotte Shelton, August 7, 1973, Oral History Program Collection, University of Virginia. Another possibility is that the suffragists hoped the threat of enfranchisement from outside would cause Virginia lawmakers to move on a state amendment. A third is that the suffragists underestimated the intransigence of Virginia lawmakers on a federal amendment; the Virginia General Assembly was the first to ratify the federal prohibition amendment, exhibiting few qualms about imposing dry laws on states whose citizens wished to remain wet. Finally, activists in the Equal Suffrage League were a relatively cosmopolitan lot who saw themselves as members of a national movement (indeed, an international one) of progressive women and men who were out to remake the world in many ways. This cosmopolitan outlook may have been what distinguished the suffragists from female antis—more than social indicators, such as formal education (hardly any of the principals on either side appear to have been college educated) or class status. In any case, the suffragists were willing to entertain arguments that the rights of the states were less important than the rights of individuals and less important than the needs of larger communities. This may help explain the seeming ease of their transition to a federal amendment.

28. Mary Mason Anderson Williams, letter to the editor, *Richmond Times-Dispatch*, September 2, 1919.

29. *Richmond Times-Dispatch*, February 11 and 21, 1920.

30. *Richmond Times-Dispatch*, September 2, 1919.

31. Virginia, *Journal of the House of Delegates of Virginia* (Richmond: Superintendent of Public Printing, 1919), 158. In the Senate, supporters of woman suffrage believed that inaction was the best course under the circumstances and succeeded in indefinitely postponing the House resolution. Virginia, *Journal of the Senate (Extra Session) of the Commonwealth of Virginia* (Richmond: Superintendent of Public Printing, 1919), 161, 166-67.

32. Lila Meade Valentine to J. Brad. Beverley, December 9, 1919, Adèle Clark Papers; Virginia, *Journal of the House of Delegates of Virginia* (Richmond: Superintendent of Public Printing, 1920), 272-73, 806; Virginia, *Journal of the Senate of the Commonwealth of Virginia* (Richmond: Superintendent of Public Printing, 1920), 172-74, 514-15.

33. Headquarters Secretary [Ida M. Thompson] to National American Woman

Suffrage Association, December 20, 1918, Adèle Clark Papers. A letter from a suffragist in Warrenton to state headquarters made a similar point: "The greatest stumbling block here is the vote of the Negro woman. . . . It is most important here." Susie F. H. Hilleary to Lila Meade Valentine, October 5, 1919, Adèle Clark Papers.

34. Anne Hobson Freeman, "Mary Munford's Fight for a College for Women Coordinate with the University of Virginia," *Virginia Magazine of History and Biography* 78 (October 1970): 481–91.

35. Robert Booth Fowler, *Carrie Catt: Feminist Politician* (Boston: Northeastern University Press, 1986), 83–90; Mari Jo Buhle and Paul Buhle, eds., *The Concise History of Woman Suffrage: Selections from the Classic Work of Stanton, Anthony, Gage, and Harper* (Urbana: University of Illinois Press, 1978), 312–13; Andolsen, *"Daughters of Jefferson,"* 21–44.

36. The leaflet is preserved in the Virginia Woman Suffrage Collection.

37. Lila Meade Valentine to Justina L. Wilson, February 17, 1919, Adèle Clark Papers. The story at the national level is told by Giddings, *When and Where I Enter,* 161–62.

38. *Newport News Daily Press,* May 6, 1915; *Winchester Evening Star,* March 19, 1918. Clippings containing all these quotations were found in the Virginia Woman Suffrage Collection. A comparable claim was made by the Advisory Committee Opposed to Woman Suffrage: "All who have had practical experience dealing with this problem know it would be ten times as difficult to deal with colored women and keep them from the polls as it ever was with colored men. The woman of the African race has her share of pertinacity too and would be exempt from fear of physical consequences." *The Virginia General Assembly and Woman Suffrage,* undated pamphlet, 8, Adèle Clark Papers.

39. On the devaluation of black women and attempts to counter it, see Beverly Guy-Sheftall, *Daughters of Sorrow: Attitudes toward Black Women, 1880–1920* (Brooklyn: Carlson Publishing, 1990), esp. chap. 3.

40. The pamphlet, entitled *Federal Amendment,* is located in the Virginia Woman Suffrage Collection. In her address to the historic 1848 women's rights convention in Seneca Falls, New York, Elizabeth Cady Stanton said, "But to have drunkards, idiots, horse-racing, rumselling rowdies, ignorant foreigners, and silly boys fully recognized, while we ourselves are thrust out from all the rights that belong to citizens, it is too grossly insulting to the dignity of woman to be longer quietly submitted to." Notice that Stanton did not target black men in this address. The *form* of her argument, however, was very much like that of later arguments used in Virginia and elsewhere. Quoted in Ellen Carol DuBois, ed., *Elizabeth Cady Stanton/Susan B. Anthony: Correspondence, Writings, Speeches* (New York: Schocken Books, 1981), 32.

41. *Richmond Times-Dispatch,* September 3, 1919. Other documents in which there is mention of white women's alleged political inferiority to black men include a letter by Mary Elizabeth Pidgeon to the *Richmond Times-Dispatch,* September 6, 1919; a letter from Adèle Clark to the *Richmond Times-Dispatch,* December 21, 1919; and an unsigned letter from Equal Suf-

frage League headquarters to Mrs. K. S. Timberlake, May 23, 1918, Adèle Clark Papers.

42. Equal Suffrage League of Virginia, *Voting Qualifications in Virginia.* The pamphlet was undated, but a ledger in the Adèle Clark Papers indicates that it was initially ordered from the printer on April 15, 1915.

43. The flier can be found in the Virginia Woman Suffrage Collection. The flier itself is undated, but the ledger in the Adèle Clark Papers indicates it was first ordered from the printer on January 19, 1916.

44. Unidentified newspaper clipping, Mary Pollard Clarke Scrapbook, Clarke Family Papers, Virginia Historical Society. A typescript version signed by Mary Pollard Clarke and dated December 19, 1915, can be found in box 1, Roberta Wellford Papers, University of Virginia. Since this article also contains the text of *Equal Suffrage and the Negro Vote,* it is reasonable to assume that Mary Pollard Clarke was the pamphlet's author.

45. *Richmond Times-Dispatch,* December 21, 1919. The same statement, indeed the entire letter, was reprinted as a broadside, "Reply to Thomas Nelson Page on the Federal Women Suffrage Amendment," Virginia Woman Suffrage Collection. The point was also made in an advertisement placed by the Equal Suffrage League, *Richmond Times-Dispatch,* September 3, 1919.

46. The article continued, "This is a white man's country and always will be, and can he be less generous than to allow his negro brother or sister the reward of citizenship which he or she has attained under the laws which the state has made?" The use of "brother" and "sister" is especially interesting in an article claiming that the grant of the vote to all black men during Reconstruction was a "crime," that woman suffrage will increase white supremacy, and that white women, outnumbering black women and men, will "raise greatly the educational and moral standard of the voters."

47. Rosalyn M. Terborg-Penn, "Afro-Americans in the Struggle for Woman Suffrage" (Ph.D. diss., Howard University, 1977), 275; Guy-Sheftall, *Daughters of Sorrow,* 99–130.

48. *Richmond Planet,* September 20, 1918.

49. The *Norfolk Journal and Guide* shared the *Planet'*s contempt for the antis; on July 29, 1922, the *Journal and Guide* summed up the antis' position: "Rather than enfranchise *some* black women, they said, we would keep the suffrage from *all* white women." For blacks, the *Journal and Guide* went on, this was "humiliating exploitation." For the period before ratification, I was unable to find in the editorials of the *Journal and Guide* any opinions on the merits of woman suffrage. Many issues are missing, however, and there may have been woman suffrage commentary in issues I was unable to locate.

50. Maggie Lena Walker, "Woman in Business," typescript, 5, Maggie Walker House, Richmond, Va.; William Anthony Aery, "National Association of Colored Women," *Southern Workman* 41 (September 1912): 537.

51. *Richmond Planet,* February 28, 1916.

52. Brown, "Womanist Consciousness," 631.

53. *Richmond Times-Dispatch,* September 23 and October 3, 1920.

54. Maggie Lena Walker Diary, September 12–23, 1920, Maggie Walker House; *Richmond News Leader,* September 17, 1920. The *Richmond Evening Journal,* September 25, 1920, reported that the black wing of the Republican party, under the direction of Mrs. E. L. Dixon-Bryan, had been organizing women in a house-to-house canvass since April.

55. The statistics were taken from the running tallies printed in the *Richmond News Leader* and the *Richmond Times-Dispatch,* September 17–October 4, 1920.

56. The text of the petition was given in the *Richmond Evening Journal,* September 23, 1920, which reported the signatories as Mrs. E. L. D. Bryan, Mrs. Bettie G. Cousins, Mrs. Margaret R. Johnson, Mrs. Lizzie E. Davis, Mrs. Sylvia L. Mitchell Scott, Giles B. Jackson, and Mrs. Ora Brown Stokes. On Walker's efforts, see Maggie Walker Diary, September 20, 1920; and *Richmond Times-Dispatch,* September 21, 1920.

57. The 2,410 black women registered slightly exceeded the number of black men registered (2,402); 2,410 was 12.5 percent of the black female population aged twenty-one and up. The 10,645 white women registered compared with 28,148 white men registered; 10,645 was 26.8 percent of the white female population aged twenty-one and up. Among black men above the age of twenty, 14.8 percent were registered. Among white men above the age of twenty, 79.4 percent were registered. Registration figures for all groups are from the *Richmond News Leader,* November 27, 1920. Population figures are from the Bureau of the Census, *Fourteenth Census of the United States Taken in the Year 1920,* vol. 2, *Population 1920* (Washington, D.C.: Government Printing Office, 1922), 357.

58. *Richmond News Leader,* September 18, 1920; *Newport News Daily Press,* September 18, 1920; *Petersburg Index-Appeal,* September 19, 1920; *Front Royal Warren Sentinel,* September 24, 1920; *Danville Register,* September 21, 1920; *Roanoke World News,* September 28, 1920; *Norfolk Virginian-Pilot and Norfolk Landmark,* September 19, 1920. The *Newport News Daily Press* had made a similar maneuver on September 8 in its report on the progress of registration locally. The headline read "Colored Women Ahead in Rush for Ballot," while the article itself went on to say that 122 white women and 36 black women had qualified so far.

59. *Richmond News Leader,* September 18, 1920.

60. The quotation from Rorer James was taken from the *Bedford Bulletin,* September 30, 1920. It appeared also in the *Culpeper Exponent,* September 23, 1920; *Roanoke World News,* September 28, 1920; *Loudoun Mirror,* September 29, 1920; and *Culpeper Virginia Star,* September 30, 1920. The quotation from the Virginia Association was taken from the *Richmond News Leader,* September 18, 1920; it appeared also in the *Culpeper Exponent,* September 23, 1920; *Front Royal Warren Sentinel,* September 24, 1920; *Staunton Evening Leader,* September 28, 1920; *Loudoun Mirror,* September 29, 1920; *Gloucester Gazette,* September 30, 1920; and *Waverly Dispatch,* October 1, 1920.

61. Statements to this effect were published in the *Norfolk Virginian-Pilot and Norfolk Landmark,* September 28, 1920; *Staunton Evening Leader,* October 4, 1920; *Brookneal Union Star,* October 29, 1920; and *Fairfax Herald,* October

29, 1920. A more personal form of expediency may also have been at work in the case of Mary Mason Anderson Williams, the president of the Virginia Association Opposed to Woman Suffrage. Her appeal to conservative women to register, which included the charge that this was needed to counter "any radical or dangerous changes which may be proposed by agitators flushed with undue self-importance and actuated by a desire for political prominence and office," was issued the day after she herself was nominated as a member of the state Democratic executive committee for the third congressional district. *Richmond News Leader,* September 18, 1920.

62. No central agency in Virginia collected registration figures. In 1921 the Virginia Association for the Common Good sent questionnaires to county and city officials asking them to report, among other things, the numbers of white men, white women, black men, and black women registered to vote in their jurisdictions. The results of this survey were published in the *Richmond Times-Dispatch,* October 30, 1921. I have attempted to cull from these reported results the most reliable figures. That is, I have eliminated counties and cities that did not return their questionnaires (the Virginia Association calculated estimates for these jurisdictions). I have also eliminated counties and cities whose reported numbers all ended in zero, assuming that these were estimates rather than actual counts. My analysis is based on the remaining counties, viz., Amherst, Bedford, Botetourt, Caroline, Chesterfield, Clarke, Culpeper, Dinwiddie, Essex, Fauquier, Fluvanna, Gloucester, Halifax, Henrico, James City, King William, Loudoun, Lunenburg, Mathews, Nansemond, Nelson, Northumberland, Orange, Powhatan, Prince George, Rappahannock, Rockbridge, Southampton, and Warren. My analysis is also based on the following cities: Alexandria, Clifton Forge, Danville, Fredericksburg, Lynchburg, Petersburg, Portsmouth, Richmond, and Suffolk.

To figure the percentage of persons twenty-one and over who registered, I used population figures from the Bureau of the Census, *Fourteenth Census of the United States Taken in the Year 1920,* vol. 2: *Population 1920* (Washington, D.C.: Government Printing Office, 1922), 1367–68. This source gives the population aged twenty-one and over, broken down by race but not by sex. I therefore divided the total adult population of a given race by two to arrive at the estimated number of women (or men). It should be noted that this skews the results somewhat, because most rural areas contained more men than women and most cities contained more women than men.

When possible I have obtained more precise population figures—which do give the actual numbers of men and women—from other sources. I have also collected registration figures from local newspapers. The remaining notes specify when these alternative sources are being used.

63. Registration figures for Richmond come from the *Richmond News Leader,* November 27, 1920. Population figures are from *Fourteenth Census,* vol. 2, 357, and do specify actual numbers of women and men.

64. Adèle Clark Interview, 20.

65. These percentages were calculated from figures derived from the survey of the Virginia Association for the Common Good, as explained in note 62. A comparable trend was observable in the cities. That is, in cities like Petersburg

and Portsmouth, which were more than 40 percent black, black women's registration rates were lower than in cities with smaller proportions of blacks in the total population. In Petersburg, 8.0 percent of the adult black female population registered (371 out of 4,645), while the comparable figure for Portsmouth was 2.8 percent (199 out of 7,167). Registration figures for both cities come from the survey of the Virginia Association. Population figures for Portsmouth are from the *Fourteenth Census*, vol. 2, 1368; those for Petersburg are from the same source, 357, and do reflect actual figures for women. In Petersburg there was an organized registration campaign led by Ida R. Harris, but the black women there seem to have been given a particularly rough time by the registrar. Harris was quoted as saying that black women were asked such questions as "Who was the man that ran the first street car?" *Petersburg Evening Progress*, September 27, 1920. Petersburg was the one jurisdiction in Virginia in which black women outregistered black men; the figure for black men was 6.3 percent (239 out of 3,793). The highest rates of black male registration in cities were in Lynchburg (42.5 percent) and Clifton Forge (38.0 percent).

66. Registration figures are from the survey of the Virginia Association for the Common Good. Population figures are from the *Fourteenth Census*, vol. 2, 1368.

67. Headquarters Secretary [Ida M. Thompson?] to Mrs. C. R. Henley, November 4, 1920, Adèle Clark Papers.

68. *Richmond Times-Dispatch*, September 23, 1920.

69. Names of the trustees were printed in the annual reports of the Virginia Industrial School for Colored Girls (titles vary), which may be found in the library division of the Virginia State Library and Archives.

70. Adèle Clark Interview, 20-21. The *Richmond News Leader*, November 2, 1920, reported that Clark and other suffragists had been visiting polling places, but it did not mention any motives having to do with violence or race.

71. Names of members of the Women's Section of the Virginia State Committee on Interracial Cooperation were listed in the *Richmond Planet*, December 3, 1921. I am grateful to John Kneebone for additional names that appeared in the Commission on Interracial Cooperation Papers, microfilm, reel 55, frames 505, 1416, 1478. Other feeders for interracial work included the Protestant churches; at least four of the thirty-four white women activists were lay leaders in the Baptist, Methodist, or Presbyterian churches. For help in identifying them, I thank John Kneebone, Brent Tarter, and Sandra Treadway of the *Dictionary of Virginia Biography* Project, Virginia State Library and Archives.

72. *Richmond Planet*, December 3, 1921.

73. *Norfolk Journal and Guide*, September 3, 1921.

74. Adèle Clark Interview, 21-22.

75. *Southern Negro Women and Race Cooperation* (n.p.: Southeastern Federation of Negro Women's Clubs, 1921), 6-7 [pamphlet located in the Maggie Walker House].

76. Adèle Clark Interview, 22. For the obvious reasons, there is not much written evidence about these efforts. Maggie Walker made a cryptic note after having been contacted by Adèle Clark: "Call from Miss Clarke, white,—political

leader—to plan the study of citizenship." Maggie Walker Diary, November 20, 1920.

77. On the political initiatives of black women nationally, see Evelyn Brooks Higginbotham, "In Politics to Stay: Black Women Leaders and Party Politics in the 1920s," in *Women, Politics, and Change,* ed. Louise A. Tilly and Patricia Gurin (New York: Russell Sage Foundation, 1990), 199-220.

78. *Richmond Planet,* September 10 and November 5, 1921.

Women's History and Political History: Some Thoughts on Progressivism and the New Deal

William H. Chafe

It has become commonplace to associate the post–World War II years of "consensus" historiography in the United States with the dominance of political history. A primary case in point is how scholars dealt with the reform periods of the early 1900s and the 1930s. Historians debated whether Progressivism represented a departure from Populism or a continuation and whether the New Deal was a reflection more of Teddy Roosevelt's New Nationalism or Woodrow Wilson's New Freedom. Graduate students struggled with controversies over the Hofstadter/Mowry thesis that status anxiety explained the upsurge of progressive reform; and careers were made or broken by how successful one was in showing that the class background of officials who voted *for* the "progressive" line differed from that of those who voted *against* it.

All these debates shared certain significant assumptions: first, issues of reform clearly fell under the rubric of traditional political history, with the focus, at least nationally, on presidential administrations; second, the most important questions involved political or economic legislation, such as direct election of senators or antitrust policy; and third, most of these "reforms" came from the top down. To be sure, such historians as Sam Hays used local studies to integrate social and political developments. For the most part, however, the discussion, even among ardent revisionists, took place within a framework shaped implicitly by the understanding that political events were the focal point of history and that these events, in turn, were defined and controlled by leaders who were white and male.[1]

Clearly, much has changed since then. Women's history, in particular, has altered dramatically the questions we ask of this era (and others), the methods we employ, and the issues on which we focus. No longer does the Mann-Elkins Act preoccupy historians. Instead, they ask where the infrastructure of America's social welfare apparatus developed, how economic and social change affected families and neighborhoods, and why and how communities of women raised such issues as child labor and social security to national prominence. Perhaps most important, women's history has caused scholars to reconsider the definition of politics itself, broadening that area of inquiry to include informal networks of influence that helped shape public policy and highlighting the intersection of the personal and the political. Moreover, a focus on women has allowed the South to gain recognition as another region in which progressivism flourished, if in more attenuated form and more isolated arenas. In the process, traditional periodization has been challenged, new questions of continuity and change have been raised, and the entire landscape of early twentieth-century political history has been redrawn.[2]

This essay represents an effort to portray, in broad strokes, some of the consequences of the new scholarship. More specifically, it speculates about how twentieth-century political history might look when informed by a perspective based on greater attention to issues of gender, race, and class. Some of these ideas remain untested; yet, in their own way, they suggest just how far women's history, especially when sensitive to issues of race and class, can alter the agenda of even such traditional fields as political history.

Many of the most important insights of women's history in this area have been summarized—and advanced—in Paula Baker's article "The Domestication of Politics: Women and American Political Society, 1780-1920." There, Baker propounded a series of arguments, all of them anchored in her central thesis that "gender, rather than other social or economic distinctions, [represented] the most salient political division" in nineteenth-century America.[3]

The language of republicanism, Baker pointed out, proved consistent with cultural norms of masculinity, such as individualism and self-reliance. Women's task, in that framework, was defined as becoming good citizens through being good mothers and imparting moral virtue to their children. Men bonded through the rituals of mass parties and public political behavior, using rallies, parades, and other displays associated with a "male sphere" to affirm their solidarity. Women, in turn, bonded around their church and household responsibilities. Yet as these extended into nurturance and care for the dependent and needy outside of the home, the politics of domesticity gradually attained a public dimension, albeit one defined as "feminine." Baker contends that during the nineteenth century "men and women operated, for the most part, in distinct political subcultures" and that women's subculture proved significant in its responsibilities and its capacity for growth. When the Fourteenth Amendment specifically inserted the word *male* to define the prerequisites for formal political participation through the franchise, the gender segregation of American political culture was legally complete; the vote constituted a prima facie definition of what united men and excluded women. There then developed a two-track system of activity that shaped public policy, one an all-male, formal process focusing on the ballot, the other a predominantly female, informal process based on women's "feminine" concern for nurturance, social welfare, and social purity. The next fifty years would witness the extension of these separate tracks, until they at least partially converged through the phenomenon of the Progressive Era. Ironically, Suzanne Lebsock has concluded, this period of informal activity also constituted "a great age for women in politics," perhaps even greater *because* of the absence of women's participation in formal political procedures.[4]

Although Baker's path-breaking article failed to recognize adequately the salience of race and class as additional crucial variables, it offered an important paradigm within which to understand better the extraordinary impact of women and their organizations on nineteenth- and twentieth-century American society. As Anne Firor Scott has shown so well, women's voluntary associations were *everywhere* in the nineteenth century, building schools and seminaries, dispensing charity, working for literacy and decent living conditions for the poor, shaping the entire social and educational infrastructure of America. When middle- and upper-class white women carried their domestic concerns outside the home, they created the quasi-public sphere of social welfare institutions. One concern inevitably led to others, so that the commitment to fight slavery, or prostitution, or alcohol abuse often led to involvement with other issues as well. As many women's historians have shown, even ventures that began with a narrow focus—such as the literary club movement or the temperance crusade—at some point carried over into questions more structural and systemic in nature. The class and race prejudices of white middle- and upper-class activists prevented many members of these movements from comprehending or identifying with the struggles of black and working-class women. But the politics of domesticity did nourish a tentative outreach that, however limited, acknowledged the problems of the oppressed far more than did most traditional male politics.[5]

It was through such "tentative outreach" that important links developed between the distinctive culture of middle-class women's lives and the public influence they were rapidly acquiring. The settlement house movement most clearly illuminates those links, even as it provides an ideal case study of Baker's thesis on the domestication of politics, and shows how much women's history can reshape our understanding of an era.

When Hull House and other settlements were opened in the late nineteenth century, they represented, in one sense, simply a logical extension of the work more traditional women's organizations had been doing. The primary difference, perhaps, was that settlement workers constituted a "class" with a distinctive experience. Mostly college educated, trained to use and value their minds, yet frustrated by the narrowing constraints of what Jane Addams called "the family claim," they chose to forge their own version of "domestic politics." Like more traditional family women in the club movement, they cared about the external environment and social disease, but unlike the club women, those in the settlement house made such issues their central preoccupation.[6]

In this sense, the settlement house constituted a particular example of other women's activities writ large. The intimacy and sharing of common values and concerns was now institutionalized in a living unit—their own home. Commitment to improve the health and educational conditions of children and other dependent people became a full-time mission. Eventually, as work on problems of safety, disease, education, and occupational conditions engaged more and more energy, the solutions to these "domestic" problems took on a more public character. When Florence Kelley saw the unregulated and dangerous factory conditions that threatened the arms and legs of industrial workers, she recognized that only a public law governing factory safety could provide any semblance of security for workers' health; it was only logical, though not automatic, that after she succeeded in pushing through such legislation, she should become the government commissioner in charge of enforcing it. When settlement house workers documented the social scandal of the abuse of children in America's new industrial ghettos, they turned to government for protection of the young, and one of them—Julia Lathrop—became the first director of the Children's Bureau. The same process occurred repeatedly. As countless women activists—joined by some like-minded men—talked to each other about the inadequacy of private solutions to the dimension of the social problems they confronted, they came to see the drive for formal political power as a helpful means of securing and implementing more humane and responsive government policies. Indeed, as Robyn Muncy argues, women reformers created a virtual "female dominion" over the area of social welfare policy.[7]

Hence the connection that Paula Baker, Suzanne Lebsock, Nancy Cott, and many others have posited between the women reformers of the Progressive Era and the battle for the suffrage. As Rheta Childe Dorr said in 1910, "Woman's place is Home. . . . But Home is not contained within the four walls of an individual house. Home is the community. The city full of people is the Family. The public school is the real Nursery. And badly do the Home and Family need their Mother." Or as Jane Addams said the same year, women were the housekeepers of America, and the nation needed to give them the vote as a means of making it possible for them to sweep the nation clean. Suffrage for women thus became simply an extension of all the public reforms with which women in the Progressive Era had become involved, an embodiment of their "domestic politics." It also became the final link between the private culture of women's separate sphere and the public culture of traditional politics.[8]

Within this framework, it makes eminent sense to see women as the heart of the progressive movement, especially if we define that movement with a small p. From today's perspective, almost everything that we find admirable about the Progressive Era appears to have been associated in one way or another with women reformers carrying out the politics associated in the nineteenth century with women's domestic concerns. (Some supporters of these efforts were men, to be sure, but men whose attitudes had largely been shaped by experience in female-centered institutions like the settlement house). The emphasis on factory safety, child labor, minimum wages, and maximum hours and the efforts to regulate tenements and sweatshops, provide day nurseries, build playgrounds, and offer adult education classes all traced their origins to institutions that were formed, governed, and largely populated by women and that, in one way or another, seemed dedicated to the ideas and values linked to the political culture of women about which Paula Baker wrote.

If women were the driving force behind the progressive movement (with a small p), what are we to make of the traditional Progressive movement (with a capital p)? Significantly, a gender-based paradigm also provides insight here, for much of the legislation that we identify with that "capital p" movement seems a product of the male political culture that Paula Baker and others have also discussed. The railroad laws, the regulation of trusts, and the effort to rationalize industry, systematize banking, and streamline government all proved much more consistent with the traditional economic and political values associated with men. As Baker observed, "The business corporation created the model for the new liberalism [or for our purposes Progressivism], while politically active women and some social thinkers took the family and small community as an ideal." The two kinds of progressivism might coexist and in some ways even be complementary. They were, after all, both using the state to intervene. In emphasis and values, however, they were dramatically different.[9]

Up to a point, then, the notion of a gender-based politics appears to provide an excellent foundation for reinterpreting the Progressive Era. Indeed, such a model may be the only vehicle for making explicable the profound contradiction between the humanistic, if limited, aims of the wage and hour movement, on the one hand, and the high-powered rationalization of the Federal Trade Commission and the Federal Reserve Board, on the other.

Yet the model, to be complete, needs to incorporate the critical dimensions of race and class. Baker's concept of "the domestication of politics" is based on the idea of gender as a universal category, allowing women, by virtue of their common domestic experiences "to cross class, and perhaps even racial lines"; however, we know from the work of Rosalyn Terborg-Penn, Jacqueline Jones, Paula Giddings, Christine Stansell, Nancy Hewitt, and others that gender solidarity was in most cases an illusion. For women who were poor or black, the realities of class and race created visions and priorities quite contrary to those held by women who were middle class and white. All too often, progressive white women failed even to consider the plight of their black sisters—even the more affluent among them. Some white women participated in the effort to disenfranchise blacks; others were willing to use the argument that white women should get the vote to lessen the influence of black or immigrant voters. Similarly, white middle-class women, however generous they might have thought they were being in their outreach to immigrant or working women, rarely respected or identified with a working-class world, where gender often meant something quite different than it did among the bourgeoisie.[10]

However, if race and class are included as forces interacting with gender, we may gain even more insight into progressivism as a whole, with a new appreciation of both its limitations and its possibilities. Take, for example, the "mother's aid" laws that were passed at the behest of women's groups during this era. On one level, such laws reflected exactly the woman-defined values that Baker had in mind. Women reformers, concerned with the health and well-being of widows and poverty-stricken mothers, sought to provide some public assistance that would sustain the family and nurture the victims of injustice or misfortune. Yet if we look at the content and implementation of these laws, we see a kind of mean-spiritedness, condescension, and class arrogance that exemplifies dramatically the limits of middle-class women's ability to reach out and encompass the perspective of their working-class sisters. These laws often provided mere scraps of aid, while imposing a system of investigation, whether by social workers or others, that undermined the dignity and self-respect of the beneficiaries. If reaching out to help represented the benevolent gender-based dynamics of progressive women, reaching down to intrude and regulate represented the malevolent, class-induced myopia of the middle and upper classes.[11]

Unfortunately, the two were more often than not inseparable when the issue was working-class women or the relations between middle-class and working-class women. Thus, notwithstanding its generous and inclusive ideology, the Women's Trade Union League (WTUL)—certainly one of the "best" of the progressive organizations—could not escape the determination of its middle- and upper-class "allies" to bring culture to working women through decorous "teas" or education classes geared to transmitting the "civilization" of the middle class. Not surprisingly, the WTUL eventually opted for a strategy of education, investigation, and legislation—not trade union organization—as its favored means of improving working women's lives. As Nancy Hewitt has pointed out, dramatically different styles of action and visions of change animated working-class women, who were far more likely to resort to spontaneous demonstrations, whether bread riots or spur-of-the-moment walkouts on behalf of aggrieved workers, than to join the hierarchical organizations and structured programs of middle-class reform groups. The worlds were not the same and understandably, since the bonds of gender counted for little when women workers encountered wives or sisters of the managerial class or when domestic servants confronted their mistresses.[12]

The same chasm divided the races, perhaps even more deeply given the ways in which class and race often reinforced each other. Again, there are examples of outreach. Certainly the eventual development of the Association of Southern Women for the Prevention of Lynching or the involvement of women reformers like Jane Addams with the founding of the NAACP spoke to a commitment to racial justice that represented the most positive aspects of white middle-class women's politics. These were probably more the exception than the rule, however. More representative, perhaps, were the exclusion of blacks, such as Ida Wells Barnett, from suffrage parades and the patronizing testimony of some woman suffrage leaders against illiterate blacks and immigrants.[13]

When these limitations of class and race are incorporated, a gender-based approach to the Progressive Era becomes much more illuminating as a means of understanding the whole period. Historians have often puzzled over three contradictions of this so-called reform period: (1) how could it be called progressive when so much of the legislation seemed designed to rationalize and systematize the dominance of corporate capitalism; (2) what is the basis for attaching a reform label to an era that witnessed the rise of racist terrorism and the calculated disenfranchisement of most black male voters in the South; and (3) what is the justification for seeing as "progress" a series of social welfare actions that were ameliorative at best and condescending at worst?

A paradigm based on the intersection of race, class, and gender at least helps to begin to make sense of these contradictions. If there were *two* progressive agendas, one of which was based on the cultural politics of middle-class white women, then we can understand why there seems to be little in common between legislation for business rationalization and laws to improve neighborhood health and safety and to protect women and children. If the women who supported these latter laws were victims of the same class and race blinders that operated on middle- and upper-class men, then we also have some explanation for why they failed to evidence solidarity with blacks and workers or to identify with their goals and experiences. It thus becomes possible to gain some appreciation of why using women's definition of politics as a departure point informs a new understanding of the Progressive Era's more reformist achievements and simultaneously illuminates the structural shortcomings of those achievements, some of which are attributable to women's inability to create a universal gender-based solidarity. In fact, if we were to pay more attention to the independent agendas supported by working-class women and black women, we would have an even better picture of the extent to which white middle-class women's activities during the Progressive Era represented only a step toward a *truly* progressive politics.

Interestingly enough, the use of women's experience as a vantage point on early twentieth-century politics also helps illuminate two other historiographical questions that bedeviled an earlier generation of scholars. In 1956 Arthur Link asked what had happened to the Progressive movement, an inquiry that reflected the widely accepted notion that the progressive impulse had died with the end of World War I and the election of Warren Harding. A second issue, related to the first, focused on the extent to which New Dealers were different from the progressives, more pragmatic and technological. Both historiographical dilemmas, however, reflected a focus on male politics and cultural assumptions, ignoring both the story and the origins of "small *p*" progressivism. If a gender-based perspective were used instead, the two queries take on an entirely different coloration, with continuity—based on women's informal networks of influence and the impact of race and class—providing the key linkage between the period before 1920 and the period afterward.[14]

As Nancy Cott and Stanley Lemons, among others, have shown so effectively, white middle-class women's participation in voluntary associations and female reform organizations did not end but continued to grow during the 1920s, especially in the South, where many progressive issues were fought for most energetically *after* World War I. Building from local club movements, educational reform ventures, new political groups like the League of Women Voters, and traditional social welfare organizations like the Consumers League, women's groups in the 1920s and 1930s carried forward the same agenda of incremental reform and humanitarian activity associated with the domestic politics of Paula Baker's nineteenth-century middle-class women and the settlement house workers of the early twentieth century. Far from ending their efforts, women activists persisted as the "spearheads of reform" even during the years when, from a male political perspective, conservatism reigned supreme. In fact, women reformers constituted a human bridge joining the indirect political influence of the settlement house generation with the formal political practices of a New Deal reform administration.[15]

Perhaps the best way to envision these connections is through the metaphor of a women's community, with interlocking links of personal friendship and association through shared membership in different voluntary associations. At the heart of the network were a few women who were situated to mobilize the constituent parts of the network. By 1933 large parts of that network were prepared to move to Washington, D.C., brought together by their common ties with Eleanor Roosevelt, the First Lady of the nation and a person who as much as anyone else exemplified the continuity of concerns and activities that constituted the core of white middle-class women's political influence.

Roosevelt's life highlights some of the features that made this community of women so important. She had been born into an aristocratic family. After a quite unhappy childhood marked by the death of both of her parents before she was ten years old, she went off to England to attend a girls' school run by an extraordinary woman, Marie Souvestre, who provided a powerful role model of intellectual and political independence. When Roosevelt returned to New York for her debutante ball in 1900, Souvestre gave her the trenchant advice not to be seduced by the life of parties and society teas but to keep her mind fixed on the serious issues of life.

Roosevelt took the advice to heart. Shortly after returning to New York, she joined the Junior League, which at the time was engaged in a series of charitable activities; she then became associated with the Rivington Street Settlement, where she learned first hand about the realities of urban and ghetto poverty. Teaching classes at the settlement house, she met a group of other women, such as Mary Rumsey Harriman, who would remain close friends throughout her life. She also joined the Consumers League, then headed by Florence Kelley, and participated in the efforts of that group to end the evils of sweatshop labor. She married her cousin Franklin in 1902 and temporarily left reform behind to raise five children and fulfill the responsibilities of the wife of a budding politician. She never forgot Souvestre's lesson or her years in the New York women's reform movement, however.

When Eleanor Roosevelt returned to New York from Washington, D.C., after World War I, she resumed these connections. Her husband had been assistant secretary of the navy during the war and in those years had engaged in a love affair with Lucy Mercer, his wife's private secretary. When Eleanor discovered the affair, it constituted such a blow to her relationship with Franklin that, for all intents and purposes, the private, intimate part of the relationship ended. In the meantime, even before her discovery of the affair, Eleanor had started to reimmerse herself in social welfare activities in Washington, working with patients at St. Elizabeth's Hospital and helping run the canteen for soldiers at Union Station. After the Roosevelts returned to New York, Eleanor steadily deepened her involvement in such activities. Nor did that commitment end when Franklin contracted polio in 1922. Eleanor spent much of her time nursing him back to a normal life and being his political ally and spokesperson, but she also continued her growing commitment to the women and the reform goals that now became the centerpiece of her life.[16]

By virtue of her distinctive background and personal situation, Eleanor Roosevelt became the critical link for a network of women reformers who combined women social workers' traditional dedication to social welfare with a new readiness to act politically. Through her own person, Roosevelt showed that direct participation in the formal political process could merge with continued dedication to women's separate reform organizations. Although earlier she had opposed woman suffrage, she now joined the League of Women Voters (LWV) and became editor of its newsletter and a lobbyist for its agenda in the state legislature in Albany. She also remained active in the Consumers League and for the first time joined the Women's Trade Union League, where she learned to overcome some of her earlier anti-immigrant and anti-Semitic prejudices. With representatives of women's trade unions, she walked picket lines. During these same years, she became a political spokesperson in her own right, heading the women's division of the Democratic party in New York, speaking at countless precinct meetings, and, in the process, keeping the Roosevelt name before the public.

Significantly, Roosevelt derived both her personal and professional raison d'etre from this community of women. She met weekly with Esther Lape and Elizabeth Reid of the LWV to talk about the league's agenda and to spend a pleasant evening together. Her friendship with

WTUL leaders thrived over the years, including personal ties with women like Rose Schneiderman, an immigrant herself, who broadened Roosevelt's social awareness substantially. Molly Dewson, a dedicated reformer in New York's Women's City Club and the National Consumers League, remained a dear and cherished friend. In the meantime, Roosevelt lived with two other women friends in a cottage she built at the Roosevelt estate in Hyde Park, taking up residence there whenever Franklin was not staying in the main house. Weekends frequently saw large segments of the reform/political community of women gather at Eleanor's cottage, swimming in the pool and conversing about their shared personal and professional concerns.

When Franklin Roosevelt was elected president in 1932, Eleanor believed that the gratifying life she had lived during the previous decade was over and that she would now be tethered by the inhibiting role of First Lady. Instead, she discovered that she could move her community to the nation's capital. The Great Depression compelled a response by the government that inevitably made social welfare measures a top priority. Programs were devised that in many ways seemed to translate into public policy the ideas and objectives that had long been advocated by women's reform groups. Who better, then, to administer and implement these programs than women from those groups—the same women who had made up Eleanor Roosevelt's community in New York and, in a larger sense, throughout America.

Within a few months, the administration witnessed an influx of women reformers that signified what Molly Dewson called an "unbelievable" change in the status of women in government. Eleanor Roosevelt herself led the way in focusing attention on women's issues, convening a White House Conference on the Emergency Needs of Women in November 1933 to force government agencies to take women seriously. Through her constant concern and omnipresent intelligence network, she discovered where women associates would be most useful and when vacancies occurred that women should fill. She held special press conferences for women reporters to give the female press corps increased status and to guarantee attention to stories, often involving women, that would otherwise go unreported. Her close friend, Lorena Hickok, operated as WPA Director Harry Hopkins's eyes and ears as she toured relief projects throughout the country, sending her memos back to both Hopkins and Roosevelt. Other women associates occupied policy-making positions in the WPA, the Social Security Administration, and the Labor Department. At times, Washington seemed like a perpetual convention of social workers, as women from the Consumers League, the WTUL, and other reform groups arrived to take on government assignments. Mary Anderson, director of the Labor Department's Women's Bureau, recalled that in earlier years women government officials had dined together in a small university club. "Now," she said, "there are so many of them they would need a hall."[17]

In effect, these women reformers were transferring to the seat of government itself the programs, priorities, and values that they—and their associates—had been promoting for more than three decades. Just as there was a direct line between Eleanor Roosevelt's experience with the Rivington Street Settlement and her commitment to social reform through various New Deal agencies, so too there was a powerful bond connecting the work of women like Ellen Woodward, who now filled federal social welfare agencies, and the WTUL, Consumers League, and other female reform groups that provided the foundation for their lives of political activism. Although few of these women exercised sufficient independent power to be singlehandedly responsible for specific New Deal reforms, it would be very difficult to imagine the more humanitarian, reform-minded programs of the New Deal without these women as prime contributors and supporters. In that sense, the women of the New Deal were the direct descendants of those who spearheaded the development of "small p" progressivism. Like those women, the New Deal's female reformers were associated with such programs as unemployment relief, social security, education, and the improvement of working conditions for women and children—not with the National Recovery Administration (NRA), Agricultural Adjustment Administration (AAA), or other agencies concerned with preserving big business or big farming. Some—like Eleanor Roosevelt—also led in creating coalitions with black women to overcome some of the racial bias of the earlier era. They thus continued the same type of work that had distinguished their foremothers, bringing it to new levels of effectiveness and success.

Such a perspective clearly has profound ramifications for how we understand New Deal historiography. The same "consensus" generation of scholars that concentrated on Teddy Roosevelt's New Nationalism and Woodrow Wilson's New Freedom also focused on the controversy over whether FDR initiated two New Deals and when the First New Deal ended and the Second New Deal began. A gendered interpretation of this reform era, however, might well lead to the conclusion that the real division within the New Deal was between those committed to an agenda of humanitarian social welfare programs and those more intent on legislation regulating businesses and utilities. Each emphasis can be found throughout the New Deal, as throughout the Progressive Era, and it may make as much sense to restructure one's understanding of the New

Deal around the struggle between these different values and priorities as it does to rely on the more traditional (and "masculine") categories of a pro-planning, pro-big business First New Deal and an anti-planning, anti-big business Second New Deal. In this sense, the influence of women's political concerns on many New Deal programs offers an important new prism through which to understand a very old historiographical issue, as well as a powerful argument for continuity between one generation of reformers and another.[18]

Yet there is an irony in this theme of gender and continuity as well. If the community of women reformers reflected the abiding strength of women's political influence from the Progressive Era through the 1930s, the community also ran the risk of seeing its influence end once its values and approach became institutionalized in government programs. Using the work of Paula Baker and Suzanne Lebsock as a frame of reference, a strong argument can be made that women's greatest political power occurred through nonelectoral activity, carried out by voluntary associations of women reformers who organized in separate groups based on a self-perception that women had distinctive interests and values. The community these women represented remained largely intact, as manifested in the personal and professional network of reformers who surrounded Eleanor Roosevelt during the 1920s and who continued to pursue the same objectives they had sought earlier. When important segments of this network moved to Washington during the New Deal, it seemed that the goals of the separate community of women's organizations had finally been achieved. Some of their programs had become established federal policy.

But there precisely was the problem. As Estelle Freedman has suggested, women's strength as political actors depended on preserving a separatist base that would be woman-controlled and that would provide a means for defining the values and concerns of women's "separate sphere." Once women's programs became absorbed into male-controlled structures, however, women could lose both their independence and their capacity for collective self-determination. They would, in other words, become *individuals,* standing alone, not part of a community with its own rationale and agenda. It could therefore be argued that the very success of women reformers in finally securing acceptance of their ideas resulted in eradication of their home base and, hence, in their own disempowerment or cooptation. Assimilation into federal social welfare bureaucracies could simultaneously signify both the triumph of women's influence and its extinction. Instead of remaining an expression of their own distinctive cultural and political worldview, women's reform agenda had been captured by a male-dominated government bureaucracy.[19]

Although many of the ideas set forth in this essay are speculative, requiring testing and refinement through further investigation, there seems little question that the scholarship of women's history has dramatically reshaped how we conceive of that bedrock of traditional historiography—political history. Some of the categories employed here remain intensely controversial. Was there a distinctive and separate culture of women's politics (at least among middle-class white women) in the nineteenth century? Should women activists be seen as individuals, or did gender create special bonds of community? How do we integrate those male progressives who focused on social justice issues into this gender-based framework? How is gender itself, as a basis for political action, shaped by race and class perspectives? The debates surrounding these questions simply highlight how far we have come in making more complex and textured our sense of what political history is all about. No longer do quadrennial campaigns and legislative encyclopedias constitute the boundaries of this discipline. Now we are free to explore informal as well as formal corridors of power, the intersection of the personal and the political, and the ongoing dialectic between social history and political events. With these new expanded boundaries come different, perhaps more exciting, questions that may lead to the kind of history that encompasses rather than excludes, that reflects diversity rather than narrow homogeneity.

There also seems a good possibility that historians' views of the Progressive Era and the New Deal will be altered as a consequence of these new boundaries. Using gender as a primary departure point, modified substantially by the impact of race and class considerations, it may become possible to develop a new synthesis about the early 1900s that unites political and social history, addresses many of the glaring contradictions that have perturbed previous generations of scholars, and offers a means of understanding the relationship between informal and formal expressions of influence. Similarly, the insights derived from this synthesis may illuminate the continuities between the New Deal and the Progressive Era and the origins of many of the reform programs that we associate with the New Deal. Finally, the perspective of women's history promises to open new horizons about what may be gained or lost by immersion in electoral politics and about what kind of power—on whose terms—is at stake when we talk about political victories and defeats. Whether or not political history has been revolutionized by women's history, it has definitely been "re-formed."

NOTES

1. Richard Hofstadter stood at the center of this debate with his magisterial review of U.S. reform movements, *The Age of Reform: From Bryan to FDR* (New York: Alfred A. Knopf, 1955), and his brilliant interpretive biographies of William Jennings Bryan, Theodore Roosevelt, Woodrow Wilson, and Franklin D. Roosevelt in *The American Political Tradition and the Men Who Made It* (New York: Alfred A. Knopf, 1948). George Mowry had also advanced the status anxiety thesis in his work *The California Progressives* (Berkeley: University of California Press, 1951). Much of the subsequent historiographical debate focused on whether class self-interest or status anxiety more adequately explained progressive legislation. See, for example, Gabriel Kolko, *The Triumph of Conservatism: A Re-interpretation of American History, 1900-1916* (New York: Free Press, 1963); and Robert Wiebe, *The Search for Order, 1877-1920* (New York: Hill and Wang, 1967). The most acute critic of prevailing views, at least within this "political" history tradition, was Samuel Hays, typified in his article "The Politics of Reform in Municipal Government in the Progressive Era," *Pacific Northwest Quarterly* 55 (October 1964): 157-69. Peter Filene presents an overview of this literature in "An Obituary for the Progressive Movement," *American Quarterly* 22 (Spring 1970): 20-34. The best political critique of Hofstadterian assumptions is Lawrence C. Goodwyn, *The Populist Moment: A Short History of Agrarian Revolt in America* (New York: Oxford University Press, 1978).

2. Anne Firor Scott helped pioneer this transformation with *The Southern Lady: From Pedestal to Politics, 1830-1930* (Chicago: University of Chicago Press, 1970), which, among other things, underlined the role of southern women in seeking progressive reform. Since then there has been a virtual flood tide of literature on women's involvement in social reform during this era. Two recent examples are Robyn Muncy, *Creating a Female Dominion in American Reform, 1890-1935* (New York: Oxford University Press, 1991); and Ellen Fitzpatrick, *Endless Crusade: Women Social Scientists and Progressive Reform* (New York: Oxford University Press, 1990).

3. Paula Baker, "The Domestication of Politics: Women and American Political Society, 1780-1920," *American Historical Review* 89 (June 1984): 630.

4. Ibid., 622; Suzanne Lebsock, "Women and American Politics, 1880-1920," in *Women, Politics, and Change*, ed. Louise Tilly and Patricia Gurin (New York: Russell Sage Foundation, 1990), 35.

5. For examples of this literature, see Anne Firor Scott, *Making the Invisible Woman Visible* (Urbana: University of Illinois Press, 1984); Anne Firor Scott, *Natural Allies: Women's Associations in American History* (Urbana: University of Illinois Press, 1991); Barbara Leslie Epstein, *The Politics of Domesticity: Women, Evangelism, and Temperance in Nineteenth-Century America* (Middletown, Conn.: Wesleyan University Press, 1981); Ruth Bordin, *Woman and Temperance: The Quest for Power and Liberty, 1873-1900* (Philadelphia: Temple University Press, 1977); and Karen J. Blair, *The Clubwoman as Feminist: True Womanhood Redefined, 1868-1914* (New York: Holmes and Meier, 1980). Nancy A. Hewitt explores the importance of class and status differences among women activists in

Women's Activism and Social Change: Rochester, New York, 1822-1872 (Ithaca, N.Y.: Cornell University Press, 1984), while Carroll Smith-Rosenberg offers insights into the rich diversity of the entire period in her collection of essays, *Disorderly Conduct: Visions of Gender in Victorian America* (New York: Alfred A. Knopf, 1985). For a series of articles dealing with black involvement (or noninvolvement), see Sharon Harley and Rosalyn Terborg-Penn, eds., *The Afro-American Woman: Struggles and Images* (Port Washington, N.Y.: Kennikat Press, 1978). Evelyn Brooks Higginbotham discusses how African American women have been left out of most women's history in "Beyond the Sound of Silence: Afro-American Women's History," *Gender and History* 1 (Spring 1989): 50-67.

6. Among the voluminous writings on Hull House and other settlements, see Kathryn Kish Sklar, "Hull House in the 1890s: A Community of Women Reformers," *Signs* 10, no. 41 (1985): 658-77; and Allen F. Davis, *Spearheads for Reform: The Social Settlements and the Progressive Movement, 1890-1914* (New York: Oxford University Press, 1967).

7. See Sklar, "Hull House in the 1890s," as well as Sklar's forthcoming biography of Florence Kelley; Allen F. Davis, *An American Heroine: The Life and Legend of Jane Addams* (New York: Oxford University Press, 1975); Blanche Weissen Cook, "Female Support Networks and Political Activism," *Chrysalis* 3 (1977): 43-61; and Muncy, *Creating a Female Dominion*. Muncy's argument clearly parallels that presented here, although the two interpretations were arrived at independently.

8. See Lebsock, "Women and American Politics"; Baker, "The Domestication of Politics"; and Nancy Cott, *The Grounding of Modern Feminism* (New Haven, Conn.: Yale University Press, 1987). Dorr is quoted in Baker, "The Domestication of Politics," 632.

9. Baker, "Domestication of Politics," 641. Progressivism, of course, consisted of more than two agendas. State regulations were different from federal actions, in motivation and politics; electoral reforms meant something different from region to region; and there was a whole movement for social purity that deserves attention in its own right. For the purposes of this essay, however, it seems useful to focus on the difference between the "small *p*" and "capital *p*" versions.

10. See, for example, Rosalyn Terborg-Penn, "Discrimination against Afro-American Women in the Woman's Movement, 1830-1920," in *The Afro-American Woman*, ed. Harley and Terborg-Penn; Jacqueline Jones, *Labor of Love, Labor of Sorrow: Black Women, Work, and the Family from Slavery to the Present* (New York: Basic Books, 1985); Paula Giddings, *When and Where I Enter: The Impact of Black Women on Race and Sex in America* (New York: William Morrow, 1984); Christine Stansell, *City of Women: Sex and Class in New York, 1789-1860* (New York: Alfred A. Knopf, 1986); and Nancy A. Hewitt, "Politicizing Domesticity: Anglo, Black, and Latin Women in Tampa's Progressive Movements," in *Gender, Class, Race, and Reform in the Progressive Era*, ed. Noralee Frankel and Nancy Shrom Dye (Lexington: University of Kentucky Press, 1991).

11. On the dual role of some social welfare legislation, see Barbara Nelson, "The Gender, Race and Class Origins of Early Welfare Policy and the Welfare

State: A Comparison of Workmen's Compensation and Mother's Aid," in *Women, Politics, and Change,* ed. Tilly and Gurin; Linda Gordon, "What Does Welfare Regulate?" *Social Research* 55 (Winter 1989): 609–30; Seth Koven and Sonya Michel, "Gender and the Origins of the Welfare State," *Radical History Review* 43 (Winter 1989): 112–19; and Linda Gordon, ed., *Women, the State, and Welfare* (Madison: University of Wisconsin Press, 1990). It should be noted that notwithstanding the origins of these laws in women's groups, they were enacted by men and administered by male-controlled bureaucracies.

12. Nancy A. Hewitt, "Varieties of Voluntarism: Class, Ethnicity and Women's Politics in Tampa, Florida," in *Women, Politics, and Change,* ed. Tilly and Gurin. On the WTUL, see Elizabeth Payne, *Reform, Labor, and Feminism: Margaret Drier Robins and the Women's Trade Union League* (Urbana: University of Illinois Press, 1988).

13. See Terborg-Penn, "Discrimination against Afro-American Women"; Rosalyn Terborg-Penn, "Discontented Black Feminists: Prelude and Postscript to the Passage of the Nineteenth Amendment," in *Decades of Discontent: The Women's Movement, 1920–1940,* ed. Lois Scharf and Joan M. Jensen (Westport, Conn.: Greenwood Press, 1983); Higginbotham, "Beyond the Sound of Silence"; Anne Firor Scott, "Most Invisible of All: Black Women's Voluntary Organizations," *Journal of Southern History* 56 (February 1990): 3–22; and Giddings, *When and Where I Enter.* For a brilliant overview of the race/gender paradigm, see Evelyn Brooks Higginbotham, "African-American Women's History and the Metalanguage of Race," *Signs* 17, no. 2 (1992): 251–74.

14. Arthur Link, "What Happened to the Progressive Movement in the 1920s?" *American Historical Review* 64 (July 1959): 883–51; on the continuity or discontinuity between the Progressive Era and the New Deal, see Otis Graham, *An Encore for Reform: The Old Progressives and the New Deal* (New York: Oxford University Press, 1967).

15. Cott, *The Grounding of Modern Feminism;* Nancy Cott, "Across the Great Divide: Women in Politics before and after 1920," in *Women, Politics, and Change,* ed. Tilly and Gurin; James Stanley Lemons, *The Woman Citizen: Social Feminism in the 1920s* (Urbana: University of Illinois Press, 1973). See also Susan Ware, *Beyond Suffrage: Women in the New Deal* (Cambridge, Mass.: Harvard University Press, 1978).

Cott's insights also help illuminate the controversy over woman suffrage. Using the Nineteenth Amendment as a benchmark, most historians have concluded that women's winning the vote did not make much difference in politics, since few women were elected to office and women neither voted as a "bloc" nor cast ballots in as large numbers as male politicos had feared. Yet if women's primary political activity occurred through voluntary associations, as opposed to the male-dominated sphere of traditional political parties, the Nineteenth Amendment would not represent an appropriate measure of women's politics. Moreover, as Paula Baker has pointed out, women had gained the vote precisely when it ceased to have the same importance it once had held. Using 1920 as a dividing line, historians thus make two mistakes: (1) they accept a male model of politics and periodization that implicitly undercuts the real nature of women's political activity; and (2) they deflect attention from the story of continuity, with women's voluntary associations and reform activities constituting, on an ongoing basis, the substantive focus of women's political activity. Once the emphasis on electoral participation is deleted, 1920 ceases to be a logical dividing line and the case for continuity is much more persuasive.

16. See Joseph Lash, *Eleanor and Franklin: The Story of Their Relationship, Based on Eleanor Roosevelt's Private Papers* (New York: W. W. Norton, 1971); and William H. Chafe, "Anna Eleanor Roosevelt," in *Notable American Women, the Modern Period: A Biographical Dictionary,* ed. Barbara Sicherman and Carol Hurd Green with Ilene Kantrov and Harriette Walker (Cambridge, Mass.: Belknap Press, 1984), 595-601.

17. Mary Anderson, "An Aid to the End," an autobiographical typescript, vol. 1, Mary Dewson Papers, Schlesinger Library, Radcliffe College, Cambridge, Mass.; see also Mary Dewson to Maude Wood Park, October 16, 1933, Mary Dewson Papers, FDR Library, Hyde Park, N.Y. On women and politics in the New Deal, see Susan Ware, *Holding Their Own: American Women in the 1930s* (Boston: Twayne, 1983); Susan Ware, *Partner and I: Molly Dewson, Feminism, and New Deal Politics* (New Haven, Conn.: Yale University Press, 1987); Joan Hoff-Wilson and Marjorie Lightman, eds., *Without Precedent: The Life and Career of Eleanor Roosevelt* (Bloomington: Indiana University Press, 1984); and William H. Chafe, *The Paradox of Change: American Women in the Twentieth Century* (New York: Oxford University Press, 1991).

18. Nancy Cott's arguments about the continuities between the presuffrage and postsuffrage eras offer the best model for this kind of interpretation, with many of the same individuals involved. See Cott, "Across the Great Divide," and *The Grounding of Modern Feminism,* chaps. 1-3.

19. See Estelle Freedman, "Separatism as Strategy: Female Institution Building and American Feminism, 1870-1930," *Feminist Studies* 5 (Fall 1979): 512-29. One of the fertile areas of inquiry still being pursued is how continuities of race and class bias among women (and men) persisted in the New Deal, even in the most "progressive" agencies. Some of these issues are highlighted in Gordon, ed., *Women, the State, and Welfare,* especially in Barbara Nelson's "The Origins of the Two-Channel State."

Women's History and Political Theory: Toward a Feminist Approach to Public Life

Sara M. Evans

Public life holds a central place in the ideals of American society. From at least the time of the Revolution, Americans have fought for the right to be not only free from oppression but also free to participate in governance. Yet in the late twentieth century it is difficult to imagine, concretely, what an active public life might mean. Media and money corrupt politics, emptying it of meaningful participation, while therapeutic languages create highly individualized and privatized images of social change. The ideal, nevertheless, remains powerful and worthy of reexamination from a feminist perspective.

This ideal, as articulated by such political philosophers as Hannah Arendt, posits "the public" as an arena of freedom and equality, a space where citizens become visible to each other as "speaker[s] of words and doer[s] of deeds" engaged in debate and decision on matters of common concern.[1] Arendt described the public as a stage on which human freedom could be enacted. Freedom, in her words, is "a worldly reality, tangible in words which can be heard, in deeds which can be seen, and in events which are talked about, remembered, and turned into stories before they are finally incorporated into the great storybook of human history. Whatever occurs in this space of appearances is political by definition."[2]

Feminist critics, however, challenged this ideal by exposing its implicit relationship to a highly gendered and unequal dichotomy of public and private. Public life could exist, as theorists from Aristotle to Rousseau to Hegel decreed, only because basic necessities and bodily needs were relegated to a sharply separate domestic arena. Women (and children and slaves as well), confined to this arena, could never gain the visibility of public participation. Moreover, once history making was defined as a characteristic of public life, women's actions could not be construed as historic. The cultural meaning of womanhood, then, constituted a fusion of "bodiliness" (those whose bodies bear children also care for the bodily needs of others) and exclusion from history (public).

Through the first two-thirds of the twentieth century a few historians of women, often working in great isolation, began the task of demonstrating women's presence in public life.[3] Since the late 1960s, however, a substantial body of work has explored the dynamic links between women's public activities and their private lives and identities.[4] Although this work lays the foundation for a new kind of theorizing, as I intend to argue here, common wisdom in the 1980s was that feminist historical scholarship had made its most significant contributions in the analysis of the private spheres of family, sexuality, domestic labor, and sociability. The insight that "the personal is political," coupled with a recognition of pervasive discrimination against and devaluation of women, challenged a new generation of politically motivated researchers to make "invisible women visible" by unearthing the realities of private life and providing theoretical frameworks to explain it.[5] At the same time, by tracing out the expansion of private concerns into public life, exploring the linkages between wage work and family, and examining the dynamics of the campaign for suffrage, many historians—including the authors in this volume—also made visible a wide array of public activity on the part of women. Yet this aspect of feminist historiography, in the absence of a fully developed feminist concept of the public, has remained theoretically undeveloped, and its full significance has not been clear.

Indeed, feminist theorists—even more than historians—through the 1970s and 1980s remained ambivalent about the public and focused their work primarily on relations of power in personal relations, family structures, child rearing, and sexuality. Theorists like Nancy Chodorow, Adrienne Rich, and Dorothy Dinnerstein explored the psychodynamics of mothering; the psychologist Carol Gilligan spelled out the different mode of moral judgment based on women's imbeddedness in personal relations; the philosopher Sara Ruddick and the political theorist Jean Bethke Elshtain asserted the political importance of "maternal thinking."[6]

By the early 1980s, then, the analysis of private life dominated feminist scholarship, though no approach or theory held uncontested sway.[7] The achievements of this effort should not be underestimated. Private life emerges as a dynamic and fundamental aspect of all human life, a locus of power. Most driving human passions—anger, grief, love, and the erotic—have deep roots in private life (which explains the widespread use of psychoanalytic theories in the 1970s), but their impact on public life has only begun to be explored.

Historians' major contribution to this debate has been to trace the emergence of Victorian conceptions of domesticity and womanhood back to the Revolutionary Era's concept of "Republican Motherhood" and the pre–Civil War "Cult of True Womanhood." They thus demonstrated that the modern ideology that proposes a sharp division between public and private emerged quite literally with the "birth" of the nation. History was essential to feminist challenges to fixed notions of public and private. By exploding any universal notion of the cultural meanings of public and private, feminists called attention to its specifically modern version, linking it to capitalism and liberal democracy and exposing both as inherently patriarchal.[8] In addition, historians have demonstrated in rich detail that women's participation in public life—whether as wage earners, club members, religious activists, or reformers—has been deeply influenced both conceptually and materially by their domestic roles.[9] Until very recently, however, historians have not used new information about women in public to theorize about public life, politics, citizenship, or the state in the way that historians who focused on women in the private sphere used *their* work to theorize about women, sexuality, and gender.[10]

The critique of a gendered and hierarchical understanding of public has left a void. According to political theorist Mary Dietz, "Few feminist theorists have confronted the question of what constitutes a feminist politics in any systematic fashion, and fewer still have attempted to outline the contours of a feminist public realm. In part, perhaps, this is because feminist theory has long had an ambivalence about matters public and political, and theoretical difficulties distinguishing 'politics' from 'the patriarchal state.' "[11]

The history of voluntary associations that women pioneered throughout the nineteenth and twentieth centuries provides historians with the basis for thinking anew about the meaning of public life and its relation to private. Female activism in the free spaces of voluntary associations subverts classic definitions of public and private. Yet it simultaneously suggests resources for retrieving the distinction itself while demonstrating their dynamic interconnection. As long as feminist scholars neglected the development of an alternative concept of public life, they operated within a model of political community conceptualized in personal terms (sisterhood) and, implicitly, sameness. Recent historical scholarship, however, illumines and challenges this theoretical void. Studies centered on struggles for power and participation, from women's labor history to the work of women of color, necessarily demand attention to questions of difference among women.[12] Indeed, the very volume of recent work on diversity, politics, and female activism provides a greater opportunity and an increased necessity for a new framework.[13]

Both historians and political theorists have recently called for greater attention to public life and a reconceptualization of politics.[14] The problem for historians is to develop a dynamic understanding of public life, drawing on political theorists' conceptual clarity about historical and contemporary definitions of public life. The dilemma for feminist political theory, however, is to understand "public," "private," and "political" in ways that recognize their historical specificity, avoid dichotomy, and reject the presumption of an underlying gender hierarchy.[15] An interdisciplinary conversation is in order here, one that can enrich both disciplines.

Why Has Private Life Been Highlighted?

In the 1960s and 1970s feminists were driven to explore private life as an extension of their fundamental challenge to cultural definitions of female and male, to the devaluation of women, and to the patriarchal state. The discovery of personal life as a new locus of history offered transformative possibilities, whereas "women in public life" in its earlier versions as studies of "great women" or "women worthies" did not seem to provide a sufficiently critical approach to the historical canon.[16]

In addition, feminists' intense focus on private relations and their reluctance to consider formal politics as a dimension or an extension of those relations reflected the inadequacy of inherited theoretical frameworks, all of which associated women with private life—domesticity—and denied its importance. At numerous points in time, gendered notions of public and private have served as conceptual tools for men engaged in the process of defining and expanding (male) public freedom. From ancient Athens to Renaissance Italy to Jacksonian America, the growth of a more participatory conception of public life has tended to implicate gendered self-understandings in concepts of "the citizen."[17] Hannah Pitkin's analysis of gender and politics in the thought of Niccolo Machiavelli, for instance, reveals a constant infusion of personal and sexual images into discussions of politics and public life. Politics, adulthood, autonomy, and citizenship are all qualities associated with manhood. They are negated by the effeminate (*effeminato*). More concretely, Pitkin argues that Machiavelli portrays women as "a danger . . . to the healthy political life of a republic. They weaken the manly self control of citizens . . . and they tend to privatize the republican citizen, drawing him out of the public square into the bedroom."[18]

One can find similar sentiments in the hyperbolic reaction against nineteenth-century suffragists. Opponents' inability to imagine public life outside of the dichotomies public/private, male/female, and reason/emotion led them to imagine women in politics as a source of chaos and corruption. They fantasized women in public settings—as legislators, judges, doctors, lawyers, or ministers—constantly and unexpectedly giving birth.[19] Charging that "women are essentially emotional," one opponent of woman suffrage argued that "what we want in this country is to avoid emotional suffrage . . . to put more logic into public affairs and less feeling. There are spheres in which feeling should be paramount. There are kingdoms in which the heart should reign supreme. That kingdom belongs to woman."[20]

By the mid-twentieth century the concept of an active public life had lost much of its meaning for most Americans. Governmental and business experts and technocrats expanded their control and appropriated authority over many more dimensions of people's lives, from politics to health care, and "citizen politics" for the enfranchised contracted to the minimal vision of a yearly trip to the voting booth. Politics, located primarily in the state, was seen as a corrupt and distant process, subject to constant media manipulation over which individual citizens had little control.[21] The dramatic forms of political activism that had their roots in the 1950s, notably the civil rights movement, virtually had to reinvent a participatory political ideal.

Many women, particularly those with roots in progressive reform, had been deeply alienated by their experience in the first three decades of direct participation in politics.[22] Through the twenties and thirties they sought to channel state power in the interests of women, children, and the family. The uneven and disappointing results were then folded into a dramatic expansion of militarized, patriarchal, and bureaucratic state power sparked by World War II and the Cold War.[23]

No wonder feminist theorists, having named the state as patriarchal, turned their attentions to theorizing from an epistemology based on motherhood, birth, and reproduction. In the process, they accepted the designation of "public" as male while attempting to turn the tables and assert the importance, indeed the moral superiority, of the private.[24] Such a theoretical direction was congruent with the formative experiences of a generation of middle-class white women raised in the fifties and early sixties and profoundly shaped by the civil rights movement, the new left, and the rebirth of feminism.

The women's liberation movement in the late 1960s was a response to, but also an extension of, the new left, whose distinctiveness lay precisely in its identification of personal liberation with political change.[25] The exhilaration that civil rights and student activists experienced in intensely committed political communities—the sense that they could *make a difference* in the world, find complete acceptance even as they broke with convention, and believe in the moral purity of their actions—forged a model of political action that dismantled the boundaries between public and private. That, in the long run, had a powerful liberating impact, especially on women. It enabled them to initiate a thoroughgoing political critique of personal life and the dynamics of gender. Within the new left, however, public life was never conceptualized as distinct from, even if dynamically related to, private life. Rather, by the late 1960s the conflation of personal and political change through dress, music, drugs, and a variety of communal experiments emerged in a full-blown counterculture.

The all-absorbing personal/political transformation offered by the intense activism of the sixties was extremely appealing to a generation of middle-class white youth raised in the privatized consumer culture of the 1950s and early 1960s. McCarthyist suppression of dissent accompanied the privatization and devaluation of women. As a result, this generation did not inherit any notion of vigorous public debate or of a public arena characterized by differences—whether of gender, race, or political point of view.[26]

For white students, the confrontation with racial difference in the civil rights movement was a central radicalizing experience, which offered the possibility of a life of meaningful action in contrast to consumerism and middle-class conformity. Though powerful, that phase of the movement was relatively brief. As a result, most students were politicized in a movement that was remarkably homogeneous in age and class. Overwhelmingly white and middle- to upper-middle-class, most student activists developed their political and personal identities in a setting of sameness. Most followed the lead of black power advocates and adopted a "politics of identity." Identity politics, in effect, proposed that political communities were conceptualized as familylike. In practice, where differences existed they were denied or subordinated.

The subsequent movements for women, gay men and lesbians, and racial and ethnic groups incorporated a tendency to make nonnegotiable, moral claims.[27] As a result, they found it difficult to negotiate, build lasting alliances, or deal with the uncertainties and moral ambiguities of actual politics.

The new left experience of the political dimensions of the personal constituted a formative, socializing experience for that generation from which many feminist scholars emerged. It opened the way to a dramatic critique of received wisdom in virtually every discipline. It also sustained a politically and intellectually vital feminist community through the 1970s and into the 1980s, a period during which many other activists floundered in a dissolving new left subculture.

The Reassertion of Public Life in the 1980s and 1990s

Against this background, feminist political language for a time accepted the conflation of public and private in a definition of politics that emphasized life-style as much as activism. You lived your politics, just as you derived those politics from who you were in terms of gender, race, and class or from a new identity born of one or more "conversion" experiences. Yet such an approach presented ever more obvious dilemmas. The more totalizing versions led to burnout and disillusionment. The problem was not that politics and personal life were linked but that they were merged. One civil rights activist who spent several years immersed in the women's movement recalled the subordination of her "personal life to this very public movement existence. I mean, I really didn't have a personal life at all."[28] An additional problem was that the moral righteousness of the victim led to absolute claims, which made coalition building extremely difficult.

By the late 1980s, however, feminist theorists and activists could no longer avoid issues of cultural and political diversity. As homogeneous political communities dissolved, new voices challenged the category "women" with its implicit modifiers (white, middle class, American or European) and demanded a more complex analysis of gender. One response of some feminist theorists has been a shift to poststructural conceptions of power and difference that operate diffusely, particularly through language, making the boundaries (or conceptual distinctions) between public and private blurred, fluid, or perhaps even irrelevant.

Faced with a conservative ascendancy at the national level, feminist theory struggled—in the absence of a clear and usable definition of public life—to develop useful strategies for political action. Indeed, feminist political action (as opposed to theory) has continued for the most part within the framework of liberal interest group and electoral politics, with its implicit, gendered, and hierarchical definitions of public and private. Alternatively, it has operated at the countercultural level, proposing separate female-centered and therefore also gendered solutions outside the political framework.[29] At the same time the nation has polarized around such issues as abortion, child care, surrogate parenting, and prayer in the schools. The difficulties of sustaining meaningful public discourse on personal issues, which tend to cut directly to people's deepest values and sources of identity, and the potential impact of state actions have highlighted the importance of effective and skillful participation in public decision making. To develop such effectiveness, feminists need a conception of the public world.

These pressures within feminist communities to rethink the nature of

public life have received added fuel in the 1990s from the claims on
democratic participation emerging throughout the developing world against
authoritarian regimes of both left and right. This renewal of democratic
ferment has called attention to the meanings of citizenship and the
nature and essential grounds of participation.[30]

A feminist reconception of public life requires first of all attention to
the relationship between public and private. It is not possible to presume
the necessary existence of a (largely unexamined) private sphere conceptualized as female and domestic, the locus of affect and bodily needs, in
the ways that both traditional and modern (nonfeminist) political theory
have done. Simply to introduce private life into the analysis calls into
question the underlying assumptions of liberal individualism and the
issue of who participates in the public. The so-called free individual owes
"his" capacity to act to the existence of this realm of inequality.[31] Those
who call for a renewal of participatory notions of public and political
life—all of whom *intend* an inclusive and gender-free definition of the
citizen—must address this relationship to be persuasive. Moreover, feminists
now face the great, though difficult, challenge of building on recent
analyses of private life to develop concepts of public and private as
distinct but related arenas.

Women's history can address this theoretical conundrum in two ways.
One explores the power of gender in political language. If one attends to
the language used to describe (and prescribe) public life, one discovers
the active presence of gender—and "woman," "womanhood," and "manliness" as metaphor—in all aspects of public life. As Joan Wallach Scott has
pointed out, gender serves as a rich source of imagery to describe
relations of power, civic virtues and weaknesses, and the body politic.[32]
In such metaphoric usage women do not generally appear as agents.
Often, indeed, they serve as counterimages against which men can
define themselves as public actors. While there is important slippage
between women as such and the metaphors of femininity, such an
analysis clarifies ongoing constructions of gender and the too frequent
conflation not only of "man" but of "manhood" with "citizen."[33]

The second contribution of women's history, and one most critical to
the task of developing a feminist reconceptualization of public life, is to
call attention to public arenas that are not governmental and to political
activity and modes of influence that political theory generally slights. The
organizational life that women created, outside of governmental institutions and structures, through the nineteenth century and into the twentieth in the United States has only recently been recognized as political,
because it does not fit prevailing definitions of politics.[34] Yet it offers a
new way to think about both the schooling of citizens—if citizenship is

understood as something that must be learned and practiced—and the linkage of public and private.

In the nineteenth century, liberal theory diverged from classical theories about public (male/political) and private (female/domestic) by recognizing the growth of a further division between politics and civil society. "The public," construed as nondomestic life, now included a "public sector"—government—and a "private sector"—civil society. Both, of course, were implicitly premised on domestic life, the proper sphere of women. The political theorist Carole Pateman argues that women have been excluded from the conceptualization of civil society as a private but nondomestic arena.[35] Such a denial of women's presence and formative role reflects both the ongoing power of gender prescriptions that define women in private/domestic terms and the consequent reluctance to confront the dynamic relation between public and private life.

Civil Society and the Feminization of Politics

In many ways the "private economy" was the dominant aspect of civil society in the nineteenth century. The dramatic growth of capitalism located enormous social and economic power in corporations and the operations of the market. Politics, in fact, was often described as simply the playground of contending economic interests, as "robber barons" and railroad companies purchased the favors of a corrupt Congress and city "bosses." Jürgen Habermas and Hannah Arendt have described the enormous loss of freedom for those who were included in the "public"—a group that was, in fact, expanding dramatically over the course of the nineteenth century. The "public"—not government but the informed citizenry—lost the capacity to discuss, criticize, and judge most fundamental aspects of communal life.[36]

Paula Baker argues that, given limited definitions of state activity and the dramatic growth of industrial capitalism, electoral politics in the nineteenth century constituted a relatively powerless public arena. Though elected officials exercised relatively little control over the expanding market and its social consequences, elections themselves became popular rituals symbolically centered on gender. Electoral campaigns served the purpose of bridging differences of class and ethnicity in an expanding electorate by emphasizing their common manhood. Military and hunting metaphors abounded, and political rallies frequently had the character of drunken brawls.[37]

As new forms of power emerged outside of government in the private economy, manhood was reconfigured primarily in terms of work and the individual freedom associated with economic independence and entrepreneurial activity, whether as merchants, prospectors for gold, western cowboys, or commercial farmers. Politics, instrumentalized by the late nineteenth century as a mechanism to be used in the pursuit of "private," mostly economic ends, lost the participatory flavor that it had only recently gained in the antebellum era.

Alongside the market economy with its emphasis on individual gain, another aspect of civil society also grew in the nineteenth century, consisting of a wide array of voluntary associations—clubs, churches, charities, and reform movements. This aspect created new possibilities for public action outside of formal politics and government.[38] It was the enormous energy generated by voluntary associations and reform movements that provided a new arena for citizenship and collective decision making and that ultimately reshaped the state. That energy was at least as much female as male. The growth of social power within the female environs of voluntary associations—an aspect of American society noted by numerous observers from Tocqueville on—may again provide the key to a reinvigorated and more participatory notion of citizenship.

Women, excluded from the electoral arena, developed a distinctive form of politics in the nineteenth century that was characterized by influence rather than direct participation and by the creation of institutions and associations through which they could act directly to achieve shared goals. Women and men alike used voluntary associations and reform movements not only as active forums for public discussion but also as schools for civic action. Women found there a new kind of free space, which offered the possibility of action outside the domestic sphere but not in formal, governmental arenas from which they were banned. They practiced the basic skills of public life—to speak and to listen, to analyze issues in relation to structures of power, and to develop agendas and strategies for action.[39] In organizations as diverse as abolition societies, the Woman's Christian Temperance Union, Knights of Labor locals, missionary societies, and immigrant associations, women drew on their privatized identities to critique male stewardship of the public realm. The domestic politics they developed shaped the creation of charitable and social service institutions—hospitals, settlement houses, orphanages— and a reform agenda that broadened the responsibilities of the state.[40]

Female voluntary associations did not achieve the classical republican ideal of a public in which the "whole people" speak and act as diverse equals; and, located between formal governmental institutions and the domestic arena, they frequently maintained homogeneities of class and race as well as gender. But they illustrate women's powerful drive to participate in governance and their historic discontent with purely private lives and private identities. Through such associations, women changed the definition of not only *who* can participate as citizens but also *what* are proper subjects for public discussion and decision and *how* people can act politically. Progressive reform, which brought to fruition decades of female activism in arenas as diverse as the Woman's Christian Temperance Union, women's clubs, crusades against lynching, and settlement houses, forced onto the political agenda a wide range of issues rooted in personal life—temperance, child welfare, occupational health and safety, widows' pensions.

The free spaces of voluntary associations need to be understood precisely in terms of their location between the state and domestic life, having characteristics of both the public and the private and providing an essential link between the two. Women themselves construed these as public not private environments, though they were often small and usually all-female. Their initial discomfort with assuming public roles is evidenced in such stories as Anne Scott's description of the first southern missionary society meetings, where women overcame their inability to speak by resorting to familiar prayers, and the famous request that James Mott chair the first women's rights convention in Seneca Falls, New York, in 1848.[41]

Can we imagine participants in these associations as Arendt's "speakers of words and doers of deeds"? They might not have had equality in more formal public realms, but it was possible for them to participate on a footing of visibility and equality with others. With astonishing swiftness, they put deference aside and took control. Two weeks after Seneca Falls, a woman presided over the women's rights convention in nearby Rochester.[42] Missionary societies moved rapidly from unison prayers to bold initiatives in which they claimed the right to control the funds they raised and to initiate projects both at home and abroad.[43] As women engaged in effective action in their own communities, they also reworked privatized definitions of femininity and demanded admission into the more formal realm of politics.

Civil society understood as the locus of free spaces is essential to effective public life, in part because it reworks the relationship between public and private. As theorist Iris Young has pointed out, much of modern political theory proposes that "the civic public expresses the Universal and impartial point of view of reason, standing opposed to and expelling desire, sentiment, and the particularity of needs and interests." Because man as citizen expresses this point of view, "someone has to care for his particular desires and feelings." This theoretical divorce between the universality of normative reason and the particularity of affect and desire reintroduces in a distinctly modern form an ancient oppositional (and hierarchical) definition of male public and female private.[44]

Within democratic voluntary associations, however, people draw directly and powerfully on private identities. Their voluntary nature makes it necessary to attend to the self-interests of participants to persuade them to devote significant time, energy, and resources. There is no illusion here of "disinterested" discourse. Rather, people speak with passion, which they do not construe as irrational; their ongoing commitment depends on it. "Self-interest" in this sense, however, should not be understood in narrowly instrumental ways.[45] People join voluntary associations to satisfy a variety of needs, including sociability and the possibility of "making a difference" by engaging in public action and receiving recognition and respect. Certainly women in the 1830s and 1840s, whether in abolition societies, charitable institutions, or workers' benevolent associations, connected such needs to other goals, such as establishing the ten-hour day, ending slavery, or challenging the social meanings of gender.

In addition, voluntary associations provide necessary places for citizens to gain the skills of public life. For white middle-class men in the United States, they have been essential training grounds for public participation, places where they gained visibility and skills that often led directly to public (i.e., political) power and action. The courts have required many private clubs, such as Rotary, to admit members without racial or sexual bias precisely because of this influential role. Female associations have for the most part been unable to provide such a direct route to traditional domains of public activity. Rather, their task in the nineteenth century was to open up the possibility of female public action by creating benevolent institutions, perfecting the politics of "influence," and gradually reshaping the responsibilities of the state.

The need for training grounds for democratic politics is most evident in the recent reemergence of the concept of civil society among theorists in Eastern Europe and the former Soviet Union, where such concepts and the practices of participation that follow from them must be revived. There it is abundantly clear that without arenas in which people can *practice* the arts of participation and experience themselves as visible and effective, democratic government cannot be rekindled and sustained. Not only must citizens learn what Harry Boyte has called political "arts"—listening, debating, exercising judgment—but they must do so in settings that provide at least minimal contact with people different from themselves. Given the intensity of long-submerged private identities—ethnic, religious, and racial—the dangers of a politics of identity in that part of the world (evidenced in renewed anti-Semitism,

Muslim fundamentalism, and ethnic separatism) are at least as evident as in our own.

Conclusion: Toward a More Useful Understanding of Public and Private Life

A feminist conception of public life will have many dimensions, including enriched understandings of participation, equality, and citizenship as well as a dynamic understanding of the links between public and private (domestic) life. The history of American women offers a clue to some of these dimensions by calling attention to the importance of civil society understood as the locus of free spaces or democratic voluntary associations, where citizens draw on their private identities and practice the basic skills of public life.

Several contemporary community-based citizen organizing experiences that have drawn key leadership from women have outlined a concept of public life as distinct from but intimately linked to private. Discussions, particularly within groups like Communities Organized for Public Service in San Antonio and BUILD in Baltimore that are associated with the Industrial Areas Foundation (IAF), explore different norms of relationships for each arena, noting that private life usually serves as the source of one's motivation for public participation. At the same time, the distinctiveness of each must be recognized and honored. For example, one *expects* similarity of ethnicity, race, religion, education, and class in private life, while differences along precisely these lines are constitutive of public life. Within private/familial life one gives and receives unconditional love. Within public life one operates out of self-interest and has a right to demand respect but not love.

Most important, in the setting of community organizations, such concepts focus on the *public* dimensions of voluntary associations. The arenas of politics, work, school, and religious associations, though strongly linked with family and friends, thus take on explicitly public characteristics. They are chosen (as opposed to given) settings in which one expects to encounter diversity and difference, where accountability and respect are fundamental to ongoing working relationships, and where people act out of their perceived self-interest. By defining voluntary associational life as "public," the IAF reinforces the necessary linkage for ordinary citizens who must have access to such free spaces to acquire and exercise the arts of political life.

Such distinctions provide a useful twist on the familiar discussions of "sameness" and "difference" by positing those as characteristics of pri-

vate and public domains, respectively.[46] Feminist perspectives call attention to the realities of power and inequality in both public and private. A
definition in which the private is characterized by sameness rather than
diversity, for example, not only ignores gender (and age) differences but
also masks male dominance. The key for feminists will be to insist that
needs met in private life—intimacy, love, unconditioned acceptance—are
human needs that cannot be incorporated into a sexual (and hierarchical)
division of labor in which men have the needs and women meet them,
without damage to the humanity of both. Furthermore, essential human
needs arising in private life—food and shelter, protection from violence,
the economic independence necessary to full and equal participation,
socialization and education of the young—can be the proper subjects of
public debate and action. This, indeed, has been women's contribution to
our political order. But the public can never substitute itself for the
private; political life cannot meet private needs, as many activists have
painfully learned in the last two decades.[47]

A feminist construction of public activity recognizes something like
Hannah Arendt's ideal as a key arena of human freedom, which offers
women and men the possibility of power, visibility, respect, and achievement basic to their humanity. Voluntary associations offer not only essential training grounds and sources of revitalization for active public life but
also the necessary arena in which to reshape our understanding of the
meaning of participation and to draw appropriately on the passions
rooted in private life. Difference, whether of gender, race, class, or
philosophical viewpoint, can be understood as constitutive of public life,
where different voices have a right to be heard and where the processes
of negotiation and decision making do not require sameness.[48] Its rewards,
then, will be freedom, achievement, and power—rather than glory (with
all its martial connotations)—and a kind of autonomy that recognizes the
centrality of private and communal relationships and accords them their
rightful claims on any individual life.

NOTES

1. Hannah Arendt, *The Human Condition* (Chicago: University of Chicago
Press, 1958), 178-79. For an exposition of this understanding of public life, see
ibid., chap. 5. Such a concept traces from Aristotle (see *The Politics,* ed. by
Stephen Everson [Cambridge: Cambridge University Press, 1988]) and was
picked up and elaborated by republican theorists from the seventeenth century to
the nineteenth, notably James Harrington, *The Commonwealth of Oceana* (London:
G. Routledge and Sons, 1887 [1656]); and Alexis de Tocqueville, *Democracy in*

America (New York: Alfred A. Knopf, 1980 [A. S. Barnes, 1856]). It has recently received renewed attention from historians, such as Mary Ryan, *Women in Public: Between Banners and Ballots* (Baltimore: Johns Hopkins University Press, 1990); Gordon Wood, *The Creation of the American Republic, 1776-1787* (Chapel Hill: University of North Carolina Press, 1969); J. G. A. Pocock, *The Machiavellian Moment: Florentine Political Thought and the Atlantic Republic Tradition* (Princeton, N.J.: Princeton University Press, 1975); James T. Kloppenberg, *Uncertain Victory: Social Democracy and Progressivism in European and American Thought 1870-1920* (New York: Oxford University Press, 1986); and Linda Kerber, *Women of the Republic: Intellect and Ideology in Revolutionary America* (Chapel Hill: University of North Carolina Press, 1980); democratic theorists, such as Sheldon Wolin, *Continuity and Vision in Western Political Thought* (Boston: Little, Brown, 1960), and the short-lived journal he edited, *democracy;* and Harry C. Boyte, *CommonWealth: A Return to Citizen Politics* (New York: Free Press, 1989); and feminist theorists, such as Carole Pateman, *Participation and Democratic Theory* (Cambridge: Cambridge University Press, 1970); Iris Young, "Impartiality and the Civic Public: Some Implications of Feminist Critiques of Moral and Political Theory," *Praxis International* 5 (January 1986): 381-401; and Mary Dietz, "Context Is All: Feminism and Theories of Citizenship," *Daedalus* 116 (Fall 1987): 1-24. For the most recent discussion, see Craig Calhoun, ed., *Habermas and the Public Sphere* (Cambridge, Mass.: MIT Press, 1992).

2. Hannah Arendt, *Between Past and Future: Eight Exercises in Political Thought* (New York: Viking, 1968), 154-55.

3. See Mary Beard, *Women's Work in Municipalities* (New York: D. Appleton, 1915), and *Woman as Force in History* (New York: Macmillan, 1946). See also Eleanor Flexner, *Century of Struggle* (Cambridge, Mass.: Belknap Press, 1959); Helen Sumner, *A History of Women in Industry in the United States,* vol. 9 of *Report on Condition of Woman and Child Wage-Earners in the United States,* Senate Doc. 645, 61st Cong., 2d sess. (Washington, D.C.: Government Printing Office, 1910). Julia Cherry Spruill, *Women's Life and Work in the Southern Colonies* (Chapel Hill: University of North Carolina Press, 1938), analyzed everyday life but with little in the way of a conceptual framework for asserting the importance of the descriptions she documented so thoroughly. In the 1960s Anne Firor Scott and Gerda Lerner opened new avenues for research in women's history with works that considered both female reform activities and personal life. See Anne Firor Scott, "After Suffrage: Southern Women in the 1920s," *Journal of Southern History* 30 (August 1964): 298-318, and *The Southern Lady* (Chicago: University of Chicago Press, 1970); and Gerda Lerner, *The Grimke Sisters from South Carolina: Pioneers for Women's Rights and Abolition* (Boston: Houghton Mifflin, 1966).

4. See, for example, the work of Anne Firor Scott, Gerda Lerner, William H. Chafe, Temma Kaplan, Kathryn Kish Sklar, Mari Jo Buhle, Anne Douglas, Linda Kerber, Mary Beth Norton, to name only a few writing in the 1970s.

5. *Making the Invisible Woman Visible* is the title of the collected essays of Anne Firor Scott (Urbana: University of Illinois Press, 1984).

6. See Nancy Chodorow, *The Reproduction of Mothering: Psychoanalysis and the Sociology of Gender* (Berkeley: University of California Press, 1978); Adrienne Rich, *Of Woman Born: Motherhood as Experience and Institution* (New York: W. W. Norton, 1976); Dorothy Dinnerstein, *The Mermaid and the Minotaur: Sexual Arrangements and Human Malaise* (New York: Harper and Row, 1976); Carol Gilligan, *In a Different Voice: Psychological Theory and Women's Development* (Cambridge, Mass.: Harvard University Press, 1982); Sara Ruddick, *Maternal Thinking: Toward a Politics of Peace* (Boston: Beacon, 1989); and Jean Bethke Elshtain, *Public Man, Private Woman: Women and Social and Political Thought* (Princeton, N.J.: Princeton University Press, 1981). Marxist-feminist theory also addressed the public/private split quite explicitly but did so largely by theorizing processes of reproduction along with those of production. Because of its emphasis on material conditions, Marxist-feminism was not very engaged with the concept of public political life per se. See, for example, Eli Zaretsky, *Capitalism, the Family, and Personal Life* (New York: Harper Colophon Books, 1976).

7. For example, an argument among historians about the importance of "women's culture" erupted in the pages of *Feminist Studies* 6, no. 1 (1980): 26–64.

8. See Carole Pateman, "Feminist Critiques of the Public/Private Dichotomy," in *Public and Private in Social Life,* ed. S. I. Benn and G. F. Gaus (New York: St. Martin's Press, 1983), 281–303. For Pateman, as for others she cites, a historical perspective was crucial to her theoretical critique.

9. Historians who explored women's work outside the home and their involvement in reform activities found, inevitably, that there were highly complex links to both the ideology and the experience of domesticity. See Alice Kessler-Harris, *Out to Work: A History of Wage-Earning Women in the United States* (New York: Oxford University Press, 1982), on the ways in which the Victorian middle-class conceptions of domesticity shaped women's wage work, their earnings, and their relationships with unions. See also Sara M. Evans and Barbara J. Nelson, *Wage Justice: Comparable Worth and the Paradox of Technocratic Reform* (Chicago: University of Chicago Press, 1989), chap. 1. Students of female reform linked the feminization of religion to the creation of new kinds of public roles for women. See, for example, Barbara Epstein, *The Politics of Domesticity: Women, Evangelism and Temperance in Nineteenth Century America* (New York: Columbia University Press, 1981); and Scott, *The Southern Lady.*

10. Ellen DuBois is one of the few who has called consistently for greater attention to politics, understood as electoral and governmental activities. Those who opposed her expressed anxiety that such an approach accepts a patriarchal model of historical significance. I am arguing that as long as public life and the patriarchal state remain conflated, feminist scholars will have difficulty conceptualizing public life, though they will find themselves inescapably working on the

boundaries of public and private. For DuBois and her critics, see *Feminist Studies*, 6, no. 1 (1980). A more recent and somewhat broader call for feminist scholarly attention to politics is Joan Wallach Scott, "Gender: A Useful Category of Historical Analysis," *American Historical Review* 91 (December 1986): 1053–75. See also Ryan, *Women in Public;* and Jan Lewis, "The Republican Wife: Virtue and Seduction in the Early Republic," *William and Mary Quarterly*, 3d ser., 44 (October 1987): 689–721.

11. Mary G. Dietz, "Hannah Arendt and Feminist Politics," in *Feminist Interpretations and Political Theory*, ed. Mary Lyndon Shanley and Carole Pateman (Cambridge: Polity Press, 1991), 246. For other feminist theoretical treatments of public life, see Pateman, "Feminist Critiques of the Public/Private Dichotomy"; Virginia Sapiro, *The Political Integration of Women: Roles, Socialization, and Politics* (Urbana: University of Illinois Press, 1983); and Young, "Impartiality and the Civil Public."

12. See Paula Giddings, *When and Where I Enter: The Impact of Black Women on Race and Sex in America* (New York: William Morrow, 1984); and Sharon Harley and Rosalyn Terborg-Penn, eds., *The Afro-American Woman: Struggles and Images* (Port Washington, N.Y.: Kennikat Press, 1978). Early studies of the Women's Trade Union League also explicitly explored tensions rooted in class and ethnic differences. See, for example, Nancy Schrom Dye, "Creating a Feminist Alliance: Sisterhood and Class Conflict in the New York Women's Trade Union League, 1903–1914," *Feminist Studies* 2, no. 2/3 (1975): 24–36.

13. For a sampler of this new work, see Ellen Carol DuBois and Vicki L. Ruiz, eds., *Unequal Sisters: A Multicultural Reader in U.S. Women's History* (New York: Routledge, 1990). On the diversity of feminisms in the twentieth century, see Nancy Cott, *The Grounding of Modern Feminism* (New Haven, Conn.: Yale University Press, 1988); Leila Rupp and Verta Taylor, *Surviving the Doldrums: The American Women's Rights Movement, 1945 to the 1960s* (New York: Oxford University Press, 1987); and Alice Echols, *Daring to Be Bad: Radical Feminism in America, 1967–1975* (Minneapolis: University of Minnesota Press, 1989).

14. In addition to Ellen DuBois and Joan Scott, see Anne Firor Scott, "On Seeing and Not Seeing: A Case of Historical Invisibility," *Journal of American History* 71 (June 1984): 7–21; Paula Baker, "The Domestication of Politics: Women and American Political Society, 1780–1920," *American Historical Review* 89 (June 1984): 620–48; Barbara J. Nelson, "Women's Poverty and Women's Citizenship: Some Political Consequences of Economic Marginality," *Signs* 10 (Winter 1984): 209–31; Frances Fox Piven, "Women and the State: Ideology, Power, and the Welfare State," in *Gender and the Life Course*, ed. Alice S. Rossi (New York: Aldine, 1985), 265–87; and works by Mary G. Dietz, Iris Young, and Carole Pateman, previously cited.

15. This definition of the agenda for feminist political theory is a contested one, of course. There are many who continue to reject the public/private distinction or a nongendered definition of any aspect of human life.

16. Gerda Lerner, "Placing Women in History: Definitions and Challenges," in *The Majority Finds Its Past* (New York: Oxford University Press, 1979), 145–59.

17. Gerda Lerner and Joan Kelly led the way in this analysis. See Gerda Lerner, "Lady and the Mill Girl: Changes in the Status of Women in the Age of Jackson," in *The Majority Finds Its Past*, 15–30; and Joan Kelly-Gadol, "Did Women Have a Renaissance?" in *Becoming Visible: Women in European History*, 2d ed., ed. Renate Bridenthal and Claudia Koonz (Boston: Houghton Mifflin, 1977), 175–202.

18. Hanna Fenichel Pitkin, *Fortune Is a Woman: Gender and Politics in the Thought of Niccolo Machiavelli* (Berkeley: University of California Press, 1984), passim (quote on 118).

19. For example: "How funny it would sound in the newspapers, that Lucy Stone, pleading a cause, took suddenly ill in the pains of parturition, and perhaps gave birth to a fine bouncing boy in court! Or that Rev. Antoinette Brown was arrested in the middle of her sermon in the pulpit from the same cause, and presented a 'pledge' to her husband and the congregation; or that Dr. Harriot K. Hunt, while attending a gentleman patient for a fit of the gout or *fistula in ano*, found it necessary to send for a doctor, there and then, and to be delivered of a man or woman child, perhaps twins. A similar event might happen on the floor of congress, in a storm at sea, or in the raging tempest of battle, and then what is to become of the woman legislator?" "The Woman's Rights Convention—The Last Act of the Drama," editorial, *New York Herald*, September 12, 1852, in *Up From the Pedestal: Selected Writings in the History of American Feminism*, ed. Aileen S. Kraditor (Chicago: Quadrangle Books, 1968), 188–91.

20. "Remarks of Senator George G. Vest in Congress (1887)," in *Up From the Pedestal*, ed. Kraditor, 196.

21. Lary May and Warren Susman, eds., *Recasting America: Culture and Politics in the Age of Cold War* (Chicago: University of Chicago Press, 1988); Elaine Tyler May, *Homeward Bound: American Families in the Cold War Era* (New York: Basic Books, 1988); Boyte, *CommonWealth*.

22. William H. Chafe, "Women's History and Political History: Some Thoughts on Progressivism and the New Deal," herein.

23. See May, *Homeward Bound*.

24. Jean Bethke Elshtain, "Antigone's Daughters," *democracy* 2 (April 1982): 46–59.

25. For two recent analyses of the "sixties experience," see Jack Whalen and Richard Flacks, *Beyond the Barricades: The Sixties Generation Grows Up* (Philadelphia: Temple University Press, 1989); and Doug McAdam, *Freedom Summer* (New York: Oxford University Press, 1988). See also Sara Evans, *Personal Politics: The Roots of Women's Liberation in the Civil Rights Movement and the New Left* (New York: Alfred A. Knopf, 1979).

26. For a critique of the ideal of community as participating "in what Derrida calls the metaphysics of presence or Adorno calls the logic of identity, a metaphysics that denies difference," see Iris Marion Young, "The Ideal of Community and

the Politics of Difference," *Social Theory and Practice* 12 (Spring 1986): 1-26 (quote on 1). On the fifties, see May, *Homeward Bound.*

27. See Claus Offe, "New Social Movements: Challenging the Boundaries of Institutional Politics," *Social Research* 52 (Winter 1985): 817-68; Linda Alcoff, "Cultural Feminism versus Post-Structuralism: The Identity Crisis in Feminist Theory," *Signs* 13, no. 3 (1988): 405-36; and Jean L. Cohen, "Strategy or Identity: New Theoretical Paradigms and Contemporary Social Movements," *Social Research* 52 (Winter 1985): 663-716; and Harry C. Boyte, "The Growth of Citizen Politics," *Dissent* 36 (Fall 1990): 513-18.

28. Quoted in McAdam, *Freedom Summer,* 223.

29. There is a long-term dilemma here regarding the effectiveness of separatist strategies. Estelle Freedman points out their use in the late nineteenth century, when separatism had both clear advantages and unresolved problems, as it did a century later. Estelle Freedman, "Separatism as Strategy: Female Institution-Building and American Feminism, 1870-1930," *Feminist Studies* 5 (Fall 1979): 512-29.

30. For discussions of participation as the focal issue in reconsiderations of citizenship, see Dietz, "Hannah Arendt and Feminist Politics"; and Pateman, *Participation and Democratic Theory.*

31. Michael Walzer has described the two definitions of citizenship as follows: "The first describes citizenship as an office, a responsibility, a burden proudly assumed; the second describes citizenship as a status, an entitlement, a right or set of rights passively enjoyed. The first makes citizenship the core of our life, the second its outer frame." His analysis grows from a series of major debates among political theorists who divide along these lines, but the entire debate for the most part perpetuates an underlying set of gendered assumptions precisely because it does not address the relationship between public and domestic life. Michael Walzer, "Citizenship," in *Political Innovation and Conceptual Change,* ed. Terence Ball, James Farr, and Russell L. Hanson (Cambridge: Cambridge University Press, 1989), 211-19 (quote on 216).

32. See Scott, "Gender." See also Joan Landes, *Women in the Public Sphere in the Age of the French Revolution* (Ithaca, N.Y.: Cornell University Press, 1988); and Lewis, "The Republican Wife."

33. This seems to have been particularly the case in periods of expanding public freedom when societal changes placed gender definitions in flux. At such times—for example, the Renaissance and the century following the American Revolution—the separation of public and private is defended most strenuously in the name of "manhood." See, for example, Paula Baker's discussion of elections in "Domestication of Politics"; Kelly-Gadol, "Did Women Have a Renaissance?"; Peter Filene's discussion of manhood in the Progressive Era in *Him/Her Self: Sex Roles in Modern America* (Baltimore: Johns Hopkins University Press, 1986), chap. 3 and 4. See also Pitkin, *Fortune Is a Woman;* and Landes, *Women in the Public Sphere.*

34. See Baker, "Domestication of Politics." When Baker described a female *politics* in the nineteenth century, she drew on a large body of historical work

from the last two decades to synthesize, clarify, and make explicit an underlying assumption.

35. Pateman, "Feminist Critiques of the Public/Private Dichotomy."

36. Habermas actually treats only one aspect of "public." Drawing on Kant and Arendt, Habermas seeks to resurrect the notion of the public as active critic and evaluator of public policy and public affairs, with its public spaces for this activity found in settings like coffee houses, discussion groups, the media, and so forth (Lyceum/Chatauqua—and the League of Women Voters—all reflect this particular view of public). He slights associational life in which citizens engage in direct problem solving, as well as insurgent reform movements, both of which were characteristically female and the source of two other senses of "public." See Habermas, *The Structural Transformation of the Public Sphere,* chap. 1-6; and Hannah Arendt, *Origins of Totalitarianism* (New York: Harcourt Brace Jovanovich, 1973), part 1. For a discussion of the three meanings of public life outlined here, see Harry C. Boyte, "The Pragmatic Ends of Popular Politics: Habermas and the New Social History," in *Habermas and the Public Sphere,* ed. Calhoun, 340-55. Mary Ryan argues that public life in the United States was at its most active and vital in the 1830s and 1840s, a turbulent time when massive gatherings of citizens debated and acted on a very wide range of public problems. Mary Ryan, "Women and the Public Sphere," in *Habermas and the Public Sphere,* ed. Calhoun, 259-88.

37. Baker, "Domestication of Politics."

38. A recent revival of interest in civil society on the right emphasizes voluntary associations as sources of social stability and privately provided social services (as in George Bush's "thousand points of light"). Peter L. Berger, with Brigitte Berger, *Facing Up to Modernity: Excursions in Society, Politics, and Religion* (New York: Basic Books, 1977).

39. See Lori Ginzberg, *Women and the Work of Benevolence: Morality, Politics, and Class in the Nineteenth Century United States* (New Haven, Conn.: Yale University Press, 1990).

40. See Baker, "Domestication of Politics"; and Sara M. Evans and Harry C. Boyte, *Free Spaces: Sources of Democratic Change in America* (New York: Harper and Row, 1986).

41. Scott, *The Southern Lady,* 140.

42. Nancy A. Hewitt, *Women's Activism and Social Change: Rochester, New York, 1822-1872* (Ithaca, N.Y.: Cornell University Press, 1984), 131-35.

43. Mary Fredrickson, " 'Each One Is Dependent on the Other': Southern Churchwomen, Racial Reform, and the Process of Transformation, 1880-1940," herein.

44. Young, "Impartiality and the Civic Public," 387, 383.

45. For a discussion of "interest," see Boyte, *CommonWealth,* 88-90.

46. For a discussion of the Industrial Areas Foundation approach and its implications for democratic political theory, see ibid., chap. 6, 7.

47. Several recent studies of sixties activists, notably McAdam, *Freedom Summer,* and Whalen and Flacks, *Beyond the Barricades,* document radicals'

attempts to construct fully politicized private lives through a variety of communal experiments. The failure of this totalizing politics led many to escape public life altogether and retreat into an apolitical private existence. See also Charlotte Bunch, "Self-Definition and Political Survival," in *Passionate Politics: Feminist Theory in Action, Essays, 1968–1986* (New York: St. Martin's, 1987), 81–93.

48. See Young, "Impartiality and the Civic Public."

Part 2

Economic Justice:
Representation and Mobilization

Women's battles for economic justice were central to the narrative composed by early feminist scholars analyzing the historical relations between class and gender. Tales of factory girls and union maids from New England to the Northwest first shaped our understanding of working-class women's activism and served as a consistent counterpoint to conceptual models framed by working-class men's and middle-class women's experiences. As they expanded definitions of politics to include struggles for power outside the electoral arena, those who explored working women's activism offered up nuanced portraits of the complex interactions between victimization and agency, familial dependency and communal militancy.

Those studying the economic dimensions of women's lives have recently added new occupational, regional, racial, and theoretical perspectives to their agenda. Highlighting the intersections of race, class, and gender, studies of working women have expanded to embrace agricultural labor (slave and free), domestic labor (unpaid and paid), clerical, sales and other service sector occupations, and industrial sites from Florida to California, the Carolinas to Colorado. Some scholars have begun evaluating the politics of shopping as well as those of the shop floor, arguing that at critical moments women's buying power was as important to campaigns for economic justice as their labor power was. Other scholars in the field have adopted postmodernist approaches, reinvigorating analyses of language and representation. Recognizing that gender often serves to signify other relations of power, we have reread texts on and by working-class women to reveal important subtexts related to race, respectability, and sexuality. Together these new perspectives on women, activism, and the economy direct our attention to the connections among material needs, social hierarchies, and moral imperatives.

Carrying us from representations of domestic upheaval in the 1830s through the mobilization of domestic power in the 1930s, the essays in this section illustrate these new approaches. Mari Jo Buhle reexamines campaigns for economic justice in the antebellum era and reminds us that the lone needlewoman—hunched over a garment in her garret or cast as the heroine of a contemporary domestic novel—was a far more common character in this period than was the "factory girl," who first garnered so much attention from women's historians. Buhle sets fictional figures next to the images devised by crusading journalists and the observations of incipient urban sociologists. In the process, she illuminates the new political economy of the emergent capitalist marketplace and its impact on women workers and those who sought to mobilize on their behalf.

Jacquelyn Dowd Hall similarly explores the links between domestic and labor relations, entanglements that become both more intimate and more intricate when cast in a biographical mode. Although the adventures of Ola Delight Smith often read like the fictional tales of antebellum northern needlewomen, they are in fact pieced together from the historical trail left by this twentieth-century southerner. Tracing Smith's career as a journalist, telegrapher, housewife, labor organizer, and amateur photographer, Hall presents a version of labor feminism that transforms our vision of the links between progressive politics and campaigns for economic justice. At the same time, informed by postmodernist perspectives, she exposes the sexual vulnerability of this disorderly woman, even as Smith herself, wielding new visual technologies, exposes the company spies who provide the sexual ammunition that discredits her. The tale is ultimately cautionary—both for the labor feminist who cannot escape either the racism of her era or the moral and material vulnerability of her sex and for the historian who fails to recognize the importance of her struggles.

In Tampa, Florida, in the same period, questions of material and moral vulnerability are configured quite differently when women are granted the suffrage just months before a local referendum on a new city charter and in the midst of a seven-month cigar strike. Nancy A. Hewitt dissects the rhetoric of "intelligent womanhood" and white supremacy brandished by rival factions of white male politicians, revealing the underlying battles over political corruption and economic control. The women of Tampa—Anglo, African American, and Latin—chose distinct, though often overlapping, strategies for voicing their concerns, including voluntarism, voting, strikes, and sexual subversion. Hewitt is less concerned than other contributors, such as William H. Chafe, with how women collectively shaped progressive politics. Rather, she explores how distinct communities of women sought to gain leverage as they pursued their own particular visions of justice, dignity, and rights within a single southern city.

For African American women in a northern city a decade later, the pursuit of justice, dignity, and rights inspired other forms of political action. Combining traditional responsibilities for domestic labor with new philosophies of economic nationalism, the founders of the Housewives' League of Detroit established "an ingenious united action organization" to "help workers, blacks, and women survive the massive economic dislocation brought on by the Great Depression." Darlene Clark Hine resurrects the organizing activities of the Detroit League and unravels the complex "communal womanist consciousness" that nurtured such efforts. Adding depth and specificity to our rapidly increasing knowledge of the work of black club women, Hine focuses on the intersection between campaigns for racial and economic justice, uplift and mutual aid. Seeking to empower women of all classes, the leaders of the Housewives' League mobilized a female-dominated consumer movement to aid black businesses, employees, and professionals communitywide.

Through the story of the Housewives' League, Hine reaffirms the critical junctures between how women represent themselves, how they mobilize others, and how such mobilization increases their economic as well as political leverage. From the antebellum era through the Great Depression, from New York to Atlanta to Tampa to Detroit, women organized around their own interests and needs; even those with the least access to formal institutions of power pursued economic justice by political means. It is clear, however, that they did so within ever-shifting but always race- and class-specific material and moral constraints.

Needlewomen and the Vicissitudes of Modern Life: A Study of Middle-Class Construction in the Antebellum Northeast

Mari Jo Buhle

"A little charity, for God's sake! my children are starving!"—so begins the title story of Caroline Mehitable Sawyer's *Merchant's Widow, and Other Tales,* published in 1841. It is a blustery winter night in New York City. A thinly clad woman, with tears streaming down her pale cheeks and shivers wracking her small body, begs for alms. On closer look, readers see that she is dressed neatly in a faded yet clean and simple calico, a sure sign that she has "seen better days." We soon learn that in fact this pitiable woman had been born to luxury. Her father, a princely merchant of Savannah, Georgia, had spared no expense in rearing his only child in comfort and refinement. By age fifteen she had blossomed into a model of Southern Womanhood and easily won the heart of a prosperous businessman. How, then, did our protagonist come upon such hard times?

Within a few years of her marriage a dark cloud descended. Both father and husband had succumbed to the temptation of easy money in the wave of speculation that swept the country, and together they met financial ruin in the Panic of 1837. The father, too ashamed to live, died within three weeks, while the husband sought redemption in New York City. The young wife tried hard to manage a household on her husband's greatly reduced income, but her ignorance defeated good intentions. Even her beloved children suffered from unintended neglect. At this point a kindly neighbor intervened and instructed the young wife in some of the simple arts of housekeeping. More important, she taught her how to sew. As the family's resources continued to dwindle, the young wife arranged to ply her needle for wages. But even after long hours of "utmost exertions," she could not earn enough to cover the family's expenses. Finally, the ultimate disaster struck: her despairing husband took ill and died.

When we meet this grieving woman, she has already reached her nadir. She explains: "I hardly know what I could do that would yield me a tolerable support. Unfortunately, I was brought up in a part of the country where females are taught scarcely anything that is useful; and until I came to this city, I had hardly learned to dress myself; and many an hour of bitter regret have I since spent at my own helplessness."

All is not lost, however, for an elderly gentleman has taken an interest in her case. Upon hearing her tale, he learns that she is the widow of the son of the woman he had once hoped to marry. That possibility lost forever, the gentleman determines to become father and grandfather to this penniless family and immediately sets himself to hire an instructor for the widow's little girl. He insists that "all know how to earn their own living, so that if fortune should desert them, they need not suffer as their mother had done."[1]

Maria L. Buckley's *Sketch of the Working Classes of New York: Or, the Sufferings of the Sewing Girls* (1856) similarly concerns a widow who has been reduced to poverty by a husband who dies prematurely after failing in the stock market. Mrs. Talbot enjoys better prospects than Sawyer's protagonist, however, because she is skilled in fine sewing. To support herself and four small children, Mrs. Talbot applies for work to an "up-town lady" who is able to pay her a living wage. Yet the wealthy patron not only offers a mere pittance but also announces her intention to pay only at the end of the season. With sums so small—fifty cents per shirt or calico wrapper—the busy society woman could not be bothered. With empty hands and broken spirit, Mrs. Talbot returns home. How would she feed her children?

The answer appears in the form of another woman. Mrs. Stevens, a widow of substantial means, knocks on the door and inquires if Mrs. Talbot would be willing to sew some mourning dresses. Mrs. Talbot is ever so eager to commission this work, of course, and quotes the price she had been promised by her former client. Mrs. Stevens responds indignantly: "Can it be possible that any lady possessed of the true feelings of benevolence toward her own sex, can demean herself so much in paying such a paltry sum?" Mrs. Stevens storms out of the modest apartment, only to return with provisions for the household and a promise that she would return. In good faith, the wealthy widow arranges to turn over to Mrs. Talbot one of the small retail establishments she had inherited from her husband's estate. She installs the less fortunate widow as manager and, assured of her well-being, places the four children in school. With loose ends tied neatly, the author nevertheless draws out the moral: "Oh, would but the rich more generally attend to the necessities of the poor, how many a pillow would be softened, and many almost broken hearts healed."[2]

By mid-century dozens of authors had created similar tales of melo-drama and morality. Between 1840 and the decade of the Civil War—a period marked as the high point of the domestic novel—American writers produced over sixty novels describing the increasing immiseration of the urban working poor. Their formulaic stories rarely concerned young women's problems in courtship, the literary staple of the early republic that Cathy N. Davidson has termed "privileging the *feme couvert.*"[3] Rather, these writers pushed the protagonist out of the domestic sphere to take stock of women's new public visibility. The predicament was that of a woman unattached to men or, in contemporary rhetoric, "thrown upon her own resources." The male seducer still lingered in the wings, ready as ever to pounce on the unprotected female and drive her into prostitution. The main antagonist appeared, however, in the form of the mercenary and dishonest employer who drove his victim if not to moral destruction then to near-death by starvation.

These stories found a ready market among the swelling literate population. Sawyer's collection, for example, sold a thousand copies within ten days of publication. While fiction depicting women out-side the home did not generate the record sales of the most popular domestic novels (Susan Warner's *Wide, Wide World,* published in 1851, is the best example of that genre), it sold well enough to attract a host of popular authors, male and female. Hoping to market their books as well as to uplift readers, popular writers, such as Charles Burdett, Maria Maxwell, and Ned Buntline (pseudonym for Edward Zen Carroll Judson), spiced their tales with adventure and romance, routinely pun-ished villains and rewarded heroes, and delivered the anticipated happy ending.[4]

Although presented as realistic tales of working-class life, these stories expressed more clearly their authors' uncertainty—and anxiety—about class relations in the first half of the nineteenth century. Like Maria Buckley, who titled her book "a sketch of the *working classes* of New York," many authors actually described their protagonists' descent into poverty from a more privileged, sometimes quite exalted, position. Like Buckley, they pointedly identified the female protagonist as a woman "who had seen better days." This common practice may have amounted to no more than a ploy to induce empathy from mainly middle-class readers who resisted crossing class lines, even in fantasy. Just as likely, this trope indicated a rudimentary construction of middle-class woman-hood outside the ascending dominant discourse of stable domesticity. These two themes played off each other, with the author's consideration of class giving license to a major reinterpretation of gender.

Indeterminate in handling matters of class, these authors clearly specified their major premise: the vicissitudes of life are problematical for all but especially so for women. They typically drew a logical parallel between woman's fortune and the seemingly unpredictable capitalist marketplace. The market for waged labor developed in tune with a highly variable and experimental consumer demand for manufactured goods and an equally capricious flow of capital indifferent to human needs. The market disrupted the traditional logic of household production, created strange forms of social relations, and forced the increasingly prevalent wageworker to depend on someone else for a livelihood. The growing tensions between masters and apprentices, the widening gap between rich and poor, and the instability and delicacy of the economy in general all suggested not only the erosion of tradition but also the incalculable hazards of modern life. And a woman removed from the family's protective network, the loving care of a husband, father, or brother—what were her chances for survival? The woman "thrown on her own resources" symbolized the manifold vagaries of the new political economy.

Needlework served to illustrate the ineluctable and shifting interplay of class and gender in the early nineteenth century. In depicting the misadventures of a wife and mother suddenly beset by poverty or the trials of a young orphan girl, writers almost invariably placed their protagonists in a struggle against the odds of earning a livelihood by woman's "traditional" occupation. The prolific melodramatist Timothy Shay Arthur, best known for his temperance tale *Ten Nights in a Barroom,* explored this theme in *Lizzy Glenn: Or, the Trials of a Seamstress,* published in 1859. Arthur presented his heroine as a victim of circumstances. He began:

> Needle-work, at best, yields but a small return. Yet how many thousands have no other resource in life, no other barrier thrown up between them and starvation! The manly stay upon which a woman has leaned suddenly fails, and she finds self-support an imperative necessity; yet she has no skill, no strength, no developed resources. In all probability she is a mother. In this case she must not only stand alone, but sustain her helpless children. Since her earliest recollection, others have ministered to her wants and pleasures. From a father's hand, childhood and youth received their countless natural blessings; and brother or husband, in later years, has stood between her and the rough winds of a stormy world. All at once, like a bird reared, from a fledgling, in its cage, she finds herself in the world, unskilled in its ways, yet required to earn her bread or perish.[5]

To Arthur and his literary peers, the life of the needlewoman epitomized the fate of women who lacked "natural," that is, *male*, providers. Only severe hardship, he surmised, would force a native-born white woman to seek a wage-earning situation. The needlewoman thus appeared the perfect object of solicitude, for it was unanticipated adversity, not ambition or convention, that drove her to wage earning.

Equally important, however, was the very conversion of a woman's skill with a needle into remunerative activity. As waged labor, sewing no longer represented a feminine vocation but rather an undesirable occupation. The transformation of needlework—a time-honored emblem of domesticity—into wage labor suggested another layer to this tragedy, the instability of domesticity itself and, accordingly, the class position of its rightful bearer. Neither factory labor nor even school teaching could serve this symbolic purpose.

In choosing needlework, these writers were, of course, attuned to a major historical development, although the problems of needlewomen were related less to the transitory character of male protection than to the changing relation of woman's labor to the market economy. The Revolution had ended British restrictions and allowed the implementation of a tariff favorable to American manufacturers, setting the scene for the growth of the clothing trade from a small custom enterprise into a major industry. New markets, such as the United States Army and Navy, the growing populations of the West, and the numerous slaves in the South created a huge demand for ready-made cheap goods. Shrewd manufacturers identified a cheap labor market in the ranks of poor women. Working primarily in their places of residence, women produced by hand and at low cost to their employers the bulk of men's clothing—their vests, pantaloons, shirts, and ties. It was estimated in 1830 that in the four major centers of the trade, New York, Philadelphia, Boston, and Baltimore, nearly thirteen thousand women sewed for wages.[6]

As the melodramatists contended, wages paid seamstresses were notoriously poor. Because employers had little capital tied up in overhead, in either machinery or rent, they regulated their profits by charging prices as high as the market would bear and, most of all, by procuring the cheapest labor. As early as 1819 New York journeymen tailors protested the policy of paying women at rates 25 to 50 percent under the prevailing standard set by men. Estimates published in contemporary newspapers and reports affirmed that even under the best conditions needlework allowed only a meager livelihood. Paid by the piece, the best grade seamstress in Philadelphia might earn in 1830 less than $1.00 per day, and that only by working sixteen to twenty hours. She might spend an entire day making a fine linen shirt and receive as a payment only 75¢.

The less skilled, the majority who managed only "plain sewing" or who made cheaper items like pantaloons, might earn as little as 12¢ or 13¢ per day. Two decades later, wages had improved slightly. In 1850 a highly skilled seamstress might bring in $1.50 or $2.00 per day.[7]

Needlework was not, however, totally devoid of advantages. The work required little formal training; most women could ply a needle well enough to handle plain sewing. Nor did needlework demand a long-term commitment. Paid by the piece or by the lot, a woman could contract on a weekly basis. Unlike domestic servants or teachers, seamstresses could establish their own calendars of employment, picking up work during times of distress and foregoing it during more prosperous intervals. Even in the best circumstances, though, the rate of payment underscored the minimal bargaining power of these workers who exchanged poor wages for the privilege of working at home. The increasing immiseration of these workers necessarily transformed their "private" labors into major "public" issues.

The novelist Maria Maxwell captured this image in her story of Lizzy Roberts, the sole caretaker of her invalid mother and her younger brother. Lizzy appeared as the protagonist of *Ernest Grey: Or, the Sins of Society; a Tale of New York Life* (1855):

> a pale, delicate looking girl about nineteen or twenty. Her fea-
> tures were rather prepossessing than beautiful, but they had a
> haggard, worn expression which told too plainly of sleepless nights
> and unremitting toil. Lizzy Roberts was a shirt maker; she worked
> for a fashionable establishment that couldn't brook disappointment,
> and therefore was she obliged to sit up night after night at her
> cheerless, monotonous employment. Long after the last sounds of
> busy life had died away, while thousands of the gay, the fashionable
> and the dissipated squandered their time and their money in the
> pursuit of foolish or criminal enjoyments, she sat and sewed, in the
> dreary miserable room which she called home, the stillness only
> broken by the heavy breathing of an invalid mother in the uneasy
> sleep of pain.[8]

Maxwell clearly linked needlework and the woman with few resources.

The sad tale of Lizzy Roberts is emblematic of the genre. The protago-
nist appears as a female representative of the working classes, although she, like so many of her fictional counterparts, had "known better days." Lizzy would have preferred to work as a governess, but the care of her ailing mother and younger brother demanded her presence at home. What else could she do? Needlework, according to the author Maria Maxwell, signified the last resort of a woman who could no

longer afford to labor without monetary compensation; it established the protagonist's plight as not only poverty but also downward social mobility.

Ostensibly tales of working-class life, these novels commonly construct intricate middle-class relationships. Authors typically linked the fictional victim of circumstance to her rescuer, invariably a beneficent representative of her former class. Male or female, the agent of salvation is also the vehicle for the author's analysis of the problem. Be it Sawyer's kindly gentleman or Buckley's good-hearted widow, this character often narrates the story or at minimum delivers the decisive interpretation of the injustice done to the protagonist, most often assigning responsibility to unscrupulous or selfish members of his or her own class. In these renditions, male employers who cheat their workers or who pay less than living wages appear the most villainous. Propertied women who evince similar qualities stand out for their insensitivity; not even greed for profits motivates their thoughtless behavior. Oppressor, rescuer, victim, as well as reader thus stand on common, middle-class ground.

The analysis of misfortune focuses, then, not on class oppression but on gender inequalities. Although working-class men and women appear in these stories, their characters function merely to illustrate the quality of life at the bottom. Concerned mainly with how their protagonists got to the bottom, the authors challenge directly the discourse of stable domesticity. A truly happy ending may gather victims and rescuers, occasionally a redeemed oppressor, into women's proper realm of the household—but not without a stern warning about its inherent fragility. For this reason, the authors routinely enjoin the presumed female reader to respond charitably to the poor while reflecting on the precarious nature of her own position. They typically conclude by superimposing the salvation of the distressed woman on the enlightenment of her benefactor.

The authors, in short, underscore in gendered terms the problems inherent in dependent relationships. Women must not rely solely on men's protection, they insist, but accept responsibility for their own welfare. Even the most well-to-do could not afford to indulge in luxury or frivolity; the love of dress and finery, the authors frequently noted, led to the exploitation of needlewomen while detracting from life's real necessities. The implicit moral embodied a host of issues more commonly associated with the mainstream woman's rights movement: better if not equal wages for work; expanded educational opportunities, including vocational training for work outside the home; and greater access to the better-paying jobs routinely held by men.

This analysis fits uncomfortably alongside other contemporary and more mainstream discussions of poverty and the plight of the poor. Traditional views of indigence, giving way to the Enlightenment-informed philosophy of laissez faire, had by the early decades of the nineteenth century been replaced by less empathetic attitudes toward the destitute. According to emerging opinion, poverty was not misfortune but the product of moral inadequacy. Charity, such as the provision of alms, only promoted idleness and extravagance, in this view, while encouraging its recipients to withhold their labor from the market. Assuming that all who were physically able could find self-support, leading social philosophers and public officials interpreted charitable assistance as morally wrong and economically unsound.[9]

This unremittingly utilitarian perspective, framed almost entirely in terms of male paupers, may have sparked the alternative literary response to the actual impoverished majority, women and their children. Whatever their inspiration, these novelists resisted its cruel implications and refused to foreswear social responsibility for new classes of the poor. They recognized the way poverty differentially affected men and women and understood that the principles of laissez faire propounded this injustice: women entered the marketplace with serious disadvantages; they could not compete fairly with men.

The melodramatists were not alone in espousing this position. They built on several decades of work by philanthropists who had responded directly to the plight of poor women. Realizing that the growing destitute population comprised a disproportionate number of women and their children, a sector of public-minded citizens refused to blame the poor for their own failures. The novelists picked up on the ideas of those reformers who had begun, as Anne Firor Scott put it, "to wonder whether vice, as they defined it, might be more the result than the cause of poverty."[10]

Scott's thorough survey and analysis of women's voluntary associations in the early nineteenth century, *Natural Allies: Women's Associations in American History* (1991), helps frame my treatment of contemporary fiction about wage-earning women. In studying the antebellum record of the numerous societies formed to assist primarily poor women, Scott points out that the differences between the patrons and clients were neither sharp nor fixed. "Class lines were not yet firmly drawn," she writes, and "members of the same family might be found on different rungs of the social ladder. Mobility was downward as well as upward." Scott notes, moreover, that the annual reports and minutes of these societies "repeatedly reminded members that they might someday be in need."[11] It was only as the century progressed that class relations came to impinge clearly and vividly on the literary imagination as well as the reform impulse.

Writers of fiction and members of female voluntary associations, by no means mutually exclusive, reconstructed a vision of womanhood in relation to developments in the market economy that were producing a new and puzzling class order in the antebellum Northeast. They were concerned at first, however, less with class inequities and divisions than with the fundamental premise of the rising ideology of female domesticity, the notion that "all men support all women." In responding to the plight of poor women—and, implicitly, to their own situation—they articulated a critique of gender relations centered on women's financial reliance on men, that is, their husbands and fathers. Novelists and reformers alike understood that women's status depended primarily on their marriage or family of origin. On the other hand, women's own relationship to the processes of capitalist production remained relatively less distinct in their analysis.

Yet this latter factor was not entirely absent. In choosing needlework as their primary point of reference, both writers and reformers grappled with the transformation of a staple of women's labor from a domestic vocation to a wage-earning occupation. While novelists told uplifting stories of downtrodden seamstresses, their contemporaries in charitable societies designed programs of work relief around traditional forms of female labor. In the late eighteenth century, philanthropists had experimented with spinning and weaving, setting up "houses of industry" to employ the growing number of destitute women. By the 1820s the commercial success of the New England textile industry undercut these programs, and needlework became the preferred system of work relief.[12] Eventually market conditions worked again to force out the philanthropic enterprises, but until the 1850s, when the factory system took hold, two systems of labor existed side by side. Many poor women undoubtedly vacillated between commercial and philanthropic establishments, procuring in both cases a mere pittance for long hours of labor. Taking charity or earning wages for needlework signified, to many women as well as their benefactors or employers, the same condition: misfortune and poverty.

Needlework proved an apt metaphor to illustrate changes in these women's relation to production during the first half of the nineteenth century. Its own history encompassed the shift from household to factory labor and symbolically women's relation first to the older family economy and eventually to the emerging commercial enterprise. Needlework, a form of production undergoing transformation, compelled women to locate themselves in class as well as gender terms.

Needlework inspired one of the earliest forms of female benevolence, the ubiquitous charities affiliated with Protestant churches. Named for the Christian disciple known for this particular act of charity (Acts 9:36–41), Dorcas societies encouraged their members to devote a portion of each day to sewing garments for the poor. Caroline Mehitable Sawyer, for example, founded a Ladies' Dorcas Society of the Universalist Church in New York City and personally shared its work until illness limited her activities to writing. In Boston, several local chapters affiliated in 1812 as the Boston Fragment Society, which in its first three decades distributed nearly forty thousand items of clothing to the city's poor. The Boston society soon began to encourage poor women to support themselves through their own needlework. Throughout the urban Northeast, many societies followed by instituting vocational programs, which offered women instruction in a high grade of sewing with the aim of improving their chances for better-paying positions.[13]

Amid the severe depression of the late 1820s, several prominent philanthropists began to discuss the relationship between these two systems of needlework. Many had previously noted the increase of women in the wage-earning population as well as on the rolls of charity organizations. The first major urban depression of 1819–20 had reduced their meager standard of living, and throughout the following decade, despite the economic upswing, women turned in large numbers to private benevolent societies and public relief agencies. Historians have since confirmed this impression, estimating in Philadelphia, for example, that between 1811 and 1829 approximately 90 percent of those adults receiving relief were women.[14]

The winter of 1828 took an even greater toll. Thousands faced unemployment, including a growing population of women who depended on their needles for a livelihood. Philanthropists perceived that many of the women asking for assistance were young, determined, yet unable to rise above a chronic state of poverty. Some sank deeper into misery; others died or "did worse." The most farsighted reformers concluded that the existing public and private charities did little more than alleviate distress for a short time.

It was within this context that a few broad-minded philanthropists established an interpretation of female poverty that linked needlework to misfortune as well as exploitation. In documenting the abysmal conditions of women's wage labor, they countered the prevailing faith in laissez-faire economics. They reviled greedy employers for taking advantage of women's inability to compete on the open market and driving them ultimately to destitution. They also nailed those charitable institutions that abided these same principles.

At the forefront of this discussion was the venerable Philadelphia publisher and philanthropist Mathew Carey. Carey had been studying the plight of the poor since before the turn of the century and had become a leading advocate of private charity. He wrote and published numerous pamphlets addressed to the leading citizens of the Northeast, imploring them to act on their Christian duty to the poor. As the 1829 depression set in, he focused on the plight of poor women, and, after reviewing their situation, he attributed the cause of their poverty to the low wages set by the clothing industry. He joined a committee of citizens who shared his concern and conducted a survey of the conditions of Philadelphia's working women. In May 1829 Carey's opinion was confirmed by the committee's public report that described wages paid to seamstresses as well as to other homeworkers as "utterly inadequate." A wage under $1.50 per week scarcely constituted a livelihood, the committee complained, even during the best times.[15]

Like the melodramatists who followed in their tracks, Carey and his colleagues shaped their arguments to appeal to middle-class sensibilities. "The highest and most exalted being that ever trod the earth," Carey warned, "has no security against the vicissitudes of fortune." He quoted from a report of the New York Society for the Relief of Poor Widows with Small Children, which illustrated his point:

> In the year 1825, I met with a family who had been reduced from a respectable life to the greatest poverty and distress. It consisted of Mrs. C——, who was left *a widow with four children, and an aged mother dependent upon her for support.* . . . Mrs. C. was extremely ill, as was also one of her children, and the poor old mother almost worn out with fatigue and anxiety; in addition to which she had become nearly blind from too close application of her needle, and was utterly unable to supply their necessary wants.[16]

Popular fiction and the official records of charitable societies thus revealed a common rhetoric and narrative. It was not unknown for writers to participate in the creation of both forms. Caroline Mehitable Sawyer, for example, turned to story writing when her active days in benevolent activity drew to a close and undoubtedly enclosed both phases of her productive life in a single philosophical framework. In both cases, sympathy for the poor barely disguised an overwhelming anxiety about middle-class domesticity.[17]

Carey played directly on these fears of downward mobility, and few novelists could improve on his rhetorical style:

> When you consider the vicissitudes of life, it is not impossible that at a future day—heaven avert such a catastrophe!—some of you may be reduced as low as those ill-fated women. And can you—will-you—resist the imperious calls of humanity, of religion—will you look with indifference on the extreme sufferings of your sex—will you not hold out the hand of protection to them, and, as far as your

power lies, avert a continuance of those miseries, by which they
have hitherto been ground down to the earth?[18]

He chastised wealthy women for not only their heartlessness but also
their foolishness.

Principal responsibility nevertheless rested, in Carey's opinion, with
the men who employed women in either commercial or philanthropic
establishments. Like the didactic novelists, his committee assumed that
information about the "real state of the case" would induce employers to
raise their rate of payment, and it therefore made a plea for voluntary
response.

Carey's indictment extended even to the ostensibly well-meaning
members of the middle class. He recognized that philanthropists often
shared with employers the blame for women's distress: they, too, failed to
pay a living wage. Many charitable organizations justified this policy,
Carey noted, on the grounds that their low rate discouraged dependency
and motivated clients to seek better-paying work in the commercial
industries. In practice, he pointed out, these charities actually set the
wage standard.

Carey identified the perfect negative example in the Provident Society
of Philadelphia. This richly endowed benevolent organization provided
work to many women during the winter months, when commercial
establishments entered their slack season, but, as Carey discovered, it
offered payments insufficient to support even a single individual. Its
original rate, set in 1824 at twelve cents per shirt, had become the
standard in the city and served five years later to keep women's wages
below a subsistence level. Carey's argument had some merit. In 1829 the
U.S. War Department contracted to pay seamstresses at twelve and a half
cents per shirt, and officials justified this low rate by referring to the
wage policy set by local benevolent societies. In response to a letter of
protest by prominent citizens, the secretary of the War Department
described the whole subject as "one of so much delicacy, and . . . so
intimately connected with the manufacturing interests, and the general
prices of this kind of labour in the city of Philadelphia" that no change in
policy could be made. Carey then turned to the Provident Society to set
a fair standard by raising its own rate of payment. As he noted, "There
will be no generosity in the rise. The present system is literally 'grinding
the faces of the poor.' "[19]

Carey spared neither philanthropists nor commercial manufacturers.
He insisted that "every individual industrially employed in a useful
occupation, has an indisputable claim to healthful and comfortable support.
Those who employ him or her, ought, in honour and justice, to yield that

support. . . . "[20] In his opinion, nothing was more morally distressing than the labor conditions of Philadelphia's seamstresses. Whereas textile operatives earned between two and three dollars a week—scarcely a living wage—seamstresses netted far less. Moreover, seamstresses faced unemployment one-third to one-half of the year, and they could not possibly tide themselves over on the mean wages paid during the bountiful season. During slack times, the "three charity months" of January through March, many turned to philanthropic organizations, only to receive the same miserable wages. Carey complained, "There is no grievance in this country that calls more loudly for redress, or is more severe in its operations, or more demoralizing in its consequences, than the paltry wages given for most species of female labor, not averaging in many cases, more than one-third of what is earned by men for analogous employments."[21]

Carey and his coterie of Philadelphia citizens strengthened the association between female wage earning and poverty, between needlework and charity. In Carey's opinion, seamstresses deserved economic justice and, failing that, solicitude. He strongly supported the committee's advocacy of "a society for bettering the conditions of the poor." He concluded, nevertheless, that if employers and philanthropists fell short of their duty, the seamstresses' case rested with members of their own sex.[22]

If tales from real life fueled reformers and litterateurs alike, they also inspired middle-class women to act on their sympathies for the poor—and on their own anxieties. Beginning in the 1830s, organizations designed to address the needs of the female poor appeared in several northern cities, some seemingly following Carey's advice to the letter. These new associations sought to halt the exploitation of their labor. Needlework once again served as the principal means of redress.

The Ladies' Depository Association of Philadelphia, founded in 1833, provides an apt illustration. Its institutional records present its own origins in a narrative similar to that of Buckley's *Sketch of the Working Classes of New York*. Although its founder, a Mrs. Stott, admitted that she had observed the operations of two similar associations in London and Edinburgh, she assigned her motivation to an incident that resembled Buckley's plot. One day while shopping in New York City, Mrs. Stott saw a genteel lady like herself present for sale some fine needlework to a retail merchant. She stood aghast as he responded rudely to the distressed woman and offered a pittance for her laboriously produced garment. This transaction allegedly fired Mrs. Stott's determination to spare other women from this fate. Mrs. Stott acted more collectively than did Buckley's Mrs. Stevens. On January 11, 1833, she called to her home twelve friends and led them in establishing the Ladies' Depository Association. This small assembly proceeded to elect a board of officers and to lay plans for opening a small retail shop for needlework. Although the founders hoped to cater primarily to "those who had seen better days," they specified that any woman who obtained a permit from one of the association's members could deposit her needlework for sale. The association in turn deducted 6 percent from the sale price to cover its operating expenses and returned the remainder to the depositor. Operating in this manner, the Depository served in its first decade between one and two hundred women per year.[23]

The Philadelphia Depository, although organized as a philanthropic society, aimed not to "reform" its clients but to intervene in the market processes to alleviate their miseries, if possible by sparing women the dangers and humiliations associated with wage earning. The managers insisted that few women were immune to the vicissitudes of fortune, even the most genteel. For this reason, they aspired to screen "the unfortunate from the unkind treatment which they too often experience in their intercourse with the world."[24]

The Ladies' Depository Association of New York, also formed in 1833, shared this goal. Four years later Rhode Island women founded the Providence Employment Society, not to save the souls of poor women but to make it possible for at least a few to receive a just wage for their honest labors. In contrast to commercial establishments, these societies determined to set a standard of just payments regardless of the market for goods. They pledged, in other words, to pay women a living wage.

Founded during an era of relative prosperity in the mid-1830s, these societies soon tested their ability to compete against capitalist employers. The business and banking systems collapsed, and between 1837 and 1843 American society passed, as one economic historian put it, "through the deep hollow of a great economic cycle, and the air became heavy with doubt and distress."[25] Within a few months New York City alone registered fifty thousand unemployed, one-third of the city's working population. With husbands and fathers lacking work, many women fell back on custom and turned to their needles. They met with little success, for businesses had failed in such numbers that the clothing industry was virtually destroyed. Orders from the South and the West had slowed to a halt, and the local markets for ready-made apparel had shrunk in kind. Most women, especially those inexperienced in wage earning and with households to maintain, had no alternatives; they scurried for the few available positions and valiantly tried to survive on the depressed wages of the era. Not since the late 1820s, when hundreds of seamstresses competed for dozens of openings, had needlework been so scarce.[26]

The Panic of 1837 further eroded the myth of stable domesticity premised on the fidelity of the male provider. It also provided both a plot and financial imperative to aspiring writers. Although some historians contend that fortunes remained surprisingly secure throughout the antebellum period,[27] the ensuing depression had a profound impact on many families, including those of later novelists. According to legend, Susan Warner's *Wide, Wide World* resulted from the author's real-life necessity to earn money. Warner's father appeared addicted to the speculative market in real estate and lost a fortune in the Panic of 1837. Unable to curb his habit, he continued to squander the family's financial resources. As the last bit of furniture was lost to public sale in 1847, Susan Warner found the inspiration for her first major and best-selling novel. Warner's subsequent writing career was one of hard labor and small earnings—out of which she supported herself and her hapless father.[28]

The Panic of 1837 also had long-range repercussions. When manufacturers began to recoup their losses in 1842, many did not return to former business practices. The most solvent and farsighted shifted from a system of out-work production to shops and factories to produce greater quantities more quickly and more cheaply. As the industry grew, the number of manufacturers actually declined, and large factories as well as small shops supplanted household production to a greater degree. By the 1850s the manufacture of men's shirts, once the mainstay of homeworkers, had shifted almost entirely to factories, some employing as many as two thousand people.[29]

The Panic of 1837 thus widened the gap between domesticity and wage labor. Although the number of jobs grew following recovery, the shift in location from home to factory left many women, like the young wife in Sawyer's story, on the short end. Opportunities for employment on an out-work basis still existed, especially in such related trades as millinery and artificial flowers, which grew apace with the garment industry, but those workers who could not enter the shops and especially those who could do only coarse handwork fared poorly indeed.

The depositories for women's work found themselves on entirely different relations with commercial industry. Taking as their "avowed and leading principle," in the words of the Providence Employment Society's secretary, *"fair wages for women's work,"* these women responded readily to women displaced by the economic crisis and its aftermath.[30] The failure of the Bank of the United States affected the well-being of the female dependents of speculators, entrepreneurs, and merchants as well as those already engaged in wage earning. Like misfortunate novelists, some members of female charitable societies also suffered from the economic reverses of the late 1830s. The records of the Philadelphia

Ladies' Depository attest that the Panic of 1837 left many "ladies" in distressed circumstances, some turning for assistance to the society that they had helped found.[31] The long depression that followed weighed heavily on the resources of these societies, as applicants for work multiplied while belt-tightening patrons bought fewer goods.

Even the business recovery of the mid-1840s did not significantly improve the situation. The secretary to the Philadelphia Ladies' Depository remarked in 1852 that it was "a matter of surprise that in a time of so much prosperity, when we hear of few disasters in the mercantile community, there should be so many individuals desirous of availing themselves of the benefits held out by the Depository. . . . "[32] The reorganization of the garment industry apparently had left many seamstresses stranded, particularly those who needed to work in their homes. Disadvantaged by the expansion of factory work in terms of both opportunity for employment and payment of wages for home-produced goods, many had no choice but to turn to alternative establishments. Organizations like the Philadelphia Ladies' Depository experienced, in turn, a drop in sales as its ability to compete with cheaply produced factory goods diminished in tandem with the rise in applicants for work.

The attempt to forge a new propriety for wage earning had stumbled over the economic realities of the time. Like the roughly contemporary workingmen's parties seeking to buttress the position of artisans, the women's societies had organized themselves for solutions that could only be short-lived. The Boston Needle Woman's Friend Society, founded in 1847, continued to uphold the principle to pay clients "justly entitled . . . as equivalent for her labor as a trader for his goods." "The guardianship of the needle may seem a small charge, but humble as is the instrument," the Boston society affirmed, "it is of the deepest moment to the happiness and well being of our sex."[33] The hard reality of the marketplace soon overpowered good intentions.

The rapid shift to the factory system in the late 1840s entailed not only the reorganization of garment production but also the utilization of new supplies of cheap labor. Urban needleworkers had for decades faced stiff competition, significantly from farm wives and daughters who accepted minimal wages on an out-work basis during the winter months. Beginning in the 1840s, however, a new source appeared in the city itself as immigrants settled in vast numbers, an estimated 4.2 million during the two decades before the Civil War. Forty percent were Irish, of whom nearly half were women. Although many became domestic servants, a considerable number entered the needle trades, usually at the lowest level. As early as 1845 the *New York Tribune* estimated that the ten thousand sewing women in the city constituted an overabundant supply, depressing the already low wages and driving many women to destitution. With the continuing influx of immigrants in the next decade, both Irish and German, seamstresses faced ever increasing competition. By 1860 one large wholesaler ascertained that only 20 percent of the women in his employ were native-born.[34]

By the 1850s the factory system depended on not only new sources of labor but also new technology. As early as 1830 the reformer Robert Dale Owen had predicted that the invention of a machine that "should do the work of thousands of women" would "take the bread from their mouths." By 1853 the *New York Tribune* advised women to look for employment along different avenues, lest they "sink back into a state of . . . abject dependence." A contemporary seamstress confirmed this impression, stating that she "was confounded at the low rates to which wages fell. The price for making a shirt was reduced to one-half. . . ." Notoriously unstable, market rates fluctuated wildly as the sewing machine wielded the final blow to the handworker—and to her allies.[35]

The women's benevolent societies had formed to deal with distressed circumstances but could hardly roll with the tide of technological development or the changing market for labor. From the beginning, the managers found it difficult to set prices for retail goods that were both realistic in terms of demand and fair in the sense of a living wage. They therefore encouraged their workers to submit items valuable primarily for their labor-intensive quality, such as fine or fancy goods, a strategy that ruled out those who most needed help. The sewing machine undercut the retail market for coarse and flat goods, while the increasing number of applicants brought fewer and fewer skills.

The managers began to construct the dilemma differently. As they now saw it, the "throng of emigrants" had reduced the opportunities for self-support "of our own people" while placing severe strains on the network of assistance. No remedy could be found. The Boston Needle Woman's Friend, for instance, emphasized the society's preference for applicants who were "American" women and residents of the city.[36] After the Civil War, women's benevolent societies drew the line even more sharply. Young women from Yankee farm villages might be accommodated, but the immigrant woman, rarely conversant in English and linked to an alien and non-Protestant culture, remained outside the reformers' imagined community.

After the Civil War, then, class clearly overtook gender in shaping the ethos of female benevolence. Poverty presumed for the victim no "better days"—save perhaps in a nationwide depression, and then only to a degree—but rather the stigma of race or ethnicity. The term *working classes* no longer signified primarily those who earned wages for their labor, or a condition of life, but a relatively fixed status.

The changed perspective surfaced in various ways and suggestively in a shift in literary genres. The plot of "she who had seen better days" rarely informed the postbellum fictional construction of women seeking a livelihood outside the domestic sphere. A rare exception was Catherine Owen's *Gentle Breadwinners,* a novel published in 1888, which offered a detailed description of an exchange for women's work similar in function to the antebellum depositories. For the most part, however, middle-class heroines nurtured professional aspirations and battled against the constraints of marriage or other barriers to their independence; discrimination rather than destitution was their plight. On the other side, the proliferation of cheap paperbacks about working-class women depended on a market of literate wage-earning women. In these stories, poverty competed with male seducers as the central threat. "Better days" appeared only in the happy ending of these "cinderella" stories. Here, the truly lower-class protagonist, like her readers, *rose* to heights she had previously only imagined, and not by hard work or benevolent assistance but by a chance romantic encounter with a man of wealth and comfort.[37]

A smaller genre, important because its authors were prominent reformers, gave the obvious hardening of class lines a remarkable twist. Each of the twin protagonists, genteel and poor, finds the "other" half of her womanhood in her opposite number. Such novels as Elizabeth Stuart Phelps's *Silent Partner* (1871) and Helen S. Campbell's *Mrs. Herndon's Income* (1886) tell the story of two women, the first compromised by an unproductive domestic life and the second suffering the exploitation of wage labor. They meet, usually by accident, and form a sisterhood of sorts. The comfortably situated but unfilled woman finds a life-purpose as she is drawn into the public sphere by her working-class alter ego. At the same time, the downtrodden hero identifies in herself the resources for survival by confronting the self-possession of her "other." Despite their mutual benefit, however—and this is a crucial distinction—class remains intact. A happy ending prevails for both characters but does not alter their class positions.[38]

The shift in the narrative structure of both fiction and the statements of philanthropic principles reflects a change in the discourse of "class" and its relation to "gender" over the course of the nineteenth century. The earliest writers perceived poverty and certain kinds of wage labor, namely needlework, as virtually synonymous, both fashioned from women's dependence on men. They recognized, of course, the exigencies of the capitalist marketplace but focused primarily on women's inability to compete with men. While acutely aware that marriage and its hallowed domesticity offered no promise of security, they could not as easily perceive wage labor in "class" terms. The reorganization of urban industry in the aftermath of the Panic of 1837 provided important lessons, widening the gap between the household and the marketplace and, consequently, between the women who occupied one sphere or the other. As the continuity between systems of production diminished, so, too, did the ambiguity of "class" as descriptive nomenclature. The later writers and benevolent reformers understood and condoned this distinction.

The differences between these two perspectives underscore E. P. Thompson's aging but still relevant dictum that class is not a category or a structure but a profoundly *historical* relationship, "embodied in real people and in a real context."[39]

NOTES

The research for this essay was supported by fellowships from the Wellesley Center for Research and Teaching on Women and the Bunting Institute, Radcliffe College.

1. Caroline Mehitable Sawyer, *The Merchant's Widow and Other Tales* (New York: P. Price, 1841), 7, 21, 56.

2. Maria L. Buckley, *A Sketch of the Working Classes of New York: Or, the Sufferings of the Sewing Girls* (New York: By the Author, 1856), 34; published with Buckley's *Amanda Willson: Or, the Vicissitudes of Life.*

3. Cathy N. Davidson, *Revolution and the Word: The Rise of the Novel in America* (New York: Oxford University Press, 1986), chap. 6.

4. Adrienne Siegel, *The Image of the American City in Popular Literature, 1820-1870* (Port Washington, N.Y.: Kennikat Press, 1981), 36-42. See also Amy Gilman Srebnick, "True Womanhood and Hard Times: Women and Early New York Industrialization, 1840-1860" (Ph.D. diss., SUNY-Stony Brook, 1979), chap. 5.

5. T. S. Arthur, *Lizzy Glenn: Or, the Trials of a Seamstress* (Philadelphia: T. B. Peterson and Brothers, 1859), 23-24. See also Arthur's two stories, "Plain Sewing: Or, How to Encourage the Poor" and "A Lesson of Patience," in *Woman's Trials: Or, Tales and Sketches from Life around Us* (Philadelphia: J. B. Lippincott, 1866), 123-25, 7-25.

6. Egal Feldman, *Fit for Men: A Study of New York's Clothing Trade* (Washington, D.C.: Public Affairs Press, 1960), 102-5. See also Christine Stansell, *City of Women: Sex and Class in New York, 1789-1860* (New York: Alfred A. Knopf, 1986), chap. 1; Christine Stansell, "The Origins of the Sweatshop: Women and Early Industrialization in New York City," in *Working-Class America: Essays on Labor, Community, and American Society,* ed. Michael H. Frisch and Daniel J. Walkowitz (Urbana: University of Illinois Press, 1983), 78-103; Helen L. Sumner, *History of Women in Industry in the United States*

(Washington, D.C.: Government Printing Office, 1910), chap. 3; and Edith Abbott, *Women in Industry: A Study in American Economic History* (New York: D. Appleton, 1910), chap. 10.

7. Feldman, *Fit for Men*, 112-13.

8. Maria Maxwell, *Ernest Grey: Or, the Sins of Society; a Tale of New York Life* (New York: T. W. Strong, 1855), 16.

9. Walter L. Trattner, *From Poor Law to Welfare State: A History of Social Welfare in America*, 2d ed. (New York: Free Press, 1979), chap. 4.

10. Anne Firor Scott, "As Easily as They Breathe . . . ," *Making the Invisible Woman Visible* (Urbana: University of Illinois Press, 1984), 266-67.

11. Anne Firor Scott, *Natural Allies: Women's Associations in American History* (Urbana: University of Illinois Press, 1991), 29.

12. Gary B. Nash, "The Failure of Female Factory Labor in Colonial Boston," *Labor History* 20 (Spring 1979): 165-88. See also Stansell, *City of Women*, chap. 1; and Abbott, *Women in Industry*, 36-41.

13. Elizabeth F. Hoxie, "Caroline Mehitable Fisher Sawyer," in *Notable American Women: A Biographical Dictionary*, vol. 3, ed. Edward T. James, Janet Wilson James, and Paul S. Boyer (Cambridge: Belknap Press, 1971), 236-37; Boston Fragment Society Papers, 1812-, Schlesinger Library, Radcliffe College, Cambridge, Mass. For a general description, see Keith Melder, "Ladies Bountiful: Organized Women's Benevolence in Early Nineteenth-Century America," *New York History* 65 (July 1967): 238. For a detailed case study, see Scott, *Natural Allies*, 27-36.

14. Michael B. Katz, *In the Shadow of the Poorhouse: A Social History of We., ..e in America* (New York: Basic Books, 1986), 41.

15. "Report on Female Wages," Philadelphia, March 25, 1829, reprinted in Mathew Carey, *Miscellaneous Essays* (Philadelphia: Carey and Hart, 1830), 267. "Situation of the Working Classes, and More Especially of Seamstresses and Others, in Philadelphia, and Work People in Cotton and Other Factories," was reprinted in *The Free Enquirer* (New York, N.Y.), May 6, 1829.

16. Emphasis in original. Mathew Carey, "Public Charities of Philadelphia," reprinted in Carey, *Miscellaneous Essays*, 197. On Carey's life and work, see Kenneth Wyer Rowe, *Mathew Carey: A Study in Economic Development*, Johns Hopkins University Studies in Historical and Political Science, Series 51, No. 4 (Baltimore: Johns Hopkins University Press, 1933).

17. Stansell, *City of Women*, 194-97.

18. Mathew Carey, "Female Wages and Female Oppression," Philadelphia, July 23, 1835, in Carey, *Miscellaneous Essays*, 2.

19. Carey, "Public Charities of Philadelphia," 167-69, 182.

20. Ibid., 162.

21. "To the Printer of the Delaware Advertiser," February 27, 1830, quoted in Sumner, *History of Women in Industry in the United States*, 131.

22. Carey, "Public Charities of Philadelphia," 270, 271. See also Mathew Carey, *A Solemn Address to the Mothers, Wives, Sisters and Daughters of Citizens of Philadelphia* (Philadelphia: n.p., 1837).

23. This history is recorded in Ladies' Depository Association, *Fiftieth Annual Report, 1882* (Philadelphia: n.p., 1883), 5-6.

24. Ladies' Depository Association, *First Annual Report* (Philadelphia: n.p., 1834), 6.

25. Samuel Reznick, "The Social History of an American Depression, 1837-1843," *American Historical Review* 40 (July 1935): 662.

26. Feldman, *Fit for Men*, 118.

27. See, for example, Edward Pessen, "Did Fortunes Rise and Fall Mercurially in Antebellum America? A Tale of Two Cities: Boston and New York," *Journal of Social History* 4 (Summer 1971): 339-57.

28. Nina Baym, *Woman's Fiction: A Guide to Novels by and about Women in America, 1820-1870* (Ithaca, N.Y.: Cornell University Press, 1978), chap. 6.

29. Alice Kessler-Harris, *Out to Work: A History of Wage-Earning Women in the United States* (New York: Oxford University Press, 1982), 45-47. On the organization of the inside shop during this period, see Feldman, *Fit for Men*, 95-102.

30. Providence Employment Society, *Fifteenth Annual Report* (Providence: n.p., 1852), 13, as quoted in Susan Porter Benson, "Business Heads and Sympathizing Hearts: The Women of the Providence Employment Society, 1837-1858," *Journal of Social History* 12 (Winter 1978): 302.

31. Nancy Hewitt noted a similar pattern in *Women's Activism and Social Change: Rochester, New York, 1822-1872* (Ithaca, N.Y.: Cornell University Press, 1984), 97-98.

32. Ladies' Depository of Philadelphia, *Nineteenth Annual Report, 1851* (Philadelphia: n.p., 1853), 4.

33. *Report for the Third Anniversary of the Needle Woman's Friend Society* (Boston: n.p., 1850), 4; *Report for the Second Anniversary of the Needle Woman's Friend Society* (Boston: n.p., 1849), 3-4.

34. Feldman, *Fit for Men*, 102. See also Srebnick, "True Womanhood and Hard Times," chap. 2; Carol Groneman, "Working Class Women in Mid Nineteenth-Century New York: The Irish Woman's Experience," *Journal of Urban History* 4 (May 1978): 260-61.

35. Both quotations appear in Feldman, *Fit for Men*, 107.

36. *Report for the First Anniversary of the Needle Woman's Friend Society* (Boston: n.p., 1848), 8-9.

37. Catherine Owen (pseudonym for Helen Alice Nitsch), *Gentle Breadwinners* (Boston: Houghton, Mifflin, 1888). For an interpretation of novels with working-class protagonists, see Michael Denning, *Mechanic Accents: Dime Novels and Working-Class Culture in America* (London: Verso, 1987), chap. 10.

38. See, for example, Elizabeth Stuart Phelps, *The Silent Partner* (Boston: James R. Osgood, 1871); and Helen Campbell, *Mrs. Herndon's Income* (Boston: Roberts Brothers, 1886).

39. E. P. Thompson, *The Making of the English Working Class* (New York: Vintage Books, 1963), 9.

O. Delight Smith's Progressive Era: Labor, Feminism, and Reform in the Urban South

Jacquelyn Dowd Hall

This is the story of a woman who almost wasn't there.[1] In the years before World War I, O. Delight Smith was the most prominent female member of Atlanta's white labor community. She wrote a hard-hitting weekly column for the local labor journal and founded and assumed the presidency of the national Ladies' Auxiliary of the Order of Railroad Telegraphers (ORT). In 1914 she helped lead one of the era's major textile strikes. By the 1920s, however, this larger-than-life woman had been blotted from history. The forces that conspired against her ranged from personal betrayal to political defeat to historians' assumptions about significance and marginality. Indeed, the preoccupations of scholars guaranteed that she, and women like her, would be trebly eclipsed, for she exemplified a brand of feminist progressivism that has been marginalized by historians of women, of labor, and of the South alike.

Womanism was the term that Smith coined to describe her brand of Progressive Era politics. Self-educated and, in important ways, self-created, she did not inherit either her feminism or her class consciousness. Nor did her passionate politics simply reflect her social location. Her consciousness was fashioned from her own experience, as that experience drew its meaning from a little-known rhetorical and political surround.[2]

While much ink has been spilled on the Populists and the Knights of Labor, exemplars of Gilded Age labor militancy, we know next to nothing about O. Delight Smith's milieu: the central labor unions, ladies' auxiliaries, and craft union locals that dotted the small towns and cities of the South after the rise of the American Federation of Labor (AFL). This neglect stems in part from the Commons school of labor history, which established the idea that the AFL was an apolitical, bureaucratic vehicle for satisfying the needs of skilled craftsmen alone.[3] There is much truth in this judgment, especially when applied to the AFL national office and the international unions. Yet revisionists have offered compelling evidence that local craft unions sometimes updated rather than abandoned the militant idealism of the Gilded Age and promoted a lively prolabor reformism in cities and industrial towns throughout the nation.[4] What these studies have failed to tell us is that women, both as workers and as workers' wives, played a vital role in this effort. In the process, working-class women articulated a labor feminism that combined communal solidarity with consumer consciousness and elements of contemporary feminist thought.[5]

Nothing in the existing scholarship would lead us to expect that such women might turn up south of the Mason-Dixon line, much less that they might play leading roles in working-class politics and join the mainstream of progressive reform. This is so in part because of the fixed idea that the South had no active working class, but it also derives from the fact that scholars have viewed southern progressivism itself through a narrow lens.

Indeed, when Anne Firor Scott set out in the 1940s to write a dissertation on southern progressives, most historians saw the subject as a contradiction in terms. The "stereotype of the Reactionary South," in C. Vann Woodward's phrase, had blinded observers to an indigenous reform movement that paralleled the "doctrines and experiments familiar to Wisconsin and Kansas and their latitudes."[6] Although Woodward's *Origins of the New South,* published in 1951, drew attention to the phenomenon, the study of southern progressivism came into its own only in the 1970s, with the reevaluation of the Age of Reform as an era of bureaucratization. Spurred by the organizational interpretation of progressivism then sweeping the field, historians documented a southern "search for order" in which elites rationalized a chaotic political system, crippled their opposition, and imposed on the region an antidemocratic accommodation to capitalism that served the interests of "middle-class whites only."[7]

Lost in this historiographical storm was the insight that transformed Anne Scott from a historian of progressivism to a founder of the field of women's history: in pursuit of southern progressives, she "kept stumbling over women." To be sure, a handful of scholars followed Scott's lead, and we now know a good deal more than we once did about southern women's activism.[8] A search of the scores of books that have grappled with the essence of the movement indicates, however, that until quite recently Scott's discovery that "women *were* there, and they made a difference" disappeared without a trace.[9]

Meanwhile, historians focused on other regions have in effect rehabilitated progressivism by showing how women reformers helped lay the foundation for the welfare state. They argue that as capitalism and urbanization erased the boundaries between the public and private spheres, women who realized that their homes were " 'chained' to city hall" used their experience as mothers and consumers to justify their entry into the formal political arena, first to fight for civic improvements on the local level and then to demand federal intervention. Men increasingly pursued their interests through issue-oriented voluntary organizations, long the province of women. Male and female political cultures converged as party loyalty and voting declined, as women got the vote, and as government took on many of the tasks that had been assigned to women's voluntary associations.[10]

This stress on maternalist thinking and the "domestication of politics" bolsters a gathering critique of the progressivism-as-social-control thesis. Revisionists concede that there *was* a fit between aspects of progressive thought and the bureaucratic revolution, but they argue that progressivism was not a unitary impulse. It encompassed a range of responses to widespread feelings of vulnerability, anxiety, and anger and found expression in ideologically fluid, issue-oriented coalitions.[11]

A narrative that features white middle-class women and turns on the domestication of politics, however, poses problems of its own. By focusing on federal action, it reinforces a traditional preoccupation with a small, tight-knit circle of prominent reformers based in New York and Chicago, obscuring the meaning and chronology of developments in the South and West and relegating them to the status of regional deviations from a putative national norm. The starting point of the story—the assumption that men and women occupied different political cultures—ignores working-class and African American women, who might act on gender consciousness but who could not and did not separate themselves from men.[12] Its culmination—the melding of those cultures in the welfare state—downplays women reformers' roles in shaping policies that were oppressive to other women and the degree to which they compromised their aims and language to make them more acceptable to men. The story's maternal imagery casts reformers as the asexual, motherly saviors of the poor, eliding the issue of sexuality in the reformers' lives as well as working-class self-activity.[13]

O. Delight Smith was anything but an asexual moral mother. Instead, she belonged to a new white-collar working class and participated, albeit at great cost, in the pre–World War I sexual revolution. She forged her politics in the spaces between social movements, but her deepest loyalties lay with those "who labored for their bread."[14] Her communal consciousness, however, was based on exclusions: neither black reformers nor black workers found a place in the cooperative commonwealth she envisioned. Her career thus brings into focus the class and race divisions among organized women as well as the geographical mobility, shifting alliances, and fluid social identities that generated much of what was "new" in the New South. Her story adds a new figure to the landscape of southern history: a labor feminist whose life confounds tidy half-truths about a conservative labor aristocracy and a middle-class monopoly on female reform.

Smith's upbringing in the South and Midwest set the peripatetic tone for her career. When her parents married in 1878, her father, John Lloyd, was farming in Scooba, Mississippi. By the time Ola Delight was born two years later, John and his wife, Lettie Long, were back in Mercer County, Illinois, where both had grown up. Lettie died when Delight was seven, and John, who had given up on farming and gone to work in a lumberyard, remarried, had three more children, and took his family on a dizzying round of moves across the American heartland. As soon as Lloyd found a job in one town, he began reading the want ads and dreaming of opportunities down the road. The family made at least twenty-nine moves in as many years, including sojourns in Nebraska, Iowa, Wisconsin, Alabama, and Georgia—where they alighted in Atlanta seven different times.[15]

Delight remembered Epes, Alabama, best, for it was there that she spent her last years at home before embarking on a disastrous marriage to Edgar B. Smith, a "traveling man" from Georgia. In Epes, Delight learned the craft she would follow for more than half a century. She began by teaching herself Morse code on a practice set at home, then took a telegraphy course at the Alabama Polytechnic Institute for Girls in Montevallo and worked relief for the Queen and Crescent Railroad. In 1900 she got a job managing a one-woman office for the Postal Telegraph Company. After their marriage in 1901, Delight and Edgar moved to Birmingham, where she became a branch manager for Western Union. From there the couple made their way to Gainesville, a mill town in the hill country fifty miles northeast of Atlanta, where Delight again worked for Postal Telegraph, Western Union's chief rival.[16]

By this time, a transportation and communications revolution had transformed Georgia and the whole Southeast. First came the railroads, with the telegraph companies following hard on their heels, planting their slender poles along the railroad rights-of-way, allowing the railroads to use their wires to control the movement of trains along the tracks, and flashing the news almost instantaneously to every decent-sized southern town. Together the railroad and the telegraph revolutionized notions of time and space, expanded each community's imaginative boundaries, and supplemented face-to-face relations with new kinds of social encounters.[17]

Telegraphers straddled two social worlds. Most were village- or country-bred, the sons and daughters of farmers, craftsmen, and, increasingly, urban blue-collar workers. Better educated than most of their peers, they traded overalls and aprons for the shirtwaists and neckties of a new low-level white-collar sector of the working class. These "kid-gloved laborers" joined the Knights of Labor during the labor conflicts of the Gilded Age, then formed craft unions that tried to hold their own against the railroads and the telegraph companies, the nation's first great modern corporations.[18]

The Brotherhood of Telegraphers, District 45 of the Knights of Labor, coalesced in 1882, welcoming into its ranks "all who created the telegraph companies' wealth," only to decline precipitously in 1883, after a ruinous nationwide strike against Western Union. The railroad telegraphers then established their own nonstriking, fraternal organization, the Order of Railroad Telegraphers, which became a full-fledged union in 1891. By 1917, when the railroads passed under wartime federal control, the ORT, like the railroad brotherhoods it resembled, had wrested "grudging tolerance from the companies and a modest but stable place on the roads." Meanwhile, organized commercial telegraphers limped along, first as a kind of annex to the ORT, then as the Commercial Telegraphers Union of America (CTUA).[19]

Telegraphy was at first a young man's craft, but the ranks of female operators increased steadily after the Civil War. By 1900 the country's 7,229 "Ladies of the Key" accounted for 12 percent of the total. Most worked in one-woman branch offices in hotels or railroad depots. Others flocked to the growing ladies' departments of large urban establishments. In both cases, the more remunerative jobs, such as operating the circuits that transmitted press or market reports or supervising the urban workrooms, were monopolized by men. Women's "dead-end berths and thin pay envelopes" led to high turnover rates, and female operators were generally young and single. Nevertheless, telegraphy demanded more training than did most other women's occupations, and few "entered the field on a lark." Telegraphers were serious breadwinners, and those who chose to work the wires did so out of a combination of necessity, adventurousness, and ambition.[20]

Railway telegraphy in particular was a male preserve, with its own raucous romance-of-the-rails mystique. The invention of railroad dispatching in the 1840s made it possible to use the invisible power of electricity to control physical processes actively, thus opening the way to the creation of the world's first integrated communications and transportation system. Railway telegraphers passed the dispatchers' orders to the conductors and engineers, and an operator's speed, accuracy, and efficiency could spell the difference between a safe trip and a tragic crash. Male telegraphers relished their reputation as a hard-drinking, "motley group of colorful characters [who] broke every rule in the book, but always turned in a good job when emergencies arose." They were also notorious "boomers"—workers who, by choice or necessity, followed rush periods of work around the country.[21]

Female railroad telegraphers, who worked long hours in isolated railroad stations and communicated with strangers through a secret code, occupied a peculiarly anomalous position. As featured in dime novels and union journals, they were notable less for their skills than for their unsupervised sexuality; the plots of these stories usually revolved around lonely young women who fell in love with their male counterparts down the line. Such fiction surely reflected—even as it scripted—aspects of women workers' lives, but its sexual subtext was more complex than at first meets the eye. Women who were doing a man's job had to prove their competence *and* their femininity, asserting both their womanliness and their place as one of "the Railroad Boys." Novels like *Wired Love* reassuringly followed a marriage plot, ending happily when their heroines were able to marry and "go housekeeping."[22] But they hinted at the existence of real-life women like O. Delight Smith, who were not presented with such easy choices. For them, dreams of romance and the stirrings of sexuality coexisted with craft loyalty, reform politics, and pride in their hard-won place in a man's rough-and-tumble world.

For Smith, that complex identity entailed a lifelong commitment to unionization. In 1904 she joined the Gainesville local of the Commercial Telegraphers Union. Two years later she became a member of the Order of Railroad Telegraphers and in 1907 was elected secretary-treasurer of the Gainesville lodge. In 1907 she moved to Atlanta and signed on with Atlanta Local 60 of the CTUA, just in time to throw herself into a nationwide strike in which the commercial telegraphers once more locked horns with Western Union.[23]

Atlanta was the South's chief railroad hub, largest telegraph relay point, and most important commercial center. It was also a city in which unionists exercised considerable political influence. The Atlanta Federation of Trades (AFT), founded in 1891, published an excellent weekly paper, the *Journal of Labor,* and furnished much of the leadership for the state's labor movement. Trade unionists helped put the printer James G. Woodward in the mayor's office four times between 1900 and 1916; other working-class men held political office as well; and between 1900 and 1903 the editor of the *Journal of Labor* spearheaded the fight against child labor. The typographers tended to dominate AFT affairs, but the railroad brotherhoods were the city's largest unions.[24]

In 1907 CTUA Local 60 claimed the allegiance of all but a handful of

Atlanta's three hundred telegraph operators, and it could count on cross-craft solidarities and public support that might, at least temporarily, offset the weakness of the international union. The *Atlanta Constitution*, the city's major newspaper, treated the strikers with the utmost respect, giving their story front-page play and providing space for their "statement of principles" and confident appeals to "our friend, the public." For all its local effectiveness, however, the CTUA was ill-prepared to pit itself against Western Union's monopolistic might, and the strike ended, like the conflict of 1883, in a crushing defeat.[25]

O. Delight Smith, who found herself blacklisted and thrown back on her own resources in the midst of the Panic of 1907, set out to make her way in a city whose population was mushrooming and whose white female labor force was climbing at an even faster pace. Georgia, like the rest of the South, remained overwhelmingly rural, but by the 1910s a mass exodus from the countryside had already begun. Atlanta and other urban areas, with their burgeoning manufacturing and service sectors, grew at the expense of a declining agrarian economy. In the four decades from 1880 to 1920, Georgia's urban population multiplied by five while its rural population, despite extraordinarily high birthrates, was inching up by only 55 percent. The flight from the countryside would eventually turn into the Great Migration of blacks to the urban North. In the years before World War I, however, displaced farm folk headed for southern cities, and whites did so in even larger numbers than blacks. Between 1900 and 1920 Atlanta's white population jumped by 154 percent, and its black population increased by 76 percent. The city as a whole expanded from 89,872 to 200,616.[26]

Among blacks especially, but among whites as well, female migrants outnumbered men. A steady stream of young women, pushed from the countryside and pulled to the city for work, transformed the urban landscape. By 1920, 42 percent of all Atlanta women aged sixteen and over had joined the work force; only the Massachusetts textile cities of Fall River, Lowell, and New Bedford and the white-collar city of Washington, D.C., had higher rates of female employment.[27]

Traditionally, a large black population accounted for the high levels of gainfully employed women in southern cities, and black women continued to work in much greater proportions than whites. From 1900 to 1920, however, the number of black women wage earners in Atlanta advanced by only 60 percent, while employment among white women almost quadrupled. This disparity was due in part to a leveling off of the laundry and household service jobs to which black women were confined and in part to the exclusion of blacks from the textile and clerical jobs that drew white women into paid labor. The result was a marked change in the racial makeup of the city's female work force. In 1900 only 28 percent of wage-earning women were white. By 1920 that figure had reached 48 percent.[28]

As a skilled worker and a craft unionist, O. Delight Smith occupied a distinctive yet revealing place within this city of women. Her husband was a traveling salesman who was usually on the road. A thoroughly unsatisfying spouse, Edgar at least provided a mantle of respectability, and Delight projected an image of determined, if wobbly, gentility. Yet she reveled in being a "lady boomer" and moved easily through a demimonde of greasy spoons, rooming houses, and cheap hotels at a time when, in many eyes, "women adrift" symbolized all that was wrong with the entry of women into the wage economy. She had to support herself, and she saw no inconsistency in blending moneymaking with homemaking, or class loyalty with pursuit of the main chance. She put her office skills to use in both the informal economy and the labor movement. Her efforts alert us to the intricacy of social identities, the inadequacy of census-based classifications, and the artificiality of distinctions between private and public spheres.[29]

To make ends meet, Smith tried her hand at a variety of economic ventures. Housekeeping was not her metier, but she hoped that running a boardinghouse in Inman Park, a fashionable streetcar suburb, would allow her the freedom to do labor work. At the same time, she set herself up as "The Eureka Letter Company," advertising her services as a letter writer and duplicator. When she found her days consumed by interruptions, she took charge of the Southern Distributing Office of the Double Fabric Tire Company and invited her friends to call on her, since she would now have more time to devote to the cause of labor.[30] On the side, she tried selling "Florida Everglades Re-Claimed Land." Six months later, in January 1912, she again launched her own business. This time she called herself "The Traveling Man's Secretary" and proposed to handle mail for the small army of commercial men who, like her husband, wove their way through southern towns. By the fall of 1913 the Smiths had saved enough money to purchase a small house in a working-class neighborhood. I have "bought me a 'dishpan' and gone to housekeeping," Delight reported. She also announced that she was again dabbling in real estate, "handling homes for the working man at prices and terms I know he can meet."[31]

Meanwhile, Smith plunged simultaneously into women's organizations and union affairs. First, she went undercover as a volunteer organizer for the ORT. In February 1908 she helped found the Dixie Twin Order Telegraphers Club to promote cooperation between the ORT and the CTUA. Soon afterward, the ORT chose Atlanta for its 1909 national convention and hired Smith to handle local arrangements; at the convention she pushed for the creation of a ladies' auxiliary and won election as its first president, a position she held until 1913. At the same time, she served as the CTUA's representative to the Atlanta Federation of Trades and the Georgia Federation of Labor. In all these positions, Smith insisted on being one of the "Brothers," yet her duties often involved such gender-coded tasks as arranging entertainment, acting as secretary, or organizing union label campaigns. She attained her highest office and greatest authority not through mixed-sex activities but as the leader of women's auxiliaries, serving not only as the national president of the Ladies' Auxiliary of the ORT but also as the head of the Georgia Federation of Labor's Union Label Committee and of Atlanta Local No. 255 of the Woman's Trade Union Label League.[32]

Smith's influence rested as much on her talents as a labor columnist as on her whirl of voluntary activities. Some years earlier, she had begun writing for the labor press under the pen name Athena, the virgin-warrior and patron of household industries. She launched her column in the *Journal of Labor* under her own byline in December 1906, and when she settled in Atlanta she became an associate editor, with special responsibility for advertising and subscriptions. Almost every week for three years, and more sporadically for five years after that, she offered a running commentary on everything from marriage to politics, from the need for labor unity to "The Penalty of Being a Woman." Her column became her platform. In it, she explained, "I always spoke my mind, and if it hurt, why, that was what I was after."[33]

Smith could not have been more loyal to the AFL, yet she relied less on the rhetoric of bread-and-butter unionism than on a language of republicanism and antimonopolism that harked back to the Populists and the Knights of Labor. There were only two classes, she believed, "Labor and Capital," those who "create the wealth of the nation and the class who enjoy the fruits of this creation." She sometimes dreamed of a utopia in which all the "money-grafters" had been banished so that everyone else could join together in "one vast web of Fraternity, which, in the end, is Unionism." But the Panic of 1907, combined with the telegraphers' defeat, convinced her that the nation was drifting toward an "Industrial War." Believing that the coming conflict would take place primarily in the halls of government, Smith ended her most apocalyptic columns by admonishing workingmen to "Wake up!" and vote.[34]

Smith's preoccupation with the ballot revealed a turn toward political action on the part of the AFL that historians have generally downplayed. By 1906 the successful lobbying efforts of the National Association of Manufacturers, the open shop drive, and the increasing use of the injunction and the Sherman Anti-Trust Act as antilabor weapons had convinced Samuel Gompers and other AFL leaders that only a "strike at the ballot box"—grass-roots mobilization of the labor vote—could break capital's stranglehold on state power. This campaign, which went against the grain of the AFL's commitment to voluntarism, had unintended consequences, for it rekindled the local activism of the 1880s and 1890s, stirring up political impulses among central labor unions and state federations that Gompers and his allies could not always control.[35]

Like many AFL activists, Smith directed those impulses along channels narrowed by ethnic and racial exclusions. She rose to prominence in the Atlanta labor community in the immediate aftermath of a race riot sparked by a vituperative disfranchisement campaign. With black voters written out of the political process and black craftsmen confined to a fixed niche in segregated unions, she apparently felt no need to address racial issues. When African Americans did appear in her writings, they did so not as women or as workers but as farcical emblems of a distinctive regional past. Her plans for the ORT's 1909 convention were a case in point. Anxious to make the entertainment for the Atlanta convention as " 'Southern' as is possible," Smith arranged an "old-fashioned barn dance." "The old plantation dancing, and pickaninny jigs will be gone through by old-fashioned plantation darkies," Smith promised, "and coon songs will be in abundance."[36] By contrast, Smith's nativism was overtly political: she lambasted "greasy . . . cast off" foreigners and devoted numerous columns to the AFL's support for immigration restriction.[37]

Such depictions of contented "plantation darkies," replicated at fairs and historical pageants throughout the region, promoted both sectional reconciliation and economic development. At Atlanta's famous Cotton States and International Exposition in 1895, for instance, scenes from the "Old Plantation" stood side by side with exhibits on Latin American villages. Equating African Americans with backward natives and wooing northern investors with the promise of a willing black labor force, this iconography linked the themes of racism, imperialism, and progress. This linkage had its class dimension as well: it helped diffuse class tensions by offering native-born white workers a vision of prosperity based on access to overseas markets while assuring them that the South had no need for immigrant labor.[38]

Smith made no such explicit connections, but her implicit blend of nativism, racism, and feminism did surface briefly in 1907, during a period of widespread alarm over an alleged labor shortage caused by black migration. The *Journal of Labor* editorialized against those who advocated replacing blacks with immigrant labor in the cotton fields. The solution to the labor problem, it suggested, was to use Georgia's vagrancy law as a "negro-prodder" to force blacks to work. Smith endorsed the idea, but with a twist that reflected the nineteenth-century feminist view of male sexuality as a pervasive threat. As a woman whose work sent her bustling about the city's male-dominated public spaces, she saw unemployed black men as part of a larger population of "Street Corner Johnnies" that included the dissolute "sons of prominent families." "Did you ever stand at a distance and watch a crowd of men and boys on the next corner?" she asked. "Did you ever notice their signs, their antics and their gestures? . . . If you have, you have heard some of the most villainous and filthy remarks." Use the vagrancy laws, she admonished, to clear "your streets and your dives, of this lazy, good-for-nothing class of men and boys—BOTH WHITE and BLACK!" We will then "have enough laborers in this country without importing any more!"[39]

Smith's labor feminism combined ideas about productive work espoused in earlier years by the Knights of Labor with the rhetoric and tactics of the Progressive Era women's movement. The Knights had acted on their inclusive vision by inviting wives to become full-fledged members and by making women the symbolic representatives of the values that motivated their movement. Similarly, when Smith addressed herself to laboring women, she meant not "only the women who earn their daily wages, but . . . those who assist in making the home for the laboring man . . . all are laborers, only in a different field." She urged men to view their wives not only as fellow workers but also as integral members of the labor movement.[40]

Smith's recuperation of the housewife as laborer could be seen as a defensive action in the face of stringent AFL membership policies that excluded nonwage-earning women as well as black and unskilled workers, male and female alike. But it also reflected an innovative—and typically "progressive"—cross-class consumer consciousness, for she chose as her political weapons the national women's auxiliary and the union label league, new types of voluntary organizations that arose in the 1890s. Through these groups, workers' wives sought to maintain their links to the labor movement, while middle-class women vied to use their power as consumers to aid women workers, curb the power of corporations, and make novel demands on the state.[41]

The ladies' auxiliaries, Smith believed, held the key both to the success of the labor movement and to the extension of private concerns into the formal political sphere. In a column on the "Influence of Womankind," she praised the astounding "rapidity with which the women of the United States are banding themselves together in organizations of all kinds," but she went on to argue that it was not middle-class feminists but class-conscious workers' wives who had "the greatest field and the grandest avenue for work." Once working-class wives, sisters, daughters, and mothers were organized, labor questions would be discussed in every worker's home, every workingman would be shamed into vigorous trade unionism, and public officials would have no choice but to respond to labor's civic concerns. If city fathers "refused to clear away rubbish heaps" or repair streets in working-class neighborhoods, "these earnest women would go before the council, for the sake of their home and the health of their family" and demand the rights of those "who labored for their bread." Libraries, rest rooms, and lunchrooms would be provided, the "sick would be cared for and the homeless looked after." The good that could be accomplished by these organized women, Smith promised, would "be beyond the most radical imagination of the day."[42]

This vision of a political culture built on civic activism and consumer consciousness and anticipating an active state bore little resemblance to the nineteenth-century tradition of politics as a proving ground for manhood and party loyalty as an end in itself. It had more in common with the domestication of politics advocated by middle-class women progressives than with the antistatism advocated by Samuel Gompers and the AFL. Yet at the center of Smith's political vision lay a politicized labor movement, purged of its sexism and thus capable of mobilizing men and women alike, not a civic maternalism dedicated to bridging class chasms or uplifting the worthy poor.

Indeed, Smith believed that organized labor deserved the credit for bringing middle- and upper-class women into public life. Union label campaigns and other cross-class efforts enlisted middle-class women as consumers in defense of the labor movement, molding them into politicized purchasing agents and saving them from the temptations of "feathers, silks . . . and—style!" Society women were raised "all unknowingly to a higher platform, and to a better knowledge of their . . . duty to themselves and those about them." The woman who once "thought of nothing but 'dress and go' is now found reading and studying economic questions of the day," and instead of occupying herself with "worthless 'teas,' 'receptions,' 'balls' and 'dinner-parties,' she is found in clubs organized for the express purpose of raising the standard of living." The goals of these clubs might be vague, but "the main good to be found is the mere fact of these women binding themselves together for the purpose of trying to help their neighbor."[43]

Club women would certainly have been surprised to find trade unionism credited with inspiring their movement. Smith's point, however, was that middle-class social concerns were aroused in part by working-class initiatives. Moreover, by stressing the centrality of working-class organizations, she sought to position herself as an equal participant in cross-class women's organizations.

Although the National Women's Trade Union League, the main vehicle for cross-class female reform endeavors, did not establish a presence in the South until the 1920s, Georgia's female labor activists and middle-class reformers shared many concerns and sometimes worked through the same organizations. Smith, for example, won appointment to the finance committee of the State Congress of Mothers because of her lobbying efforts in behalf of a kindergarten bill, a state health bill, and a probation bill aimed at forcing husbands to support their families. She decried prostitution, lobbied for laws barring women from drinking clubs, and urged the creation of a reformatory for girls. As head of an Atlanta Federation of Trades committee charged with investigating the "conditions under which children are plying street trades in this city," she advocated compulsory education, sought the cooperation of women's clubs and ministerial groups in lobbying for a child labor law, and served as the Georgia Federation of Labor's delegate to the Southern Conference on Woman and Child Labor.[44]

In these efforts, Smith drew on a rhetoric of assistance and sexual danger that characterized progressivism generally, but she gave that familiar language a distinctive working-class gloss. Middle-class observers in Atlanta responded to the surge of white women into wage labor with pity, puzzlement, and disapproval. They assumed that black women should work and would probably be sexually active, but the independent, and possibly promiscuous, white working girl was a new and frightening phenomenon, and the anxieties she aroused helped put prostitution and juvenile delinquency at the center of the progressive agenda. Smith, too, decried the "depravity of our boys and the ruination of our girls," but she blamed those problems on "poor wages, long hours and bad working conditions," and she pinned her hopes for change on the "Herculean efforts" of trade unionists to bring women into the "House of Labor." In the meantime, unionists should not leave to "churches and charitable organizations" the task of turning the fallen "from the error of their ways." Young people who would shun well-meaning reformers would welcome the help of "one from their rank and file."[45]

The campaign against child labor, which Smith joined, exemplified both the cross-class nature of progressive concerns and the class-based tensions within the progressive coalition. The initiative for regulating child labor in Georgia came first from the Knights of Labor and then from the AFL. This effort gained national AFL backing in 1900, when Samuel Gompers sent Irene M. Ashby, a young English woman who had been active in the London settlement house movement, to the South, charging her with the unenviable task of attracting nonlabor support without snubbing local labor leaders. In Georgia the Federation of Women's Clubs and various ministerial associations endorsed the cause, but they viewed Ashby with suspicion and tried to keep their distance from organized labor. Attempts to discredit the movement as the hobbyhorse of "dreadful labor and busy-bodied women" contained a grain of truth.[46] But at the turn of the century, middle-class women's groups played only a secondary role.

This uneasy alliance achieved its first success in 1906, when the Georgia legislature finally passed a child labor law. The next victory came in 1914, when Atlanta textile workers, on strike against the Fulton Bag and Cotton Mills, crowded the galleries to witness a successful fight for a stronger bill. After World War I, middle-class women seized the initiative, and in 1925 the Children's Code Commission, composed primarily of women's groups and represented by a female legislator, succeeded in passing the state's first effective legislation. By that time, however, changes in technology and managerial strategies had already eliminated many children from the mills. In Georgia, as in other parts of the country, women took the lead in promoting state responsibility for society's most vulnerable members. But Smith would have pointed out that the Fulton Mills strikers, acting in their own behalf, helped undermine the mill owners' contention that they employed children only at the millhands' behest and that it was unionists, not reformers, who persistently linked child labor restrictions to demands for a living wage.

It was the working-class woman, however, not the child laborer who inspired Smith's most original and impassioned columns. Her strategy for empowering workers' wives rested on premises as old as those of "republican motherhood" and as widespread as the notion of "municipal housekeeping." Those assumptions could be summed up in a title she favored for columns on the ladies' auxiliaries: "The Hand That Rocks the Cradle Rules the World."[47] When she turned from the "Housewife" to the "Industrial Woman," though, she offered a critique of gender hierarchy that marked her as a modern feminist, a member of a small band of rebels who, in the 1910s, put economic independence at the center of their challenge to the social order.[48]

Smith rooted both her notion of consumption as an arena of struggle and her advocacy of wage work for women in a distinctive Progressive Era version of the female past. Like Charlotte Perkins Gilman, Olive Schreiner, and other late nineteenth-century feminist thinkers, she saw current problems and opportunities as the outcome of a long and inevitable process of social evolution.[49] The plantation mistress and the slave were notably absent from the story; Smith's populist rendition turned instead on the transformation of white yeoman farm wives from the

" 'manufacturers' of the day" into consumers. Writing in 1911, the same year in which Olive Schreiner published her influential *Woman and Labor,* Smith argued that in the 1840s "our grandmothers were workers." They canned, spun cloth, sewed, milked, churned, and labored in the fields. By the 1870s factories were producing canned food and ready-made cloth. Women no longer hoed and plowed. Today, "everything comes to the household ready to eat, ready to wear." Men, with their technological inventions, appropriated women's labor. Yet when women attempted to use their power as consumers for political purposes or to enter the industrial and commercial world, they were beaten back "by some man-of-the-house, who says, 'A woman's place is in the home!' "[50]

The precariousness of that home was one of Smith's major themes. Indeed, her idealization of the working-class family and her prescriptions for political harmony between the sexes stood in sharp contrast to acerbic descriptions of domestic life, which were drawn, perhaps, from her own unhappy experience as measured against prevailing ideas of romantic love and companionate marriage. Like middle-class feminists who saw reform radiating outward from the home, she liked to inspire her readers with the image of an exemplary family in which the wife understood that she owed her standard of living to the labor movement and urged her husband to active trade unionism, while the husband appreciated his wife's productivity and encouraged her self-education. But as soon as Smith shifted from future ideal to present reality, she conjured a family that resembled a battleground rather than a little commonwealth. Putting utopian visions aside, she berated nagging, "simper-headed" wives for complaining when their husbands attended union meetings and excoriated the "blind fool" who says his wife "has no business dabbling in union affairs" and "preaches 'eight hours' to his union brothers and then works his wife to death."[51]

If marriage was a woman's destiny, moreover, the "Penalty of Being a Woman" was that she could not actively seek it out; nor could she be assured that marriage would bring security, much less "married bliss." In any case, not every woman was suited to the role or willing to stay "within four walls; without ambition." "We must remember," Smith wrote, "that there are homes ... where nothing but strife, or where nothing but poverty and misery, resides. ... There are women forced to make their own living on account of the poor wages of the father or the poor wages of the husband. There are women born with just as independent spirit as was ever born in any of the 'Lords of Creation,' as they style themselves!"[52]

Whether they worked from necessity or out of a desire for independence, wage-earning women found themselves doubly disadvantaged: exploited by employers and held back by the jealousy and shortsightedness of trade union men. Instead of welcoming the entry of women into the work force as an evolutionary necessity, male craft unionists viewed their sisters as competition. Smith acknowledged the problem that women's cheap labor posed, but she argued that the solution was to organize women, not push them out of the labor force. Yet even when men grudgingly admitted as much, they made little effort to welcome women to their ranks. A woman who managed to screw up her courage and attend a union meeting, Smith explained, "feels out of place; she feels that she is not wanted. . . . I have ladies almost every day tell me that they do not go to their union meetings because they feel like the men don't want them there."[53]

Neither Smith's keen awareness of the shortcomings of individual men nor her advocacy of female ambition shook her faith in the labor movement as the agent of women's emancipation. For too long, she argued, woman had allowed herself to be seduced by the pernicious idea that she had to be protected, that she was "a dependent, a weakling, a necessary protectionable appendage hung to the coat-tails of mankind. . . . What we need is not so much protection, but to be taught to protect ourselves!" Trade unionism was the means by which that lesson could be hammered home. Through wage work and self-organization, the modern woman had at last realized that she was "a human being, with life, with brain, with a soul, and with the right of independence." In the union and union auxiliary, she gained "that self-possession . . . which goes to make up a true woman." She found that she had not only the right but also the ability "to stand shoulder to shoulder with man."[54]

Womanism was Smith's word for the change of character that allowed women to combine class solidarity and consumer consciousness with the fight for economic autonomy. She used the term to distinguish between the "True-Woman" and the "lady, who is nothing but a 'lady.' " Centuries of being "pampered . . . and sat-down-upon" had made ladies dependent, frivolous, and selfish; they did nothing but gossip and spend their husbands' money. "Womanism" resulted "when our girls get out into public life and bump up against the world, and know humanity and feel the responsibility of life."[55] The transformation Smith envisioned was far-reaching. Every woman must learn a trade; every man must acquire a "knowledge of house-keeping." Both men and women must lay aside the "petty prejudices of the present day, deeply set customs must be broken and thrown aside."[56]

No brief for women's sexual freedom accompanied Smith's demand for economic emancipation. Yet between the lines of some of her columns ran a sharp awareness of the ways in which traditional notions of female honor inhibited women's participation in public life. For Victorian women, honor meant, above all, sexual restraint; an honorable woman was a chaste daughter or a faithful wife. For men, honor had less to do with the private than with the public self.[57] Smith attacked that double standard: such civic virtues as solidarity and political courage, she argued, should be the hallmarks of manhood and womanhood alike. Writing in 1911, after a national wave of women garment workers' strikes, Smith warned her fellow trade unionists that female honor was becoming a political issue that called for the utmost vigilance. She believed that "organized capital" had determined to wage an all-out war on trade union women, using as its chief weapon their susceptibility to a special form of character assassination. Now that women were "armed and standing at [men's] side in the battle front for the cause of labor," capital was turning to private detectives to "destroy a woman's name" and thus her "influence in the rank and file."[58]

As it happened, Smith's fears proved eerily premonitory, for three years later she found herself victimized by the very tactics against which she had cautioned her readers. In 1914, when workers at the Fulton Mills joined the United Textile Workers Union (UTW) and walked off their jobs, Smith secured a commission as a paid organizer. Equipped with that coveted imprimatur, she plunged into a major textile strike.[59] She did not see herself as breaking ranks or acting inconsistently, for the "vast web of Fraternity" she envisioned included white women as well as men, unskilled and unorganized white workers as well as the labor aristocracy. She would soon learn, however, that it was one thing to move in the interstices between the women's movement and the labor movement, to berate craft unionists for their sexism and women reformers for their classism while building alliances with both. It was quite another to exchange the role of volunteer for that of paid organizer and to cross the line between the world of the ladies' auxiliaries and that of the South's most despised white workers. Making that leap, Smith found herself the target of a smear campaign, orchestrated by company detectives ("beings in human flesh devoid of character or conscience") who lived in the mill village and infiltrated the union.[60]

Smith had no experience in organizing textile workers, but she moved quickly to capitalize on her skills as a publicist, combining the pen with the camera in a campaign designed to encourage collective self-confidence among the workers and to garner public support. Working closely with the UTW organizer Charles Miles, Smith recruited a moving-picture company to film the picket line and invited the workers to free screenings in a local theater. Sporting a hand-held "detective camera," she darted about the mill village, snapping pictures of child laborers, evicted families, defiant workers, and undercover agents. She also hired local commercial photographers to help document the strike. She then captioned those images, mounted them on cardboard, and displayed them in store windows to expose the bosses' sneering arrogance and the strikers' poverty and respectability.[61]

Smith's use of photography placed her squarely in the progressive tradition, for the camera furnished the movement's preeminent mode of proof. Lewis Hine had traveled through Georgia for the National Child Labor Committee in 1913, and Smith was surely familiar with his work.[62] Like him, she created ensembles of images and words. Her most widely circulated photograph featured an emaciated, barefooted boy seated alone on a curb. The caption, hand-lettered on the negative, identified the child as Milton Nunnally, "Age 10 Years," a Fulton Mills worker who had "received for 2 weeks wages only 64 cents." This picture, distributed as a postcard throughout the country and reprinted by numerous newspapers and journals, drew child labor reformers to the strikers' cause.[63]

It would be a mistake, however, to view Smith's visual broadsides simply as appropriations of established formulas. Hine saw himself less as an individual innovator than as a reformer, and he urged others "in the thick of battle" to "get a camera" as well. Social workers led the battle he envisioned, and the camera was the means by which they persuaded middle-class viewers to support legislative reforms. Smith's photographs had a similar purpose, insofar as they aimed at marshaling middle-class backing for the union. But by showing the strikers to themselves, in action and as a collectivity, she sought to foster class consciousness, not to heal class divisions. Her candid shots of company spies, or "spotters," reversed the usual power relations between the seer and seen. "The pictures were taken by myself," Smith wrote, "while thugs and spotters were ever around me." Several cameras, she continued, were "knocked from my hand and smashed before I succeeded in collecting these." Smith certainly found herself "in the heat of battle," but her position in that battle—as an insider/outsider and as a woman in an arena dominated by men—gave her photographs both a reformist purpose and a radical edge.[64]

The spies, in turn, sought to undermine the workers' solidarity and the public's sympathy by casting the union in a disreputable light. They singled out O. Delight Smith for special vilification. Their tactics ranged from rumormongering to blackmail and entrapment. They staked out her house, peeping through the windows until the lights went off. They observed her drinking beer in the German Cafe "until long past midnight" and having a "jolly good time" with the UTW organizer Charles Miles. A man claimed that he saw the couple registering at a hotel under an assumed name but promised to keep the secret if Smith would have "intercourse" with him. He said that she refused but procured another woman—a member of the King's Daughters, no less—from whom he promptly caught gonorrhea.[65]

To make matters worse, Smith's husband apparently colluded with those who sought to do her in. In the midst of the strike, Edgar initiated divorce proceedings, represented by the counsel for Fulton Mills. He withdrew his petition, but the following summer Delight sued for divorce, charging her husband with cruelty and failure to provide. Edgar counter-sued, upping the ante by claiming that he had found Delight, drunk and "about half dressed," at home with a drifter named Pat Calahan. But his main charge was that Delight refused to stay at home, "where all good women ought to be."[66]

Delight disputed his allegations and "introduced a number of women witnesses in her behalf." She accused him of being remote, morose, and disagreeable. She had worked out of necessity, yet he placed "every obstacle possible" in the way of her success. He complained "in the presence of others that she neglected her domestic duties and him," circulated rumors detrimental to her "reputation of chastity," and "advised and abetted" those who were trying to force her out of her job.[67] In the end, the jury refused her request for a divorce with alimony and granted her husband a divorce instead. It went further, giving him but denying her the right to remarry.[68]

Until this domestic scandal erupted, the spies' campaign of sexual innuendo seems to have had little effect on Smith's standing in the labor community. Eventually, however, John Golden, the conservative Catholic president of the UTW, decided that she had to go. He fired her on November 18, 1914, despite her protests that while professional UTW organizers had come and gone, she had held the strike together under extraordinarily difficult circumstances. Even after her dismissal, Smith seems to have maintained the strikers' support. Less concerned with sexual propriety or more skeptical of her detractors' accusations, they urged Golden at least to retain her and assign her elsewhere, as she would be "Superior to Many in Organising in the South."[69]

With Smith gone, the strikers held out through the winter, but with dwindling hopes and diminishing support. On May 15, 1915, the UTW admitted defeat. By that time Smith had vanished from the pages of the *Journal of Labor* and the records of the Atlanta Federation of Trades.[70] Her departure remained unmarked and unexplained.

Vanished perhaps, but not quite blotted out of history. Smith still had her craft—she could walk into a railroad office and say, "Here you fellows, I can deliver the goods[,] now put me on your payroll"—and she found a job in Texas with the Santa Fe Railroad, traveling back and forth to Atlanta until she finally succeeded in convincing the court to remove the disabilities that prevented her from remarrying. Meanwhile she threw herself into a passionate affair and then married again, albeit again disastrously, since her husband unaccountably disappeared two years later. In 1920 she surfaced in Portland, Oregon, where she took refuge with the Young Women's Christian Association. Eventually, she got a job at Western Union, became a charter member of the Portland local of the Commercial Telegraphers Union, and flung herself heart and soul into the labor movement once more. By the time she died thirty-eight years later, she was known as the "first lady of Oregon labor." "I have 'cast my bread on the waters' all through my half-century in the LABOR MOVEMENT," she exulted. "[I]t has 'returned to me ten fold.'"[71]

Like her nom de plume Athena, O. Delight Smith celebrated women's household arts; yet she was also a warrior, embroiled simultaneously in what she saw as a "Mighty Conflict" between capital and labor and in a struggle for sexual equality. She fought on two fronts, with workingmen against their class enemies and with women against the "petty prejudices of the present day." Her concern for such issues as prostitution and child labor, her commitment to consumer organizing, and her use of the camera to disclose the city's hidden truths reflected values that she and her middle-class allies shared. She, however, sought footing on more ambiguous and treacherous terrain. The fact that she could so quickly cross the border between respectable women and wayward girls, reformers and the women they were trying to reform, speaks volumes about the precariousness of low-level white-collar life. It also suggests the dangers women faced when they abandoned the metaphorical protection of the parlor to grapple directly with men and trespass on male-dominated public space.

In private and in public, Smith displayed the creativity that boundary crossing often inspires. Her limitations, however, demonstrate the power of those boundaries to impoverish the reform imagination of her times. Her nativism and racism circumscribed her vision of both sisterhood and class unity; exclusions underlay the advantages of the labor aristocracy to which she belonged. Similar exclusions influenced her fate, for when she transcended the craft barriers that limited the reach of the AFL and took her stand with the city's textile workers, she lost the fragile immunities her race and skill conferred.

Re-creating the past is a delicate enterprise, prey to the contingencies that can crush an individual and erase her name from history. The attack on Smith's sexual reputation, the collapse of her marriage, and her banishment from Atlanta's craft community helped ensure that in the written accounts of the period her name cannot be found. By recovering the lives of such unremembered people, we do more than honor forerunners who gave much and got little in return; we also expand our own imaginative boundaries. With women like Smith at the center of the story, labor history reveals itself as doubly emplotted: a narrative of love as well as work, sexuality as well as class consciousness. The South becomes less aberrant. And feminism grows more capacious, as do our conceptions of reform.

NOTES

This essay owes a great deal to the research assistance of Todd Benson, Frances Rivers, Misti Turbeville, Karen Leathem, and, especially, Lawrence Boyette. My quest for O. Delight Smith would not have been nearly so fruitful—and so enjoyable—without the generosity and enthusiasm of Jay A. Lloyd of Long Beach, California, who shared with me his painstaking genealogical research. I thank Leon Fink, Julia Greene, Nancy Hewitt, Robert Korstad, Suzanne Lebsock, Susan Levine, Dale Martin, Kathleen Much, Mary Murphy, David Thelen, and the members of a delightful ad hoc graduate seminar—Georg Leidenberger, Marla Miller, and Laura Moore—for their incisive comments. My greatest debt is to Glenda Gilmore, who worked with me on this project from start to finish. I am also grateful for a research grant from the Institute for Research in Social Science of the University of North Carolina at Chapel Hill and for the financial support of the National Endowment for the Humanities and the Andrew W. Mellon Foundation, which enabled me to complete this essay at the Center for Advanced Study in the Behavioral Sciences.

1. This trope of the historian as rescuer of a woman "who—almost—wasn't there" is drawn from Claire Tomalin's biography of Charles Dickens's mistress, *The Invisible Woman: The Story of Nelly Ternan and Charles Dickens* (New York: Viking, 1990), 3.

2. *Journal of Labor,* April 10, 1908, 5. Alice Walker, Elsa Barkley Brown, and others have used the term *womanism* to describe the mixture of feminism and communal consciousness among African American women. Alice Walker, *In Search of Our Mothers' Gardens: Womanist Prose* (New York: Harcourt Brace Jovanovich, 1983), xi-xii; Elsa Barkley Brown, "Womanist Consciousness: Maggie Lena Walker and the Independent Order of Saint Luke," *Signs* 14 (Spring 1989): 610-33. For the contested meanings of *experience,* see Joan W. Scott, "Experience," in *Feminists Theorize the Political,* ed. Judith Butler and Joan W. Scott (New York: Routledge, 1992), 22-40.

3. Michael Kazin, *Barons of Labor: The San Francisco Building Trades and Union Power in the Progressive Era* (Urbana: University of Illinois Press, 1987), 3-4; Maurice Isserman, " 'God Bless Our American Institutions': The Labor History of John R. Commons," *Labor History* 17 (Summer 1976): 309-28.

Reflecting this view, Dewey Grantham provided much evidence of labor's contribution to social reform yet reserved the term *progressive* for middle-class elements and characterized southern unions as job-conscious and apolitical. Dewey Grantham, *Southern Progressivism: The Reconciliation of Progress and Tradition* (Knoxville: University of Tennessee Press, 1983), 290-301.

4. See J. Joseph Huthmacher, "Urban Liberalism and the Age of Reform," *Mississippi Valley Historical Review* 44 (September 1962): 231-41; and John D. Buenker, *Urban Liberalism and Progressive Reform* (New York: Scribner, 1973), for the importance of working-class voters to urban progressivism. Revisionist studies, such as Gary M. Fink, *Labor's Search for Political Order: The Political Behavior of the Missouri Labor Movement, 1890-1940* (Columbia: University of Missouri Press, 1973), and Kazin, *Barons of Labor,* show that on the local level AFL trade unionists were more politically active than the Commons school suggested. Neither Fink nor Kazin, however, dispute the received interpretation of the AFL generally. Julia Greene, "Striking at the Ballot Box: The American Federation of Labor, Local Trade Union Leadership, and Political Action, 1881-1916" (Ph.D. diss., Yale University, 1990), offers a more general challenge to the notion that the AFL opposed political action. For recent reevaluations of John R. Commons and the Wisconsin School of labor history, see Leon Fink, "'Intellectuals' versus 'Workers': Academic Requirements and the Creation of Labor History," *American Historical Review* 96 (April 1991): 395-421; and Ellen Fitzpatrick, "Rethinking the Intellectual Origins of American Labor History," ibid., 422-28.

5. Kazin, *Barons of Labor,* for instance, argues that the leaders of San Francisco's building trades excluded women from union culture. Yet historians of women, focusing mainly on the 1920s and broadening their definition of labor activism to embrace such consumer-oriented strategies as boycotts and union label campaigns, have begun to show that in many situations women did play a central role in the AFL. See Susan Levine, "Workers' Wives: Gender, Class, and Consumerism in the 1920s United States," *Gender and History* 3 (Spring 1991): 45-64; Dana Frank, "Gender, Consumer Organizing, and the Seattle Labor Movement, 1919-1929," in *Work Engendered: Toward a New History of American Labor,* ed. Ava Baron (Ithaca, N.Y.: Cornell University Press, 1991): 273-95; Maurine Weiner Greenwald, "Working-Class Feminism and the Family Wage Ideal: The Seattle Debate on Married Women's Right to Work, 1914-1920," *Journal of American History* 76 (June 1989): 118-49; and Dorothy Sue Cobble, "Rethinking Troubled Relations between Women and Unions: Craft Unionism and Female Activism," *Feminist Studies* 16 (Fall 1990): 519-48. For "communal" or group consciousness, see Nancy Hewitt, "Beyond the Search for Sisterhood: American Women's History in the 1980s," *Social History* 10 (October 1985): 299-321; and Nancy F. Cott, "What's in a Name? The Limits of 'Social Feminism'; or, Expanding the Vocabulary of Women's History," *Journal of American History* 76 (December 1989): 827-29. For earlier studies delineating the tensions between working- and middle-class feminism, see Mari Jo Buhle, *Women and American Socialism, 1870-1920* (Urbana: University of Illinois Press, 1981); Nancy Schrom

Dye, "Creating a Feminist Alliance: Sisterhood and Class Conflict in the New York Women's Trade Union League," *Feminist Studies* 2, no. 2/3 (1975): 24-38; and Alice Kessler-Harris, "Where Are the Organized Women Workers?" *Feminist Studies* 3 (Fall 1975): 92-110.

6. Anne Firor Scott, "A Historian's Odyssey," in Scott, *Making the Invisible Woman Visible* (Urbana: University of Illinois Press, 1984), xv, xviii-xix, and "A Progressive Wind from the South, 1906-1913," *Journal of Southern History* 29 (February 1963): 51-70; C. Vann Woodward, *Origins of the New South, 1877-1913* (Baton Rouge: Louisiana State University Press, 1951), 371. Woodward was elaborating on a theme introduced by Arthur S. Link, "The Progressive Movement in the South, 1870-1914," *North Carolina Historical Review* 23 (April 1946): 172-95. Woodward titled his chapter on progressivism, "Progressivism—for Whites Only," underlining the era's paradoxical coupling of reform and racism and noting that the paradox had its "counterpart in the North, where it was not uncommon for one man to champion both progressivism and imperialism." The chapter itself, however, stressed the movement's originality and vigor, not its racial conservatism. Woodward, *Origins of the New South*, 369-428 (quote on 373). By contrast, the outpouring of scholarship that crested in the 1970s was dominated by the argument that southern progressivism was, in John Dittmer's words, "conservative, elitist, and above all racist." John Dittmer, *Black Georgia in the Progressive Era, 1900-1920* (Urbana: University of Illinois Press, 1977), 110. There were, however, notable exceptions. Dewey Grantham, for example, downplayed racism and lauded the reformers' success in persuading individualistic southerners to accept a more vigorous regulatory state. Grantham, *Southern Progressivism*. Others took Woodward's paradox as their central thesis. See, for example, Jack Temple Kirby, *Darkness at the Dawning: Race and Reform in the Progressive South* (Philadelphia: Lippincott, 1972).

7. The most influential statements of this thesis were Gabriel Kolko, *The Triumph of Conservatism: A Re-Interpretation of American History, 1900-1916* (New York: Free Press, 1963); and, from a less critical perspective, Robert H. Wiebe, *The Search for Order, 1877-1920* (New York: Hill and Wang, 1967). For the South, see Peter H. Argersinger, "The Southern Search for Order," *Reviews in American History* 3 (June 1975): 236-41; J. Morgan Kousser, *The Shaping of Southern Politics: Suffrage Restriction and the Establishment of the One-Party South, 1880-1910* (New Haven, Conn.: Yale University Press, 1974), and "Progressivism—For Middle-Class Whites Only: North Carolina Education, 1880-1910," *Journal of Southern History* 46 (May 1980): 169-94; and George B. Tindall, *The Persistent Tradition in New South Politics* (Baton Rouge: Louisiana State University Press, 1975).

8. Scott, "Historian's Odyssey," xviii. The first wave of studies of southern women's activism centered primarily on white women in the 1920s. George B. Tindall coined the term "Business Progressivism" to describe what he saw as the metamorphosis of progressivism in this period, when development-minded reformers continued to press for social order and economic growth while the social justice impulse declined. Focusing on the trajectory of white female reform, Scott

argued instead that "the progressive movement came fully into being in the South" only after World War I. George B. Tindall, "Business Progressivism: Southern Politics in the Twenties," *South Atlantic Quarterly* 62 (Winter 1963): 92-106; Anne Firor Scott, "After Suffrage: Southern Women in the 1920s," in Scott, *Making the Invisible Woman Visible*, 222-43, and *The Southern Lady: From Pedestal to Politics, 1830-1930* (Chicago: University of Chicago Press, 1970), 191-211 (quote on 191). For a survey of this literature, see Jacquelyn Dowd Hall and Anne Firor Scott, "Women in the South," in *Interpreting Southern History: Historiographical Essays in Honor of Sanford W. Higginbotham,* ed. John B. Boles and Evelyn Thomas Nolen (Baton Rouge: Louisiana State University Press, 1987), 454-509.

9. Scott, "Historian's Odyssey," xix. Women have long been associated with the "social justice" wing of progressivism, and Dewey Grantham, with his optimistic view of the movement, noted their contributions. A handful of excellent recent studies, which do not necessarily share Grantham's perspective on progressivism, have focused specifically on white women and gender issues: James L. Leloudis, "School Reform in the New South: The Woman's Association for the Betterment of Public School Houses in North Carolina, 1902-1919," *Journal of American History* 69 (March 1983): 886-909, and " 'A More Certain Means of Grace': Pedagogy, Self, and Society in North Carolina, 1880-1920" (Ph.D. diss., University of North Carolina, 1989); Joseph F. Kett, "Women and the Progressive Impulse in Southern Education," in *The Web of Southern Social Relations: Women, Family, and Education,* ed. Walter J. Fraser, Jr., R. Frank Saunders, Jr., and Jon L. Wakelyn (Athens: University of Georgia Press, 1985), 166-80; LeeAnn Whites, "The De Graffenried Controversy: Class, Race, and Gender in the New South," *Journal of Southern History* 54 (August 1988): 449-78; Nancy Hewitt, "Politicizing Domesticity: Anglo, Black, and Latin Women in Tampa's Progressive Movements," in *Gender, Class, Race, and Reform in the Progressive Era,* ed. Noralee Frankel and Nancy S. Dye (Lexington: University Press of Kentucky, 1991), 24-41; Elizabeth Turner, "Women, Religion, and Reform in Galveston, 1880-1920," in *Urban Texas: Politics and Development,* ed. Char Miller and Heywood T. Sanders (College Station: Texas A & M Press, 1990), 75-95; and Marjorie Spruill Wheeler, "New Women of the New South: The Leaders of the Woman Suffrage Movement in the Southern States" (Ph.D. diss., University of Virginia, 1989). See also David E. Whisnant, *All that Is Native and Fine: The Politics of Culture in an American Region* (Chapel Hill: University of North Carolina Press, 1983).

10. Maureen A. Flanagan, "Gender and Urban Political Reform: The City Club and the Woman's City Club of Chicago in the Progressive Era," *American Historical Review* 95 (October 1990): 1048 (quote). The most influential statement of this argument is Paula Baker, "The Domestication of Politics: Women and American Political Society, 1780-1920," *American Historical Review* 89 (June 1984): 620-47.

11. Examples of this critique include Daniel T. Rodgers, "In Search of Progressivism," *Reviews in American History* 10 (December 1982): 113-32;

David P. Thelen, "Social Tensions and the Origins of Progressivism," *Journal of American History* 56 (September 1969): 323-41; Richard L. McCormick, "The Discovery that 'Business Corrupts Politics': A Reappraisal of the Origins of Progressivism," *American Historical Review* 86 (April 1981): 247-74; and William A. Link, "Privies, Progressivism, and Public Schools: Health Reform and Education in the Rural South, 1909-1920," *Journal of Southern History* 54 (November 1988): 623-42.

12. For a sympathetic but critical look at this reform network, see Robyn Muncy, *Creating a Female Dominion in American Reform, 1890-1935* (New York: Oxford University Press, 1991). For an insightful study of Western reformers, see Peggy Pascoe, *Relations of Rescue: The Search for Female Moral Authority in the American West, 1874-1939* (New York: Oxford University Press, 1990). Linda Gordon, "Black and White Visions of Welfare: Women's Welfare Activism, 1890-1945," *Journal of American History* 78 (September 1991): 559-90, shows convincingly how the very definition and periodization of welfare activism obscures the efforts of minority women. Still needed are studies that emphasize the importance of regional environments (from the streets of Chicago to the plains of Kansas to the farms and upstart cities of Georgia) in influencing people's choices and options. In the South, for instance, reformers operated in the shadow of slavery, building such institutions as public schools from the ground up and using them as sites for public health and other welfare programs. Black southerners embraced the spirit of reform in a struggle to create their own private institutions, gain access to these newly established state and local services, and stop lynching. Both black and white women worked through the church, rendering their efforts invisible to scholars focused on secular organizations. Fortunately, students of black women's history have begun to clarify the inadequacy of interpretations that fail to take African American initiatives into account. For a pioneering anthology of research on black women's activities, see Sharon Harley and Rosalyn Terborg-Penn, eds., *The Afro-American Woman: Struggles and Images* (Port Washington, N.Y.: National University Publications, 1978). Recent examples include, in addition to Gordon, Rosalyn Terborg-Penn, "African-American Women's Networks in the Anti-Lynching Crusade," in *Gender, Class, Race, and Reform*, ed. Frankel and Dye, 148-61; Jacqueline Anne Rouse, "Atlanta's African-American Women's Attack on Segregation, 1900-1920," ibid., 10-23, and *Lugenia Burns Hope: Black Southern Reformer* (Athens: University of Georgia Press, 1989); Brown, "Womanist Consciousness"; Cynthia Neverdon-Morton, *Afro-American Women of the South and the Advancement of the Race, 1895-1925* (Knoxville: University of Tennessee Press, 1989); Dorothy C. Salem, *To Better Our World: Black Women in Organized Reform, 1890-1920* (Brooklyn: Carlson, 1990); Anne Firor Scott, "Most Invisible of All: Black Women's Voluntary Associations," *Journal of Southern History* 56 (February 1990): 3-22; Glenda Elizabeth Gilmore, "Gender and Jim Crow: Women and the Politics of White Supremacy in North Carolina, 1896-1920" (Ph.D. diss., University of North Carolina, 1992); and Elizabeth Dan Lasch, "Black Neighbors: Race and the Limits of Reform in the American Settlement House Movement, 1890-1945" (Ph.D. diss., University of Massachusetts, 1990).

13. Michael McGerr, "Political Style and Women's Power, 1830-1930," *Journal of American History* 77 (December 1990), 864-85, and Sarah Deutsch, "Learning to Talk More Like a Man: Boston Women's Class-Bridging Organizations, 1870-1940," *American Historical Review* 97 (April 1992): 379-404, point out the costs of the convergence between male and female political cultures. For a shrewd critique of maternalist interpretations of Progressive Era reform, see Eileen Boris, "From Parlor to Politics: Women and Reform in America, 1890-1925," *Radical History Review* 50 (Spring 1991): 191-203, esp. 199-200.

14. *Journal of Labor,* August 5, 1909, 5.

15. Register of Marriage, John A. Lloyd and Lettie Long, June 27, 1878, and Certificate of Record of Birth, Ola Delight Lloyd, January 21, 1880, Mercer County Clerk's Office, Mercer County, Ill.; Register of Marriage, John A. Lloyd and Alta K. Jackson, June 18, 1891, Shelby County Clerk's Office, Shelbyville, Ill.; Ruth (Hood) Osterhout to Margaret Lloyd, May 2, 1982; Margaret Lloyd to Jay Lloyd, January 10, 1982; and O. Delight Cook to Alta Lloyd, December 11, 1932, in Jacquelyn Hall's possession. I thank Jay A. Lloyd, Delight's nephew, for sharing these documents with me. See also [O. Delight Cook], "Record," entry for April 24, 1920, box 6, no folder, and "History of a Female-Boomer-Operator," [1950], box 3, folder 6, Ola Delight (Lloyd) Cook Papers, Oregon Historical Society, Portland, Oreg.

16. Isa (Lloyd) Osterhout to O. Delight Cook, December 28, 1933, box 3, folder 3; [O. Delight Cook], "History" and untitled biographical sketch, box 3, folder 1, Cook Papers; Manuscript Census, Epes, Sumter County, Alabama, Schedule No. 1, Population, Twelfth Census of the United States, June 13, 1900; Register of the Alabama Polytechnic Institute for Girls, 1898-1899, in author's possession (by 1903 the school was calling itself the Alabama Girls' Industrial School for White Girls; it is now the University of Montevallo); Cook, "History of a Female-Boomer-Operator"; Delight Lloyd to S. A. Duncan, February 1900; Duncan to Lloyd, April 29, 1900, box 3, folder 2, Cook Papers. For a published version of Delight's early history, which differs in some details from this account, see *Journal of Labor,* April 7, 1950, 1-2; also in *Oregon Journal,* March 23, 1950, 10.

17. Edwin Gabler, *The American Telegrapher: A Social History, 1860-1900* (New Brunswick, N.J.: Rutgers University Press, 1988), 40-41; Carolyn Marvin, *When Old Technologies Were New: Thinking about Electric Communication in the Late Nineteenth Century* (New York: Oxford University Press, 1988), 3-8; James W. Carey, "Technology and Ideology: The Case of the Telegraph," in *Communication as Culture: Essays on Media and Society* (Boston: Unwin Hyman, 1988), 201-30. Relatively little has been written on the relationship between the railroads and the telegraph companies or on the cultural impact of telegraphy, despite the vast scholarship on the transportation and communications revolutions. The principle history of Western Union is Robert L. Thompson, *Wiring a Continent: The History of the Telegraph Industry in the United States, 1832-1866* (Princeton, N.J.: Princeton University Press, 1947), and it takes the story only to 1866. For an original and provocative account of the timing and pace of social change in the turn-of-the-century South, see Edward L. Ayers, *The Promise of the New South:*

Life after Reconstruction (New York: Oxford University Press, 1992). As Ayers points out, between 1870 and 1910 the South outstripped national rates of growth in its labor force in transportation and communication (173 percent to 99 percent).

18. For the social origins and ambivalent class position of these pioneering technical workers, see Gabler, *American Telegrapher.* The term *kid-glove laborers* is his. In similar fashion, Ileen A. DeVault, *Sons and Daughters of Labor: Class and Clerical Work in Turn-of-the-Century Pittsburgh* (Ithaca, N.Y.: Cornell University Press, 1990), 6, argues that the "collar line" did not serve as a "major social marker for the nineteenth-century working class."

19. Archibald M. McIsaac, *The Order of Railroad Telegraphers: A Study in Trade Unionism and Collective Bargaining* (Princeton, N.J.: Princeton University Press, 1933), 5-7, 33; Gabler, *American Telegrapher,* 7, 172 (quotes); F. Ray Marshall, *Labor in the South* (Cambridge, Mass.: Harvard University Press, 1967), 51; Vidkunn Ulricksson, *The Telegraphers: Their Craft and Their Unions* (Washington, D.C.: Public Affairs Press, 1953), 60-61.

20. Gabler, *American Telegrapher,* 107-30 (quotes on 115-16).

21. Carey, "Technology and Ideology," 202-4, 215; Thompson, *Wiring a Continent,* 212-16. In small-town depots, the railroad telegrapher might also manage a commercial telegraph branch office and serve as station manager, ticket agent, and baggage clerk, all rolled into one. *Railroad Telegrapher* 24 (April 1907): 540-42; Richard Reinhardt, ed., *Workin' on the Railroad: Reminiscences from the Age of Steam* (Palo Alto, Calif.: American West Publishing, 1970), 191, 198-99; *Commercial Telegraphers Journal* 43 (November 1945): 33 (quote); Minnie Swan Mitchell, "Railroad Terms," *American Speech* 12 (April 1937): 154-55; Cook, "History of a Female-Boomer-Operator." I am grateful to Dale Martin for guiding me to appropriate sources and sharing with me his vast knowledge of railroad lore.

22. Ella Cheever Thayer, *Wired Love: A Romance of Dots and Dashes* (New York: W. J. Johnston, 1853); "By Telegraph," *Railroad Telegrapher* 24 (March 1907): 385-88; Marvin, *When Old Technologies Were New,* 26-32; [O. Delight Cook], "The Everyday Diary," entry for January 31, 1950, box 6, Cook Papers (quote); Gabler, *American Telegrapher,* 114 (quoting an article in *Electric Age*). For a contemporary account of such tensions, see Linda Niemann, *Boomer: Railroad Memoirs* (Berkeley: University of California Press, 1990), 35 and passim.

23. *Journal of Labor,* February 8, 1907, 3, April 7, 1950, 4; *Atlanta Constitution,* August 17, 1907, 2, 5; *Journal of Labor,* December 13, 1907, 4.

24. Franklin M. Garrett, *Atlanta and Environs: A Chronicle of Its People and Events,* vol. 2 (Athens: University of Georgia Press, 1982 [1954]), 191-93. As might be expected, the literature on labor politics in Atlanta is quite thin. For the salience of class issues and the participation of skilled workers in city politics, see Eugene J. Watts, *The Social Bases of City Politics: Atlanta, 1865-1903* (Westport, Conn.: Greenwood, 1978); Mercer Griffin Evans, "A History of the Organized Labor Movement in Georgia" (Ph.D. diss., University of Chicago, 1929), 34, 45, 258-59, 262; Thomas Mashburn Deaton, "Atlanta during the Progressive Era" (Ph.D. diss., University of Georgia, 1969), 120, 135-36; Thomas M. Deaton,

"James G. Woodward: The Working Man's Mayor," *Atlanta History: A Journal of Georgia and the South* 31 (Fall 1987): 11-23; and Elizabeth H. Davidson, *Child Labor Legislation in the Southern Textile States* (Chapel Hill: University of North Carolina Press, 1939), 76.

25. *Atlanta Constitution*, August 10, 1907, 1, August 19, 1907, 6, August 14, 1907, 1, August 17, 1907, 2, 5 (quote); *Journal of Labor*, May 29, 1908, 5; *Oregon Journal*, December 17, 1958, 10b. For the national union's internal conflicts and its lack of AFL support, see Ulriksson, *The Telegraphers*, 69-88. According to John Bertram Andrews, *History of Women in Trade Unions*, vol. 10 of *Report on Condition of Woman and Child Wage-Earners in the United States*, Sen. Doc. 645, 61st Cong., 2d sess. (Washington D.C.: U.S. Government Printing Office, 1911), 195, in the wake of the strike the telegraph companies set out to "extirpate unionism among their women employees."

26. Jack Temple Kirby, "The Southern Exodus," *Journal of Southern History* 49 (November 1983): 585-600; Neil Fligstein, *Going North: Migration of Blacks and Whites from the South, 1900-1950* (New York: Academic Press, 1981), 79; Steven Wayne Wrigley, "The Triumph of Provincialism: Public Life in Georgia, 1898-1917" (Ph.D. diss., Northwestern University, 1986), 31-40; Donald B. Dodd and Wynelle S. Dodd, *Historical Statistics of the South, 1790-1970* (University: University of Alabama Press, 1973), 18-19; Bureau of the Census, *Twelfth Census of the United States, 1900*, vol. 1 (Washington, D.C.: U.S. Government Printing Office, 1901), 612; Bureau of the Census, *Fourteenth Census of the United States, 1920*, vol. 2 (Washington, D.C.: U.S. Government Printing Office, 1922), 222.

27. Dolores Janiewski, *Sisterhood Denied: Race, Gender, and Class in a New South Community* (Philadelphia: Temple University Press, 1985), 55-56; Jacqueline Jones, *Labor of Love, Labor of Sorrow: Black Women, Work, and the Family from Slavery to the Present* (New York: Basic Books, 1985), 110-27; Julia Blackwelder, "Mop and Typewriter: Women's Work in Early Twentieth-Century Atlanta," *Atlanta Historical Journal* 27 (Fall 1983): 24; Joseph A. Hill, *Women in Gainful Occupations, 1870 to 1920*, Census Monographs, 9 (Washington, D.C.: U.S. Government Printing Office, 1929), 11, 146. In 1910 the city's sex ratio stood at 92.7 (i.e., there were 92.7 men for every 100 women). Bureau of the Census, *Thirteenth Census of the United States, 1910*, vol. 2 (Washington, D.C.: U.S. Government Printing Office, 1913), 367.

28. Hill, *Women in Gainful Occupations*, 145-46.

29. Untitled biographical sketch; Joanne J. Meyerowitz, *Women Adrift: Independent Wage Earners in Chicago, 1880-1930* (Chicago: University of Chicago Press, 1988); *Journal of Labor*, June 30, 1911, 4; Mrs. O. L. Smith v. Edgar B. Smith, Libel for Divorce, Depositions of Defendant, August 17, 1915, Superior Court of Fulton County, Fulton County Courthouse, Atlanta, Ga., 12 (hereafter, Depositions of Defendant). For the notion of a "city of women," see Christine Stansell, *City of Women: Sex and Class in New York, 1789-1860* (New York: Alfred A. Knopf, 1986). For other studies that take the complexity of women workers' identities as a central concern, see Susan Porter Benson, *Counter Cultures: Saleswomen, Managers, and Customers in American Department Stores,*

1890-1940 (Urbana: University of Illinois Press, 1986), 229 and passim; Jacquelyn Dowd Hall, "Disorderly Women: Gender and Labor Militancy in the Appalachian South," *Journal of American History* 73 (September 1986): 354-82; Alice Kessler-Harris, "Gender Ideology in Historical Reconstruction: A Case Study from the 1930s," *Gender and History* 1 (Spring 1989): 31-49; Ardis Cameron, *Radicals of the Worst Sort: The Laboring Women of Lawrence, 1860-1912* (Urbana: University of Illinois Press, 1993); and Carole Turbin, "Beyond Dichotomies: Interdependence in Mid-Nineteenth-Century Working-Class Families in the United States," *Gender and History* 1 (Autumn 1989): 293-308.

30. Atlanta Historical Society, *Atlanta in 1890: "The Gate City"* (Macon, Ga.: Mercer University Press, 1986), xxii-xxiii; *Journal of Labor,* May 29, 1908, 5, October 2, 1908, 4 (quote), November 13, 1908, 5, June 30, 1911, 4.

31. *Journal of Labor,* July 28, 1911, 5, January 12, 1912, 4, October 24, 1913, 5 (first quote), October 10, 1913, 3 (second quote).

32. Ibid., April 7, 1950, 1-2, February 14, 1908, 8 (quote), September 18, 1908, 4, October 17, 1913, 5, November 24, 1911, 3, July 24, 1908, 5, July 2, 1909, 6, July 1, 1910, 6; *Railroad Telegrapher* 26 (June 1909): 915-17, 929-30.

33. *Journal of Labor,* January 11, 1907, 4, December 12, 1906, 6, November 1, 1907, 4, February 5, 1909, 5 (first quote), December 11, 1908, 5 (second quote).

34. Ibid., April 19, 1907, 5 (first quote), June 7, 1907, 5 (second quote), November 1, 1907, 5 (third quote), January 31, 1908, 2 (fourth and fifth quotes), March 27, 1908, 5. For the antimonopoly strain in progressive thought, see Rodgers, "In Search of Progressivism," 123-24.

35. Greene, "Striking at the Ballot Box"; Julia Greene " 'The Strike at the Ballot Box': The American Federation of Labor's Entrance into Electoral Politics, 1906 to 1909" (Yale University, 1989, unpublished paper in Julia Greene's possession). For the 1880s and 1890s, see Leon Fink, *Workingmen's Democracy: The Knights of Labor and American Politics* (Urbana: University of Illinois Press, 1983).

36. *Journal of Labor,* April 16, 1909, 1.

37. Ibid., February 7, 1908, 5 (quote), May 1, 1908, 5. Gwendolyn Mink, *Old Labor and New Immigrants in American Political Development* (Ithaca, N.Y.: Cornell University Press, 1986), argues that nativism and racism were key to the AFL's evolution. For a critique of this view, see Julia Greene's review in *International Labor and Working-Class History* 34 (Fall 1988): 120-23.

38. Robert W. Rydell, *All the World's a Fair: Visions of Empire at American International Expositions, 1867-1916* (Chicago: University of Chicago Press, 1984), 72-104; David Glassberg, *American Historical Pageantry: The Uses of Tradition in the Early Twentieth Century* (Chapel Hill: University of North Carolina Press, 1990).

39. *Journal of Labor,* February 8, 1907, 4 (first quote), July 14, 1911, 8 (second quote), February 15, 1907, 3 (remaining quotes). Between 1906 and 1911 the state's leading newspapers clamored for more drastic enforcement of a law passed in 1866 "to prevent vagrancy and to compel free persons of color to

labor in the state" and strengthened in 1903. Aimed originally at forcing the ex-slaves to acquire the habit of wage labor, vagrancy laws were promulgated by reformers throughout the country and served as important tools of labor control. Wrigley, "Triumph of Provincialism," 85, 90-92; Deaton, "Atlanta during the Progressive Era," 148-49; Evans, "The Labor Movement in Georgia," 316-20; *Acts and Resolutions of the General Assembly of the State of Georgia* (Atlanta: Franklin Printing and Publishing, 1903), 45-47 (quote); Eric Foner, *Reconstruction: America's Unfinished Revolution, 1863-1877* (New York: Harper and Row, 1988); 161-67.

40. Susan Levine, "Labor's True Woman: Domesticity and Equal Rights in the Knights of Labor," *Journal of American History* 70 (September 1983): 323-39; *Journal of Labor,* June 28, 1907, 5 (quote), October 25, 1907, 2.

41. Levine, "Workers' Wives." For the centrality of consumer consciousness to progressivism, see David P. Thelen, "Patterns of Consumer Consciousness in the Progressive Movement: Robert M. La Follette, the Antitrust Persuasion, and Labor Legislation," in *The Quest for Social Justice: The Morris Fromkin Memorial Lectures, 1970-1980,* ed. Ralph M. Aderman (Madison: University of Wisconsin Press, 1983), 19-47. For the National Consumers League, see Kathryn Kish Sklar, *"Doing the Nation's Work": Florence Kelley and Women's Political Culture, 1860-1930* (New Haven, Conn.: Yale University Press, forthcoming).

42. *Journal of Labor,* August 5, 1909, 5.

43. Ibid., January 11, 1907, 7 (first quote), March 26, 1909, 6 (remaining quotes), January 16, 1914, 3, February 26, 1909, 5.

44. Ibid., August 22, 1913, 4, July 12, 1912, 7, July 18, 1913, 6, February 13, 1914, 5 (quote), August 2, 1907, 5, December 6, 1907, 5, November 24, 1911, 3; *Atlanta Georgian,* July 2, 1914, 2. For the Southern Conference on Woman and Child Labor, see Davidson, *Child Labor Legislation,* 145-47; *AFL Weekly News Letter,* no. 53, April 6, 1912; *Atlanta Constitution,* April 25 and 26, 1911.

45. *Journal of Labor,* November 10, 1911, 3.

46. Davidson, *Child Labor Legislation,* 70-71, 81, 194 (quote).

47. Ibid., 73, 75, 211-14; Deaton, "Atlanta during the Progressive Era," 164; Samuel Gompers, "Georgia's New Child Labor Law," *American Federationist* 21, pt. 2 (October 1914): 869-70; Scott, *Making the Invisible Woman Visible,* 228-29; *Journal of Labor,* April 26, 1907, 5, June 10, 1909, 2, January 4, 1907, 7.

48. For a definition of feminism, see Cott, "What's in a Name?" 821, 826.

49. Charlotte Perkins Gilman, *Women and Economics: A Study of the Economic Relation between Men and Women as a Factor in Social Evolution,* ed. Carl Degler (New York: Harper and Row, 1966 [1898]); Olive Schreiner, *Woman and Labor* (London and Leipzig: Unwin, 1911). See Greenwald, "Working-Class Feminism," 135-38, for the influence of these writers on working-class feminists in Seattle during World War I.

50. *Journal of Labor,* July 28, 1911, 7. See also ibid., February 5, 1909, 5.

51. O. Delight Cook, untitled journal, box 6, no folder, and "My Life's Story, 1917 to 1925," box 3, folder 3, Cook Papers; *Journal of Labor,* January 4, 1907,

7, July 5, 1907, 5, June 10, 1909, 2, August 7, 1908, 5 (first quote), June 25, 1909, 5 (second quote), May 8, 1908, 5 (third quote).

52. *Journal of Labor,* February 5, 1909, 5 (first and third quotes), August 4, 1911, 3 (second quote). Smith's opinions on these matters were considerably in advance of the AFL. By 1914, however, Samuel Gompers had bowed to the inevitable and was espousing ideas about women's work that—on paper at least—closely paralleled Smith's 1909 line. Samuel Gompers, "Working Women, Organize!" *American Federationist* 21, pt. 1 (March 1914): 231-34. For the AFL's hostility toward women workers, see Kessler-Harris, "Where Are the Organized Women Workers?"; Alice Kessler-Harris, *Out to Work: A History of Wage-Earning Women in the United States* (New York: Oxford University Press, 1982), 152-66; and Ann Schofield, "Rebel Girls and Union Maids: The Woman Question in the Journals of the AFL and IWW, 1905-1920," *Feminist Studies* 9 (Summer 1983): 335-58.

53. *Journal of Labor,* February 12, 1909, 2.

54. Ibid., August 20, 1909, 5 (first quote), February 19, 1909, 2 (second and fourth quotes), February 26, 1909, 5 (third quote), February 19, 1909, 2.

55. Ibid., April 10, 1908, 5 (first, third, and fifth quotes), February 19, 1909, 2 (second quote), February 5, 1909, 5 (fourth quote). See also ibid., February 26, 1909, 5.

56. Ibid., February 5, 1909, 5, August 20, 1909, 5.

57. Bertram Wyatt-Brown, *Honor and Violence in the Old South* (New York: Oxford University Press, 1986), 85-115; Edward L. Ayers, *Vengeance and Justice: Crime and Punishment in the Nineteenth-Century American South* (New York: Oxford University Press, 1984), 9-33.

58. *Journal of Labor,* January 18, 1907, 3, September 15, 1911, 5 (quote); *New York Times,* May 8 and August 6, 1911.

59. The AFL at the time employed few official organizers, and women organizers in particular were few and far between. For Smith, the commission was both an honor and a windfall; it meant that she could support herself through labor work instead of scrambling to make a living while volunteering on the side. For a more detailed treatment of this strike, see Jacquelyn Dowd Hall, "Private Eyes, Public Women: Images of Class and Sex in the Urban South, Atlanta, Georgia, 1913-1915," in *Work Engendered,* ed. Baron, 243-72. Pages 182-84 are drawn, with revisions, from that essay.

60. *Journal of Labor,* June 12, 1914, 7, September 15, 1911, 5 (quote).

61. Operative H.J.D., June 3, 1914, box 2, file 15; Operative J.W.W. and A.E.W. 10, June 6, 1914, box 1, file 2, Fulton Bag and Cotton Mills Papers, Price Gilbert Memorial Library, Georgia Institute of Technology, Atlanta, Ga. (hereafter Fulton Mills Papers). Smith compiled and annotated three small albums of these photographs, numbering 120 in all, which she titled "Conditions," "Evictions," and "Tent City." The original albums, along with sixteen additional photographs, can be found at the George Meany Memorial Archives in Washington, D.C. Copies are available at the Southern Labor Archives, Special Collections, Georgia State University, Atlanta, Ga. Copies of some of the photographs are also

located in "Exhibits," Fulton Bag Company, Case File 33/41, Record Group 280, Federal Mediation and Conciliation Service Records, Suitland Branch, National Archives, Washington, D.C. See Clifford M. Kuhn, "Images of Dissent: The Pictorial Record of the 1914-15 Strike at Atlanta's Fulton Bag and Cotton Mills" (Paper prepared for the annual meeting of the Organization of American Historians, St. Louis, Mo., April 6, 1989, in Clifford Kuhn's possession), for an analysis of this photographic record. I thank Kuhn for drawing my attention to these materials. For other worker-filmmakers who used silent movies to promote their cause, see Steven J. Ross, "Struggles for the Screen: Workers, Radicals, and the Political Uses of Silent Film," *American Historical Review* 96 (April 1991): 333-67. According to Robert E. Mensel, the term *detective camera* was used to describe any camera that could be "concealed on one's person and used surreptitiously to take pictures of the unwilling or unknowing." Robert E. Mensel, " 'Kodakers Lying in Wait': Amateur Photography and the Right of Privacy in New York, 1885-1915," *American Quarterly* 43 (March 1991): 43, n. 41.

62. Peter B. Hales, *Silver Cities: The Photography of American Urbanization, 1839-1915* (Philadelphia: Temple University Press, 1984), 163. The National Child Labor Committee apparently supplied copies of Hine's Georgia child labor photographs to the *Atlanta Georgian*, which reprinted them without attribution during its 1914 anti-child labor campaign. The photographs published in the *Child Labor Bulletin* 2 (August 1913): 24, and 3 (February 1915): 35, appeared in the *Atlanta Georgian*, June 29, 1914, 1.

63. Alan Trachtenberg, *Reading American Photographs: Images as History, Mathew Brady to Walker Evans* (New York: Hill and Wang, 1989), 168; Fulton Bag and Cotton Mill Strike Photograph Album, Meany Archives (quote); Kuhn, "Images of Dissent," 3-6; *Atlanta Georgian*, June 25, 1914, 1.

64. Trachtenberg, *Reading American Photographs*, 227-28 (first quote); Fulton Bag and Cotton Mill Strike Photograph Album, Meany Archives (second quote).

65. Operative 12, July 25, 1914, box 2, file 16; Operative 39, July 25, 1914, box 2, file 17; Operative 39, July 26, 1914, box 2, file 17; Operative 12, July 26, 1914, box 2, file 16; Operative 15, August 1, 1914, box 2, file 18; Operative 39, August 1, 1914, box 2, file 17; R. H. Wright to Harry G. Preston, September 23, 1914, box 1, file 6 (first quote); Operative 16, December 27, 1914, box 3, file 31 (second quote), Fulton Mills Papers. The International Order of the King's Daughters and Sons was a charity organization to which Smith was devoted. Founded in 1886, it was a nondenominational, interracial organization, which in 1887 admitted men as members. The Atlanta circle was probably doing relief work among the strikers.

66. Depositions of Defendant, 4. See also Mrs. O. L. Smith v. Edgar B. Smith, Divorce Suit, Fulton Superior Court, September Term, 1915, August 27, 1915; and Mrs. O. L. Smith v. Edgar B. Smith, Divorce Suit 34067, Fulton County Superior Court, August 27, 1915, Fulton County Courthouse, Atlanta, Ga. The evidence indicates that Smith was not having an affair with a Pat Calahan. It is possible, however, that she was involved with Almond A. Cook, the man she eventually married. Almond Cook to O. Delight Smith, May 18, 1917, box 3,

folder 2, Cook Papers. When the Smiths' case went to court in August 1915, Edgar was no longer being represented by Rosser, Brandon, Slaton, and Phillips.

67. *Atlanta Georgian,* January 19, 1917, 8 (first quote); Petition of Mrs. O. L. Smith, August 3, 1915, Superior Court of Fulton County, Fulton County Courthouse, Atlanta, Ga. (remaining quotes). For evidence that Smith probably did play a role in getting his wife fired, see E. B. Smith to American Federation of Labor, November 29, 1914, vol. 401, Frank Morrison Letterbooks, Perkins Library, Duke University, Durham, N.C.

68. Foreman's report, Mrs. Ola L. Smith v. Edgar B. Smith, January 18, 1917; Mrs. O. L. Smith v. E. B. Smith, Petition for Divorce, and Cross-bill by deft. and second verdict for defendant upon his cross-bill in Fulton Superior Court, June 7, 1917, Fulton County Superior Court, Fulton County Courthouse, Atlanta, Ga. According to state law, three terms of court were necessary in divorce actions. The court impaneled a special jury for each term of court. Absolute divorce was granted only on the verdict of two concurring juries; the second jury determined the rights of the parties and could impose "disability of remarriage on the guilty part." Disabilities could be removed in subsequent proceedings. Franklyn Hudgings, *What Everybody Should Know about the Law of Marriage and Divorce* (New York: New Century Company, 1935), 23; Orville A. Park, *Civil Code,* vol. 2 of *Park's Annotated Code of the State of Georgia* (Atlanta: Harrison, 1918); *Atlanta Georgian,* January 8, 1917, 3, January 19, 1917, 8.

69. Frank Morrison to Mrs. E. B. Smith, October 20, 1914, vol. 397; Smith to Morrison, November 28, 1914, vol. 401, Morrison Letterbooks; Strike Committee to Frank Morrison, November 28, 1914, vol. 401 (quote), Morrison Letterbooks. A month later, Golden fired Charles Miles as well.

70. *Journal of Labor,* June 12, 1914, 7.

71. Almond A. Cook to O. Delight Smith, n.d. [Spring 1918], box 3, folder 2, Cook Papers (first quote); *Oregon Journal,* March 23, 1950, section 2, 10, January 24, 1956, 3, December 17, 1958, 10b; *Oregon Labor Press,* December 12, 1958, 1; *The Oregonian,* December 7, 1958, 37, December 18, 1958, 13 (second quote); O. Delight Cook, untitled, undated speech, box 3, folder 9, Cook Papers (third quote). Smith's phoenixlike rise in the West places her in the broad and continuous tradition of working-class women's activism documented by Annelise Orlect, *Common Sense and a Little Fire: Working-Class Women's Organizing in the Twentieth Century United States* (Chapel Hill: University of North Carolina Press, forthcoming). Orlect, who traces the careers of activists who came of age amid the radical ferment at the turn of the century and died or retired from the labor movement in the 1950s, argues that this tradition has been obscured by studies that focus on single decades rather than whole life trajectories.

In Pursuit of Power:
The Political Economy of Women's
Activism in Twentieth-Century Tampa

Nancy A. Hewitt

On September 21, 1920, Wallace Stovall, the editor of the *Tampa Morning Tribune,* decried the "unexpected and uncouth treatment of the white women of Tampa" by opponents of the proposed city charter. The attack was aimed most directly at the *Tribune's* journalistic rival, the *Tampa Daily Times,* which supported the existing system of electing councilmen by ward. Stovall granted that the registration of women to vote was newsworthy, but he cried foul when the *Times* embarrassed socially prominent and "home-loving" ladies by making fun of their anxiety at the registration office, ridiculing them as "potential candidates for the office of commission," and, worst of all, printing "the age of those offering to register." Such actions are "certainly indicative," argued Stovall, "that among a certain class the old-time chivalry, deference and honor, reverence and protection, which the Southern gentlemen throw about woman has decayed most lamentably." In explaining the ill-treatment of white women registrants, Stovall pointed to the opposition's concomitant deference to potential black voters. As evidence, he noted, "Not one negro woman of Tampa has been embarrassed or humiliated by having cheap fun poked at her" in the *Times.* "Can it be that the opposition knows it can count on Negro women's vote to help defeat the charter . . . adoption of which means a cleaner Tampa, a better governed Tampa, a Tampa such as we have dreamed of?"[1]

The local battle over ward-based versus city commission government had raged for several years. Commission supporters wanted to reduce the power of African American and immigrant voters who, under the ward system, could influence the choice of representatives from racially homogeneous districts. In June 1920 a charter committee was finally elected through the white primary system. In July it proposed replacing the ward-based city council with a commission, all five members of which would be elected at large. They scheduled a binding referendum for October. Then on August 26 Tennessee became the thirty-sixth state to ratify the Nineteenth Amendment to the Constitution, granting women suffrage. Though the Florida legislature did not ratify the amendment until 1969, the state's Democratic party chairman immediately began urging white women to register to counterbalance the feared influx of their black counterparts. By September Tampa officials had been informed by the state's attorney that the charter issue could not be resolved through the white Democratic primary but must be introduced to the general electorate and that women would be eligible to participate.[2]

Overnight, Tampa civic leaders traded in their antisuffrage posture for paeans to "intelligent" womanhood and simultaneously inserted racist diatribes directed at African American voters and their white "collaborators." Over the next month, each side accused the other of courting black ballots, and each side worked vigorously to attract white female support. City officials aided in the effort to recruit women voters by assuring local residents that blacks would be assigned to separate lines at the polling places, thereby forestalling fears of racial mingling. Women themselves joined the battle. Mrs. Amos (Julia) Norris, for example, a sixth-generation Tampan and past president of the Florida United Daughters of the Confederacy, spoke "eloquently" on behalf of the proposed charter and, pointing to the heavy registration of Negro women, "emphasized the necessity of white women to accept it as their duty to register and vote since equal suffrage is now the policy of the country."[3]

The white women fulfilled their duty. On October 20 the *Tribune* headline blared, "Charter Wins by 770, Commission Plan Triumphant Despite a High Vote Cast Against in the Town's Black Belt." The story credited the victory to white women who recognized "that it was largely a contest between their votes and those of negroes" and that the new charter provided "a weapon by means of which they could protect their homes and children." "Tampa women," the report concluded, "have shown they are able to rock the cradle and the politicians at the same time."[4]

As part of the mosaic of difference being crafted by those studying the intersection of race, class, and gender, the Tampa case helps us plot the differential effects of political change on black and white women in the South. It demonstrates how white women wielded their power in support of seemingly progressive reforms that in practice often muted the voices of their black neighbors. It reminds us, moreover, that the enfranchisement of white women occurred in the aftermath of the disfranchisement of black men across the South and that such timing doubly victimized black women.[5]

Looking beneath the rhetoric, however, it becomes clear that the real battle was not between white and black women but between local party factions composed of white men. This was a struggle for control of not just politics but also profits—from bars, brothels, and bolita (a Cuban numbers game) based in the Latin enclave of Ybor City. In posing the conflict as one between white and Negro women, male opponents offered up a racialized and sexualized landscape of fear familiar across the South. Such a black and white portrait obscured the racially variegated composition of the city, for Tampa was not biracial but multiracial, linked as much to the Caribbean as to the cotton South. It was also a city characterized by political corruption on the level of that in other, mainly northern, metropolises with large immigrant populations. It was partly the desire to deny the centrality of the Latin connection in the city's political struggles that encouraged politicians to employ common southern shibboleths—white supremacy and intelligent womanhood—as vehicles for consolidating support.

During the 1920 charter fight, local politicians lavished attention on Anglo women and vigorously attacked African Americans, but they ignored their Latin counterparts, claiming that "very few Latin women voted, apparently taking little interest in government."[6] Yet if city fathers denied Latin women's significance in the electoral arena, they had long recognized them as the most effective among Tampa's women in pursuing power by other means. Having gained control over ballot boxes, bars, and brothels, city fathers struggled to assert their authority over the city's most important resource—Latin labor—by replacing Latin women and men with "American girls." On the very day that Tennessee legislators assured the ratification of the suffrage amendment, *Tobacco Leaf* (a manufacturers' journal) also declared a new day for women. Responding to a two-month strike in Tampa led by the male-dominated cigar packers' union, the *Leaf* assured its readers that "girl packers" from across the country were pouring into the "cigar city" and finding "working conditions superior to their expectations." These young Anglo women, "earning twice as much as they have been accustomed" to, were declared the wave of the future by both leading manufacturers and local politicians.[7]

Yet the wave proved insufficient to dislodge union solidarity. As the charter fight threatened to overtake union demands in the minds of Anglo and African American residents, Latin women and children regained center stage by leading the "biggest labor parade ever seen in Tampa." As politicians sought support from local voters, strikers sought assistance from workers nationwide. When the charter battle came to a close in October, workers called a mass meeting to confirm their commitment to continuing the strike.[8]

If it was illegal profits from bolita that fostered political corruption and shaped citywide politics in the electoral arena, it was conflict over legal profits from the cigar industry that fostered labor exploitation and union militancy in the Latin districts. Political corruption *and* labor exploitation—and the racial injustice inhering in each—pulled women from all racial and ethnic groups into public activism in Tampa, leading to the creation of new political agendas, institutions, and discourses. By examining the different political and economic agendas of Anglo, African American, and Latin women in 1920 and the ways in which these were inscribed and characterized by city fathers, Latin unionists, and women themselves, we can illuminate more fully the connections and contradictions between representation and mobilization, moral rhetoric and material needs, electoral power and economic justice.

To make sense of the events of 1920, we must step back into late nineteenth-century Tampa. In 1886 the establishment of the cigar industry had begun attracting Cubans, Spaniards, and Italians to the city, and by the 1890s local residents were becoming keenly aware of the complicated mix of race, class, and gender identities that boomtown life offered. In the summer of 1898 the encampment of African American and white soldiers in Tampa before the U.S. invasion of Cuba resulted in a tirade of racist epithets and, on June 6, the city's first race riot. A year later, however, when cigarmakers entered a float in the local Labor Day parade featuring an Afro-Cuban "Queen of Labor" and white Cuban attendants, the *Tribune* simply reported it as "somewhat of a startling innovation."[9]

At the time of the 1899 parade, Anglo Tampans were willing to look the other way, cheered by the economic prosperity provided by cigar manufacturing and by the U.S.-Cuban victory over Spain, but the glow of military alliances and industrial profits faded quickly as labor militancy and "race suicide" seemed to threaten the political, economic, and social hierarchy. By the turn of the century, native-born whites comprised only 44 percent of Tampa's population, while the foreign-born (white, black, and mulatto) totaled 32 percent and African Americans another 24 percent.[10] In this context, the repeated characterization of Latin workers as a race, usually as "an excitable and undependable race," suggested the ease with which local Anglos could translate ethnic difference, particularly among the working classes, into racial antagonism.[11] Such translations were facilitated by the race suicide rhetoric promulgated by Tampa's favorite military hero, Teddy Roosevelt, who lent national sanction to local prejudices. One of the darkest images of Latins came from an officer in the Rough Riders, who, while stationed in Cuba, characterized the island's residents as "a treacherous, lying, cowardly, thieving, worthless, half-breed mongrel . . . born of a mongrel spawn of Europe, crossed upon the fetiches of darkest Africa and aboriginal America."[12]

Paternalistic constructions of local Latins as "fun-loving" and "colorful" were generally more popular among Tampans, who preferred not to see their future as a choice between race suicide and economic suicide; they were after all dependent on this "mongrel race" for the labor that fueled the factories in this one-industry town. Such paternalistic characterizations, along with Anglos' long-standing belief in the sexual desires and desirability of Caribbean women, allowed, indeed encouraged, their investment in bars, brothels, and bolita in Ybor City.[13] Manuel Suarez, a Spaniard, is credited with introducing bolita into the community in the late 1880s. In Cuba the game functioned under the auspices of the state as the Cuban National Lottery, but in Tampa it flourished as part of a free enterprise system of gambling and graft. Bolita was closely connected with the saloon trade, and by 1900 there were more taverns in Ybor City than in all the rest of Tampa. Soon bolita games were being run from grocery stores and coffeehouses as well as from lavish gambling emporiums, such as the El Dorado Club, which also housed prostitutes. The clubs were generally owned and managed by Spaniards (as were the cigar factories) and "protected" by Anglo politicians and police. After the passage of prohibition, bootlegging was added to bolita and brothels as a source of enormous profits and payoffs. Anglo sheriffs, county commissioners, mayors, and newspaper editors were all linked to the system, alongside newer Italian and older Spanish and Cuban immigrants.

In 1912 the *Jacksonville Dixie*—a reform paper—proclaimed, "Tampa is reeking in crime, and gamblers in the open operate in various parts of the city. . . . " The king of crime in the city, the report claimed, was Charlie Wall, descendant of prominent pioneer political families and brother of circuit court judge Perry Wall.[14] In 1916 the *Tribune* accused rival editor D. B. McKay of being the beneficiary of Wall's machine through gambling connections and vote fraud. McKay, married to the daughter of one of the largest cigar manufacturers, was then serving his second term as mayor of the city and running for a third. His victory that year, dependent on ballots cast in Ybor City's Sixth and Seventh wards, inspired the formation of the coalition that finally effected charter reform in 1920.

The most ardent opposition to political corruption and gambling in Ybor City came not from Anglo editors and reformers, however, but from Latin labor leaders. *El Internacional,* the journal of the cigarmakers' union, continually crusaded against organized crime, claiming that bolita only served to immiserate the workers. Still, most workers were less concerned with eradicating bolita or bars than with improving shop-floor conditions. Of those who sought change, few viewed the electoral arena as a likely vehicle for reform. Florida's poll tax and residency requirements discouraged immigrants as well as African Americans from registering. Indeed, far more blacks than Latins registered to vote in early twentieth-century Tampa. African American registration peaked in 1920 when 18.5 percent of local blacks signed up to vote, including nearly 22 percent of newly enfranchised black women.[15] Though no separate registration figures exist for Latins in 1920, in 1910 fewer than 10 percent of the city's adult Cubans and Spaniards and fewer than 3 percent of adult Italians were citizens. By 1930 Tampa ranked at the bottom of American cities with over 100,000 population in terms of the percentage of foreign-born adults who had acquired citizenship and thus voting privileges; Latin women were even less likely than their male kin to become citizens.[16]

Still, during strikes in 1901, 1910, 1919, and 1920–21, these same immigrants—women and men, Italians and Cubans, white Cubans and Afro-Cubans—demonstrated their power to reshape the city's political and economic agenda. In the midst of strikes, for instance, warring Anglo politicians were forced temporarily to suspend their factionalism and join forces. In 1910 Wallace Stovall called for action by the "best citizens of Tampa" and warned "agitators to understand they will not have the [police] officers alone to deal with, but an organization of determined citizens."[17] McKay and his supporters promptly forgot old political rivalries and joined the newest citizens' committee. Even without wielding the ballot, Latin workers could disrupt politics as usual in the city.

Political leaders returned the favor by using citizens' committees to create crises in union ranks. These committees appeared during every major strike from 1901 to 1931. Drawing support from members of the Anglo-dominated Board of Trade and the Spanish-dominated Cigar Manufacturers' Association (the latter founded in response to a successful cigar strike in 1899), the committees used vagrancy laws, violence, and evictions to disrupt union ranks. During October 1910 such vigilante groups broke up gatherings of workers, sacked the offices of *El Internacional* and the Labor Temple, assisted in the arrest of union leaders, and closed down worker-run soup kitchens. Yet having declared on October 20 that "the backbone of the strike was broken," Anglo civic leaders and cigar manufacturers faced three more months of working-class resistance.[18]

In the final months of the strike, more activities were orchestrated by women as their male comrades fell victim to arrests and deportations. A typical scene that November found a group of Italian women gathered near the Arguelles factory to keep strikebreakers out. Six were arrested, and each was fined fifty dollars by Judge E. B. Drumright, who claimed that though the women were probably "enticed" to do what they did "by someone behind [them]," they must be punished the same as "any other violator of the law." Soon after, a circle of twenty-eight Cuban and Italian women strikers published a manifesto declaring that women held the "premiere place in class struggle." Calling on the legacies of Joan of Arc, Louise Michel, and the Spanish syndicalist Teresa Claramunt, they proclaimed, "It is our duty" to protest against those "who degrade our sons," for degradation of them "is degradation of us."[19]

Though the 1910 strikers were finally defeated, over the next decade the rising tide of women in the cigar labor force became increasingly critical to union success. And Latin women were not alone. In the decade preceding the charter vote, Tampa women from all race, class, and ethnic groups pursued power in increasingly public ways and with increasingly well-articulated political and economic agendas. Collectively, they demonstrated a new sophistication regarding political action that drew on a range of resources—the Latin heritage of labor militancy, northern models of social housekeeping and the social gospel, African American and Latin traditions of self-help and mutual aid, newly won political rights, and popular ideals of the New Woman. Anglo, African American, and Latin women each developed autonomous organizations and institutions in this period, and they joined more visibly and vocally in efforts promoted by the men of their communities.

Such an extended burst of female activism on the eve of women's enfranchisement may have made some men wary of furthering the formal political clout of their sisters. Moreover, such recognition of women's heightened influence in the public sphere occurred at a moment when male civic leaders were already anxious about female autonomy in other areas of life. During July and August of 1920, for instance, articles and advertisements in the *Tribune* evidenced a certain unease with changing gender roles: "Shall women propose?" asked one editorial; "Woman believes man a better husband if he knows some other females," claimed a feature story; "Has 'undressing' reached the limit?" queried a full-page clothing ad.[20]

Still, throughout the summer local business and political leaders were far more concerned with strikers' solidarity than with women's emancipation. Once woman suffrage was granted, the focus shifted to the charter battle and concerns about "what the woman voter [will] do with her newly acquired rights and privileges." In the two most threatening scenarios, male politicians and editors envisioned black women flocking to the polls and their white counterparts forming "a party run and managed by women only."[21]

To quiet their gravest fears, many civic leaders eagerly sought to bring women under the control of a male-dominated electoral system. They praised the continued involvement of wives and mothers in church and charitable activities, and they reiterated and sought to reinforce women's supposedly natural inclination for consumption by running such features as the three-page "news" story on the opening of Cracowaner's, "Florida's biggest and best equipped exclusive woman's shopping emporium."[22] At the same time, male party leaders applauded white women's "intelligent interest in public affairs," evidenced in the educational campaigns under-taken by the local Business and Professional Women's Club and women's attendance at meetings arranged for them by local Democratic and Republican officials.[23] They also assured each other that women *would* "affiliate with one of the two old parties in this country" and that the new type of woman in politics "is not afraid to be charming. She works with, not against, men."[24]

The dynamics of sexual politics were changing within Latin and black as well as Anglo communities in Tampa in the years preceding the passage of the Nineteenth Amendment. The issues and timing varied by race, class, and ethnicity, but in each case a shift (or attempted shift) in the balance of public power between women and men occurred *before* women gained voting rights. One key event was a brief strike in 1916, which proved as unsettling to Latin union leaders as to their Spanish and Anglo foes. On November 10 women tobacco strippers from the Lozano and Sidelo Company walked out, demanding higher wages. They marched to other factories, calling out the workers, and by nightfall some fifteen hundred cigarmakers had left their benches and another eighty-five hundred threatened to join them. The spontaneity and militancy of the movement were recognized as the work of women. Factory owner Celestino Vega sought "protection" for his male rollers when they were accosted by a "disorderly mob of strikers," who "rushed into the factory deriding and hooting workers. . . . women, leading the mob, called the men at work 'females' and offered their skirts to those who refused to quit." Mayor McKay assured Vega that police would be on hand the next day to secure the premises and protect the male rollers.[25]

This strike was opposed by not only the factory owners and city fathers but also the male leaders of the cigarmakers' union. *El Internacional* derided the wildcat venture from the beginning and singled out women for their "blind enthusiasm." The Cuban editor asked his readers, "May a man now say what he thinks without exposing himself to the dangers of being insulted by his female comrades who offer him their skirts?"[26] The strike was soon settled, though the greatest benefits went to the cigar rollers (mostly men) rather than to the strippers (mainly women) who had initiated the action.

The 1916 walkout might be considered just an interesting anecdote if it stood alone; instead, it marks a turning point in the redefinition of women's public and political roles in the Latin community. In the 1901 and 1910 strikes Cuban and Italian women had become politically active—petitioning the governor and the Anglo wives of vigilantes and marching on the mayor's office—but they had justified their actions largely in the language of motherhood. Then in 1913-14 Luisa Capetillo, a working-class feminist and union organizer from Puerto Rico noted for dressing in men's clothing, arrived in Tampa. She achieved the unusual distinction of being hired as a reader in a cigar factory, the most prestigious position for a cigarworker and the most influential politically.[27] She spent a year organizing working women around a range of economic and political issues before moving on to Havana. Over the next several years, two local socialist women, Mrs. A. Kossovsky and Mrs. José De La Campa, published frequent letters in *El Internacional* that combined demands for workers' and women's rights.

It was in this context that the women wildcatters of 1916 chose sexual ridicule over maternal rhetoric as a means of "inspiring" their male coworkers. At the same time, domesticity became the practical basis for organizing consumer protests rather than the rhetorical justification for women's extra-domestic militancy. In the late 1910s some two dozen food and clothing cooperatives were founded in Ybor City in which women held positions of leadership. In 1915 Cuban and Italian housewives mobilized against an ordinance that threatened to increase the price of bread, and in 1917 they sustained a potato, meat, and onion boycott.[28]

Then in 1919 they organized a rent strike, just as Latin workers walked out as part of a nationwide wave of cigar strikes. This time, however, male labor leaders recognized the importance of women's support and refused to accept a settlement that would have raised wages for the most skilled workers, mainly men, leaving the "clerks, strippers, and banders [mostly women], to 'paddle their own canoe.'" Claiming that "labor will ever be subservient . . . so long as they stand divided," union leaders gradually accepted women as more equal partners in the public realm.[29]

The same appears to be true in the African American community, though here the evidence is more fragmentary. From the 1880s until the early 1900s, most information related to organizing in the black community recounts the activities of men; from then on, women receive at least as much and often more attention as public advocates for community self-help.[30] For African Americans, the turning point may have been 1908, when Z. D. Greene, a black lawyer, attempted to run for municipal judge. After obtaining sufficient signatures to place his name on the ballot, Greene was informed the night before the filing deadline that his petition had been lost. The city council then resolved that only original petitions would be accepted. After unsuccessfully seeking a resolution with the council, Greene petitioned the circuit court, asking that the city be forced to place his name on the ballot. Greene lost his bid to become the first black candidate in Tampa when Judge Perry Wall found that Greene was guilty of neglect for delaying his appeal for ten days, and he dismissed the case. In the aftermath of the Greene case, white civic leaders organized the White Municipal party (Judge Wall was selected as chair of the executive committee), and within two years they instituted the white primary system for all elections.[31]

At the same time that Z. D. Greene was challenging white city councilmen for political office, Clara Frye, a black nurse, was seeking their support for medical services. Clara Frye converted her home into a hospital as segregation closed other facilities to needy blacks. With support from the black community, local white physicians, the city's white and black women's clubs, and, after 1921, the Urban League, the Clara Frye Hospital served the African American community for four decades. It was the first of several health care, childcare, and educational institutions founded by local black women in the 1910s and 1920s, the period when they also first entered the electoral arena.[32]

The leading black club woman in this period was Blanche Armwood, the daughter of Tampa's first black sheriff, who graduated at age fifteen from Atlanta's Spelman Seminary. In 1915 she founded the School of Household Arts, funded by Tampa Gas Company, a program that continued under the auspices of the Colored Women's Clubs of Tampa. As head of one of only eight such citywide federations in the country, Armwood (later Armwood Beatty) became active in Republican politics and the National Association of Colored Women's Clubs, traveling the country on behalf of congressional candidates and woman suffrage.

During her extended absences from the city in the late 1910s, a small circle of black teachers, cooks, and businesswomen took the lead in community organizing. Christine Meachem, principal of Harlem Academy; Emma Mance, a teacher at the West Tampa School; hairdressers Gertrude Chambers, Lila Robinson, and Annie House; and Preston Murray, the wife of a prominent local undertaker, were among the most active club women in Tampa during the 1910s and 1920s. Aware of movements elsewhere, these club women voiced concern about the "forces among our own people and outside of the Black community [which] tend to humiliate and destroy" black womanhood.[33] They also were aware of more positive developments and eagerly embraced an African American version of the New Woman that emphasized cultural pride and civic activism.

Like her white counterpart, the African American New Woman was encouraged to adopt new fashions in clothing, hair care, and cosmetics. In 1920 the African-American Beauty Culture Association held its national meeting in Tampa, and many local black hairdressers attended. These women were not substituting fashion for uplift; rather, they were using the business prospects offered by the former to fund the latter. At the time of the convention, Chambers, Robinson, and House—all of whom worked in the same shop—served as officers in three local black women's clubs; three years later they helped to found the Helping Hand Day Nursery, which provided services for African American children. The director of the day nursery was Inez Alston, a teacher who gained recognition throughout Tampa when she presided over a series of debates on the city charter held in black churches during the fall of 1920. She and other black club women had become charter members of the Urban League in 1921, along with Blanche Armwood Beatty, who served as the local league's first executive secretary.

Perhaps, then, the concern voiced by white civic leaders about the potential political power of black women was not simply a convenient trope for inspiring racial fears and inducing white women to vote. Moreover, male charter advocates might have inadvertently recognized—if only to denigrate—the economic plight of local African American women (over 53 percent of whom were in the paid labor force in 1920) when they charged that those opposing the charter were trying to overcome the white women's vote "by the suffrage of the purchaseable colored women of the city."[34] Of the 1,298 black women who registered to vote in 1920 (over 60 percent of the total black registrants, including Afro-Caribbeans), many came to the polls having already pursued power through voluntarist channels for more than a decade.[35]

Awareness of such activism in African American neighborhoods and its potential for upsetting the racial status quo helps explain why so many Anglos, already in control of elections through the white primary, still felt it necessary to dilute minority voting power further through at-large elections. These fears of black political power, aroused even before woman suffrage was passed, ensured that white civic leaders would rush to enlist the electoral aid of their female counterparts immediately upon their enfranchisement.

White women, of course, were already publicly active. A few of the 2,462 white women who registered in 1920 (32 percent of all whites registered to vote that year, including Latins categorized as white) could trace their careers back to the 1880s and 1890s.[36] Beginning in 1886 white women in Tampa had founded an array of organizations and institutions like those in other large urban areas. The Woman's Christian Temperance Union, the Emergency Hospital, the Children's Home, the Working Woman's Mission, the Old People's Home, the Day Nursery Association, the Tampa Woman's Club, the Tampa Civic Association, and the Door of Hope Rescue Home were all in place a decade before women won the vote. Several of these organizations undertook explicitly political work, even though they shied away from advocating suffrage. The Tampa Woman's Club, for instance, hosted a speech by William Jennings Bryan in 1900, and a coalition of white women's organizations campaigned throughout the 1910s for state legislation to raise the age of sexual consent, institute social purity and child labor laws, and mandate prohibition.[37]

In 1916, when female tobacco strippers initiated the first woman-led walkout, Anglo women activists had just completed campaigning for the first woman school board member, who ran as a candidate in District Two, which included Ybor City. A year earlier the Florida legislature had passed a Municipal Reform Act that allowed for local option on a number of electoral matters.[38] Neighboring cities, including St. Petersburg, had instituted municipal suffrage for women; Tampa did not, so women remained dependent on male voters to make their case. Yet in the context of their previous years of public activity, they agreed that it was time to adopt a more explicitly electoral agenda. They learned a valuable lesson. When the votes in the school board election were counted, Alice (Mrs. Fred) Snow had lost to the Reverend Irwin Walden by only fifteen out of the nearly four thousand votes cast, the margin of defeat provided by a set of contested ballots from Ybor City's Twenty-sixth Precinct.[39]

Women entered no more electoral races until 1920. In 1917, however, a statewide suffrage meeting was held in Tampa, after which twenty-one local women, including Mrs. Snow, organized an Equal Suffrage League. At the founding meeting, held in the council chamber at city hall, the members elected Mrs. I. O. (Ada) Price to the presidency and agreed to circulate petitions to be sent to Florida's delegation in Congress urging passage of the Nineteenth Amendment.[40]

The Equal Suffrage League received little public notice over the next two years, but as soon as the suffrage amendment was ratified, white club women met to discuss their new responsibilities. Led by the president, Mrs. D. B. (Annie) Givens, the members of the Tampa Woman's Club seemingly overnight published a pamphlet entitled *An Open Forum on Our Government for Women Voters.* This served as the basis for a series of meetings designed to prepare women to cast their first ballots. Ada Price, presiding over one of these gatherings, noted that both Democrats and Republicans now claimed the honor of having produced suffrage for women. She warned her partisan male counterparts, however, that "neither party has us roped and branded . . . and they will never get us gagged."[41]

Women spoke out on both sides of the charter debate. Several dozen joined the newly formed Commission Government Club to promote passage of the proposed charter, including Julia Norris and Mrs. R. G. (Minnie) Albury, a prominent Tampa club woman. Others became members of the Home Rule Club, opposing the change. Prominent among them were Kate Jackson, founder of the all-female Tampa Civic Association, and Annie Givens, whose husband was the city's street and sidewalk inspector.[42] Throughout October white women organized, attended, and spoke at dozens of political meetings and rallies on both sides. When the charter passed and elections for city commissioners were announced, Julia Norris—who had teamed up with Judge Drumright and Minnie Albury in a series of procommission speeches presented at black churches —placed her name in nomination. Though some white club women thought placing a woman's name on the ballot so soon was "an unfortunate mistake," she stayed in the race, polling 957 out of over 22,000 votes cast.[43]

Even after women's formal entry into electoral politics, most white women continued to rely on voluntarism instead of voting as the best vehicle for promoting social reform in the city. This was partly because of the widespread corruption that often made voting in local elections meaningless until the 1950s and partly because of the array of perceived problems that seemed to defy electoral solutions, such as strikes. Even in the midst of the charter battle, Anglo women and men were as concerned about controlling Latin labor, this time through a combination of voluntarism and vigilantism, as they were about implementing a new system of municipal government.

The Anglos found the unity among the nearly eighty-seven hundred cigarworkers astounding. The union did not even bother to post pickets around the factories: "the committee says they don't need any as they have no fear that strikers will desert the ranks."[44] Such unity inspired extra-electoral activities among whites while the charter committee was completing its work. In July Mayor McKay, at the behest of Anglo women leaders, offered the Children's Home as a refuge for the children of strikers. The workers rejected the offer, refusing to "leave [their] children to the tender mercy of men [or women] who will try to squeeze the lifeblood out of [us] while living."[45] The links between Anglo women reformers and cigar manufacturers were all too clear to Latin laborers. Mayor McKay was married to the daughter of a Spanish factory owner; the Children's Home, after a devastating fire the previous year, was

located in a refurbished cigar factory; one of the vice presidents of the
Children's Home was Mrs. Celestino Vega, whose husband's factory had
been raided by unruly women four years earlier; and several board
members had petitioned the state the previous year for a compulsory
education statute with the intention of forcing stricter enforcement of
child labor laws in Ybor City.

Moreover, families who needed assistance had an array of more palat-
able alternatives, most of which had been created by the collective efforts
of Latin women and men. The union, as in previous strikes, offered
monetary benefits, soup kitchens, and moral support; the local Labor
Temple provided a place where strikers could meet to exchange not only
information but also food, clothing, and other necessities of life. During
the 1920 battle, in which the key issue was the closed shop, local
branches of the Cigar Makers International Union—representing packers,
pickers, rollers, banders, and stemmers—each appointed one representative to the Committee of Public Health to coordinate relief efforts. The
vice president of the committee was Elizabeth Law, head of the tobacco
stemmers union.[46] The committee received donations not only from
Latin shopkeepers and community leaders but also from union locals
across the country.[47]

Individual strikers could also seek help from one of the several mutual
aid societies located in Ybor City and West Tampa. Centro Asturiano, for
instance, founded in 1902, offered meeting rooms, medical services,
emergency relief, and recreational activities for children throughout the
strike. The church-sponsored missions and settlement houses in the Latin
enclaves provided another source of support, with the Methodists alone
opening five Cuban and two Italian missions, a clinic, and two settlement
houses by 1920. Here urban missionaries, many of them women, offered
day nurseries, sewing classes, medical assistance, mother's clubs, and
recreational facilities to local Latin families.[48]

On October 14, 2,500 to 3,000 striking workers, "about 50 per cent of
them women, crowded the Centro Asturiano Club house to the doors" for
a mass meeting called by the Committee of Public Health. Mutual aid
society officers and missionaries joined the ranks of those eager to hear
the remarks of José Rojo, secretary of the Havana branch of the Federation of Labor. Assuring the strikers of the "hearty support" of their Cuban
compatriots, Rojo turned the platform over to a stream of speakers,
including Mrs. Candida Bustamente, a widow who roomed with the cigar
bander Maria Cosa. Perhaps she was the "old lady," described by an *El
Internacional* reporter, who "electrified" the audience. Combining traditional paeans to women's familial roles with recognition of their new
militancy, she declared, "We, the wives and mothers, must choose to die,

together with our children and our husbands, rather than submit to the unparalleled condition of servitude which the manufacturers impose upon us."[49] Though "no vote was taken," the *Tribune* reported that the participants demonstrated their support for the leaders of the strike and their confidence in achieving victory.[50]

During the following week, as the day for the charter vote approached, local newspapers avoided further coverage of the strike. Candida Busta-mente, however, gained the *Tribune's* attention again on October 20, when she presented a report on the activities of the Methodist Women's Home Missionary societies of Ybor City and West Tampa to the Latin District Conference of the Methodist Church.[51] Still, most of the space that day was devoted to the victory for charter reform. For several days the *Tribune* and the *Tampa Daily Times* devoted column after column to analyses of the charter vote and women's role in the outcome.

The *Tribune* claimed that "out of 2,999 votes cast against the charter, 1,976 were cast by Negroes and Latins leaving but 1,023 white Ameri-cans in Tampa who voted against the adoption of the charter. In other words, out of a white American vote of approximately 3,100, only 1,023 voted against the adoption of the charter. A three to *one* majority."[52] Discounting the votes of African Americans and Latins (men and women), Anglo city leaders could reassure themselves of their continued control of the city. They did not dismiss the importance of their Anglo sisters, however, noting that the high registration totals for the charter election were largely due to "the advent of women into politics and to the negro registration." White women, a *Tribune* reporter claimed, were so eager to participate on election day that they "brought their babies with them in many instances to the polls." Moreover, civic leaders tried to reassure them-selves that even among Latins and Negroes, "the better and more intelligent . . . the higher class, better informed, honest set . . . helped to win the election by counterbalancing the votes" of the "idle and worthless."[53]

Of course, the *Tribune* reporters could only guess at how any group of city residents had actually voted. They based such speculations partly on wishful thinking—wanting to believe that most white women and "honest" Latins and blacks had followed the path to the polls carved out for them by white procharter men. They also analyzed vote totals from precincts throughout the city. The largest number of black registrants, for instance, lived in Precinct Two and Nine, which were among the three areas with the highest anticharter vote margins. (The third was Precinct Twelve in Ybor City.) The highest procharter margins came from precincts Three, Five, and Eighteen, where white women had registered in particularly large numbers. Indeed, in Precinct Five, including sections of Tampa's affluent Hyde Park neighborhood, white women constituted nearly half of the registrants and reportedly turned out in larger numbers than did men on election day. Only two African Americans, one man and one woman, were on the registration lists in that precinct, and they may not have been among the 825 individuals who participated in the balloting.[54]

It was thus with some basis in fact that the newspapers applauded the "efficiency and intelligence" of white women who cast their first ballots. They still could not resist poking fun at the length of time it took women to vote—up to three hours if you included the hours it took a woman to get ready to go out to the polling place. Still, city fathers had to admit that the "number of women voting was larger than expected in many precincts." Hafford Jones, an inspector in predominantly white Precinct Seventeen, declared that "the women had voted 99 percent strong in that precinct and that he believed the women of the city deserved great credit for the way they had taken hold of things. He thought that at least one member of the city commission should be a woman."[55] Perhaps he was among those voting for Julia Norris in November.

African American voters, including women, received more vituperative coverage. Amos Norris—a leading merchant, husband of the commission candidate, and an inspector in heavily black Precinct Nine—claimed that the "worst class of negroes imaginable were present." Norris rejected the ballot of a black man, who purportedly gave the wrong address, and of several black women who he thought "were under age." He also swore out a warrant against "Julia Sacio, negress," for "paying off" voters at his polling station. Throughout the city, it was reported, "a large number of negroes had been systematically herded into the registration and poll tax offices by a negro policeman, and it is presumed that all of these voted against the charter." In addition, the members of the "old political ring" were accused of "forgetting their color and standing in life sufficiently as to engage in taking negro men and women to the polling places."[56] Despite more than a decade of local organizing by African Americans for voting rights, economic justice, and social services, Anglo civic leaders rejected the possibility that black women and men might justifiably pursue political power on their own terms.

Latin women, too, pursued power for their own reasons, but for them the ballot box held little interest. On November 2, for instance, as women and men in other sections of the city turned out to vote in the national presidential election, members of the union's Committee of Public Health launched a publicity campaign. They sought to offset a series of lurid stories appearing in the local press that they believed were intended "to stir up mob spirit among the people of Tampa."[57] On November 6 American Federation of Labor unions around the country participated in a "National Donation Day" in support of Tampa cigarworkers. The

Tribune ignored the effort, focusing instead on the activities of the White Municipal party in selecting a slate of candidates for the city commission. Still, perhaps in reaction to the nationwide outpouring of union support, Wallace Stovall did entitle his November 7 editorial "Bring It to an End at Once." In it, he claimed that "the willing and needy industrious workers have been forced to lie idle" by "trouble-makers" who are only interested in taking home their union paycheck.[58]

In the years following the 1920 charter vote, both Latin and African American women became more active in the public sphere, in their own communities and throughout the city. They founded more schools, day nurseries, and clinics. Latin women formed auxiliaries within Centro Asturiano and other mutual aid societies to coordinate their fundraising efforts and increase their influence over society policies. Black women expanded their base within the Urban League while continuing their activities in separate women's clubs and in the churches and schools. Increasing numbers of African American women also took jobs in the cigar factories; indeed, according to the *Tampa Citizen*, a local labor paper, it was African American, not Anglo, women who had entered cigar packer ranks during the 1920 strike. Manufacturers' hopes of filling up the cigar benches with white "American girls" were "swiftly fleeting," claimed the *Citizen*, since "American girls cannot be secured as long as they are forced to work at the same benches with negro girls."[59]

Latin women were more willing to work alongside African Americans in the factories or in public political efforts. Throughout the 1920s increasingly strong alliances were formed between Latin and black women in Tampa, particularly between African American and Afro-Cuban women activists. The Helping Hand Day Nursery, for instance, opened its doors to Afro-Cuban children in 1923, and for the next decade many of the Day Nursery's fundraising and social events were held in the Union Martí-Maceo, the Afro-Cuban clubhouse in Ybor City. Although these groups maintained distinct identities, members of the two communities continued to cooperate throughout the Great Depression and into the civil rights era.

The choice of allies, agendas, strategies, and priorities differed among Anglo, African American, and Latin women in Tampa, but women in each community pursued power in increasingly public ways. The year 1920 was pivotal, a moment when the efforts of women on behalf of political reform and economic justice were illuminated with special clarity under the glare of constitutional change and labor strife. When the charter vote occurred in late October, few Latin women turned out to vote, but thousands helped sustain the strike for another three months. They did vote on February 5, 1921, when the strike was finally declared over.[60] We do not know how women influenced the outcome of the vote to return to work, but we do know that the following fall women strippers initiated a general strike by walking out in protest over "short pay." When the union called a strike vote a few days later, the strippers proclaimed that they "would stay out on strike regardless of the outcome of the vote."[61] For Latin women, the ballot became—at least for a moment—an instrument for wielding power within workers' ranks rather than within the larger community.

For many Anglo women, particularly those who remembered that fraudulent ballots cast in the Latin precinct kept Mrs. Snow from office and who recognized that brothels and bolita were protected by the ward system, commission government seemed the best answer to Tampa's problems of political corruption. At the same time, such a system helped calm their fears of the rising tide of activism among their African American neighbors. Of course, the minority of native-born white women and the majority of African American women who backed the ward system did so not as a means of protecting bolita and bootlegging profits but in hopes of expanding the roles of women now that they finally had the opportunity to enter the electoral arena. Through ties with Anglo ward politicians, through cooperative efforts at civic reform, or through a recognition that ward politics increased the leverage of minority residents, anticharter women pursued power by supporting the political status quo.

Their failure in this attempt did not end their public efforts, but it assured that they would participate in electoral politics in addition to, not as a substitute for, voluntaristic efforts. At least for a few, this meant engaging in interracial organizing through the Urban League, where such diverse women as Blanche Armwood Beatty, Julia Norris, and Gertrude Chambers all found a political home in the early 1920s. At the same time, Anglo women activists invited more of their affluent Latin sisters—the wives of cigar factory owners and professionals—to join them on the boards of the Children's Home, the Hillsborough County Federation of Women's Clubs, and the Friday Morning Musicale.

As Anglo, African American, and Latin women moved into the public and political arena in Tampa in the decades before and after 1920, they found themselves working in distinct but overlapping circles of activity. So, too, did they find themselves responding to common images of womanhood and racially and economically specific representations of women's nature. Though the granting of woman suffrage in conjunction with the referendum on charter reform momentarily highlighted one form of female activism seemingly accessible to all women, the rhetoric surrounding the 1920 vote obscured as often as it illuminated women's pursuit of power. This was not only because white men sought to subsume their own power struggles within the battle between newly enfranchised white and black women but also because so many Tampa residents, black and white, accepted a definition of politics that was restricted to the electoral arena. At the same time, the emphasis within the Latin community on union solidarity generally obscured the gendered character of labor politics, representing women as either workers first and women second or as martyred wives and mothers supporting their union men.

The meanings behind such representations of women can be fully understood only by examining the actions and listening to the voices of women themselves. This does not eliminate the need to analyze representations, since women also offered complex visions of their public roles. Anglo women supporting the charter, for instance, presented themselves as part of the wave of progressive reform breaking over a benighted South. Only in the context of events in the African American and Latin communities can we see the ways that such social justice campaigns also reinforced the racial status quo. Similarly, the significance of the New Woman for female activism in Tampa can be fully comprehended only by examining the different uses to which it was put by Anglo and African American women with distinct economic and political agendas. For Latin women, the New Woman was perhaps best represented by the wildcatters of 1916. Yet in offering their skirts were these women denigrating femaleness as well as recalcitrant male workers, or were they following in the footsteps of Luisa Capetillo by removing their skirts to put on the pants? And how did the import of this action change when reported to the Latin community by *El Internacional* and to the Anglo community by the *Tampa Morning Tribune?*

The political economy of women's activism in Tampa, and in other cities as well, cannot be understood without comparing the organizations and campaigns of women in various racial, ethnic, and economic communities. For each group individually and for all collectively, the connections between images and actions, representation and mobilization, moral rhetoric and material needs were complex and always in flux. Only within the historically specific web of race, class, and gender relations that existed in Tampa can we understand what was political and for whom. It is only rooted in this understanding that we can comprehend how the various groups of women pursuing power—each in response to a different set of representations and material realities—reinforced barriers or created openings for themselves and each other regarding political access and economic justice.

NOTES

The author wishes to thank the faculty and graduate students at Duke University, and the participants in the Works-in-Progress Colloquium Series at the Afro-American Studies Center, Princeton University, for their interest and insights. A National Endowment for the Humanities Fellowship for College Teachers provided critical support as I began research for this study. Gary Mormino and George Pozzetta have generously shared their knowledge of early Tampa politics. Steven Lawson continues to improve my analysis by simultaneously challenging my approach to the study of politics and offering me his deft editorial touch.

1. *Tampa Morning Tribune,* September 21, 1920. The copy of the *Times* to which Stovall refers is unfortunately not available.

2. On charter battle, see Randy Gardner and Steven F. Lawson, "At-Large Elections and Black Voting in Tampa/Hillsborough County, 1910-1984," manuscript in author's possession; and *Tampa Morning Tribune* and the *Tampa Daily Times* for July through October 1920, especially July 24, August 25, and October 2, 6, 14, 20, and 21, 1920.

3. *Tampa Daily Times,* October 6, 1920. When introducing women into the story, I have used the form of the individual's name that most often appeared in the press, such as Mrs. Amos Norris. In parentheses I have supplied the other name by which the person was known locally.

4. *Tampa Morning Tribune,* October 20, 1920.

5. This is not to deny the important role that white women had in advancing progressive reforms in the South. One of the best analyses of white women's progressive use of the suffrage remains Anne Firor Scott, *The Southern Lady: From Pedestal to Politics, 1830-1930* (Chicago: University of Chicago Press, 1970), chap. 8. Still, the very definition of particular reforms as "progressive" was based on specific race, class, and gender experiences and assumptions.

6. *Tampa Morning Tribune,* October 20, 1920.

7. *Tobacco Leaf,* August 26 and September 23, 1920.

8. On workers efforts between August and October 1920, see, for example, *Tampa Morning Tribune,* September 7 and October 15, 1920; *Tampa Citizen,* November 12, 1920; *El Internacional,* September 10, 1920; and *Cigar Makers International Journal,* September 15, 1920.

9. On 1898 encampment, see Willard B. Gatewood, Jr., "Negro Troops in Florida, 1898," *Florida Historical Quarterly* 49 (July 1970): 1-15; on the Labor Day parade, see *Tampa Morning Tribune,* September 5, 1899.

10. U.S. Bureau of the Census, *Abstract of the Fourteenth Census of the United States* (Washington, D.C.: Government Printing Office, 1923), 114-15, 130-31.

11. On racial, ethnic, and class antagonisms in twentieth-century Tampa, see Robert P. Ingalls, *Urban Vigilantes in the New South, 1882-1936* (Knoxville: University of Tennessee Press, 1988); and Nancy A. Hewitt, " 'The Voice of Virile Labor': Labor Militancy, Community Solidarity and Gender Identity among Tampa's Latin Workers, 1880-1921," in *Work Engendered: Toward a New*

History of American Labor, ed. Ava Baron (Ithaca, N.Y.: Cornell University Press, 1991), 142–67.

12. A Fifth Army Corps officer, quoted in Louis A. Pérez, Jr., *Cuba between Empires, 1878–1902* (Pittsburgh: University of Pittsburgh Press, 1983), 206.

13. The following section on bolita and political corruption is based on Gary Mormino and George Pozzetta, "The Political Economy of Organized Crime, Bolita and Bootlegging in Tampa," n.d., manuscript in author's possession.

14. Charles E. Jones, "Sodom or Gomorrah—or Both," *Dixie,* June 27, 1912, quoted in Mormino and Pozzetta, "The Political Economy of Organized Crime," 417.

15. For registration figures, see *Tampa Morning Tribune,* October 18, 1920. For population figures, see U.S. Bureau of the Census, *Abstract of the Fourteenth Census of the United States, 1920,* 114-15, 130-31.

16. For figures on citizenship, see Mormino and Pozzetta, "The Political Economy of Organized Crime," 426.

17. *Tampa Morning Tribune,* October 17, 1910, quoted in Ingalls, *Urban Vigilantes,* 103. For membership and activities of the 1910 Citizens' Committee, see his chap. 4.

18. *Tampa Morning Tribune,* October 20, 1910. On the activities of citizens' committees in Tampa, see Ingalls, *Urban Vigilantes.*

19. *Tampa Morning Tribune,* November 16, 1901; "A Los Trabajadoras de Tampa," 1910, Labor Union Manifestos, microfilm of *El Internacional* and related papers, reel 1, University of South Florida, Tampa, Fla.

20. *Tampa Morning Tribune,* July 25, July 30, and August 14, 1920. These are only a few of many articles, editorials, features, and advertisements focused on changing gender roles during this period that appeared in both the *Tribune* and the *Tampa Daily Times.*

21. *Tampa Morning Tribune,* August 25, 1920; *Tampa Daily Times,* October 2, 1920. From August 25 through the coverage of the charter vote on October 20, the *Tribune* and *Times* ran far more articles on women and woman suffrage than on the strike, with a large number discussing the "problem" of Negro women voters. After October 20, with the strike in its fourth month, the papers refocused attention on Latin labor agitators.

22. See Social Scene and What's Happening Today columns in the *Tribune* throughout 1920; for the special feature on Cracowaner's store, see *Tampa Morning Tribune,* October 17, 1920.

23. See, for example, *Tampa Daily Times,* October 2 and 6, 1920.

24. Ibid., October 2, 1920. The final quote was reprinted in the *Times* from an article in *Good Housekeeping* magazine.

25. On the 1916 incident, see *Tampa Morning Tribune,* November 11, 17, and 25, 1916; and *El Internacional,* December 1, 1916. Quote is from *Tribune,* November 11, 1916.

26. *El Internacional,* December 1, 1916.

27. On the career of Luisa Capetillo, see Yamile Azize, *La Mujer en La Lucha* (Rio Piedras: Editorial Cultural, 1985). The reader was chosen by the other

workers in the factory to entertain and inform them during working hours. The reader's time was generally divided between reading news items, political tracts, and novels. I have found only one other reference to a woman reader in the cigar factories of Tampa, Key West, or Havana.

28. On consumer issues, see Gary Mormino and George Pozzetta, *The Immigrant World of Ybor City* (Urbana: University of Illinois Press, 1987), 151, 152, 157–59; *El Internacional,* September 5 and 12 and November 7 and 14, 1919.

29. *El Internacional,* December 1919 (date illegible).

30. The main sources for information on African Americans in Tampa prior to 1945 are the *Tribune* and the *Times.* There were two black newspapers in Tampa during the earlier part of the century, the *Tampa Bulletin* and the *Florida Sentinel,* but the only extant copies of the *Sentinel,* later the *Sentinel-Bulletin,* cover the post-1945 period. There were also a few other papers, such as the *Afro-American,* published for brief periods in the city; these papers are quoted in other sources, but no extant copies are available to researchers.

31. Gardner and Lawson, "At-Large Elections."

32. Material on black women's activism is based on Nancy A. Hewitt, "Politicizing Domesticity: Anglo, Black and Latin Women in Tampa's Progressive Movements," in *Gender, Class, Race, and Reform in the Progressive Era,* ed. Noralee Frankel and Nancy Shrom Dye (Lexington: University of Kentucky Press, 1991), 24–41.

33. Quoted from an article on "Womanhood," printed in the *Afro-American Monthly* in 1915, published by the Afro-American Civic League. The article is cited in Otis R. Anthony and Marilyn T. Wade, comps., *A Collection of Historical Facts about Black Tampa* (Tampa: Tampa Electric Company, 1974), 11.

34. *Tampa Morning Tribune,* October 8, 1920.

35. For an analysis of black women's importance in electoral politics nationally, see Evelyn Brooks Higginbotham, "In Politics to Stay: Black Women Leaders and Party Politics in the 1920s," in *Women, Politics, and Change,* ed. Louise Tilly and Patricia Gurin (New York: Russell Sage Foundation, 1990), 199–220.

36. If you eliminate the Latin precincts from these totals, the percentage of women registrants among all non-Latin whites registered rises to just over 37 percent. In the heavily Latin precincts, only 69 white women registered, compared with 153 "colored" women, though we do not know how many of the latter were Afro-Cuban and how many African American.

37. On black and white women's activism in early twentieth-century Tampa, see Hewitt, "Politicizing Domesticity"; and Nancy A. Hewitt, "Varieties of Voluntarism: Class, Ethnicity and Women's Activism in Tampa," in *Women, Politics, and Change,* ed. Tilly and Gurin, 63–87.

38. Gardner and Lawson, "At-Large Elections," 3.

39. *Tampa Morning Tribune,* September 19, 1916.

40. On Equal Suffrage League, see Doris Weatherford, *A History of Women in Tampa* (Tampa: Athena Society, 1991), 92–93.

41. *Tampa Morning Tribune,* October 8, 1920. Mr. I. O. Price was a Republican party candidate for sheriff in 1920. Mrs. Price apparently shared her husband's

party affiliation, which made her an interesting choice for president of the Equal Suffrage League in this heavily Democratic community and region.

42. Of the small number of women identified with the Equal Suffrage League, most were members of the Tampa Civic Association, as were many of the outspoken women opponents of charter reform. Like their male counterparts, most women on both sides of the debate were Democrats. Indeed, despite taking opposing positions on the benefits of commission government, Mrs. D. B. Givens and Mrs. Amos Norris shared the stage at a Cox-Roosevelt rally just days before the charter vote.

43. *Tampa Daily Times,* November 6 and 16, 1920.

44. R. S. Sexton to Samuel Gompers, July 31, 1920, reel 36, American Federation of Labor Papers, University of Maryland, College Park, Md. Sexton was the CMIU organizer on the scene.

45. *Tampa Citizen,* July 20, 1920, letters column.

46. On Committee of Public Health, see *Tampa Morning Tribune,* October 15 and November 2, 1920. The editors of *El Internacional,* in disputing the characterizations of local cigarmakers unions by the mainstream press, claimed that 30 percent of the city's 8,125 cigarworkers were American-born, many of American-born parents, and that the president of the stemmers union was an American woman. The only Elizabeth Law listed in city directories for the period is an African American woman who lived on Garcia Street in Ybor City with her husband, William, a fireman. No occupation is listed for her. Manufacturers and Anglo civic leaders always used the term "American girls" to mean white women only; union leaders used the term to mean any native-born woman, white or black.

47. The *Cigar Makers' Official Journal* of September 15, 1920, included a list of those unions donating to the AFL Fund in Aid of the Tampa Strikers between August 10 and September 10, 1920. The donors ranged from the Garment Workers No. 26 of St. Louis, through the Cracker Packers and the Laundry Workers of San Francisco to the Tobacco Strippers of Bayamon, Puerto Rico. Other contributors included locals of bricklayers, mine workers, switchmen, and bookbinders from all over the United States and the Caribbean.

48. On missions, see the report on the Methodist conference in the *Tampa Morning Tribune,* October 20, 1920.

49. The presence of Candida Bustamente as a speaker is recorded in ibid., October 15, 1920. The description of the electrifying speech appeared in *El Internacional,* October 22, 1920.

50. The *Tampa Daily Times,* October 14, 1920, claimed that a vote was taken and that women strikers voted with the majority to continue the strike. A photograph of the mass meeting reveals that despite the shared vision of striking women and men, certain social and sexual conventions were retained. The women are all sitting on the main floor of the meeting room, and the men are all sitting in the balcony or standing along the back wall.

51. *Tampa Morning Tribune,* October 20, 1920.

52. Ibid., October 31, 1920. It is not clear how the editors determined who

cast which votes, other than assuming that all those voting against the charter in
certain precincts must have been Negro or Latin.

53. Ibid., October 20, 1920.

54. For registration totals, see *Tampa Daily Times,* October 18, 1920; on
procharter and anticharter vote margins by precinct, see ibid., October 21, 1920.
Since the *Times* was opposed to the charter, they would have little reason to
report favorably on the heavy procharter vote from predominantly white precincts and the heavy anticharter vote in black precincts. See also *Tampa Morning
Tribune* coverage of voter turnout, October 20, 1920.

55. *Tampa Morning Tribune,* October 20, 1920.

56. Ibid.

57. Letter from Committee of Public Health to *Tampa Morning Tribune,*
published November 2, 1920.

58. *Tampa Morning Tribune,* November 6 and 7, 1920.

59. *Tampa Citizen,* August 13, 1920, responding to claims in *Tobacco Leaf*
that "American girls," meaning native-born white women, were pouring into
Tampa to take jobs left vacant by striking Latin men.

60. See report of union meeting in *Tampa Morning Tribune,* February 6,
1921. The vote was 2,514 for ending the strike and 1,054 against, but there was
no report on differences in women's and men's position on the issue.

61. Quote from *Tampa Morning Tribune,* November 27, 1921; see also
Tampa Daily Times, November 26, 1921. For an overview of this period of labor
strife, see Hewitt, " 'Voice of Virile Labor,' " 164–66.

The Housewives' League of Detroit: Black Women and Economic Nationalism

Darlene Clark Hine

The Great Depression of the 1930s was one of the most catastrophic periods in American history. All Americans suffered massive economic dislocation but none more than African Americans. For blacks who had always occupied a subordinate position in the American economy, the tenuous economic gains of the World War I era rapidly evaporated. Indeed, the economic deterioration among black Americans had commenced shortly after the cessation of hostilities and the return of white servicemen from European fronts. Employers lost little time firing black workers and replacing them with white veterans. As their economic status plummeted, blacks in cities across the Middle West and Northeast encountered increased incidences of violence, blatant job discrimination, and housing segregation. The thousands of black men and women who had quit the Jim Crow, lynching, and rape-infested South for northern urban areas in search of a better future found themselves (as early as the mid-twenties) embroiled in a fierce and sometimes deadly struggle for jobs and housing.

Some scholars have argued the Great Depression affected blacks less severely than it did their white counterparts simply because black economic conditions had deteriorated long before 1929. Such arguments, however, fail to take into consideration the reality of some short-lived postwar gains and the hopes and heightened expectations of improvement that had motivated thousands of black migrants in the first place. In short, few of the southern migrants were strangers to poverty, political powerlessness, segregation, or discrimination, but the promises of access to relatively well-paying jobs in northern industries and the (albeit limited but real) success some blacks had achieved during World War I made the depression conditions even more unbearable.

It was during these dire times that black women in Detroit founded an ingenious united action organization based on principles of economic nationalism. Established in 1930, the Housewives' League of Detroit had

as one of its mottos "Stabilize the economic status of the Negro through
directed spending." For the next thirty years, the members of the league
adhered to five basic tenets, all intended to retain higher proportions of
material resources within their own communities. They pledged to patronize all organized Negro businesses; to patronize "stores that employ
Negroes in varied capacities and that do not discriminate in types of work
offered"; to support and encourage institutions training Negro youth for
trades and commercial activities; to teach "Negro youth that no work
done well is menial"; and finally to conduct "education campaigns to
teach the Negro the value of his spending."[1]

The Housewives' League of Detroit is best understood as part of a
cluster of nationwide grass-roots movements that cut across racial and
gender lines to help workers, blacks, and women survive the massive
economic dislocation brought on by the Great Depression. Throughout
this era, blacks in key urban centers, including Chicago, Baltimore,
Washington, D.C., Detroit, and Harlem, launched a series of "Don't buy
from where you can't work" boycott and picketing movements against
white-owned businesses.

Throughout the 1920s, in a similar vein, white workers and unions in
various parts of the country organized consumer movements that articulated an independent, working-class political perspective on consumption.
These consumer cooperatives and boycotts united workers across lines of
gender, skill, and trade, and they helped bridge the gap between paid
and unpaid labor. Union leaders across the North, but especially in
Seattle, Washington, put considerable pressure on housewives to "shop
union" labels. Many women needed little encouragement to consume in
accordance with their families' best interests.[2]

In many communities women's auxiliaries to male-dominated unions
initiated and sustained consumer protests. These groups embraced immigrant and native-born white women as well as black women, though in
separate campaigns. In assessing women's involvement in public activism,
the historian Nancy Cott suggests three dimensions of consciousness:
feminism, female consciousness, and communal consciousness. It is her
third form of consciousness that best describes black and white women's
involvement in consumer activism and "directed spending" campaigns
during the 1920s and 1930s. According to Cott, "Women's communal
consciousness ought to be explicitly recognized for its role in women's
self-assertions, even while those self-assertions are on behalf of the
community that women inhabit with their men and children." For black
women in the Housewives' League, such communal consciousness was
reinforced by "womanist" consciousness. The historian Elsa Barkley
Brown states the point well: "many black women at various points in

history had a clear understanding that race issues and women's issues were inextricably linked, that one could not separate women's struggle from race struggle."[3] To be a womanist was a big order, because it required holding together many constituencies and multiple purposes all at once. Perhaps it is fair to say black women developed a communal womanist consciousness that enabled them to fight one struggle on many different fronts, using strategies according to their effectiveness in a given space and time.

The economic program, the communal womanist consciousness, and the organizing activities of the Housewives' League of Detroit were logical outgrowths of the national black women's club movement that flourished throughout the opening decades of the twentieth century. That movement, along with its white counterpart, has received considerable attention in recent years.[4] In July 1895 Josephine St. Pierre Ruffin of Boston presided over the first National Conference of Colored Women in America. Out of this meeting emerged the National Association of Colored Women's Clubs (NACW) in 1896. NACW was incorporated in 1904, and its constitution was ratified in 1926. The preamble conveyed the purpose of the organization: "We the Colored Women of the United States of America feeling the need of united and systematic effort, and hoping to furnish evidence of moral, mental, and material progress made by our people, do hereby unite in a National Association." As the historian Anne Firor Scott has demonstrated, the heretofore invisible but significant work of black club women contributed to the survival of regional black communities in myriad ways. The schools, hospitals, clinics, orphanages, homes for the elderly, employment agencies, day-care centers, libraries, playgrounds, and settlement houses they founded addressed the needs of diverse black constituencies.[5]

Ida Wells Barnett of Chicago, Jane Edna Hunter of Cleveland, Sallie Wyatt Stewart of Evansville, Indiana, and Rosa L. Slade Gragg of Detroit are but four examples of midwestern black women who established settlement or community houses and opened training schools during the Progressive Era. Throughout the twenties black women in communities above and below the Mason-Dixon line also mobilized support for the establishment of black branches of the Young Women's Christian Association (YWCA). This work was particularly important given the widespread discrimination practiced by the white YWCA. Typically, single black women could not secure living accommodations and did not have access to the social facilities and employment bureaus in existing YWCAs.

These institution-building activities reflected the same spirit of voluntarism seen among white women in American society during the Progressive Era. Entrenched racism in the society as a whole and among white women in particular, however, gave black women additional incentives to create both parallel and distinctively new social welfare structures. No social history of twentieth-century America is complete without analysis of the role these women played in erecting an infrastructure of social welfare agencies; community institutions, such as penny saving banks and credit unions; protest organizations; and cultural programs. Although largely ignored in earlier histories of black civil rights organizations, the work of the club women, along with that of the National Association for the Advancement of Colored People (NAACP) and the National Urban League, helped ease the transition and accelerated the adaptation of rural black migrants to their urban environments.[6]

The black women's clubs were important in at least two major regards. Black women were able to put into actual practice the ideologies of self-help and racial solidarity advocated by such national leaders as Booker T. Washington of the Tuskegee Institute; Marcus Garvey, founder of the Universal Negro Improvement Association; and W. E. B. Du Bois, editor of the NAACP's *Crisis* magazine. A desire to alter negative images of black womanhood was a second, perhaps even more compelling, motivation for club formation. The clubs, in short, became the chief vehicles for implementing black women's determination to serve and uplift their race. Simultaneously, they allowed black women the space and means whereby they could develop positive images of themselves as women and thereby challenge the prevalent negative stereotypes of their virtue.[7]

In 1900 attorney D. Augustus Straker, the political leader of black Detroit, addressed the first convention of the Michigan State Association of Colored Women's Clubs, organized by Lucy Smith Thurman. Voicing approval of the political implications of black women's organizing, Straker challenged the group to "Agitate! Agitate! Agitate!" He declared, "I hope before you close your labors you will establish a committee in every city of the State to get employment for our young women and thus protect them against the evil results of idle hands."[8] Straker's emphasis on the need for protection against the evil of idle hands was a thinly veiled reference to the prevailing negative stereotypes of black women's morality. Straker advised the women, "What you need to do is to create American sentiment for equal opportunity for black women in the development of true womanhood." He exhorted them to "open the stores and the factories, and the millineries, and the school houses, and the counting house for our young women, as well as the kitchen, the washtub, the nursery and the scrub room. . . . "[9] Of course, Straker's remarks simply echoed what Michigan's black women knew had to be done.

Although several exemplary studies, including Deborah Gray White's essay in this volume, have outlined the larger history of the club women's movement, one theme in need of further exploration is the intersection between the work of black urban club women and the development of strategies for economic housekeeping. Throughout the Great Depression and World War II the Housewives' League of Detroit and the leagues that sprouted in other cities directed the spending of black families into businesses owned and operated by blacks. The Housewives' League of Detroit was the sister organization of the Booker T. Washington Trade Association, an affiliate of the National Negro Business League. So successful was the Detroit League that in 1933 it became the model for the newly formed National Housewives' League of America. The organization flourished in the thirties and forties but finally folded in the late sixties.

Two decades after the founding of the Michigan State Association of Colored Women's Clubs, a strong club women's movement flourished in Detroit. Although black women's clubs with various social and cultural purposes had existed in the city since the antebellum period, the recent influx of large numbers of migrants and the expansion of Detroit's black middle class stimulated greater club formation and collaboration. By 1920 black women leaders in the city deemed it wise to gather all of the disparate clubs under the umbrella of one large organization, the Detroit Association of Colored Women's Clubs. Under the strong leadership of President Rosa Gragg, who in 1926 had joined the Current Topic Study Club, the Detroit Association peaked in 1945, with a membership of seventy-three clubs and approximately three thousand individual members. In recognition of her indomitable spirit, untiring effort, and commitment to club work on the local level, Gragg was elected president of the National Association of Colored Women's Clubs in 1958.[10]

A brief survey of the severe employment discrimination black women endured in seeking work other than in domestic service underscores the economic and political significance of the clubs they created. The majority of black women, regardless of regional location, worked in domestic service throughout the opening decades of the twentieth century. Census studies for 1920 reveal that from one-third to one-half of all black women worked in domestic service jobs. In the South, where the number employed was greater than in any other region, their backbreaking work brought low pay and low status. Given the often marginal and seasonal employment of so many southern black men and the ravages of the Great Depression, black women's meager earnings often proved critical to the survival of their families. Although many white women worked to attain middle-class status and then "retired" once they achieved it, black women tended to remain in the labor force even after marriage or the start of a family.[11]

Like their male counterparts, many black women had quit the South during World War I with the hope that in such cities as Detroit, Chicago, Milwaukee, and Cleveland they would have access to the factories and shops that provided new employment opportunities for increasing numbers of white women.[12] The reminiscences of the author Mary Helen Washington provide poignant testimony to the dashed hopes of many female migrants:

> In the 1920s my mother and my five aunts migrated to Cleveland, Ohio, from Indianapolis and, in spite of their many talents, they found every door except the kitchen door closed to them. My youngest aunt was trained as a bookkeeper and was so good at her work that her white employer at Guardian Savings of Indianapolis allowed her to work at the branch in a black area. The Cleveland Trust Company was not so liberal, however, so in Cleveland she went to work in what is known in the black community as "private family."[13]

The employment discrimination and racial exclusion of black women from certain occupations in Detroit were strikingly similar to those experienced by their sisters in other major cities. Detroit's black women encountered virtually insurmountable barriers to employment in the automobile industries. The Ford Motor Company remained one of the nation's largest employers of black men, even during the depression, but it was adamant in its refusal to hire black women. The incipient defense orders in 1940 suggested that the tide might turn, but, as the historians August Meier and Elliott Rudwick point out, "when turning to female labor to staff the assembly lines at their new Willow Run bomber plant, they [Ford managers] fought hard to keep the work force there lily-white." Ford's policy toward black women was not an aberration. Other corporations in the Detroit defense industries also refused to hire black women. According to Meier and Rudwick, "Black civic leaders and trade unionists fought a sustained and energetic battle to open Detroit war production to black women, but because government manpower officials gave discrimination against Negro females low priority, the gains were negligible when compared with those achieved by the city's black male workers." Actually, by the end of World War II, black men and women constituted a mere 3.5 percent, or 735, of the work force at Willow Run.[14] In other words, neither group fared particularly well.

One of the major challenges to black women during the economic crises of the 1930s and World War II was finding adequate and respectable jobs for themselves and for their sons and daughters. The destructiveness of underemployment, forced firings, and sexual stratification in the labor force spurred many black women to embrace the idea that economic progress was impossible without concomitant change in their political consciousness. The powerful combination of racial discrimination and the sexual stratification of labor imprisoned them at the bottom of the economic ladder. All traditional patterns of protest and the objections of black rights organizations seemed powerless to alter their exclusion or continued exploitation. The convergence of racial, sexual, and class oppression made it difficult for black women to advance through traditional economic channels. The very complexity of their oppression dictated the need to develop a new political consciousness. Black women, like their nineteenth-century forebears, mainly had to depend on their own resources in the ongoing fight for equality of opportunity and social change.

The greatest weapon Detroit black club women had at their disposal during the height of the Great Depression was the leadership and organizing skill they had cultivated during decades of involvement in club work. If there was one thing these women knew well, it was how to mobilize their members, how to develop persuasive arguments, how to conceptualize issues, and how to fight for their families and communities. Although it may be tempting to view poor black women as powerless to combat overwhelming and seemingly intractable racial and sexual discrimination, they were better prepared to do battle than one might expect. Well grounded in a tradition of social welfare and club work, Detroit's communally conscious black women appreciated the necessity for collective action. When called upon, they were even prepared to blur class lines and transcend color stratification to overcome economic and educational barriers to black advancement.

The Detroit Study Club was but one of many organizations that reflected the transition from a strictly cultural orientation to one focused on racial uplift work. This club had been organized on March 2, 1898, as the Browning Study Club. Within a decade the club had shifted from "just a self culture club and branched out into the broader field of Philanthropy and civil social work," according to one of its earliest members, Lillian E. Johnson. "The club was established as a purely literary club, however, the members soon realized the need of sharing in the social welfare work in the city, so a department of philanthropy was established sometime during the first ten years," she elaborated, and "the Club contributes liberally to the many charities, civic organizations and education movements in the city, and cooperates with the National, State and City Association of Colored Women."[15]

As black women in Detroit experimented with new strategies to serve their people and to enhance their status as women, they seized on the idea of harnessing and targeting their economic power, perhaps influenced by the ideas advanced by consumer activism movements and by such black leaders as Du Bois. As the woes of the depression deepened, Du Bois urged that the NAACP adopt a program of "systematic 'voluntary segregation' in the form of a separate black cooperative economy."[16] He advocated that blacks pool their resources and develop businesses and engage in other self-help endeavors while continuing their pressure for full integration and equality within the larger society. In response to growing levels of national black unemployment and welfare dependency, the NAACP *Crisis* editor W. E. B. Du Bois advised that the "2,800,000 families in the United States must systematically organize their $106,000,000 a month, consumer purchases" for blacks to become an economic power capable of demanding and protecting their own interests.[17] To a great extent throughout the 1930s, Du Bois echoed the ideas that had been espoused in the early 1920s by Marcus Garvey, one of the most renowned black nationalists of the twentieth century.[18] Black women in Detroit, however, put an altogether different spin on these ideas.

On June 10, 1930, a group of fifty black women responded to a call issued by Fannie B. Peck, wife of the Reverend William H. Peck (1878-1944) who was pastor of the two-thousand-member Bethel AME Church and president and founder of the local branch of the Booker T. Washington Trade Association. Fannie B. Peck was born August 15, 1879, in Huntsville, Missouri, to Thomas and Leanna Campbell. She married William H. Peck in 1899, and the couple moved to Detroit in June 1928. Out of the initial meeting called by Fannie Peck and held in the gymnasium of Bethel Church emerged the Detroit Housewives' League. Fannie Peck had conceived the idea of creating an organization of housewives following a lecture by Albon L. Holsey, secretary of the National Negro Business League. Holsey had described the successful efforts of black housewives in Harlem, who consolidated and concentrated their considerable economic power in support of Colored Merchant Association Stores. Peck, like many ministers' wives, exercised considerable influence in her community, and she was convinced that if an organization "to support Negroes in business and professions" worked in New York, it was worth replicating in Detroit. According to one handwritten account of the first meeting, Peck "explained to those present the purpose and need of such an organization. She stated that it would be a pioneering organization in its field as there was not in existence a pattern by which to plan and govern its activities. Therefore members would learn by doing."[19] The first group of elected officers included Peck as president, Ethel L. Hemsley as first vice president, Mamie C. Boone as second vice president, Wilma Walker as recording secretary, Christina Fuqua as assistant secretary, and Hattie Toodle as treasurer. In 1933 the Detroit Housewives' League would send two delegates to a major meeting convened in Durham, North Carolina, to form the National Housewives' League.

The leaders of the individual leagues sought to empower black women across the economic spectrum. Peck lectured to large numbers of black women in Detroit, declaring they were not without real economic power. In her opinion, their power simply had to be harnessed.[20] At one point Peck recounted some of the early thinking that underlay the founding of the Housewives' League. "It has been in the minds of our women that they, their husbands and children were the victims of a vicious economic system," she wrote. "They were denied employment in many places where they spent their money, and that even when employed no opportunities for advancement were given." As her successor extolled, "Peck had focused the attention of women on the most essential, yet most unfamiliar factor in the building of homes, communities, and nations, namely—The Spending Power of Women."[21]

The Detroit Housewives' League grew with phenomenal speed. From the fifty members who attended the first meeting, its membership increased to ten thousand by 1935, embracing all segments of the black community. In explaining the "marvelous growth," Peck maintained that it was due to the realization on the part of the black woman of the fact "that she has been travelling through a blind alley, making sacrifices to educate her children with no thought as to their obtaining employment after leaving school." Mary L. Beasley subsequently organized the first junior unit of the league as a "definite step in helping youth develop a greater appreciation for business owned and controlled by Negroes." Laura Dounveor, as chair of the league's Dramatic Committee, inspired members "to write plays, and skits depicting the struggles and progress of business and professional people."[22]

Essentially, the Housewives' League combined communal womanist consciousness and economic nationalism to help black families and black businesses survive the depression. In Detroit at the outset of the depression, blacks operated 51 of the 147 grocery stores, 18 of the 31 drug stores, and 5 of the 27 haberdasheries in their neighborhoods. By 1932, however, over forty-eight thousand black families in Detroit depended on the city's welfare system. They were not alone.[23]

The only requirement for league membership was a pledge to support black businesses, buy black products, patronize black professionals, and keep one's money in the community. As one leader of the Housewives' League argued, black women were the group positioned most strategi-

cally to preserve and expand the black internal economy. The members
heard frequent exhortations along the lines that "it is our duty as women
controlling 85 percent of the family budget to unlock through concentrated spending closed doors that Negro youth may have the opportunity
to develop and establish businesses in the fields closest to them." The
league officers promised members that in exchange for their support and
work they would instruct and inform them on "prices of merchandise,
family budget, food values, and all things pertaining to the management
of the home."[24]

Actually, members of the Housewives' League sometimes received
material rewards for their work as well as advice on home management.
When Lincoln Gordon, a manufacturer of Quality Cleanser, contacted
the Housewives' League in 1939, he made it clear he was willing to share
profits: "I shall be very pleased to have this body of business makers
select or recommend to me one or more of your group to sell Quality
Cleanser. I formally state and announce openly as the business increases,
each person will be paid as his or her ability merits." Gordon promised to
return to the "agent" one-fifth, or five cents, of every twenty-five cents
earned in selling the cleanser. Gordon pledged, "I shall function for the
mutual benefit of business for the race and trust that the reciprocity of
the race will be the same as far as it is possible to influence the activity of
your exemplary body."[25]

League members took great pains defining their objectives and assuring
potential critics and competitors that they intended to restrict their
activity to matters relating to the home, family, and community: "We see
the great need of our social education, religious and economic improvement,
and we have selected the economical as our field of endeavor. The great
loss of employment upon the part of our people has reduced us to the
place where we have not the sustenance for our bodies, clothes to wear,
homes to live in, books to read, and none of the many things which are
not any longer luxuries, but are prime necessities to the home life of
modern standards." The Housewives' League adopted the slogan "Find a
job, or Make one and make your dollar do Triple duty." A dollar doing
triple duty would "get you what *you* need. Give the Race what it needs—
Employment, and Bring what all investments should bring—*Dividends.*"[26]

The Housewives' League's constitution contained several artfully crafted
declarations of independence that emphasized how it differed from traditional advancement agencies and existing institutions in the black
community. Their promises to confine their work to carefully defined
"female spheres" reflected an awareness of the broad needs of the race.
These somewhat muted statements also hint at a deeper understanding
of the politics of gender roles in the black community. Women seldom

occupied visible leadership roles in the churches, nor did any hold or run for elective office in this period. The world of public politics and religious leadership they acquiesced to belonged to the men of the community. The one exception in Detroit was Rosa Gragg. In 1941 President Franklin D. Roosevelt appointed her to the volunteers' participation committee in the Office of Civil Defense. In 1948 Mayor Eugene I. Van Antwerp appointed her president of the Detroit Welfare Commission, which had 1,947 employees and an operating budget of twenty million dollars. Still, Gragg adhered to convention in that she did not hold or seek an elective political position.[27]

In section seven of the Housewives' League's constitution the women inserted yet another qualification: "We recognize the place of the church and allied organizations among us for the advancement of our group. We are in full sympathy with their purposes, but are not a religious organization and shall not permit any discrimination for or against to in any way enter our thought or determine our action on any question of policy in our organization." Moreover, in section eight they declared, "We are mindful of achieving political solidarity among us, increasing our opportunity of representation in bodies that control the activities in our city, state, and nation—but we are not a political organization."[28] By disclaiming religious and political involvement, the women disarmed potential male critics who might have felt their authority threatened.

Essentially, the women cleverly let it be known that they were not in competition with other organized black advancement groups. This did not, however, prevent Gertrude J. West, secretary of the Housewives' League, from appropriating the rhetoric of black male leaders like Booker T. Washington. She proclaimed, "This is a challenge to Negro women, who control largely the finance that comes into the home. It offers an opportunity to make Christianity a reality by letting down your bucket where you are, knowing that you must first set your house in order before going out to help your neighbor."[29]

The Housewives' League's attempt to eliminate a sense of competition with other black organizations and institutions was apparently effective, for I was unable to locate evidence that proved male hostility to the goals and strategies employed by the women. The statements that disarmed and avoided antagonizing male leaders in politics and the churches are, perhaps, one facet of successful communal womanism. League leaders effectively practiced a politics of reassuring that they had taken to heart the entire community's interests, a reassurance that was reflected in the league's structure as well as its statements.

Each neighborhood had its own Housewives' League unit. The different units all belonged to the Central Committee. This organizational structure permitted maximum participation on neighborhood levels. The neighborhood officers attended meetings of the executive board, usually held on the second Tuesday of each month. Any woman who pledged to "help build bigger and better Negro businesses and to create and increase opportunities for employment" was welcomed to membership in her neighborhood unit. One card declared, "A belief in the future of Negro business and a desire to assist in every way by patronizing and encouraging the same is all that is necessary to become a member."[30] The organization took pains to make sure that all interested women had the opportunity to join and participate in the league's work.

Becoming a member was the easy part; keeping up with league activities required considerable effort and commitment. Members of each unit canvassed their neighborhood merchants demanding that they sell black products and employ black children as clerks or stockboys. Unit leaders also organized campaigns to persuade their neighbors to patronize specific businesses owned by blacks or white businesses that employed blacks. In 1946 the Housewives' League launched a bulletin and solicited paid advertisements from local businesses. They charged twelve dollars for half-pages and twenty dollars for whole pages. In 1950 the bulletin was enlarged to include "a new feature . . . which will better call to the attention of the reader, the kind of businesses owned by you." Potential advertisers were urged to "take the buying public to your business through pictures."[31] Throughout the city, league officers organized lectures, planned exhibits at state fairs, discussed picketing and boycott strategies, and disseminated information concerning the economic self-help struggles of blacks across the country. Accurate, timely communication was imperative for the smooth operation of the league. The head of the Research Committee gathered data and made recommendations about the types of businesses needed in various communities and neighborhoods and reported on the results of "directed spending" tactics.[32]

By 1946 the members of the Housewives' League of Detroit no longer had to maintain the fiction of being apolitical. In the post–World War II years, both male and female leaders boldly informed their people that it was wise to employ the ballot in the war for racial advancement. One letter by a league officer observed that "it has become necessary for other racial groups to become more and more concerned about entering politics as candidates for public office, and as organized groups, to see that the masses are educated to their responsibility as voters."[33] The heightened political consciousness of blacks undoubtedly reflected their frustration with the federal government's hypocritical denunciation of German and Italian fascism while maintaining rigid adherence to stateside segregation policies.

As late as 1963 the Housewives' League was still going strong. In a letter to Mayor Jerome P. Cavanagh, league president Naomi Jefferies declared that "we recognize the economic power which the housewife possesses, and we believe that through the constructive efforts, we hold the key to the doors of opportunity that will make it possible to 'Stabilize our economic status and be instrumental in placing us in a position where, by virtue of efficiency the Negro Race will be within and not without this great American Business World.' "[34] By the late 1960s the Housewives' League would run its course. The success of the civil rights movement, expanding employment opportunities made possible through affirmative action legislation, and the failure to find women to take the places of the aging founding leaders probably contributed to the league's demise.

While the Housewive's League was a force for black nationalism, the leaders also deserve recognition for their early appeals to women's solidarity. The leaders concluded that "certainly the Negro woman whose home must suffer most, ought become concerned and join hands with other women who realize what happens in party politics affects homes as directly as what happens in her block. . . . Housing, economic equality, education opportunity for children and security are all affected by government."[35] Black women's activism and womanism remained securely attached to concern for home, family, and community uplift, although in one revealing speech Peck urged black women to participate in the Housewives' League's programs to win the respect of white women, asserting that "if we are to be respected by other women, if we are to walk side by side with them, we cannot continue to spend thoughtlessly and buy the things we want and beg for the things we need." By the dawn of the modern civil rights movement, then, black women in Detroit consciously perceived their advancement along both sexual and racial lines as being inextricably connected to and grounded in the tripartite base of home, family, and community.

It is impossible to calculate the full impact of the Housewives' League of Detroit on the city's economic life. The historian Jacqueline Jones does, however, venture an assessment of the overall impact of the leagues:

The struggles in Chicago, Baltimore, Washington, Detroit, Harlem, and Cleveland relied on boycotts sponsored by neighborhood "Housewives Leagues," whose members took their grocery and clothes shopping elsewhere, or did without, rather than patronize all-white stores. These campaigns captured an estimated 75,000 new jobs for blacks during the depression decade, and together they had an economic impact comparable to that of the CIO in its

organizing efforts, and second only to government jobs as a new
source of openings. In the process women's energies at the grass-
roots level were harnessed and given explicit political expression.[36]

Certainly the Housewives' League of Detroit made a significant difference in the political consciousness of the women who attended the
meetings. They could scarcely avoid becoming more confident and aggressive in their confrontations with neighborhood businessmen and more
insistent in demands for jobs and opportunities for their children. In
assessing the performance of the Housewives' League, one member
wrote, "The League feels that its greatest accomplishments have been
the vision of self-help it has given the Negro woman; the confidence it
has inspired in Negro business and professional men and women, the
courage it has imparted to our young people to continue their education."[37]

This brief sketch of the Housewives' League of Detroit raises many
questions about power and the intersection of race, gender, and ideology
in the black community. Black women extended into the public arena
their collective concerns for social reform and the problems confronted by
poor, uneducated, infirm, aged, and unemployed black people. Most
studies ignore the importance women, particularly black women, place
on economic self-determination. Clearly, more scholarly investigation is
sorely needed. As yet there is no full-length study of the history of black
women workers in America. Moreover, our understanding of the participation of black women in labor unions remains incomplete. Other questions come to mind. Were there costs to economic nationalism? Were
working poor black women torn between buying black and buying
cheaper from white-owned businesses with higher inventories and
volume—a conflict that would have been less severe for the better-off
league members? The connection between the club women's movement
and the fashioning of economic and political strategies based on the
subordinate position black women occupied by virtue of their race and
sex promises to increase our understanding of the dynamic processes of
black institutional development throughout the nation. Although they were
excluded, discriminated against, and enjoyed little respect in the larger
society, these women never gave up the struggle. The Housewives' League
of Detroit teaches us that even those at the bottom of the social, political,
and economic ladder often have resources with which to effect change.

NOTES

The author wishes to thank Linda Werbish for her assistance with the preparation of this essay.

1. "Constitution of Housewives' League of Detroit and Declaration of Principles," n.d., box 1, Housewives' League of Detroit Papers, Burton Collection, Detroit Public Library, Detroit, Mich. The league was structured into a central league and units. Twelve distinct committees made up the central league: organizing, membership, program, social, publicity, ways and means, sick, sanitary, research, filing, music and drama, and budget. The president, officers, and chair of all committees from the central league and all individual units constituted the executive board. Each neighborhood unit had eight committees: membership, program, social, publicity, sick, research, sanitary, and budget. According to the constitution, the duties of, for example, the Sanitary Committee were as follows: "to suggest better means of sanitation, to raise the standard in any place where needed, to encourage more artistic and attractive arrangement of merchandise by offering placards of approval or endorsement to those who reach the highest standards proposed and to educate the merchant to appreciate endorsements of the League as other merchants do that of Good Housekeeping." Space does not permit inclusion of more detailed descriptions of the duties and functions of all of the committees. Suffice it to say there was sufficient variety to permit virtually every woman the opportunity to participate on a central or unit committee in a meaningful capacity.

2. Dana Lynn Frank, "At the Point of Consumption: Seattle Labor and the Politics of Consumption, 1919-1927" (Ph.D. diss., Yale University, 1988), 519. See also Maurine Weiner Greenwald, "Working-Class Feminism and the Family Wage Ideal: The Seattle Debate on Married Women's Right to Work, 1914-1920," *Journal of American History* 76 (June 1989): 118-49; Susan Levine, "Workers' Wives: Gender, Class and Consumerism in the 1920s in the United States," *Gender and History* 3 (Spring 1991): 45-64; and Nancy A. Hewitt, "Beyond the Search for Sisterhood: American Women's History in the 1980s," *Social History* 10 (October 1985): 299-321.

3. Nancy F. Cott, "What's in a Name? The Limits of 'Social Feminism': Or, Expanding the Vocabulary of Women's History," *Journal of American History* 76 (December 1989): 827; Elsa Barkley Brown, "Womanist Consciousness: Maggie Lena Walker and the Independent Order of Saint Luke," *Signs* 14 (Spring 1989): 610-33. Brown defines *womanism* as a consciousness that incorporates racial, cultural, sexual, national, economic, and political considerations. My discussion of the multifaceted economic role of black women during the 1930s particularly benefited from reading Robin D. G. Kelley, *Hammer and Hoe: Alabama Communists during the Great Depression* (Chapel Hill: University of North Carolina Press, 1990).

4. Gerda Lerner, "Early Community Work of Black Club Women," *Journal of Negro History* 59 (April 1974): 158-67; Karen J. Blair, *The Clubwoman as Feminist: True Womanhood Redefined, 1868-1914* (New York: Holmes and Meier, 1980); Nancy F. Cott, *The Grounding of Modern Feminism* (New Haven, Conn.: Yale University Press, 1987); Cynthia Neverdon-Morton, *Afro-American Women in the South and the Advancement of the Race* (Knoxville: University of Tennessee Press, 1989); Darlene Clark Hine, *When the Truth Is Told: A History*

of Black Women's Culture and Community in Indiana, 1875-1950 (Indianapolis: National Council of Negro Women, Indianapolis Section, 1981).

5. Preamble quoted in Darlene Clark Hine, *Black Women in the Middle West: The Michigan Experience,* 1988 Clarence M. Burton Lecture (Ann Arbor: Michigan Historical Society, 1990), 13; Anne Firor Scott, "Most Invisible of All: Black Women's Voluntary Associations," *Journal of Southern History* 56 (February 1990): 14, 16. See also Dorothy Salem, *To Better Our World: Black Women in Organized Reform, 1890-1920* (Brooklyn: Carlson, 1990), 103-44; Darlene Clark Hine, " 'We Specialize in the Wholly Impossible': The Philanthropic Work of Black Women," in *Lady Bountiful Revisited: Women, Philanthropy, and Power,* ed. Kathleen D. McCarthy (New Brunswick, N.J.: Rutgers University Press, 1990), 70-93; Darlene Clark Hine, "Lifting the Veil, Shattering the Silence: Black Women's History in Slavery and Freedom," in *The State of Afro-American History: Past, Present and Future,* ed. Darlene Clark Hine (Baton Rouge: Louisiana State University Press, 1986), 224-49; and Susan Lynn Smith, "The Black Women's Club Movement: Self-Improvement and Sisterhood, 1890-1915" (M.A. thesis, University of Wisconsin-Madison, 1986).

6. For an analysis of voluntary associations, see Anne Firor Scott, "On Seeing and Not Seeing: A Case of Historical Invisibility," *Journal of American History* 71 (June 1984): 9-18; and Edith V. Alvord, ed., *A History of the Michigan State Federation of Women's Clubs, 1895-1953* (Ann Arbor, Mich.: Ann Arbor Press, 1953), 5-9. For a discussion of impact of migration on black women's lives, see Darlene Clark Hine, "Black Migration to the Urban Midwest: The Gender Dimension, 1915-1945," in *The Great Migration in Historical Perspective,* ed. Joe W. Trotter (Bloomington: Indiana University Press, 1991), 126-44.

7. Hine, "Lifting the Veil, Shattering the Silence," 245; Beverly Guy-Sheftall, *Daughters of Sorrow: Attitudes toward Black Women, 1880-1920* (Brooklyn: Carlson, 1990), 72-75.

8. D. Augustus Straker, "Manhood and Womanhood Development," *Colored American Magazine,* February 1901, 312-13. For discussion of the three black male leaders, see Louis R. Harlan, "Booker T. Washington and the Politics of Accommodation," in *Black Leaders in the Twentieth Century,* ed. John Hope Franklin and August Meier (Urbana: University of Illinois Press, 1982), 1-18. In the same volume, see Elliott Rudwick, "W. E. B. Du Bois: Protagonist of the Afro-American Protest," 63-83; and Lawrence W. Levine, "Marcus Garvey and the Politics of Revitalization," 105-38.

9. Straker, "Manhood and Womanhood Development," 313.

10. Additional information on Rosa Slade Gragg is contained in her manuscript collection located in the Burton Historical Collection, Detroit Public Library, Detroit, Mich. See also Hine, *Black Women in the Middle West,* 20-22.

11. William H. Harris, *The Harder We Run: Black Workers since the Civil War* (New York: Oxford University Press, 1982), 64-65.

12. Florette Henri, *Black Migration: Movement North 1900-1920* (New York: Anchor Press, 1975), 141-43; Hine, "Black Migration to the Urban Midwest," 126-44. According to the historian James R. Grossman, Chicago was one of the

few cities in which fewer than half (43.9 percent) of all employed black women were classified by the 1920 census as servants or hand laundresses. Over 12 percent, or 2,608 black women, found work in Chicago's factories before World War I. The packing industry, Grossman points out, was probably the greatest single employer of black women during the war. James R. Grossman, *Land of Hope: Chicago, Black Southerners, and the Great Migration* (Chicago: University of Chicago Press, 1989), 184-85. In his study of employment trends in Milwaukee during the depression years, the historian Joe Trotter observed that black women were basically excluded from the industrial sector. He found that "60.4 percent of their numbers labored in domestic service as compared to only 18.6 percent of all females." Trotter calculated that following the end of World War II the number of unskilled black females in industry in the city dropped from 620 in 1945 to 249 by 1947. For these women, the readjustment from industrial to domestic service was painful. As Trotter noted, "A mother of eight dependent children was laid off from her defense industry job in mid-August 1945. Unable to find factory work, she finally took a domestic service position at $0.50 per hour compared to the $1.10 per hour she made as a war worker." The woman explained, "I don't see how I can keep my family on such a low income as this domestic job offers. But if I don't take it they might deny my unemployment benefits." Joe William Trotter, Jr., *Black Milwaukee: The Making of an Industrial Proletariat, 1915-45* (Urbana: University of Illinois Press, 1985), 157, 173.

13. Mary Helen Washington, *Invented Lives: Narratives of Black Women 1860-1960* (Garden City, N.Y.: Doubleday, 1987), xxii.

14. August Meier and Elliott Rudwick, *Black Detroit and the Rise of the UAW* (New York: Oxford University Press, 1979), 136, 156.

15. Lillian E. Johnson, "History of the Detroit Study Club," May 1949, typescript, box 2, Detroit Study Club Papers, Burton Historical Collection, Detroit Public Library, Detroit, Mich. Karen J. Blair has written extensively on the literary clubs white women established that eventually became concerned with social action. This process is often contrasted with black women's clubs that were assumed to have always, from inception, focused on social action or political issues. Actually, as the history of the Detroit Study Club illustrates, the pattern was more complex. Only some black women's clubs moved from being literary to involvement with and concern for broader social issues. Blair, *The Club Woman as Feminist*, 66-67; Lerner, "Early Community Work of Black Club Women," 160-62. For recent examinations of the work of black club women, see Jacqueline Anne Rouse, *Lugenia Burns Hope: Black Southern Reformer* (Athens: University of Georgia Press, 1989); and Stephanie Shaw, "Black Club Women and the Creation of the National Association of Colored Women," *Journal of Women's History* 3 (Fall 1991): 10-25.

16. Quoted in Rudwick, "W. E. B. Du Bois," 81.

17. W. E. B. Du Bois, "N.A.A.C.P. and Segregation," *Crisis* 41 (February 1934): 53.

18. Amy Jacques-Garvey, ed., *Philosophy and Opinions of Marcus Garvey*, vols. 1 and 2 (New York: Atheneum, 1969); E. David Cronon, *Black Moses: The*

Story of Marcus Garvey and the Universal Negro Improvement Association (Madison: University of Wisconsin Press, 1969 [1955]).

19. Fannie B. Peck, "History and Purpose of Housewives League," May 1, 1934, box 3, folder "Speeches and Cards," Housewives' League of Detroit Papers; "History of Housewives League of Detroit," July 27, 1944, box 1, Housewives' League of Detroit Papers. See also Richard W. Thomas, "From Peasant to Proletarian: The Formation and Organization of the Black Industrial Working Class in Detroit, 1915-1945" (Ph.D. diss., University of Michigan, 1976), 264ff.

In July 1928 Albon Holsey, president of the National Negro Business League, launched the Colored Merchants Association (CMA) in Montgomery, Alabama. It lasted until 1934. The CMA organized local associations to purchase collectively wholesale products at discount prices by forming buyer cooperatives of at least ten black retail stores. The CMA then encouraged the development of housewives' leagues to promote patronage of the stores in particular and black businesses and professionals in general. Gary Jerome Hunter, "Don't Buy from Where You Can't Work: Black Urban Boycott Movements during the Depression, 1929-1941" (Ph.D. diss., University of Michigan, 1977), 53-54. See also Albon Holsey, "The C.M.A. Stores Face the Chains," *Opportunity* 7 (July 1929): 210.

20. Fannie B. Peck, "Negro Housewives, What Now?" reprinted from *Service Magazine,* November 1942, box 4, Housewives' League of Detroit Papers.

21. Christine M. Fuqua, president, National Housewives' Leagues of America, "Declaration of May 18, 1948 as Fannie B. Peck Day," box 4, Housewives' League of Detroit Papers.

22. Typewritten and handwritten undated speeches and fragments of minutes of meetings, box 3, folder "Speeches," Housewives' League of Detroit Papers; "History of Housewives' Leagues of Detroit," July 27, 1944, box 1, Housewives' League of Detroit Papers.

23. Hunter, "Don't Buy from Where You Can't Work," 52, 220.

24. Peck, "History and Purpose of Housewives' League."

25. Lincoln Gordon to Mrs. Christine Fuqua, November 14, 1939, box 1, Housewives' League of Detroit Papers.

26. Peck, "History and Purpose of Housewives' League." This change in strategies to "home sphere" improvements is discussed with considerable sophistication in Earl Lewis, *In Their Own Interests: Race, Class and Power in Twentieth-Century Norfolk, Virginia* (Berkeley: University of California Press, 1990).

27. See Rosa Slade Gragg Collection.

28. "Constitution of Housewives' League of Detroit and Declaration of Principles."

29. Ibid.; "Constitution and Bylaws," box 1, Housewives' League of Detroit Papers.

30. "Slogan" of Housewives' League of Detroit, box 1, folder "Constitution and Bylaws," Housewives' League of Detroit Papers.

31. Catherine Pharr to Advertiser, July 31, 1950, box 1, folder "Letters," Housewives' League of Detroit Papers.

32. "Constitution of Housewives' League of Detroit and Declaration of Principles."

33. Gertrude J. Tolber, secretary of the Housewives' League of Detroit, "What Now that the War Is Over," n.d., box 3, folder "Speeches," Housewives' League of Detroit Papers.

34. Naomi Jefferies, Christiana Fuqua, and Dolores Crudup to Jerome P. Cavanagh, May 1, 1963, box 1, folder "Letters," Housewives' League of Detroit Papers.

35. Tolber, "What Now that the War Is Over."

36. Jacqueline Jones, *Labor of Love, Labor of Sorrow: Black Women, Work and the Family, from Slavery to the Present* (New York: Basic Books, 1985), 215.

37. Report and notes of the Research Committee of the Housewives' League of Detroit, box 3, Housewives' League of Detroit Papers.

Part 3

The Politics of Reform: Tensions and Contradictions

Among the scholars establishing the field of women's history, those recovering the voices of women involved in movements for social reform provided a common refrain. Focusing first on suffrage and then alternating between analyses of antebellum and Progressive Era campaigns, scholars charted a vast array of institutions, organizations, and actions initiated, sustained, and transformed by collectivities of women. The earliest works tracked women's entry into the formal political arena, but the emphasis soon shifted to studies of the paths that led women to consider political power their right. In the antebellum case, the trail wound from woman's rights conventions through antislavery, temperance, and moral reform associations to late eighteenth-century church and charitable societies. At the turn of the twentieth century, women's clubs, labor unions, temperance societies, associations dedicated to urban reform, social welfare, and birth control, and socialist and anarchist movements presaged and fed the demand for direct access to political power.

Since the 1980s we have used the attainment of formal political power less often as the index of women reformers' success. Instead, as studies of organized women expanded to embrace various regions, races, religions, nationalities, and classes, we have attended more closely to the internal dynamics of specific movements, the tensions and contradictions among women activists, and the impact of mass mobilization on particular communities. At the same time, we have become more aware both of the common ground claimed by women and men who share social and economic circumstances and of those special moments when women from quite different circumstances manage to bridge the gap.

The most recent work in the field, represented by the essays in this section, demonstrates the continued saliency of the study of women's distinct political culture and the distinctions among women rooted in race, class, and region. Deborah Gray White and Dolores Janiewski press beyond analyses of tensions and contradictions *between* groups of women activists to examine them *within* a single group and *within* a single activist. Marion W. Roydhouse and Mary E. Frederickson, on the other hand, begin with the assumption that women reformers differed in their politics and priorities depending on their race and class, and they then move on to explore some rare moments of cooperation and coalition building.

White focuses on the tensions produced by black club women's feminist commitments and middle-class status as they sought to define a race politics that addressed the needs of the entire African American community. White is especially sensitive to the ways that racism and sexism shaped, and sometimes misshaped, club women's agendas and the role that the relative affluence of women leaders played in their definitions of respectability and race progress. In addition, she explores the ambivalent reactions of activist men to women's race leadership, pointing to the shared terrain of race and the troublesome dynamics of gender.

Shifting the lens back to relations among women activists from different racial and class communities, Roydhouse and Frederickson scrutinize two of the most important institutional arenas for southern women's activism—the Young Women's Christian Association and the Methodist church. Drawing on the same rich historiographical literature that informs the analyses of Hine and White, these authors focus on the autonomous organizing efforts of African American women in the racially charged atmosphere of the twentieth-century South. They also consider the ways that the industrialization and urbanization of the South in the early twentieth century shaped a new set of social relations, intensifying women's reform activities and setting the stage, or at least making the need more visible, for cross-class and interracial work.

Covering the years from the turn of the century to World War II, Roydhouse details the tensions created by the national YWCA's commitment to overcoming "racial, economic and social divisions endemic in the wider society" when confronted with the virulent antiunionism and racism of southern communities. Focusing first on the disappointing record of southern Ys in achieving interracial cooperation in this period, Roydhouse then turns to their more successful efforts at cross-class organizing. The most effective bonds seem to have been created between young white working-class women and the campus Ys in areas where both industry and higher education flourished, foreshadowing perhaps the development of interracial organizing among campus Y members in the 1960s.

The religious roots of the YWCA's vision are explored in greater depth by Frederickson, who traces the conflicts and cooperative ventures between white and black women in the Methodist Episcopal Church, South, and the Colored Methodist Episcopal Church. Detailing the autonomous efforts of Euro-American and African American churchwomen to address the "human costs of rapid industrial development, rural transformation, and racial segregation," Frederickson then explores the instances when the two groups made common cause. She emphasizes the ways that black Methodist women "converted their concerns . . . into a format that was accessible to white women," creating an interdependence in interracial efforts that often went unrecognized by their white counterparts. Still, by the 1940s the dual religious traditions rooted in race had begun, at least among the women, to meld into common concerns for widespread social reform.

In tracing developments among Methodist women, Frederickson notes the forms of dissemblance employed by black activists to sustain white women's interest and cooperation and the forms of self-delusion adopted by white women to sustain their own sense of power and control. In contemplating Alice Fletcher's career as a feminist advocate and Indian reformer, Dolores Janiewski probes the contradictory impulses of self-assertion and self-delusion within a single life. Aware of women's traditional power in many Native American societies, traditions used by woman's rights advocates since the 1840s to counter claims for women's "natural" dependence on men, Fletcher nonetheless sought to persuade Indian women and men of the benefits of modern civilization. A pioneering ethnographer, Fletcher drew on evolutionary models of human development to calm her own doubts about the benefits of introducing Euro-American political, economic, and gender relations into Native American communities. At the same time, she used her prestige in the women's movement to advance a version of Indian reform that ultimately undermined native women's power. Alternating between metaphors of motherhood and sisterhood, Fletcher sought to work out "internal conflicts between her feminist, reformist, and professional selves" through her public role as an advocate for the oppressed. Janiewski sympathetically and deftly negotiates the complicated commitments of this formidable figure. She reminds us, as do the other authors in this section, of the constraints of class, race, and gender shaping the lives of women reformers and the importance of highlighting those moments when such constraints are challenged, overcome, or cast aside to reveal a broader vision.

The Cost of Club Work,
the Price of Black Feminism

Deborah Gray White

Both scholars and the public have generally assumed that because black women have historically been the victims of racism and sexism, they have been more sensitive to injustice and more tolerant of difference among people than have other groups. This assumption encourages the complementary notion that tolerance and sensitivity somehow come easier to black women than to other groups and that they do not struggle with the complex issues of race, class, and gender as others do. Nothing could be further from the truth, as becomes clear when we explore how black female leaders, usually from the middle classes, have attempted to reconcile race, class, and gender.

Addressing all the questions while meeting all the needs on all three fronts has been an almost impossible task for those who are themselves victims of institutionalized racism and sexism. This essay explores the ideology and reality of the late nineteenth- and early twentieth-century club movement, with an eye on the complexity of the relationship between race, class, and gender. It argues that the National Association of Colored Women (NACW), a federation of black women's clubs, adopted a feminism that was unprecedented in its militancy and well suited for race work. It shows, however, that black club women paid a price for their feminist race work. The class and gender tension that was the cost of club work demonstrates it was difficult, if not impossible, for late nineteenth- and early twentieth-century black middle-class women to synchronize race, class, and gender so the needs of the race as a whole and the particular needs of black men and women were addressed in a just and equitable way.

That the first truly national secular black association organized around the principle of racial self-help was an organization founded by black women in the interest of black womanhood and race progress is usually overlooked in the history of black activism. The National Association of Colored Women was founded in 1896 to fight lynching and to defend black women against defamation of character. The Colored Women's League of Washington, D.C., was perhaps the first of the clubs that would later form the future NACW. Organized in 1892 by Mary Church Terrell, Anna Julia Cooper, and Mary Jane Patterson, the Women's League called on black women to unite to solve race problems. The Women's League established branches in the South and as far west as Kansas City, Missouri. A few months after the founding of the Women's League, the Woman's Loyal Union, under the leadership of the journalist Victoria Matthews, united seventy women from Brooklyn and Manhattan in support of Ida B. Wells and her antilynching crusade. The Woman's Loyal Union formed sister clubs in Charleston, Memphis, and Philadelphia. Not long after the New York women organized, the community activist Josephine Ruffin founded the New Era Club in the Boston area. This association proved the prototype for similar organizations in other areas of New England. By the fall of 1893 there were numerous black women's clubs, including one in Chicago with over 300 members and one in Kansas City with 150 members. When the NACW was finally organized in 1896 under the leadership of Mary Church Terrell, it actually combined two seminational organizations, the Women's League and the National Federation of Afro-American Women, representing a total of two hundred clubs from across the country. In response to the need for coordinated activities, club leaders formed state and eventually regional federations. By 1909 there were twenty state federations, a Northeastern Federation, and a Southern Federation.[1]

Notwithstanding regional peculiarities, the goals of these clubs were basically the same across the country. Black club women believed they could solve the problems of the race through intensive social service, particularly self-help activity aimed at improving the home and the community. Some of their programs focused on increasing the skills and intellectual ability of club members, while other programs sent members into local neighborhoods to assist black people, particularly black women and children. Some organizations, like the Woman's Musical and Literary Club of Springfield, Missouri, were first established as self-improvement clubs and then added a charity component to their activities. The Springfield women raised money for a black hospital. Similarly, the Semper Fidelis Club of Birmingham, Alabama, was initially organized as a literary society but later also provided scholarships to students at the local high school and donated money and clothing to the Old Folks and Orphan Home of the city.[2]

Other clubs were founded on the principle that one improved oneself by helping others. The vast majority of these clubs was organized around some charity or goodwill project. For instance, the Harriet Tub-

man Club of Boston founded a home for working girls, and the women of
Vicksburg, Mississippi, bought a residence, repaired it, and established a
nursing and orphan home. Women in Indianapolis, Indiana, turned their
club into a kind of employment agency, securing work for black women
in the canning factories of the city. As of 1909 they had found work for
more than 150 black women. In accordance with the goal of racial uplift,
black women also formed mothers' clubs. Across the country but especially in the South, where the masses of black women lived, mothers'
clubs were formed by middle-class black women to teach the fundamen-
tals of child rearing, homemaking, and self-improvement to their poorer
counterparts. Other clubs provided day care for the children of working
mothers, established reformatories for delinquent children, built community settlement houses, raised money for church projects, or pressured
city officials for playgrounds, sidewalks, and sewer facilities.[3]

Clubs were also active in the antilynching movement led by Ida B.
Wells. They helped finance her 1892 speaking tour of the United States
and the British Isles, and in the wake of World War I mob violence
against blacks, club women launched speaking and petition campaigns
against lynching. Working in tandem with the National Association for
the Advancement of Colored People, the NACW raised thousands of
dollars, testified before Congress, and generally mobilized the black
population in an effort to end the terror of lynching.[4]

That the NACW took up antilynching is not surprising since Wells's
success at revealing the horrors of lynching to the British public provided
the spark leading to the first federation. The NACW was founded after a
series of meetings first organized to defend black women against the
slanderous attack of a Missouri columnist incensed by British outrage
over lynching. The NACW, therefore, owed much to Wells, and although
most club work was in the realm of self-help social service, members paid
their debt to Wells many times over.[5]

Given the NACW's multifaceted program, it is difficult to break club
work into categories of race, class, and gender without oversimplifying
and distorting its efforts. Club women did not usually compartmentalize
their program. As they saw it, what they did for women they did for the
race, what they did for the race they did for all classes of the race, and
when they worked for all classes they worked for black women and black
men. Josephine Bruce spoke for the majority of club women when she
said that "it is difficult to separate the woman problem from the general
problem."[6] The general problem was, of course, the race problem, and
although the historian, in the interest of clarity, can distinguish the
separate elements of club ideology, to Bruce and other black women,
race, class, and gender issues were so inseparable that one could not

work on one front without working on all three. Club women used the
same master plan for black women, for the poor, and for the race.

Black women were, however, the principal actors in their master plan,
and this is the key to understanding the black feminism of the period. So
strong was the club woman's confidence in women that she believed
solutions to the race problem (which inherently included class problems
and poverty) began and ended with black women. "The Negro woman
has been the motive power in whatever has been accomplished by the
race," argued Addie Hunton, an Atlanta club woman who later became
an active NAACP member.[7] Echoing that sentiment, Anna Jones, a
Kansas City club woman and University of Michigan alumna, declared
that the "colored people realize that in the development of their women
lie the best interest of the race."[8] Organizing was also in the best interest
of the race, and club women never missed an opportunity to remind themselves and the public of that fact. According to Josephine Silone Yates,
one-time president of the NACW, since organizing was essential to race
progress and since the NACW was the only truly national black organization,
the NACW was for black people the "first step in nation-making."[9]

No doubt the confidence these women exhibited was partly grounded
in nineteenth-century ideology, which declared women to be the more
nurturant, moral, and altruistic sex. As a group, club women endorsed the
popular belief that women were better suited than men for social welfare
work because man's nature was belligerent, aggressive, and selfish. Frances
Ellen Watkins Harper, a mid-nineteenth-century suffragist, frequently lectured club women on their duty to the race and the advantages of womanhood. She insisted that woman had to be "the companion of man, must
be a sharer" in the social and moral development of the human race. Yet
she criticized men for their greed for gold and lust for power. She
declared that "men had destroyed, dashed in pieces, and overthrown. . . . "
Woman's work, however, she deemed "grandly constructive." Harper
proclaimed the latter part of the nineteenth century to be the "woman's
era," a sentiment endorsed by one of the earliest black club women,
Josephine St. Pierre Ruffin. Founder of the Boston-based New Era Club,
Ruffin published the first black woman's newspaper and appropriately
titled it *Woman's Era.*[10] Anna Julia Cooper also saw the possibilities of
the period. In 1892 she claimed it was up to women to mold "the
strength, the wit, the statesmanship, the morality, all the psychic force,
the social and economic intercourse" of the era. It was the "colored
woman's office" to stamp weal or woe on the history of her people.[11] So
ingrained was the feeling that the woman's era was upon them that by
the time Fannie Williams announced the advent of a "woman's age" in
1904, most club women had already accepted it as a fait accompli.[12]

The black club woman's confidence in her ability to tackle race problems was also nourished by her sense of equality with black men. This sentiment did not grow out of the tradition of enlightenment rationalism or the liberal tradition it spawned. Rather, it was based on the knowledge that black women, just like black men, had endured incredible hardships during slavery and that neither sex had gained any advantage in the nearly two and a half centuries of enslavement. "In our development as a race," argued Fannie Williams, "the colored woman and the colored man started even." She continued, "The man cannot say that he is better educated and has had a wider sphere, for they both began school at the same time. They have suffered the same misfortunes. The limitations put upon their ambitions have been identical. The colored man can scarcely say to his wife 'I am better and stronger than you are,' and from the present outlook, I do not think there is any danger of the man getting very far ahead."[13]

Williams was not alone in this kind of thinking. As a member of the white Chicago Woman's Club and as the first woman to serve on the Library Board of the City of Chicago, she had unique opportunities; however, she shared with other club leaders the idea of equality of black men and women. For instance, Anna Cooper, a founder of the D.C. Women's League and author of *A Voice from the South* (an early treatise on race and womanhood), sounded a similar chord when she argued that gender equality grew from the denial of the franchise to the race. Cooper observed that neither black men nor women had the vote. The black man had been driven from the polls by repression, and the black woman had never been given the franchise. Cooper was dismayed but not discouraged by the harsh and exclusionary politics of late nineteenth-century white America. She thought it might be God's way of preparing the race for something nobler than what white Americans had wrought. Like Williams, she evoked the same image of a new and equal beginning for men and women, declaring that "the race is young and full of the elasticity and hopefulness of youth, all its achievements are before it."[14]

For Williams, Cooper, and the many women who announced the "woman's era," the fact that black men functioned in a wider arena than black women did was clearly inconsequential. Racism severely limited the life chances of black men, but some black men voted, particularly those in the North, and a few held political positions. Black men also held the most powerful positions in the black church, and most, although not all, business people were males.[15] Of course, club women could have pointed to their steadier employment, a few very successful businesswomen, and the host of school founders and educators in their ranks.

Yet women like Cooper and Williams did not see black men as significantly more advantaged than women. The economic successes of individual black men and the positions of power a few held in black and white society did not matter as much as the ineffectualness of black men as a group when it came to the race problem. If club women saw either sex as advantaged, it was their own, a product of the endurance of black women during slavery, the higher development of women's humane sensibilities, and the debilities of black men in white society. For the women who proclaimed the "woman's era," the standard formula was the superiority of women in matters concerning the moral welfare of black people and the equality of black men and women in everything else.

This sense of real equality with black men made the black woman's club movement qualitatively different from the white woman's club movement of the period, even though black and white women seemed to be doing and saying the same things and embracing the same philosophy of womanhood. Some scholars have argued that the essential difference was that black club women worked for their race while white club women worked primarily for self-improvement and only occasionally for their communities.[16] Yet white women's clubs created makeshift libraries, worked for better schools and medical care of children, and lobbied for improved streetcars, sewerage, and garbage collection. They also argued that women brought a greater sense of humanity to the public sphere than men did.[17] But because the context of the black and white women's efforts was different so were the implications of their movements, even when they pursued similar goals and used similar rhetoric.

At the end of the nineteenth century black people were responding not only to the new industrial environment but to racial repression as well. The period was remarkable for black peonage, lynchings, disfranchisement, white primaries, race riots, and a white supremacist ideology that on the national level supported imperialistic expansionist policies. The race was under assault from all sides. Black men were especially challenged because they voted and were, by and large, the direct victims of the convict-lease system and lynch mobs.

It was during what has been called the nadir in the black experience that black club women, with full knowledge of the ravages being wrought, proclaimed the advent of the "woman's era" and came forth with a plan that made black women the primary leaders in the regeneration of the race. Black women argued for their solutions from a position of perceived equality with black men. Looking back, one can see that the most important differences between the white and black club movement went beyond the different emphasis given to self-improvement and community assistance. The black club woman's work went to the heart of the race's leadership. To the extent that black men considered race leadership their own domain, the black club woman's proclamations of equality of condition and superior moral sensibilities challenged male predilections toward black patriarchy.[18]

Club women, however, did not mean to mount a malevolent attack against black men. They argued their position under the banner of race progress. Moreover, their gender-based philosophy synchronized well with the predominant race ideologies articulated by Booker T. Washington and W. E. B. Du Bois. Washington, for instance, argued that progress and uplift began with the individual in the home and the community, precisely the arena in which club women operated. Although Du Bois opted for more public articulation of political rights, he insisted that the most talented blacks were obligated to uplift their less fortunate counterparts. Club women had been doing this for quite some time *before* Du Bois put forth his "talented tenth" philosophy. Moreover, like Du Bois, club women were vocal in their antilynching posture.[19]

While the feminism of the club movement was not at odds with the prevailing race strategies, it did threaten to deny black men an arena in which they could predominate. Women came to community self-help from the home, the traditional woman's sphere. In essence, club women expanded their mother role to the community. Black men, however, did not function from so solid a base. In the traditional male spheres of politics, business enterprise, and professional occupations, they were peripheral. Wholesale terror, the centerpiece of which was lynching, forced most black male spokesmen to adopt an accommodationist race posture, and the majority actually retreated from American politics altogether.[20] Black men therefore exercised most of their political power within the black community. Yet this was precisely the arena in which club women proclaimed their supremacy. When black men did community work, they found themselves in the precarious position of vying with women for leadership in an arena where black women were strong.[21] Even though the race and gender strategies of the club movement were not at odds with predominant race tactics or philosophies, the foundation for tension between male leaders and female club leaders was laid.

Tension was not eased by club women's assertions of race leadership. Although southern club women tended to be less militant in their language, club women from both the North and the South made their feelings known. Margaret Murray Washington was not known for her militancy in either the race or club movement. The third wife of Booker T. Washington, she asked his permission to continue to teach after their marriage, and once married she lived in his shadow, endorsing his philosophy of industrial education and race accommodation and serving almost in the capacity of a secretary. In the club movement, however, she walked in no one's shadow. As a president of the Southern Federation of Colored Women and as editor of the NACW newspaper, *National Association Notes,* Margaret Murray Washington was a preeminent exponent of the philosophy that the rural woman who developed her home and family held "the solution to the so called race problem." In summing up her thinking on the role of women in race advancement, she quipped, "As the woman, so the man is."[22]

Fannie Williams, Anna Cooper, and others were less subtle. Anna Cooper suggested that black men in the South had sold their vote "for a mess of pottage," something the black woman would never do, since she was ever "orthodox on questions affecting the well-being of her race." According to Cooper, it was the southern black woman who kept men united in their support of the Republican party and made men fearful of voting Democratic. Without the women, black men were "apt to divide on local issues" and forget that it was a Republican president who freed the slaves.[23] Fannie Williams was in total agreement. She thought that although men proclaimed their race work, they did very little. In 1894 she told club women not to follow the example of black men "whose innumerable conventions, councils and conferences during the last twenty-five years have all begun with talk and ended with talk."[24]

Club leaders were critical of black men and adamant about female leadership in part because they tied the issue of race progress to the protection of black women against sexual exploitation. Most club leaders found the black male's defense of black womanhood sorely wanting. They understood that violent racism had rendered black men powerless to protect women against rape, but many thought that black men should give black women more vocal support. Anna Cooper wrote of being hampered and shamed by black men who would not admit that women could influence anything, and Fannie Williams faulted black men for not exalting the black woman's character.[25] According to Williams, black women had to rely on themselves for their own defense because there were "too many colored men who hold the degrading opinions of ignorant white men, that all colored girls are alike. . . . How rare are the reported instances of colored men resenting any slur or insult upon their own women." Fannie Williams directly challenged black men: "Is the colored man brave enough to stand out and say to all the world, 'Thus far and no farther in your attempt to insult and degrade our women?' "[26]

The call for black men to show support for black women came from many corners of black middle-class society. Ida B. Wells, like Williams, thought that too many black men shared white society's stereotyped notions about black women. She once confronted a southern black minister who alleged that southern black women lacked virtue. When she finished her defense of black womanhood, he made a public apology before his congregation.[27] Similarly, Addie Hunton, in a 1904 article entitled "Negro Womanhood Defended," upbraided William Hannibal Thomas for his outrageous charge that "not only are fully ninety per cent of the negro women of America lascivious by instinct and in bondage to physical pleasure, but . . . the social degradation of our freedwomen is without parallel in modern civilization." Hunton called Thomas a "Judas Iscariot" and warned against what she perceived as a tendency to blame black women "for every weakness of the race."[28] Hunton insisted that black women needed protection, a sentiment expressed also by the editors of such black newspapers as the *Savannah Tribune* and the *Washington Bee*. The editor of the *Tribune* praised a black man who defended a black woman against a white assailant and suggested that the man's action serve as a model for all black men. W. Calvin Chase, editor of the *Bee*, criticized black men in Washington, D.C., who he felt took sexual advantage of black women because they lacked respect for the black woman's morality.[29]

For club leaders, and for others as well, defense of black womanhood had a meaning deeper than chivalry; it struck at the very heart of the question of race leadership. They reasoned that the direct descendants of whites who had degraded their female slaves now misrepresented the black woman's character to debase her further and to oppress the race as a whole. For club women and their supporters, there was no doubt that the sexual exploitation of black women and the oppression of black people were connected. So closely were gender and race bound in this area that Fannie Williams predicted that "there will never be an unchallenged vote, a respected political power, or an unquestioned claim to position of influence and importance" among Negroes "until the present stigma is removed from the home and the women of its race."[30] Black women therefore had to be protected, not only to prevent their physical assault but also to gain equal rights for blacks.

This line of reasoning was not unique to club women but was the accepted belief of many black men and women. It was not unusual for a late nineteenth-century black person to claim that "a race can rise no higher than its women." Monroe Majors, a black physician from Texas, found three such quotes to grace the title page of his 1893 book on the achievements of black women:

"A race, no less than a nation, is prosperous in proportion to the intelligence of its women."

"The criterion for Negro civilization is the intelligence, purity and high motives of its women."

"The highest mark of our prosperity, and the strongest proofs of Negro capacity to master the sciences and fine arts, are evinced by the advanced positions to which negro women have attained."[31]

The book, *Noted Negro Women*, was a defense of black womanhood and the race. In presenting almost four hundred pages of names and achievements of black women, Majors hoped to prove not just that black women were worthy of recognition but that their progress made the race itself worthy. As Majors put it in his preface, the book was written as a "signification of Negro progress."[32]

Also in his preface was a veiled reference to the debate over race leadership. Majors noted that an important question was "whether our leading women have cleared the culminating point and out-distanced our great men. . . . "[33] In the minds of many club women, the answer was undeniably affirmative. That is why Fannie Williams confidently said that men's conventions began and ended with talk, and Josephine Silone Yates claimed that the NACW was the "first step in nation-making."[34]

It is hard to say how widespread it was, but there was considerable support for the contention that women were more capable race leaders. For instance, the male editorial board of *The Voice of the Negro*, an early twentieth-century race periodical, advised the NACW to "set their faces like a flint against the political methods of our men." They further advised, "Eschew 'Resolutions,' 'Petitions' and 'Memorials' to congress, governors or anybody else. The men in the religious, political, social and educational conferences and conventions have filled up the Book of Resolutions. There is not a single page left. But the Book of Acts has not had the first page or chapter written in it. Women of the Negro Race!! Write a Book of Acts for the race."[35]

Although there was support for female leadership, there was also opposition. The noted educator John Hope opened a speech to an Atlanta woman's club by chastising them for caustic remarks they had made about men. Hope regretted that an eminent Georgia clergyman delighted in the saying that "all the men we have are women," and while he conceded that the preacher meant well, Hope was sure the sentiment was "dangerous" for black women because the black race needed its men to be more manly and women to be more womanly. For women to act as substitutes for men would, according to Hope, amount to "calamity."[36] Other men echoed Hope, accepting the dogma that a race can rise no higher than its women but interpreting the phrase very narrowly. A contributor to James Haley's *Sparkling Gems of Race Knowledge Worth Reading* thought that if black women pursued intellectual activity over child rearing, the race would raise dangerous citizens.[37] Even W. E. B.

Du Bois, whose support and praise of black women was unfailing, believed that women exercised their greatest influence in the home, as keepers of the hearth and socializers of future generations.[38]

The point of this discussion, however, is not how much support there was for female leadership or who among black men supported or opposed such roles, but that for club women the issue of female leadership turned on whether black men were willing to defend black women against physical and verbal abuse. The club leadership's belief that refuge from sexual exploitation could materialize only when the issue took priority in race matters, that black men either did not take the issue seriously or had been co-opted by white propaganda, led them to conclude that women had to take the helm of race leadership. They did not doubt they were equal to the task, for, as discussed earlier, their feminism gave them the utmost confidence in women and reinforced their belief in the actual equality of black men and women.

Of course for club leaders to make protection of black women the test of race leadership was to place black men between the proverbial rock and a hard place. For women to assume the traditional male protectionist role and make themselves, as Addie Hunton asserted, their own emancipators, was to create tension.[39] To ridicule male leadership that was already under violent assault was to add insult to injury. No doubt the black club movement and the "woman's era" were greeted with a degree of suspicion by black men. That some men found shelter in the acceptance of the promiscuous black woman stereotype and that some cautioned black women not to extend their influence beyond the home should come as no surprise, for around the turn of the century it was easier to do battle with black women than with white racists. Black women might have made life for black men psychologically uncomfortable, but white supremacists made the black male's life pure hell.

On the other hand, gender tension was the price black women paid for their feminism. No matter how much they succeeded in synchronizing race and gender in ideology, there would always be blacks, particularly black men, who would regard female leadership with suspicion and resentment. There would always be the competing notion that patriarchal norms, not feminist principles, were the foundation on which race progress had to be built. No matter how much they needed protection, black women would seldom be able to insist on it, for in doing so they implicitly challenged black men to risk the lynch mob, judicial retribution, or psychological belittlement. In the context of racism, feminism set black men and women at further odds with each other. In tackling racism, they did battle not only with white America but unfortunately with each other as well.

Gender tension was not the only by-product of turn-of-the-century women's activism. Fannie Williams challenged black men to protect black women, but she also challenged them to recognize that all black women were not alike. Addie Hunton said almost the same thing. In her defense of black womanhood, Hunton was upset not only because a black man had joined forces with the white race to insult black women but also because "those who write most about the moral degradation of the Negro woman know little or nothing of that best element of our women. . . ."[40] This argument was made frequently. Black club women drew distinctions among black women. Sylvania Williams of New Orleans, Louisiana, found the white person's blanket condemnation of all black women to be the "darkest shadow and deepest wound." She wanted whites to recognize class differences: "We could not, nor would not feel aggrieved, if in citing the immorality of the Negro, the accusation was limited to the pauperized and brutalized members of the race."[41]

The entire issue of sexual exploitation thus spoke to the issue of class. Succinctly put, club women correctly believed that the sexual exploitation of black women originated during the slavery era, when white men used black women like cattle to reproduce the slave population. When white men forbade legal slave marriages, separated families, and took sexual advantage of female slaves, they further debased black women. Club women believed they could, and to some extent had, overcome their history, indeed that it was a prerequisite to race progress.

One aspect of their plan of action was to lecture to anyone who would listen on the unbridled lust of white men, the helplessness of black women, and the complicity of white women. Mostly, though, their program was directed inward. The goal of many clubs was to teach black women how to lead moral lives and make their homes a bulwark in defense of black womanhood. The motto of the NACW, "Lifting As We Climb," emphasized this bond between the middle and lower classes. The duty of the middle-class club woman was to provide not just social services for the poor but services that in one way or another educated blacks, particularly black women, on the means and benefits of achieving the moral life. In the club leaders' thinking, moral purity was the key to social improvement. Social improvement meant everything from music appreciation to civic responsibility, but the first step was chastity. Chastity would liberate black women from their "blighted past," and because it would fend off the advances of white men, it would, according to Sylvania Williams, preserve race integrity.[42]

For club women, then, chastity was the litmus test of middle-class respectability. As a group, black people were prevented from ownership of property and upward mobility in the traditional economic and political sense of the terms. At least through the first quarter of the twentieth century, middle-class status in black society was therefore associated more with "style of life" than with gross economic income. Adoption of a particular "style" qualified one for the middle class. Manners, morality, a particular mode of consumption, race work—these were the criteria for middle-class status.[43] For club women, chastity was at the top of the list. It could be nowhere else, for only by giving it highest priority could the NACW fulfill its pledge to protect black women against slander. If all black women were chaste, then clearly all of the onus, either for exploiting black women or for failing to protect them, was on men.

Yet in making chastity the foremost requirement for middle-class status, club women established an orthodoxy bound to drive a wedge between themselves and the masses of black women. Unwittingly, club women placed the burden of sexual exploitation on the shoulders of the victim—the black woman. Even though they sympathized and empathized with the masses of black women, called on white men to stop taking advantage of them, and chastised black men for not defending them, the educational programs of most clubs were aimed at reforming the very persons on whose behalf they spoke. Reform of black women was essential to their program, not only because it was a way of preventing sexual exploitation but also because club women believed that it was a "woman's age" and that black women themselves could and should solve the race problem. If the Atlanta educator and school founder Lucy Laney was correct, the veil of "ignorance and immorality" had "intensified prejudice," and the educated black woman's "burden" was to lift that veil.[44]

Many club women believed it would take a lot of work. Anna Jones declared that some women of the race had made progress in refining their social life but that most black women had not yet followed their example. In fact, she regretted that the moral standard of "our average is lower than that of the people by whom we are surrounded."[45] Most club women were not as negative as Jones, but they almost universally confessed a belief that slavery had left black women devoid of moral character and that the most difficult struggle in the years since slavery had been the establishment of moral principles. In the homes they established for troubled or delinquent girls, in mothers' clubs, and in their speeches, club leaders set about reversing what they saw as the most detrimental consequence of slavery. In the process, they opened a gulf between a small circle of club leaders and the masses by insisting that black girls who transgressed the moral law be "shut off from the best class of people, and looked askance by ordinary people."[46]

There was another reason that club women were so earnest about chastity. Morality would have to prevail for the sake of not just the race but middle-class educated black women, who were not free to reach their potential as long as the masses of black women were judged to be immoral.[47] Their oft repeated pleas for whites and blacks to distinguish between the different classes of black women suggest that while club women worked to reform and educate working-class and rural black women, on some level club leaders regretted being classed with them and resented the women they set out to reform. This suggests that turn-of-the-century black female unity was a political concept born of the exigencies of the times. It was not a social reality and was not proclaimed to be.[48] Mary Church Terrell, the first president of the NACW, was quite succinct about the tactical and strategic nature of the union of middle-class and poor black women. Of educated black women, she wrote that "they know that they cannot escape altogether the consequences of the acts of their most depraved sisters. They see that even if they were wicked enough to turn a deaf ear to the call of duty, both policy and self-preservation demand that they go down among the lowly, the illiterate and even the vicious, to whom they are bound by ties of race and sex, and put forth every possible effort to reclaim them."[49] Addie Dickerson, a Philadelphia club woman, shared Terrell's perspective. In *National Association Notes*, she wrote that the black women on Philadelphia's sleazy South Street attracted more attention from the white media than club women did. Issuing a warning similar to that made by Terrell, Dickerson told NACW women that "until we shall have helped this class, until we have raised them to our standard, there is danger of our being dragged to their level in the public eye by our enemies. . . . If we can save and help this class we are saved and helped ourselves to all eternity."[50]

These sentiments compel an analysis of the NACW that goes beyond a rehearsal of their altruism. Without belittling the NACW and its myriad accomplishments, we need to understand that the different classes of black women were allied, not united; that their alliance was based on race and sex sameness and the sentiments that flowed from this kinship, not on social or cultural unity. Given their program, the NACW motto, "Lifting As We Climb," presumed race and sex sameness and social and cultural distance.

That distance was manifested in other aspects of club work and philosophy. For instance, among the clubs affiliated with the NACW were numerous literary, art, and music appreciation clubs aimed at cultural improvement.[51] Formed for the sole benefit of their members, these clubs were founded on the belief that character development was dependent on intellectual growth and that black people had been denied such growth even while they were unfairly penalized for lack of it. Charlotte Hawkins Brown, president and founder of North Carolina's Palmer Memorial Institute, established one such literary club in 1909.[52] Years later, in a speech entitled "The Quest of Culture," she explained the importance of culture and, by implication, the purpose of improvement clubs. On the practical level, she thought that "Nordics" would give black people more social recognition if blacks adopted the social practices and customs of "peoples of refined tastes." On a more esoteric level, Brown explained the meaning culture had for her: "Culture is the discipline of the mental and moral powers manifest in the ease, grace and poise one exhibits in the performance of one's life. It is the result of the development of the intellect and the appreciation of the aesthetic. Culture may be achieved through intensive training and continued practice."[53]

The purpose of the literary, art, and music clubs, therefore, was to provide intensive training and continued practice, not in black culture, which was implicitly judged inadequate, but in the dominant high culture of the period.[54] The Kansas City Book Club, for instance, read Confucius and discussed the moral philosophy of Athens. In addition, their meetings were social occasions, where members felt compelled to wear the finest fashions and exhibit the finest social graces. The "fashionette promenades" held by the book club were not events open to ordinary black women, and there is little question that the majority of the black female masses would have felt more than a little uncomfortable at such events.[55]

Another area where difference was manifest between middle-class club women and the black female masses was religion. The emphasis leaders put on intellectual development and cultural refinement was inconsistent with the emotionally charged religious services in which most blacks participated. Anna Cooper found the emotionalism of black worshippers "ludicrous," and Mary Church Terrell found it "discouraging and shocking to see how some of the women shout, holler and dance" during services. To Cooper and Terrell, such behavior only reinforced the pervasive negative images of black women. Cooper, in particular, found the Protestant Episcopal church more to her liking. Predictably, she found "its quiet, chaste dignity and decorous solemnity" infinitely more proper than the "semi-civilized religionism" of most black churches.[56] Fannie Williams attacked black religion on other grounds. For her, black religion had not caught up with the age of science and reason that characterized the late nineteenth century. Although encouraged by black women's acceptance of the many different religious doctrines, "from the Catholic creed to the no-creed of Emerson," Williams regretted that black women adapted only slowly to "the growing rationalism in the Christian creeds."[57]

Besides the class differences, a crucial gender issue was raised by club leaders' religious practices and beliefs. To their concern over image and reason, they added their fear that most black ministers retarded race progress. Ida B. Wells described black preachers as "corrupt" and "ignorant."[58] Margaret Murray Washington agreed. Of Quaker background, she shared her husband's belief that black ministers were self-aggrandizing opportunists. Suggesting that black women could use their time more profitably, she cautioned them against spending too much time in church.[59] From the NACW leader's perspective, black preachers, especially southern itinerants, were negative role models. Many agreed with Fannie Williams's assessment that the race was "more hindered by a large part of the ministry intrusted with leadership than by any other single cause."[60] From the club leaders' vantage point, preachers preached the "new day" sermon but, unlike club women, did little to usher it in. Instead of initiating self-help programs and executing plans to eliminate race prejudice, they avoided hard work and lived off the contributions of the more industrious. By eschewing reason in favor of emotion, ministers not only retarded the progress of the black masses but also proved an embarrassment to the race. This made them, in the club leaders' view, part of the race problem, part of that male leadership that did so little to advance the race.[61]

Of course, not everyone shared this outlook. Most blacks continued to prefer the emotionally charged congregational churches over the more sedate Catholic and Calvinist denominations. In black communities ministers remained a force to be reckoned with, and many blacks just ignored the NACW or ridiculed the positions it took on race leadership, culture, and religion.[62]

For their part, NACW leaders were aware that there were alternative voices in black America. Indeed, they knew that some blacks thought they mimicked white women and that others felt club activity was merely an excuse to socialize. Added to these criticisms was the argument that there were just too many clubs for the NACW to be effective. Others claimed that clubs promising kindergartens, reading rooms, and other charities did not always deliver on their promises and that those purporting to study art, music and literature did no such thing.[63]

In response, NACW leaders either denied the charges or urged individual women and clubs to make good on their promises, suggesting in the process that the criticism was not unfounded. Anna Jones, for instance, flatly denied charges that NACW members only socialized, insisting "there are no society butterflies among them."[64] On the other hand, Josephine Yates lamented that some club women seemed to forget the uplift purpose of the NACW. What the organization needed, she wrote, were women to "work, work, work," not women who were "so much show and talk."[65] Fannie Williams concurred. She was just as demanding of club women as she was of black men and the poor. The NACW, she warned, "is of little value unless it can and does actually do the thing for which it was called into being." She cautioned against the tendency of some clubs to adopt the constitutions, bylaws, and programs of white clubs, and as early as 1904 she called on the clubs of the NACW to abandon programs that its members had neither the talent nor money to implement.[66]

What the criticism of the clubs pointed to, and what Yates and Williams were guarding against, was the proclivity of various clubs toward a separatism that was contrary to the NACW motto, "Lifting As We Climb." Only two years after the NACW's founding, Margaret Murray Washington urged club women to resist the temptation to set themselves apart. "We can not separate ourselves from our people," she warned, "no matter how much we try."[67] Twenty-two years later at the organization's 1920 national convention, Katherine Macarthy issued a stinging criticism that suggested more than a few clubs had been unsuccessful in following Washington's advice. Speaking before the general assembly, she observed, "It seems to be getting more and more the tendency of the club women to hold themselves aloof from others, to move around in a prescribed circle and to ostracize everybody else who does not happen to be in that circle." If, as she further alleged, there were "many places in which there are federated clubs, and in those very places there are hundreds of women, good women, intelligent women, who have never heard of our federation, either state or national," then an unanticipated consequence of club activity had been the development of social cliques.[68] Macarthy's charges, and the advice that came from Washington, Yates, and Williams, suggest that while the NACW's feminist strategy of race uplift gave some black women the opportunity to prove women could work effectively against racism, it also encouraged an exclusiveness and eventually an aloofness that proved damaging to the NACW's program and image. There is no doubt the clubs spawned sorority and friendship that helped its members accomplish the often lonely work of social uplift. Sisterhood provided the necessary underpinning of black feminist race work.[69] Yet, for an organization whose prominent members had denounced black male leadership and set themselves up as examples for the working poor, exclusive social cliques were a regrettable development.

But such was the cost of club work and the price of feminism. Black club women were earnest about their abilities to solve the race problem. Their feminism served them well in this regard, for it provided the confidence and the ideological basis for their leadership in the uplift of the race. Indeed, their accomplishments were many. When neither the government nor white social workers would lend blacks a helping hand, NACW women came forward with settlements for women and girls, hospitals and nursing homes, reading rooms, kindergartens, and antilynching race work. Nevertheless, their feminism was divisive because it challenged black men, because the solutions prescribed belittled less fortunate black women, and because it encouraged club women to associate only with one another. Given the problems they tried to solve, however, it is difficult to imagine that they could have chosen another path or that there could have been a different result. If there was a culprit, it was the discrimination they fought on all fronts—race, class, and gender. As blacks and as women, they could not ignore the discrimination against all blacks, the problems of poverty, and the exploitation of black women. They had to tackle problems of race, class, and gender and come up with solutions on all fronts. That they could not juggle all three variables and be perfect is not surprising, for the problems they could not solve, as well as the problems their programs gave rise to, have been among the most tenacious in the twentieth century.

NOTES

1. Loretta Barnett Floris Cash, "Womanhood and Protest: The Club Movement among Black Women, 1892-1922" (Ph.D. diss., SUNY-Stony Brook, 1986), 55-76, 85; Paula Giddings, *When and Where I Enter: The Impact of Black Women on Race and Sex in America* (New York: William Morrow, 1984), 89-95. For additional studies on the club movement or aspects of the club movement, see Adrienne Lash Jones, *Jane Edna Hunter: A Case Study of Black Leadership, 1910-1950,* vol. 12 of *Black Women in United States History,* ed. Darlene Clark Hine (Brooklyn: Carlson, 1990); Beverly Washington Jones, *Quest for Equality: The Life and Writings of Mary Eliza Church Terrell, 1863-1954,* vol. 13 of *Black Women in United States History,* ed. Hine; Gerda Lerner, *The Majority Finds Its Past: Placing Women in History* (New York: Oxford University Press, 1979), 83-93; Cynthia Neverdon-Morton, *Afro-American Women of the South and the Advancement of the Race, 1895-1925* (Knoxville: University of Tennessee Press, 1989); Jacqueline Anne Rouse, *Lugenia Burns Hope, Black Southern Reformer* (Athens: University of Georgia Press, 1989); Dorothy Salem, *To Better Our World: Black Women in Organized Reform, 1890-1920,* vol. 14 of *Black Women in United States History,* ed. Hine; Anne Firor Scott, "Most Invisible of All: Black Women's Voluntary Associations," *Journal of Southern History* 56 (February 1990): 3-22; and Stephanie J. Shaw, "Black Club Women and the Creation of the National Association of Colored Women," *Journal of Women's History* 3 (Fall 1991): 10-25.

2. W. E. B. Du Bois, ed., *Efforts for Social Betterment among Negro Americans* (Atlanta: Atlanta University Press, 1909), 47-64.

3. Ibid.

4. Cash, *"Womanhood and Protest,"* 176-206; *Woman's Era,* May 1894, 8; June 1894, 6, 14; July 1894, 4.

5. Giddings, *When and Where I Enter,* 93.

6. Josephine Bruce, "What Has Education Done for Colored Women," *Voice of the Negro* 1, no. 7 (1904): 297. Historians and social scientists who study black feminism have reiterated Bruce's comments in their discussions of black feminism. See, for instance, Elsa Barkley Brown, "Womanist Consciousness: Maggie Lena Walker and the Independent Order of Saint Luke," *Signs* 14, no. 3 (1989): 610-32; Patricia Hill Collins, *Black Feminist Thought: Knowledge, Consciousness, and the Politics of Empowerment* (New York: Routledge, Chapman and Hall, 1990); and Deborah K. King, "Multiple Jeopardy, Multiple Consciousness: The Context of a Black Feminist Ideology," *Signs* 14, no. 1 (1988): 42-72.

7. Addie Hunton, "Negro Womanhood Defended," *Voice of the Negro* 1, no. 7 (1904): 280.

8. Anna Jones, "The American Colored Woman," *Voice of the Negro* 2, no. 10 (1905): 692.

9. Josephine Silone Yates, "Woman's Clubs," in *Efforts for Social Betterment,* ed. Du Bois, 47.

10. Bert James Loewenberg and Ruth Bogin, eds., *Black Women in Nineteenth Century American Life: Their Words, Their Thoughts, Their Feelings* (University Park: Pennsylvania State University Press, 1976), 243-45.

11. Anna Julia Cooper, *A Voice from the South* (New York: Negro Universities Press, 1969 [1892]), 143, 145.

12. Fannie Barrier Williams, "The Woman's Part in a Man's Business," *Voice of the Negro* 1, no. 11 (1904): 544.

13. Ibid., 546.

14. Cooper, *Voice from the South,* 138, 144.

15. For general overviews of black life with reference to this topic, see Jacqueline Jones, *Labor of Love, Labor of Sorrow: Black Women, Work, and the Family from Slavery to the Present* (New York: Basic Books, 1985), 180-81; articles in *Black Women in United States History,* vols. 1 and 2, ed. Hine; Julius F. Nimmons, "Social Reform and Moral Uplift in the Black Community 1890-1910: Social Settlements, Temperance, and Social Purity" (Ph.D. diss., Howard University, 1981); August Meier and Elliott Rudwick, eds., *From Plantation to Ghetto* (New York: Hill and Wang, 1970), 177-212; and Allan H. Spear, *Black Chicago: The Making of a Negro Ghetto, 1890-1920* (Chicago: University of Chicago Press, 1967).

16. Cash, "Womanhood and Protest," 8-11; Giddings, *When and Where I Enter,* 96-100.

17. Karen J. Blair, *The Clubwoman as Feminist: True Womanhood Redefined, 1868-1914* (New York: Holmes and Meier, 1980), 93-115.

18. This subject is explored in this essay. See remarks by John Hope, W. E. B. Du Bois, and others later in this essay.

19. Washington's *Up From Slavery* offers testimony to his ideas about the place of the community, home, and school in the uplift of the race and gives Washington's version of how he came to his beliefs. See Booker T. Washington, *Up From Slavery* in *Three Negro Classics* (New York: Avon Books, 1965 [1901]), esp. 122–23. See also Louis R. Harlan, "Booker T. Washington and the Politics of Accommodation," in *Black Leaders of the Twentieth Century,* ed. John Hope Franklin and August Meier (Urbana: University of Illinois Press, 1982), 3–4; W. E. B. Du Bois, *The Souls of Black Folk,* in *Three Negro Classics* [1903], 280, 326.

20. Joel Williamson, *A Rage for Order: Black-White Relations in the American South since Emancipation* (New York: Oxford University Press, 1986), 60; Meier and Rudwick, eds., *From Plantation to Ghetto,* 177, 188, 194.

21. Nimmons, "Social Reform and Moral Uplift," 20–23, 52–60, for evidence that men, as ministers, deacons, masons, and concerned citizens, worked in much the same manner as women for uplift of the community.

22. Mrs. Booker T. Washington, "Social Improvement of the Plantation Woman," *Voice of the Negro* 1, no. 7 (1904): 290.

23. Cooper, *Voice from the South,* 139, 140.

24. *Woman's Era,* June 1894, 5.

25. Cooper, *Voice from the South,* 135.

26. Fannie Williams, "The Colored Girl," *Voice of the Negro* 2, no. 6 (1905): 403.

27. Alfreda M. Duster, ed., *The Autobiography of Ida B. Wells* (Chicago: University of Chicago Press, 1970), 43–45.

28. William Hannibal Thomas, *The American Negro: What He Was, What He Is, and What He May Become* (New York: MacMillan, 1901), 195; Hunton, "Negro Womanhood Defended," 280.

29. *Savannah Tribune,* April 13, 1907; *Washington Bee,* May 27, 1893. Quoted in Nimmons, "Social Reform and Moral Uplift," 245, 258.

30. Fannie Williams, "The Club Movement among the Colored Women," *Voice of the Negro* 1, no. 3 (1904): 102.

31. Monroe A. Majors, *Noted Negro Women: Their Triumphs and Activities* (Chicago: Donohue and Henneberry, 1986 [1893]).

32. Ibid., x.

33. Ibid., viii–ix.

34. See notes 9 and 24.

35. Editorial, *Voice of the Negro* 1, no. 7 (1904): 310–11.

36. Alton Hornsby, ed., *The Papers of John and Lugenia Hope* (Frederick, Md.: University Publications of America, 1984), 2–3, reel 21, 0213.

37. James T. Haley, *Sparkling Gems of Race Knowledge Worth Reading* (Nashville: J. T. Haley, 1897), 123.

38. See Beverly Guy-Sheftall, *Daughters of Sorrow: Attitudes toward Black Women, 1880–1920,* in *Black Women in United States History,* vol. 11, ed. Hine, 72.

39. Addie Hunton, "The Southern Federation of Colored Women," *Voice of the Negro* 2, no. 12 (1905): 850.

40. Hunton, "Negro Womanhood Defended," 280.

41. Sylvania Francoz Williams, "The Social Status of the Negro Woman," *Voice of the Negro* 1, no. 7 (1904): 299.

42. Ibid.; Hunton, "Negro Womanhood Defended," 280.

43. Bart Landry, *The New Black Middle Class* (Berkeley: University of California Press, 1987), 18-66. The black middle class also conforms to what Max Weber called a status group. See Max Weber, *Essay in Sociology,* trans. and ed. H. H. Gerth and C. Wright Mills (New York: Oxford University Press, 1946), 186, 194, 300-301. For a comprehensive study of the black upper and middle class, see Willard B. Gatewood, *Aristocrats of Color: The Black Elite, 1880-1920* (Bloomington: Indiana University Press, 1990). For his discussion of the transformation that occurred in the 1920s, see 325-48; see also August Meier, "Negro Class Structure and Ideology in the Age of Booker T. Washington," *Phylon* 23, no. 3 (1962): 258-66; and August Meier and David Lewis, "History of the Negro Upper Class in Atlanta, Georgia, 1890-1958," *Journal of Negro Education* 28 (Spring 1959): 128-39.

44. Lucy Laney, "The Burden of the Educated Colored Woman," in *Black Women,* ed. Loewenberg and Bogin, 299.

45. Jones, "The American Colored Woman," 694.

46. Bruce, "What Has Education Done for Colored Women," 295.

47. See also Giddings, *When and Where I Enter,* 95-102.

48. For instance, in speaking of upper-class social circles in Washington, D.C., Terrell noted that there were "subdivisions ad infinitum" but that there was "one general rule of admission into all, to which there has never been an exception. . . . It would be as difficult for a bore or a moral leper to obtain social recognition among the educated, refined, colored people at Washington, as it would be for a camel with a hump to pass literally through a cambric needle's eye." See Mary Church Terrell, "Society among the Colored People of Washington," *Voice of the Negro* 1, no. 4 (1904): 152.

49. Quoted in Sharon Harley, "Mary Church Terrell: Genteel Militant," in *Black Leaders in the Nineteenth Century,* ed. Leon Litwack and August Meier (Urbana: University of Illinois Press, 1988), 311.

50. *National Association Notes* 17, no. 3 [n.d., probably 1914], 7.

51. Du Bois, ed., *Efforts for Social Betterment,* 47-64.

52. Letter from Grace Deering Literary Society to Charlotte Hawkins Brown, n.d. 1909, Series 1, Charlotte Hawkins Brown (CHB) Papers, Library of Congress, Washington, D.C.

53. Speeches, 1929, Series 1, CHB Papers.

54. See Laney, "Burden of the Educated Colored Woman," 299.

55. Kansas City Federation of Colored Women's Clubs, Frederick Douglass Collection, Moorland-Spingarn Research Center, Howard University, Washington, D.C.

56. Cooper, *Voice From the South,* 34; Mary Church Terrell, diary entry May

24, 1936, reel 7-8, Mary Church Terrell Papers, Library of Congress, Washington, D.C.

57. Fannie Williams, "The Intellectual Progress of the Colored Women of the United States since the Emancipation Proclamation," in *Black Women*, ed. Loewenberg and Bogin, 272.

58. Letter from Ida B. Wells to Booker T. Washington, November 30, 1890, in *The Booker T. Washington Papers*, vol. 3, ed. Louis Harlan, Stuart Kaufman, and Raymond Smock (Urbana: University of Illinois Press, 1974), 108.

59. Speech given by Mrs. Booker T. Washington in 1898 in Charleston, S.C. See *The Booker T. Washington Papers*, vol. 4, ed. Louis Harlan, Stuart Kaufman, Barbara Kraft, and Raymond Smock (Urbana: University of Illinois Press, 1975), 467.

60. Fannie Williams, "Religious Duty to the Negro," in *Black Women*, ed. Loewenberg and Bogin, 269. See also Williams, "The Intellectual Progress of the Colored Women," 272.

61. For general information on the relationship between class and religion in black society, see Vattel Elbert Daniel, "Negro Classes and Life in the Church," *Journal of Negro Education* 13, no. 1 (1944): 19-29; St. Clair Drake and Horace R. Cayton, *Black Metropolis: A Study of Negro Life in a Northern City*, vol. 2 (New York: Harcourt, Brace, 1945), 535-40; Norval Glenn, "Negro Religion and Negro Status in the United States," in *Religion, Culture and Society: A Reader in the Sociology of Religion*, ed. Louis Schneider (New York: John Wiley and Sons, 1964), 623-39; and Spear, *Black Chicago*, 91-97.

62. To undertake a discussion of the alternative voices in black America during this period would take this essay far afield of its stated purpose. To explore this topic, one should probably begin with the list of life-styles cited in Williamson, *A Rage for Order*, 53-57; and then proceed to such studies as Lawrence Levine's *Black Culture and Black Consciousness: Afro-American Folk Thought from Slavery to Freedom* (Oxford: Oxford University Press, 1977), 136-446.

63. It is difficult, if not impossible, to obtain from the average black woman an opinion or evaluation of the club movement. They did not leave personal records that give an account of their feelings on the subject. The criticism cited here comes from the writings and speeches of club women who were aware of, and sensitive about, their standing in black communities. Fearful of rebuke from those they were trying to help, these women guarded against negative characterizations of club women. It is probably safe to assume that if club women picked up on a criticism, they picked it up from nonclub members and/or average working-class black Americans. In this case see Williams, "The Club Movement among Colored Women," 100.

64. Jones, "The American Colored Woman," 693.

65. Letter from Josephine Silone Yates to Margaret Murray Washington, May 16, 1904, box 132, Booker T. Washington and Margaret Murray Washington Papers, Tuskegee Institute Library, Tuskegee, Ala.

66. Williams, "The Club Movement among Colored Women," 101-2.

67. Speech given by Mrs. Booker T. Washington in 1898 in Charleston, S.C. See *The Booker T. Washington Papers,* vol. 4, ed. Harlan et al., 464.

68. Katherine Macarthy, "The Club and the Community," *National Association Notes* 23, no. 4/5/6 (1923): 12.

69. For instance, in her 1930 address to the Kansas City Federation of Colored Women's Clubs, the outgoing president, Rosabelle S. Jones, tied service to sisterhood this way: "if to 'LIFTING AS WE CLIMB' we add to this quotation ... 'Add to kindness amiability/Subtract good from evil/Multiply duty by love/Divide cheerfulness to its lowest denomination and/The result will be TRUE FRIENDSHIP.' " See Kansas City Federation of Colored Women's Clubs, folder 92, Frederick Douglass Collection.

Bridging Chasms:
Community and the Southern YWCA

Marion W. Roydhouse

In 1924 the national staff of the Young Women's Christian Association's Industrial Department issued a bulletin that laid out its thinking about women workers in industry. Since most Americans felt that those who could escape ought to "leave the working class group" behind, women workers had a "cramping sense of social inferiority" that needed to be eradicated if American society was to become truly egalitarian. If industrial workers sat on the boards of the Y and were members of its committees, there would be not only "democratic control" of the association but also contact among different groups within the organization. This would lead to a sense of fellowship and community that would "help bridge the chasms of racial, class, and religious prejudice" and eliminate that sense of inferiority.[1]

Y leaders thus made clear their expectation that workers were going to gain political power. The YWCA's role in this change was to create a place where "women of all kinds [could] discuss industrial problems in the light of the teachings of Jesus." The national staff, convinced that discussion by itself was not enough, added that "such discussion, if it is to have vitality, does of course result in action such as legislation, in many instances."[2]

The extent and the exact nature of this "action" would cause a debate in southern YWCAs before World War II that would tug at the delicate threads of community the women's organization had carefully woven. What follows is an exploration of these tensions and the ways women found to hold together southern YWCAs despite the "chasms" created by racial, class, and religious divisions.

The YWCA aimed to be an organization in which women could come together to carve out a social and physical space where the racial, economic, and social divisions endemic in the wider society might be overcome by a combination of the social gospel, feminism, and progressive reform spirit. An examination of the Industrial Department, organized by and for industrial working women, can reveal both the limits and the successes of a women's community in the early twentieth century.

An investigation of the YWCA Industrial Department in the southern states, where the cramping force of racism was at its height and where anti-union and antilabor feeling was virulent, can give us a sense of the kinds of constraints placed on women's public activism. The focus is on one region, but in many ways the same elements were at work in other parts of the nation in the years between the turn of the century and World War II.

The YWCA in the South was able to forge a place in the local community, but it was not able to overcome segregation and could only create an extremely limited interracial movement. The YWCA was more successful in its efforts to support labor legislation and labor activism, despite enormous opposition. The pressures on the women's community that undercut labor reform efforts will be explored, but we also need to examine the hard-won efforts to overcome differences created by the wider social and economic structure that were a part of the Industrial Department's work. In the small towns and cities scattered across the Piedmont landscape, where the "dark, satanic mills" had erupted in the late nineteenth century, women workers from the tobacco factories and the textile mills joined the Y, as did college women and their older compatriots, many of them married and now members of influential families. After 1908 an internal division of structure in the YWCA emerged that allowed industrial workers to organize separately within the organization and to address the particular needs and interests of this group of women. While an element of uplift and condescension born of class difference was endemic in the organization, the YWCA was commit-ted to creating a place where women from vastly different social groups could communicate their concerns.

The Young Women's Christian Association had originated not in the heavily Protestant and evangelical southern states but in the North during the process of industrial and commercial growth and urbanization that took off after the Civil War. A parallel set of associations emerged in the Midwest when women began to meet in prayer groups on college campuses. The southern states came late to this social movement.

Protestant college women insisted that members of the YWCA must be "in good standing" in an "evangelical church."[3] The city Ys, however, focused less on religious qualification and more on a social mission rooted in the desire to provide a Christian home, and thus moral support, for young women newly arrived in the urban milieu. In the 1880s and 1890s the two wings of the movement fought over the fairly restrictive require-ment for voting membership, but they reached an official compromise in the winter of 1906 that allowed for the creation of one directorate and thus one national organization, which would be headquartered in New York. Well into the 1930s, however, debate continued over who could be a voting member of the YWCA.

This long conflict between the American (or student and midwestern) Committee and the International (or city-centered) Board left the YWCA divided over the relative importance of its several goals. The debate over membership was only part of a wider conflict concerning the extent to which the organization would be an active proponent of social reform. Should the YWCA be a group focusing exclusively on spiritual outreach and restricted to Protestant young women, or would its mission be to reach as many as possible, regardless of their religious affiliation and racial or ethnic background? After World War I the national organization became increasingly more ecumenical and moved toward social activism, but this did not prevent regional divergence because the association maintained a very democratic and rather loose structure.[4] This debate was especially important in the South, with its overwhelmingly evangelical climate; this conflict was played out continually in each local branch, especially in the Industrial Departments. When local branches emerged in the southern states at the turn of the twentieth century, the national leadership was determined they would advance the broader goal of assuring "the physical, social, intellectual, moral and spiritual interests of young women" rather than simply minister to spiritual needs or provide only social uplift.[5]

The Young Men's Christian Association took a different philosophical turn at this point and remained much more evangelical and much less reform-minded. This lead to a constant undercurrent of tension between the two organizations that was often reflected in competition between the two groups at the local level.[6]

To understand the impact of the Industrial Department as a separate group within the YWCA in the South, we need to explore briefly the threefold vision of its national leadership. Propelled principally by the energy of a young midwesterner, Florence Simms, who was the leader of the Industrial Department until her early death in 1923, these women wanted to provide for a "more abundant personal life," which meant both intellectual and physical development. Equally important was the "creation of fellowship within the industrial group and between it and other groups within and without the Association." This community was to be driven by the social gospel, not simply evangelical fervor. The YWCA was to transform the larger society in the hope that "relations between classes, races and nations may be controlled by the principles of brotherhood."[7] Class and racial conflict would be erased by women whose energy flowed from a commitment to social change.

The Industrial Department stood firmly committed to the idea that women who worked in industry had special needs as a consequence of their "living close to the margins and realities of life." The leadership was well aware that even within the walls of the association industrial workers were regarded as somewhat less valuable members than others and were seen as "bettering themselves" if they moved into office work. Yet, Simms and her colleagues argued, these women had a "greater potential group consciousness than any other group in the Association," and they should be encouraged to explore the causes and consequences of the social, economic, and political structure. "Clear thinking and sane judgment on the social and industrial problems with which they are surrounded" would lead to a new and better "social order."[8]

With this vision, Y organizers sallied into the South soon after 1900. As social activists, they stood ready to transform attitudes and to create a women's fellowship in the former Confederacy. Given the difficulties the social gospel and progressive reform movements had making headway in the New South, the task of a women's reform movement seemed doubly difficult. By World War II, however, almost every major southern city had a YWCA, and many smaller towns did too. Most of this expansion occurred during the 1920s. Major membership campaigns took place in the upper South and in other places where industry had had substantial impact. In Virginia, North Carolina, South Carolina, Georgia, and Alabama, YWCA organizers tried hard to recruit industrial workers to their programs.

National staff and women in the New South forged a particular accommodation to the YWCA vision that was shaped by forces peculiar to that region—notably tense race relations, religious conservatism, and expansive industrial hopes—combined with all the burden of southern history and southern difference. Here especially distinct sex roles encouraged separate women's institutions, but racial barriers militated against communities based solely on sex. Yet the YWCA did manage to foster a women's community created for and by industrial workers, and at least for some women workers it served as an arena that coexisted with the home, the church, and the workplace as one of the central social institutions of the era.

While the workplace provided one cornerstone in the edifice of the southern community, the evangelical church provided another. Many writers have explored the central role of the Protestant church in the South, including its opposition to the tenets of the social gospel movement, its resistance to women's participation in governance, and its bifurcation by race.[9] Nevertheless, there emerged in the South a progressive movement that was partly rooted in the social gospel, a women's movement that partly emanated from women's organizational work in church societies, and an interracial movement that largely grew out of church-based women's missions.[10]

Joining a church had been the usual way to get integrated into a community; the YWCA offered an alternative way to meet other young women. The YWCA leadership hoped their institution could supplement activities of the local church, where women were the mainstays of the congregation. The YWCA, however, was to be a training ground in independence for women whose participation in southern religious institutions was limited by men's unwillingness to allow women any significant control. There does not seem to be any evidence of tension between the major denominations in the South and the YWCA, and at the local level it seems that initial suspicions about YWCA clubs were dispelled by the creation of prayer groups and the spotless reputations of the middle-class board women, whose imprimatur could be placed on the YWCA's recruiting campaigns.

The South after 1900 was still a region in flux. The Great Depression and mechanization sounded the death knell for an overwhelmingly rural society, although many southerners remained both poor and rural until well after World War II.[11] For men and women in the burgeoning towns and cities, dominated increasingly by bourgeois values and middle-class entrepreneurs, the New South brought a world of industrial work and urban values that competed with the agrarian ethos. Families that had toiled together on the parched or worn-out soil of tenant farms or on holdings run on shares simply moved the whole family work force into the industrial community. Women and girls, wives and daughters, worked in the mills, contributing to the family wage.[12]

This embryonic work force was clearly divided by race. Most African American southerners were shut out from industrial work or employed in the dirtiest and most dangerous tasks in the tobacco factories and cotton mills. Racial lines were drawn inside as well as outside the factory. The majority of black women who moved into the towns worked in domestic service, not in the textile or tobacco industry. The range of available work for white women was much greater, if still limited. The herculean efforts of Henry Grady and his followers to attract industry provided major new opportunities. White women stood behind counters in the new department stores and began to work in secretarial and other white-collar jobs in the expanding state and local bureaucracies.

From the start the issue of race relations prevented the Y from reaching its objective of being a women's community that bridged all barriers. Despite the goodwill of those at national headquarters at the turn of the century, no one there was able to muster enough national support to achieve local integration in the South. The explanation (or rather the rationalization) went like this. After the 1906 merger of the two national groups, it was decided that in any town there should only be one entity identified as the YWCA. To foster this goal, any "colored" women's Y would be a "branch" of the main—or white—YWCA, and the staff of all branches would consult on programs and would work toward a unity of membership. The reality was that most African American women worked in branches that were isolated from the white organization, and the "Colored" or "Branch" YWCAs were founded and run by women's groups from within the African American community.[13]

At the national level, the YWCA stood against lynching, worked with the Interracial Commission in the South, undertook careful studies of employment patterns, and tried to address issues like that of employers who brought in African American strikebreakers during labor unrest. Yet despite some racially progressive leaders at the national level and a handful of African American traveling secretaries who worked in the South, local Ys in the southern states refused even to consider integration. Race would remain a barrier never truly breached in the pre–World War II years.[14]

The records of local associations in the South reveal instances in which African American women who wanted to start a YWCA branch were told that they could not do so unless a central (that is, "white") association already existed. In Goldsboro, North Carolina, for example, a request for authorization to organize came from a schoolteacher—a position of influence in the African American community.[15] A negative or equivocal reply probably did not come as a surprise to those intrepid leaders of African American communities who had already endured much at the hands of the planter South, but it was evidence of the ambiguity within the YWCA as to the role of African American women. Relations between local action and national directives were most strained in the South over the issue of race, and the national staff could do little more than cajole local branches.[16]

One state's experience can illuminate further the racial policies of southern Ys. In North Carolina in the twenties there were "colored branches" in Durham, Charlotte, Greensboro, and Asheville; in the thirties a branch was established in Raleigh. There were few industrial programs for African Americans in North Carolina, despite the fact that it was one of the more industrialized southern states. Some cities had a small industrial pool from which to draw; in those cities African American women were generally domestic workers, and there seems to have been some ambivalence about whether these were "industrial" workers. Domestic workers tended to be served by the general programs of the African American YWCA rather than by those of the Industrial Department. In defining African American women as standing outside the Industrial Department, North Carolina was probably typical of the southern states. Industrial organizing by the YWCA was essentially for white women in the South, with African American women remaining on the periphery, connected to the national organization by indefatigable traveling secretaries but too often ignored at the local level.

The situation in the heart of the tobacco industry is illustrative of this segregation. In the early thirties the Durham branch had two industrial clubs in a building funded by the African American–owned North Carolina Mutual Insurance Company. This branch struggled unsuccessfully with the white community to get funding from the Community Chest on a par with the central YWCA. Its program continued, but it was largely funded by the African American community.[17] Despite efforts by African American women, the YWCA would remain almost completely segregated and its funding unequal to the white Y's. This seems to have been a pattern for other cities.

On occasion the wall between the races was acknowledged and discussed in the YWCA, even if it was never scaled. In 1926, for example, white women at a summer industrial conference in the Carolina mountains listened to a representative of the Interracial Commission in Atlanta. Another evening a group of African American women from the Phillis Wheatley Branch in Asheville came with Adele Ruffin, a strong-minded African American Y secretary. The women sang at evening vespers, and then Ruffin spoke on black "poetry, art and business." The white women noted in their report of the conference that "we must watch ourselves to see that we are willing to give justice to other races who are God's children."[18]

Such contacts between the races in southern YWCA branches were limited, but they represented a departure from the status quo. In this sense the southern YWCA was ahead of most of its neighbors. Although northern regional conferences for industrial workers were integrated in the twenties, it was not until the mid-forties that southern YWCA summer camps for industrial workers were desegregated.[19] African American women from southern associations went to northern camps during the pre–World War II period. At the local level, segregation often lasted several decades longer.

The realities of southern society defeated the national vision of racial cooperation. In 1946 the national YWCA adopted a report recommending a greater focus on the issue of race and a more determined effort to integrate its program and membership and bring African American women into the "main stream of Association life."[20] The implication is, of course, that such a situation did not exist in 1946. It seems clear that the women's community represented by the YWCA did not eradicate racial prejudice, although it should be emphasized that it did not ignore the problem and that the YWCA was viewed as dangerously radical by many southerners. The racial mores of the South shaped the institution as they did the surrounding society.

Race created virtually impassable barriers, but class was almost as divisive. To explore this, we turn to a close analysis of the Industrial Departments in the South as they fostered a sense of community among the more homogenous group of white women. If we view the lives of southern white women as lived in a series of circles, rather like a Venn diagram, where some segments overlap or intersect but others remain discrete, we can get a sense of the reach of this women's community. The white members of the Young Women's Christian Association may have come from different economic "circles" and from Baptist or Methodist churches, but they met at the Y in an atmosphere of mutual support. The demands of family, workplace, local churches, and religious communities all vied for space in women's lives, but the YWCA provided a women's community that was singular in trying to forge a common meeting ground for women across class and religious affiliation, if not race.

Before World War I several YWCA workers started recruiting efforts in southern mill villages and industrial communities. The first campaigns for membership among industrial workers seem to have taken place after 1904, when one or two organizers went into mill villages in South Carolina. By 1909 South Carolina had four well-organized mill village associations, employing some ten professional staff.[21] In the 1920s North Carolina had the highest concentration of branches with Industrial Departments, followed by Virginia, South Carolina, and Georgia. Industrial workers in Charlotte, Durham, Winston-Salem, Asheville, High Point, Salisbury, and Greensboro were invited to join the YWCA, as were those in Richmond, Roanoke, Macon, Atlanta, and a handful of other southern industrial or manufacturing cities.[22]

Young women workers as a group formed the basic constituency of the YWCA, but it proved far easier to recruit young white-collar workers than industrial workers. In the social and economic hierarchy of southern urban communities, it was women from the "five and dimes" who moved most easily into the Y community. The Y also attracted young secretaries and others in commercial positions.[23]

The YWCA staff reached young industrial workers by organizing groups and clubs that provided a concrete purpose for stepping into the Y buildings. It was hoped that once drawn in, the women would find that the YWCA community offered much more than just a place to enjoy gymnastics or swimming classes or more than just room and board. The backbone of this effort was the ubiquitous "club," which drew young women to the industrial program. Each class attracting industrial workers represented a culmination of long hours of work recruiting members.[24] In town after town, in mill village after mill village, groups of women met together. In Tampa, Florida; Lexington and Ashland, Kentucky; Durham, North Carolina; Richmond, Virginia; Parkersburg, West Virginia; and Meridian, Mississippi, the local Industrial Committee and the local industrial secretary helped young women decide how best to spend some of their limited free time. Women danced, discussed poetry, learned mathematics, and led prayers. They created pageants, took part in exercise classes, and played basketball. They prepared for workers' education schools at Bryn Mawr and the Southern Summer School, or they raised money to attend a YWCA conference. In 1923 alone southern YWCA industrial programs included classes in dressmaking, millinery, basketry, etiquette, homemaking, piano, ukulele, business English, composition, American literature, legislation, labor problems, race relations, current events, dancing, dramatics, church history, running a meeting, typing, gymnasium, and swimming. It was through these classes that most young women workers first encountered the YWCA.[25]

The YWCA was successful in helping these white working women understand the economic and social structure of their communities. This, in turn, helped these same women question the status quo. At least occasionally then, these workers questioned the world of board women who provided the funds to support the organization. The very success of the industrial program caused tensions in the organization. The only way to survive this built-in contradiction in the industrial program was to engage in a delicate balancing act. At its worst the association could appear to the more labor-minded workers as a place where "nice, middle-class ladies" attempted to understand the needs of the working class. To some women workers, Y leaders often seemed to lack activist spirit in dealings with labor reformers or organized labor. At the other extreme, as Lucy Carner of the national staff put it, "the ties of fellowship in a common task can break down many of the barriers of time and space."[26] Yet despite this hope, as white working-class women gained a sense of their own power and abilities, they posed a problem to the YWCA's more affluent leaders and thus to the ties and bonds of the overall community. The southern YWCA would never be as active in labor issues as the most "advanced" working women or staff wanted it to be.

As industrial workers grew older and as they became more aware of the economic infrastructure in which they toiled, some began to look for more thoroughgoing reform institutions. Because the labor movement in the twenties and early thirties in the South did not really welcome women or provide a reasonable alternative for large numbers of them, only a relatively few members of the YWCA moved into the labor movement. Those who did came from both the professional staff and the rank-and-file membership. Lucy Randolph Mason is the best known of the industrial secretaries who went on to organize for the CIO, but she was not the only one.[27] The lists of women who went to the Southern Summer School contain the names of many who went into the field in the thirties and forties in the struggle to organize workers in the South.

The *commitment* to a women's community and thus to the process of resolving conflicts within that community was what allowed the YWCA to continue. This process never functioned without strain, however. The industrial program was most successful in establishing local clubs and providing activities for white working women and in introducing them to workers' education. It was particularly successful with younger women, but it did not provide a long-term solution to the needs of industrial workers or function as an active advocate for structural economic change. It was, however, an important arena in which middle- and upper-class women could begin to see the lives of working women and to understand the kinds of barriers that economic divisions produced in the society. In the South such opportunities were few.

The industrial clubs were the mainstay of the everyday work of the local community, but the reach of the women's community extended beyond the limits of the local building. In each of several regions "industrial conferences" were held during the summer to bring together young white industrial workers from all over the South to introduce them to workers' education and the Y's innovative educational and organizational practices.

Borrowing from the workers' education movement, these ten-day conferences (summer camps) held in the Blue Ridge Mountains aimed to make women aware of and articulate about their position in the industrial economy. The YWCA's social gospel heritage contributed the desire to help women transform working conditions. Young women in freshly laundered cotton dresses with borrowed bathing suits in their luggage trooped to Lake Junaluska, high in the Blue Ridge Mountains. Often traveling on funds raised by their local clubs, they arrived at camp not knowing quite what to expect. At the end of two weeks they had gone swimming in the lake, hiked across the mountains, sat out the June rains, and acted in plays or pageants that the campers themselves wrote. The young women had listened to speakers who told them where the profit from industry went and who discussed with them the problems of long hours, low wages, and poor working conditions. They had listened to women in other industries tell tales of their hardships and hopes. The 1925 conference motto—"To Break Down Barriers, Change Thinking, and Widen the Reach of Our Love"—was typical. The theme was constantly discussed and its implications examined during the long summer days. Poetry and swimming, economics and hiking, brought thirty or forty young women together that year for a brief interlude before they returned to the drudgery of the textile mills of Spartanburg or the tobacco factories of Durham.[28]

Women who had been to the summer sessions were expected to bring in new industrial members, join student-industrial groups, and volunteer to work with legislative committees. They served as "interpreters" to the "leisure woman" on the local industrial committee and led study groups with their newfound "sense of responsibility."[29] There is evidence that these summer camps produced results. The camps revived the flagging morale of industrial workers and YWCA staff alike and provided a means of overcoming the isolation felt in associations scattered across the small towns of the South.[30] The camps also served as recruiting grounds for women who went on to further workers' education. The Bryn Mawr Summer School for Women Workers in Industry and the Southern Summer School founded in 1927 both emerged from the interests and concerns of the YWCA industrial staff. Some women went to the Brookwood Labor School in the foothills of the Catskills above Katonah, New York, or in later years the Highlander Folk School in Tennessee, both in the forefront of the workers' education movement.[31]

In consolidating their mission to break down barriers, Y organizers often arranged conference dates so college student YWCA members attending their own divisional summer conferences could spend some time in the camps with industrial workers. It was hoped that each section of the organization would reinforce and reinvigorate the other. The ongoing "student-industrial program," which brought together college students and industrial workers in a variety of ways, reveals the national organization's larger vision of a women's community. In college towns across the South small groups of college students and industrial workers met to get to know one another and to discuss industrial and economic conditions. Some groups met only twice a year, some met often, but at the least these meetings provided a way to "break down the barriers" for women who were otherwise isolated and insulated by the class structure. These structural means of creating community reveal the depth of the commitment to creating allies across economic divides.

Key to all this activity was the YWCA's salaried staff—the "secretaries." Any one association might have several secretaries, but only those with a substantial number of industrial workers could afford to hire an "industrial secretary." These women formed the bonds or conduits between the older, married women on the boards and volunteer committees, on one hand, and the younger working "girls," on the other. They were pulled in different directions by the two constituencies. Their mandate was broad. They were to try to educate middle- and upper-class women about the needs and concerns of working-class women, and they were to work with working-class women to allow them to develop intellectually and spiritually. At the same time these women were to function as a liaison with other social agencies and interest groups. Local staff members, like the headquarters staff, were largely young, college-educated, single women, only a handful of whom were African American.

The activities of the local branches and local staff were monitored, encouraged, and applauded by the national organization. The physical manifestation of this connection was the cadre of energetic and devoted women who made up the traveling national staff. Both local and national staff came from the same recruiting grounds as the women who went into the settlement house movement. Their job title was "secretary," but they made up the executive and professional officers of the organization.

To sustain the loose connections between the national headquarters and the local YWCAs, national staff members were sent across the country. Industrial Department staff members Louise Leonard, Lucy Carner, and Eleanor Copenhaver crisscrossed the southern states between the wars and were almost never without their "carpetbag." In 1928 Eleanor Copenhaver made twenty-two visits to local southern branches and spent the late summer in eastern Europe attending two international conferences. The next year, she made forty-nine visits to local associations as well as attending several regional meetings.

As they journeyed by train or car from Nashville to New Orleans and from Savannah to Richmond, the industrial secretaries served as the connecting thread of the southern industrial program. At each stop they wrote extensive reports on the local situation. One typical comment read, "Miss E. Margaret Johnson who is the general secretary is just right for this position. She was a personnel worker in a steel plant at Middletown, Ohio. . . . She is well aware of the limitations of welfare work. Her personality and enthusiasm are absolutely irresistible."[32] The national staff also reported on the local climate for labor relations and carefully noted the number of working women in every community. They interviewed local staff, talked to various volunteer women on the board and Industrial Committee, and then wrote detailed recommendations for future action.

They also commented on wider economic and social issues pertinent to the organization's social conscience. Eleanor Copenhaver wrote an incisive analysis of the cotton mill strikes of 1929. Her commentary on the power of the church and manufacturers to control southern labor reveals her intimate understanding of what it meant to be a southerner and a worker in the New South. Her insights were typical of the national staff as she detailed the elements at work in labor unrest and provided a cogent analysis of the causes and consequences of the strikes. National industrial secretaries were astute analysts of the political, economic, and social structure of the South. It was their political acumen that often shaped local strategies, and it was they who were the most supportive of labor activism and political campaigns for protective labor legislation.

Local secretaries could be equally supportive on labor questions, often at the risk of losing their jobs. Their stances bordered on the heroic, given the political milieu in which they worked. The industrial secretary in Durham, North Carolina, in the mid-twenties arranged for Y members to testify before the state legislature on working conditions and child labor in factories.[33] The industrial secretary in Charlotte lost her job after she publicly supported a request by several women's groups for a survey of women's working conditions in North Carolina. In Richmond, Virginia, the industrial secretary resigned when the local board refused to take a public stand in favor of a survey of working conditions for women.[34]

The underpinning for this activism in labor reform lay in the training of the professional staff. The extent and impact of industrial programs depended heavily on the skill and enthusiasm of the local staff, as well as on the support and direction provided by national representatives. A national training school was started soon after the 1906 merger, and until 1928 staff were brought to New York City and put up in the elegant residence at 600 Lexington Avenue while they were schooled in the goals and methods of the movement. In this way the ideals of the national leadership percolated to the regions. A great deal of this time was spent discussing the biblical basis for their Christian mission, but they were also trained in contemporary social work methods. From New York the trained staff would venture into the field to persuade and educate local volunteers, newly appointed staff, and the women who ate in Y cafeterias, lived in their boardinghouses, and joined the myriad clubs. Local branches, too, were encouraged to produce their own "scientific" studies of the job market and housing for young women.[35]

The recruiting grounds for the professional staff of the Industrial Department were often women's colleges. Local campus Ys frequently sponsored programs that sought ways to bring young women together across class lines. For college students in these programs, whose numbers were relatively few, such work had a greater significance than their numbers would indicate. It was part of the wider program of "student-industrial cooperation" that brought together college students and industrial workers.

In Atlanta in the summer of 1923, as the textile industry was begin-

ning to sink into the long decline that marked the twenties, a young
college student from South Carolina named Lois MacDonald applied for
a job on the night shift in one of the city's many mills. She was hired as a
learner, making $3.50 a week to start. Before she left at the end of the
summer she had begun to bring back a pay packet of $7.00. She paid half
of this meager wage for her room and board at the Church Home for
Girls, a boardinghouse.

The wealthy women who subscribed to the Church Home in Atlanta
were stunned when this forthright, but soft-spoken southerner told the
board women that they were in effect subsidizing the textile industry by
making it possible for employers to pay less than a living wage. Lois
MacDonald's rent did not cover the actual cost of her room, which
was overrun with bedbugs. Nor did it cover the cost of her food, which
she found almost inedible. Moreover, MacDonald said, none of these
"comfortable" middle-class women would accept these living conditions,
and it was unreasonable of them to expect that the working women
in the mills should be grateful for their largess. MacDonald, who
thought that many of these women from Atlanta were also volunteers
at the local Y, had discovered that kindly intentions were insufficient;
middle-class women needed to be made aware of the reality of industrial conditions.[36]

MacDonald's experience was not unique. She was one of many college
students who ventured into factories in summer programs organized by
the YWCA to broaden the understanding of the middle class. Young
women went into working-class communities unheralded to discover
firsthand what it was like to work for a living at less than a living wage.
Armed with a list of books to augment their practical experience, the
young women were surprised to find that at the end of the day's work
they had not a whit of energy left to focus on intellectually demanding
texts. They quickly came to understand and empathize with the plight of
women who came to the YWCA too worn out to undertake heavy educational programs. They also began to appreciate the strength of will of
active industrial members of the YWCA.[37]

Moreover, these women now knew why individualism and individual
solutions to what were called "social problems" in the sociological parl-
ance of the day simply could not work. One woman commented in 1928
that these college students had had their "illusions shattered on how to
help the working class." They became convinced that "it is not important
to teach the workers how to live properly" but that collective action was
necessary to change the economic and social system.[38]

The kind of results that emerged from this experience can be seen in
the work of the campus Y groups across the South. When Lois MacDonald
became a secretary for the YWCA branch on the campus of the North

Carolina College for Women in Greensboro, she arranged for students to tour one of the Cone mills. Some of these women had been to the joint student-industrial meetings held in the Blue Ridge Mountains and were eager to do more research. With ten students in tow, Lois MacDonald drove to the mills to investigate conditions in the production of denim. Not wanting to appear rude, the young women kept their reactions to themselves until the oppressive heat of the dyeing room caused one to blurt out, "This seems terrible that all these people have to work in this. I can hardly stay here, I'm about to faint!" The manager conducting the tour hastened to reassure her. "Oh," he said, "you needn't worry. These people are like animals." The young woman, taken aback by this condescension, looked as if her face had been smacked, recalled MacDonald. When they got out of the mill, the group "just went to town. They would have beaten this young man up, if they could have gotten hold of him."[39] It was this sort of experience in empathy that the YWCA was able to foster. Moreover, these programs also helped recruit professional staff and volunteers.

The right of laboring men and women to organize or to lobby for protective legislation was, however, an explosive issue that threatened to unravel the carefully constructed Y community, despite such student-industrial programs. Tension existed between the national board staff, which promoted discussion of industrial relations and women's place in the economic structure of the South, and some local branches, which were hesitant to deal with the one subject beyond race that would and did cause immediate uproar in the mill-driven and mill-dominated world of the Piedmont South.

Just before World War I, the national board of the YWCA reported that it believed young women were paid "utterly inadequate wages."[40] Accordingly, the women argued for legislation to provide a minimum wage and regulation of hours. Such a stance put the YWCA in the forefront of labor reform nationally, which caused much consternation at the local level. It meant that the organization as a whole stood clearly in favor of restricting the power of employers over their work force, even while the Y expressed its sympathy with the plight of the capitalists by pointing out that "the Association, while endeavoring to improve the industrial condition of the working girl shall point steadfastly to a higher standard of faithful service and achievement for the worker and of justice and consideration for the employer."[41] The language of the Y women was equivocal because the advocates wanted to avoid confrontation between employer and employee and hoped to eradicate class antagonism by promoting a spirit of "Christian" unity, as did many progressives. Yet they recognized that pragmatically such cooperation would not immediately be possible.

The national board, even before World War I, urged that local Ys should avoid meeting inside factory gates. Although employers were to be solicited for funds, the YWCA's primary focus and loyalty had to be to the women who were members. Local associations were advised to rent space in industrial neighborhoods if they could not build their own centers, and they were urged not to continue holding meetings on shop floors, as had been the initial practice. This was in marked contrast to the position of the Young Men's Christian Association, which remained much closer to employers and consequently took far fewer political stances that would potentially alienate.[42]

In the 1920s the Industrial Department as a collective entity came out squarely on the side of protective legislation and encouraged workers to testify before legislators. Local branches were urged to hold classes that would make women understand the economic structure of industry. They were also urged to prepare women for workers' schools so they would be even more capable of leadership in the local community. A 1924 bulletin of the Industrial Department couched its message about political activism in the language of the social gospel: "we are organized to be a movement of industrial women of the Young Women's Christian Association to try to permeate the womanhood of industry with a Christian idea and to help build a Christian order, to try to educate public opinion by our own experience as to what the needs of that order are and as to the conditions today which must be changed if we are to give women the fullest kind of life."[43] This statement reflected the belief that the "Christian" world would be one without marked inequalities in the economic, racial, and political orders and that the "fullest kind of life" meant one that not only was bound by work and sleep but also allowed for intellectual pursuits, leisure time, and the development of each woman's talents and interests. Such a new world could be reached only by active involvement in the public arena. The programs of the local clubs in the southern states reveal women who were trying to reach this goal but were hampered by the mores and economic interests of local notables and by the ever-present walls of segregation.

In the South tensions over workers' rights posed particular dilemmas since many of the middle-class and upper-class women who raised funds and sat on the local boards were drawn from the ranks of the owning and employing class. In the Piedmont South this meant that board members came from families who controlled the tobacco and textile industries in a political climate extremely sensitive to labor unrest, families actively hostile to efforts by workers to improve working conditions and easily offended by suggestions that hours or wages should be controlled by state or federal legislation.

In Prichard, Alabama, like other southern towns, the YWCA had difficulty overcoming the separations created by class backgrounds and education during the twenties. As one worker wrote, "When I was employed in the _____ Cotton Mills, [it] seem[ed] to me that the interest that the Y.W.C.A. secretaries took in the Cotton Mill workers, or shall I say girls, was done in a sort of condescending way, more from the idea of having a report to turn in than for any real help that might be rendered the girls in the Mill Villages. Of course I like to think and hope I was wrong but if I got that impression it's possible other girls did too. Anyway for some reason we do not have very much interest shown here to industrial girls as I have lately learned is done in many other cities and some of them are pretty far south."[44]

The records of local branches in North Carolina, one of the states most hostile to protective legislation, reveal that the industrial and manufacturing sectors did dominate local association boards. In Charlotte three of the women on the committee that oversaw the industrial program for white women in the mid-twenties were "directly" connected to the "cotton industry."[45] In Winston-Salem the president of the local white board in the 1930s, Mrs. M. Bahnson, came from a family "connected with knitting mills," and her husband had recently "acquired cotton mills in Fries, Virginia."[46] In Durham at least two of the women who chaired the Industrial Committee in the twenties were the wives of men who controlled the town's tobacco industry.

Yet at times middle-class women could be found supporting the interests of the working class despite their financial and family ties. For ten years the wife of the son of the president of Liggett and Myers supported the YWCA in its fundraising and its efforts to bring together women workers and middle-class volunteers. Moreover, she was described as "amazingly liberal" in reports by the national staff, and she was opposed to the "narrowness" of the middle-class vision in the city.[47] In 1928 the secretary in Winston-Salem found jobs for women who were fired for trade union activity, and the board did not censure her. The board president even took one of the fired unionists into her home.[48]

National and local staff, energetic working women, and empathetic middle- and upper-class board women could forge a strong local Industrial Department. In towns where industrial working women became fairly long-term members of the YWCA and attended industrial conferences or one of the workers' schools, the local industrial program could reflect a strong sense of what the national board literature referred to as a "group consciousness," a sense that industrial women were part of a larger group of "industrial women of many nations and races."[49] The central branch in Durham, North Carolina, is one example of a strong Industrial Department—and of the strains that eventually undermined its best work. In Durham, the women's community functioned effectively for white women across class lines for much of the period before the Great Depression. The Industrial Department flourished, and there was a good deal of communication among women from differing economic and social backgrounds. By the middle of the twenties a number of Durham women had attended summer regional workers' conferences, ten had gone to Philadelphia for the Bryn Mawr Summer School for Women Workers, and in subsequent years others would go there or to the Southern Summer School in the Carolina mountains.[50] A handful of these women were leaders of the Industrial Department throughout the twenties and thirties. That they formed a close-knit group was evident when the replacement of an industrial secretary in the mid-twenties caused rifts in the branch because the "old guard" industrial members refused to work with the new staff member.

The energetic efforts of Durham's Industrial Department also produced a strong "student-industrial discussion group," with women students from Duke University. The YWCA staff commented that since there were "so many advanced girls [workers] who have studied economics this class is unusually effective."[51]

Esther Peed, one of the industrial workers in this student-worker group, was a member of the Industrial Committee that ran the industrial program for the white central Durham Y, which was largely composed of middle-class volunteers. Her presence on the committee testified to the success of this branch in creating a flourishing cross-class women's community during the twenties, despite much tension over labor issues in the community. Over half the women at the annual membership dinner in 1931 were industrial workers, and the industrial secretary noted that they were the "backbone" of the association. Over 140 women were regular industrial club members, and the industrial programs reached over 1,200 young women. Industrial workers were creating plays with the Carolina Playmakers, and others served on the YWCA board. Women who had suffered wage cuts were found places in the residence hall even though the building was full.

Eventually, however, class divisions undermined the women's community so carefully constructed. By the late 1930s it appeared that the plight of women workers was not sufficiently understood by wealthier women on the board. The 1937 reports noted "no contact" between the industrial workers and the board women. Town and gown tensions had undermined the branch's industrial work because the wives of Duke University professors were viewed by wealthy manufacturers as too radical.

The board itself was divided over the question of social activism. Esther Peed complained bitterly that the working women were told that "the businessmen of the town will not allow the YWCA to have anything to do with legislation." Noting that the chair of the YWCA board held stock in the factory where Peed worked, she commented further that it was "a farce to say that there is any relationship between the board and the girls who work in the factory which lets them understand each other at all. The community at large does not know that the YWCA is interested in working conditions and does not understand at all."[52]

Ruth Culberson, another woman whose start in the workers' education movement began in the Durham YWCA, felt that in the thirties the organization failed to make its stand on labor issues public. Fearing loss of funds, board women muzzled themselves, undercutting the efforts of the Industrial Department. By the late thirties the middle-class woman who headed the Industrial Committee in Durham stated privately that industrial workers were by nature inferior, that it was a matter of "biology." This same chairwoman refused to allow a former member of the Durham industrial group who was employed in state government to come in and talk to Y members, because this woman now "spoke the patois of labor."[53] In this tobacco-producing town facing the Great Depression, the interests of the industrialists won out over the desire to bridge class interests. There were still industrial clubs throughout the thirties, but the energy that had marked the twenties had waned. Clearly the YWCA had not been able to overcome prevailing beliefs and mores of the entrepreneurial world outside the institution's walls.

A further example of such class conflict can be seen again in North Carolina, where in 1923 a segment of the state YWCA leadership began asking the state government to undertake a survey of the conditions of work for women and children in North Carolina's factories. The campaign to get either the Women's Bureau or the state Department of Labor to do such a survey consumed the energies of many women and many women's organizations for much of the twenties. Active in the effort were the League of Women Voters, the Federation of Women's Clubs, and the Business and Professional Women's Club, along with the women from the YWCA.

In a lengthy report on the wave of textile strikes in 1929, a national board secretary noted the central question for the YWCA: would the women of the local boards allow the industrial women to determine their own programs and actions, or would the fact that these boards were made up of the "wives of men who are their industrial overlords" erode the Y's sense of community in a period when workers were themselves becoming more class conscious?[54] The tensions thus engendered were never resolved and probably could not be, but it is significant that at least some Y leaders recognized that the central issue was to reach a middle ground, where the YWCA could continue to mediate between groups. It is also testimony to the strength of this newfound sense of community that these same Y leaders could be found agonizing over the conflicts induced when their family and class loyalties were at odds with the political or social stances of the YWCA and the interests of working women.

After several years of negotiations, much of it in bad faith on the part of the governor, himself a mill owner, Eleanor Copenhaver reported to New York headquarters on the status of the survey campaign. Clara Cox (a leading Quaker) is effective, "but her family oppose her," Copenhaver noted, adding, "Miss Cox feels the women are standing out against their husbands. . . . Mrs O'Berry's husband is President of an overall factory and against the survey yet she stood at the door of the factory and delivered hand bills."[55] A board member in Charlotte was pressured to give up YWCA work when her husband was visited by a deputation from the mills (his machine tool business depended on orders from these mill men).[56] Yet this same woman continued to persevere for some time in her work with the YWCA. Eventually, the women gave up on the survey request and in the late twenties worked instead for protective labor legislation, finally succeeding in 1931 in a measure that curtailed night work and shortened the hours women could work. In this instance and others the needs of the community of women that the YWCA represented overcame class interests and indeed family pressure.

The central issue here was whether the Y membership could directly campaign for reform of the workplace. Could middle- and upper-class women accept working women actively pursuing collective bargaining or protective legislation? Mathematics, labor drama, and writing were acceptable topics for club nights, but a speech from a local striking worker posed many more difficulties to the institution. In places where "breaking down barriers" of class had been seriously undertaken in the 1920s, the strains and stresses of class and economic conflict quickly showed during the thirties, when the rise of the CIO and an active labor movement heightened tensions in the South.

The historian Thomas Bender argues for our seeing community as something separate from a particular locale or structure and defines community as something created by "a network of social relations marked by mutuality and emotional bonds."[57] Such a way of viewing the construction of community is helpful in the YWCA context, in light of the separate world that the YWCA leadership sought to create. They aimed to shape an institution that could meet the needs of young women, and within that structure they tried to create a community of interest for young industrial workers, which would encompass not only these women workers but also other groups of young women, as well as the professional staff and volunteers.

In the YWCA, community did not mean an absence of conflict. Rather, conflict was contained within a network of bonds, which meant that the participants felt the responsibility to work at, or work out, the causes of the conflict. Differing class interests posed severe tests to the Y's vision of sisterhood. The white YWCA, at least in this one region and for this time period, did represent an institution that provided a highly unusual meeting ground, one that was created for and by women. It was an intensely female community, and its language and actions reflect a sense of concern for the problems and delights of women's lives.

That women could be a part of several communities seems to be a reasonable reading of these southern women's lives in the early twentieth century. To be a member of one particular class did not exclude one from also being a part of a community of women in the YWCA. Class, race, ethnicity, and regional origin divided women and made it difficult to communicate, but it did not stop the YWCA from creating that "network of social relations marked by mutuality and emotional bonds" for the white women in the organization.

If we turn this definition of community on its head and consider that we can also define community by what is excluded as well as what is included, we can see the YWCA as a place where African American women also created a community across class lines, even though race continued to be the major unbridged chasm in the Y, as it was in the wider society. The YWCA was a step closer to interracial harmony than most other organizations in the South were, but this did not mean that the YWCA was able to overcome local prejudice or create an interracial community within the local branches.

The national staff was acutely aware of tensions between local and national YWCA attitudes and action. In 1929 the national board secretary for the southern states noted that "there is the continual question of national and local autonomy which impinges on the whole southern situation. There are bound to be many times when the industrial membership in line with the national Industrial Department will want to take part in local issues and when the local community will defend its autonomy as strictly as the Confederate States defended their sovereign rights. This dilemma is not confined to the industrial field. It is just as acute in racial problems and in some instances in international problems as well as in such minor matters as the right to dance."[58] In the long run local and regional mores overwhelmed the hopes of the national organization, and southern difference held sway over national unity.

The YWCA's stance on labor relations and its activism in shaping working women's lives implicitly threatened the southern status quo but did not directly confront it. The Y was not ultimately successful in its goal to bring all women together in search of a more spiritual and more socially active life, but at times it did provide a place where some women could focus on the needs and concerns of women alone. In this sense it formed a distinct, if embattled, women's community.

NOTES

The author would like to thank the Chester Avenue Seminar for its help and succor in this project.

1. Industrial Department of the YWCA, *Bulletin*, June 1924, n.p., Young Women's Christian Association Papers, Sophia Smith Collection, Smith College, Northampton, Mass. (hereafter YWCA Papers, Smith College).

2. Ibid.

3. Mary S. Sims, *The Natural History of the Social Institution: The Young Women's Christian Association* (New York: Womans Press, 1936), 23ff. There has been no analytical history of the YWCA overall, although there were three "in-house" histories produced: Elizabeth Wilson, *Fifty Years of Association Work among Young Women, 1866–1916: A History of Young Women's Christian Associations in the United States of America* (New York: National Board of the Young Women's Christian Association, 1916); Sims, *The Natural History*; and Mary S. Sims, *The Young Women's Christian Association: An Unfolding Purpose* (New York: Womans Press, 1950). See also Grace H. Wilson, *The Religious and Educational Philosophy of the Young Women's Christian Association*, Contributions to Education, No. 54 (New York: Teachers College of Columbia University, 1933). Such scholars as Frances Saunders Taylor, Ken Fones-Wolf, Karen Mittelman, Nancy Robertson, and Regina Bannan have begun to look at aspects of the organization or have made studies of Ys in specific cities.

4. Regina Bannan's forthcoming dissertation on the managerial style of the YWCA examines this issue.

5. Sims, *The YWCA*, 25. Much time was spent after World War I debating who should be a voting member of the organization. No one ever seems to have been turned away from programs or clubs because of their religious beliefs or background, and in the Northeast especially many outside of the Protestant pale came to the YWCA. Mary Frederickson has elsewhere recounted the impressive record of the national Industrial Department of the YWCA. No other women's organization at the time reached as many young working women to provide resources that could lead women into the labor movement. See Mary Frederickson, "Citizens for Democracy: The Industrial Programs of the YWCA," in *Sisterhood*

and Solidarity: Workers' Education for Women, 1914-1984, ed. Joyce L. Kornbluh and Mary Frederickson (Philadelphia: Temple University Press, 1984), 75-106.

6. See Ken Fones-Wolf, *Trade Union Gospel: Christianity and Labor in Industrial Philadelphia, 1865-1915* (Philadelphia: Temple University Press, 1989): 122-44; David I. Macleod, *Building Character in the American Boy: The Boy Scouts, YMCA and Their Forerunners, 1870-1920* (Madison: University of Wisconsin Press, 1983); and C. Howard Hopkins, *History of the Y.M.C.A. in North America* (New York: Association Press, 1951).

7. "Work among Young Girls in Business and Industry," Industrial Department, *Bulletin,* May 1924, 1, YWCA Papers, Smith College.

8. Ibid., 2-3.

9. Jean E. Friedman, *The Enclosed Garden: Women and Community in the Evangelical South, 1830-1900* (Chapel Hill: University of North Carolina Press, 1985); Noreen Dunn Tatum, *A Crown of Service: A Story of Woman's Work in the Methodist Episcopal Church, South, from 1878-1940* (Nashville: Parthenon, 1960); Sara Estelle Haskin, *Women and Missions in the Methodist Episcopal Church, South* (Nashville: Methodist Publishing House, 1925); John Patrick McDowell, *The Social Gospel in the South: The Woman's Home Mission Movement in the Methodist Episcopal Church, South, 1886-1939* (Baton Rouge: Louisiana State University Press, 1982); Donald G. Mathews, *Religion in the Old South* (Chicago: University of Chicago Press, 1977). See also Mary Frederickson's essay, herein.

10. Marion W. Roydhouse, "'The Universal Sisterhood of Women': Women and Labor Reform in North Carolina, 1900-1932" (Ph.D. diss., Duke University, 1980); Anne Firor Scott, *The Southern Lady: From Pedestal to Politics, 1830-1930* (Chicago: University of Chicago Press, 1970); Anne Firor Scott, *Making the Invisible Woman Visible* (Urbana: University of Illinois Press, 1984); Anne Firor Scott, "Most Invisible of All: Black Women's Voluntary Associations," *Journal of Southern History* 56 (February 1990): 3-22.

11. Jack Temple Kirby, *Rural Worlds Lost: The American South, 1920-1960* (Baton Rouge: Louisiana University Press, 1987); Pete Daniel, *Breaking the Land: The Transformation of Cotton, Tobacco, and Rice Cultures since 1880* (Urbana: University of Illinois Press, 1985); James C. Cobb, *Industrialization and Southern Society, 1877-1984* (Lexington: University of Kentucky Press, 1984).

12. The nature of the family economy and the institution of the southern mill village is finely drawn by Jacquelyn Dowd Hall, James Leloudis, Robert Korstad, Mary Murphy, LuAn Jones, and Christopher B. Daly, *Like A Family: The Making of a Southern Cotton Mill World* (Chapel Hill: University of North Carolina Press, 1987). See also Marion W. Roydhouse, "Weeds from the Beans: The Impact of Industrial Life on Women in the South," in *The South Is Another Land: Essays on the Twentieth-Century South,* ed. Bruce Clayton and John Salmond (Westport, Conn.: Greenwood, 1987), 85-106; Allen Tullos, *Habits of Industry: White Culture and the Transformation of the Carolina Piedmont* (Chapel Hill: University of North Carolina Press, 1989).

13. It would seem that cross-class alliances existed in both white and African

American branches, but we know too little about the dynamics of this situation in the industrial South at this point to be certain. Certainly from what we know in northern communities the black women had their own agenda, and it did not always coincide with that of the central "white" organization. See Scott, "Most Invisible"; Cynthia Neverdon-Morton, *Afro-American Women of the South and the Advancement of the Race, 1895-1925* (Knoxville: University of Tennessee Press, 1989); Frances Saunders Taylor, "'On the Edge of Tomorrow': Southern Women, the Student YWCA, and Race, 1920-1944" (Ph.D. diss., Stanford University, 1984); and Karen Mittelman, "'A Spirit that Touches the Problems of Today': Women and Social Reform in the Philadelphia YWCA, 1920-1945" (Ph.D. diss., University of Pennsylvania, 1987).

14. In 1930 the YWCA cooperated with Mabel Byrd of Fisk University in a study of employment of African American women, but the focus of the investigation was on the need for vocational training, a focus that smacked of Washingtonism. Biennial Report, 1931, YWCA Papers, Smith College.

15. Mary V. Brown to Eva Bowles, November 1926, Local Association Files, Young Women's Christian Association Papers, Young Women's Christian Association National Board Archives, New York (hereafter YWCA Papers, National Board).

16. There has been little work done on the African American experience in the southern Ys, and my investigations have only scraped the surface. The records of the institution itself reflect the orientation of local branches toward the historic "invisibility" of black women, especially black women workers. See Neverdon-Morton, *Afro-American Women,* 207-22.

17. Local Association Files, North Carolina, YWCA Papers, National Board.

18. Southern Industrial Conference Report, Lake Junaluska, 1926, YWCA Papers, Smith College.

19. In 1942 the southern conferences were desegregated, but in 1946 they still faced hostile mobs from Hendersonville. Brooks Creedy, Report, June 1946, YWCA Papers, Smith College; Eleanor Copenhaver Anderson to Southern Branch Secretaries, December 10, 1942, YWCA Papers, Smith College; Wilson, *Religious and Educational Philosophy,* 47-87; George L. Collins, "Southern Students and Race Relations," *Woman's Press,* June 1928, 399-400.

20. Sims, *The YWCA,* 72.

21. "The Work of the Young Women's Christian Association in the Cotton Mill Villages of the South," 1909, Industrial Department Files, YWCA Papers, Smith College.

22. The industrial work competed with other programs at the YWCA building. In any one town the YWCA might have a residential building that could provide room and board for young women, a swimming pool and a gymnasium frequented by Girl Reserve members (high school students), and a well-used cafeteria. The Industrial Department might compete with the business clubs for workers.

23. A subsequent offspring of the YWCA was the Business and Professional Women's Club, which was the direct result of the YWCA's efforts to create organizations for women when they felt that the Y's reach had been overextended.

The Business and Professional Women's Club was to serve white-collar workers who had grown too old for the Y's mandate. There was no equivalent organization for female industrial workers.

24. Minnie Kimball, aware that she faced a community of workers who were unused to any organization except church-affiliated ones, set about her task in Winston-Salem with great care, organizing women into visiting groups that welcomed newcomers into the mill community and offered help when someone was ill. Industrial Department, *Bulletin,* June 1925, YWCA Papers, Smith College.

25. Industrial Department, *Bulletin,* June 1924, 4–5, YWCA Papers, Smith College.

26. Ibid., 2.

27. See John Salmond, " 'Miss Lucy of the CIO': A Southern Life," in *The South Is Another Land,* ed. Clayton and Salmond, 107–21; Mary Frederickson, " 'I Know which Side I'm on': Southern Women in the Labor Movement in the Twentieth Century," in *Women, Work and Protest: A Century of U.S. Women's Labor History,* ed. Ruth Milkman (Boston: Routledge and Kegan Paul, 1985), 156–80; and Kornbluh and Frederickson, eds., *Sisterhood and Solidarity.*

28. Lucy Carner, "Working Girls Talk It Out," *Survey,* October 1922, n.p.; Industrial Conference Reports, box 19, YWCA Papers, Smith College. The workers' education movement provided informal educational opportunities to men and women whose formal education was limited. Copied in part from British models, the movement in this period believed that students had to participate in their own learning. Discussion and active participation in the subject matter made these classes particularly effective. See Theodore Brameld, ed., *Workers' Education in the United States* (New York: Harper and Bros., 1941).

29. Lucy Carner, "An Educational Opportunity for Industrial Girls," *Journal of Social Forces* 1 (November 1922): 612–13.

30. Louise Leonard, "The Industrial Workers Power over Life," Camp Greystone Report, 1927, YWCA Papers, Smith College.

31. Kornbluh and Frederickson, eds., *Sisterhood and Solidarity.*

32. Eleanor Copenhaver, Ashland Kentucky, Visitation Reports, 1928, YWCA Papers, National Board.

33. Mary O. Cowper Papers, William R. Perkins Library, Duke University, Durham, N.C.

34. Lucy Carner, Report, 1926, YWCA Papers, Smith College.

35. Report of Inquiry Commission, 1924–1927, YWCA Papers, Smith College. See also the forthcoming dissertation by Regina Bannan of the University of Pennsylvania, which contains discussion of the training of Y staff.

36. Lois MacDonald, taped interview by author, Stockton, N.J., June 24, 1975. See also Industrial Department, *Bulletin,* April 1923, YWCA Papers, Smith College; and Sadie Goodman, "Students Who Work and Workers Who Study," *Woman's Press,* July 1928, 464–65.

37. Industrial Department, *Bulletin,* January 1923, YWCA Papers, Smith College. The program began in the West in 1922, and in 1923 college students went into the industrial workplace in Denver, Cleveland, and Atlanta.

38. Goodman, "Students Who Work and Workers Who Study," 464–65.

39. Lois MacDonald, taped interviews by Mary Frederickson, August 26, 1977, Stockton, N.J., transcript, 53, in possession of author. The North Carolina College for Women had a tradition of making women think independently and making them aware of the economic and political structure outside the campus walls. Greensboro produced many active suffrage workers and many women who went on to long involvement in politics and social causes.

40. Sims, *The Natural History,* 210.

41. Ibid.

42. At this point very little has been written on the connections between the two organizations. See Ken Fones-Wolf, "Gender, Class and the Transformation of the Philadelphia YM and YWCA Industrial Work, 1900-1920," in author's possession.

43. Industrial Department, *Bulletin,* June 1924, 7, YWCA Papers, National Board.

44. "Mill Village Study," 1932, YWCA Papers, Smith College.

45. Local Association Files, Durham, N.C., 1928, YWCA Papers, National Board.

46. Local Association Files, Winston-Salem, N.C., 1931, YWCA Papers, National Board.

47. Local Association Files, Durham, N.C., 1937, YWCA Papers, National Board.

48. Local Association Files, Winston-Salem, N.C., 1928, YWCA Papers, National Board.

49. Industrial Department, *Bulletin,* June 1927, 4, YWCA Papers, Smith College.

50. Mary Frederickson, "'A Place to Speak Our Minds': The Southern Summer School for Women Workers" (Ph.D. diss., University of North Carolina at Chapel Hill, 1981).

51. Local Association Files, Durham, N.C., 1927, YWCA Papers, National Board.

52. Local Association Files, Durham, N.C., 1937, YWCA Papers, National Board.

53. Local Association Files, Durham, N.C., 1920-1940, YWCA Papers, National Board.

54. Eleanor Copenhaver, Biennial Report, 1928, 1929, YWCA Papers, National Board.

55. Eleanor Copenhaver, Visitation Reports, 1927, YWCA Papers, National Board.

56. Mary O. Cowper Papers. See also Roydhouse, "The Universal Sisterhood," 279ff.

57. Thomas Bender, *Community and Social Change in America* (Baltimore: Johns Hopkins University Press, 1982), 7.

58. Eleanor Copenhaver, Biennial Report for 1928, 1929, YWCA Papers, National Board.

"Each One Is Dependent on the Other": Southern Churchwomen, Racial Reform, and the Process of Transformation, 1880-1940

Mary E. Frederickson

In the last two decades of the nineteenth century, as the South underwent enormous economic and social changes, black and white churchwomen became increasingly aware of the human costs of racial segregation. Empowered by their belief in women's civic and religious responsibility, thousands of southern churchwomen decided to play a part in redressing the numerous inequities evident in their society. By the 1920s white southern churchwomen had become widely recognized regionally, and even nationally, as leaders in interracial reform. They became part of an amalgam of white religious and secular women's groups working for social change in the South. At the same time, black southern churchwomen, faced with building a free society within the post-Emancipation boundaries established by southern whites, saw the church as an institution through which they could successfully gather resources, create and sustain schools, deal with housing and social welfare concerns, and address political and economic issues crucial to the well-being of black southerners. As social activists, black churchwomen also participated in a broad social reform movement organized by southern black women beginning in the 1880s.[1]

As historians have examined patterns of interaction among black and white southern women during the period between 1880 and 1940, several distinct models have emerged. Anne Firor Scott, following on the work of church historians, many of whom were women, first identified the importance of interracial work by white churchwomen. She argued that white women's sympathy for black women derived from their shared roles as mothers and homemakers and that white and black women had relationships that were "quite unlike those common between white and black men."[2] In contrast, Dolores Janiewski, Darlene Clark Hine, and Rosalyn Terborg-Penn have emphasized the lack of sisterhood between black and white women and the adversarial relationship that existed between black women and the larger society.[3] Jacquelyn Dowd Hall expanded Scott's model by documenting cooperation between the southern white and black women politically involved in antilynching reform, while at the same time exploring tensions and misunderstandings among southern women divided by race. Evelyn Brooks Higginbotham also incorporated both perspectives, underscoring "the very real barrier of white racism," while recognizing "parallels and cooperative efforts, which also existed between black and white women's organizations," collaboration that reflected "shared interests among women regardless of race." In her study of Baptist women, Higginbotham found black southern churchwomen who developed sustaining alliances with northern white women, ties that strengthened their position as they worked for social reforms in the southern region.[4]

Taken collectively, this work clearly indicates that patterns of interracial cooperation and racial animosity coexisted. It also shows that one specific pattern of relationships could dominate in a particular context, at a specific time, or around certain issues, while at other times, in different places, or in response to other concerns another, completely different, pattern of interactions could prevail.

Building on earlier scholarship, a fresh analysis of interactions between black and white churchwomen in the South between 1880 and 1940 reveals that while patterns of interracial cooperation and interracial animosity coexisted, white and black churchwomen also developed relationships based on neither collaboration nor enmity but mutual dependence. This type of relationship can be seen clearly in interactions between women in the white Methodist Episcopal Church, South (ME), and women in the Colored Methodist Episcopal Church (CME). This relationship developed primarily because of a strategy employed by CME women, which we can call the process of transformation. Through this process, CME women, most of whom were grass-roots leaders based in small towns or rural areas, converted their concerns about the economic and social conditions faced by black southerners into a format that was accessible but not threatening to white women, one that could be incorporated into the white agenda for social change. Because of this process, actively practiced by black women but almost always invisible to whites, white churchwomen came to rely heavily on their counterparts in the black church for help in developing reform agendas and in carrying out interracial programs, and black women came to rely on white churchwomen for needed resources to be used in their own communities.[5]

Interactions between these southern churchwomen, white and black, consistently took place in ways that let white women preserve the power they derived from their race and class. For decades white women refused to acknowledge the help they received from black women. White church-women were consistently described in both ME and CME records as "teaching" and "helping" the black women with whom they met. CME women controlled their interactions with ME women in such a way that they always appeared to be "learning" from and "being assisted" by whites. These ritualized interactions reinforced white dominance, while simultaneously allowing black women to maintain the dynamics of dissemblance, defined by Darlene Clark Hine as "behavior and attitudes of Black women that created the appearance of openness and disclosure but actually shielded the truth of their inner lives and selves from their oppressors."[6] Self-imposed deference afforded black women the protec-tion they needed to survive in a repressive, white-dominated society. Through the process of transformation, by which black women cast their ideas for reform such that white women would incorporate them into the white reform agenda, black women actively shaped the interracial pro-grams sponsored by white women reformers. Taken together, dissem-blance and the process of transformation provided black women with effective mechanisms for producing a balance between survival and accomplishment. Unable to act directly in a society that severely restricted their behavior, black women developed complex strategies that allowed them to transcend the economic and social barriers placed in their way. By working indirectly to influence white churchwomen, who commanded resources that far surpassed their own, black women achieved their own reform goals and obtained funding for the programs they deemed important.

A close examination of the dual religious traditions of blacks and whites in the Methodist Episcopal churches (South and Colored) reveals the interaction of southern women who were bound together in a com-mon church tradition that was racially segregated but organizationally connected and theologically united. These black and white Methodist Episcopal churches were inextricably linked; neither was completely autonomous. Before 1870 the churches had been one, with southern whites ministering to congregations that included slaves and then increas-ing numbers of free blacks. With the founding of the Colored Methodist Episcopal Church in Jackson, Tennessee, on December 12, 1870, south-ern white Methodists were forced to recognize black religious autonomy.[7]

Unwilling to sever all connections with black Methodists and wanting to retain some contact and control, white southern Methodists offered "assistance" to newly formed black congregations. They furnished the first editor for *The Christian Index,* the official CME publication. They encouraged CME congregations to hold services in white churches. In some communities white pastors preached to CME congregations, and black ministers were regularly requested to speak to white congregations. ME congregations were encouraged to donate land and to assist in building CME church buildings. Stewards of the white churches "assisted the Colored stewards and trustees in understanding the law and polity of Methodism." These same stewards encouraged loyalty to the CME, clearly viewed by whites as a more acceptable alternative than the northern-based African Methodist Episcopal (AME) or African Methodist Episcopal Zion (AME Zion). White Methodists frequently provided CME pastors for black tenants on their plantations or worked with CME preachers to help build a church for local blacks. These forms of assistance perpetuated white control and extended black dependence on, and allegiance to, nearby white congregations.[8]

The system cut two ways, however. Continued white control also meant that the Methodist Episcopal Church, South, could not separate from its black counterpart. Whites had to acknowledge openly the existence of black Methodists who were part of the same religious tradition, who were in theory "brother and sister Methodists." As CME editor J. A. Martin proclaimed, "The C.M.E. Church was seen side by side with the Methodist Church, South, in almost every small town and rural section."[9] This fact was a persistent thorn in the side of most southern white Methodists, men and women who lamented the defeat of slavery and were actively involved in redefining limited political and economic roles for free black southerners. At the same time though, the shared rituals, liturgy, and administration of the Methodist Episcopal Church provided a common language and organizational structure that facilitated interracial contact and perpetuated white involvement in the black church and vice versa.

The Methodist Episcopal Church, South, and the Colored Methodist Episcopal Church also shared a tradition of male domination. Women church members could not vote or serve as lay leaders or ministers. Women were expected to perform the regenerative tasks that held a congregation together: running church schools, furnishing parsonages for ministers, cleaning the church, and preparing food for church suppers. Women also formed a social service network within the churches, ministering to the sick and caring for grieving families, needy children, and the elderly. Both black and white Methodist women raised substantial amounts of money to build and maintain churches and parsonages. Both provided funds for ministers' pensions and cared for ministers' widows.[10] More than any other common aspect of their lives, this shared patriarchal tradition had the potential of uniting black and white southern churchwomen.

Within this context of male leadership and female service, Methodist women activists organized sisterhoods, divided by race, that confirmed them personally and professionally. These black and white churchwomen working in southern communities had much in common, yet there were also great differences between them. Their interaction, sustained for over half a century, took place under circumstances of accelerating racial segregation, sustained extralegal racial violence, and the steadfast refusal of politically powerful whites to incorporate black southerners into the body politic and to accept them as full citizens of the South.

Despite these outside pressures, southern churchwomen established a record of cooperation across racial lines. Their visions of southern progress shared a number of common elements, and over the years they associated in ways that mutually sustained them. As Dr. Mattie Coleman, the first president of the CME Woman's Connectional Missionary Council, claimed when addressing the council's first meeting in 1918, "There has always been a close relationship between the sisters of the M.E. Church, South and the sisters of the C.M.E. Church. . . . We have long since realized that each one is dependent on the other."[11]

Understanding the similarities and differences between these two groups of southern women and the nature of their interaction is our purpose here. Mattie Coleman's characterization of the relationship between black and white churchwomen as interdependent was precise and on target. But mutual dependency is always a complicated way of relating, and in the historical context of slavery and the racial climate of the early twentieth-century South, the interactions between black and white women were extraordinarily complex, emotionally charged, and laden with political and economic significance.[12] Clearly, white ME women developed the interracial reform programs for which they became well known because of their relationship with, and dependence on, women in the CME Church. Conversely, black CME women chose not to confront injustice head on, an impossible option for them in the segregated South of the period, but rather to work behind the scenes and use their connections with white women to benefit their own people.

The relationship between southern churchwomen of different races must be examined in the context of the parallel development and growth of women's missionary organizations in the Methodist Episcopal Church, South, and the Colored Methodist Episcopal Church. Women's home mission work in the Methodist Episcopal Church, South, began in 1882, when Laura Askew Haygood, arguing that local missionary work should take precedence over foreign missions, established the Trinity Home Mission Society, a group of sixty churchwomen who ministered to poor women and children of both races in downtown Atlanta. Haygood was the daughter of an influential Methodist couple in Georgia and the sister of Atticus Haygood, a Methodist minister, the president of Emory University, and an enthusiastic proponent of New South industrialization. In 1883 Laura Haygood led a broad movement to organize white Methodist Episcopal women across the South for home mission work. She guided a strong female countercurrent that focused attention on the exploitative and dehumanizing aspects of the region's new economic system so touted by her brother and his supporters. In 1886 these efforts resulted in the formation of the Woman's Department of Church Extension. The Woman's Department expanded rapidly as southern white churchwomen set up homes for unwed mothers, boardinghouses for women in industrial jobs, mission homes for foreign immigrants in southern cities, and schools for young black and Appalachian women. By 1908 almost 60,000 Methodist women had joined the ranks; by 1940 the network included more than 300,000 women, or one-tenth of the entire denomination.[13]

The state of Georgia was also the site of the first organized local Woman's Missionary Society of the Colored Methodist Episcopal Church, founded in Fort Valley in 1894. Peggie Lesure, a church activist, had earlier reported to the area bishop, L. H. Holsey, that she had dreamed of "a great gathering of Missionaries, ministers and Bishops." In her dream, it seemed "as if the women were the center of attractions." The sermons and discussions were wonderful in this dream, and "the Holy Ghost swept the audience." The startled bishop, having grown concerned about the number of women who consistently attended the district and annual conferences called by the men of the church, saw in Peggie Lesure's dream a way to address the needs of the women. "Yes," he replied to her when she had finished, "that is a great revelation and I am going to organize that vision." To him, the women "manifested the Missionary spirit" and were "waiting and looking for a place" in the work of the church. In 1890 Bishop Holsey spoke to the CME South Georgia Conference in Macon, urging that "some such department as the Woman's Missionary Society should be created at the coming General Conference, in order that our women be given greater opportunities to work for the Kingdom of God." In Columbia, South Carolina, at the General Conference of 1898, the department was created. By that time local CME women already had organized in ten states, including California, Kansas, Missouri, and Illinois, as well as Georgia, Florida, Alabama, Mississippi, North Carolina, and Kentucky. After the women organized, the Missionary Society grew rapidly, and in 1918 the CME General Conference approved an expanded role for the Woman's Connectional Missionary Council. By 1930 over 3,200 local societies had been established, with 37,000 members (out of a church membership of 241,000).[14]

These parallel histories underscore the common experience faced by women who lived in a hierarchical society organized by gender. Both black and white women sought to expand their work in their churches, to be recognized for their contributions, and to make their invisible work visible. Both groups of women began by campaigning for voting (laity) rights within the church; both argued for the ordination of women ministers; and both fought against men in the church, ministers and laymen, who opposed equal rights for women parishioners. Gradually, white and black churchwomen crossed the thin line separating congregational service and what came to be defined as home mission work. They began by teaching Sunday school and caring for sick church members; they ended up addressing regional public health issues, the dual system of southern education, women's working conditions, child welfare, and racial inequities.

While it was obvious to both black and white southern women involved in church missionary work that many of the South's people were in need, these women were also motivated by their deep desire to undertake meaningful work for their *own* benefit. As early as 1861 a white Alabama woman wrote to Bishop James O. Andrew regarding the role of women in the church's mission work, both domestic and foreign. She pleaded, "Bishop, give us work! We can do it, not at once, perhaps, but let us begin." Three generations later, a speech by CME president Mattie Coleman contained a similar plea: "Give us an equal chance, that we may do more effectively the work that is justly ours by the decree of our Heavenly Father." When requested by the Board of Church Extension in the mid-1880s to prepare plans for a woman's department in the Methodist Episcopal Church, South, Lucinda Helm of Kentucky recalled, "I knew many of my sisters must feel as I did. An impetus, a light, a propelling power beyond me had lighted a fire within my soul, and was moving with an irresistible force to throw my life into the work . . . of establishing the kingdom of my Lord." In strikingly similar language, Peggie Lesure, one of the first CME women involved in missionary work, wrote in 1894, "We were a little band of women . . . with burning zeal, outstretched hands, eager hearts, and tearful eyes, longing in our hearts for a place to work."[15]

Beyond opportunities for service and self-development, black and white southern women remained committed to missionary work because of the deep sense of sisterhood that developed within their own separate missionary societies. Women in the Methodist Episcopal Church, South, realizing that "in organized effort there is strength," engaged in common work over the years. They created a body of rituals, ceremoniously consecrating as deaconesses the young, single women trained for work in the home mission movement and presenting life memberships to honor women who had served especially well. They gained strength from communicating with one another, finding a "kinship of soul" among women sharing their lifework. CME women also viewed their organization as a "Sisterhood," which "called the women from every corner of the Church 'To Arms' to build up the kingdom of God in the world." CME women saw themselves as supported by "noble spirited mothers," who "have been and are loyal and faithful pioneers" in the church. Younger CME women chosen to "travel this Highway of Missions, Love and Service" felt the support of those "who have passed to the Great Beyond," women who "labored amidst derision, criticism and oppositions, but with an inexpressible love and faith in the work."[16]

Many commonalities thus bound black and white southern churchwomen together. Within the church, women of both races developed as individuals, while at the same time they worked as members of a collective committed to sustaining the church and shaping the world around them. In this work, both sets of women encountered opposition from the male-dominated church leadership. Although there were many similarities, there were important differences as well. The two organizations diverged with respect to the economic and demographic profiles of their members, their organizational structures, their programmatic goals, and the public issues they were willing to endorse. In many ways, then, black and white southern churchwomen stood on different ground.

White Methodist congregations were made up of middle- or upper-middle-class professionals, merchants, and small planters. Economically comfortable, ME members came neither from the ranks of the most affluent nor from among the poorest of southern whites. After 1870 CME church leaders, often ex-slaves themselves, organized former slaves in rural areas. In urban centers they brought together younger black men and women who had left the countryside in search of work. CME congregations in cities like Atlanta, Memphis, and New Orleans competed with AME and AME Zion missionaries who came South to establish congregations. CME congregations did not draw black intellectuals, who responded to the AME Church, or urban political or business leaders, who tended to join AME Zion congregations, but had their base among the urban middle and working classes and the farmers and sharecroppers in rural communities.[17]

The economic disparity between the women's missionary societies of the CME and Methodist Episcopal Church, South, was a stark reflection of vast differences in both the size of the denominations and the economic status of ME and CME women. Black CME women took tremendous pride in raising several thousand dollars; white ME women routinely boasted of fund drives that yielded *hundreds* of thousands of dollars. As CME leader Mattie Coleman pointed out, "A great difference has been made between those who have been forced to labor for a living and those who have not."[18]

Black and white southern churchwomen also came from demographically dissimilar backgrounds. Southern white women who became heavily involved in church reform activities generally had few children and tended to become church activists after their children were grown. Only a few of these women had had careers, usually as businesswomen or teachers; the vast majority had never worked outside their homes and were married to merchants, doctors, lawyers, school superintendents, or successful farmers. All of the white women involved in church missionary work employed black women and men as domestic servants, as was the norm for white middle-class southerners before 1940. Their homes were kept, their children tended, and their meals cooked by African American women, often by a staff of several African American women and men. Middle- and upper-class southern white women were free to engage in church work precisely because black women, paid next to nothing, did the domestic work involved in running white households. Dependency on this personal level was mirrored in the larger work of the women's organizations. A number of well-known southern Methodist activists were single or widowed; others worked in the church over the protests of their husbands, some of whom were Methodist ministers. For these women, the sisterhood they enjoyed in the church often took the place of relationships they did not have at home.[19]

Black churchwomen, on the other hand, generally had somewhat larger families, and the vast majority were employed outside their own homes. Schoolteachers and principals dominated the CME missionary society leadership. A small percentage of CME women were businesswomen or professionals; a significant proportion labored as domestic workers. In addition to raising their own children, some CME women church leaders adopted needy or abandoned children as part of their work in the church community. Widows formed a substantial minority of CME women leaders. Unlike their white counterparts, black women who were married to ministers or bishops seem to have had fewer open conflicts over their independent activism.[20]

At the time the ME and CME Woman's Missionary societies were founded, the two churches were at very different stages of development. Organizationally, the Methodist Episcopal Church, South, was older and well established, having formed in 1844 by breaking off from the Methodist Episcopal Church over the issue of slavery. The CME Church was newly founded and rapidly growing. This meant that from 1880 to 1940 the opportunities for white women to participate in the founding of new congregations were limited to rapidly expanding urban areas. CME women, on the other hand, were needed to build new churches in communities throughout the South. "Building churches" in this period meant not only constructing buildings but also establishing congregations. Building and supporting churches that were independent of white control; founding mission congregations; locating, educating, and supporting ministers; and establishing organized women's groups took the time and energy of thousands of CME women.[21]

For example, CME church member Mrs. V. K. Glenn of Alabama first traveled to Florida in 1887, where she found that "there were no churches established, nor anyone that claimed to be a part in Christ." On Sundays, Glenn found that everyone she met was "engaged in bathing, boat and bicycle-riding." Glenn found gambling widespread, and she believed she "was the only one to sing, pray and preach to the folk." Glenn decided to build a church and sent back to Alabama for a preacher. In the meantime, she held church meetings in the rented room she occupied near the beach. She would begin by singing and then start to pray. After a while, she wrote, "people would stop on the outside and listen to my services. At last they came to my little room to the service that I held." Finally, a minister came, and together, Glenn wrote, "we worked and all those sinners" joined the church. In 1904 Glenn, the widowed mother of two sons, began traveling across the state of Florida organizing Woman's Missionary boards in communities large and small. Once organized, these women's groups raised the money to build CME churches in eight Florida cities, including Jacksonville, St. Augustine, West Palm Beach, Orlando, Miami, Pensacola, St. Petersburg, and Tampa. In most cases the missionary women "were the only dependence by which these brick and stone churches were built in these places."[22]

Glenn's experience in Florida was similar to that of other black churchwomen throughout the region. CME missionary women in Kansas and Missouri came together for the first time in 1893, and after that consistently raised 50 percent of the church's annual budget. Wrote one man, "We ministers in the Missouri and Kansas Conference thank God for the Missionary Societies." In Kentucky the same was true; black churchwomen organized in 1894 and became the foundation of the church. The state bishop said of them, "Whatever I want done in this Conference, I whisper it to the Missionary ladies and they put the program over."[23]

The level of organizational development in the ME and the CME churches affected the work that women activists undertook. Supporting mission preachers was always a priority of CME missionary women. Women like Glenn in Florida served as temporary ministers, holding a new congregation together until a permanent pastor could be located. Black missionary women routinely recruited male ministers and frequently took responsibility for paying their salaries. Because of a shortage of well-trained ministers, missionary women also supported seminary courses and training programs for preachers at CME schools that they had helped found throughout the South. Sometimes CME women themselves served as ministers. "We have produced many Missionary lady preachers," wrote the Woman's Missionary Society's historian Sara McAfee in 1934. Official licensing of women ministers came in 1954, after years of campaigning by CME missionary women, who first raised the issue in 1902. Clearly, however, from 1870 on CME women preached, ran congregations, and used the title "reverend." For instance, Rev. Ida E. Roberts was elected president of the Woman's Missionary Society in North Carolina in 1892 and served for twenty-three years. It was reported that "Sister Roberts had the advantage of most women, being a minister and State Evangelist, she was called by all the pastors to hold their revivals and organize the Woman's Missionary Society." Roberts spent several years traveling across the state with her three children in tow.[24]

While CME missionary women served as ministers more frequently than their white counterparts, there were other important programmatic differences in the two female missionary societies. Southern white missionary women struggled constantly to shift the focus of church mission work from foreign lands to local enterprises. For many ME parishioners, foreign work was less threatening than local philanthropy. If southern Christians directed their attention to the alleviation of poverty and disease in China or India, it was easier for them to ignore the needs of mill workers in Macon, the unemployed in Atlanta, or sharecroppers in rural Alabama.[25]

In contrast, CME congregations were not divided in their commitments to missions. Between 1870 and 1933 *all* CME mission work was done in the United States; foreign missions were not an issue. Discussed occasionally by CME groups in the early 1900s, the first CME foreign mission was not established until 1933, when the Woman's Missionary Society voted to support a station on the Island of Trinidad. Without exception, CME women focused their greatest attention on African Americans.[26] They organized congregations and Woman's Missionary societies in the southern region and established mission churches in the North. Southern CME church members were concerned that "many of our people had settled in northern cities, without a church home." Laywomen were asked to fund mission preachers "to get our scattered people together who were wandering around with no church home, like sheep without a shepherd."[27] While white Methodists argued over whether to channel resources into foreign or home missions, southern African American Methodists readily opened missions for their own people throughout the United States.

Another programmatic difference between the two groups involved the elaborate reform agendas and political programs developed and endorsed by white missionary women. After the turn of the century, white women shifted their emphasis from the prevention of social problems to a more active political program designed to achieve social change. Eventually, they resolved to focus on three regional concerns: industry, rural development, and interracial cooperation. ME women developed bureaus, commissions, study groups, and committees to examine social issues and determine the ME Woman's Missionary Society's official position on such questions as child labor, protective legislation for hours and wages, collective bargaining, rural conditions, convict-lease, and racial segregation.[28]

Development of such a bureaucracy and public reform platform held little appeal for CME missionary activists, who shared with their members ideas for programs that could be easily adapted by the diverse woman's groups, small and large, urban and rural, educated and uneducated, that constituted the CME Woman's Missionary Connection. CME women saw their role as one of "Christianizing" their people. Christianization was a full-fledged program spoken in a one-word code. It meant becoming literate and economically secure. It meant being counted as a citizen, voting, and having access to public resources, as well as following a set of standards that restricted alcohol and gambling and emphasized an individual's responsibilities to spouse and children. Christianization was also acceptable, at least superficially, to whites. CME women protected themselves by *not* taking official stands on public issues. To shield themselves and their families from attacks by whites, black churchwomen kept their own agendas hidden and were circumspect about their goals. For instance, they did not publish the proceedings of their meetings as the ME women did, and their few publications rarely included articles on controversial subjects. They did, however, openly applaud the progressive public positions taken by the white ME women. When ME women spoke out against lynching, for example, or in favor of improving black schools, CME women supported the white reform platform.[29]

This indirect form of speaking out was especially important for southern black women working at the grass-roots level who were not well known—women who were not protected by position, northern connections, or reputation. When prominent black, non-CME women, like Margaret

Murray Washington, Lugenia Burns Hope, Charlotte Hawkins Brown, or
Nannie Burroughs, took sides on an issue, they did so knowing that their
role as public figures provided some degree of protection.[30] This is not to
say that these well-known black southern women were ever completely
safe from threats, humiliation, or extralegal violence; they certainly were
not. But CME missionary activists were for the most part known only
locally and consequently were at greater risk as they advocated for
African Americans at a time when white animosity was intensifying.
CME women did not hesitate to employ the strategy of showing their
support for certain social or economic changes by endorsing a platform
put together by white women. In part this was dissemblance; black
women took the position of endorsing an agenda created by white
churchwomen. But African American women also affirmed the white
agenda because they had played an instrumental, albeit indirect, role in
its shaping.

Over the years, meetings between CME and ME women were reported
by both groups. These chronicles followed a prescribed format, used by
both races, in which white women were consistently portrayed as giving,
teaching, aiding, assisting, and supporting the black women with whom
they met. Black women, on the other hand, were always reported as
learning, receiving aid, and appreciating the assistance they were given.
This "helping"/"learning" posturing, as it were, covered up the most
essential aspects of the relationship between these women of different
races: their mutual dependence and the process of transformation by
which black women converted their concerns and priorities into a form
that could be understood and adopted by white reformers.

For black women, the process of transformation filled the gap between
perceived needs and successful programs. Within their own organizations
black churchwomen debated, agonized over, and prioritized what needed
to be done in their communities, knowing that white churchwomen had
the resources to underwrite the work. The self-conscious process of
transformation was an effective way of mobilizing white resources for use
in the black community. A crucial part of the process involved black
women allowing white women to take credit for drawing up innovative
agendas and progressive interracial programs. But without input from
CME women and without the willingness of black women to run ME-
sponsored programs in black communities, the interracial ministry
sponsored by the ME sisters would have been very limited.

As it was, black churchwomen, usually assisted by one or two white
missionary women, actually implemented the programs funded by the
ME Woman's Missionary Council. In 1902 the ME board completed
construction of a women's annex to Paine Institute, an ME-sponsored

school for blacks in Augusta, Georgia. Black churchwomen served as faculty and staff at the Paine Annex and staffed eight community centers, called Bethlehem Houses, in various southern cities.[31] Women in the CME sisterhood ran ME-sponsored day nurseries and health programs, organized Negro PTAs, community clubs, and social service committees, and distributed Methodist literature in the black community. CME women welcomed ME missionaries into their homes and neighborhoods, cooperating with them as they intervened in the courts on behalf of individual blacks and petitioned municipal governments and public schools for additional resources for the black community. Addressing the vast majority of ME women, whose involvement in interracial work rarely extended beyond their pocketbooks, Bertha Newell emphasized that "your generous appropriations made [the work] possible," and she underscored how leadership schools and Bethlehem Centers "create a spirit of mutual helpfulness between Southern Methodist women and women of colored churches."[32]

Initially, white Methodist women's concern for southern blacks was acted on within the context of missionary programs directed at all races and many ethnic groups. White Methodist women spoke out against racial prejudice directed toward Asians in California and Mexicans in Texas and New Mexico more often than against that affecting African Americans in the South. In 1907 Paine Institute was only one of fifteen schools supported by the Woman's Home Mission Society across the southern tier of states from Georgia to California, with a total of 2,156 pupils. One-third of the institutes' students were "mountaineers" in Appalachia, and one-tenth were "Orientals" in California, where white Methodist women reported that "racial prejudice and exclusion laws have created a great agitation against Japanese and Chinese" and "made the work difficult." The remainder were in cities, which white Methodist women considered in dire need of "evangelization" because of the large number of "foreign people" who flooded southern ports of entry, such as Charleston and Savannah. Methodist Episcopal women argued that 65 percent of the "conglomerate population" of the United States was non-Christian. They believed that without a personal ministry to these "aliens," it would be impossible for the United States to remain a Christian country, "for their indifference, their opposition, will sap our strength, and we will become a nation which has no God or Redeemer."[33]

Gradually, this orientation to "all races" changed, largely because of the influence of black churchwomen themselves. As CME women organized into local missionary societies, white Methodist women intensified their focus on southern African Americans, whom the ME Woman's Board president Belle Bennett saw in 1909 as "the dark faces of the alien race that looked daily into theirs."[34] Endorsement of the social platform of the Federal Council of Churches in 1913 had an important impact on the ME Woman's Missionary Society's work with southern black women. That year, President Belle Bennett reiterated the platform's first plank, a commitment to stand "for equal rights and complete justice for all men in all stations of life." At the same time she endorsed the work of Deaconess Mary DeBardeleben in the black community in Augusta, Georgia, and issued a strong statement against "the barbarous crime of lynching": "We therefore, as an organized and representative body of Southern women, should declare our disapproval and abhorrence of the savagery that provokes this crime, and by tongue and pen and, in those States where our women have the power of suffrage, by the ballot arouse and develop a public sentiment that will compel a rigid enforcement of the law against such violence until it is no longer known among us."[35]

Following Bennett's lead, the ME Woman's Missionary Council reported in 1915 that "earnest women are praying and planning for a broader, kinder ministry to this backward race." One sister implored, "They are our very own charge, what are we going to do about it?" The following year twenty auxiliaries were reported "helping the black sister," and the council's Bureau of Social Service argued that "this field in our Southland [Africa at Home] is very broad, and the cultivation of it is our own peculiar charge." ME women called for "a larger and a more kindly ministry to the negro," arguing that "the white South *for its own self-interest* [emphasis added], if for no more noble reason must respect the negro's desire to help himself where the desire exists and must help him to find himself when it does not." The Woman's Missionary Council believed that "in a spirit of friendly cooperation the two races must march . . . in separate companies, but a solid phalanx to the stirring notes of a better humanity." In 1918 ME women argued that "the 9,000,000 negroes located in the South constitute the biggest opportunity for the Church to build up a citizenship which will make this country God's country."[36]

Clearly, then, by 1918 white Methodist women saw working with black southerners as the central focus of their domestic missionary program, although their approach to this work was condescending toward African Americans and oppressively maternalistic. White women were surprised at their "discoveries of negro efficiency" and claimed southern blacks their "own peculiar charge." It was only after Mattie Coleman became president of the CME Woman's Missionary Society in 1918 that, at *her* initiative, direct contact between the two women's groups began to occur at regular intervals. Coleman asked permission to attend ME Woman's Missionary Council meetings on a regular basis as a delegate, and gradually, because of Coleman's influence, the ME's orientation to what they called "negro work" began to change, in both substance and tone.[37]

Mattie E. Coleman was born in Tennessee on July 3, 1870. She finished high school at fifteen and continued her education at Central Tennessee College, which later became Walden University. In 1902 she married Rev. P. J. Coleman and joined the CME Church. A graduate of Meharry Medical College, she practiced medicine in Clarksville, Tennessee, where her husband was sent to pastor Wesley Chapel CME. Coleman served as medical examiner of the court in Calanthe, Tennessee, for more than twenty years. She was the only black woman physician to ever work as a state tuberculosis adviser and counselor. For several years she served as dean of women at Lane College. An energetic missionary worker, she urged the CME General Conference, meeting in Chicago in 1918, to give her and the missionary women permission to organize the Woman's Connectional Missionary Council, of which she became the first president. She held that position for twenty-one years, from 1918 to 1939.[38]

Organized, articulate, well-educated, and dynamic, Coleman provided strong leadership for CME women and, at the same time, indirectly guided the ME sisterhood as well. Coleman never failed to praise the work of the ME women in lavish tones. For example, at the first meeting of the CME Woman's Missionary Society she was reported to have delivered "a glowing tribute to the women of the M.E. Church, South, setting forth the various ways in which they had helped in this movement." Later in the same meeting Coleman called for the establishment of a social service department, "where we might join our sisters in the M.E. Church, South, in building more Bethlehem Houses. . . . " First dissembling in a manner acceptable to whites, she deliberately acknowledged the "help" received from the white women. Once this ritual was complete, however, Coleman called for a new program initiative, a CME-controlled social service department, and spoke of "joining" together as sisters, implying a relationship based on equality, not racial hierarchy.[39]

Whenever black women interacted with their white Methodist sisters, although they postured deference, praising the white women and thanking them profusely for their help and assistance, they also transmitted unmistakable messages, sometimes veiled in a prayer, a Bible verse, or in the words of a hymn, that they expected fair treatment. Black churchwomen often dissembled in one breath and demanded in the next. For example, CME women reported their genuine hope of working with the ME women toward "a full life without restrictions." Black churchwomen wrote that "they [the ME women] do not come to us thinking we are not capable of doing our work, but they heard a voice ringing out from the humble homes of our C.M.E. Sister workers." In other words, the white women helped us because we asked them to do so. In the context of discussing the parallel fight for church voting rights waged by ME and CME women, black women used words laden with double meaning. The battle for women's rights clearly reflected the ongoing struggle for racial justice, and the words aimed at the men also contained a message for the white sisters: "Give us a larger sphere; open the door of opportunity. . . . Give us an equal chance, that we may do more effectively the work that is justly ours. . . ."[40]

When the CME missionary worker Theresa Dent delivered a sororal message at the ME Woman's Missionary Council annual meeting in 1931, she followed the pattern of speaking whereby dissemblance was followed by directives. Dent reported trying "to impress upon the consciences and hearts of that great body of women the vast need for a new interpretation of the Kingdom of God." Dent then outlined the specific interpretation she thought best: "I asked that they consider work at home as well as abroad; give our women in their employ a living wage; encourage them to send their children to school; assist in getting better streets and lights, and living conditions for our people." In a similar mode, when the ME group was reconsidering its funding of leadership schools, CME women voted "much appreciation and thanks" for the ME women and then passed a resolution that was nothing short of a demand: "Be it resolved that these schools be continued from year to year."[41]

Southern women's church records, both ME and CME, contain many examples of black women transforming their own agreed-upon needs into a format that became part of the white women's reform agenda. Tracing the patterns of black-white interactions requires a binocular reading of both the extensive records published by white Methodist Episcopal women and the relatively few extant records left by Colored Methodist Episcopal women, with an eye for both what was recorded and what was left unsaid. Some examples of the process of transformation are immediately obvious, such as when Sara McAfee reported in 1933 that the white ME missionary women had labored hard "to instruct, influence and help" the black population of Columbus, Georgia. After having carefully repeated the helping/teaching mantra, as ritual demanded, McAfee then revealed how the white women "have worked side by side with me in making this County School Missionary work a success." Following McAfee's suggestions rather than instructing her, the white women had furnished speakers and contributed books to "every Colored School" in Muscogee County.[42] In other situations we can only speculate about how the process of transformation worked, understanding that this was a pattern of interaction that became second nature for both whites and blacks.

One of the most striking examples of the process of transformation at work is included in the only history of women in the CME church, written in 1934. There, Sara McAfee tells the story of "Mother Sawyer," an elderly black woman who lived in Nashville, Tennessee, at the turn of the century. This woman was said to have opened "her great mother heart" to every child in the community. She cared for children whose parents worked from dawn to dusk. Frequently she wept for her people, who suffered from unjust racial discrimination, inadequate schooling, and low wages and were thus vulnerable to unhappiness, hopelessness, and despondency. One evening after the last child had gone home, so the story goes, Mother Sawyer "lifted her soul in fervent prayer," asking for a way to help. Then, "as if in answer to her prayer, Mother Sawyer learned of the work that the Southern Methodist women were doing for her neglected white people of the city through their Wesley Houses," and "a hope was born in her heart for similar work for her own people."[43]

Certain that she had the answer, Sawyer made an appointment to see Tochie MacDonell, the white general secretary of the Methodist Episcopal Church, South, Woman's Board of Home Missions. MacDonell sent her to see Estelle Haskin, in charge of community service, and Haskin heard her out. Sawyer presented her case, revealing evidence of crowded living conditions, children with no place to play except back alleys, babies left helpless while mothers worked, and children with curable diseases but no treatments. Haskin's heart "was touched," and she promised to help. Shortly after this, Haskin reportedly "walked through the Negro section of Nashville in search of a place" to begin solving these problems. As she walked, she happened to notice "the flood of sunlight" in the basement of a local church. She asked the pastor if he would be willing to help sponsor a kindergarten in the basement of his church. He was willing, and the school was opened, funded by the ME Woman's Missionary Society.

Mother Sawyer saw all this and was said to be "delighted with the progress being made." She was not satisfied, though. Eager to enlarge the work "in order for it to reach more people," Mother Sawyer continued to pray. This time "her prayers were answered" when the ME Woman's Missionary Society of the Tennessee Conference became interested and asked permission to contribute money. When the appropriation came in, Mother Sawyer rented a house and "was made the house mother." There she worked "with her people, opening up larger and larger opportunities for them."

Mother Sawyer ministered to her people as a CME churchwoman, and through the church she obtained the resources needed to carry on her work to improve the community. Sawyer's story, told so eloquently in the CME's history, does not appear in the ME Woman's Missionary Council records, where there is simply a reference to "the mission being developed in Nashville, Tennessee, by Miss Haskin, of the Methodist Training School."[44] Sawyer and hundreds of women like her in communities across the South were involved in this process of transformation. These women regularly translated the massive economic and social needs of individuals and groups in the black community into a format that could be clearly understood by white women reformers. They gave lists of specific social problems and suggestions for their solution to white churchwomen (as Sawyer gave MacDonell and Haskin information about her community). White reformers then took this information and incorporated it into their own agenda. Black women, in a way largely invisible to whites, controlled the process: they determined which needs were most pressing, they suggested solutions, and in most cases they did the work of setting up and running the programs. If a specific outcome was desired, starting a kindergarten in a particular church basement or renting a house out of which Mother Sawyer could work, then the process of transformation included some direct intervention: Haskin did not just walk past the church with the sunlit basement by accident, and that minister, no doubt, had been notified to watch for her.

Whether self-consciously or not, white churchwomen learned a great deal from black churchwomen and depended on them as they designed and implemented interracial programs. White women also followed the lead of black women in fighting for laity rights and in campaigning for the ordination of women ministers. CME women "began to agitate the question of woman's rights" within their church in 1906; ME women began in 1909. CME women started working for the ordination of women in 1902; ME women first pressed the issue in 1930.[45]

CME women looked to white Methodist women for financial backing, funding they saw as their due, no doubt because of the unpaid wages of slavery and the low wages they had received after freedom. For instance, black women attended ME-sponsored leadership training schools, reporting that "these schools have been much help to us, to the extent that we feel we are due. . . . " CME women also looked to ME women for critical support at specific times and even used the power of white womanhood to coerce the male CME leadership into meeting the demands of the churchwomen's organization. For example, when CME men opposed the formation of the CME Woman's Connectional Missionary Council, CME missionary society women invited ME member Mrs. Hume Steele to speak in favor of the proposal at a CME conference. Black women saw themselves as willing to "join our sisters in the M.E. Church." They said white women worked "side by side" with them, and as they expanded their role in the church, CME women stated that they were "well assisted by the missionary women of the M.E. Church, South."[46]

Increased contact with organized CME women had a major effect on the work of the ME Woman's Missionary Council. In 1920 ME women formed the Committee to Establish Policy for Negro Work, and the following year they began to organize interracial committees in communities throughout the South. Two years later they issued a new call to abolish mob violence and lynching. By 1923 they reported that 445 interracial committees had been organized; by 1927 there were 666, with most classified as "working in a spirit of cooperation, confidence, and mutual respect." During the 1920s ME women redefined what they meant by interracial cooperation, arguing for "face-to-face and hand-to-hand work with our Negro neighbors." They insisted that charity was *not* interracial cooperation, and they recognized that "fear, the closed mind and heart, the credulity of the masses, sentimentalism, emotionalism, patronizing attitudes and low standards" impeded constructive interracial work. Step by step, they began to speak in different tones, saying that "the race problem in America must be solved," not for white self-interest but because they recognized "all human beings as children of God with a right to a chance to make their lives all possible to them." In 1924 ME women called for equal resources and services for black southerners in housing, schools, and benefits from state agencies. In 1928 they recommended that the missionary societies, in cooperation with black citizens in each community, "engage in a definite study of Negro public schools" for the purpose of "making every Negro elementary school what any school for any child ought to be, and, further, of placing a high school education within the reach of all Negro boys and girls who aspire to larger usefulness."[47]

As white churchwomen followed the lead of their black counterparts, ME women leaders sought to guide and enlighten their own membership. As they studied conditions, tallied social and economic inequities between southern blacks and whites, and worked to educate the women within their organization, forward-thinking leaders on the ME Woman's Missionary Council encouraged white southern women to "see their social environment as it affects and controls the lives of others," in other words, to understand the impact of white domination and their own power as white southerners. They wanted white women "to use their own initiative in carrying out their own decisions," to take responsibility for existing conditions and act to change them. It was not an easy task. Responding to this challenge required women "running counter to public opinion, to popular prejudice, and, hardest of all, in opposition to members of their own households."[48]

According to Bertha Newell, an ME leader who was born in Wisconsin and educated at the University of Chicago, the obstacles were formidable: widespread indifference, "positive antagonism to the idea of working *with* Negroes," and the most fundamental effort of all, getting whites to acknowledge "the Negro as a *person* with feelings." Newell's vision, unusually farsighted for the period, came from her ability to place southern race relations in a national context, arguing that "the history of the Negro as related to the American people at once places it as one of the most grave and perplexing national problems." Along with other committed white Methodist leaders, Tochie MacDonell, Estelle Haskin, Carrie Parks Johnson, and Thelma Stevens, Newell regularly pushed for the endorsement of interracial goals that were no doubt often passively ignored, if not vigorously opposed, in local missionary societies throughout the South.[49]

Because of the support and indirect guidance of CME women, interracial work undertaken by white Methodist women, in sharp contrast to their industrial and rural reform efforts, actually increased in intensity during the Great Depression. By 1932 Bertha Newell reported that "the variety in services is so great we could not even list them [and] the change in attitudes is a constant surprise." As these southern women of both races came together for institutes and interracial committee meetings, white women were being educated by the CME women they were supposed to be "teaching." In these meetings, ME women reported being almost overwhelmed as they learned of "the difficulties colored families have in getting an education, of the disparity in division of funds between schools for the two races in given counties, of ominous lacks in sanitation for schools and homes." "On both sides of the color line," Newell declared, "new understandings are arrived at and misconceptions brushed away." Gradually, some white women began to acknowledge what was happening, and by 1938 white women teaching in leadership schools for CME women reported that "they came to help and were helped."[50]

In the context of a program centered on leadership training and interracial community-based meetings, ME women also supported the work of the Commission on Interracial Cooperation, Women's Division, and, after 1930, of the Association of Southern Women for the Prevention of Lynching (ASWPL). Having publicly spoken out against lynching since 1913, ME women did not hesitate to endorse the Costigan-Wagner antilynching bill in 1933, although it was never endorsed by the ASWPL. In 1933 ME women recommended studies of the "white primary" to find out "to what extend the right of voting in primaries is limited to white citizens and to discover methods to correct abuses." That same year they launched a study of domestic service, which they viewed, optimistically, as "Christian interracial opportunities within our own households."[51]

By 1935 ME women acknowledged that members of the CME Woman's Connectional Missionary Council "have met us more than half way," and both groups of women continued to applaud the benefits of holding interracial Bible schools and supporting interracial teaching staffs. Women delegates to interracial missionary meetings, black and white, were regularly welcomed as guests in the homes of CME women, who studiously and courageously ignored existing racialized codes of behavior. ME women funded schools and institutes and paid boarding fees for black delegates, but they never entertained black women as overnight guests. As the thirties drew to a close, ME and CME women increased their efforts to improve black schools, and for the first time ME women spoke in favor of college training for southern African Americans, long a CME priority.[52]

The work of these women, black and white, made a difference in hundreds of local southern communities, where conditions for black southerners were improved or at least did not deteriorate further, and on the regional level, where such secular groups as the Commission on Interracial Cooperation and the Southern Conference on Human Welfare came to depend on the support of a large constituency of reform-oriented churchwomen. As interracial work between ME and CME women developed and changed across decades of increasing racial segregation, some of these black and white women reached out and called each other "Sister." They communicated, albeit in a discourse filled with innuendos and allusions. Through the process of transformation, CME women recast the white women's agenda for social change and gave public expression to their visions of a more just and humane society.

In 1939 ME women wrote about their work with CME women in words confirming that the dual Methodist sisterhoods, at least in a certain sense, had become one: "As experiences were exchanged it became clear that as individuals and as a group we were seeking a greater awareness of our common needs and resources and building confidence among ourselves and a belief in the ultimate triumph of the power of God."[53] By 1940 Methodist Episcopal women expressed their desire to infuse their reform program into the church at large, where it could transform a broader constituency. When that did not happen, they continued to bear witness to their own ideals. In this they had the steadfast support of the Colored Methodist Episcopal women, whose beliefs in racial justice and economic opportunity they had adopted as their own. As Mattie Coleman knew well, to realize this vision, each one had been dependent on the other.

NOTES

I would like to thank Sharon Lane, Roslyn Ware, Jenny Presnell, and Clint Joiner for their assistance. Mattie Jackson and her staff at the Miles College Library in Birmingham, Alabama, generously helped in my search for CME records. I am also grateful to Suzanne Lebsock and Nancy Hewitt for their thoughtful comments on the manuscript.

1. These organizations spanned a broad political spectrum. Protestant religious reformers, led by the Methodists, joined with the American Association of University Women, the League of Women Voters, the Young Women's Christian Association (YWCA), and the National Women's Trade Union League to constitute the center; they were flanked on the right by the Woman's Christian Temperance Union (WCTU) and the General Federation of Women's Clubs and on the left by the Southern Summer School, union women, and women active in groups supported by socialists and communists. For a study of interactions among the groups along this spectrum, see Marion Winifred Roydhouse, "The 'Universal Sisterhood of Women': Women and Labor Reform in North Carolina, 1900-1932" (Ph.D. diss., Duke University, 1980). Black women's organizations included the National Association of Colored Women's Clubs, the National Council of Negro Women, and the International Council of Women of the Darker Races. Southern black women joined southern affiliates of national organizations, such as the YWCA and the WCTU, as well as neighborhood and community women's clubs, such as the Tuskegee Woman's Club in Alabama, the Woman's Industrial Club of Louisville, Kentucky, and the Neighborhood Union in Atlanta. See Paula Giddings, *When and Where I Enter: The Impact of Black Women on Race and Sex in America* (New York: William Morrow, 1984), 95-117; Cynthia Neverdon-Morton, *Afro-American Women of the South and the Advancement of the Race, 1895-1925* (Knoxville: University of Tennessee Press, 1989); and Jacqueline Anne Rouse, *Lugenia Burns Hope: Black Southern Reformer* (Athens: University of Georgia Press, 1989), 1-10.

2. Anne Firor Scott first discussed the work of the women of the Methodist Episcopal Church, South, in *The Southern Lady: From Pedestal to Politics, 1830-1930* (Chicago: University of Chicago Press, 1970), quote on 199. She reemphasized the importance of this group as leading advocates of social change in "Women, Religion and Social Change in the South, 1830-1930," in *Religion and the Solid South,* ed. Sam S. Hill, Jr. (Nashville: Abingdon, 1972), 92-121. Scott based her analysis in part on church histories, such as those compiled by Mary Noreen Dunn, *Women and Home Missions* (Nashville: Cokesbury, 1936); Sara Estelle Haskin, *Women and Missions in the Methodist Episcopal Church, South* (Nashville: Methodist Publishing House, 1920); and Mrs. R. W. [Tochie] MacDonell, *Belle Harris Bennett: Her Life Work* (Nashville: Board of Missions, Methodist Episcopal Church, South, 1928); and Noreen Dunn Tatum, *A Crown of Service: A Story of Woman's Work in the Methodist Episcopal Church, South, from 1878-1940* (Nashville: Parthenon, 1960). More recent works include John Patrick McDowell, *The Social Gospel in the South: The Woman's Home Mission*

Movement in the Methodist Episcopal Church, South, 1886-1939 (Baton Rouge: Louisiana State University Press, 1982); Jacquelyn Dowd Hall, *Revolt against Chivalry: Jessie Daniel Ames and the Women's Campaign against Lynching* (New York: Columbia University Press, 1979); Mary E. Frederickson, "Shaping a New Society: Methodist Women and Industrial Reform, 1880-1940," in *Women in New Worlds: Historical Perspectives on the Wesleyan Tradition,* vol. 1, ed. Hilah F. Thomas and Rosemary Skinner Keller (Nashville: Abingdon, 1981), 345-61. The history of women in the CME church has received little attention from scholars. See Mrs. L. D. [Sara] McAfee, *History of the Woman's Missionary Society in the Colored Methodist Episcopal Church* (Jackson, Tenn.: Publishing House, CME Church, 1934).

3. Dolores Janiewski, *Sisterhood Denied: Race, Gender, and Class in a New South Community* (Philadelphia: Temple University Press, 1985); Darlene Clark Hine, "Rape and the Inner Lives of Black Women in the Middle West: Preliminary Thoughts on the Culture of Dissemblance," *Signs* 14 (Summer 1989): 294; Rosalyn Terborg-Penn, "Discrimination against Afro-American Women in the Woman's Movement, 1830-1920" in *The Afro-American Woman: Struggles and Images,* ed. Sharon Harley and Rosalyn Terborg-Penn (Port Washington, N.Y.: Kennikat Press, 1978), 17-27.

4. Hall, *Revolt against Chivalry,* esp. chap. 3; Evelyn Brooks Higginbotham, "Beyond the Sound of Silence: Afro-American Women in History," *Gender and History* 1 (Spring 1989): 60, and "Unlikely Sisterhood: Black and White Baptist Women's Cooperation during the Era of Jim Crow" (Paper delivered at the Organization of American Historians Meeting, Louisville, Ky., April 12, 1991).

5. Patricia Hill Collins's discussion of black women's activism focuses on the struggle for group survival and "the struggle for institutional transformation," which she defines as "those efforts to change existing structures of oppression," including "all individual and group actions that directly challenge the legal and customary rules governing African-American women's subordination, such as participating in civil rights organizations, labor unions, feminist groups, boycotts, and revolts." See Patricia Collins, *Black Feminist Thought: Knowledge, Consciousness, and the Politics of Empowerment* (New York: Routledge, Chapman and Hall, 1991), 141-42. The process of transformation that I am defining here is different from that identified by Collins but not unrelated. Black churchwomen, at least within the CME, did not directly challenge the rules and mores shaping their subordination. Rather they participated, both as individuals and as members of a group of women, in a process of transformation whereby their concerns and needs were translated into a form that could be adopted by white reformers. Of course, participation in this process of transformation, along with concomitant acts of dissemblance, did not preclude joining in direct challenges of institutional transformation.

6. Hine, "Rape and the Inner Lives," 294.

7. *AME Year Book, 1918* (Philadelphia: AME Book Concern, 1918), 4; McAfee, *History,* 32. On the formation of the CME Church, see C. Eric Lincoln and Lawrence H. Mamiya, *The Black Church in the African-American Experi-*

ence (Durham, N.C.: Duke University Press, 1990), 60-65; "Work with Negro Members," in *The History of American Methodism*, vol. 2, ed. Emory Stevens Bucke (New York, Nashville: Abingdon, 1964), 279-87; Manning Marable, "Religion and Black Protest Thought in African American History," in *African American Religious Studies: An Interdisciplinary Anthology*, ed. Gayraud S. Wilmore (Durham, N.C.: Duke University Press, 1989), 330-31; Darlene Clark Hine, *When the Truth Is Told: A History of Black Women's Culture and Community in Indiana, 1875-1950* (Indianapolis: National Council of Negro Women, Indianapolis Section, 1981), 18; John B. Boles, *Black Southerners, 1619-1869* (Lexington: University of Kentucky Press, 1983), 201-2; and Glenn T. Eskew, "Black Elitism and the Failure of Paternalism in Postbellum Georgia: The Case of Bishop Lucius Henry Holsey," *Journal of Southern History* 58 (November 1992): 637-66. For the white response, see Kenneth K. Bailey, *Southern White Protestantism in the Twentieth Century* (New York: Harper and Row, 1964), 4-7; and Erskine Caldwell, *Deep South: Memory and Observation* (New York: Weybright and Talley, 1968), 194-98.

8. J. A. Martin, "Background of Missionary Activities," in McAfee, *History*, 33-35. From 1870 to 1890, 50 to 60 percent of the rural church house lots of the early CME Church were given with conditional clauses, stipulating that the property would revert to the original donor when the land or building was no longer used for religious services by the CME.

9. Ibid., 35.

10. See McDowell, *Social Gospel*, chap. 1; and McAfee, *History*, 41-64. In *When the Truth Is Told*, Darlene Clark Hine writes of the "most 'invisible' constituency within the black church—the women" (17).

11. McAfee, *History*, 145.

12. Eugene Genovese, *Roll, Jordan, Roll: The World the Slaves Made* (New York: Pantheon Books, 1974).

13. Oswald Eugene Brown and Anna Muse Brown, *Life and Letters of Laura Askew Haygood* (Nashville: Publishing House of the Methodist Episcopal Church, South, 1904), 1-98; Frederickson, "Shaping a New Society," 346-48; McDowell, *Social Gospel*, 9-10.

14. McAfee, *History*, 41-46; Woman's Connectional Missionary Council membership figures are from the *Handbook for Adult Missionary Societies* (Nashville: Woman's Connectional Council of the Colored Methodist Episcopal Church, 1930), 3; denominational figures are from the *AME Yearbook, 1918*, 67. For a parallel movement among black Baptist women, see Evelyn Brooks, "The Feminist Theology of the Black Baptist Church, 1880-1900," in *Class, Race, and Sex: The Dynamics of Control*, ed. Amy Swerdlow and Hanna Lessinger (Boston: G. K. Hall, 1983), 31-59.

15. Quotations, in order, from Tatum, *Crown of Service*, 16-17; McAfee, *History*, 146; Tatum, *Crown of Service*, 26; McAfee, *History*, 41.

16. Quotes on ME women in Brown and Brown, *Life and Letters of Laura Askew Haygood*, 87; quotes on CME women in McAfee, *History*, 194, 197; on ME rituals, see Frederickson, "Shaping a New Society," 350-51.

17. In the last decades of the nineteenth century, because of the close affiliation between CME and ME congregations, other black Methodists "suspected C.M.E. leaders and openly charged them with being leaders of the Uncle Tom type and would have Negroes be mere tools for former masters." CME leaders agreed that "upon the face of things this looked possible," and over the years, "this charge, though dead, left its mark of division upon the Negro group." CME church members were pulled two ways: affiliation with the ME Church separated them from other black Methodists and maintained a tie with whites; combining with nonsouthern denominations, such as the AME, provided more independence vis à vis whites but involved giving up the autonomy won in 1870 when the CME Church was founded. Quotation from McAfee, *History*, 35; see also Lincoln and Mamiya, *The Black Church*, 47–75.

18. Coleman quoted in McAfee, *History*, 142. Belle H. Bennett, "Address of the President," in *Twenty-third Annual Report of the Woman's Home Mission Society* (Nashville: Publishing House of the Methodist Episcopal Church, South, 1909), 48, reported that for the two years between 1907 and 1909 the ME Woman's Home Mission Society and Foreign Missionary Society had raised $400,000 annually, or two-thirds of the total amount collected for mission work by the entire church membership. CME leaders were more affluent than the general membership. The difference between the wealth of white and black congregants was greater than between white and black women leaders. Nevertheless, black women, even when in the same occupational category as whites (e.g., as a schoolteacher or principal), were paid 50 percent of the salaries paid to whites.

19. McDowell, *Social Gospel*, 146–47; Hall, *Revolt against Chivalry*, 180–86; Frederickson, "Shaping a New Society," 349–52.

20. Life history material on individual CME women is available in McAfee, *History*, 41–64. Schoolteachers and principals seem to be the most numerous professionals among CME women leaders. Information about the occupations of rank-and-file women in the CME Woman's Missionary Society can be found in an ME list of the occupations of women attending a Leadership School for Colored Church Women at Texas College, Tyler, Texas, in 1931: "Three dressmakers, two preachers, a notary, funeral director and florist, a real estate dealer, three saleswomen, three beauty culture specialists, three farmers, a nurse, several cooks, laundresses, and maids, were enrolled, with many who gave no occupation." *Report of the Twenty-Second Annual Meeting* (Nashville: Publishing House of the Methodist Episcopal Church, South, 1932), 111 (hereafter cited as numbered *Report of Council*). Paula Giddings found similar occupational patterns among the first generation of black club women. See Giddings, *When and Where I Enter*, 108.

21. McAfee, *History*, 75–117.

22. Ibid., 79, 88.

23. Ibid., 101, 116.

24. Ibid., 202, 101. Date on official licensing from Lincoln and Mamiya, *The Black Church*, 73. On black women ministers, see Cheryl J. Sanders, "The Woman as Preacher," in *African American Religious Studies*, ed. Wilmore,

372-91; Jacquelyn Grant, "Womanist Theology: Black Women's Experience as a Source for Doing Theology, with Special Reference to Christology," 372-91 in the same volume; Cheryl Townsend Gilkes, " 'Together and in Harness': Women's Traditions in the Sanctified Church," *Signs* 10 (Summer 1985): 383; Jualyne E. Dodson and Cheryl Townsend Gilkes, "Something Within: Social Change and Collective Endurance in the Sacred World of Black Christian Women," in *Women and Religion in America, 1900-68*, vol. 3, ed. Rosemary R. Ruether and Rosemary S. Keller (San Francisco: Harper and Row, 1986), 85; and Jualyne Dodson, "Nineteenth-Century A.M.E. Preaching Women: Cutting Edge of Women's Inclusion in Church Polity," in *Women in New Worlds*, vol. 1, ed. Thomas and Keller, 276-89.

25. Frederickson, "Shaping a New Society," 348-49; McDowell, *Social Gospel*, 7-10.

26. McAfee, *History*, 70. The first CME churches north of the Mason-Dixon line were founded as blacks began to migrate from southern states to northern cities. The first northern missions were established in Washington, D.C.; others followed in St. Louis and eventually in Chicago and as far west as California. The AME Church, unlike the CME, supported numerous foreign missions, primarily in Africa, beginning in the nineteenth century.

27. Ibid., 112.

28. *Twenty-first Report of Council* (1931), 126.

29. McAfee, *History*, 149-56; 142-46; *Handbook for Adult Missionary Societies*, 51-55; *The Messenger* (Jackson, Tenn.: Woman's Connectional Council of the Colored Methodist Episcopal Church), published monthly, 1940-49.

30. See Evelyn Brooks, "Religion, Politics, and Gender: The Leadership of Nannie Helen Burroughs," *Journal of Religious Thought* 44 (Winter/Spring 1988): 7-22; and Rouse, *Lugenia Burns Hope*, 133. For use of a strategy based on collective economic development, see Elsa Barkley Brown, "Womanist Consciousness: Maggie Lena Walker and the Independent Order of Saint Luke," *Signs* 14 (Spring 1989): 208-23.

31. Paine Annex discussion in *Fifteenth Annual Report, Woman's Parsonage and Home Mission Society* (Nashville: Publishing House of the Methodist Episcopal Church, South, 1901), 51-52 (hereafter cited as numbered *Report*). Donations to build the annex were made by individual women in memory of their "old nurses." For example, Belle Bennett donated money in memory of "Mammy Ritta," and Mary Helm made a donation in memory of "Aunt Gilly." On Bethlehem Houses, see McDowell, *Social Gospel*, 86-87. He refers to them as Bethlehem Centers, although both ME and CME women called them Bethlehem Houses.

32. *Twenty-sixth Report of Council* (1936), 123.

33. Quotation on "conglomerate population" from *Tenth Report of Council* (1920), 60; other quotations from *Twenty-first Report* (1907), 39.

34. *Twenty-third Report* (1909), 47.

35. Belle Bennett, "President's Message to the Woman's Missionary Council," in *Third Report of Council* (1913), 293-99.

36. Fifth *Report of Council* (1915), 101; *Sixth Report of Council* (1916), 131-32; *Ninth Report of Council* (1919), 80.

37. *Sixth Report of Council* (1916), 131; McAfee, *History*, 148.

38. *Missionary Messenger* (Women's Missionary Council, CME Church) 43 (February 1989): 3.

39. McAfee, *History,* 130, 142.

40. Ibid., 146.

41. Ibid., 191 (first two quotes), 159-60 (second two quotes).

42. Ibid., 174. As a schoolteacher and principal in segregated black schools, McAfee, like many other teachers among the CME female leadership, was adept at negotiating with white superintendents and school board members. No doubt, a process of transformation took place in those negotiations similar to those between black and white churchwomen.

43. Ibid., 177-80. Quotes concerning Sawyer in subsequent paragraphs also from ibid., 177-80. McAfee's history provides the only written record of the early years of women's organizing in the CME Church. McAfee wrote that she had "but little record from which to get my information" (6). She relied on her firsthand experience as a young member of the congregation in which the first local Woman's Missionary Society was organized, in Fort Valley, Georgia, in 1894, as well as a lifetime of service in the church. To collect material for her book, a record for "unborn generations that our efforts will not be branded as all failures" (6), McAfee interviewed women church leaders and wrote to local missionary societies throughout the region for information about their founding and subsequent activities.

44. *Third Report of Council* (1913), 298.

45. McAfee, *History,* 121; on ME laity rights see McDowell, *Social Gospel,* 130-40; and Virginia Shadron, "The Laity Rights Movement, 1906-1918: Woman's Suffrage in the Methodist Episcopal Church, South," in *Women in New Worlds,* vol. 1, ed. Thomas and Keller, 261-75.

46. Quotations in order from McAfee, *History,* 159, 129, 174, 197.

47. Quotations in order from *Thirteenth Report of Council* (1923), 169; *Fourteenth Report of Council* (1924), 130; *Eighteenth Report of Council* (1928), 142; *Fourteenth Report of Council* (1924), 135-139; *Fifteenth Report of Council* (1925), 155; *Nineteenth Report of Council* (1929), 117. In forming interracial committees in local communities, ME women, under the direction of Bertha Newell, relied heavily on the expertise and "insight, and practical ability" of Jessie Daniel Ames, director of women's activities for the Commission on Interracial Cooperation. Ames, in turn, depended on white southern Methodist women for support in the antilynching campaign. See *Twenty-third Report of Council* (1933), 109; and Hall, *Revolt against Chivalry,* 176.

48. *Eighteenth Report of Council* (1928), 139. Elsa Barkley Brown has underscored the fact that "women's history, thus far, has gone a long way toward reaffirming the notion that only people of color have race." She has emphasized that "we have to accept the fact that one cannot write adequately about the lives of white women in the United States *in any context* without acknowledging the way in which race shaped their lives." Elsa Barkley Brown, "Polyrhythms and Improvisation: Lessons for Women's History" (Roundtable presentation, American Historical Association, New York City, December 28, 1990).

49. *Eighteenth Report of Council* (1928), 142. It is difficult to measure the impact of the ME Woman's Missionary Council programs on white southern women. In one North Carolina study, Anastasia Sims found that few local missionary societies implemented the interracial programs of the ME Woman's Missionary Council. See Anastasia Sims, "Sisterhoods of Service: Women's Clubs and Methodist Women's Missionary Societies in North Carolina, 1890-1930," in *Women in New Worlds: Historical Perspectives on the Wesleyan Tradition,* vol. 2, ed. Rosemary Skinner Keller, Louise L. Queen, and Hilah F. Thomas (Nashville: Abingdon, 1982), 196–210.

50. *Twenty-third Report of Council* (1933), 108; Twenty-eighth *Report of Council* (1938), 146.

51. *Twenty-fourth Report of Council* (1934), 123. As an issue lynching clearly united southern white women. It was hard for middle- and upper-class southern women *not* to agree that lynching was deplorable and that legislation punishing lynching as a crime should be passed. Focusing on lynching also involved a secondary gain. The issue was so powerful that it gave reluctant interracial reformers, and there were many in the ME sisterhood, the perfect rationale for shifting their attention away from the arduous and controversial work they had taken on: improving black schools and opening playgrounds, libraries, health clinics, day nurseries, hospitals, and bus lines to southern African Americans. The ME leadership was aware of the lure of lynching as an issue, and while they supported all antilynching efforts to the fullest extent, they steadily continued to push their broad-based interracial program forward. They supported the Costigan-Wagner antilynching bill over the objections of ASWPL Director Jessie Daniel Ames, a ME activist herself, who steadfastly opposed federal antilynching legislation. See McDowell, *Social Gospel,* 100; and Hall, *Revolt against Chivalry,* 87, 176.

52. *Twenty-sixth Report of Council* (1936), 123–24.

53. *Twenty-ninth Report of Council* (1939), 153. At this juncture, in 1939, both churches were on the brink of change. In 1939 the northern and southern branches of the Methodist Episcopal churches reunited, forming the United Methodist Church. The CME Church remained a separate entity, changing its name in 1954 to Christian Methodist Episcopal Church. The racial designation was eliminated to avoid any exclusionary suggestion in an era of integrationist thinking. The CME Church grew more slowly than the African Methodist churches from the late nineteenth century on. By 1890 the CME Church had a membership exceeding 103,000, 75 percent of which was in Alabama, Georgia, Mississippi, and Tennessee. The Christian Methodist Episcopal Church remains the smallest of the three black Methodist denominations, with a national membership in 1989 of 900,000 in the United States and 75,000 overseas. See Lincoln and Mamiya, *The Black Church,* 63. After 1940 the organizational ties that had united black and white Methodist women, CME and ME, no longer existed, and although some local interracial committees no doubt remained active, most gradually dissolved.

Giving Women a Future:
Alice Fletcher, the "Woman Question,"
and "Indian Reform"

Dolores Janiewski

The *Woman's Journal* of February 11, 1882, carried a letter from Alice Cunningham Fletcher reporting her encounter with the imprisoned Sitting Bull at Fort Randall.[1] Fletcher, having journeyed to Nebraska to "study the life of Indian women" and to learn about the "historical evolution of the 'woman question,'" endorsed Sitting Bull's views on this topic.[2] In a quotation that would gain poetic embellishment as she retold it over the years, Fletcher recalled Sitting Bull's words: "You are a woman. You have come to me as a friend. Pity my women. We men owe what we have to them. They have worked for us. They are good; they are faithful, but in the new life their work is taken away. For my men I see a future; for my women I can see nothing. Pity them; help them, if you can."[3] As she repeated the words, they grew more dramatic.[4] She later quoted Sitting Bull as saying, "They will be stripped of all which gave them power and position among the people," and ending with an eloquent plea, "Give a future to my women!" In the newer version, the Sioux leader gave her a ring and said, "Take this to remind you of my request. Help my women." That scene, she informed her readers, "was a vivid illustration of the problem . . . that confronted woman the world around during the development of society." Woman needed a future to replace the past that was being "taken from her."[5] In fidelity to her vow to Sitting Bull, Fletcher would create for herself a career as a champion of "Indian reform," while urging Native American women toward a future that women like herself were trying to escape.

After that fateful encounter with Sitting Bull, Fletcher, already an active member of Sorosis, the New England Woman's Club, and secretary for the Association for the Advancement of Women, pursued her feminist, reformist, and vocational commitments in often profoundly contradictory ways. In her original 1882 report, she proposed a solution to the "woman question" that pointed to problems she would encounter in combining a concern for the situation of women like herself, Native American women, and the condition of Native Americans as a whole. She assured the readers of the *Woman's Journal* that the answer lay in making Native American men "manly" so they would take up the industries women had "done in times past." She saw that development as teaching them the "power which has made the white race the dominant people," the power of "new and higher wants" that led to "United labor," her term for the division of labor in a market economy, which would allow them to rise "out of the natural plane of brotherhood." She preached the same doctrine to her readers, promising that the division of labor would bring "freedom and power and prosperity for all" because it was "brotherhood in the thought and in the market, in the field and in the home."[6] Wavering between defining *brotherhood* as something to be transcended or as something inherent in a market-based economy, her words suggested an intellectual and ideological confusion that would characterize Fletcher's attempts to reconcile commitments to a laissez-faire political economy, the "woman question," and the needs of Native American men and women.

The contradictions between Fletcher's public commitments mirrored internal conflicts between her feminist, reformist, and professional selves. Kinship, as befitted an aspiring amateur ethnographer and veteran of a women's movement that aspired to expand "enlightened motherhood" and sisterhood into public activities, offered Fletcher the essential vocabulary to discuss her affiliations. In her private life, she formed a close personal relationship with Francis La Flesche, son an Omaha chief, whom she adopted and lived with in Washington, D.C., until her death. Like the adoption itself, the reforms she championed sought to transform Native American society from one based on broad kinship groupings to one revolving around individual, private households containing only parents and children.[7] Recurrently, she referred to herself as "mother" to "the little ones" or proclaimed herself "sister" to Native American women facing "difficulty and hardship" at being "called to enter our civilization."[8] The reformist language, which Fletcher also embraced, celebrated the emancipation of the individual male from the bonds of kinship, tribal authority, and government control. Fletcher's alternate embrace of terms that emphasized a fraternal, maternal, or sisterly stance or celebrated the possessive individual competing freely in the impersonal marketplace revealed incompatible beliefs, commitments, and languages.

After her remarkable encounter with Sitting Bull, the forty-three-year-old Fletcher returned to the Omaha reservation, where she was conducting one of the first ethnographic observations after Frederick Putnam and his assistants at the Peabody Museum at Harvard University had given her informal tutelage.[9] On the Omaha reservation she moved in the circle surrounding Chief Joseph La Flesche, whose members described themselves as the "citizens' party" because of their eagerness to assimilate into the dominant culture and market-based economy. Responding to their concern about insecure land titles, she drew up a petition to Congress signed by a minority of the Omaha men, whom she declared to be "the true leaders among the people."[10] Taking the petition to Washington, she became involved in a coordinated effort to secure a law allotting Omaha land, that is, dividing it into individual holdings, awarding title to male household heads, and opening the remainder to sale and white settlement. Soon she was meeting with prominent women involved in the Washington chapter of the Women's National Indian Association, government officials, and Indian reformers. As a result of her testimony, lobbying, and lectures and publications on the Omaha, Sioux, and Winnebago, Fletcher acquired a reputation as a scientific expert on Native Americans. In 1883 she received an unpaid appointment as a special agent of the Bureau of Indian Affairs to allot the Omaha lands and to implement the law whose passage she had secured.[11] Stricken by a serious illness while engaged in her duties, Fletcher was nursed by Francis La Flesche, who would become her lifelong associate and collaborator. The symbolic marriage with Sitting Bull had produced a son.

As a result of her practical experience in the allotment process, Fletcher was often a featured speaker at annual meetings of the Friends of the Indian, held at Lake Mohonk, where she "was made quite a heroine."[12] Fletcher received accolades as someone who had "added fresh luster to American womanhood" and represented a combination of "scientific student" and "practical humanitarian."[13] Seeking a future for Native American women, she had developed a place for herself as an expert and honored reformer in a group whose beliefs reinforced her own laissez-faire and antistatist assumptions. She shared the organization's determination to "save the Indians from themselves" and their "fatal tendency . . . to fixed tribal life."[14] Like other participants, she saw her mission as instilling "manliness" and encouraging "good order and individual enterprise" amidst the "disintegrating process" that made "the incoming of new life possible" by teaching men to become possessive, property-owning, yeoman farmers and women to become domestic helpmates.[15] Forming a close relationship with Electra and Anna Dawes, Fletcher became an important part of the group of reformers who won congressional support for the division of all Native American lands into individual homesteads in an 1887 law that would become known as the Dawes Act, named after its senatorial champion, Henry L. Dawes. At the end of the decade she secured paid employment for allotting the lands of the Winnebago and the Nez Perce. After her active career as an allotting agent had ended, she summed up her labors as "taking by the hand the people of an alien race and helping them to step across the deep chasm that lies between their past and our present" in a 1895 letter to the members of the Women's National Indian Association, with whom she had cooperated in her reform activities.[16]

At the same time Fletcher pursued her professional aspirations as a pioneering anthropologist. She became a Fellow of the American Association for the Advancement of Science in 1882 and attended the American Social Science Association. Financial support from the wealthy William Thaw of Pittsburgh allowed her to begin an ethnographic partnership with Francis La Flesche, who was employed as a clerk at the Indian Bureau, which would lead to the publication of *The Omaha Tribe* two decades later.[17] Forced by financial necessity to continue with allotment work, she assured her scholarly mentor, Frederick Putnam at the Peabody, that "I will get the work done and before long."[18] After Thaw's death, his widow endowed a Thaw Fellowship at the Peabody Museum that allowed her to resign from active service for the Bureau of Indian Affairs after the Nez Perce allotment was completed in 1892.[19] She joined the Women's Anthropological Society of America, founded at a time when women were excluded from the Anthropological Association of Washington.[20] Fletcher served as its president and as president of the new society formed after its merger with the once male-only organization, the American Anthropological Association.[21] Publications in *Science, Proceedings of the American Association for the Advancement of Science,* and *American Anthropologist* and the reports of the Smithsonian Bureau of American Ethnology perpetuated her scholarly reputation until her death in 1923.

Fletcher's interests in Native American women also received a warm reception from the women's movement, with which she had been associated since her involvement in the founding of the Association for the Advancement of Women in the 1870s. Her activities received enthusiastic mention in the pages of the *Women's Tribune,* where she was praised as an "enthusiastic idealist," and the *Woman's Journal.*[22] Introduced at the 1888 International Council of Women by Susan B. Anthony, Fletcher spoke about the "legal status of Indian women" to an audience of attentive feminists and female reformers. According to Fletcher, Omaha women had told her, "As an Indian woman, I was free. I owned my home, my person, the work of my hands; and my children could never forget me. I was better as an Indian woman than under white law." Following her, Matilda Joslyn Gage and Lucy Stone commented that Fletcher's examples had shown that Native American law was "more just" than "the

family laws of the white men for women."[23] Fletcher's efforts to seek
answers to the "woman question" by observing Native American women
followed the work of Lydia Maria Child, who had examined gender and
racial issues in her novel *Hobomok* in the 1820s and in her editing of
Harriet Jacobs's *Incidents in the Life of a Slave Girl.*[24] Perhaps influenced by Fletcher, Elizabeth Cady Stanton drew insights about the
situation of women by studying the history of Native American women.
Stanton's "Matriarchate or Mother-Age," an address prepared for the
1891 National Women's Council, utilized the works of Johann Jakob
Bachofen and Lewis Morgan, one of Fletcher's inspirations, to demonstrate the "period of woman's supremacy." She urged "every woman
present" to "have a new sense of dignity and self-respect feeling that our
mothers during some periods in the past have been the ruling power" and
to believe that "our turn will come again."[25] Fletcher's addresses to
women's groups contributed to the construction of a feminist discourse
that used knowledge of Native American women to criticize the patriarchal nature of their own society.

Fletcher's enthusiastic advocacy of Indian reform and her connections
to the women's movement, including a close relationship with Caroline
Dall, apparently equipped her to act as a bridge between two groups of
women reformers. Doubtless Anthony was hopeful that just such a link
might aid in the creation of a single, unified "woman movement" when
she attended the meeting of reformers and missionaries held by the
Indian commissioners in 1885.[26] Such indeed was the intention for the
convening of the International Council of Women, where Fletcher's
remarks were so warmly received in 1888, and the National Council of
Women, which she would address in 1891.[27] But Fletcher found it as
difficult to reconcile her interest in the "woman question" and her advocacy of "Indian reform" as Anthony did in trying to unite all the female
reform organizations in support of the campaign for suffrage. Indian
reformers and feminists did not necessarily speak the same language,
even when they used the same words.

Speaking to the International Council of Women, Fletcher referred to
Native American women as "sisters," whose traditional freedoms other
women might emulate.[28] Amelia Quinton of the Women's National Indian
Association pleaded for the "legally oppressed, intellectually-pinioned,
and hand-tied woman" and also referred to them as "sisters" who needed
help entering American civilization.[29] Despite their common invocation
of sisterhood, they had very different assessments of Native American
women. As expressed by Fletcher, echoing Sitting Bull's lament, Native
American women had controlled resources and had escaped the legal
restrictions that denied civilized women autonomy. She told her audience,

"Her influence in the growth and development of tribal government, tribal ceremonies, and tribal power show that her position had always been one of honor rather than one of slavery and degradation."[30] Where Gage, Fletcher, Stone, and Stanton utilized the example of Native American women's greater autonomy to criticize the patriarchal structures of their own society, reformist discourse used their situation to illustrate the blessings of the civilization to which they were benevolently transporting the victims of "abject slavery." Yet Fletcher, despite her disagreements with the reformers' assessment of the Native American women's position, remained committed to the reforms that involved her in the ironic situation of implementing the law that resulted in "the absorbing of the wife's right to land in that of her husband's."[31]

Feminism gave Fletcher the chance to interrogate critically the male-dominated social order that had frustrated her own aspirations. Adopting the vocabulary of a reformer gave her access to prestige and power in that same society. A childless woman acquired the ability to operate as a powerful "mother" who could nurture "manhood" among her adopted sons and lead them "to the happiness that awaits man in a 'free society.' "[32] Refusing to take up the Thaw Fellowship until she had finished her work among the Nez Perce, Fletcher wrote Putnam that she was involved in "the worst struggle of my life" but "the Indians cling to me like children and I must and will protect them."[33] She also gained an opportunity to carry on "scientific work" at "government expense," as she wrote Frederick Putnam.[34] According to Martha Goddard, active in Boston Indian reform and women's circles, Fletcher readily succumbed to the temptations of power. Reporting the critical comments of Susette La Flesche Tibbles and her husband concerning Fletcher's visit to the Omahas in 1886, Goddard complained to the Indian Reform Association, "She has fallen into a wretched sentimental way of calling the Omahas her children—her babies & such pet names—this is well enough in private talk with a friend . . . but it is mischievous as a habit & in public, and she is frankly foolish about her heavy, hearty, twice-married 'boy' [Francis La Flesche]. . . . She has been invested with altogether too much irresponsible power."[35] To expect Fletcher to relinquish that power to give the "woman question" absolute priority in her actions and her commitments was an impossible demand.

Like a good mother, Fletcher greeted Native Americans on their "new birth," which had occurred with the passage of the Dawes Act that she had helped secure after the "success" of the Omaha allotment. She praised the granting of "land, law, citizenship and manhood" at a special celebration of Indian Emancipation Day at Hampton Institute.[36] Fletcher's assignments in allotting land for the Winnebagos and the Nez Perces only gave her further encouragement to act as the "mother" to these new citizens. Infusing anthropological theory with her maternalist metaphor, Fletcher told the 1900 conference of reformers at Lake Mohonk, "In the suggestive words of one of the speakers last evening we were cautioned to think of the native Hawaiians as children among the family of races. That is a very good thought in dealing with the so-called dependent races. The life of the nations and of the people of the world is like the life of the human being; it has the childhood period, the adolescent period and the mature period . . . so we speak of savagery, barbarism, and civilization."[37] As Joan Mark, her biographer, concluded, Fletcher had a tendency "to relate to other people as a dependent child or as a mother" because she found it difficult to deal "with people as equals."[38] Inevitably, her professional and personal involvement in "Indian emancipation" that gave "every individual Indian . . . a home and a wife and children just as white men" encouraged a greater identification with the reformist agenda. Her deep and enduring relationship with Francis La Flesche would only strengthen her tendency to see herself primarily as "Mother to the Indians" rather than as a "sister" to Native American women.[39]

Fletcher's maternalist preference was reinforced by the absence of Native American women in reformist circles. The few Native American women "heard" by reformers endorsed "progress." Susette La Flesche, of mixed French, Ponca, and Omaha parentage, was the person whose eloquence had originally led Fletcher to embrace the Native American cause when La Flesche came to Boston in 1879 with her younger brother Francis. La Flesche wrote in an introduction to Tibbles's *Ploughed Under: The Story of an Indian Chief* that the "solution of the vexed 'Indian Question' is *Citizenship.*"[40] Sarah Winnemucca Hopkins, befriended by Elizabeth Peabody and Mary Peabody Mann, toured eastern cities in the 1880s advocating citizenship and individual land tenure for Native Americans until rumors about her gambling, drinking, and sexual misconduct led to her rejection by Indian reformers, except the loyal Peabody.[41] Elaine Goodale Eastman, a teacher at Hampton Institute who lived among the Sioux in the 1880s, spoke before the Friends of the Indian in 1895 and gave a possible explanation for reformers' reluctance to pay heed to Native American women's opinions: "The Indian woman . . . ends as a feminine autocrat . . . determined always to have the last word; and, if that last word is not for progress, but, as it usually is, for the old-time thought, she becomes a barrier, a real hindrance and obstacle in the way of civilization. . . . She is invariably suspicious of the white man and takes no pains to hide her dislike of him. She revives some of the worst features of the old Indian life in her songs, her death-dirges, and songs upon every possible occasion."[42] Only women who spoke in the reformist "tongue" found a ready audience among reformers.

Like other reformers, Fletcher communicated primarily with Native Americans eager to embrace the advancing civilization. In an 1884 letter announcing the "presentation to the Peabody Museum . . . of the entire belongings of one of the Sacred Tents of the Omaha Tribe," she told Frederick Putnam, "It is the first time a people have parted peaceably . . . with such peculiar sacred symbols and signs of authority." This action "marks a firmness in stepping forth toward a future unknown and inevitable wherein the Indian must be merged in the American that indicates a people of more than ordinary gifts of character."[43] Conversely, Fletcher scorned the Omaha who met "together and have resolved they would be and remain Indians forever." By the time Susette La Flesche Tibbles had begun to question the "great deal of trouble" allotment had caused the Omahas, Fletcher and Tibbles were no longer listening to each other.[44] Fletcher's Native American correspondents were usually the graduates of the boarding schools at Hampton, Carlisle, or Chemenwa, who had been initially recruited by Fletcher.[45] Harriet and James Stuart, her Nez Perce interpreters, represented the "best Indians I can find." She repeated Harriet Stuart's words approvingly to an audience of Indian commissioners, missionaries, and reformers: "I don't want to build a house 'til James has money enough to build a fence around it, for I am to have a flower garden and a canary bird." Fletcher added, "This is a girl who has stood with her husband . . . laboring for severalty and progress."[46] Listening only to Native Americans who expressed similar desires, Fletcher reinforced her understandable tendency to applaud the results of the work to which she had devoted so much energy in the 1880s and early 1890s.

Fletcher's assignment as an allotting agent to the Nez Perce in northern Idaho, which occupied her summers from 1889 to 1892, confirmed her reformist inclinations but also elicited a feminist commentary on her activities. E. Jane Gay, who had attended the Brooklyn Female Academy with Fletcher in the 1840s and then Emma Willard's Academy, had renewed her acquaintance with her fellow student in the 1880s, after a career as a teacher in Knoxville, Tennessee, and Macon, Georgia; as a nurse serving under Dorothea Dix; and as a clerk in the Dead Letter Office of the U.S. Post Office.[47] Gay's unpaid position as cook and unofficial photographer for the Idaho expedition seemingly awakened feminist sensibilities, which Fletcher's power and pay as an official allotting agent silenced. Gay's letters from the field played openly with notions of gender. She identified her own character as alternatively male or female, depending on whether she quoted "The Photographer" or "The Cook." Fletcher, often called "Her Majesty," carried out her official duties in apparently masculine self-absorption, while Gay took pictures, cooked nourishing meals, and occasionally anguished over the effects of their activities on the Nez Perce. Gay's shrewd eye sometimes perceived contradictory aspects in a process that would bring the "blessings of civilization" to a reluctant people.

Gay described the scene when Fletcher met the Nez Perce in council to tell them "manhood" would come from individual land titles under the provisions of the 1887 "Land in Severalty," or Dawes Act: "They are all men, the women staying at home in an exemplary manner, just like civilized white women, when any matter particularly affecting their interests is being discussed by the men." Fletcher told them that their land must be allotted. "The law must be obeyed," she told the protesting Nez Perces, who responded, "We are content to be as we are." Momentarily assuming the position of the Nez Perce, Gay explained, "They could scarcely be blamed for their incredulity. That reasonable human beings, thought worthy of having citizenship thrust upon them, should have no say whatever in matters, which so exclusively concern themselves, was an idea too difficult for the untutored mind to grasp." Accidentally or deliberately, Gay, "untutored" in feminist theory, equated the situation of "civilized white women" and Native Americans.[48]

Writing to a female correspondent, Gay noted the "hopelessness upon the faces of the women" in the settler communities surrounding the reservation and the "lonesome life they led" and contrasted this with the freedom enjoyed by Nez Perce women. Paraphrasing Fletcher, she wrote, "The Indian woman can take down the tent, if she so pleases, and depart with all her property, leaving the man to sit helpless upon the ground, for her husband is only a guest in the lodge of the wife." Gay added, "Civilization has been built up largely upon the altruism of the woman, at the cost of her independence, and it is still an expensive luxury to her." The same letter revealed, however, that Gay also spoke the language of reform, mingled with feminist skepticism about male pretensions. Like Fletcher, she denounced the "old chiefs" who held back the "progressive Indian," describing them as "petty tyrants as every man is tempted to be when in the possession of a little power."[49] Perhaps her readers could detect the irony of Fletcher's administering a law that would cost Native American women their independence in exchange for a "civilization" that both women had taken the occasion to escape.

On the journey that would bring them back to the Nez Perce reservation for a second summer in 1890, Gay and Fletcher visited the Omahas and the Winnebagos. In writing about that part of their trip, Gay sometimes adopted the reformist voice. She described the Winnebagos as "slow to perceive the justice of the white man's law" and as having "raised, some of them, their small moccasined feet to kick against the iron-shod inevitable." She described "Her Majesty" as wrapping "about these nascent citizens her ample robe of charity," giving "impetus to the halting, and hope to the dependent." But then Gay took ironic delight in Fletcher's discomfiture when the "children" rebelled against their mother. Gay accompanied Fletcher to see the Omahas "with the pleasing picture in mind of a happy hen brooding a lot of helpless chickens." That evening she saw "a disconsolate, puzzled hen" because the Omahas had refused to accept her advice. "We are not children. We are citizens," they told Fletcher. Gay's tone shifted again when they reached the Nez Perce reservation. Now Fletcher had to deal with "refractory sick children," who "*must* take the medicine that is best for them."[50]

Gay was thus also torn between the "unholy pleasure" of maternal power operating in the name of "civilization against barbarism" and a feminist discourse applauding those aspects of "barbarism" that gave women greater freedom. Certainly Gay, who had less invested in the reformist project, indicated greater ambivalence than Fletcher. After the visit of Chief Joseph, the exiled leader of the Nez Perce War of 1877, Gay wrote, "It was good to see an unsubjugated Indian. One could not help respecting the man who still stood firmly for his rights, after having fought and suffered and been defeated in the struggle for their main- tenance." Comparing Protestant and Catholic conversion techniques, she declared that Catholic missionaries "are wiser than some of us. They do not wrench the man too suddenly from all he has hitherto held sacred. . . . Perhaps the miscarriage of many of our efforts in behalf of the race come from our ignorance of its own ideals."[51] When a Nez Perce woman was given a "white woman's burial," Gay mused, "Would not their own old funeral song cheer the departing spirit more truly? Were the white people's ways better for the Indian than his own? The unmoved faces of the women told us nothing. Were they dumb all through? Who could tell?"[52] Gay predicted "the suffering which will follow this sort of open- ing up of the reservation" but fatalistically saw "wrongs for which there is no practical remedy." She described "Her Majesty, calmly writing," while Gay herself was "whirled by the endless revolution into confusion of spirit."[53] Unable to occupy herself with the duties that Fletcher performed, Gay wrote about the conflict among the Nez Perce, about which Fletcher remained silent.

Fletcher expressed complete certainty in her mission to lead the Nez Perce "to work and manly independence of outside help." Whatever the sources of opposition, Fletcher insisted that "the work of allotting would go on." She was sustained by "the conviction that God has placed me here where I stand apparently the sole bulwark between the progressive Christian Indian and the helpless ones on this reservation and the corrupt forces marshalled against them."[54] The energy not demanded by the task of persuading recalcitrant Nez Perce went toward her efforts to remove antagonistic government agents. She welcomed the visit of Chief Joseph for the "first time since the Nez Perce war." Fletcher described him as "full of power to work but I doubt if he is ever able to go much further in progressive ideas."[55] Only later, after she was able to observe the effects of the reforms she had implemented, did Fletcher privately express a doubt about the success of her efforts.[56]

Fletcher never expressed any public doubts about the essential worth of the progress she had brought to the Omaha, the Winnebago, or the Nez Perce.[57] As she described "the helpfulness of our work" in an 1895 letter to the Women's National Indian Association, she explained the conviction that had hardened her against the doubts that afflicted Gay. She acknowledged the terrible stress reform involved "for the Indian" who was forced to give "up of his native tongue, his social and religious ideas, in fact . . . be recreated mentally." She assured her readers, however, "We cannot stop the rush that is engulfing the Indians, but if we are faithful and persevere, we shall help and save hundreds of struggling individuals in the future."[58] In 1898 in the pages of *Southern Workman,* the Hampton Institute organ, she stressed the importance of keeping "the past life of the Indian . . . a closed book."[59] More than a decade later she was still expressing publicly the same faith in the worthiness of her efforts. Having returned to the Omaha reservation in 1909, she reported prosperity, comfortable homes, and the disappearance of an "era of drunkenness and debauchery, which followed the sudden accession to citizenship and freedom."[60] She kept her sympathies for women subjected to "a domination that did not exist in the olden times" and her belief that "no people can be helped if they are absolutely uprooted" from intruding on her public assessment of the reforms to which she had devoted more than a decade of her life.[61]

That same year Gay finished a compilation of her letters and photographs for the period she had spent with Fletcher among the Nez Perce. Twenty years after she had encountered the Nez Perce, Gay optimistically concluded, "The Reservation has been opened, the tribe has been scattered, and, thanks to the prescience of Her Majesty, the red man is separated from his white neighbors only by the breadth of his own allotment. . . . With tribal bonds broken away and the individual man standing, more and more responsible for his own future, we may hopefully leave our Indian friends to work out their own salvation."[62] Gay's use of the masculine gender prevented the resurfacing of her earlier anguish about the cost to women that would accompany the arrival of this particular "future."

Fletcher's feminist voice, which surfaced in her instructions to an 1883 biographer to "write me as one who loves her fellow-women," was submerged in reformist discourse but never extinguished. When she visited Hampton in 1882 to talk to the "Indian class," she insisted that girls learn to raise vegetables because "I don't believe in any special rights of knowledge. I like to have girls know how to strike a nail square on the head and how to fix things about a house; boys to learn how to cook and sew. . . . Don't think that now when you go home the boys must do all the out-door work and the girls stay in the house all the time. . . . Both must work indoors and outdoors."[63] Attending the annual meeting of the Board of Indian Commissioners with reformers and missionaries, she reflected on her experiences with the Omaha and the Winnebago: "Three years ago I thought that it was sufficient that the Indian woman should be united to her husband in property matters. . . . [Now] I think it would be much better for the wife to be independent in a property point, of her husband. She would fare better and her children would fare better. But I found, when I came here, that I ran into the 'woman question,' and, if the Indian woman were given rights that were peculiar to her, it might give some rights to the white women that are not quite ready yet and so I must withdraw. I am told it is quite enough to give the Indian woman what the white women have. Well, I am sorry that the Indian woman can not hold her own property, yet I submit that she ought to."[64] She expressed similar opinions in letters to the Indian commissioners and the commissioner of Indian Affairs concerning the Dawes Act: "In the law as it was written, women are losers. They own nothing in their own right and yet they are as truly heirs to the tribal heritage as the men."[65] By the time she finished allotting the Nez Perce, she had succeeded in her campaign to place some land in women's hands.

Nor did Fletcher cease her criticisms of the "edge of our laws," under which Native American women had lost their accustomed freedom. "It has been my task," she told her audience at the 1888 International Council of Women, "to explain to Indian women their legal conditions under the law. In bringing these lines down upon their independent lives I have been led to realize how much woman has given of her own freedom to make strong the foundations of the family and to preserve the accumulations and descent of property" and to make possible "the devel-opment of civilization."[66] In asking her audience to "take pity on the Indian woman," she was implicitly asking them to think about their own situation: "They must lose much they hold dear and suffer wrongs at the hands of those, whose added legal powers, when untempered by an unselfish, cultured spirit, makes the legal conditions of woman akin to slavery. I crave for my Indian sisters, your help, your patience, and your unfailing labors, to hasten the day when the laws of all the land shall know neither male nor female, but grant to all equal rights and equal justice."[67] Eleven years later, in 1899, her article "The Indian Woman and Her Problems," published in *Southern Workman,* echoed the themes of her 1888 address. Referring to the Native American woman, "There is now no public reward for her work; there are now no tribal ceremonies at the time of planting.... The picturesque has gone out of her life. The black cooking stove, the wash-tub, the glinting needle are her silent and inexorable companions.... There are also new laws to distress her." The article closed by asking men and women to work together to help Indian women, because it was "impossible to bisect the body politic along the line of sex" and any solution demanded "mutual respect, mutual regard, mutual help, both in thought and in action."[68] Two years later Fletcher told the readers of the *Women's Tribune* about the Indian woman who "finds herself under a domination that did not exist in the olden times" and with whom she expected them to sympathize.[69] Clearly Fletcher regretted the necessity that caused these difficulties for Native American women.

Yet her empathy could not prevent her from insisting that it was necessary to journey to "a future unknown and inevitable where the Indian must be merged in the American."[70] As a result, the Native American past must be placed for "safekeeping" in sympathetic hands like her own. She applauded the "voluntary burial of the tribal past" by progressive leaders so the "people may be freer to enter into the new life of civilization."[71] Once again, a conflict emerged between her reformist insistence that freedom was "the product of civilization" and her recognition that civilization was a costly blessing. When she spoke with a "maternal" voice, she celebrated her children as "men whom . . . I feared would live and die Indians . . . now pushing out into better modes of living and thinking."[72] She found it harder to insert daughters into this celebratory mode.

Fletcher's major ethnographic work, *The Omaha Tribe,* written in collaboration with Francis La Flesche, departed from most of her writing in only one major regard—the conflicts between the reformer and the "other voice" emerged in a single text.[73] Writing as the reformer, Fletcher introduced the work declaring, "To-day, towns with electric lights dot the prairies where the writer used to camp amid a sea of waving grass and flowers.... The past is overlaid by a thriving present. The old Omaha men and women sleep peacefully on the hills while their grandchildren farm beside their white neighbors, send their children to school, speak English, and keep bank accounts." The ethnography itself paid scrupulous attention to gender relations and placed women "on a moral equality" with men in the "overlaid past." In contrast to the introduction, the concluding sections raised questions about the cost of progress. The two authors referred to the Omaha as becoming "less strong to resist the inroad of new and adverse influences which came with his closer contact with the white race." They pointed out the "contradiction between the principles taught as belonging to Christianity and the conduct of most of the white people with whom the Indian came into contact" and expressed sympathy for the person "slow to change his native point of view of justice and of truth."[74] Like Gay in her assessment of "white man's civilization," Fletcher and La Flesche conveyed ambivalence about a future that had been constructed over the bones of the culture they so carefully detailed.

One way to complete an assessment of Fletcher's work would be to examine the effect of the reforms she sponsored on peoples like the Omaha. Two decades after the publication of *The Omaha Tribe* an anthropological "daughter" retraced Fletcher's journey to the Omaha. Margaret Mead, trained by one of Fletcher's associates, Franz Boas, was sent west in pursuit of the same question that initially brought Fletcher to the Omaha. Mead wrote, "My task was to look at the women, and I had the unrewarding task of discussing a long history of mistakes in American policy toward the Indians and of prophesying a still more disastrous fate for them in the future." Mead's assessment of the results of Fletcher's work was highly critical:

> But this was a culture so shrunk from its earlier style . . . that there was very little out of the past that was recognizable and still less in the present that was aesthetically satisfying. . . . They lived in the small, now ramshackle houses that had been built for them in the period in which each man was given 160 acres of land on which to farm. But few farmed. Instead, they lived on their rents, drove around in battered old cars, and took what comfort they could from meeting to play games. . . . They had met anthropologists before whom they had come to regard primarily as a source of revenue.[75]

Fletcher's memory lingered only in a tale of cultural retribution. Chief Joseph La Flesche's untimely death was described as his punishment for having given the sacred treasures of the Omaha to Alice Fletcher.[76] Measured by Mead's observation, Fletcher's lifework had resulted in transforming a "living" culture into a shrunken culture still contained in the depressing "atmosphere of the Indian agency."[77] Mead believed that Omaha women had fared better than the men because "it is impossible to strip her life of meaning as completely as the life of the man was stripped," but her analysis suggested that the future Fletcher brought to the Omaha was not the one she had promised Sitting Bull.[78]

When considered in the context of her time, Fletcher's work deserves to be evaluated more positively. She was, of course, an agent of "empire" who helped the American state, the market economy, and the patriarchal social order penetrate and absorb Native American cultures, territory, and resources, but she was not just that. In violation of the scholarly convention of the "outside Western ethnographer-observer," she encouraged Francis La Flesche, one of the "others," to share with her the study of his people in "modes not always circumscribed and defined by force."[79] Her use of kinship as the predominant metaphor for her relationships with Native Americans was in stark contrast to the racist discourse that predominated in the late nineteenth century. She sought to overcome "ethnological ignorance" that lay "at the root of much of our mistaken action toward this Race." Among these mistakes, she included "treating the Indians all alike, simply as Indians, not as men or circumstances." She rejected the primacy of biology over culture. In that sense, her evolutionary optimism served as a precursor to the notion that culture, gender, and race are socially constructed identities rather than biologically determined fates.[80] Fletcher, despite her inability to confront the contradictions between "Indian reform" and the "woman question," made it easier for the others who followed.

The problem that Fletcher identified as the central one facing Native Americans was also her own. As she told her 1899 readers, Native Americans were now 'learning with difficulty to work in new ways, to think new thoughts, to speak a new language."[81] Her language did convey an intensely subjective engagement with the "others" that contemporary scholars are now being urged to rediscover. In 1896, in a brief account of her "journey into Indian country," Fletcher wrote about the emotional bonds that tied her intimately to the people she came to study. Describing her desolation on a vast and treeless plain, she wrote, "I could find nothing to connect myself with nature so unaltered by man; there was nothing here on my own plane of life; and thus, alone and self-centered, a sense of loneliness began to oppress me." Yet suddenly she was rescued: "A sound fell upon my ear— a strange sound but with a human tone in it . . . an Indian on horseback. The easy figure, the wayward song . . . the absence of all concern with time, of all knowledge of the teeming life out of which I had come, and which was even now surging toward him . . . touched a new thought-center and awoke a new interest. . . . I had crossed the line, another race had welcomed me with a song. . . . "[82] Her ability to hear music where other agents of "empire" heard only barbarous noises was one of Fletcher's gifts.

Fletcher summed up her life's work in two passages, whose opacity contributes to the perplexity about assessing her intentions and her achievements. In an early letter to Frederick Putnam, Fletcher, just returned from her first encounters with Native Americans, declared it "strange to read the books that have been written about the people. The white man sees only himself . . . I have taken much pains to get at the Indian sense of property . . . and family relation . . . and have sometimes succeeded in twisting around to the Indian view."[83] Can such a passage be read as a feminist critique of the "authoritative, explorative, elegant, learned voice" that "analyses, amasses evidence, theorizes, speculates about everything—except itself?" Yet a contradiction intrudes. Is Fletcher trying to claim for herself that same power over the "passive, dependent" others only she can understand?[84] Is Fletcher a feminist or a maternalist?

Fifteen years later Fletcher wrote another testimonial to her life's work: "I have never ceased to strive patiently for more knowledge of the Indian. I have gone back with him into the distant past, have shared with him the changing present, have tried to forecast his future, have alternately hoped and despaired with him, pressed always by the desire which is sure to arise in those who succeed in catching a glimpse of his real character—the intense desire to 'do something' for his betterment: his protection, if you will."[85] Is this a maternal lament for a beloved son that obscures the presence of women and the effects *his* "betterment" would have on women? Is it English grammar or Fletcher's unwillingness to face the conflicts between her beliefs, ambitions, and the results of her actions that make women invisible in this passage? Pulled between "powerful systems of meaning" and antagonistic commitments, Fletcher achieved no harmonious synthesis of her feminist, reformist, and professional aspirations.[86] Certainly Fletcher's life can point to the difficulties in achieving such a synthesis between careerist and feminist commitments, but it can also serve as an inspiration. Creating *other* ways of telling about men's and women's lives will require us to cross boundaries of gender, ethnicity, and class, as Alice Fletcher did more than a century ago. As Fletcher's writing indicates, she was engaged in creating a language that could express her vision of a future, where the "laws will know neither male nor female but grant to all equal rights and equal justice."[87] Her society did not allow her to succeed. Only when that future arrives can Fletcher's achievements be fairly assessed.

NOTES

The research on which this essay was based was supported by a grant from the John Calhoun Smith Fund at the University of Idaho, Moscow, Idaho.

1. *Woman's Journal,* February 11, 1882.

2. Alice C. Fletcher to Lucian Case, August 3, 1881, Peabody Museum Papers, Harvard University Archives, Pusey Library, Harvard University, Cambridge, Mass. (hereafter PM/HU).

3. *Woman's Journal,* February 11, 1882.

4. Alice C. Fletcher to Frederick W. Putnam, November 7, 1881, PM/HU; Women's National Indian Association, *In Memoriam: Harriet W. Foote Hawley* (Washington, D.C.: National Indian Association, Washington Auxiliary, 1886), 21-22; Alice C. Fletcher, quoted in the *Women's Tribune,* March 31, 1888; Alice C. Fletcher, "The Indian Woman and Her Problems," *Southern Workman* 28 (May 1899): 172-76.

5. Alice C. Fletcher, "The Indian Woman and Her Problems," n.p., Alice C. Fletcher-Francis La Flesche Papers, National Anthropological Archives, Smithsonian Museum of Natural History, Washington, D.C. (hereafter Fletcher/NAA).

6. *Woman's Journal,* February 11, 1882.

7. See, for example, *Papers and Letters Presented at the First Woman's Congress of the Association for the Advancement of Woman, Held in the Union League Theater, October 1873, New York* (New York: Mrs. Wm. Ballard, Book and Job Printer, 1874), where the talks included, "Enlightened Motherhood" by August Cooper Bristol, "Enlightened Motherhood—How Attainable" by Lucinda B. Chandler, "Enlightened Motherhood" by Mrs. Elizabeth C. Lovering and Mrs. H. M. Tracey Cutler, M.D., and "The Co-Education of the Sexes" by Mrs. Elizabeth Cady Stanton, National Institutions Collection, American Antiquarian Society, Worcester, Mass.

8. Alice Fletcher to Ednah C. Cheney, December 20, 1888, New England Hospital Papers, Sophia Smith Collection, Smith College, Northampton, Mass.; Alice Fletcher, quoted in *Women's Tribune,* March 31, 1888.

9. Joan Mark, *A Stranger in Her Native Land: Alice Fletcher and the American Indians* (Lincoln: University of Nebraska Press, 1988), 34-38.

10. Alice C. Fletcher and Francis La Flesche, *The Omaha Tribe,* Twenty-seventh Annual Report of the Bureau of American Ethnology, 1905-6 (Washington, D.C.: Government Printing Office, 1911), 637-39; Alice C. Fletcher to John Morgan, December 31, 1881, Fletcher/NAA.

11. Hiram Price, Commissioner of Indian Affairs, to Honorable Secretary of the Interior, April 20, 1883, Fletcher/NAA.

12. Alice C. Fletcher to Caroline S. Dall, October 1884, Caroline S. Dall Papers, microfilm edition, University of Massachusetts, Amherst, Mass.

13. U.S. House of Representatives, "Report of the Commissioner of Indian Affairs," *Executive Documents,* 48th Congress, 2d session, 1884-85, 722.

14. "Notes from the Indian Conference at Lake Mohonk," *Southern Workman* 13 (November 1884): 117.

15. Alice Fletcher to Dr. J. E. Rhoads, President, Indian Rights Association, April 7, 1887, Fletcher/NAA.

16. Alice C. Fletcher to Sarah T. Kinney, President of the Connecticut Auxiliary of the Women's National Indian Association, November 20, 1895, Fletcher/NAA.

17. Alice Fletcher to Frederick Putnam, January 20, 1883, PM/HU.

18. Alice C. Fletcher to Frederick Putnam, August 3, 1889, PM/HU; Fletcher and La Flesche, *The Omaha Tribe.*

19. Alice Fletcher to Frederick Putnam, September 28, 1890, PM/HU.

20. Anita McGee, *Organization and Historical Sketch of the Women's Anthropological Society of America* (Washington, D.C.: Judd and Detweiler, 1889).

21. Mark, *A Stranger in Her Native Land,* 290.

22. *Women's Tribune,* January 1, 1884.

23. Ibid., March 31, 1888.

24. Lydia Maria Child, *Hobomok and Other Writings on Indians,* ed. Carolyn L. Karcher (New Brunswick, N.J.: Rutgers University Press, 1986), xi–xxxiv; [Harriet Brent Jacobs], *Incidents in the Life of a Slave Girl, Written by Herself,* ed. Lydia Maria Child (Boston: For the Author, 1861).

25. Elizabeth Cady Stanton, "The Matriarchate or Mother-Age" (read at the Women's National Council, Washington, D.C., February 1891 by Miss Susan B. Anthony), Stanton-Anthony Papers, University of Massachusetts, Amherst, Mass.

26. U.S. House of Representatives, "Report of the Commissioner of Indian Affairs," 727.

27. Ellen Carol DuBois, Introduction to *Elizabeth Cady Stanton/Susan B. Anthony: Correspondence, Writings, Speeches,* part 3, 1874-1906 (New York: Shocken, 1981), 171-81.

28. Alice Fletcher, International Congress of Women, quoted in *Women's Tribune,* March 31, 1888.

29. *Women's Tribune,* March 17 and 23, 1888.

30. Fletcher, "The Indian Woman and Her Problems," Fletcher/NAA.

31. Alice C. Fletcher to the Honorable Commissioner of Indian Affairs, June 1884, Fletcher/NAA.

32. Alice C. Fletcher, "The Indian and the Prisoner," Winnebago Indian Agency, January 12, 1888, Fletcher/NAA.

33. Alice Fletcher to Frederick Putnam, November 11, 1891, PM/HU.

34. Alice Fletcher to Frederick Putnam, August 6, 1891, PM/HU.

35. Martha L. B. Goddard to Herbert Welsh, Indian Rights Association, August 2, 1886, Indian Rights Association Papers, microfilm edition, Library, Smithsonian Museum of Natural History, Washington, D.C. (hereafter IRA/DC).

36. "The Indian's Emancipation Day Programme," Fletcher/NAA.

37. *Proceedings of the Eighteenth Annual Meeting of the Lake Mohonk Conference of Friends of the Indian (1900),* ed. Isabel C. Barrows (Boston: Lake Mohonk Conference, 1901), 73.

38. Mark, *A Stranger in Her Native Land,* 14.

39. "The Indian's Emancipation Day Programme." "Mother to the Indians" is the title Joan Mark applies to part 2 of *A Stranger in Her Native Land.*

40. Thomas Henry Tibbles, *Ploughed Under: The Story of an Indian Chief* (New York: Fords, Howard, and Hurlbert, 1881), 4-5, quoted in Mark, *A Stranger in Her Native Land,* 127.

41. Elizabeth Peabody to Henry L. Dawes, November 12, 1883, Henry Laurens Dawes Papers, Library of Congress, Washington, D.C. (hereafter Dawes/ LC); C. C. Painter to Herbert Welsh, December 11, 1885, IRA/DC.

42. *Proceedings of the Thirteenth Annual Meeting of the Lake Mohonk Conference of the Friends of the Indian (1895)*, ed. Isabel C. Barrow (Boston: Lake Mohonk Conference, 1895), 93.

43. Alice Fletcher to Professor Putnam, June 7, 1884, Fletcher/NAA.

44. U.S. House of Representatives, "Report of the Indian Commissioner," *Executive Documents*, 49th Congress, 1st session, 1885–86, 1035–37.

45. See, for example, Julia St. Cyr to Alice C. Fletcher, July 20, 1885, Fletcher/NAA.

46. U.S. House of Representatives, "Report of the Board of Indian Commissioners," *Executive Documents*, 51st Congress, 1st session, 1887–88, 944–45.

47. Jane Gay Dodge, "Brief Biography of E. Jane Gay," Jane Gay Dodge Papers, Schlesinger Library, Radcliffe College, Cambridge, Mass. (hereafter Dodge/SL).

48. E. Jane Gay to Jean, July 26, 1889, and E. Jane Gay to Captain P. (Richard H. Pratt), June 29, 1889, in E. Jane Gay, "Choup-nit-ki: With the Nez Perces," manuscript, Dodge/SL.

49. E. Jane Gay to "E," July 15, 1889, in Gay, "Choup-nit-ki."

50. E. Jane Gay to "B," May 11, 1890, in Gay, "Choup-nit-ki."

51. E. Jane Gay, Letter Fifteen, June 24, 1890, in Gay, "Chou-nit-ki."

52. E. Jane Gay, Letter Eighteen, September 24, 1990, in Gay, "Choup-nit-ki."

53. E. Jane Gay, Letter Twenty-One, May 30, 1891, in Gay, "Choup-nit-ki."

54. Alice C. Fletcher to Honorable Commissioner of Indian Affairs, July 25, 1889; Fletcher to Honorable Commissioner, December 26, 1889; Fletcher to Gen. Thomas J. Morgan, Commissioner of Indian Affairs, November 2, 1891, Fletcher/NAA.

55. Alice C. Fletcher to Electra S. Dawes, October 2, 1890, Dawes/LC.

56. According to Joan Mark, in 1897, after a visit to the Omahas, and in 1907, Fletcher began to reach the private conclusion that her work among the Omahas had been "a failure." See Mark, *A Stranger in Her Native Land*, 265, 310.

57. Ibid., 267.

58. Alice C. Fletcher to Sarah T. Kinney, President of the Connecticut Auxiliary of the Women's National Indian Association, November 20, 1895, Fletcher/ NAA.

59. Alice C. Fletcher, "The Indian at the Trans-Mississippi Exposition," *Southern Workman* 27 (November 1898): 217.

60. *Report of the Twenty-seventh Annual Meeting of the Lake Mohonk Conference of the Friends of the Indian and Other Dependent Peoples (1909)*, reported by Lillian D. Powers (Boston: Lake Mohonk Conference, 1909), 88.

61. Fletcher, "The Indian Woman and Her Problems," Fletcher/NAA; quoted from a 1905 letter, Alice C. Fletcher to Albert Smiley, the host at Lake Mohonk, in Mark, *A Stranger in Her Native Land*, 268.

62. E. J. Gay, January 1909, in Gay, "Choup-nit-ki."

63. Alice C. Fletcher, "Incidents of Indian Life at Hampton: A Friend's Counsel," *Southern Workman* 11 (August 1882): 8.

64. U.S. House of Representatives, "18th Annual Conference with Representatives of Missionary Boards and Indian Rights Association," *Executive Documents*, 50th Congress, 2d session, January 17, 1889, 840.

65. Alice C. Fletcher to Commissioner of Indian Affairs, April 4, 1889, Special Cases, Record Group 75, National Archives, Washington, D.C.

66. Alice Fletcher, quoted in *Women's Tribune*, March 31, 1888.

67. Alice Fletcher, quoted in *Report of the International Council of Women Assembled by the National Woman Suffrage Association, March 25 to April 1, 1888* (Washington, D.C.: Rufus H. Darby, 1888), 241.

68. Fletcher, "The Indian Woman and Her Problems," Fletcher/NAA, which was published in *Southern Workman* 28 (May 1899): 172-76.

69. Alice C. Fletcher, "The Indian Woman Problems," *Women's Tribune*, August 31, 1901.

70. Alice Fletcher to Frederick Putnam, June 7, 1884, Fletcher/NAA.

71. Alice C. Fletcher, "Indian Life, Personal Studies of Tribal Life among the Omahas," *Century*, new series, 29 (January 1896): 455.

72. Alice C. Fletcher to J. E. Rhoads, President, Indian Rights Association, April 7, 1887, Fletcher/NAA.

73. Fletcher and La Flesche, *The Omaha Tribe.*

74. Ibid., 30, 269, 615, 628, 629.

75. Margaret Mead, *Blackberry Winter: My Earlier Years* (New York: William Morrow, 1972), 191, 190.

76. As described in Alice Fletcher to Professor Putnam, June 7, 1884, Fletcher/NAA.

77. Mead, *Blackberry Winter,* 190.

78. Margaret Mead, *The Changing Culture of an Indian Tribe* (New York: Columbia University Press, 1932), 134.

79. Edward W. Said, "Representing the Colonized: Anthropology's Interlocutors," *Critical Inquiry* 15 (Winter 1989): 216-17.

80. Alice C. Fletcher to Senator Henry Dawes, February 4, 1882, Dawes/LC; see, for example, Rosalind Rosenberg, *Beyond Separate Spheres: Intellectual Roots of Modern Feminism* (New Haven, Conn.: Yale University Press, 1982), xiii.

81. Fletcher, "The Indian Woman and Her Problems," Fletcher/NAA.

82. Fletcher, "Tribal Life among the Omahas," 450-51.

83. Alice Fletcher to Frederick Putnam, August 10, 1881, PM/HU.

84. Said, "Representing the Colonized," 212.

85. Fletcher, "Tribal Life among the Omahas," 451.

86. James Clifford, "Introduction: Partial Truths," in *Writing Culture: The Poetics and Politics of Ethnography*, ed. James Clifford and George E. Marcus (Berkeley: University of California Press, 1986), 1-26.

87. Fletcher, *Women's Tribune*, March 31, 1888.

Part 4

The Politics of Knowledge:
Exemplary Lives

For the past quarter-century, women's historians have been discovering the rich heritage, the often bittersweet legacies, and the transformative power of a female perspective on the world. They have also been recovering the lives of individual women whose achievements, though often marginalized in their own time, provide inspiration, as well as warning, to succeeding generations. Given women's restricted access to institutions of higher learning, few of these foremothers were academics, though many were educators and activists. Among the most well known of these early activist educators is Mary Ritter Beard. In the introduction to a collection of Beard's private letters, editor Nancy Cott notes that "Beard spent the better part of her life trying to prove the utility of history, especially by recovering women's past. She insisted that history was not whole without women's story. . . . Never an academic, always an organizer through ideas, Mary Beard spoke to and wrote for the community at large."

The two women whose careers are the focus of this section—Alice Mary Baldwin and Anne Firor Scott—exemplify many of the ideas Beard held dear. Both explored the lives of exemplary women in earlier periods of American history, and both examined not only the formal institutions of education open to women but also the alternate sites, where far more women found opportunities for discussion and debate. Like Beard, Baldwin and Scott were writing about women before there was a field of women's history, and like her and those they studied, they carried the weight of centuries of discrimination against thinking women.

Linda K. Kerber, investigating the two centuries from 1750 to 1950, contrasts the safe haven for women thinkers created through literary clubs, reading circles, and salons with the precarious positions they held in the academy. Nancy Weiss Malkiel focuses on the last half-century as higher education opened to women and, more reluctantly, to feminist perspectives. She traces the ways Scott and scholars like her expanded such openings, while sustaining alternate sites so conducive to women's intellectual growth.

Despite similarities in the careers of Baldwin and Scott, these two essays remind us of the marked changes in the environments in which they constructed those careers. Baldwin was completing her tenure at Duke just as Scott was beginning to imagine such a possibility. Unable to obtain the full-time faculty position she desired in the history department, Baldwin struggled against the odds as dean of women in a male-dominated system that refused to give ground. The energy absorbed by her administrative duties limited her achievements as an academic, where her research on women cut against the grain of her chosen field. Kerber notes the stubborn barriers confronted by Baldwin and the generations of women scholars before her who functioned "without the matrix of support on which we can now rely." Anne Scott became a Duke faculty member in an environment that had changed only slightly in the two decades since Baldwin's retirement, yet she spent most of her career creating and working within a matrix of support that her predecessors lacked.

Kerber uses Baldwin's life and writings as a springboard for exploring the continuities and changes in the experience of intellectual women from the eighteenth century to the twentieth. Though she necessarily emphasizes the constraints within which women scholars functioned, Kerber's analysis of Baldwin's unpublished work reveals the light at the beginning of the tunnel. From such beginnings, feminist historians would soon illuminate a whole new terrain of knowledge, much of it first circulated through underground channels before breaking to the surface and remaking the academic map. As Nancy Weiss Malkiel shows, Scott provides a critical link between Baldwin's era and our own. Venturing into uncharted territory in her study of southern women progressives and initially happy to obtain even a temporary post as a visiting professor, she became one of the founders of a whole new field of scholarship. Over the next two decades, Scott not only gained a permanent position at Duke University—eventually ascending to a named chair—but also was elected to the presidencies of the Organization of American Historians and the Southern Historical Association, served on numerous editorial boards and professional committees, had prizes and scholarships named in her honor, and was recognized many times for her achievements as teacher, mentor, and scholar.

Scott has conducted the growing chorus of women's historians and happily joined in the singing. She has also given voice to eighteenth- and nineteenth-century women intellectuals and educators, many of the same women who attracted Baldwin's attention, and to twentieth-century women activists. She did so in a stream of books and essays rather than, as Baldwin did, in the hidden pages of a sealed archive. This alone reflects the profound shifts in the production and politics of knowledge that has occurred over the course of this century.

These two essays capture the ways in which individual women and a collective women's vision can alter our understanding of the world. Yet many questions remain. How does one's identity—race, class, gender, regional background, and sexual orientation—shape research interests and scholarship? How does the relationship between women's academic opportunities and their activist commitments change over time? In what ways are representations of women and womanhood affected by women's entry into higher education and other occupations long dominated by men? Finally, to what extent will the new scholarship produced by American women's historians transform our understandings of activism in the past and inform our participation in activism in the present and the future?

"Why Should Girls Be Learn'd and Wise?": The Unfinished Work of Alice Mary Baldwin

Linda K. Kerber

> Col. [Thomas Wentworth] Higginson said that one of the great histories yet to be written is that of the intellectual life of women.
> —Anna Garlin Spencer, *Women's Share in Social Culture*, 1925

Alice Mary Baldwin was a formidable American educator. A historian who received her Ph.D. from the University of Chicago in 1926, she is best known as the author of a long-standard monograph on New England ministers in the era of the American Revolution.[1] Baldwin spent most of her career as dean of the Woman's College of what is now Duke University. Overworked and underpaid, she had trouble fitting research projects into her day and published little after her doctoral dissertation.

Baldwin's life and work exemplify some of the key issues and major patterns in the history of the intellectual life of American women. In the course of her career she was forced to reflect on the position of intellectual women and on women's formal education; at the end of her life this restrained, discreet woman set on paper her own bitter criticism of the way Duke University had treated its women's college and its dean. She ordered this account sealed for twenty years; it has only recently been opened. In the fraction of her time that she could devote to research in early American history, Baldwin found herself increasingly drawn to the study of women's experience. Through her notes and drafts of essays, we can watch a fine mind struggling to write women's history without the matrix of support on which we can now rely. In 1938 she could not command attention for her narrative of two colonial sisters who hungered for intellectual challenge except by offering them as "quaint." By the time she died, in 1961, she was no longer treating women's experience apologetically. Left unfinished among her papers were notes and drafts for an essay tentatively called "The Reading of Women in the Colonies before 1750." In this essay she set herself to defend colonial women from the charge that they "ordinarily read very little" and that "intellectual accomplishments were not expected of the weaker sex."[2]

I do not know whether Baldwin suspected that her own career and the research on which she embarked were parts of the same large story, that she was in effect a character in a late chapter of a narrative featuring her heroine, the eighteenth-century Bostonian Jane Colman Terrell, in its first chapter. For all its complexity, the intellectual history of women in America has been at base a single story: a continuing quest by determined women to claim access to books, instruction, and opportunity to interpret, always resisting the assumption—as much a part of our legacy from the Greeks and Romans as is the architecture of the Parthenon—that women's minds are naturally limited to the trivial. Individual women had to struggle to clear a space for their own intellectual activity and to defend themselves against the charge that intellectual effort was inappropriate, even dangerous, when attempted by a woman. What they knew was, in Michel Foucault's terms, treated as "subjugated knowledges"— knowledges "disqualified as inadequate to their task or insufficiently elaborated"—knowledges instantly devalued once claimed by a woman.[3] African Americans were systematically excluded from Western systems of literature, learning, and publication; as Henry Louis Gates recently pointed out, fifty-six years elapsed between the publication of Phillis Wheatley's *Poems on Various Subjects, Religious and Moral* in 1773 and the next book of poetry published by an African American, George Moses Horton, in 1829. The first book of essays published by an African American was Ann Plato's in 1841.[4] Before a black woman could claim Virginia Woolf's "room of her own," she had first to claim her own body, her own mind, and her own house—physical as well as metaphoric—in which to place that room.

As David Hollinger has shrewdly observed, intellectual history in America has traditionally been written in a manner that "treats . . . ideas, for the most part, as a structure, and attributes the structure to a community of interacting minds." The paradigm for intellectual history has long been Perry Miller's *New England Mind,* published in 1953. What was novel and exciting about *The New England Mind,* Hollinger observes, was that the life of the mind was "depicted as a *life,*" conveyed through "a succession of disputes, of discussions, of arguments" rather than as "a set of discrete units of thought," like the idea of progress or the Great Chain of Being.[5] Indeed, Hollinger observes, intellectual history as it has been written in America "focuses on arguments made by people whose chief business it was to argue. . . ."[6] What for a long time went virtually unnoticed was that although Miller was describing the arguments carried on by New England's ministers and political leaders, he offered and his readers accepted this as an account of an entire *generation:* "the premises," Miller said, "of all Puritan discourse."[7]

Hollinger's connection of intellectual history to the discourse of intellectuals suggests questions about the extent to which communities of intellectuals—"people whose chief business it was to argue"—have fashioned themselves in large part by class and by gender. If the site of intellectual life in colonial New England is understood to be the arguments of ministers and women were excluded from the ministry—even, as Anne Hutchinson tragically discovered, from informal claims to theological authority—then women were neither part of a profession nor part of an intellectual community. If women are not "people whose chief business it was to argue," then we are unlikely to find the intellectual history of women in the usual places. The theater for women's intellectual life has rarely been institutional. Its locus was necessarily wherever women gathered to argue: in antislavery societies, where they wrestled with ideas about the limits of individualism, or in social meetings, where they struggled with concepts of the authentic relationship between labor and capital, or around kitchen tables, where, after a day of labor, they gathered informally to discern the essential elements of the social and economic system in which they felt trapped. The task of constructing themselves into something called "an intellectual" was different for women than it was for men because as a group women were understood to be differently situated in relation to argument, reason, and particularly abstraction. The culture of argument involved also a culture of oratory, a culture as old as Demosthenes. The "learned" professions—the ministry, law, and the professoriate—involved not only reason and argument but also forceful public speaking, barred to women by law and custom. With few exceptions, women would not begin to insert themselves into public space as orators until the antislavery and women's rights movements of the second third of the nineteenth century; indeed, the presence of women in public argument has only recently begun to be normalized.

To write women into intellectual history as American historians have traditionally understood it, we would have to wait for the creation of institutions in which women can carry on argument. That is, the history of women's intellect, unlike the history of women thinking, would have to wait for the building of institutions in which women argued and in which they exercised authority.[8] Those institutions were built only gradually, at first informally, and always with many variations. A wide range of sites in which argument took place was developed—the lyceum lectures women attended and discussed, the literary societies in boardinghouses in Lowell and other mill towns, women's literary and debating societies at coeducational colleges. Women's study and book discussion groups, which flourished from the 1880s through the twentieth century, have only recently been understood to be a site of intellectual development and argument.[9] Until quite recently, whether women were included in historians' narratives of intellectual history depended heavily on whether they had intense personal relationships with men's intellectual communities, from Margaret Fuller among the transcendentalists to Mary McCarthy among the *Partisan Review* circle.[10]

We may discern four distinct periods or stages in the framing of women's formal intellectual claims. To evaluate each, we need to know something about the levels of literacy—both elementary and sophisticated—among women as compared with men; their opportunities to participate in formal and informal intellectual practices—access to books and newspapers, correspondence, schooling—and the extent to which they were able to establish formal and informal communities of colleagues who examined ideas critically. Despite their usual claim to be free of social inequities—to be an "ivory tower"—these communities have reflected patterns of racial, ethnic, and gender segregation at work in the societies of which they have been a part. It is still the very rare intellectual community in which the men and women participate in equal numbers on equal terms.

In the first era, the colonial period, female literacy grew slowly and erratically, and there were no formal institutions of higher education for females. Literacy was tightly tied to race and class and was connected to residence in an urban commercial environment. By the end of the period, basic literacy was widespread among white women in the Northeast; some authors have argued that it was close to universal in that region by the time of the Revolution.[11] Women who aspired to an education more complex than the three Rs, however, had to find their own mentors in a culture that was highly skeptical of their efforts.

The years between the Revolution and 1833, the opening of Oberlin College to women, might be labeled the Era of the Great Debate over the Capacities of Women's Minds. These years were marked by continuing improvement in female literacy, a political revolution that articulated the need for the education of succeeding generations of moral citizens, and the assertion by some articulate women of their need for institutional support. Inherited assumptions about women's incapacity for higher education were questioned; schools for girls with serious aspirations, whether for learning or for upward social mobility, were established. The founding of Oberlin marked the end of one era and the beginning of another. Although Oberlin offered somewhat different tracks to white men, to white and black women, and to black men, it created the first coeducational and interracial student body and made an important statement about the range of people in whom genius might be found.[12]

The years between Oberlin's founding and roughly the turn of the century may be thought of as a third era, characterized by women's increasing access to institutions of higher education. State colleges and universities were opened to women; some followed the model of the University of Iowa, founded in 1847, which was coeducational and admitted women from the moment of its founding. In the Reconstruction years, institutes and colleges for black students were established, and virtually all were coeducational. Among the most exciting were Wilberforce University in Ohio, founded in 1856; Atlanta University, founded in 1865; Fisk University, founded in 1866; and Howard University, founded in 1867. Indeed, despite the fame of the women's colleges established in the last quarter of the century—Wellesley and Smith in 1875, Spelman in 1881, Bryn Mawr and Randolph-Macon in 1884, and Barnard in 1889—coeducational institutions would always account for the largest number of women students. (In the South, however, women were most likely to attend women's colleges.) In 1775 not a single institution of higher education included women among its students; a century later over a hundred allowed white women to enter, and a handful—Oberlin, Antioch, Fisk, Atlanta—admitted black women. Not many by today's standards, certainly, but an extraordinary contrast with a century before.

A fourth period in women's higher education may be said to extend from the first decade of the twentieth century, when strong backlash against women's intellectual claims frequently excluded them from the newly developing research universities, to the 1970s, when Title 9 of the Higher Education Act of 1972 prohibited sex discrimination in most schools that receive federal financial assistance, and one after another elite colleges and universities admitted women to their student bodies.[13] The first two decades of the twentieth century were characterized by, in Barbara Miller Solomon's words, an "explosion in female enrollments"; between 1900 and 1920 women moved from constituting one-third of all students enrolled in institutions of higher education to nearly one-half.[14] Their more visible presence, coupled with their academic success, "precipitated yet another round in the cycle of criticism."[15] The opening years of the twentieth century were notable for the complaint that women were "taking over" the universities; it sometimes seemed that the higher their achievement, the more opposition was expressed to their equal access to educational institutions. When women students earned more awards than men did, writes Solomon, Stanford University ignored "the university statute requiring 'equal advantages in the University to both sexes' "; between 1904 and 1933 it maintained an admissions ratio of three males to each female, and admissions on a roughly equal basis was not established until the 1970s. The University of Chicago went to the length of establishing a separate junior college to push women out of the undergraduate college when, in 1902, it realized women accounted for a majority of those achieving Phi Beta Kappa status. The segregated system was short-lived. An effort to segregate women into a separate teachers' college at the University of Wisconsin in 1907 was only narrowly defeated, as was a similar effort at the University of South Carolina in 1913. Women were admitted only to upper-division courses at the University of North Carolina in 1898, and they would not be admitted on an equal basis with men until a court order in 1972; no women at all were admitted to the University of Virginia in Charlottesville until the threat of a court order in 1970.[16]

Even when efforts to resegregate academic institutions failed, they left behind a general sense that women had entered into space controlled by men and stayed only so long as men found it convenient. When wartime conscription, particularly during World War II, drew men out of the pool of prospective students, colleges vigorously welcomed women, but when men flooded back after the war, hostility to women's presence was again expressed. Women's enrollment in institutions of higher learning declined after 1920, reaching a twentieth-century low of 30 percent in 1950, when space was given to veterans and popular magazines ran articles questioning whether women should take up spaces that would otherwise go to men.[17] Moreover, coeducation in universities extended only to the student body; faculties, administrators, boards of trustees were overwhelmingly male. During the twentieth century, it could be said that women's relationship with academic intellectual communities has intensified but generally been uneasy.

Through all these years there hummed, like the steady continuo of the harpsichord, the constant complaint versified by John Trumbull at the end of the eighteenth century:

> Why should girls be learn'd and wise?
> Books only serve to spoil their eyes.
> The studious eye but faintly twinkles
> And reading paves the way to wrinkles.[18]

In the late 1930s Alice Mary Baldwin wrote a narrative she called "Two Sisters of Old Boston." It serves well as an introduction to our first era, when most women had only the most marginal literacy and those who acquired more than the rudiments did so through informal instruction in their own families.[19] Although Baldwin did not explicitly mark the Colman sisters as emblems of the fate of the colonial woman who hungered for learning, that implication is embedded in her account.[20]

Jane and Abigail were the daughters of Benjamin Colman, a graduate of Harvard in 1692 and the minister of the Brattle Street Church in Boston. Jane, the older, was born in 1702. The girls read the poems of Elizabeth Singer Rowe, Alexander Pope, Richard Blackmore, and Edmund Waller. Jane probably was familiar with some of the Latin poets as well, since later she wrote a poem in imitation of Horace. Jane's poems testified to her hunger for learning:

> Come now, fair Muse, and fill my empty mind,
> With rich ideas, great and unconfin'd . . .
> O let me burn with *Sappho's* noble Fire,
> But not like her for faithless man expire.

Benjamin Colman respected Jane's quest for "great and unconfin'd" ideas; in 1725 he admitted that "with the Advantages of my liberal Education at School & College, I have no reason to think but that your genius in writing would have excelled mine." At the same time, however, he warned her that writing poetry was indulgent; she should spend her time in reading and in devotion.

But Jane Colman was unlucky in her husband. Ebenezer Terrell was a minister at Medford; Baldwin assessed him as a smart but humorless man who monopolized control of the books and ideas circulating in their household.[21] "The story," wrote Baldwin, "told in the old letters and in the phrasing of the day, makes very clear the demands upon her young body and the conflicts of her mind and spirit." By the time Jane was twenty years old she had come to be fearful for her salvation and to regret her reading of fiction. When she died at the age of twenty-seven, her father's colleague, the Reverend John Adams, thought he was doing her honor by praising her as

> Free from ambition . . .
> Nor was she vain, nor stain'd with those Neglects,
> In which too learned Females lose their Sex—

The story of the younger sister, Abigail, is even more tormented. "Nabby," as she was called, was twelve when Jane gave up romances to please her husband. Abigail nevertheless "gave herself to reading from her Childhood," reported her father, "and soon to writing. She wanted not a Taste for what was excellent in Books, more especially of a Poetical Turn or Relish. . . . Thus run her too soon and too far into the reading of Novels, &c., for which God in his righteous Providence afterwards punished her by suffering her to leave her Father's House, to the grief of her Friends and the Surprise of the Town."

Colman assumed a clear connection between Nabby's reading and her elopement with the young rake Alfred Dennie, who took her to New Hampshire, where, to the family's horror, they were married by "a Priest of the Church of England." There were desperate fights over Nabby's inheritance and Dennie's expenditure of her money; Dennie was accused of giving his wife "a foul disease." Nabby claimed that she loved Dennie "with a Love stronger than Death"; she did indeed die shortly thereafter, but not before observing that "I ought to be the subject of a Tragedy as noble as that of Cato's."

Stories like Abigail's would be told and retold for at least another century as a way of warning young girls to avoid misalliance. The genre would reach its apogee in the 1790s in Susannah Rowson's *Charlotte: A Tale of Truth* (1791) and Hannah Webster Foster's *Coquette* (1797). Each is a political cautionary tale in which the price of sexual adventure is death. Each is also a bitter criticism of a world in which upwardly mobile men use women for their own purposes. In a commercial society in which all rests on promises and credit, marriage promises themselves could not be trusted.[22] Young women read fiction literally to save their own lives.

Baldwin understood both sisters as emblems of caution against reading. Abigail's reading was thought to have drawn her into irresponsible behavior. Jane managed to maintain her intellectual interests without discrediting her character, but it seemed, as the Reverend John Adams put it, a near thing. In 1961 Baldwin decided to find out how typical the Colman girls had been. She suspected that the worry about novel reading had been overstated and not only for poor Nabby: "In the wills and inventories which I have been able to find [in New York] there is no mention of any novel or romance." In fact, there were few novels or romances in the colonies before 1750. "Usually authors have been contented to say that for the most part women were interested in household affairs, in embroidery, painting, perhaps a smattering of French. . . . " Baldwin was skeptical; she also suspected that these authors were repeating each other. She embarked on a search of wills, printed library lists, and diaries. She found women reading *The Spectator,* William Shakespeare, Robert Burton's *Anatomy of Melancholy,* Joseph Addison, Richard Price, William Congreve, Alexander Pope, and John Dryden. She even found a woman who supervised the studies of her descendants after death: in 1780 one Mrs. Latham saw "the specter of an elderly woman," an ancestor who had willed her books to her descendants and who now appeared "to reprove her for reading a novel on the Sabbath Day."[23]

Baldwin died before she could finish this essay, but she had clearly established that the range of women's reading was far wider than her contemporaries had thought.

In *The Wealth of Nations,* published in 1776, Adam Smith sensitively noted that there were few institutions in England dedicated to the education of women. He suggested that this was because women were not thought to need an education that would draw them into a world of commerce, politics, and the unpredictable. Boys, in contrast, required an education that gave them the skills needed to respond to the public world. Smith wrote, "There is nothing useless or absurd or fantastical in the common course of women's education. They can be taught what their parents or guardians judge necessary or useful for them to learn. They are taught nothing else."[24] Since parents, in effect, can predict what a woman is going to need to know, she can be trained at home to face that life. It was not anticipated that women would encounter the uncertain and the unexpected, "the absurd or the fantastical." A reasonably sophisticated level of literacy is the crucial means of access to the community of argument, but in the first era the girl who, like Jane Colman, hungered for more literacy and argument than she "needed" was incomprehensible to her contemporaries.

Beneath a veneer of stability, major changes were under way throughout the eighteenth century and would come with breathtaking speed at the end. A second era in women's intellectual history may be discerned in the years of the early Republic—roughly including the Revolution and the first decades of the nineteenth century—when competence in skills increased markedly, especially for white middle-class women, and claims were made with some frequency that women's intellect was at least comparable to men's. A virtual revolution in literacy was under way, encouraged by the transition of the economy to a print culture and reinforced by a technology that made printed materials more widely available and injected them into new areas of life, and by an ideological campaign that linked reading to rationality, upward mobility, and control of one's own life. Although literacy did not increase at the same rate for each class or each sex within each class, what might be called a "literacy gap" between free white men and women gradually closed during the first half-century of the Republic's history. This gap had been a double one; reading and writing were differently gendered. As Jennifer Monaghan has shown, in the colonial era reading was understood to be appropriate for girls as well as boys and was normally taught to children by women, whether their mothers or other adult women in "dame schools." But "writing was considered a craft . . . a male job-related skill, a tool for ministers and shipping clerks alike."[25] Studying towns in the upper Connecticut River Valley for the years of the early Republic, William Gilmore reports nearly universal literacy for men of all classes by the 1780s and 80 percent female literacy for the richest eight-tenths of the population.[26] Skills once regarded as those of the powerful—reading and writing—were distributed among American women to an unprecedented extent. White women in New England seem to have been the most literate women in the Western world.

These figures cannot be generalized for the entire United States. They are specific to region: the South lagged far behind; as late as 1850 one out of five white women in the South was illiterate.[27] They are specific to race: literacy was denied to slaves by law; free blacks lacked both opportunity and institutional support for extended study. Yet the literacy of free blacks was much higher than, until recently, it has been assumed, and urban African Americans quickly narrowed the gap between the races after the Civil War. In 1910, when 36 percent of all rural African Americans were illiterate, less than 6 percent of urban African Americans in western cities were, a slightly lower level of illiteracy than prevailed among white foreign born in the same cities.[28]

For people on the margins of society, achieving literacy could mean the opening of wonderful, even magical new horizons. But not necessarily. Nowhere is the ambivalence of the marginal person toward reading—and toward the life of the intellect in general—expressed with more precision than by Harriet A. Jacobs in her thinly disguised autobiography, *Incidents in the Life of a Slave Girl*.[29] In that account, literacy is no predictor of moral integrity. When Jacobs's grandmother stands on the auction block, placed there by her privileged and literate masters, she is saved by "a feeble . . . maiden lady, seventy years old, the sister of my grandmother's deceased mistress. . . . [She] could neither read nor write; and when the bill of sale was made out, she signed it with a cross. But what consequence was that, when she had a big heart overflowing with human kindness? She gave the old servant her freedom."[30]

The generations of women who lived through the American Revolution and the first years of the early Republic were aware—to varying degrees—that they were living through a strategic moment in the history of the female intellect. The republican ideology of the revolutionary years made literacy a moral obligation; the diffusion of knowledge was the responsibility of a republican society. There was understood to be a reciprocal relationship between an informed people and a virtuous people—an ideology given its classic expression in Thomas Jefferson's remark to the effect that he would choose a free press over other republican institutions. Believing as they did that republics rested on the virtue of their citizens, revolutionary leaders needed to believe that Americans of subsequent generations would continue to display the moral character that a republic required. The role of a guarantor of civic virtue, however, could not be assigned to a particular branch of government. Instead, it was hoped that other agencies—churches, schools, families— would fulfill that function. Within families, the crucial role was thought to be the mother's, a role combining political and educational obligation that I have called the "Republican Mother."[31]

Republican ideology thus combined with Protestant encouragement of Bible reading and the increasingly print-oriented commercial trading networks to sustain not only basic literacy but an enlarged range of knowledge, for girls as well as boys, women as well as men. Formal facilities for teaching girls multiplied; it is estimated that "nearly four hundred exclusively female academies were founded between 1790 and 1830."[32] In New York City, as Carl Kaestle has shown, "common pay schools" charged modest fees, enrolled approximately one girl for every two boys, and were accessible to students from a wide range of social classes.[33] In Philadelphia Sarah Mapps Douglass opened a school for African American children in 1820; by 1853 she was in charge of the girls' primary department of the Philadelphia Institute for Colored Youth. Quaker women formed societies to support the education of girls and black children and hired younger women to teach.[34] Moravians established pairs of schools for boys and girls. New England schools began to hold summer sessions for girls and younger children. As public moneys were allocated to pay female teachers' salaries, the functions of the summer schools were gradually integrated into the year-round public grammar school.

Many interesting things might be said about the girls' schools of the early Republic: their size; their social composition; the extent to which they opened careers to talented teachers and administrators like Sarah Pierce, Emma Willard, and Sarah Mapps Douglass; the impact they had on the women of the next generation. These schools provided the requisite groundwork for a subsequent demand for even more advanced, or "higher," education. Before there could be colleges, there would have to be elementary schools, academies, and seminaries.[35] For the young women who taught and managed schools in the early Republic, Joan Jensen argues, teaching "provided an essential transition—for some women at least—from a functional to a liberating literacy through which they could interact with the social and intellectual life of the new nation in ways that only males had done earlier. . . . The teaching daughters were an essential link between Republican motherhood and feminist sisterhood."[36]

These new opportunities—to move "from a functional to a liberating

literacy"—were regarded with great ambivalence. They could be welcomed with excitement, but they were also met with profound distrust.
Indeed, they became the subject of a bitter debate—in student essays, in
graduation orations, in newspaper columns—on the merits of female
education. The hostility with which educated women were greeted is
akin to the skepticism with which upper classes have traditionally regarded
the spread of literacy among the poor or the fear whites displayed of
freed black people's drive for learning before and after the Civil War.
Approval of the new competence was balanced by a fear that new
knowledge might make its holders more troublesome. As literate women
moved into a male world of print and the professions, they found themselves criticized for transforming the roles that were initially theirs by
virtue of their sex. They encountered a variant of the anti-intellectualism
that Richard Hofstadter identified as a distinctive feature of American
life in times of stress.[37] This consisted of the assertion that women did
not need learning, for they could not be wise. This idea can be found in
Plato; it retained its vigor down through the centuries. The complaint
that the learned woman crossed the boundaries of her sex, a complaint
lodged against Jane Colman Terrell, received fresh energy during the
anxious years of the early Republic. Indeed, that it was made shows us,
as in mirror image, that women were reaching for access to higher
education and gaining enemies in the process. "Women of masculine
minds," thundered the Boston minister John Sylvester John Gardiner,
"have generally masculine manners, and a robustness of person ill calculated to inspire the tender passion."[38]

Still, virtually no one explicitly defended marginal literacy for women.
Education for girls began to be welcomed as a path to an upwardly
mobile marriage, and, increasingly, there were those who took Mary
Wollstonecraft's arguments to reflect the common sense of the matter:
that is, limits on female intelligence were more a matter of educational
opportunity than the result of nature.[39]

Finally, and perhaps most significantly, women welcomed learning as
a route to power and as an expression of ambition. One is struck by some
women's hunger for learning and for access not only to skills but also to
wisdom and by their expression of resentment for being excluded from
the world of books. The distinguished playwright and novelist Susannah
Rowson wrote in 1794, "There is no reason why we should stop short in
the career of knowledge, though it has been asserted by the other sex
that the distaff, the needle, together with domestic concerns alone should
occupy the time of women. . . . The human MIND, whether possessed by
man or woman, is capable of the highest refinement and most brilliant
acquirements."[40]

In an era in which Jefferson was shocked to find Hamilton acknowledging his hunger for fame frankly and openly, it was the more startling to find Judith Sargent Murray writing that young women's minds ought to be taught to aspire. Murray did not arrive at that conclusion easily or without pain; indeed her major work, three volumes of essays published as *The Gleaner* in 1798, originally had been offered with a male authorial voice.[41] Not until the final installment, "The Gleaner Unmasked," did Murray identify herself as the Constantia who had "filled some pages" in the *Boston Magazine* and the *Massachusetts Magazine.* She had passed "in the masculine character" because, she said, she was "ambitious of being considered *independent as a writer*"; she had kept her secret even from her own husband.[42] In so misogynist a culture, "observing . . . the contempt, with which female productions are regarded," she even now feared that "it will be affirmed, that the *effeminacy* and *tinsel glitter* of my style could not fail of betraying me at every sentence which I uttered."[43] The political voice was so deeply understood to be specific to men that a woman who wished to enter into the dialogue needed, as it were, to dress in men's clothes. The secret, however, was soon out, and an increasingly wide audience knew Murray's columns as those of a woman. In these columns she argued that ambition was a noble principle and urged that girls be taught "to reverence themselves. . . . that is, their intellectual eminence," insisting that self-respect and intellectual power went together. She warned against attempts by parents to eliminate pride; properly understood, pride (or "self-complacency") seemed to her a useful defense against false flattery and manipulation by others, especially men.[44]

"There are some ambitious spirits," observed Emma Willard comfortably in 1819, "who cannot be confined in the household and who need a theatre in which to act. . . . " Instead of being distressed at the possibility of ambition in women, she proposed they use their energies to establish and direct female academies.[45] A female poet, writing an attack on Alexander Pope, claimed:

> In either sex the appetites' the same
> For love of power is still the love of fame. . . .
> In education all the difference lies;
> Women, if taught, would be as learnd and wise
> As haughty man, improved by arts and rules. . . . [46]

A recurrent theme in these prescriptions for women's education was, as Murray had said, that a woman ought to be taught "to reverence herself." The study of history had an important role in this and was often commended as an antidote to novels. Women harbored some doubts, however. Miss Morland, in Jane Austen's *Northanger Abbey,* explains why she prefers popular novels to history: "I read it [history] a little as a duty, but it tells me nothing that does not either vex or weary me. The quarrels of popes and kings, with wars or pestilences, in every page; the men all so good for nothing, and hardly any women at all."[47]

Feminist writers and teachers responded to such skepticism by compiling lists of accomplished women and anthologies of historical episodes. Women's history as a subject of study in the United States may be said to have begun with the late eighteenth-century search for a usable past, one that would link girls to heroic women of the past and attempt, however hesitantly, to provide women a place in the civic culture. Compilers of "ladies repositories," ladies' magazines, and textbooks for girls' schools ransacked their libraries, tumbling historical examples about. They were often heedless of chronology: Charlotte Corday might be paired with Lady Jane Grey, Margaret of Anjou with Catherine of Russia. Not until Oberlin's opening years were coherent histories of American women available for the female audience. Samuel L. Knapp's *Female Biography* appeared in 1834, Lydia Maria Child's *History of the Condition of Women in Various Ages and Conditions* in 1835, Elizabeth Ellet's great compilation of the activities of women during the American Revolution in 1848, and Sarah Josepha Hale's *Woman's Record* in 1853. The generation of antebellum activist women could read histories that challenged the canon and made claims for women's presence and the significance of women's actions. Ellet's *Domestic History of the American Revolution*, published in 1850, was perhaps the very first history of any war to give men's and women's activities equal space, offering accounts of civilian women's steady patriotic resistance and occasional heroism interchangeably with accounts of male battles.

Hesitantly, carefully, it became possible for a young woman, growing to maturity in the early nineteenth century, to contemplate advanced education as an attractive option. The curriculum of the girls' seminaries was, of course, not often rigorous; even the "Ladies' Course" at Oberlin would now appear to be that of a secondary school rather than a college. But the path of Mary Ann Shadd, daughter of a leading free African American abolitionist and educated in a West Chester Quaker school, who spent her career as a teacher, lecturer, antislavery and emigration advocate and, at the age of sixty, earned a law degree from Howard University, epitomizes not only an individual woman's own educational quest but also women's use of institutional options that Jane Colman Terrell could not have imagined.[48]

In the third era, from 1833 to the early twentieth century, formal supports for intellectual communities of women were created by the

establishment of institutions. The number of schools grew steadily—
seminaries at a faster pace than colleges. The temptation for the modern
observer to tell an institutional story here is very great. It is easy enough
to chart intellectual opportunity in terms of the growth in the number of
classrooms, teachers, and growing access to professions. The dramatic
expansion of public "common" schools, initiated in the 1840s and nurtured
by regional leaders like Horace Mann, created a substantial community
of solidly instructed girls, a small proportion of whom continued on to
high school, seminaries, and even college. Their numbers steadily increased
throughout the nineteenth century; in many communities girls tended to
stay in schools longer than boys did. Selwyn Troen has charted this
growth between 1840 and 1880 for St. Louis, where more than half of
the children between ages seven and twelve attended schools and where
a free high school was available to whites. St. Louis did not, however,
establish a public high school for black students until 1875.[49] That high
school was one of only four such schools open to black students in all of
the South; as late as 1915 twenty-three of the forty-two southern cities
with populations over twenty thousand lacked even a single public high
school for African Americans. There was no public high school for
African Americans in Atlanta until 1924.[50] On the other hand, many of
the high schools that were open to African Americans in the years
1880-1916 offered challenging college preparatory curricula, including
Latin, Greek, and advanced mathematics; all were coeducational.[51]

But there was an extra-academic, extra-institutional aspect of American intellectual life, as there still is; it was very strong in the nineteenth
century, and it had particular relevance for women. In a world in which
only a few thousand women were in college or university in any given
year, most "higher" education was necessarily self-education.[52] Women
shaped their intellectual lives out of their own reading, diary keeping,
and letter writing. Their study was squeezed in between the domestic
tasks that their families—even the most supportive—required of them.
"Dear Friend," wrote Sarah Bradford to Mary Moody Emerson in 1814,
"You will have me write—what? The interesting detail of mending,
sweeping, teaching? What amusement can you reasonably require at the
hand of a being secluded in a back chamber, with a basket of stockings on
one side, and an old musty heathen on the other?" Yet her letters testify
to a wide and dense range of reading: Josephus, Virgil, Friedrich Klopstock,
David Hume. "Oh, how I envy the scholar, the philosopher, whose
business, whose profession, is science!" Bradford observed. Like Mary
Moody Emerson's, her studies were undisciplined; years later Sarah
Bradford was to recall accurately of her friend, "She has read, all her life,
in the most miscellaneous way. . . . " One may be permitted to wonder

whether Mary Moody Emerson would have rambled on in her writing had there been a public audience for it, as there was for the writing of her nephew?[53]

Justifications for study fell into three categories, only two of them considered respectable: religious self-appraisal of the sort especially sanctioned by Calvinist tradition, service to the family by preparing oneself to teach one's children, and self-indulgence. "I am sometimes almost tempted to wish I knew nothing about Latin, and had not a taste for studies that subject me to so many inconveniences; for the time I now employ in study I should then spend in reading books which would enable me to join in the conversation and partake of the pleasures of fashionable ladies, but now I am as careful to conceal my books and as much afraid of being detected with them as if I were committing some great crime," Sarah Bradford confessed.[54] In the private writing of mid-century women, we can sense this need for a justification for learning that was self-fulfilling as well as self-indulgent, a rationale for learning that enabled one to shape one's own self or affect one's own community. This wish and this need may well have been embedded in the choice that thousands of women made by reading Mme. de Staël's *Corrine*. One of the most popular novels of the early nineteenth century, *Corrine* offered, as almost no other novel did until George Eliot began to publish, a woman who sought to please herself and who made demands on the society of men.[55]

The experiences of Lydia Maria Child and Margaret Fuller suggest some of the pains of trying to structure an intellectual career without institutional support. Child's formal education extended no further than dame school, though her brother Convers Francis, to whom she was very close, graduated from Harvard and studied at the Harvard Divinity School. Yet she read widely and seriously. At fifteen she was complaining to her brother about "Milton's treatment of our sex" in *Paradise Lost;* at eighteen she was teaching school in Maine and searching for a religious identity, which she found in the Unitarian church; and at twenty-two she was writing her first novel. *Hobomok: A Tale of Early Times* (1824) was political fiction that entered into public argument about the status of Indians, interracial marriage, and Puritan history.[56] The success of *Hobomok* prompted the Boston Athenaeum to offer Child an honorary membership that provided free access to its library; it was an unusual compliment, signaling that as an intellectual woman she could literally enter male space. When, a few years later, she offended conservatives with her trailblazing antislavery pamphlet, *An Appeal in Favor of That Class of Americans Called Africans* (1833), her library privileges were abruptly withdrawn.[57] Thereafter she would proceed—as did most of her male and all of her female contemporaries—without institutional support for her studies. She found intellectual and political sustenance in the overlapping communities of transcendentalists and abolitionists and in friendship and dialogue with women who became informal colleagues— Margaret Fuller among them.[58]

Everyone who knew Margaret Fuller seems to have agreed that she had a fine mind; she spent much of her life restlessly searching for a context in which to exercise it effectively and consequentially. Unlike Child, she was deeply skeptical of voluntary associations; unlike Catharine Beecher, she found teaching girls' schools deeply frustrating.[59] Her "Conversations," an effort to guide the learning of other women, were constructed in criticism of women's educational options. She opened the first session in 1839 with the following declaration:

> Women are now taught, at school, all that men are; they run over, superficially, even *more* studies, without being really taught anything. When they come to the business of life, they find themselves inferior, and all their studies have not given them that practical good sense, and mother wisdom, and wit, which grew up with our grandmothers at the spinning-wheel. But, with this difference; men are called on, from a very early period . . . to put to use what they have learned. But women learn without any attempt to reproduce. Their only reproduction is for purpose of display.[60]

Fuller's relationship with the transcendentalist writers, exhibited through shared work on *The Dial* and in the volume of memoirs that her American male friends compiled after her untimely death, has seemed to suggest she was their colleague. But this collegiality is problematic; Caroline Healey Dall reported on one set of "Conversations" offered to both men and women, where Emerson was present. "Emerson pursued his own train of thought. He seemed to forget that we had come together to pursue Margaret's."[61]

In 1885 Annie Nathan, an eighteen-year-old New York girl, began to read the *Memoirs of Margaret Fuller* and not long thereafter organized a reading group called the Seven Wise Women. "The idea came to me last year while reading of M. Fuller's social gatherings. . . . The idea is to study these women carefully—& write an essay upon each: Hannah More, Mary Wollstonecraft, E. B. Browning, Mary Somerville, M. Fuller, Harriet Martineau, Caroline Herschel, Geo. Eliot."[62]

By 1885, however, there was a substantial institutional context for the aspirations of girls like Annie Nathan. She knew of authentic colleges for women: Vassar was already twenty years old, Smith and Wellesley had opened ten years before, Spelman had been in operation for four years and Bryn Mawr for a year. The 1870s were something of a "take-off" decade for coeducational, especially public, institutions in the North and women's colleges in the South; often the increased need for women's higher education was ascribed to a superfluity of young women, whose male peers had been killed in the Civil War and who therefore needed to be self-supporting.[63] In 1885 the Mississippi State College for Women, the first female public institution in the South, opened its doors.[64] In 1896 Washington Duke gave $100,000 to Trinity College in Durham, North Carolina, with the provision that the college admit women, "placing them in the future on an equal footing with men, enabling them to enjoy all the rights, privileges and advantages of the college. . . . "[65] At the University of Wisconsin and the University of Missouri women reasserted their claim to a liberal education in the same classes with men, instead of segregated in a normal school; at the University of Michigan a fundraising campaign to provide the $100,000 necessary to establish the female department promised by the university's charter finally succeeded. In Nathan's own city of New York the options were more constricted, but Columbia College had just established an "Annex" through which women could be examined by Columbia professors, although they could not take courses. Annie Nathan entered this marginal academic setting. Within a few years she had committed herself to a major fundraising campaign to endow a women's college. Before five years were up, Barnard College was in existence, and Annie Nathan was writing, "Felt happy and proud to see evidence of my work. I can always look to Barnard College even if I am only 23 & feel if I die tomorrow, I have not lived in vain. I do hope that next year this time we have an endowment of $250,000."[66]

The intensity of young Annie Nathan's feelings about her college experience seems characteristic of her generation. College women in the late nineteenth century knew they had made an unusual commitment. "We worked in those years," Jane Addams recalled of her time at Rockford in the 1870s, "as if we really believed the portentous statement from Aristotle . . . with which we illuminated the wall occupied by our Chess club[:]. . . . There is the same difference between the learned and the unlearned as between the living and the dead."[67] Yet they still had to defend their access to learning. "The world of thought," Anna Julia Cooper ruefully observed in 1892, "moved in its orbit like the revolutions of the moon; with one face (the man's face) always out, so that the spectator could not distinguish whether it was disc or sphere." Cooper counted herself among the mere thirty African American women to whom B.A. degrees had ever been awarded; gently she challenged African American men to raise funds to increase that number: "While our men seem thoroughly abreast of the times on almost every other subject, when they strike the woman question, they drop back into . . . the idea that women may stand on pedestals or live in doll houses, (if they happen to have them) but they must not furrow their brows with thought to attempt to help men tug at the great questions of the world." Cooper called for scholarships earmarked for "ambitious" girls "with pluck and brain . . . to offset and balance the aid that can always be found for boys who will take theology."[68]

African American women who founded schools, as Mary McLeod Bethune did in 1904, often began them as elementary schools because of the absence of good facilities for black children. By 1922 Bethune's school, which had begun with an enrollment of five girls aged eight to twelve whose parents paid fifty cents weekly tuition, had merged with Florida's first college for black men to become Bethune-Cookman College. "When I walk through the campus," Bethune wrote in 1941, "with its stately palms and well-kept lawns, and think back to the dump-heap foundation, I rub my eyes and pinch myself."[69] Mary Church, the daughter of one of the very few wealthy black businessmen in the country, was sent to study languages at Oberlin and in Europe; her father wished her education to be an ornamental one. Her commitment to teaching other black students—first at Wilberforce, then at the high school for Negro students in Washington—required gumption. "As some girls run away from home to marry the man of their choice," Mary Church Terrell wrote in her memoirs, "so I left home and ran the risk of permanently alienating my father from myself to engage in the work which his money had prepared me to do."[70]

Many, like Cooper, Terrell, and Addams, felt a strong sense of obligation that their learning be used for some larger social good, but it also began to be possible to be part of a "group of women who have gone on acquiring knowledge for themselves," as one Vassar alumna put it in 1895. By the 1920s the struggles of these women had begun to fade from consciousness. "Don't ever dare to take your college as a matter of course," Alice Duer Miller admonished the students at Barnard, "because, like freedom and democracy, many people you'll never know anything about have broken their hearts to get it for you."[71]

The opening of research universities to women brings us back to Alice Mary Baldwin. Baldwin graduated from Cornell University in 1900. She had chosen to transfer there after a year at coeducational Bates College because Cornell, also coeducational, offered more career options, but coeducation at Cornell was contested; although classes were open to women, many male students thought women did not belong in college activities. Baldwin joined a women's student organization that fought vigorously to protect the right of women students to participate in elections, publications, and committees.[72] She stayed on at Cornell for two years after her graduation to earn a master's degree, with a thesis on enlightened despotism in Sweden. A traveling fellowship offered by the Association of Collegiate Alumnae gave her the chance to study briefly at the Sorbonne and the University of Berlin and to travel in Europe. She enrolled in the history department at Columbia in 1903.[73] Financial difficulty following the death of her father seems to have forced her to drop graduate school, briefly take a job teaching languages in a New Jersey high school, and then spend an unhappy two years as dean of women and instructor in history at Fargo College in North Dakota. In 1906 she returned to the East to teach history at the Baldwin School, one of the best preparatory schools in the country, founded explicitly as a "feeder school" for Bryn Mawr. She remained there for fifteen years. In 1921, when it appeared that she was likely to be named headmistress, she took a leave of absence and enrolled at age forty-two in the history department of the University of Chicago.[74]

The University of Chicago was, along with Columbia University in New York, one of the few research universities that made women graduate students reasonably welcome.[75] Baldwin's advisers at Chicago knew how to take advantage of the skills of such a mature and experienced student. She was awarded a graduate research assistantship and studied with the distinguished historian Andrew McLaughlin. Her dissertation on the New England clergy in the era of the American Revolution was a search for her own roots, although she would have said it was less a search than an appreciation. In the introduction to the published version, she situated herself in a male line of intellectual descent: "The following study has not been for me one of merely academic interest. My grandfather . . . my father . . . and my uncle . . . were all congregational clergymen; and it was through them that I first learned to appreciate, in some measure, the ministers of New England."[76]

In her second year Marion Talbot, the innovative dean of women, appointed Baldwin head of a women's residence hall. It was a role Baldwin viewed with ambivalence. Her career goal was a faculty appointment in a college history department, preferably in a research institution; Talbot might be offering Baldwin opportunities to train herself to be a dean elsewhere, but it was not an opportunity Baldwin welcomed. She had already spent enough of her career arranging the lives of the young.

When she came close to achieving her Ph.D., however, the jobs open to her involved administration. The one everyone *but* Baldwin thought she ought to accept was the position of dean of women at Trinity College, a small coeducational institution in Durham, North Carolina. As she hesitated, McLaughlin undertook the duty of telling his student the facts of academic life. "The . . . question relates to the future at Chicago, the most distant future," he observed in response to her letter. "I am afraid there is not any future. . . . You and I agreed in our conversation that whether it be just or not, the fact is that in the University there is not much opportunity for women. I would not wish to have such a sentiment proclaimed aloud from the housetops; and I am not sure that I should lay it down as a policy. You know the conditions as they actually exist, and as I have said, I understand that you look upon those conditions very much as I do. . . ." [77] Forty-four years old, with substantial administrative experience and a Ph.D., Baldwin was in demand for a job that, remembering her unhappy years in North Dakota, she emphatically did not want. Trinity College in North Carolina recruited her vigorously as dean of women; she accepted because she had no other options, but only after she followed McLaughlin's advice to insist on an appointment to the faculty as well as the deanship. It was well that she did. [78]

The very next year a $40 million bequest from James B. Duke transformed Trinity into a university with law, medical, and graduate schools. The male undergraduate college was formed of the men who had formerly attended Trinity; a Woman's College—it bore the generic name until its demise in 1972—was formed of their female counterparts. The creation of the Woman's College in 1927 reflected a widespread reaction against coeducation and a break with Washington Duke's instruction of less than thirty years before that the women of Trinity be placed "on an equal footing with men." [79]

In the new configuration, Baldwin was dean of the Woman's College; her job would be to fight for "equal footing" of the single-sex colleges within the coeducational university. "My chief aims," she wrote, "were to have full opportunities for the women to share in all academic life." [80] She was warmly welcomed by the older male historians, and she was the first woman to teach an upper-level course in history to a mixed class of men and women. [81] She encountered more resistance from administrators, who had trouble dealing with her "as a fellow administrator, not simply as a woman to be treated with Southern courtesy." [82] Just as she had insisted on a faculty appointment for herself, she now insisted that the women students in the college be understood to be students in the university, receiving their degrees from the university. [83] As dean of the Woman's College, she claimed "the same authority" that the dean of Trinity had. Moreover, she set herself absolutely against the addition of home economics courses to the women's curriculum. [84]

Yet as even the architecture of the newly configured campus made clear, the new Duke University was really two separate institutions.

The firm of Frederick Law Olmsted, the nineteenth century's greatest landscape architect, designed the male university with collegiate gothic buildings claiming an implicit link to medieval learning; the phallic towers of the central chapel aggressively pointed skyward. The Woman's College, two miles away, was placed on a space less than one-quarter the size of the university campus, in neoclassic buildings whose lines emphasized peacefulness and repose; its major buildings no more than three stories high, capped not by towers but by rounded womblike domes.[85] Only with difficulty did Baldwin dissuade President William Preston Few from adding "a big, decorative iron fence around the quadrangle to be locked at night for the safety of the girls."[86] Alice Mary Baldwin intended to forge a women's intellectual community at Duke—and she did succeed in hiring a number of women faculty (Katherine Gilbert in philosophy, Hertha Spooner in botany, Julia Dale in mathematics)—but she had to do it in an institutional setting that denied women the opportunity to argue with men.[87] President Few assumed that women's persuasive options were confined to the narrow range between the simple request and the tearful appeal to emotions. Among his first questions to Baldwin was whether she "could take criticism and disappointment without weeping."[88] Years later Baldwin assured a colleague "that she had never cried at any of their meetings."[89] Baldwin was caught in the trap of a status that required forthright argument but an institution that required decorum—her original fears were not off the mark.

Required by her vulnerable position to exercise the greatest discretion, Baldwin offered her criticisms of the state of women's education only in passing, interweaving them between the lines of carefully guarded accounts of her own college. Occasionally, it is possible to see what she really thought. In 1932 Baldwin called for "real coordination rather than subordination" when a women's college was part of a university. "There should be women on the board of trustees." The budget should not be wholly in the hands of men. There should be "a reasonable number of women of fine personality and ripe scholarship" on the faculty.[90] By 1949 she had concluded that "in the larger coeducational institutions . . . the interests of the women students, always in the minority, tend to be submerged in those of the men. . . . Perhaps the most serious loss is in the part played by the women themselves; in their sense of unity, of belonging to a college which is peculiarly their own and for which they are in large part responsible. . . . " Her posthumous memoir provides the evidence that she knew herself to be undervalued and underpaid throughout her life at Duke, and she was outraged not only for herself but also for the women of the college whom she served.[91]

Alice Mary Baldwin's world was far removed from that of her predecessors, Jane Colman Terrell, Judith Sargent Murray, Emma Willard, and Margaret Fuller, or even that of Anna Julia Cooper and Mary Church Terrell in her own time. One theme linked them, however. They all lived in a culture deeply skeptical of learned women. It is true that as time went on, levels of literacy improved, opportunities for its active use—especially in correspondence and in print—increased, informal and institutional sites for argument expanded, and women found more allies in their quest for intellectual freedom and opportunity. Skepticism was voiced with more delicacy; no minister thundered from the pulpit that the learned woman was necessarily masculine. But such women were still regarded as oddities. As learned women, they were still viewed with suspicion. Baldwin's memoirs show that, though she spent her entire life as an intellectual and a scholar, she knew she was not welcomed to fellowship with her male colleagues, and it hurt.[92]

For two hundred years it was assumed that learning in men and learning in women could not be quite the same. Women had to find room for their educations and for critical thinking without eliciting male hostility and contempt. It was assumed that the learning for women required special justification; the standard question was, "What studies are appropriate for the female mind?" Adam Smith said that women needed a continuation of what had been learned in the home and could be used directly and practically in adult life; he called for "no absurdities." In the nineteenth century the list of appropriate studies lengthened; it became respectable for women to contemplate a widening range of activities. But few would say with Margaret Fuller, "Let them be sea-captains if they will," and fewer still would maintain that women might properly indulge in any form of study. As recently as 1956 it was fresh and unusual for the Harvard sociologist David Riesman to propose for women an education that would be *discontinuous* with what had come before, that would "put pressure on life," open up new worlds of learning, encourage new ambitions, make room for the problematic and, in Adam Smith's word, the "fantastical."[93] Even in the twentieth century, communities of male scholars based in research universities maintained distanced and ambivalent relationships with the most distinguished women intellectuals—Charlotte Perkins Gilman, Mary Ritter Beard, Margaret Mead, Hannah Arendt—who, in a mixture of choice and necessity, built their careers outside of the academy.[94] The renewed women's movement of the early 1970s had an often unappreciated intellectual and institutional component in what Adrienne Rich has called the "women's university-without-walls," which burst into life in the early 1970s and continues to thrive "in the shape of

women reading and writing with a new purposefulness, [in] . . . feminist
bookstores, presses, bibliographic services . . . libraries, art galleries . . . all
with a truly educational mission. . . . "[95] When the Ivy League colleges
opened their doors to women in the 1970s, they responded to the claims
that women were making, answering the question of what studies are
appropriate for the female mind by taking Riesman's, Judith Sargent
Murray's, and Margaret Fuller's positions: all studies are appropriate for
the female mind; no one need any longer fear undermining her own
character by what she chooses to study.

But if we have resolved in this generation the question of whether
women's minds are fit for serious thought, we have not yet fully resolved
the related issue of whether women's experience is as important a part of
our cultural inheritance as the medieval cathedral and whether it is as
important for men to study women's experience as it has been for women
to study men's. The revolution that is feminist studies addresses that
issue; the hyperbolic response that women's texts destabilize the canon of
the great work of Western thought is evidence of the vigor and complexity of that revolution.

The educational challenge before us is to transform our institutions of
higher education so they not only accept both men and women as students
but also provide an understanding of the world in which the record of
women's experience, needs, and accomplishments is regarded with as much
respect and as much pride as the record of men is. The story of Jane
Colman Terrell is of interest not because it was "quaint" but because she
was silenced. Her story is as much a part of American educational history
as the story of Harvard College is. Alice Mary Baldwin was seeking to
find a way to tell us this when she died. I think she would be pleased to
know that many voices have now been added to hers and that the issues
she had to tiptoe around are now being contested and directly confronted.

NOTES

This essay is a revised and expanded version of " 'Why Should Girls Be Learn'd and
Wise?' Two Centuries of Higher Education for Women as Seen through the
Unfinished Work of Alice Mary Baldwin," originally published in John Mack
Faragher and Florence Howe, eds., *Women and Higher Education in American
History* (New York: W. W. Norton, 1988). I am greatly indebted to Kenneth
Cmiel, Mary Ann Dzuback, Leon Fink, and Barbara Sicherman for thoughtful
and helpful comments, to Leslie Taylor for smart research assistance, and to the
National Humanities Center for collegial surroundings.

1. Alice Mary Baldwin, *The New England Clergy and the American Revolution* (Durham, N.C.: Duke University Press, 1928). Alice Mary Baldwin was born

in 1879. The most complete account of her life is found in Dianne Puthoff Brandstadter, "Developing the Coordinate College for Women at Duke University: The Career of Alice Mary Baldwin, 1924-47" (Ph.D. diss., Duke University, 1977).

2. All references to Baldwin's work are based on the Alice Mary Baldwin papers in the Duke University Archives and are quoted by permission of the Duke University Archives. See especially the typescript "Two Sisters of Old Boston," circa 1938; her miscellaneous notes on cards and on sheets of paper, filed as "The Reading of Women," circa 1961; and her typescript memoir, "The Women's College as I Remember It," 1959, opened in 1980.

3. Michel Foucault, "Two Lectures," in *Power/Knowledge: Selected Interviews and Other Writings, 1972-1977*, trans. Colin Gordon, Leo Marshall, John Mepham, and Kate Soper; ed. Colin Gordon (New York: Pantheon Books, 1980), 82. For an example, see discussion of the gendered dimensions of social science knowledge in the early twentieth century in Barbara Laslett, "Gender In/And Social Science History," *Social Science History* 16 (Summer 1992): 177-95.

4. Henry Louis Gates, Foreword to *The Schomburg Library of Nineteenth-Century Black Women Writers* (New York: Oxford University Press, 1988), x-xi.

5. David Hollinger, "Historians and the Discourse of Intellectuals," in *New Directions in American Intellectual History*, ed. John Higham and Paul K. Conkin (Baltimore: Johns Hopkins University Press, 1979), 47.

6. Ibid., 49.

7. Ibid., 47.

8. Mary Kelley is now exploring the connections between women's improved learning and their intrusion into the public sector. See especially " 'Vindicating the Equality of Female Intellect': Women and Authority in the Early Republic," *Prospects* 17 (1993): 1-27.

9. Mary Ann Dzuback, personal communication. On sites of argument, see Theodora Penny Martin, *The Sound of Our Own Voices: Women's Study Clubs 1860-1910* (Boston: Beacon, 1987). Adrienne Rich, "Toward a Woman-Centered University," in *On Lies, Secrets and Silence: Selected Prose 1966-1978* (New York: W. W. Norton, 1979), 125-55, is a bitter and insightful indictment.

10. Even the book in which Hollinger's essay appeared—itself marking an important historiographic moment for intellectual history—and in which many authors paid obeisance to Merle Curti's pioneering work on the social context of American thought, failed to identify gender as part of that social context. Yet Curti's own work and career has been marked by a receptivity to women scholars and to women's history.

11. See, for example, William Gilmore, "Elementary Literacy on the Eve of the Industrial Revolution: Trends in Rural New England 1760-1830," *Proceedings of the American Antiquarian Society* 92, part 1 (1982): 87-178.

12. Lori D. Ginzberg, " 'The Joint Education of the Sexes': Oberlin's Original Vision," in *Educating Men and Women Together: Coeducation in a Changing World*, ed. Carol Lasser (Urbana: University of Illinois Press, 1987), 67-80. See

also Barbara Miller Solomon, "The Oberlin Model and Its Impact on Other Colleges," in *Educating Men and Women Together,* ed. Lasser, 83. African Americans entered Oberlin in the early 1860s.

13. Exceptions from Title 9 were made for single-sex and religious institutions. See statistics on number of colleges open to men and women 1870-1981 in Solomon, "The Oberlin Model," 44.

14. Ibid., 63.

15. Barbara Miller Solomon, *In the Company of Educated Women: A History of Women and Higher Education in America* (New Haven, Conn.: Yale University Press, 1985), 58.

16. Ibid., 58-61, is the best brief summary of these developments. Lynn D. Gordon's shrewd chapters on women at the University of California and the University of Chicago are indispensable. See Lynn D. Gordon, *Gender and Higher Education in the Progressive Era* (New Haven, Conn.: Yale University Press, 1990), chap. 2, 3. For the southern institutions, see Amy Thompson McCandless, "Maintaining the Spirit and Tone of Robust Manliness: The Battle against Coeducation at Southern Colleges and Universities, 1890-1940," *NWSA Journal* 2 (Spring 1990): 199-216. For the University of Virginia, see *Kirstein v. Rector and Visitors of the University of Virginia,* 309 F. Supp 184 (1970), in which a three judge panel approved a consent order.

17. On the exclusion of women from postwar enrollments, see Alma Lutz, "Women Need Education, Too," *Christian Science Monitor,* July 20, 1946. On the persistence of this perspective, see Philip Ward Burton, "Keep Women Out of College!" *This Week,* February 9, 1958.

18. John Trumbull, "The Progress of Dulness," in *Satiric Poems: The Progress of Dulness and M'Fingal,* ed. Edwin T. Bowden (Austin: University of Texas Press, 1962), 88.

19. See Joel Perlmann and Dennis Shirley, "When Did New England Women Acquire Literacy?" *William and Mary Quarterly,* 3d ser., 48 (January 1991): 50-67; and response by Mary Beth Norton, *William and Mary Quarterly,* 3d ser., 48 (October 1991): 639-45.

20. This summary of the story draws on Baldwin's draft and on her 1961 notes.

21. Tom Leonard at the School of Journalism, University of California-Berkeley, is exploring the control of printed matter in the household and also examining painting and prints for depictions of the use of reading to reinforce hierarchy.

22. See Linda K. Kerber, *Women of the Republic: Intellect and Ideology in Revolutionary America* (Chapel Hill: University of North Carolina Press, 1980), chap. 8, esp. 240-52. See also Cathy N. Davidson, "The Life and Times of Charlotte Temple: The Biography of a Book," in *Reading in America: Literature and Social History,* ed. Cathy N. Davidson (Baltimore: Johns Hopkins University Press, 1989), 157-79; and Carroll Smith-Rosenberg, "Engendering Virtue," in *Literature and the Body: Essays on Populations and Persons,* ed. Elaine Scarry, Selected Papers from the English Institute, 1986, new series, no. 12 (Baltimore: Johns Hopkins University Press, 1988), 160-84.

23. The book at issue was Giovanni Paolo Marana's *Letters Writ by a Turkish Spy . . .* (London: G. Strahan, 1734), which may have been the model for Montesquieu's *Persian Letters* and which included a passage supporting extended education for women.

24. Adam Smith, *An Inquiry into the Nature and Causes of the Wealth of Nations,* ed. Edwin Canaan (New York: Modern Library, 1937), bk 5, chap. 1, pt. iii, part 2, 734.

25. E. Jennifer Monaghan, "Literacy Instruction and Gender in Colonial New England," in *Reading in America,* ed. Davidson, 60–61.

26. William Gilmore, *Reading Becomes a Necessity of Life: Material and Cultural Life in Rural New England, 1780–1835* (Knoxville: University of Tennessee Press, 1989). See also Linda Auwers, "Reading the Marks of the Past: Exploring Female Literacy in Colonial Windsor, Connecticut," *Historical Methods* 13 (Fall 1980): 204–14; and Richard D. Brown, *Knowledge Is Power: The Diffusion of Information in Early America, 1700–1865* (New York: Oxford University Press, 1989).

27. Maris Vinovskis and Richard Bernard, "Beyond Catharine Beecher: Female Education in the Antebellum Period," *Signs* 3 (Summer 1978): 856–69.

28. Bureau of the Census, Department of Commerce, *Negro Population, 1790–1915* (Washington, D.C.: Government Printing Office, 1918), 417.

29. Harriet A. Jacobs, *Incidents in the Life of a Slave Girl, Written by Herself,* ed. L. Maria Child (1861); ed. Jean Fagan Yellin (1987) (Cambridge, Mass.: Harvard University Press, 1987 [1861]).

30. Ibid., 12.

31. See Kerber, *Women of the Republic,* chap. 7, 9; Linda K. Kerber, "The Republican Mother: Women and the Enlightenment—An American Perspective," *American Quarterly* 28 (Spring 1976): 187–205; and Linda K. Kerber, "The Republican Ideology of the Revolutionary Generation," *American Quarterly* 37 (Fall 1985): 474–95.

32. Kelley, " 'Vindicating the Equality of Female Intellect,' " citing Lynne Templeton Brickley, " 'Female Academies Are Every Where Establishing': The Beginnings of Secondary Education for Women in the United States, 1790–1830" (Qualifying paper, Harvard Graduate School of Education, 1982).

33. In 1796 thirteen-year-old Washington Irving, whose father was assessed for £1500 in real estate and £350 in personal property, had as a classmate Catharine Steddiford, daughter of an auctioneer who had no real estate at all and only £250 in personal property. In New York, charity schools also enrolled girls as well as boys. Carl F. Kaestle, *The Evolution of an Urban School System: New York City, 1750–1850* (Cambridge, Mass.: Harvard University Press, 1973), 44–49.

34. Joan Jensen, *Loosening the Bonds: Mid-Atlantic Farm Women 1750–1850* (New Haven, Conn.: Yale University Press, 1986), 170–71, 181–82.

35. Ibid., 172; see also Kaestle, *The Evolution of an Urban School System,* 38–40.

36. Jensen, *Loosening the Bonds,* 182–83.

37. Richard Hofstadter, *Anti-Intellectualism in American Life* (New York: Alfred A. Knopf, 1963).

38. *Massachusetts Mercury and New-England Palladium* (Boston), September 18, 1801. See also verses headed "To a Lady, Who Expressed a Desire of Seeing a University Established for Women," *American Museum* 3 (February 1788): n.p. On the long tradition in Western thought in which "women out of their place—in tropes subject to decorum and to warnings against 'excesse' or abuse—are part of a potentially dangerous invasion of linguistic into social responsibility," see Patricia Parker, *Literary Fat Ladies: Rhetoric, Gender, Property* (London: Methuen, 1987), esp. chap. 6 (quote on 111).

39. See, for example, the graduation debate between Mr. Little and Mr. Bannister in 1797, Dartmouth College Archives. For a classic statement of progressive male students' attitudes at the time, see James Iredell, Jr. (son of the Supreme Court Justice), "On the Female Sex," February 18, 1805, Iredell Papers, University of North Carolina, Chapel Hill, N.C. I am grateful to Don Higginbotham for this reference. I have commented on the exclusion of women from classical studies in *Women of the Republic,* 190-93.

40. Susannah Rowson, *Mentoria: Or the Young Ladies Friend* (Philadelphia: n.p., 1794), preface.

41. Judith Sargent Murray, *The Gleaner,* vol. 1 (Boston: I. Thomas and E. T. Andrews, 1798), 13.

42. Ibid., vol. 3, 314-15.

43. Ibid., 313.

44. Judith Sargent Murray, "Desultory Thoughts upon the Utility of Encouraging a Degree of Self-Complacency, Especially in Female Bosoms," *Gentlemen and Ladies Town and Country Magazine,* October 1784, 251-52.

45. Emma Willard, *An Address to the Public . . . Proposing a Plan for Improving Female Education* (Middlebury: n.p., 1819), 34.

46. "On Pope's Characters of Women," by a Lady, *American Museum* 11 (June 1792): Appendix 1.

47. Jane Austen, *Northanger Abbey and Persuasion,* ed. John Davie (London: Oxford University Press, 1971), 97.

48. Shadd's career is summarized in Jensen, *Loosening the Bonds,* 181-82, and in *Notable American Women, 1607-1950: A Biographical Dictionary,* vol. 1, ed. Edward T. James, Janet Wilson James, and Paul S. Boyer (Cambridge, Mass.: Belknap Press, 1971), 300-301, under "Mary Ann Shadd Cary." Another example of use of the new options is the career of Lucy Stone, which took her from her town school, to rather marginal female seminaries, to Mount Holyoke Female Seminary, and finally to Oberlin, where she became the first Massachusetts woman to take a college degree.

49. Selwyn K. Troen, *The Public and the Schools: Shaping the St. Louis System, 1838-1920* (Columbia: University of Missouri Press, 1975), 119-24. Troen persuasively links the disparity in length of school attendance to the wider range of remunerative and skilled work available to boys when they left school. Eighteen percent of the boys of sixteen who were not in St. Louis schools had

white-collar jobs, but fewer than 2 percent of the girls did; on the other hand, 26 percent of the boys were unskilled workers, but nearly 40 percent of the girls were in unskilled occupations ranging from domestic service to prostitution.

50. Among these cities were Atlanta, New Orleans, Charleston, and Montgomery. See James D. Anderson, *The Education of Blacks in the South, 1860-1935* (Chapel Hill: University of North Carolina Press, 1988), 186-237, esp. tables 6.3 and 6.4.

51. Ibid., 199. By the early 1920s, however, most of these schools had been transformed into "industrial" schools offering only limited vocational training.

52. The usually cited figure is 11,000 in 1870, but that includes seminaries; 3,000 is closer to the mark for colleges. See Solomon, *In the Company of Educated Women*, 63, 44; and Helen Lefkowitz Horowitz, *Alma Mater: Design and Experience in the Women's Colleges from Their Nineteenth Century Beginnings to the 1930s* (New York: Alfred A. Knopf, 1984).

53. Sarah Bradford to Mary Moody Emerson, November 9, 1814, and Sarah Bradford Ripley to Mr. Simmons, October 7, 1844, in *Worthy Women of Our First Century*, ed. Sarah Butler Wister and Agnes Irwin (Philadelphia: Lippincott, 1877), 130, 175. See also Phyllis Cole, " 'The Advantage of Loneliness': Mary Moody Emerson's Almanacks, 1802-1855," in *Emerson: Retrospect and Prospect*, ed. Joel Porte (Cambridge, Mass.: Harvard University Press, 1983), 1-32.

54. Sarah Bradford to Mary Moody Emerson, circa 1810, in *Worthy Women of Our First Century*, ed. Wister and Irwin, 126-27.

55. As Gail Parker has observed, "Madame de Stael had suggested that it was possible for a woman to be Byronic—at least if she were willing to die young." Gail Parker, *The Oven Birds: American Women on Womanhood* (New York: Doubleday, 1972), 13.

56. The novel has recently been reprinted with a thoughtful introduction. See Lydia Maria Child, *Hobomok and other Writings on Indians*, ed. Carolyn L. Karcher (New Brunswick, N.J.: Rutgers University Press, 1986). See also Linda K. Kerber, "The Abolitionist Perception of the Indian," *Journal of American History* 62 (June 1975): 271-95, esp. 271-73.

57. Lydia Maria Child to Samuel J. May, n.d., 1867, in *Letters of Lydia Maria Child with a Biographical Introduction by John G. Whittier and an Appendix by Wendell Phillips* (New York: Negro Universities Press, 1969 [1883]), 195, and comment on the affair by Wendell Phillips, 264.

58. See Milton Meltzer and Patricia C. Holland, eds., *Lydia Maria Child: Selected Letters, 1817-1880* (Amherst: University of Massachusetts Press, 1982), chap. 1, 2.

59. See her letters on teaching in Providence in 1837 in Robert N. Hudspeth, ed., *The Letters of Margaret Fuller*, vol. 1 (Ithaca, N.Y.: Cornell University Press, 1983), 288ff.

60. In *Memoirs of Margaret Fuller Ossoli*, vol. 1 (Boston: Phillips, Sampson, 1852), 329. See Charles Capper, "Margaret Fuller as Cultural Reformer: The Conversations in Boston," *American Quarterly* 39 (Winter 1987): 509-28, and his splendid biography, *Margaret Fuller—An American Romantic Life: The Pri-*

vate Years (New York: Oxford University Press, 1992). Fuller intended, she wrote to Sophia Ripley in a letter extensively quoted by Capper, "to systematize thought . . . [and to] give a precision in which our sex are so deficient" and to enlarge the range of subjects about which women thought so that they might "make the best use of our means of building up the life of thought upon the life of action" (513).

61. Caroline Healey Dall, *Margaret and Her Friends: Or Ten Conversations with Margaret Fuller upon the Mythology of the Greeks and Its Expression in Art* (Boston: Roberts Bros., 1897), 46.

62. Journal of Annie Nathan Meyer, October 18, 1885, box 12, folder 5, Annie Nathan Meyer Papers, American Jewish Archives, Cincinnati, Ohio. For shrewd observations on the meaning of reading to women of Meyer's generation, see Barbara Sicherman, "Sense and Sensibility: A Case Study of Women's Reading in Late-Victorian America," in *Reading in America,* ed. Davidson, 201-25.

63. Patricia Palmieri, "From Republican Motherhood to Race Suicide: Arguments on the Higher Education of Women in the United States 1820-1920," in *Educating Men and Women Together,* ed. Lasser, 49-64, esp. 53.

64. Solomon, *In the Company of Educated Women,* chap. 4.

65. Brandstadter, "Developing the Coordinate College for Women," 31.

66. Journal of Annie Nathan Meyer, October 6, 1890, Annie Nathan Meyer Papers. See also Lynn D. Gordon, "Annie Nathan Meyer and Barnard College: Mission and Identity in Women's Higher Education 1889-1950," *History of Education Quarterly* 26 (Winter 1986): 503-22.

67. In *Twenty Years at Hull House,* quoted in *The American Woman: Who Was She?* ed. Anne Firor Scott (Englewood Cliffs, N.J.: Prentice-Hall, 1971), 65-66. See also Palmieri, "From Republican Motherhood to Race Suicide," 56, on the ambiguous experience of the first generation of college women.

68. Anna Julia Cooper, "The Higher Education of Women," in *A Voice from the South* (New York: Oxford University Press, 1988 [1892]), 56, 75, 78-79. I am indebted to Elizabeth Alexander of the University of Chicago for sharing her unpublished work on Cooper.

69. Mary McLeod Bethune, "Faith that Moved a Dump Heap," *Who: The Magazine about People* 1 (1941): 54.

70. Mary Church Terrell, *A Colored Woman in a White World* (Washington, D.C.: Ransdell, 1940), 63.

71. Quoted in Marian Churchill White, *A History of Barnard College* (New York: Columbia University Press, 1954), 139.

72. Brandstadter, "Developing the Coordinate College for Women," 12.

73. Ibid., 10-13.

74. Ibid., 13-15.

75. See Rosalind Rosenberg, *Beyond Separate Spheres: Intellectual Roots of Modern Feminism* (New Haven, Conn.: Yale University Press, 1982), esp. chap. 2; Gordon, *Gender and Higher Education in the Progressive Era,* esp. chap. 3; and Ellen Fitzpatrick, *Endless Crusade: Women Social Scientists and Progressive Reform* (New York: Oxford University Press, 1990).

76. Quoted in Brandstadter, "Developing the Coordinate College for Women," 16.

77. Andrew McLaughlin to Alice Mary Baldwin, July 6, 1923, quoted in ibid., 22-23.

78. On her recruitment, see her memoir, "The Woman's College as I Remember It," 1-5 (hereafter AMB Memoir).

79. Brandstadter, "Developing the Coordinate College for Women," 31.

80. AMB Memoir, 16. Her fellow administrators were all men, "none of [whom]," she wrote later, "had worked with a woman who had any real authority or faculty standing. . . . " Ibid., 4.

81. Ibid., 35. She was touched when, at the first faculty meeting that she "rather hesitatingly" attended in 1924, two elderly members made a point of rising and "welcomed me, sat me between them . . . [and] old Dr. Pegram said, 'Miss Baldwin, I have longed to see this day.' " Ibid., 14.

82. Ibid., 15.

83. This required her to resist the university president, who entertained the idea that it ought to be "possible for a woman to receive a degree for work done entirely on our campus." Ibid., 16-18.

84. Brandstadter, "Developing the Coordinate College for Women," 58ff, 88. She was not fully successful. "In 1936-38 questions arose concerning the desirability of differentiating in any way between the courses offered men and women: for example, in physical education, home economics, etc. I remember talking with Prof. Hatley about making the experiments in the physics classes for women somewhat different, tho not in any way less difficult, than those in the men's classes, and with Dr. Robert Smith about work in Economics dealing especially with questions likely to arise in a woman's life. For a time a course in what might be called household economics was offered, but it did not become especially popular." AMB Memoir, 59.

85. See Annabel Wharton, "Gender, Architecture, and Institutional Self-Presentation: The Case of Duke University," *South Atlantic Quarterly* 90 (Winter 1991): 175-217.

86. AMB Memoir, 21.

87. See Anne Firor Scott, "Duke Women: Visible and Invisible," in *Proceedings, the Changing Patterns of Our Lives: Women's Education and Women's Studies, A Sesquicentennial Symposium,* Duke University, March 3-5, 1989, 7-15, Duke University Archives.

88. Soon after this question was posed by Few, "Mr. Flowers and Dr. Wannamaker came also, asking identical questions, including my ability to refrain from tears." AMB Memoir, 4-5.

89. Brandstadter, "Developing the Coordinate College for Women," 60.

90. "Proceedings," Association of Colleges and Secondary Schools of the Southern States, 1932, box 17, Alice Mary Baldwin Papers. On petty problems that could nevertheless be demoralizing, see AMB Memoir, passim (e.g., the failure of Trinity College administrators to inform her of changes in their class schedule, 50-51).

91. "History of Woman's College on Its Twenty-fifth Anniversary," box 17,

Alice Mary Baldwin Papers. On being underpaid, see AMB Memoir, 38, 78-80. The configuration of Baldwin's career is not idiosyncratic. Mary Ann Dzuback of Washington University, St. Louis, who has intensively studied the careers of women social scientists, has identified a long list of scholars of Baldwin's genera-tion who found that the only academic situations open to them were primarily administrative ones. Among these women might be included Lucy Flower, Violet Jayne, and Ruby Mason, deans of women at the University of Illinois; Sarah Gibson Blanding, dean of women at the University of Kentucky (1923-41), dean of Cornell's College of Home Economics (1941-46), and president of Vassar; and Eleanor Harris Rowland, dean of women at Reed College. Personal Communication, April 30, 1991. See also Paula A. Treichler, "Alma Mater's Sorority: Women and the University of Illinois, 1890-1925," in *For Alma Mater: Theory and Practice in Feminist Scholarship,* ed. Paula A. Treichler, Cheris Kramarae, and Beth Stafford (Urbana: University of Illinois Press, 1985), 5-61, esp. 23ff.

92. The general pattern of Baldwin's career, as well as the human pain that was inescapably part of such a career, was not limited to the discipline of history. See especially the exemplary account of the career of the distinguished American philosopher Suzanne Langer offered by Bruce Kuklick, *The Rise of American Philosophy: Cambridge, Massachusetts, 1860-1930* (New Haven, Conn.: Yale University Press, 1977); and the ironic Marjorie Nicolson, "Scholars and Ladies," *Yale Review* 19 (September 1929): 775-95.

93. David Riesman, "Continuities and Discontinuities in Women's Education" (Bennington College commencement address, 1956). See also David Riesman, *Constraint and Variety in American Education* (Lincoln: University of Nebraska Press, 1956), 139-43. Riesman's position was contested; two years later, in a commencement address at Smith, Adlai Stevenson would counsel the women graduates to use their learning to soothe the cares of "western man." Smith College Archives, Sophia Smith Library, Smith College, Northampton, Mass.

94. Mead had an adjunct appointment at Columbia; her base was the Museum of Natural History. Mary Beard scorned the academy. See Nancy F. Cott, *Mary Beard: A Woman Making History* (New Haven, Conn.: Yale University Press, 1991), 39-40. Hannah Arendt held occasional visiting and part-time academic appointments throughout her American career, but she identified herself as one *"nicht vom Fach,* not from the profession." Elizabeth Young-Bruehl, *Hannah Arendt: For the Love of the World* (New Haven, Conn.: Yale University Press, 1982), 410.

95. Rich, "Toward a Woman-Centered University," 126.

Invincible Woman:
Anne Firor Scott

Nancy Weiss Malkiel

For each of the authors in this volume, Anne Firor Scott has served as an inspiration and guide through her research, her teaching, and her mentorship. Carrying forward the challenges to traditional scholarship offered by Alice Mary Baldwin, Scott not only has demonstrated through her own work that "women's experience is as important a part of our cultural inheritance as the medieval cathedral" but also has opened the doors of academic cathedrals to many other women scholars. In "A Historian's Odyssey," the prefatory essay in her widely read book *Making the Invisible Woman Visible* (1984), Scott recounts the personal circumstances, intellectual influences, and professional opportunities and obstacles that have been most important in her own evolution as teacher and scholar. Because Scott has claimed that territory so effectively, this essay takes a different approach. What do we, Anne Scott's students, colleagues, and friends, have to learn from her odyssey? What has been her effect on *our* lives and on our professional careers?

In addressing these questions, the essay focuses on four of the many attributes that make Anne Scott distinctive: her gifts as a communicator; her keen political sense; her talent for seizing opportunities and running with them; and her exceptional generosity to younger scholars.

Anyone who has ever read or studied with or listened to Anne Scott knows about her skill as a communicator: her gifts of literary craftsmanship; her creativity as a teacher; her ability to establish personal and intellectual rapport with an audience; her instinct for asking the right questions. The craftsmanship is partly a matter of inspiration, partly the product of plain hard work. Sitting at the typewriter or, more recently, the computer, she shapes her prose through intense, focused effort. She communicates to students and colleagues alike the importance of working at writing. In talking to Anne Scott about one of Scott's essays that she particularly admired, Marion Roydhouse was startled to learn that Scott had been reading Virginia Woolf as she wrote the piece and had tried consciously to reproduce Woolf's cadences. "Like a bolt of lightning, it struck me," Roydhouse reflected, "you could try to write well, and still be a historian!"

Anne Scott is, quite simply, a remarkable teacher. It is commonly believed that, unlike many senior scholars, she enjoys undergraduates, perhaps even prefers them to graduate students, and she has frequently taken her turn at the introductory American history survey. Her delight in the enterprise is contagious. "This fall will be the first time in seven years that I have taught the survey," she wrote to me in the spring of 1979, "so I am busy devising what will be a new course—an attempt to link political and social history. I'm having fun getting the material together (though the copyright law is giving me fits as I try to put together multiple copies of documents for the students to use)." What might she recommend by way of summertime preparation for a middling student who would be taking the survey that fall, I asked, and she responded:

> This course will work best for students who already have a firm grasp on the traditional "story" of American history, but I'm a little hesitant about suggesting that [he] tackle Morison's Oxford History of the U.S., say, on his own, since if he is beginning to incline toward intellectual effort one doesn't want to turn him off. How about giving him Turner's Essay on the Significance of the Frontier ...for a start and suggest he try his hand at making a one page outline of Turner's argument—and ask if he can find any holes in the argument.
>
> If he does that and enjoys it, another useful exercise might be to read Franklin's *Autobiography* asking himself how many of the elements of the American identified by Turner he can find in Franklin.
>
> After this much warm up you could suggest Morgan's *Puritan Dilemma* which will be assigned for class discussion.

Sara Evans, who took an earlier version of Scott's American history survey course as an undergraduate at Duke, captured her approach in the classroom: "Her teaching was absolutely inspired. I still use it as a model, though I have never been able to bring myself to call on students who don't raise their hands with the same authority [that Anne displayed]. We didn't dare come to class unprepared, because she was likely to ask a question based on the reading, look you in the eye, and say, 'Miss Evans?'" Marion Roydhouse, a graduate student at Duke who sat in on Anne Scott's undergraduate course in the social history of American women, described it this way: "It was a riveting experience. I have never seen anyone who could bring out the best in students and who could get discussion going and keep it flowing in the same way that Anne could.

She could manipulate a class and inspire them in a truly magnificent fashion."

Committed to, in Roydhouse's words, "active learning" in the classroom, Scott eschewed lectures in favor of spirited exchange between students and professor, textbooks in favor of primary sources. "She told us the first day," Evans recalled, "that lectures became obsolete with the invention of the printing press." Her style was always to ask questions, teasing ideas out of students, prodding and provoking them until they came to understand, not by her telling them but by their own hard-won comprehension. She taught students to make sense of the past by grappling with the original sources from which history is fashioned—diaries, letters, census data, public records. In her words, "My students and I practice 'doing' history as well as reading about it . . . finding out what history is and how historians go about their work." As Scott's retirement approached, colleagues and former students recognized Scott's exceptional effectiveness as a teacher by endowing the Anne Firor Scott Research Fund in Women's History, which supports Duke undergraduates and graduate students conducting independent research projects in women's history; at the same time, the university established Anne Scott House, a dormitory for undergraduate men and women taking a certificate in women's studies, where the programming encourages discussion of women's issues.

The knack for asking the right questions that inspired Anne Scott's teaching carries over into her scholarship and her professional exchanges as well. By posing such questions—in books, articles, review essays, papers, and comments—Scott has shaped a scholarly agenda well beyond her own work. In so doing, she has laid much of the groundwork for the emergence of American women's history as an important field of scholarly inquiry. As Darlene Clark Hine has observed of her influence, with Scott, as with other academics of her stature, "the questions are more revealing, perhaps, than the answers." The gift for asking questions that recast problems, that push the limits of others' understanding, is by no means confined to historical matters; Anne Scott's talent in this respect is so highly developed that, it is said, when the Scott children were growing up, the family dinner table resembled a seminar meeting.

As for political instincts—knowing which battles to fight, which not to fight, and how to maneuver most effectively—Anne Scott displays a sureness and a skill worthy of the best of the women civic leaders and social reformers about whom she has written. Like them, she understands how to take strong positions, often in behalf of women's causes, without alienating the male colleagues who need to be brought along. One ought not be misled by her collegial style and southern graciousness— here is a political operator of the first order. Honed through her work for the League of Women Voters and her roles as chair of the North Carolina Governor's Commission on the Status of Women, the Duke faculty council, and her own department, she possesses an acute political sense that leads many of us to turn to her for advice on how to handle the stickiest, most complicated professional situations we encounter. It is rumored, as a consequence, that she knows more highly confidential information about more institutions other than her own than anyone else in the profession.

That political skill has paid off especially on behalf of other women. Anne Scott's leadership of the Organization of American Historians' Committee on the Status of Women is a case in point. Formed in 1970, at the height of the contemporary women's movement, the OAH committee gave Scott a platform from which to push for opportunities for women in the historical profession. The committee operated as an informal placement service, putting women in touch with departments newly interested in hiring them. It drafted a code, subsequently adopted by the organization and circulated to history departments, which spelled out guidelines for the fair treatment of women in admission to graduate school, grants, awarding of degrees, and faculty employment. Within the OAH, the committee worked for equitable representation of women in appointive and elective offices, committee assignments, and convention panels. Simple objectives, one might think in retrospect, but they were not easily accomplished. "I was shocked to hear the list of new editors [of the *Journal of American History*] announced," Scott wrote to a fellow committee member in the spring of 1971. "I had thought we'd made enough dent so they wouldn't *think* of not including a woman, and was only wondering who she would be!" Although progress came slowly, the changes were unmistakable, as women began to show up more often on convention panels and committees. Scott herself won election to the OAH executive board in 1972 (and, years later, the OAH presidency), a visible symbol that women's hopes for real inclusiveness might someday be realized.

As for seizing opportunities and running with them, Anne Scott has been doing that all of her professional life. It is hard to imagine what path her career might have taken had she not had an instinct for operating that way and a healthy dose of buoyancy and resilience. She grew up professionally in a world without the financial, emotional, and peer group support that so many of us depend on today. There were many obstacles and diversions. In the ten years between her general examinations at Harvard and the completion of her dissertation, three children came; that's very nice, her mentor, Oscar Handlin, replied in response to each birth announcement, but where is the next chapter? It was a world in which, as Anne Scott has written in her "Historian's Odyssey," she for many years saw her work "as something to be picked up and laid down as the family needs and [her husband] Andrew's career dictated."

That meant that it took a special canniness to recognize and take advantage of her own opportunities. Her first teaching job, at Haverford College in 1957-58, is a case in point. She tells the story this way:

Coming out of the library on a beautiful spring day, I met one of Haverford's two historians who said that he was about to take a leave and wondered if I could suggest some young man who might like a one-year appointment in American history. I agreed to think about the question and started home. As I walked across the campus it suddenly came to me: here was a Job. I turned back and intercepted my friend: "Tom, why not me?" He looked surprised, but thoughtful: after all he was a committed Quaker and Quakers have long been given to treating men and women equally. He agreed to consult the acting-president (who was, fortunately, a sailing companion of my husband's) and that is how I became a lecturer in history. My career as a historian had begun.

This ability to recognize and seize opportunities, along with the pragmatic philosophy that getting your foot in the door and doing a good job might well bring other opportunities, explains much of what Anne Scott has been able to accomplish. Add to it what she once described as a "general characterological disposition never to say No to a new opportunity," along with great good judgment and a gift for getting things done, and one begins to understand the profusion of opportunities and responsibilities that have come her way. These have included executive board memberships and subsequent presidencies of both the Organization of American Historians and the Southern Historical Association; memberships on advisory councils of numerous institutions, among them the Danforth Foundation and the Radcliffe (later the Bunting) Institute; memberships on many boards, including the Carnegie Corporation of New York, the National Humanities Center, and the Woodrow Wilson International Center for Scholars; appointment as a Phi Beta Kappa Visiting Scholar; and visiting professorships at the University of Washington, Johns Hopkins, Stanford, Marquette, Radcliffe, Harvard, and Universität Bonn. There have also been offers of deanships and presidencies, opportunities declined to give priority to family and to scholarship.

These many opportunities might overwhelm, but in Anne Scott's case, they reinforce each other, to excellent effect. That is true, in part, because of her unusual energy and talent for juggling. "Since you saw me departing for the train," she wrote me, "I have (1) met with a group average age 75 at Mystic . . . , (2) gotten some serious work done at the

Schlesinger, (3) joined a bit in the planning for the Schlesinger anniversary celebration ... , (4) listened to the complaints of a fistful of ... fellows ... , (5) taken part in a disastrous conference ... , (6) spent 22 days in Nova Scotia."

Anne Scott also displays an unusual—one might go so far as to call it single-minded—ability to focus on the task at hand. To a prospective holiday guest, she wrote, "Do bring something you need to read or work on, because—alas—we both have a considerable list of To Do Over Vacation"; once the visit was done, she penned, "Glad to hear that all the work you were forced to do in this concentration camp paid off. Someday we'll be less driven—I hope." Of a colleague who urged her to fly to New York for a dinner marking the release of a major report by a foundation where she was a trustee, she observed, with some exasperation, "I wonder what he thinks we *do* in universities?" This ability to focus on the work that needs to be done, reinforced by remarkable self-discipline and a long-standing distaste for self-indulgence, sometimes makes Anne Scott appear austere. Friends with a taste for the romantic once coached Andrew Scott in planning a special dinner to celebrate an important wedding anniversary. The next day, they were dismayed to discover that she had turned down his invitation. With their sabbatical year drawing to a close, she had insisted instead on spending the evening at the computer.

Anne Scott's unusual relationship with younger scholars deserves special comment. Particularly (but by no means exclusively) for younger women, Anne Scott's very presence in the profession has provided a powerful message about future possibilities. Here was a widely respected senior woman of accomplishment, influence, and standing, a rarity in the 1960s and 1970s, not yet common even in the 1980s. She had succeeded in putting everything together—marriage, family, civic activism, career. She showed her women students that they, too, could become historians without treading, in Marion Roydhouse's words, "a straight and narrow line of focus on professionalism at the expense of one's private life." She gave younger women scholars reason to be hopeful about their place in the profession. Linda Kerber felt that encouragement in an unexpected way. The occasion was a limousine ride to the airport at the conclusion of an OAH convention in the early 1970s. Finishing a one-year teaching appointment without the prospect of another position, Kerber was feeling particularly beleaguered and alone, "very aware of being a young woman in a men's profession." There, in front of her in the car, was a woman she did not know who was talking easily and confidently about professional matters to the men with whom she was riding. To Kerber, the scene was "inspiriting"—the charm and authority the woman exuded were "wonderful to observe." In that simple limousine ride, Anne Scott provided the rare example of a woman dealing comfortably with men as colleagues—a mode of relating professionally that Kerber had never before seen.

Even more significant than Anne Scott's influence as a role model is her exceptional generosity in nurturing younger scholars. As she herself put it in "A Historian's Odyssey," "It is hard to overestimate the importance of encouragement to anyone embarking uncertainly upon a new terrain." Ask those younger scholars embarking on the new terrain of American women's history with Anne Scott's encouragement, and you hear the same refrain: "Anne Scott put more energy into me than any of my teachers did"; "She takes graduate students from institutions not her own in hand, helps them out, sees them through"; "I consider her to be my intellectual and professional mother." The point is not simply that Scott played a critical role in helping younger scholars establish themselves as professionals but that she made it possible, in Suzanne Lebsock's words, "for us to engage in discovery in a risky new area in which we were passionately interested, to participate in the creation of a field, and to imagine that scholarship and teaching and the place of women in the world would be better for our efforts." The personal experiences of some of the contributors to this anthology illustrate the point.

Anne Scott has a striking habit of reaching out to, and promoting the careers of, younger scholars who are not formally her students. She discovers them by evaluating their fellowship applications, reading their work, and meeting them at conferences. She goes out of her way to help scholars of promise develop professionally, offering advice, opening doors, sharing opportunities that come her way, making their work visible to others. Suzanne Lebsock described the phenomenon: "She carried on something like an underground graduate program across long distances, identifying people with talent, reading dissertations, sitting on fellowship committees, contacting publishers, writing letters, putting one scholar in touch with another." As a result, she not only has made a significant difference in the careers of individuals but also has had a real impact on the growth of American women's history as a scholarly field.

Lebsock herself first met Anne Scott at a Southern Historical Association convention in the mid-1970s, while she was still a graduate student at the University of Virginia. Scott had learned about Lebsock's work in the course of reviewing women's studies dissertation fellowship proposals for the Woodrow Wilson National Fellowship Foundation, and she made a point of seeking Lebsock out. "I don't remember exactly what happened after that initial meeting," Lebsock wrote. "What I do remember is an extraordinary rush from having been recognized by her—I thought of Anne as a sort of fairy godmother who appeared from the clouds and

bibbity-bobbity turned me into a legitimate historian." As Lebsock pursued her research at Duke and the University of North Carolina, Scott
helped her find places to stay, invited her to talk to one of her classes,
and introduced her to other scholars working in women's history—"all the
while making me feel as though I was doing her a favor." Along with the
practical assistance went regular advice—when to stop doing research
and start writing, how to develop most effectively as a professional
scholar. As Lebsock matured professionally, the intensity of the advice
diminished; as she put it, "Anne has a great knack for making transitions
from patronage to friendship." But at crucial moments, Scott provided
essential assistance: reading and criticizing drafts, writing letters of
recommendation for fellowships, and, with Lebsock's tenure deadline
looming, putting her in touch with the publisher W. W. Norton, which
resulted in a contract on her unfinished manuscript that "made all the
difference."

Ellen DuBois first met Anne Scott when they both happened to be
invited to participate in a radio show on women's history in Chicago.
DuBois was a graduate student at Northwestern; Scott had just published *The Southern Lady*. Interested immediately in DuBois's work,
Scott urged her to send chapters of the dissertation. Before long, Scott
was functioning, in effect, as the codirector of DuBois's thesis. For DuBois,
as for others working in the new field of American women's history, Anne
Scott "provided just enough of that legitimating authority" to make them
believe that what they were doing was historically significant. Her relationship with them was in some ways that of student as well as teacher.
She had a "genuine scholarly hunger," DuBois said, and she was as
anxious to learn from them what she did not know as to teach them what
she knew. Scott's openness and graciousness about younger people, her
"ability to welcome, connect to, and respond to the next generation,"
struck DuBois as "extremely important and very rare."

For Deborah White, the first—and most crucial—connection to Anne
Scott came through the mail, in one of the letters of encouragement that
Scott frequently sends to younger scholars whose work she has read and
admires. The letter came at a critical moment. As White tells the story, at
first she thought the envelope from North Carolina must hold another
letter rejecting something she had submitted for publication. She had
gotten so many of them that she put off opening it. "I was really quite
discouraged about my career as a historian," she said; "I had had incredible difficulty getting the dissertation accepted for the Ph.D., I was
commuting to the University of Wisconsin–Milwaukee from Chicago, and
was facing tenure in a year and a half with as yet no book contract and no
articles." Walking across campus, she finally read the letter, not bothering

to look to see who it was from. "I was stopped dead in my tracks by its comments. It praised my dissertation, and told me to keep up the good work." When she got to the end, she discovered that the letter was from Anne Scott. "I had had no previous contact with Anne and this was so out of the blue. Believe me, it was the first glimmer of hope in a long time and I truly clicked my heels. I was on cloud nine for-a couple of days and faced the fifth rework of the dissertation with renewed confidence." A few months later, White heard from W. W. Norton, whom Scott had encouraged to look at the manuscript. Shortly thereafter, White had a book contract. "I had never met Anne," White marveled, "did not meet her for another year and a half. She went to bat for me even though she did not know me and had never met me."

For Linda Kerber, Anne Scott's sponsorship came through comments on the manuscript and ultimately a quotation for the dust jacket of her new book, *Women of the Republic.* Kerber's publisher had looked for senior scholars who could help launch the book. It was not directly in Scott's field, and Kerber had not been her student; it would have been easy to decline to help. Instead, Scott read the manuscript, offered Kerber good advice, and wrote a comment for publicity purposes. Kerber felt that she had been "adopted" by an important person who was helping present her to the scholarly world. The sponsorship, Kerber said, reflected "pure generosity of spirit."

Nancy Hewitt, whom Anne Scott discovered when she evaluated her dissertation for a university press, made a similar point:

more than her suggestions on writing and analysis, it was her willingness to open doors, to open the field, and always to keep an open mind that provided me an entree to the profession that almost no one else could have, and certainly no one else did. To me she has been both a senior mentor and a scholar among equals, both maternal and collegial, both teacher and student—it's that ability to use her status and experience to assist junior scholars while treating their ideas and interpretations as equally valid and interesting as her own that makes Anne so special.

Anne Scott's generosity has manifested itself as well in an eagerness to share professional opportunities and to put younger scholars forward to benefit from a limelight that might otherwise have been exclusively hers. My own experience, after being recruited by Scott as the junior member of the OAH Committee on the Status of Women, was to find myself appointed as the chair of the committee two years later, when Scott won election to the OAH executive board—a move startling in light of the seniority of the other committee members but accomplished nevertheless because of Anne Scott's sponsorship. Nancy Hewitt has often been the beneficiary of invitations to give lectures or participate in special projects where Scott—the first choice—recommended her instead. (The people who invited her "clearly knew almost nothing about me or my work," Hewitt said, "but . . . were willing to have me at Anne's recommendation.")

William Chafe's experience provides another case in point. In the mid-1970s, when Anne Scott was invited to give the keynote address at a National Archives conference on women's history, she proposed instead that she and Chafe, a junior colleague at Duke, have a public dialogue about what they wished they knew about women's history. To Chafe, that was "a marvelous example of generosity and inclusiveness" that showed Scott's "willingness to share her own status and prestige." Suzanne Lebsock remembered an occasion when she heard Anne Scott speak to the Southern Association of Women Historians: "During the question-and-answer period, someone asked her a question, which she quickly threw to me. . . . This seems very Anne-like—the incorporation of others, the deferring to another person with knowledge, the highlighting of younger people—in short, making a dialogue into a roundtable." In Anne Scott's presidential address to the Southern Historical Association in 1989, she began, characteristically, by naming younger scholars whose dissertations and published work had provided the "bricks" from which she had built the account she was about to give of black women's voluntary associations.

To be sure, one ought not to romanticize mentorship beyond its due. Mentoring sometimes spilled over into mothering, with admonitions to speak up, cut one's hair, eat properly, and dress warmly—all of which, depending on one's point of view, could be appealing or overbearing. One such exchange with Nancy Hewitt ended with Scott laughing and confessing, "I know, I know, it's not my job, but I can't help worrying about you—I can see you and your mother can't." Academic mothering could also foster sibling rivalry or daughterly disappointment. Favored daughters were sometimes dismayed to find the warmly supportive mentor assessing them with a coolly professional eye. Sometimes Scott's own students thought that scholars from other institutions had the best of the mentorship.

These sensitivities might describe any relationship between graduate student and adviser, beginning and senior scholar. In American women's history in the 1970s and early 1980s, however, there were reasons for them to be especially acute. For some time, as the field developed, senior scholars whose reach extended beyond their own institutions were extremely rare. Anne Scott, together with Gerda Lerner, played an unusually important role. (Witness the establishment in 1991 of the

Lerner-Scott Prize in U.S. Women's History, awarded annually by the Organization of American Historians for the best doctoral dissertation in that field.) Younger scholars invested a great deal in their approval, probably more than might otherwise have been the case. That was true not only because of the paucity of senior scholars in the field but also because American women's history itself was not yet widely perceived to be a legitimate, serious area of scholarly inquiry. Those circumstances undoubtedly increased the feeling of younger scholars that their careers were at risk, making them especially sensitive to affirmation from established figures. In this context, Anne Scott forged remarkably positive relationships.

The balance between maternalism and camaraderie, candid criticism and collegiality is always difficult to strike. Here, too, we can learn much from Anne Scott. She makes no secret when she believes work suffers from irredeemable flaws of spotty research or sloppy argument. Yet she is deeply concerned not to offend. To Nancy Hewitt, along with pages of detailed, handwritten comments on the draft of an article, she attached a note: "Reading this [my comments] over, I suspect it was an effort to clarify my own thinking as much as to suggest things to you—but it will be interesting to talk to you about all these things." She offered Hewitt the chance to make the same sort of assessment of essays she was working on, "if you are willing!" "I won't write you any more forlorn letters to know if I've alienated people whose work I've had occasion to read," Scott wrote to me after confiding her fears about not having heard from someone whose manuscript she had critiqued. "I very shortly got a long and friendly letter from her. I guess I'm just unduly worried about these things."

The scholars represented in this volume, like many others, have benefited immeasurably from Anne Scott's gift for teaching, supporting, and engaging the next generation. We are grateful for her eagerness to hear us, her generosity in giving us space of our own, her willingness to entertain ideas and support scholarly efforts that may criticize, take issue with, or supersede her own work. We owe her a particular debt for her role in legitimating a new field of scholarly inquiry and for enabling us to pursue intellectual discovery in new, uncharted territory. Jacquelyn Hall speaks aptly for all of us in concluding,

> One of the things I admire most about Anne is that as she approached retirement, a time when people often grow more querulous about the younger generation and less open to new people and experiences, she moved in just the opposite direction. She might have reacted defensively when women's history took off and "revi-

sionism" inevitably began. Instead, she has taken great pride in the accomplishments of those who came after. What she seems to want from us is not deference but good work and friendship. And because of that she has become an ever more highly respected and warmly regarded figure in the women's community. Perhaps also as a result, she seems not to have aged at all; she has lost none of her optimism or her amazing energy.

We applaud this remarkable woman for all she has done to make invisible women visible.

Contributors

MARI JO BUHLE is a professor of history and American civilization at Brown University. She is the author of *Women and American Socialism* and the coeditor (with Paul Buhle and Dan Georgakas) of the *Encyclopedia of the American Left*.

WILLIAM H. CHAFE, Alice Mary Baldwin Professor of History at Duke University, is author of *Civilities and Civil Rights, Unfinished Journey,* and *Paradox of Change: Women in Twentieth Century America*. He is currently completing work on *Never Stop Running: Allard Lowenstein and the American Political Tradition*.

ELLEN CAROL DuBOIS is a professor of history at the University of California, Los Angeles. She is the author of *Feminism and Suffrage* and the coeditor (with Vicki Ruiz) of *Unequal Sisters*. A new edition of her edited volume, *Elizabeth Cady Stanton-Susan B. Anthony: A Reader* is now in press as well as a new edition of Stanton's *Eighty Years and More,* with an introduction by DuBois.

SARA M. EVANS is a professor of history at the University of Minnesota. She is the author of *Personal Politics* and *Born for Liberty: A History of Women in America,* the coauthor (with Harry Boyte) of *Free Spaces: Sources of Democratic Change in America,* and the coauthor (with Barbara Nelson) of *Wage Justice: Comparable Worth and the Paradox of Technocratic Reform*.

MARY E. FREDERICKSON is an associate professor of history at Miami University. She has coedited (with Joyce Kornbluh) *Sisterhood and Solidarity: Workers' Education for Women* and has authored the forthcoming book, *A Place to Speak Our Minds: The Southern School for Women Workers in Industry*.

JACQUELYN DOWD HALL is the Julia Cherry Spruill Professor of History at the University of North Carolina-Chapel Hill. She is the author of *Revolt against Chivalry,* which is forthcoming in a new edition, and coauthor (with Robert Korstad, James Leloudis, LuAnn Jones, Mary Murphy, and Christopher B. Daly) of *Like a Family.* She is currently working on class and sex in the turn-of-the-century South.

NANCY A. HEWITT, a professor of history at Duke University, is the author of *Women's Activism and Social Change* and the editor of *Women, Families, and Communities: Readings in American History.* She is currently completing a study of work and politics among Anglo, African-American, and Latin women in Tampa, Florida, 1885–1945.

DARLENE CLARK HINE is the John A. Hannah Professor of History at Michigan State University. She is the author of *Black Victory* and *Black Women in White* and the coeditor (with Thomas Holt) of *The State of Afro-American History: Past, Present and Future.* Recently, she has edited the two-volume *Black Women in America: An Historical Encyclopedia.*

DOLORES JANIEWSKI is a professor of history at the Victoria University of Wellington. She is the author of *Sisterhood Denied: Race, Class and Gender in a New South Community* and is currently pursuing a study of gender and race in North Carolina, 1865–1930.

LINDA K. KERBER is the May Brodbeck Professor in the Liberal Arts and a professor of history at the University of Iowa. She is the author of *Federalists in Dissent* and *Women in the Republic* and co-editor (with Jane DeHart) of *Women's America: Refocusing the Past.* She is at work on a book entitled *Paradoxes of Women's Citizenship.*

SUZANNE LEBSOCK is a professor of history at the University of North Carolina–Chapel Hill. The author of *The Free Women of Petersburg* and *"A Share of Honour": Virginia Women, 1600–1945,* she is currently working on an 1895 Virginia murder case.

NANCY WEISS MALKIEL is a professor of history and dean of the college at Princeton University. She is the author (as Nancy J. Weiss) of *Whitney M. Young, Jr., and the Struggle for Civil Rights* and *Farewell to the Party of Lincoln: Black Politics in the Age of FDR.*

MARION W. ROYDHOUSE is an associate professor of history and director of the College Studies Program at Philadelphia College of Textiles and Science. She has written articles on workers' education and industrialization in the South and is author of a forthcoming book on women and political reform in North Carolina.

DEBORAH GRAY WHITE, an associate professor of history at Rutgers University, is the author of *Ar'n't I a Woman? Female Slaves in the*

Plantation South and the forthcoming *Too Heavy a Load: Race, Class and Gender in Black Women's Associational Activities, 1896-1980.*

LEEANN WHITES is an assistant professor of history at the University of Missouri-Columbia. She is the author of the forthcoming book *Gender and the Origin of the New South: Augusta, Georgia 1860-1900.*

Index

Abolitionism: as arena where women challenged male leadership, 128
Adams, John, 355, 356
Addams, Jane, 2, 11, 12, 104, 105, 107, 366, 367
Addison, Joseph, 356
Affirmative Action, 235
African-American Beauty Culture Association, 209
African Americans: attitudes toward, in Progressive Era, 3, 106–7; gender politics among, 6, 207–9, 250–57; and suffrage movement, 8–9, 17, 65–66, 69, 75, 80–82, 208; and definitions of citizenship, 22, 24; men perceived as sexually dangerous, 46, 51, 176; disfranchisement of, 66–67, 200, 251; and identity politics, 124, 235; and segregation of labor movement, 168, 175; and Great Migration, 172, 223; as voters, 199–201, 204, 213–14; economic dislocation after World War I, 223; discriminated against in industrial jobs, 274; educational opportunities of, 350, 353, 363, 366–67; literacy rates among, 358. *See also* African American women; Freedmen; Interracial Cooperation; Race; Racism
African American women: and "womanism," 5, 81, 143, 224–25, 231, 233, 235; limits of cross-class unity among, 6, 258–64; and segregation of YWCAs, 8, 275–77, 290; as victims of racism and sexism, 27, 56, 200, 247; and suffrage movement, 80–82; and Great Migration, 172, 228; and work, 172–73, 227–29, 304; and the "New Woman," 209; and domestic service, 227, 274, 304; and sexual exploitation, 255, 258–59; criticism and resentment of as leaders, 257, 262–63; and dynamics of dissemblance, 298, 308; educational opportunities of, 350, 353, 366–67. *See also* African Americans; Interracial Cooperation; Race; Racism
—activism among, 142–43, 244, 296, 297, 367; in Detroit, 4–5, 223–36; and inseparability of race, class, and gender issues, 5–6, 168, 249–50; in Tampa, 205, 208–9, 215–16; through the National Association of Colored Women (NACW), 247–64; and demand for chastity, 258–60. *See also* Colored Methodist Episcopal Church (CME); Housewives' League of Detroit; National Association of Colored Women (NACW)
—as voters: images of, 76–77, 199, 200, 201, 205, 209; voter registration among, 83–87, 204
—stereotypes about: as slaves, 46; as promiscuous, 77, 178; combated by club women, 226, 249, 258–60; held by black men, 254–55, 257
African Methodist Episcopal (AME) Church, 299, 303
African Methodist Episcopal Zion (AME Zion) Church, 299, 303
Afro-Cubans, 202, 204, 215. *See also* Latins; Latin women
Agricultural Adjustment Act (AAA), 112
Alabama, 169, 273, 277, 301, 305, 306
Alabama Polytechnic Institute for Girls, 169
Albury, Minnie, 211
Alston, Inez, 209

American Academy for the Advancement of
Science, 328
American Anthropological Association, 328
American Anthropologist, 328
American Federation of Labor (AFL): considered apolitical and bureaucratic,
166–67, 174–75, 177; exclusionary mem-
bership policies of, 176; and child labor
laws, 178; supported Tampa cigar-
workers' strike, 214
American Indians. *See* Native Americans
American Revolution: Alice Mary Baldwin's
study of, 10, 349, 368; effects on gar-
ment industry, 149; and education for
women, 352, 357–59
American Social Science Association, 328
American Woman Suffrage Association, 20,
23. *See also* National American Woman
Suffrage Association (NAWSA)
Anatomy of Melancholy (Burton), 356
Anderson, Mary, 111
Andrew, James O., 302
Anglo Saxon Leagues, 89
Anthony, Susan B., 75, 328, 329; direct-
action voting by, 25, 31; arrested and
tried for violation of Enforcement Act,
31–32; on Reconstruction amendments,
33, 34
Anthony Amendment. *See* Nineteenth
Amendment
Anthropological Association of Washington,
328
Antilynching campaigns. *See* Lynching
Antioch College, 353
Anti-Semitism, 110, 130
Antisuffragism: and white supremacy, 8, 17,
54–55, 63–90; women as antisuffragists,
16; and southern gender politics, 54–55;
and states' rights, 54, 73; in Virginia,
64–90; and perceptions of African
American women, 76–77; and women's
public roles, 122–23
Antiunionism: in Tampa, 204; of southern
communities, 244, 271
*Appeal in Favor of That Class of Ameri-
cans Called Africans, An* (Child), 364
Arendt, Hannah, 119, 127, 129, 132, 371
Aristotle, 119
Armwood, Blanche. *See* Beatty, Blanche
Armwood

Arthur, Timothy Shay, 148, 149
Ashby, Irene M., 178–79
Asheville, North Carolina, 275, 276, 277
Ashland, Kentucky, 278
Asians: prejudice against, 309
Association for the Advancement of Women,
325, 328
Association of Collegiate Alumnae, 368
Association of Southern Women for the
Prevention of Lynching (ASWPL), 107,
316
Atlanta, Georgia, 5, 9, 166–86, 250, 256,
259, 276, 277, 283, 300, 303, 306, 363
Atlanta Constitution, 172
Atlanta Federation of Trades (AFT), 171,
174, 178, 184
Atlanta University, 353
Augusta, Georgia, 309, 310
Austen, Jane, 361

Bachofen, Johann Jakob, 329
Bahnson, Mrs. M., 286
Baker, Paula, 102–3, 104–5, 109, 127
Baldwin, Alice Mary, 345–47, 371, 372,
381; career and scholarship of, 10–11,
349–50; and "Two Sisters of Old Boston,"
354–57; and study of colonial women's
reading, 356–57; educational background
of, 367–69; became dean of women at
Trinity College (later dean of the
Woman's College of Duke University),
369–70
Baldwin School, 368
Baltimore, Maryland, 131, 149, 224, 235
Bank of the United States, 159
Baptists, 297
Barnard College, 353, 366, 367
Barnett, Ida B. Wells, 107, 225, 248, 249,
254, 262
Barrett, Janie Porter, 11, 88, 89
Bartow County, Georgia, 46, 47
Basch, Norma, 34
Bates College, 367
Beard, Mary Ritter, 345, 371
Beasley, Mary L., 231
Beatty, Blanche Armwood, 208, 209, 216
Beecher, Catharine, 365
Bender, Thomas, 289
Bennett, Belle, 309–10
Bethlehem Houses (Detroit), 309, 311

Bethune, Mary McLeod, 367
Bethune-Cookman College, 367
Bingham, John, 27
Birmingham, Alabama, 169, 248
Blackmore, Richard, 355
Blacks. *See* African Americans
Board of Indian Commissioners, 336
Board of Trade (Tampa), 204
Boas, Franz, 338
Bolita, 201, 202, 203, 216
Booker T. Washington Trade Association, 227, 230
Boone, Mamie C., 230
Boston, Massachusetts, 149, 154, 225, 248, 249, 330, 331, 354, 355, 360
Boston Athenaeum, 364
Boston Fragment Society, 154
Boston Magazine, 361
Boston Needle Woman's Friend Society, 160, 161
Boycotts, 5, 207, 224, 235. *See also* Economic nationalism
Boydton, Virginia, 69
Boyte, Harry, 130
Bradford, Sarah, 363-64
Bradwell, Myra, 30. *See also Bradwell* case
Bradwell case, 30-32, 33
Brooklyn Female Academy, 332
Brookwood Labor School, 280
Brotherhood of Telegraphers, 170
Brown, Charlotte Hawkins, 261, 308
Brown, Elsa Barkley, 5, 81, 224
Brown, Mary Olney, 24, 25
Browning, Elizabeth Barrett, 365
Bryan, William Jennings, 210
Bryn Mawr College, 278, 353, 366, 368
Bryn Mawr Summer School for Women Workers in Industry, 280, 287
Bruce, Josephine, 249
Buckley, Maria L., 146, 147, 151, 157
BUILD (Baltimore), 131
Bunting Institute (formerly Radcliffe Institute), 385
Buntline, Ned (Edward Zen Carroll Judson), 147
Burdett, Charles, 147
Bureau of Indian Affairs, 327, 328
Burnham, Carrie, 23
Burroughs, Nannie, 308
Burton, Robert, 356

Business and Professional Women's Club, 206, 288
Bustamente, Candida, 212, 213
Butler, Benjamin, 26, 27
Butler Report. *See* Minority Report

Calahan, Pat, 184
Calanthe, Tennessee, 311
California, 301, 309
Campbell, Helen S., 162
Campbell, Leanna, 230
Campbell, Thomas, 230
Capetillo, Luisa, 207, 217
Capitalism: sharpened division between public and private spheres, 121; growth in nineteenth century, 127; impact of on women, 142, 148, 153, 162; and women's public activism, 167-68. *See also* Market economy
Carey, Mathew, 154-57
Carnegie Corporation of New York, 385
Carner, Lucy, 278, 281
Carolina Playmakers, 287
Caroline County, Virginia, 86
Carpenter, Matthew, 30
Cartersville, Georgia, 44
Cartter, Judge, 29
Catherine the Great, 362
Catt, Carrie Chapman, 73, 75
Cavanagh, Jerome P., 235
Centro Asturiano (Tampa), 212, 215
Chambers, Gertrude, 208, 209, 216
Charleston, South Carolina, 248, 309
Charlotte, North Carolina, 275, 277, 282, 286
Charlotte: A Tale of Truth (Rowson), 356
Charlottesville, Virginia, 354
Chase, W. Calvin, 255
Chicago, Illinois, 30, 168, 224, 225, 228, 235, 248, 311, 388
Chicago Woman's Club, 251
Child, Lydia Maria, 329, 362, 364-65
Child labor, 178
Children: confined to private sphere, 119
Children's Bureau, 104
Children's Code Commission (Georgia), 179
Children's Home (Tampa), 210, 211, 212, 216

Chodorow, Nancy, 120
Christian Index, The, 298
Church, Mary. *See* Terrell, Mary Church
Cigar industry, 5, 201, 202
Cigar Makers International Union, 212, 214
Cigar Manufacturers' Association (Tampa),
    204
Cigarworkers, 5, 201, 206, 210, 211; union
    activity among, 201, 202, 203, 206
Citizens Suffrage Association of Philadel-
    phia, 23
Civil rights movement: as a model of politi-
    cal action, 123–24; supplanted volun-
    tary associations, 235
Civil society: as private, nondomestic arena,
    127, 129; and voluntary associations,
    128, 131
Civil War: and women's public roles, 2, 41,
    44; and race attitudes, 7; as defining
    factor in southern social and political
    scene, 16; and decline of southern patri-
    archy and "protection," 43–44, 45–46,
    48; effects on women's educational
    opportunities, 366
Clara Frye Hospital (Tampa), 208
Claramunt, Teresa, 205
Clark, Adèle, 68, 79, 86, 88, 89
Clarke, Mary Pollard, 79
Clarksville, Tennessee, 311
Class: and women's activism, 4, 103, 106–7;
    and Progressive Era historiography, 102,
    106–8, 114; divisions among African
    Americans, 258–64. *See also* Poverty;
    Social mobility; Working classes;
    Working-class women
Cleveland, Ohio, 225, 228, 235
Clifton Forge, Virginia, 86
Cold War: and expansion of bureaucratic
    state, 123
Coleman, Mattie, 300, 302, 304, 310–11,
    317
Colman, Abigail, 355–56
Colman, Benjamin, 355
Colman, Jane. *See* Terrell, Jane Colman
Colored Merchant Association Stores
    (Harlem), 230
Colored Methodist Episcopal Church (CME),
    296–317; founded, 298; theological and
    organizational ties to Methodist Episco-
    pal Church, South (ME), 298–99; male

dominance within, 299, 302, 314; demo-
    graphics of membership, 303–4; expan-
    sion of, 305. *See also* Methodist
    Episcopal Church, South (ME)
— women's missionary organizations: and
    interracial cooperation with Methodist
    Episcopal Church, South (ME), 7–8,
    296–317; development of, 300–303;
    activities of, 305–7; transformed agenda
    of ME women, 307–8, 311–14; finan-
    cial dependence on ME women, 314
Colored Women's Clubs of Tampa, 208
Colored Women's League of Washington,
    D.C., 248, 251
Columbia, South Carolina, 301
Columbia University, 366, 368
Columbus, Georgia, 312
Commercial Telegraphers Union of
    America (CTUA), 170, 171, 172, 173,
    174, 185
Commission Government Club (Tampa),
    211
Commission on Interracial Cooperation, 89,
    316, 317
Commons, John R., 166
Communities Organized for Public Service
    (San Antonio), 131
Congress of Industrial Organizations (CIO),
    235, 279, 289
Congreve, William, 356
Connecticut, 358
Consumers League, 109, 110, 111, 112
Consumption: as a form of social activism,
    5, 141, 176–77, 224; and Cold War
    culture, 124; effects of on antebellum
    labor market, 148; as palliative for
    women, 206. *See also* Economic
    nationalism
"Conversations" (Fuller), 365
Convict-lease system, 252, 307
Cooper, Anna Julia, 248, 250, 251, 254,
    261, 366, 367, 371
Copenhaver, Eleanor, 281, 289
Coquette (Foster), 356
Corday, Charlotte, 362
Cornell University, 367
Corrine (Staël), 364
Cosa, Maria, 212
Costigan-Wagner antilynching bill, 316
Cott, Nancy, 104, 108, 224, 345

Cotton States and International Exposition, 175
Coverture: in *Bradwell* case, 30
Cox, Clara, 289
Crisis, The, 72, 80, 226, 230
Cuba, 202, 203, 212
Cubans, 202, 203, 204, 205, 206, 207, 212; labor activism among, 5. *See also* Latins; Latin women
Culberson, Ruth, 288
"Cult of True Womanhood," 121. *See also* Domesticity
Current Topic Study Club (Detroit), 227

Dale, Julia, 370
Dall, Caroline Healey, 329, 365
Danforth Foundation, 385
Danville Register, 84
Davidson, Cathy N., 147
Davis, Paulina Wright, 29
Dawes, Anna, 327
Dawes, Electra, 327
Dawes, Henry L., 327
Dawes Act, 327, 330, 333, 336
Day Nursery Association (Tampa), 210
DeBardeleben, Mary, 310
DeKalb County, Georgia, 42
De La Campa, Mrs. José, 207
Democratic party, 110; and woman suffrage, 54, 85, 200; in Virginia, 66, 67, 71, 85, 86; in Tampa, 206, 210–11; African American women's support for, 254
Demosthenes, 351
Dennie, Alfred, 356
Dent, Theresa, 312
Depression of 1819–20: effects on garment workers, 154
Detroit, Michigan, 4, 25, 143, 223–36
Detroit Association of Colored Women's Clubs, 227
Detroit Study Club, 229
Detroit Welfare Commission, 233
Dewson, Molly, 111
Dial, The, 365
Dickerson, Addie, 260
Dietz, Mary, 121
Difference (Diversity): and women's history, 6; as source of political tensions, 16, 124–25, 244; and rights activism, 19; and need for new theory of public life, 121, 131–32; Tampa as case study of, 200; within African American community, 261. *See also* Identity politics
Dinnerstein, Dorothy, 120
Dinwiddie County, Virginia, 86
Direct-action voting, 23–26, 29, 34. *See also* New Departure
District of Columbia. *See* Washington, D.C.
Dix, Dorothea, 332
Dixie Twin Order Telegraphers Club, 173
Domestic History of the American Revolution (Ellet), 362
Domesticity: instability of, 10, 44, 149, 151, 153, 159, 163, 180; threatened by market economy, 45, 48–49, 50, 53; and threat of intemperance, 48, 49; and suffrage movement, 53; vs. public life, 119, 120–21, 127, 128, 159; and consumer protest, 207; rhetoric of in Indian reform, 327, 333. *See also* Separate spheres
Domestic novels, 142, 147
Domestic service, 227, 274, 275, 304, 316–17
Door of Hope Rescue Home (Tampa), 210
Dorcas societies, 153
Dorr, Rheta Childe, 104
Douglass, Sarah Mapps, 359
Dounveor, Laura, 231
Drumright, E. B., 204, 211
Du Bois, W. E. B., 226, 230, 253, 256
Duke, James B., 369
Duke, Washington, 366, 369
Duke University (formerly Trinity College), 10, 11, 287, 346, 349, 366, 368, 369–70, 382, 383, 384, 388, 390
Durham, North Carolina, 231, 275, 276, 277, 278, 280, 282, 286, 287–88, 366, 368
Dryden, John, 356

Eastman, Elaine Goodale, 331
Economic nationalism, 143, 223–24, 230, 231, 236. *See also* Housewives' League of Detroit
Education: among African Americans, 308–9, 315, 317, 350, 353. *See also* Workers' education
—for women: opposition to, 16, 74–75, 353–54; as domestic reform, 51, 52;

Education for Women (*Continued*)
    ambivalence toward in early Republic,
    352–53, 359–60; expanding oppor-
    tunities in nineteenth and twentieth
    centuries, 353, 362–62, 365–67; sex dis-
    crimination prohibited by Higher Educa-
    tion Act, 353; and American Revolution,
    359; and ambition, 360–62, 364; over-
    view, 371–72. *See also* Women's history —
    intellectual history
El Dorado Club, 203
El Internacional, 203, 204, 206, 207, 212,
    217
Eliot, George, 364, 365
Ellet, Elizabeth, 362
Elshtain, Jean Bethke, 120
Emerson, Mary Moody, 363–64
Emerson, Ralph Waldo, 365
Emory University, 301
Enforcement Act: and woman suffrage
    movement, 25–26, 29, 31, 33; declared
    unconstitutional, 33
Epes, Alabama, 169
Equal Suffrage and the Negro Vote, 78
Equal Suffrage League of Richmond, 67
Equal Suffrage League of Tampa, 210
Equal Suffrage League of Virginia, 62, 66,
    68–69, 70, 71, 72; and white
    supremacy, 67, 75–76, 77–80, 82,
    87–88; supported "Winning Plan," 73;
    and interracial cooperation, 83, 88–89
*Ernest Grey: Or, the Sins of Society, a Tale
    of New York Life* (Maxwell), 150
Essex County, Virginia, 86
Evansville, Indiana, 225

Factory girls: as focus of women's history,
    141, 142
Fall River, Massachusetts, 172
Fargo College, 368
Fauquier, Virginia, 74
Federal Council of Churches, 310
Federal Reserve Board, 106
Federal Trade Commission, 106
Federation of Women's Clubs, 179, 288
Felton, Rebecca Latimer, 6–7, 16; became
    first female senator, 41, 55–57; accepted
    traditional southern gender relations,
    42–43; blamed male greed for loss of
    protection, 43, 45, 48, 50, 53; and

women's need for male protection,
    43–44, 45, 48–54; Civil War experience
    of, 44; and white farm women, 44,
    49–50, 51; blamed freedmen for loss of
    male protection, 45–46, 50–51; assisted
    in husband's political career, 46–47; and
    Woman's Christian Temperance Union
    (WCTU), 47–48, 49; and empowerment
    of white motherhood, 49, 51, 52, 53, 56;
    called for domestic legislation, 49, 51–53;
    use of rape imagery by, 51; racist reform
    agenda of, 52–53, 56; supported woman
    suffrage, 53–55
Felton, William, 42, 44, 46, 47
Female Biography (Knapp), 362
Femininity: in political discourse, 122–23,
    127
Feminism: and labor movement, 5; histori-
    cal perspectives on current debates,
    19–20; vs. womanism, 81; and identity
    politics, 123–24; of African American
    women, 247, 250, 253, 257, 263–64. *See
    also* Feminist theory
Feminist theory: and definitions of public
    and private, 119–26
Few, William Preston, 370
Fifteenth Amendment: and woman suffrage,
    3, 16, 19–34; narrowing interpretations
    of, 33; and southern fears of black voters,
    54, 73
Fisk University, 353
Fitzhugh, George, 43
Fletcher, Alice Cunningham, 9, 245,
    325–40; encounter with Sitting Bull,
    325; found it difficult to reconcile femi-
    nism and Indian reform, 326, 328–29,
    336–37, 339; used kinship metaphors to
    describe her relationships with Native
    Americans, 326, 330–31, 334, 337,
    339–40; supported land allotment, 327,
    328, 332, 334–35; wanted to instill
    "manliness" in Native American men,
    327, 330, 333; work assessed, 338–39;
    questioned cost of progress, 338
Flexner, Eleanor, 15
Florida, 200, 204, 301, 305, 306
Florida United Daughters of the
    Confederacy, 200
Ford Motor Company, 228
Fort Valley, Georgia, 301

Foster, Hannah Webster, 356
Foucault, Michel, 350
Fourteenth Amendment: and woman
    suffrage, 3, 16, 19–34; as first reference
    to sex in Constitution, 20–21, 103;
    contrasted with Bill of Rights, 22;
    narrowing interpretations of, 32, 33; and
    gender segregation of U.S. political
    culture, 103
Francis, Convers, 364
Franklin, Benjamin, 2, 382
Freedman, Estelle, 113
Freedmen: and Fifteenth Amendment, 21,
    33; political rights supported by Enforce-
    ment Act, 25; hostility toward in Recon-
    struction South, 45–46, 50, 51
Freedmen's Bureau, 25
Free love: and woman suffrage movement,
    28–29
Friday Morning Musicale (Tampa), 216
Friends of the Indian, 327, 331
Fries, Virginia, 286
Front Royal, Virginia, 84
Frye, Clara, 208
Fuller, Margaret, 352, 364, 365, 371, 372
Fulton Bag and Cotton Mills, 179, 182, 183,
    184
Fuqua, Christina, 231

Gage, Matilda Joslyn, 328, 330
Gainesville, Georgia, 169, 171
Gandhi, Mohandas Karamchand
    "Mahatma," 2
Gardiner, John Sylvester John, 360
Gardner, Nanette, 25
Garment industry. See Textile industry
Garment workers. See Seamstresses
Garvey, Marcus, 226, 230
Gates, Henry Louis, 350
Gay, E. Jane, 332–34, 335, 338
Gay rights movement, 124
Gender: and segregation of political culture,
    102–3, 114; in language of public life,
    126; and working classes, 141, 147; in-
    equalities depicted in domestic novels,
    151. See also Femininity; Gender
    relations; Gender roles; Masculinity;
    Womanhood
Gender relations: and "stable domesticity,"
    10; among antebellum southern elite,

41–42, 43; ruptured by Civil War, 43;
    in postbellum South, 46–47, 56, 57, 199;
    in working-class families, 180–81. See
    also Gender; Gender roles
Gender roles: among antebellum southern
    elite, 42–43; in 1920 Tampa, 205;
    among African Americans, 232–33,
    250, 256–57; in New South, as basis
    for women's activism, 273, 299; in
    rhetoric of Indian reform, 327. See also
    Gender; Gender relations
General Assembly of Virginia: and woman
    suffrage, 66, 70, 72, 73, 74, 78, 80;
    ratifies Nineteenth Amendment in 1952,
    73
Gentle Breadwinners (Owen), 162
Georgia, 6, 16, 41, 169, 273, 277, 301, 309
Georgia Federation of Labor, 174, 178
Giddings, Paula, 106
Gilbert, Katherine, 370
Gilligan, Carol, 120
Gilman, Charlotte Perkins, 179, 371
Gilmore, William, 358
Givens, Annie, 210, 211
Gleaner, The (Murray), 361
Glenn, Mrs. V. K., 305, 306
Goddard, Martha, 330
Golden, John, 184
Goldsboro, North Carolina, 275
Gompers, Samuel, 175, 177, 178
Goode, Nannie, 69
Gordon, Lincoln, 232
Grady, Henry, 274
Gragg, Rosa L. Slade, 225, 227, 233
Grannis, Elizabeth, 34
Grant, Ulysses S., 31
Great Depression, 111, 143, 274; and Afri-
    can Americans, 5, 143, 223, 224, 227,
    231; effects on social activism, 288, 316
Great Migration, 172, 175; consequences of,
    for African Americans, 223; and growth
    of women's voluntary associations, 227;
    and women, 228
Greeley, Horace, 31
Greene, Z. D., 207–8
Greensboro, North Carolina, 275, 277
Grey, Lady Jane, 362

Habermas, Jürgen, 127
Hale, Sarah Josepha, 362

Haley, James, 256
Hamilton, Alexander, 361
Hampton, Virginia, 80
Hampton Institute, 81, 330, 331, 332, 335, 336
Handlin, Oscar, 384
Harding, Warren, 108
Hardwick, Thomas, 55, 56
Harlem, 224, 230, 235
Harper, Frances Ellen Watkins, 250
Harriet Tubman Club, 248
Harriman, Mary Rumsey, 109
Harvard University, 327, 355, 364, 372, 384, 385
Haskin, Estelle, 313, 314, 316
Haverford College, 385
Haygood, Atticus, 301
Haygood, Laura Askew, 300–301
Hays, Sam, 101
Hegel, Georg Wilhelm Friedrich, 119
Helm, Lucinda, 302
Helping Hand Day Nursery (Tampa), 209, 215
Hemsley, Ethel L., 230
Henry, Patrick, 68
Herschel, Caroline, 365
Hickok, Lorena, 111
Higginbotham, Evelyn Brooks, 297
Higginson, Thomas Wentworth, 349
High Point, North Carolina, 277
Higher Education Act of 1972, 353
Highlander Folk School, 280
Hill, Peter, 25
Hillsborough County Federation of Women's Clubs, 216
Hine, Lewis, 183
History of the Condition of Women in Various Ages and Conditions (Child), 362
Hobomok: A Tale of Early Times (Child), 329, 364
Hofstadter, Richard, 101, 360
Hollinger, David, 350
Holsey, Albon L., 230
Holsey, L. H., 301
Holt, Saxon W., 70
Home Rule Club, 211
Hooker, Isabella Beecher, 27, 29
Hope, John, 256
Hope, Lugenia Burns, 308
Hopkins, Harry, 111

Hopkins, Sarah Winnemucca, 331
Horace, 355
Horton, George Moses, 350
House, Annie, 208, 209
"Houses of industry," 153
Housewives' League of Detroit, 4–5, 143, 223–36; activities of, 230–35; impact of, 235–36
Houston, Nora, 88
Howard University, 353, 362
Hull House, 104
Hume, David, 363
Hunter, Jane Edna, 225
Hunton, Addie, 250, 255, 257, 258
Huntsville, Missouri, 230
Hutchinson, Anne, 351

Idaho, 332
Identity politics: and women's activism, 16; and civil rights movement, 124, 125; in voluntary associations, 128, 130, 131
Illinois, 12, 301
Immigrants: as voters, 63, 199, 204; and progressive reform, 106, 128; in needle trades, 160–61; as labor force, 175, 202–3; consumer activism among, 224. See also Afro-Cubans; Cubans; Italians; Latins; Latin women; Nativism; Spaniards
Incidents in the Life of a Slave Girl (Jacobs), 329, 358
Indianapolis, Indiana, 249
Indian reform, 245, 325, 326, 327, 333. See also Native Americans
"Indian Woman and Her Problems, The" (Fletcher), 337
Industrial Areas Foundation (IAF), 131
Industrial Home School for Girls, 88
Intellectual history: traditional paradigms of, 350–51; of women, 351
"Intelligent womanhood," 142, 200, 201
International Council of Women, 328, 329, 336
International Order of the King's Daughters and Sons, 184
Interracial Commission, 275, 276
Interracial cooperation, 8; between Colored Methodist Episcopal Church and Methodist Episcopal Church, South, 7–8, 296–317; in Virginia, 83, 88–89; in

Interracial cooperation (*continued*)
Tampa, 216; in southern YWCAs, 244,
271, 290; among southern churchwomen, 245, 274, 296, 297
Interracial marriage: as argument against
woman suffrage, 70, 73
Iowa, 169
Italians, 202, 203, 204, 205, 207, 212. *See
also* Latins; Latin women

Jackson, Giles B., 83
Jackson, Kate, 211
Jackson, Tennessee, 298
Jacksonville, Florida, 305
Jacksonville Dixie, 203
Jacobs, Harriet A., 329, 358
James, Rorer, 85
Jefferies, Naomi, 235
Jefferson, Thomas, 2, 68, 358, 361
Jeffrey, Mrs. R. Jerome, 75
Jenson, Joan, 359
Joan of Arc, 205
Johns Hopkins University, 385
Johnson, Carrie Parks, 316
Johnson, E. Margaret, 281
Johnson, Lillian E., 229
Johnston, Mary, 62, 72
Jones, Anna, 250, 259, 262
Jones, Hafford, 214
Jones, Jacqueline, 106, 235
Joseph, Chief, 334–35
Josephus, 363
Journal of American History, 384
Journal of Labor, 174, 175, 184
Junior League, 109

Kaestle, Carl, 359
Kansas, 167, 301, 305
Kansas City, Missouri, 248, 250
Kansas City Book Club, 261
Katonah, New York, 280
Kelley, Florence, 104, 109
Kentucky, 301, 305
King William County, Virginia, 86
Klopstock, Friedrich, 363
Knapp, Samuel L., 362
Knights of Labor, 128, 170, 174, 176,
178
Knoxville, Tennessee, 332
Kosovsky, Mrs. A., 207

Kraditor, Aileen S., 15, 63–64, 76
Ku Klux Klan, 89

Labor activism: among Tampa cigarworkers,
5, 201, 202, 204; and sexuality, 5,
206–7; role of women's auxiliaries in,
176–77
Labor feminism, 5, 167; of O. Delight
Smith, 142, 176
Ladies Aid Society (Cartersville, Georgia),
44
Ladies' Depository Association of New York,
158
Ladies' Depository Association of Phila-
delphia, 157, 158, 159–60
Ladies' Dorcas Society of the Universalist
Church (New York City), 154
La Flesche, Francis, 326, 327, 328, 330,
331, 337, 338, 339
La Flesche, Chief Joseph, 327, 338
La Flesche, Susette. *See* Tibbles, Susette La
Flesche
Laissez-faire economics, 326; and disadvan-
tages of women in the marketplace, 152,
154
Lake Junaluska, 279
Lake Mohonk, 327, 331
Lane College, 311
Laney, Lucy, 259
Lape, Esther, 110
Latham, Mrs., 356
Lathrop, Julia, 104
Latins: labor activism among, 201, 203,
204, 206, 211, 212, 217; as voters,
201, 204, 213; Anglos' attitudes
toward, 202–3; and bolita, 203; and
women's public roles, 206–7. *See also*
Latin women
Latin women, 5, 142; labor activism among,
5, 201–2, 204–7, 214–16; gender con-
sciousness of, 5, 206–7; as voters, 201,
204; sexual stereotypes of, 203. *See also*
Latins
Law, Elizabeth, 212
League of Women Voters (LWV), 89, 109,
110, 288, 384
Lee, Robert E., 68
Lemons, Stanley, 108
Leonard, Louise, 281
Lerner, Gerda, 15, 390

Lesure, Peggie, 301, 302
Lexington, Kentucky, 278
Liberal Republicans, 31
Library Board of the City of Chicago, 251
Liggett and Myers, 286
"Lily Blacks," 90
Lincoln, Abraham, 2
Link, Arthur, 108
Literacy: among women, 352, 357–59
Lizzy Glenn: Or, the Trials of a Seamstress (Arthur), 148
Lloyd, John, 169
Lloyd, Lettie Long, 169
Loughridge, William, 27
Lowell, Massachusetts, 172, 351
Lozano and Sidelo Company, 206
Lynchburg, Virginia, 87
Lynching, 6, 252; activism against, 89, 275, 297, 307, 310, 315; as impetus for Great Migration, 223; activism against among African American women, 247, 248, 249, 253, 307

McAfee, Sara, 306, 312–13
Macarthy, Katherine, 263
McCarthy, Mary, 352
McCarthyism, 124
MacDonald, Lois, 9, 283–84
MacDonell, Tochie, 313, 314, 316
Machiavelli, Niccolo, 122
McKay, D. B., 203, 204, 206, 211
McLaughlin, Andrew, 368, 369
McNeill, Martha Chamberlayne, 87–88
Macon, Georgia, 44, 277, 301, 306, 332
Madison, Georgia, 42
Maine, 364
Majority Report, 27, 32
Majors, Monroe, 255–56
Mance, Emma, 208
Mann, Horace, 363
Mann, Mary Peabody, 331
Mann-Elkins Act, 101
Margaret of Anjou, 362
Mark, Joan, 331
Market economy: as a threat to women, 10, 148, 149, 162; and developing class order in antebellum Northeast, 153; and Native Americans, 326, 327, 339

Marquette University, 385
Marriage licenses, 52
Marshall, John, 68
Martin, J. A., 299
Martineau, Harriet, 365
Masculinity: in rhetoric of temperance movement, 49; and politics, 102–3, 122–23, 127, 177; in rhetoric of Indian reform, 326, 327, 333
Mason, George, 68
Mason, Lucy Randolph, 68, 89, 279
Massachusetts Magazine, 361
"Matriarchate or Mother-Age" (Stanton), 329
Matthews, Victoria, 248
Maxwell, Maria, 147, 150
Meachem, Christine, 208
Mead, Margaret, 338, 371
Mecom, Jane, 2
Medford, Massachusetts, 355
Meharry Medical College, 311
Meier, August, 228
Memoirs of Margaret Fuller, 365
Memphis, Tennessee, 248, 303
Mercer, Lucy, 110
Mercer County, Illinois, 169
Merchant's Widow, and Other Tales, The (Sawyer), 145
Meridian, Mississippi, 278
Methodist church, 7–8, 212, 213, 244. *See also* Colored Methodist Episcopal Church (CME); Methodist Episcopal Church, South (ME)
Methodist Episcopal Church, South (ME), 296–317; theological and organizational ties to Colored Methodist Episcopal Church (CME), 298–99; male dominance in, 299, 302, 314; demographics of membership, 303–4; founding and growth of, 304–5. *See also* Colored Methodist Episcopal Church (CME)
—women's missionary organizations: and interracial cooperation with Colored Methodist Episcopal Church, 7–8, 296–317; development of, 300–303; activities of, 306–7, 309–11; reform agenda transformed by CME women, 307–8, 311–14, 315–17
Methodist Women's Home Missionary societies, 213

Mexicans: discrimination against, 309
Miami, Florida, 305
Michel, Louise, 205
Michigan State Association of Colored
    Women's Clubs, 226, 227
Middle class: depicted in domestic novels,
    10, 151, 155
Middletown, Ohio, 281
Miles, Charles, 182, 183
Miller, Alice Duer, 367
Miller, Perry, 350–51
Milton, John, 364
Milwaukee, Wisconsin, 228
Minor, Francis, 22–23, 26
Minor, Virginia, 22–23, 25, 26, 33. *See also*
    Minor v. Happersett
Minority Report, 27–28
Minor v. Happersett, 32–33, 34
Mississippi, 301
Mississippi State College for Women, 366
Missouri, 22, 33, 249, 301, 305
Monaghan, Jennifer, 357
Montevallo, Alabama, 169
Moravians, 359
More, Hannah, 365
Morgan, Edmund, 382
Morgan, Lewis, 329
Motherhood: empowered by temperance
    movement, 49; and white supremacy,
    51; used as metaphor in Indian reform,
    245, 326, 330–31, 334, 337, 340; as
    basis for social activism, 253, 296
Mother's aid laws: as example of contradic-
    tions of progressivism, 106
"Mother Sawyer," 313–14
Mothers' clubs, 249
Mott, James, 129
Mountaineers, 309
Mowry, George, 101
Mrs. Herndon's Income (Campbell), 162
Muncy, Robyn, 104
Murray, Judith Sargent, 361, 371, 372
Murray, Preston, 208
Muscogee County, Georgia, 312

Nansemond County, Virginia, 86
Nashville, Tennessee, 281, 313–14
Nathan, Annie, 365, 366
National American Woman Suffrage Associa-
    tion (NAWSA), 73, 75, 76
National Association for the Advancement

of Colored People (NAACP), 107, 226,
    230, 249, 250
National Association Notes, 254, 260
National Association of Colored Women
    (NACW), 80, 208, 225, 227, 247–64
National Association of Manufacturers,
    174
National Child Labor Committee, 183
National Conference of Colored Women in
    America, 225
National Council of Women, 329
National Federation of Afro-American
    Women, 248
National Housewives' League of America,
    227, 231
National Humanities Center, 385
National Negro Business League, 227, 230
National Recovery Administration (NRA),
    112
National Woman's Party, 55
National Woman Suffrage Association, 20,
    21, 27–28. *See also* National American
    Woman Suffrage Association (NAWSA)
National Women's Trade Union League. *See*
    Women's Trade Union League
Native Americans: traditional power of
    women among, 9, 245; and land allot-
    ments, 9, 327; and assimilation, 9, 327,
    331, 332, 335; and "manliness," 326.
    See also Native American women
Native American women: traditional
    autonomy of, 9, 245, 329–30, 333;
    dislocated by assimilation, 9, 325,
    328–29, 337; and "woman question,"
    325; as symbols for women's rights
    activists, 328–29, 330; opposition to
    reform among, 331
Nativism, 106, 111, 161, 175. *See also*
    White supremacy
Nebraska, 169, 325
Needle trades. *See* Textile industry
Needlewomen. *See* Seamstresses
Needlework: as metaphor for women's
    changing relations to production, 148,
    149, 153
New Bedford, Massachusetts, 172
New Deal, 108, 109, 112; links with
    Progressive Era, 3, 112, 114; histori-
    ography, 17, 108–14; women's roles in
    administering, 111–12

New Departure: Constitutional arguments of, 21–23; as impetus for women's direct-action voting, 23–26, 34; supported by Victoria Woodhull, 26; Congressional response to, 27; and election of 1872, 31; defeated by Supreme Court in *Minor v. Happersett*, 33, 34
Newell, Bertha, 309, 316
New England Mind, The (Miller), 350
New England Woman's Club, 325
New Era Club (Boston), 248, 250
New Freedom, 101, 112
New Hampshire, 356
New Jersey, 368
New Left, 123, 124, 125
New Mexico, 309
New Nationalism, 101, 112
New Orleans, Louisiana, 258, 281, 303
Newport News, Virginia, 70
Newport News Daily Press, 77, 84
New Woman: images of, 70, 205, 217; African American version of, 208–9
New York City, 34, 109, 110, 111, 145, 147, 149, 150, 154, 157, 158, 168, 248, 272, 282, 289, 356, 359, 365, 366, 386
New York Society for the Relief of Poor Widows with Small Children, 155
New York Tribune, 28, 160, 161
Nez Perce tribe, 9, 328, 330, 332–35, 336
Nez Perce War of 1877, 334
Nineteenth Amendment: as culmination of suffragists' constitutional claims, 21; opposition to in southern states, 41, 54, 55, 57, 74; ratified by Tennessee, 68, 200; ratified by General Assembly of Virginia, 73; and changing sexual politics in Tampa, 206
— effects of ratification: on African Americans, 8, 65–66; in Georgia, 55; in Virginia, 65, 68, 82–87
Norfolk Equal Suffrage League, 67, 72
Norfolk Virginian-Pilot, 84
Norris, Amos, 214
Norris, Julia, 200, 211, 214, 216
Northanger Abbey (Austen), 361
North Carolina, 11, 261, 273, 277, 286, 301, 306
North Carolina College for Women, 284
North Carolina Governor's Commission on the Status of Women, 384

North Carolina Mutual Insurance Company, 276
North Dakota, 368, 369
Northeastern Federation of Women's Clubs, 76
Northwestern University, 388
Noted Negro Women (Majors), 256
Nunnally, Milton, 183

Oberlin College, 352–53, 362, 367
O'Berry, Mrs., 289
Old People's Home (Tampa), 210
Olmsted, Frederick Law, 370
Olympia, Washington, 25
Omaha tribe, 9, 326–38
Omaha Tribe, The, 328, 337–38
Open Forum on Our Government for Women Voters, An, 210
Order of Railroad Telegraphers (ORT), 166, 170, 171, 173, 174, 175
Organization of American Historians, 346, 384, 385, 386, 389, 391
Orlando, Florida, 305
Out-work, 159, 160
Owen, Catherine (Helen Alice Nitsch), 162
Owen, Robert Dale, 161

Paine Institute, 308–9
Palmer Memorial Institute, 261
Panic of 1837, 145, 158–60, 163; effects on garment industry, 158–60; eroded myth of stable domesticity, 159
Panic of 1907, 172, 174
Paradise Lost (Milton), 364
Parker, William Watts, 70
Parkersburg, West Virginia, 278
Participatory politics, 131, 132; growth of in Age of Jackson, 122; reinvented in civil rights movement, 123; demand for in developing nations, 126, 130; decline of in late nineteenth century, 128
Partisan Review, 352
Pateman, Carole, 127
Patterson, Mary Jane, 248
Paul, Alice, 55
Peabody, Elizabeth, 331
Peabody Museum, 327, 328, 332
Peck, Fannie, 230–31, 235
Peck, William H., 230

Peed, Esther, 287, 288
Pensacola, Florida, 305
Petersburg Index-Appeal, 84
Phelps, Elizabeth Stuart, 162
Philadelphia, Pennsylvania, 23, 149, 154-57, 248, 260, 359
Philadelphia Institute for Colored Youth, 359
Pierce, Sarah, 359
Pitkin, Hannah, 122
Pittsburgh, Pennsylvania, 328
Plato, 360
Plato, Ann, 350
Ploughed Under: The Story of an Indian Chief (Tibbles), 331
Poems on Various Subjects, Religious and Moral (Wheatley), 350
Political history: and women's activism, 3; and women's history, 15, 17, 101-14; and class, 102, 106-8, 114
Politics. *See* Identity politics; Participatory politics; Political history
Ponca tribe, 331
Pope, Alexander, 355, 356, 361
Popular sovreignty: and woman suffrage, 22, 26
Populism, 101, 174
Portland, Oregon, 185
Postal Telegraph Company, 169
Poverty: public views on, 10, 151-52, 154, 161-62, 162-63
Powhatan County, Virginia, 86
Price, Mrs. I. O. (Ada), 210
Price, Richard, 356
Prichard, Alabama, 286
Proceedings of the American Association for the Advancement of Science, 328
Progressive Era: historiography, 1, 3, 15, 17, 101-8, 112-14; links with New Deal, 3, 108-14; and gender-based politics, 103-6, 107-8; and race and class barriers to reform, 106-8. *See also* Progressivism
Progressivism: origins of, 3; historiography, 3, 101-8, 112-14, 167-68; and race and class biases, 3, 106-8; links with New Deal, 3, 108-14; as product of distinct masculine and feminine political cultures, 105
Prohibition, 203

Protection: male protection of white women in the South, 16, 41, 43-44, 45, 48, 49, 51, 53, 56; and temperance movement, 48; from the vicissitudes of market economy, 148, 149, 151; of African American women, 254-55, 257, 308
Providence, Rhode Island, 158
Providence Employment Society, 158, 159
Provident Society of Philadelphia, 156
Putnam, Frederick, 326, 328, 330, 332, 340

Quakers, 262, 359
Quarles, Benjamin, 25
Queen and Crescent Railroad, 169
Quinton, Amelia, 329

Race: and women's activism, 4; and political history, 102, 106, 114; and women's history, 102, 106, 114. *See also* Racism; White supremacy
—and suffrage movement, 53; historiography, 62-64; in Virginia, 62-90
"Race degeneration," 51
Race riots, 73-74, 202, 252
"Race suicide," 202, 203
Racism: characteristic of Progressive Era, 3, 106, 252; in New South, 52-53, 56, 200-201, 271, 273, 274-77; in labor movement, 175; and black women's activism, 225-26, 249, 252; divided black men and women, 257. *See also* White Supremacy
Radcliffe College, 386
Radical Republicans, 20
Raleigh, North Carolina, 275
Randolph-Macon College, 353
Rape, 6, 51, 254
"Reading of Women in the Colonies before 1750, The" (Baldwin), 350
Reconstruction: and race attitudes, 7; and definitions of citizenship, 16; suffrage movement in, 19-34; egalitarianism of, 21, 22, 23; and women's public roles, 41; set precedent for federal enforcement of Constitution, 73; education for African Americans during, 353
Reconstruction amendments. *See* Fifteenth Amendment; Fourteenth Amendment
Reid, Elizabeth, 110

Religion: and interracial cooperation among southern Methodist churchwomen, 7, 296–317; as source of division in African American community, 261–62; and YWCA, 271, 273

Republicanism: and masculinity, 102; and education for women, 358–59

"Republican Motherhood," 121, 179, 359

Republican party: and African American women, 23, 86, 90, 254; and woman suffrage, 27, 30–32; and election of 1872, 31; in Virginia, 66, 67, 79; in Tampa, 206, 210–11

Rhode Island, 158

Rich, Adrienne, 120, 371

Richmond, Virginia, 69–88, 277, 278, 281, 282

Richmond City Democratic Committee, 85

Richmond Evening Journal, 70

Richmond Neighborhood Association, 84

Richmond News Leader, 67, 69, 83, 84

Richmond Planet, 80, 81

Richmond Times-Dispatch, 67, 70, 72, 73, 83, 87

Riesman, David, 371, 372

Rivington Street Settlement, 109, 112

Roanoke, Virginia, 277

Roanoke World News, 84

Roberts, Ida E., 306

Robinson, Lila, 208, 209

Rochester, New York, 25, 129

Rockbridge, Virginia, 72

Rockford College, 366

Rojo, José, 212

Roosevelt, Eleanor, 109–12, 113

Roosevelt, Franklin, 110, 111, 233

Roosevelt, Theodore, 101, 112, 202

Roseville, New Jersey, 23

Rough Riders, 202

Rousseau, Jean-Jacques, 119

Rowe, Elizabeth Singer, 355

Rowson, Susannah, 356, 360

Ruddick, Sara, 120

Rudwick, Elliott, 228

Ruffin, Adele, 276

Ruffin, Josephine St. Pierre, 225, 248, 250

Rutherford, Mildred, 54

Sacio, Julia, 214

St. Augustine, Florida, 305

St. Francis, 2

St. Louis, Missouri, 25, 363

St. Petersburg, Florida, 210, 305

Salisbury, North Carolina, 277

San Antonio, Texas, 131

Santa Cruz, California, 25

Santa Fe Railroad, 185

Sappho, 355

Savannah, Georgia, 145, 281, 309

Savannah Tribune, 255

Sawyer, Caroline Mehitable, 145, 147, 151, 153–54, 155, 159

Scalawags, 45

Schneiderman, Rose, 111

School of Household Arts (Tampa), 208

Schreiner, Olive, 179, 180

Science, 328

Scooba, Mississippi, 169

Scott, Andrew, 386

Scott, Anne Firor: as pioneer and mentor, 1, 11, 381–92; scholarship of, 1–2, 6, 7, 11–12, 103, 129, 152, 167, 225, 296; academic career of, 10–11, 345–47, 381–92; *The Southern Lady,* 2, 6, 12, 15, 42, 388; *Natural Allies,* 2–3, 152; *Unheard Voices,* 12; *Making the Invisible Woman Visible,* 381; "A Historian's Odyssey," 381, 384, 387

Scott, Joan Wallach, 126

Seamstresses, 10, 142, 145; as representatives of working classes, 150

Seattle, Washington, 224

Semper Fidelis Club (Birmingham, Alabama), 248

Seneca Falls, New York, 129

Separate spheres: in American political culture, 20, 102–3, 114; as model for historical scholarship, 20, 126; as source of political strength for women, 113; model challenged by new theory of public life, 126; absence of in working-class and African American political cultures, 168, 253. *See also* Domesticity

Settlement houses, 212, 280; and middle-class women, 103–4; founded by African American women, 249, 264

Seven Wise Women, 365

Sexuality. *See* Women's sexuality

Shadd, Mary Ann, 362

Shakespeare, William, 356

Shaw, Anna Howard, 75
Sherman Anti-Trust Act, 175
Silent Partner, The (Phelps), 162
Simms, Florence, 272, 273
Sioux tribe, 325, 327, 331
Sitting Bull, 325, 326, 327, 329, 339
Sketch of the Working Classes of New York: Or, the Sufferings of the Sewing Girls, A (Buckley), 146, 157
Slaughterhouse cases, 32, 33
Slavery: and southern domesticity, 46, 48, 49; and growth of garment industry, 149; and gender equality among African American women, 251; and sexual exploitation of African American women, 258, 259; issue divides Methodist Episcopal Church, 304–5
Slaves: confined to private sphere, 119
Smith, Adam, 357, 371
Smith, Edgar B., 169, 173, 184
Smith, Ola Delight, 5, 142, 166–86; and "womanism," 5, 166, 181; excluded African Americans from reform agenda, 168, 175, 185; early life and education, 169; work as telegrapher, 169; labor activism of, 171, 173–85; reform agenda of, 174–81, 185; nativism of, 175–76, 185; perceived male sexuality as a threat, 176; and role of women in labor movement, 176–77; and women's sexual freedom, 181–82; involved in domestic scandal, 182–84
Smith College, 353, 365
Smithsonian Bureau of American Ethnology, 328
Snow, Alice, 210, 216
Social mobility: depicted in domestic novels, 147, 151, 152, 155
Solomon, Barbara Miller, 353
Somerville, Mary, 365
Sorbonne, 368
Sorosis, 325
South: historiography of progressivism in, 1, 6, 167; social and political landscape of, 6, 16, 168–69, 200, 244, 273, 300; YWCA activities in, 8, 269–91; and women's need for "protection," 41–57; gender relations in, 42–43, 56, 57, 199; failure of patriarchy in Civil War, 45–46; growth of voluntary associations in after World War I, 108–9; labor activism in, 166–86; and employment of African American women, 227; and urbanization, 244, 274, 301; black women's club work in, 248–49; female literacy rates in, 358
—and education: for women, 353, 358, 366; for African Americans, 363
—and religion: central role of Protestant church in, 273; activities of black and white churchwomen in, 296–317
—and woman suffrage: southern opposition to, 41, 42; southern suffragists blamed for white supremacist arguments, 62–64. *See also* Suffrage movement: in Virginia
Southampton County, Virginia, 86
South Carolina, 25, 273, 277
Southern Association of Women's Historians, 390
Southern Conference on Human Welfare, 317
Southern Conference on Woman and Child Labor, 178
Southern Federation of Colored Women, 254
Southern Historical Association, 346, 385, 387, 390
Southern Summer School, 278, 279, 280, 287
Southern Workman, 81, 335, 337
Souvestre, Marie, 109, 110
Spaniards, 202, 203, 204, 206. *See also* Latins; Latin women
Sparkling Gems of Race Knowledge Worth Reading (Haley), 256
Spartanburg, South Carolina, 280
Spectator, The, 356
Spelman College, 208, 353, 365
Spencer, Anna Garlin, 349
Spencer, Sara, 29
Spooner, Hertha, 370
Springfield, Missouri, 248
Staël, Madame de (Anne Louise Germaine Necker), 364
Stanford University, 353–54, 385
Stansell, Christine, 106
Stanton, Elizabeth Cady, 28, 30; on Fourteenth Amendment, 20; and matriarchal example of Native American women, 329, 330
State Congress of Mothers (Georgia), 178

States' rights: and woman suffrage, 31, 54–55, 68, 73, 74
Stebbins, Catherine, 25
Sterilization: of "erring" women, 52–53
Stevens, Thelma, 316
Stewart, Sallie Wyatt, 225
Stokes, Ora Brown, 84, 88
Stone, Lucy, 23, 328, 330
Stott, Mrs., 157
Stovall, Wallace, 199, 204, 215
Straker, D. Augustus, 226
Stuart, Harriet, 332
Stuart, James, 332
Suarez, Manuel, 203
Suffrage movement: and New Departure, 3, 16, 19–34; and white supremacy, 8, 53–55, 62–90; split over Reconstruction amendments, 20–21; and "free love," 28–29; conservatism of after New Departure defeat, 34; and women's need for protection, 53–54; historiography, 62–64; in Virginia, 62–90; and women's "domestic politics," 104–5; in Tampa, 205, 210. *See also* New Departure; Nineteenth Amendment
Supreme Court, U.S.: and woman suffrage, 3; as guardian of sexual and racial hierarchy, 15; in *Bradwell,* 30–32; in *Slaughterhouse,* 32; in *Minor v. Happersett,* 32–34

Talbot, Marion, 368
Tampa, Florida, 5, 142, 199–217, 278, 305
Tampa Citizen, 215
Tampa Civic Association, 210, 211
Tampa Daily Times, 199, 213
Tampa Morning Tribune, 199, 200, 202, 203, 205, 213, 215, 217
Tampa Woman's Club, 210
Telegraphers: work culture of, 169–71; women as, 170–71; labor activism among, 170, 171–72, 173–74
Temperance, 8, 48, 148. *See also* Woman's Christian Temperance Union (WCTU)
Tennessee, 200, 201
Ten Nights in a Barroom (Arthur), 148
Terborg-Penn, Rosalyn, 106, 297
Terrell, Ebenezer, 355

Terrell, Jane Colman, 350, 355–56, 357, 360, 362, 371, 372
Terrell, Mary Church, 248, 260, 261, 367, 371
Texas, 185, 255, 309
Textile industry: commercial success of in early nineteenth century, 149, 153; working conditions in, 149–50; reorganization after Panic of 1837, 159, 160, 163; increased importance of factory system in, 160–61; decline of in 1920s, 282
Textile workers, 157, 179, 182, 184
Thaw, William, 328
Thomas, William Hannibal, 255
Thompson, E. P., 163
"'Three Immediate Women Friends' of the Anthony Family, The," 75
Thurman, Lucy Smith, 226
Tibbles, Susette La Flesche, 330, 331, 332
Title 9, 353
Tobacco Leaf, 201
Tocqueville, Alexis de, 128
Tolstoy, Leo, 2
Townsend, Jessie, 72
Trade unionism: as inspiration for women's activism, 177. *See also* Labor activism
Trevelyan, G. M., 15
Trinity College. *See* Duke University
Trinity Home Mission Society (Atlanta), 300
Troen, Selwyn, 363
Trumbull, John, 354
Turner, Frederick Jackson, 382
Tuskegee Institute, 226
"Two Sisters of Old Boston" (Baldwin), 354

Unemployment: during Panic of 1837, 158
Union label campaigns, 224
Union Marti-Maceo, 215
United Daughters of the Confederacy, 51, 200
United States v. Cruikshank, 33
United States v. Reese, 33
United Textile Workers Union (UTW), 182, 183, 184
Universal Negro Improvement Association, 226
Universität Bonn, 385

University of Berlin, 368
University of Chicago, 316, 349, 354, 368
University of Iowa, 353
University of Michigan, 366
University of Missouri, 366
University of North Carolina, 354, 388
University of South Carolina, 354
University of Virginia, 354, 387
University of Washington, 385
University of Wisconsin, 354, 366, 388
Urban League, 89, 208, 209, 215, 216, 226

Vagrancy laws: used to create labor force, 175–76; used against striking cigar-workers, 204
Valentine, Lila Meade, 62, 72, 74, 76, 79, 87
Van Antwerp, Eugene I., 233
Van Valkenberg, Ellen, 25–26
Vassar College, 365, 367
Vega, Celestino, 206
Vega, Mrs. Celestino, 212
Vicksburg, Mississippi, 249
Vineland, New Jersey, 23
Virgil, 363
Virginia, 7, 8, 16–17, 62–90, 273, 277; disfranchises blacks and lower-class whites, 66–67, 80. See also General Assembly of Virginia
Virginia Association Opposed to Woman Suffrage, 69, 73, 85
Virginia Federation of Colored Women's Clubs, 88
Virginia League of Women Voters, 89
Virginia Suffrage News, 67
Voice from the South, A (Cooper), 251
Voice of the Negro, The, 256
Voluntary associations: prevalence of in nineteenth-century America, 2, 103; as source of women's greatest political power, 2, 103, 113; as link between public and private, 3, 17, 121, 128–29; as schools for public participation, 3, 17, 126–27, 128, 130, 131, 132; and legislative reform, 52; growth of after World War I, 108–9; and identity politics, 128, 130–31, 132; and social mobility, 152; and consumer activism,

176; black and white women's club movements compared, 252
Voting Qualifications in Virginia, 78

Walden, Irwin, 210
Walden University (formerly Central Tennessee College), 311
Walker, Alice, 5
Walker, Maggie Lena, 80–82, 83, 84, 90
Walker, Wilma, 231
Wall, Charlie, 203
Wall, Perry, 203, 208
Waller, Edmund, 355
Warner, Susan, 147, 159
Washington, Booker T., 226, 233, 253
Washington, D.C., 7, 29, 41, 109, 110, 111, 113, 172, 224, 235, 255, 326, 327, 367
Washington, George, 12
Washington, Margaret Murray, 253–54, 262, 263, 307–8
Washington, Mary Helen, 228
Washington Bee, 255
Washington Territory, 24–25
Watson, Georgia Durham, 55
Watson, Tom, 55
Wealth of Nations, The (Smith), 357
Welfare state, 3, 17, 167
Wellesley College, 353, 365
Wells, Ida B. See Barnett, Ida B. Wells
West, Gertrude J., 233
Western Union, 169, 170, 171, 172, 185
West Palm Beach, Florida, 305
West Tampa, Florida, 212, 213
Wheatley, Phillis, 350
White, Hugh, 72, 80, 82
White House Conference on the Emergency Needs of Women, 111
White Municipal party (Tampa), 208, 215
White primary system, 200, 201, 208, 209, 252, 316
White supremacy: as characteristic of Progressive Era, 6, 252; in reform agenda of Rebecca Latimer Felton, 7, 51–55, 56–57; in Tampa charter debate, 142, 200–201. See also Racism
—and suffrage movement, 53–55, 62–64; in Virginia, 8, 62–90
Wide, Wide World, The (Warner), 147, 159
"Wife's Farm," 50

Wilberforce University, 353, 367
Willard, Emma, 2, 10, 11, 332, 359, 361, 371
Willard, Frances, 47
Williams, Alfred, 70–71, 72
Williams, Fannie, 250, 251, 254, 255, 256, 258, 261, 262, 263
Williams, Sylvania, 258
Wilson, Woodrow, 68, 101, 112, 385
Winchester Evening Star, 77
Winnebago tribe, 9, 327, 328, 330, 333, 335, 336
"Winning Plan," 73
Winston-Salem, North Carolina, 277, 286
Wired Love, 171
Wisconsin, 167, 169, 316
Wollstonecraft, Mary, 360, 365
Womanhood: defined by "bodiliness" and exclusion from public life, 120; as political metaphor, 126; southern womanhood depicted in domestic novels, 145; traditional definitions of accepted by black club women, 250. *See also* "Intelligent womanhood"
Womanism: defined, 5; of O. Delight Smith, 5, 166, 181; and white supremacy of Rebecca Latimer Felton, 7; and suffrage movement in Virginia, 81–82; and Housewives' League of Detroit, 143, 224–25, 231, 233, 235
Woman's Christian Temperance Union (WCTU), 47, 48, 49, 52, 128, 129, 210
Woman's Era, 250
Woman's Journal, 325, 326, 328
Woman's Loyal Union (New York City), 248
Woman's Musical and Literary Club (Springfield, Missouri), 248
Woman's Record (Hale), 362
Woman's Trade Union Label League, 174
Woman suffrage movement. *See* Suffrage movement
Women: as opponents of women's rights, 15–16; and feminine political sphere, 20, 102–3, 128, 244; and need for protection, 41, 43, 48, 49, 51, 53, 56; roles in farm families, 49–50, 51; as voters, 83, 85–87, 199, 200, 205, 211, 213–14; change in political status of under Roosevelt administration, 111; and public life, 119–22; and labor movement,

167, 176–77, 204, 206; as telegraphers, 170, 171; intellectual history of, 349–65; and literacy, 352, 356, 357–58. *See also* African American women; Latin women; Native American women; Womanhood; Women's activism; Women's history
"Women adrift," 173
Women's activism: historiography of, 1–3, 126, 243–44;.and constraints of race and class, 4, 271; and identity politics, 16; absorbed in government bureaucracy, 113; black and white women's club movements compared, 252. *See also* Suffrage movement
Women's Anthropological Society of America, 328
Women's Bureau (U.S. Labor Department), 112
Women's City Club, 111
Women's colleges, 282, 353
Women's history: and women's activism, 1–2; and political history, 15, 17, 20, 101–3, 105, 114; and class, 102, 106–8, 114; and study of public life, 119–22; and study of private life, 120, 122; eighteenth-century beginnings of, 362
—intellectual history, 349–65; noninstitutional character of, 351–52; four periods of, 352–54
—labor history: recent developments in, 141–42; and role of women in labor movement, 166–67; and sexuality, 186
Women's liberation movement, 123–24
Women's National Indian Association, 327, 328, 329, 335
Women's rights: changing definitions of, 19–20; and collective exercise of individual rights, 20, 25; and inspiration of Native American women, 328–29. *See also* Suffrage movement; Women's liberation movement
Women's sexuality: and woman suffrage debates, 28–29; and work culture, 171; and labor movement, 182, 206–7; and status in African American community, 258–59
Women's Share in Social Culture (Spencer), 349
Women's Trade Union League (WTUL), 107, 110, 111, 112, 178

Women's Tribune, 328, 337
Woodhull, Victoria, 26–29, 30
Woodrow Wilson National Fellowship
    Foundation, 387
Woodson, William S., 83
Woodward, C. Vann, 167
Woodward, Ellen, 112
Woodward, James G., 171
Woolf, Virginia, 350, 381, 382
Workers' education, 278, 279, 280, 288
Working classes: attitudes toward in Progres-
    sive Era, 3, 9, 106–7; disfranchised in
    Virginia, 66; gender roles among, 180.
    See also Cigarworkers; Seamstresses;
    Telegraphers; Working-class women
Working-class women: social activism of, 4,
    141, 176–77, 224; attitudes toward in
    Progressive Era, 106–7, 178, 270; and
    YWCA, 244, 270–80, 287–88
—fictional representations of: seamstresses,
    10, 145–52, 162–63; telegraphers, 171
Working Woman's Mission (Tampa), 210
Works Progress Administration (WPA), 111
World War I: and suffrage movement, 68,
    73; and progressivism, 108, 109; and
    sexual revolution, 168; and economic
    gains of African Americans, 223; as
    impetus for Great Migration, 228; and

mob violence against African Americans,
    249
World War II: and expansion of bureaucratic
    state, 123; and exclusion of African
    American women from defense jobs,
    228; effects on women's educational
    opportunities, 354

Yates, Josephine Silone, 250, 256, 262–63
Ybor City, Florida, 201, 203, 207, 210, 212,
    213, 215
Yeoman farmers, 7, 44, 46, 50, 51, 179–80,
    303
Young, Iris, 129
Young Men's Christian Association (YMCA),
    272, 285
Young Women's Christian Association
    (YWCA), 7, 8, 9, 185, 225, 244, 245;
    and race relations, 8, 271, 275, 276; goal
    of fostering women's community, 270,
    271, 272; Industrial Department of,
    270–80, 287–88; origins of, 271; and
    labor activism, 271, 278–79, 282,
    284–86, 288–89, 291; internal organiza-
    tion of, 272, 280–82, 286, 290–91;
    student-industrial program of, 280,
    282–84, 287

Books in the Series Women in American History

Women Doctors in Gilded-Age Washington: Race, Gender, and Professionalization
Gloria Moldow

Friends and Sisters: Letters between Lucy Stone and
Antoinette Brown Blackwell, 1846–93
Edited by Carol Lasser and Marlene Deahl Merrill

Reform, Labor, and Feminism: Margaret Dreier Robins and
the Women's Trade Union League
Elizabeth Anne Payne

Private Matters: American Attitudes toward Childbearing and
Infant Nurture in the Urban North, 1800–1860
Sylvia D. Hoffert

Civil Wars: Women and the Crisis of Southern Nationalism
George C. Rable

I Came a Stranger: The Story of a Hull-House Girl
Hilda Satt Polacheck
Edited by Dena J. Polacheck Epstein

Labor's Flaming Youth: Telephone Operators and Worker Militancy, 1878–1923
Stephen H. Norwood

Winter Friends: Women Growing Old in the New Republic, 1785–1835
Terri L. Premo

Better Than Second Best: Love and Work in the Life of Helen Magill
Glenn C. Altschuler

Dishing It Out: Waitresses and Their Unions in the Twentieth Century
Dorothy Sue Cobble

Natural Allies: Women's Associations in American History
Anne Firor Scott

Beyond the Typewriter: Gender, Class, and the Origins
of Modern American Office Work, 1900–1930
Sharon Hartman Strom

The Challenge of Feminist Biography: Writing the Lives
of Modern American Women
Edited by Sara Alpern, Joyce Antler, Elisabeth Israels Perry,
and Ingrid Winther Scobie

Working Women of Collar City: Gender, Class, and Community in Troy, 1864–86
Carole Turbin

Radicals of the Worst Sort: Laboring Women
in Lawrence, Massachusetts, 1860–1912
Ardis Cameron

Visible Women: New Essays on American Activism
Edited by Nancy A. Hewitt and Suzanne Lebsock